From Revivals to Removal

Portrait of Jeremiah Evarts
(*American Quarterly Register*, November 1831;
Courtesy Philip Schaff Library,
Lancaster Theological Seminary)

From Revivals to Removal

JEREMIAH EVARTS,
THE CHEROKEE NATION,
AND THE SEARCH
FOR THE SOUL OF AMERICA

John A. Andrew III

THE UNIVERSITY OF GEORGIA PRESS
Athens and London

Paperback edition, 2007
© 1992 by the University of Georgia Press
Athens, Georgia 30602
www.ugapress.org
All rights reserved

Designed by Erin Kirk
Set in Baskerville by Tseng Information Systems, Inc.
Printed digitally in the United States of America

The Library of Congress has cataloged the hardcover edition of this
book as follows:
Library of Congress Cataloging-in-Publication Data
Andrew, John A.
From revivals to removal : Jeremiah Evarts, the Cherokee Nation,
and the search for the soul of America / John A. Andrew III.
x, 434 p. : port. ; 24 cm.
ISBN 0-8203-1427-7 (alk. paper)
Includes bibliographical references (p. 339-417) and index.
1. Evarts, Jeremiah, 1781-1831. 2. Missionaries--Biography.
3. Trail of Tears, 1838-1839. 4. Cherokee Indians--Missions.
I. Title.
BV3705.E7 A53   1992
277.3'081'092 B 20   91-36846

Paperback ISBN-13: 978-0-8203-3121-8
ISBN-10: 0-8203-3121-X

British Library Cataloging-in-Publication Data available

For Roz

Contents

Acknowledgments ix

Prologue 1

1. The Formative Years 9
2. More Than a Revival: The Second Great Awakening and New England Society 30
3. "If the Gangrene Strike the Vitals": Jeremiah Evarts, Benevolent Reform, and the Organizing Impulse 48
4. Apocalyptic Visions: Jeremiah Evarts and Postwar Reform, 1815–1821 74
5. Taking Control, 1821–1825 107
6. Clouds on the Horizon, 1825–1829 133
7. The General and the Missionary 169
8. "The Torches Are at Hand": The Removal Battle in Washington 199
9. The Aftermath 229
10. Epilogue 259

Abbreviations 269

Notes 271

Bibliography 339

Index 419

Acknowledgments

✺

All historians owe a great debt to archives and those archivists who not only gather and preserve materials of the past but make them readily available for research. Like those before it, this study was possible only because of individuals and institutions who had the foresight to consider the written ephemera of the past significant. Numerous archival staffs aided immeasurably my pursuit of materials from the early republic. I would particularly like to thank the staffs at the American Antiquarian Society in Worcester, Massachusetts; at the Congregational Library in Boston, Massachusetts; at Sterling Library, Yale University; and at the American Board of Commissioners Archives in Houghton Library, Harvard University, for their kind assistance. My research trips to each of those institutions proved rewarding in large measure because of them. The staffs at the other libraries cited in my bibliography provided efficient responses to my queries through the mail. Mary Rutherford and her interlibrary loan colleagues at Franklin and Marshall College were persistent and creative in their pursuit of various odd volumes that I seemed to keep requesting. The staff and the Franklin and Marshall College Center for Academic Computing helped solve numerous computer "glitches" that arose during final preparation of the manuscript.

Financial support is important, and I would like to thank the American Philosophical Society for an early grant that allowed me to probe several key archives as well as the Grants Committee of Franklin and Marshall College, which provided funding for a substantial research swing through New England.

Several colleagues read various parts of the manuscript. David Schuyler and Louise Stevenson read early drafts of the first chapter, and James Curtis gave an earlier version of the manuscript a close and critical reading. Anonymous university press referees provided critical commentary that helped polish the manuscript. At the University of Georgia Press, Malcolm L. Call, Jane Weldon Powers, Matt Brook, and Kelly Caudle scrutinized the manuscript carefully as it made its way toward publication. I also want to thank Laura Moss Gottlieb for preparation of the index. Whatever problems remain, of course, are solely mine.

Finally, I would like to express my appreciation for the support of my family. My wife, Roz, and my children, John and Lea, retained an interest in this project and consistently supported my work even though they would have preferred that I write science fiction or a racy adventure novel that would have returned large royalties. Such is life.

From Revivals to Removal

Prologue

We are, indeed, an afflicted people! Our spirits are subdued! Despair has well nigh seized upon our energies! But we speak to the representatives of a christian country; the friends of justice; the patrons of the oppressed. And our hopes revive, and our prospects brighten, as we indulge the thought. On your sentence, our fate is suspended; prosperity or desolation depends on your word. To you, therefore, we look! Before your august assembly we present ourselves, in the attitude of deprecation, and of entreaty. On your kindness, on your humanity, on your compassion, on your benevolence, we rest our hopes. To you we address our reiterated prayers. Spare our people! Spare the wreck of our prosperity! Let not our deserted homes become the monuments of our desolation! But we forbear! We suppress the agonies which wring our hearts, when we look at our wives, our children, and our venerable sires! We restrain the forebodings of anguish and distress, of misery and devastation and death, which must be the attendants on the execution of this ruinous compact.

These words, written by Chief John Ross as the Cherokees in Georgia faced despair and removal along the Trail of Tears, signaled the end of an era and the failure of a cause.[1] They also marked the failure of one man—Jeremiah Evarts—to convince public and politician alike that humanitarian and moral precepts demanded obedience to treaty obligations and Christian principles. Only months earlier Ross had told Congress that "The Cherokees were happy and prosperous under a scrupulous observance of treaty stipulations by the Government of the United States, and from the fostering hand extending over them, they made rapid advances in civilization, morals, and in the arts and sciences. Little did they anticipate that when taught to think and feel as the American citizen, and to have with him a common interest, they were to be *despoiled by their guardian,* to become strangers and wanderers in the land of their fathers, forced to return to the savage life, and to seek a new home in the wilds of the far west, and that without their consent."[2]

To understand what had happened, historians have studied various aspects of Andrew Jackson's Indian removal policy. But no one has looked closely at the man who stood most firmly against that policy, Jeremiah Evarts. This study seeks to examine Evarts and the society that shaped his beliefs and principles, a society in the midst of significant change and nurturing various (often conflicting) interpretations of reality.

In the spring of 1837 Andrew Jackson, one of the country's last remaining links to its revolutionary beginnings, stepped down as president after eight turbulent years in the White House, to be succeeded by Martin Van Buren. That same year, an ocean away, Victoria ascended to the throne of England. These changes, continents apart, symbolized the end of one era and the onset of another. By mid-century a new generation had come to maturity in both England and the United States, what came to be called the Victorian generation. Where did it come from? What were its formative influences? In the United States it was fathered in part by men like Lyman Beecher and Jeremiah Evarts, by the experiences and values of a generation which in turn had matured in the decades following the American Revolution. This postrevolutionary generation drew sustenance from and sought to marry a moderate evangelicalism with secular success in the professions to promote a Christian republic permeated by a moral ethos and to bequeath that legacy to sons like Henry Ward Beecher and William Maxwell Evarts.

That sensibility, soon to be called Victorian, that began to emerge in the 1830s developed from a fusion of republicanism, capitalism, and revivalism that suffused the new nation in the decades following the revolution. It took shape as the men and women of Jeremiah Evarts's generation (1781–1831) sought to blend political ideals with religious millennialism, social change, and economic growth. No one pattern emerged, for the proportions in this mixture varied with individuals, each of whom drew upon its elements to form and shape particular attitudes—attitudes toward private matters as well as public morality. Competing visions frequently sprang from shared assumptions, as leaders of the post-revolutionary generation became self-conscious about their role in shaping the American future. The ethos that emerged was increasingly behavioristic, one that believed public actions to be a reflection of private belief and which often used the former to judge the latter.

Victorian culture emerged in the United States, as Daniel Walker Howe has observed, at a time of expansion, industrialization, urbanization, and evangelicalism. Equally important, it appeared at a time when a post-revolutionary generation worried that these very forces might undermine the legacy and values of that revolution as they understood them. To dissect those forces and try to claim that one was more important than another is futile, for in fact each element at once reinforced and challenged the others. To many people capital expansion and economic growth indicated God's benevolence and Americans' virtue, while to others they signaled a luxury and self-centeredness that threatened the public good. To a generation confident that purposeful human activity could make or destroy political institutions, one person's nectar was another's poison. Character formation and proper motives were thus essential to the preservation of the public good.[3]

Public good, moreover, rested on acceptance of a republican synthesis that embraced a particular political language but quarreled over behavioral fundamentals. Such disputes were inherently interpretive in nature and therefore not usually amenable to easy solution. For instance, was economic change and growth a positive sign of market forces and the corporate growth so indicative of a vigorous people, or was it instead a signal that a greedy acquisitiveness had come to blight the land and threaten republican values? Did individual self-interest naturally advance in accord with and foster the public good, or was the increasing emphasis on individualism destructive of a community ethos and a sign of dangerous centrifugal forces that threatened to fragment American society? Was there an inherent conflict between the twin themes of individualism and institutionalism? Whether the differences were between what Robert Shalhope called the radicals (traditionalists) and the social reformers (moralists), or Republicans and Federalists, or Jacksonians and Whigs, they reflected differing visions for the American future.[4]

All purported to embrace republicanism, but the synthesis became increasingly ambiguous as the distance from the revolution increased. What joined both sides, what focused debates on issues ranging from political rights to social reform, was a conviction that politics could be a mechanism for either good or evil. This belief, together with the emphasis on character and virtue, ensured that judgments on the course of events could at any time turn conspiratorial. The generation of Jeremiah Evarts remained convinced that ultimate truths existed as much in economics and politics as in religion and that the human mind could discover those truths.[5]

A feeling that their generation was breaking away from the past led Americans in two directions. Some quickly embraced all or selected elements of change and dismissed the past as old-fashioned and stultifying. Others, like Jeremiah Evarts, sought to define and perpetuate what they believed to be the essence of the American spirit—to search for the soul of America. Alive in what seemed to them a rapidly changing environment, these individuals often became traditionalists and sought to articulate an underlying ethos that they hoped would permeate the American experience. With hindsight, we can see that they stood between two worlds, the Age of the Revolution and Victorian America. They often had a foot in each yet were fully a part of neither. If they were reactionaries, then they reacted against a growing belief that freedom was autonomy, that individuals could manipulate their lives without influence or interference from outside forces. Evarts and his colleagues feared that this new freedom meant casting off traditional institutions that stabilized society: family, community, religion, morality.

At the outset, Evarts hoped that the reformation of individuals' internal consciousness would lead to a proper and moral public behavior. He believed that the soul of America was to be found not only in the ideological, philosophical, or religious beliefs of the American people, but was reflected in their behavior as well. It was an inner conviction about what mattered, about what lay at the center of things—the *primum mobile*. This essence was an intangible web of belief and conscience that ignited private conviction and a sense of public duty.

During the early years of the nineteenth century, accordingly, he placed his hopes on the revitalizing and transformative power of the Second Great Awakening. Converted individuals, he believed, would instinctively advance a Christian republicanism. By the second and third decades of the century, however, his expectations had changed. The change was subtle and apparently unconscious, but it led him to promote and lead a network of institutionalized benevolent societies. While these societies sprang from religious convictions and continued to emphasize the need for conversions to fuel a basic moral ethos, they nonetheless stressed above all else the need for proper public behavior regardless of its cause. This change from inward conviction to outward expression paralleled the disappearance of a deferential world; behavioral characteristics replaced family and background as symbols of propriety and morality for an emerging middle class. In the increasingly free-wheeling world that would become Jacksonian America, a growing emphasis on unfettered individualism, free-market capitalism, and political democracy led men like Evarts to urge their fellow citizens to steady their moral compass.

Evarts and many of his colleagues hoped to be proactive, to embrace change while at the same time maintaining traditional moral underpinnings before they eroded, but frequently their critics perceived them as reactive, opposing all change and trying to retain a world that had since passed. Evarts's own career reveals an individual whose primary concern always remained focused on law and morality rather than on particular social or cultural arrangements. There was a remarkable continuity between his senior address at Yale in 1802 and his "William Penn" essays in 1829 and 1830. What changed over these years, however, was his perspective on Christian republicanism. In 1802 Evarts clearly believed that his audience would be the leaders of the future. Because they were moral, the country and its laws would reflect that same ethos. Three decades later he was not so sure. Indian removal and the politics of Jacksonian America demonstrated to him that one could no longer assume the existence of an underlying moral ethos. Legislation was apt to reflect the pressures of party or self-interest; Americans had to be reminded that national honor rested on a shared morality. Evarts's death in 1831 coincided with yet another transition in this process. After that date the persistent but moderate cries for temperance, sabbatarianism, and the preservation of the rights of Indians turned into insistent and radical demands for the abolition of slavery.

What Evarts had appeared to discover was that human nature was not naturally benevolent when freed from restraint. This discovery led him to embrace missionary work at home and abroad, but his controlling vision was always larger than "merely" temperance or the individual conversion of the "perishing heathen." Specific reforms were, for him, more than an end in themselves. They were part of his search for the soul of America and part of his hope that his fellow Americans would recognize the importance of that search and join his efforts. His search often led him to look back to the revolution and has frequently led historians who chronicle early nineteenth-century reform to see men like Evarts as full of status anxiety and afraid of the future. Evarts did look back, but he also looked forward. He sought to shape the future as well as to preserve the past.

This linkage of past and future sharply separated Jeremiah Evarts from many of his fellow citizens. Evarts was more concerned with development through time than he was with development across space. While other men and women of the early national period embraced geographic expansion, Evarts searched for the soul of America through a continuity of conscience, honor, and morality. He pursued that constant which citizens could clutch as a moral compass while they traveled through time, as they traveled from the revolutionary world of farming and commerce to the Jacksonian world of commerce and industry. And he sought to create organizational networks, webs of cultural cohesion, to orient and comfort those citizens as they made the journey. In an increasingly transient society, Evarts hunted for pillars of permanence. Change seemed everywhere; the future seemed not only to supplant the past but to make it irrelevant.

> "What a triumph of art is the steam engine," says the capitalist, who supplants a thousand young women by a spinning jenny, a thousand young men by a fly wheel; and grinds down the wages of a twelve hours worked infant to six-pence a day! "What a noble system is civil law," says the attorney, "which prevents men from settling their own quarrels, and offers justice to all who can pay for it!" "What a glorious invention is religion," says the priest, "which builds large houses, in which to levy contributions by fear of the devil and in the name of almighty God!" "What a noble principle is competition," says the merchant, "which lays the producer at my mercy, and gives every man a chance of ruining his neighbor!" "What a transcendent contrivance is a circulating medium," says the economist, "which facilitates accumulation, encourages speculation, substitutes wealth for employment, and imparts an ideal value to objects the most worthless!" "Oh, what a compound of blessings," shouts the civilized world, "is CIVILIZATION! . . . old laws without justice, new laws without meaning . . . founding of churches and enlarging of jails, improvements in machinery and distress of the population, ordination of ministers and condemnation of criminals. . . . Oh, CIVILIZATION!"[6]

In view of the society in which he lived, it is perhaps fitting that the story of Jeremiah Evarts begins in western Vermont, a region that spawned many reformers throughout the nineteenth century, moves to Connecticut, the land of steady habits, and then proceeds to Boston, a worldly port town that embraced the marketplace of ideas as well as commerce. From his offices in Boston, Evarts sought to reach across the seas with his missionary zeal through the *Panoplist* (and later the *Missionary Herald*) and through his work at the American Board of Commissioners for Foreign Missions. It was from Boston that Evarts sought to preserve symbols of his own cultural rootedness even as they appeared to lose their meaning in the larger society. And it was to Boston that he returned after death, to be buried beneath historic Park Street Church on brimstone corner.

By that time he was out of step with much that defined national culture. He had attempted to ground the soul of America in a moral ethos, but by 1836 Francis J. Grund defined it in a different manner, arguing that business was "the very soul of an American."[7] Evarts was religious in an age of increasing religiosity. He believed in a behavioral ethos of Christian republicanism in a time when this had largely been supplanted by an ideology of virtue. He believed in the economic and political parameters of republicanism at a time when liberal capitalism had begun to seize the American economic and political imagination. He sought to inculcate a moral ethos at the same time that many Americans sought an unfettered individualism. The result, to his dismay, was often conflict. This combination of emergent discord and search for harmony became a hallmark of Evarts's generation. In the words of one nineteenth-century poet:

> The *drawing heads* admonitory move,
> And narrow, selfish *singleness* reprove;
> They intimate Fredonia's favorite plan,
> Political equality of man;
> They bid us rule our lives with even sway,
> And neither weak, nor haughty points display,
> While rolling years, to level frame, reduce
> Our tempered minds—thus only fit for use.
> Methinks they call for virtue's cleansing aid,
> Where joys can dwell, or fearful woes invade;
> To wasteful idleness their works declare
> The pressing need of vigilance and care.
> These busy samples may we all embrace,
> And mend our lives at every broken place.
> . . . .
> And while you closely scan each laboring frame,
> For rising profit, or instructive aim,
> Remark the moral order reigning here,
> How every part observes its destined sphere;
> Or, if disorder enter the machine,
> A sweeping discord interrupts the scene!

Learn hence, whatever line of life you trace,
In pious awe your proper sphere to grace.[8]

The first chapter outlines Evarts's early years and the social and religious influences that shaped them. By far the most transformative influence, not only for Evarts but for many of his generation, was the Second Great Awakening. Chapter two details its impact as a force to revitalize society as well as revive religion. Chapter three examines Evarts's early years as editor of the *Panoplist*, years when he plunged into various activities to reform and revitalize American society. After the War of 1812, those efforts took on new meaning as the millennium beckoned, and Chapter four looks at his visions for a future America. Then, in 1821, he took over as corresponding secretary of the American Board of Commissioners for Foreign Missions after the death of Samuel Worcester. The next two chapters examine his unstinting efforts on behalf of the missionary cause. Increasingly he found himself drawn to the board's North American Indian missions, and the remaining chapters focus on those missions—first his conflict with President Andrew Jackson, then his battle with Congress over removal, and finally his efforts to salvage what he could from defeat at the hands of Jacksonians. If the Indian issue seems to dominate Evarts's later years, it was because it was central to Jacksonian America and symbolic of the many forces that coursed through the life of Jeremiah Evarts. His death in 1831 concluded his struggles, but efforts to infuse politics with Christian principles persisted. Under the leadership of the abolitionists, those efforts led in the next generation to a clash far more convulsive than Indian removal.

CHAPTER ONE

The Formative Years

"We were sure to hear the voice of Evarts on the side of law, order, respect for constituted authorities, for superiors in age and office, and for the principles of virtue." With these words a Yale classmate characterized Jeremiah Evarts, an angular Vermont farm boy whose pursuit of Christian republicanism led him from a career in the law to a lifetime commitment to benevolent reform.[1] Evarts's own convictions about the necessity of virtue to preserve a moral society coalesced by 1802, the year he graduated from Yale, and his essay for those graduation exercises revealed an attitude and a concern that shaped the rest of his life. In an essay titled "On the Execution of the Laws," the Yale senior wrote: "Whoever is in the least acquainted with the state of morals in our country, cannot but confess that much depends upon the execution of the laws. Who does not know that national calamities are the legitimate offspring of national vice and abandonment? And who will not acknowledge that our nation ought to be purified from sin, that the judgments, which hang over us, and which we so justly deserve, may be averted?"[2] Throughout his career Evarts consistently argued that laws should reflect and defend a mixture of legal, moral, and religious principles if the nation was to retain its republican heritage and realize its millennial expectations.

Seizing the opportunity of a graduation address, and drawing strength from his recent conversion, the twenty-one-year-old pupil of Timothy Dwight impressed upon his audience the necessity for swift punishment to deter both moral and secular crimes. Vices, he insisted, were especially repugnant because they "deform the human character," thereby encouraging poverty, contempt, drunkenness, and other excesses that eroded the bonds of community. Vigilance was essential, for the slightest relaxation led to further inattention, "til the whole code becomes the object of neglect and ridicule." Social harmony would then dissipate and diminish public confidence in government and the men who held public office. That would subvert the parameters of republicanism itself and dislodge the nation from its lofty position of moral eminence in the world community. These themes—opposition to vice, moral vigilance, social harmony—would command Evarts's attention throughout his life. That this triumph of vice and immorality was possible Evarts was convinced. Look around you, he urged his commencement audience. "Hear curses uttered by children unconscious of their meaning. . . . View the drunkard, forfeiting all claim to human society. . . . See the Sabbath . . . converted into a day of sloth. . . . See adultery proved in our courts . . . for the purpose of obtaining a divorce. . . ." Elsewhere the intrigues of faction polluted politics, and a grubbing for profit and wealth governed economic relationships, leading men to sacrifice their dignity as well as their right to the public trust.

Evarts urged his listeners to "consider yourselves as always responsible to your country." They were entrusted with a precious and vital charge: "You are to purify the public morals; you are to guard our youth against the numerous temptations, which lie in wait to devour them." If people maintained a responsibility to God, they could guard the vitals of the republic and protect the soul of America. It was, moreover, their duty to do so—for themselves, their country, and their God. These alarms and admonitions retained their vitality for Evarts throughout his life, a life dedicated to public watchfulness and reform. Indeed, they infected many young men and women of his generation—a generation that came of age at the onset of the Second Great Awakening amid the party battles of the early national period and one that in its twilight witnessed the adoption of Victorian social mores.

Jeremiah Evarts was born in Sunderland, Vermont, on February 3, 1781. His father, James, was from Guilford, Connecticut, a conservative, agrarian town located east of New Haven. The Guilford community was noted for its stability; young sons generally remained on the parental farms or located close by. Throughout the eighteenth century families that persisted in the town intermarried and clustered on neighboring farms. When these families left, they transferred their land to Guilford relatives.

The Evarts family was no exception. From their arrival from Yorkshire, England, in 1650 as one of the first settlers of Guilford until the last third of the eighteenth century, they reared successive generations in this tradition. But by the close of the French and Indian War, the growth of population and the accompanying decrease of available fertile land convinced many of Connecticut's young males to emigrate. They hoped to perpetuate traditional habits in a different setting.[3]

Among those deciding to seek a better livelihood elsewhere was James Evarts, who moved with his young wife, Sarah (the daughter of Timothy Todd of East Guilford), to Sunderland, Vermont. Accompanied by other Connecticut emigrants, James Evarts hoped to find more hospitable conditions for farming in the wilderness of southwestern Vermont. He quickly discovered, however, that Sunderland was better suited as a water power site than as an agrarian haven. The town was too mountainous to fulfill many settlers' expectations, and in 1787 James and Sarah Evarts left with their young son to help settle Georgia, Vermont.[4]

Lying north of Burlington along the shores of Lake Champlain, Georgia possessed good timber resources and a rich, productive soil. Settled largely by Baptists and Congregationalists, the town grew quickly. By 1790 it was one of the most populous and prosperous communities in northern Vermont. Mills and schools appeared rapidly, although when Jeremiah passed his eleventh birthday his parents sent him to school in Burlington, twelve miles to the south.[5]

The Vermont farmer's son found himself more attracted to books than to the plow. Slight of frame, and with a delicate constitution, he had neither the robust physical qualities nor the intellectual inclination for a life of labor in the fields. His hardy pioneer father, busy clearing the forest to make a new life for his family, must have felt some pangs of disappointment. James Evarts nonetheless encouraged his son's intellectual pursuits, although later letters revealed the father's deeply held hope that his eldest son might return to manage the Vermont homestead. An unspoken but deepening rift developed between father and son, a rift undoubtedly born of unmet expectations and lingering guilt. New Englanders still emphasized the duty of children to their parents in practice, and celebrated it in verse.

> See the young stork his duteous wing prepare
> His aged sire to feed with constant care;
> O'er hills and dales his precious load conveys

And the great debt of filial duty pays
Careful return! By nature's self design'd.
A fair example set to human kind.
Shouldst thou refuse they parent's needful aid,
The very stork might the foul crime upbraid:
Be mindful how they rear'd their tender youth,
Bear with their frailties, serve them still with truth.[6]

But Jeremiah Evarts was bent on following a different path. Whether or not his precarious health, his fragile frame, an intellectual bent, or some maternal influence led him to look beyond the farm we can never know, for Evarts left few personal papers and wrote little about his childhood or private life. Like many young men of his generation, he chose to turn his back on agriculture, move to a city, and pursue a profession. His ambitions embraced a future beyond his father's desire for more land and the prosperity of the family farm. This was, as Joseph Kett has so ably remarked, a critical transition.[7] It was a change rather than a reform, but a change that itself became a focal point for later reform activity.

After attending school in Burlington, Jeremiah began serious preparation for college. With his father's blessing (and his company for the journey), in January 1798 the young man traveled on horseback to East Guilford, Connecticut, to study with the Reverend John Elliott (Yale, 1786), minister of his mother's native parish. The following October, at age seventeen, he entered the freshman class at Yale.[8]

Yale at that time was under the superintendence of Timothy Dwight, who had succeeded to the presidency after the death of Ezra Stiles in 1795. In addition to his administrative responsibilities, Dwight also preached from the pulpit in the college chapel. And Timothy Dwight was neither bashful nor circumspect in his use of authority. He believed that his responsibility was to train the minds of his students, and to do this meant the establishment of character, emphasis on the function of religion, and instruction in public and private morality. Students encountered strict discipline, a ban against dancing assemblies and dancing schools, more than forty pages of college regulations, a new Moral Society, and insistent attacks on French philosophers and "infidelity."[9]

Dwight stood as a parent, a strict parent, to Yale's undergraduates. It was a role he welcomed, even sought, for he intended that graduates be diligent, methodical in their work, and morally upstanding. He had no wish to turn out refined gentlemen, vain in their manners and fashionable in their vices. Disorder, litigation, and artful pandering to popular prejudices were to be avoided, and Dwight looked askance at lawyers and Jeffersonians. During Evarts's college years the only Republican member of Yale's faculty would be forced out—exiled to the University of Georgia in 1800.[10] Timothy Dwight was an active and open supporter of Federalist principles, believing with men like the Reverend Nathaniel Emmons that "there is even a present prospect of perilous times, which will require the friends of virtue, of religion, and of government, to make more vigorous exertions in support of these important objects than they have yet been called to make. It seems that piety and patriotism will be put to the severest trials."[11] Students heard such admonitions periodically from the college pulpit. They were central to the character of both the institution and its president at the opening of the nineteenth century.

During his presidency Dwight bore sole responsibility for the instruction of the senior class. Possessed of a dynamic mind, he also served as a professor of English and oratory and as professor of divinity. Herein lay his influence. Through his sermons and lectures he brought to Yale undergraduates the legacy of New England Congregationalism drawn from his grandfather, Jonathan Edwards, and modified by Dwight's own theological system. Published posthumously as *Theology Explained and Defended, in a Series of Sermons*, Dwight's system rested on a cornerstone of morality, virtue, benevolence, and regeneration.[12] From those sermons Jeremiah Evarts would later internalize a set of moral and evangelical values which led him to search for the soul of America amid the conflicting tensions of the early nineteenth century. Central to Evarts's ideology would be a theory of moral agency that emphasized the power of regeneration. Timothy Dwight expressed it best in his sermon "Regeneration: Its Nature," when he said: *"Regeneration is a change of the temper, or disposition, or in other words, of the heart, of man; and, by consequence, of his whole character.* The heart is the great controlling power of a rational being; the whole of that energy, by which he is moved to action. The moral nature of this power, therefore, will be the moral nature of the man. If this be virtuous, all his other faculties will be rendered means of virtue; if sinful, the means of sin. Thus regeneration will affect the whole man; and govern all his character, powers, and conduct."[13] In the hands of men like Jeremiah Evarts this theory would prove to be a powerful force in an effort to shape American society and culture.

Dwight's series of 173 sermons, with topics such as "The Law of God Perfect," "Love to Our Neighbour," "On Personal Happiness," "The Perpetuity of the Sabbath," "The Duty of Subjects," or "Regeneration," formed a system which gave Yale students of Jeremiah Evarts's generation a millennial vision. Although he divided his *Theology* into three parts—a system of doctrines, a system of duties, and a system of dispensations—he particularly focused on the social effects of Christianity. Dwight argued that God enjoined benevolence as an active principle; he insisted that Christians should concentrate on doing good to others if they wished to fulfill God's plan. "In whatever sphere of life you are placed," he wrote in Sermon 97 ("On Personal Happiness"), "employ all your powers and all your means of doing good, as diligently and vigorously as you can."[14] The transformation of individuals would eventually transform society, and students of Dwight in Jeremiah Evarts's generation came to believe that individual moral reformation would inculcate virtue and elevate the conduct of public affairs. They believed, as Dwight himself argued, "that the whole vindicable conduct of Rulers toward their Subjects, and of Subjects toward their Rulers, is nothing but a mere collection of duties, objects of moral obligation, required by God, and indispensably owed to Him by men."[15] Jeremiah Evarts's undergraduate years at Yale would be a prolonged course of instruction in this new moral ethos.

When Jeremiah Evarts arrived for the fall term in 1798 he was only a year off the farm. Yet he was not completely out of place in New Haven with his rustic garb and simple, stiff manners. Yale students were generally the sons of farmers, although few (like Evarts) came from the newer settlements. Most were from Connecticut, from families beginning to feel the pinch of inadequate local land resources for the rising generation, and were at Yale to prepare for the professions, especially the ministry or the law. In this respect Evarts *was* different, for his father had land but not wealth; his family hoped that he would return to Vermont, not join the professional ranks of New Haven or Boston. This sense of difference seems to have impressed his classmates, for they described him as rural in dress, stiff and a bit awkward in demeanor, and honest in his countenance. They quickly discovered that he was a determined competitor as well.[16]

Evarts himself was not completely unprepared for his classmates. His Guilford relations provided some advice and assistance. He had taken an entrance examination in July and at that time met the tutors and some of the faculty. During the summer he had acquired a wardrobe and received a warning about college behavior from the Reverend Elliott. Referring to the student riots then common at colleges, Evarts reflected on this advice and confided that "we should not be found in scandalous tricks and plots which are a disgrace to human nature, but on the one side of order and sobriety . . . we should always be the friends of virtue, humanity and religion. . . ."[17]

Evarts's diary reveals that his experiences in New Haven rivaled those of any other Yale freshman. The Yale Corporation had prohibited students from boarding at New Haven taverns, and incoming students applied to President Dwight's office, which routed them to a tutor for assistance in finding room and board. In the course of this procedure a new student often received a lecture on some topic of interest to Dwight; only afterward did the president give the proper directions. Evarts complained about "supercilious" looks from college officials and a seemingly irrelevant "discourse upon vegetable animalculine putrefaction" but thoroughly enjoyed the room and board provisions at tutor Atwater's. In keeping with Americans' tendency to gastronomic excess, meals were large and the portions hefty.[18]

Throughout his freshman year the Vermont farm boy explored New Haven, a metropolis teeming with economic, political, and social activity. Fascinated by the urban environment, he quickly discovered the state's general assembly, then meeting in the city. Within a month of his arrival Evarts was attending the debates and dining with the representatives, including the governor and lieutenant governor. This sparked a lifelong interest in political affairs, although he never ran for public office. These encounters broadened his perspectives and shaped his future. They planted in him a conviction that men might embrace politics even while they avoided partisan divisions. New Haven contributed as much as Yale to his education. His studies and other college activities occupied the remainder of his time and energy. With his classmates he listened to the preaching of Dwight, heard speakers on current social and political questions, and occasionally played some football.[19]

He also suffered through less pleasant aspects of college life, for although American society was slowly losing its deferential character, democracy had not yet reached the colleges, and lower classmen received periodic reminders of their status. "In the afternoon," Evarts wrote on November 3, 1798, "the Senior Class assembled in the library and sent for ours, where, having locked us in, they gave us some directions how to behave with deference, decency, &c."[20] Rowdyism was rampant at American colleges in these years, and like other institutions Yale did its best to discourage the wholesale destruction of its facilities. Tutors bore the primary responsibility for vigilance, much to their dismay. In the Yale commons this meant "the presence of unhappy tutors feeding on elevated platforms, and by such devices as the exclusive use of pewter instead of glass and china." New Haven witnessed the added attraction of full-scale brawls when soldiers came to the college to attack the students.[21]

Evarts fully enjoyed his collegiate experience, however. Despite his feeling awkward and ill at ease when speaking before his class, his intellectual curiosity and quick mind led him to investigate the varieties of academic life. Two new tutors had been hired, Charles Denison and Benjamin Silliman, and he became acquainted with both. He joined the music society, visited President John Adams when he passed through New Haven, and saw the "philosophical apparatus and was shocked with electricity."[22] His formal studies included Virgil, Cicero's orations, Pike's arithmetic, and Greek. During short holidays he visited relatives in Guilford, but following his freshman year he undertook the two-week ride to Vermont, accompanied by his uncle, John Todd, to see his parents. There he encountered a smallpox epidemic and rode twenty miles to be innoculated, only to be reinnoculated two days later. He became very sick and went to the "pest house" for two weeks. "In my face there are 450 pustules. My mouth very sore, being filled with variolae, as well as my tongue, and some even came partly on my teeth." He reported for his sophomore year more than two months late.[23]

On his return to New Haven, Evarts immersed himself in his studies. He prepared several essays, each of which explored a theme to which he would later return. In his sophomore essay, "A Dissertation on *Amor Patriae*," he supported the beneficial effects of literary societies, arguing that, along with a love of one's country, they civilized man and prevented him from becoming a mere savage. Support for these societies was important, he insisted, because institutions to which people profess no attachment were useless.[24] His junior year essay, in 1801, discussed the question "Are the Abilities of Females Inferior to Those of Males?" Although he insisted that the constitutions of the sexes prepared them for different pursuits, that difference was not proof of inequality. He argued that the mental endowments of the sexes were equal, as children, although the education of women had been neglected. Women were equal to men, he concluded, but each sex had its primary sphere of activity.[25] These essays indicated not only his love for ideas but also a fascination with behavioral matters, a conservative inclination, and a humanitarian sentiment.

That spring the dark-complexioned junior was elected president of the Brothers' Society, was chosen orator by the Moral Society, and received election to Phi Beta Kappa. This series of honors punctuated a steady intellectual growth and a mounting concern for the nature of American society. His activities in the Moral Society especially reflected this awareness. The Yale Moral Society, a secret organization formed in 1797, was one of the earliest societies for moral reform. It mirrored, in part, the proclivities of Timothy Dwight's Yale to utilize voluntary moral and religious societies instead of politics to combat infidelity and foster public morality. Members, even as students, had to pass an admissions test in which they promised to use the Bible as their code of moral conduct, take all "prudent measures" to suppress vice and promote morality at Yale, avoid all use of profane language, and refrain from playing cards.[26]

By his senior year Evarts's routine consisted of going to prayers, studying, attending the meetings of various societies, and observing sessions of the General Assembly. He was also active in the New Haven community and taught school part-time. The latter, he declared, was "dull business."[27] Religion absorbed more and more of his attention, and Dwight's dictum that religion "is the chief end of man" preyed on his mind. He passed examinations in the "Greek Testament, Horace, Cicero de Oratore, English Grammar, Geography, Surveying, Algebra, Pike's Geometry, Conic Sections, Mensuration, Trigonometry, and Navigation" that September and a month later faced examinations in "Priestly, Philosophy and Astronomy." Meanwhile he published some poetry (a version of the twenty-ninth chapter of Job), became interested in literary criticism, and ventured out to see a dwarf on exhibit.[28]

But the centrality of religion and morality to assure republican virtue and the American future dominated his thoughts. Here the influence of Dwight was inescapable. The Yale president had warned his students as well as New Haven residents that the state of society was "disturbed." Although standard fare for many of the Federalist clergy after the election of Jefferson in 1800, Dwight's jeremiad nonetheless highlighted an increasingly self-conscious probing of the American experiment. America had been blessed, Dwight's contemporaries argued, but what would be the result? They observed that while God had aided our cause in the revolution, we now had a responsibility and a duty to curb ambition, avarice, and discord. "Whether we shall have wisdom and virtue enough," warned another clergyman, "to legislate by the man of our choice, and peaceably to obey as subjects; or whether we shall be rent and torn by party spirit and faction, until we fall under despotic rule, can be determined only by experience."[29] In his senior year at Yale Jeremiah Evarts underwent this same kind of introspective searching and in so doing drew together a perspective of society and his postgraduate objectives. His conversion in a revival that swept the college in 1802 sparked these convictions and shaped his adult life.

Revivals rose like spring freshets throughout New England in the early years of the nineteenth century. Some emerged amid a flurry of frenzied revivalism; others appeared suddenly and without warning, the product of extended anxiety and private religious experience. As quickly as they surfaced they received attention in the public and religious press. In a sense, therefore, these revivals all had a quasi-public character that commingled hopes and fears to produce an expectant air of fulfillment about them. For the converts, the revival was at once an easing of psychic tension and a rush of expectation. Converts both found answers and received direction. Like many other youths, Evarts grappled with this psychic dilemma. "From my own experience," he wrote, "I am induced to believe that evil spirits are continually present on this earth, and that they tempt and lead astray the minds of men. Else, whence does it so frequently happen to me, and to many others, that, when we are thinking seriously on any subject, the bent of our minds is suddenly turned aside, and something seems to force itself forward on purpose to attract attention."[30] Satanic intrusions swirled in youthful minds, and young men and women struggled for self-control and guidance.

The revival at Yale began in the spring of 1802, perhaps touched off by Timothy Dwight's sermon "The Youth of Nain." Urging the young men to repent before they died, Dwight sought to provoke conversions. Student after student testified to saving experiences, and in April Jeremiah Evarts joined the college church. More than eighty undergraduates had undergone this intense introspection and experienced conversion when the revival ended in August. At the same time that he encouraged the revival, however, Dwight sought to control it. He hoped to bring religion, order, and discipline to Yale without any raucous enthusiasm. What resulted, wrote junior Noah Porter, was a sudden and great "change in individuals, and in the general aspect of the college." This was no doubt welcome, for violence seemed the norm. Tutor Moses Stuart complained that students customarily rolled barrels down his stairs, cut bell ropes, and launched a "broadside at one of my windows, which popped off without ceremony six squares of glass."[31] New Haven, however, remained largely unaffected for the time being. The residents, Evarts lamented, were just too busy earning money to worry about spiritual matters.[32] At graduation he joined a mutual covenant with other converts among his classmates to "pray for each other, to learn one another's circumstances, and to correspond with, and counsel one another in subsequent life."[33]

Evarts's conversion experience was peaceful but pronounced. It marked a watershed in his life and set him on a course from which he would rarely stray. A concern for private and public morals and religious conviction remained with him until death. His conversion, as well as his contact with the preachings of Dwight, forever sensitized him to the need for character, trust, and virtue in public as well as private life. For Evarts, the conversion experience led to a new world, a world far different from that of his parents, and beckoned him to find a calling at once moral and influential. Conversion marked, therefore, a definitive break with the past, even though it did not yet settle his future. For the next few years Evarts struggled with that problem, first amid traditional family surroundings and then on his own in the urban atmosphere of New Haven.

Following graduation he returned to the family farm in Georgia, Vermont, to read, write, and ponder future employment. He clearly had no intention of becoming a farmer, but his recent conversion had led him to consider his life's work from a new perspective. Many of his classmates had entered the ministry, but while Evarts wanted to acquire some "professional knowledge," he had no particular course in mind. His health remained fragile, but he was intent on following an occupation that provided more than private rewards. In early 1803 he postponed a final decision and took a job as principal of the Caledonia County Grammar School in Peacham, Vermont.[34]

To superintend a school in rural Vermont, however, was not Jeremiah Evarts's purpose in life. He longed for the hustle and invigorating atmosphere of the city, despite his concern for vice and immorality. Politics attracted him too, but not for the joys of office holding or personal recognition. David Fischer has demonstrated that as political awareness spread, deference faded, and politics became more hotly contested and divisive throughout New England. With this upsurge, religion and politics frequently overlapped—as when dissenting sects petitioned to support only their own ministers and during periodic clashes between established churches and increasingly heterogeneous parishes. The postrevolutionary generation, the generation that came of age with Evarts, witnessed a social, political, and economic transformation. Public discussion of basic issues such as liberty and prosperity was heated, and Evarts feared that ephemeral concerns rather than civic virtue would be decisive. Before leaving for Peacham he had lamented: "I was at the Democratic Festival in New Haven. It was really a melancholy spectacle to any person who prefers truth, honesty and freedom, to falsehood, public fraud, and Jacobinic persecution."[35]

With his own recent religious conversion as a throbbing reminder, Evarts resolutely rejected the "vain amusements" and irreligion so rampant in Peacham and after only a few months began to look elsewhere. Admitting that his poor health seemed to preclude preaching, he nonetheless confessed that he was in "considerable doubt with respect to my duty as to a professor for life."[36] Tormented by self-doubt, his health precarious, his commitment to duty strong, Evarts finally decided to become a lawyer. His friends were surprised, almost shocked. Few had suspected that he would become anything but a preacher. But Evarts sought influence, so that he might advance the cause of religion and morality. The low state of religion in Vermont and elsewhere, coupled with the growing importance of the bar as Americans became increasingly prone to litigation, convinced him that one pious lawyer could become more influential than a host of clergymen. "If it is not right for a good man to study law," he wrote in reply to some criticism, "it certainly cannot be right for any man. . . . The law then must be given up as a . . . collection of harpies polluting everything by their impure touch."[37]

Seizing the theme he had articulated in his commencement address a year earlier, Evarts argued that lawyers and judges were essential to carry the laws into speedy execution. He would join their ranks. Commitment to virtue, not mere choice of a profession, determined those who were useful in the Christian cause. In a letter to a classmate at Yale, however, the young Vermonter confided the difficulty of the decision: "The great temptation to a lawyer is worldly-mindedness, and with it comes desire to conform to the world. Where these gain a prevalence, religion is cut up by the roots. My great fear would be, therefore, that I should not live a religious life, and consequently that I should never do any good in the world. These considerations repel me from the bar many times, but I am driven to seek for a third alternative. But the instruction of youth would be a confinement for life, if I could go through with it; for merchandize or agriculture I have no stock, and am ignorant of both."[38] His mind made up, Evarts returned to New Haven in April 1804 to study law under Judge Charles Chauncey.

This was, nonetheless, a rather paradoxical choice. Evarts was nothing if not a cultural traditionalist. Yet he had successively abandoned his parents and their farm, rejected teaching and the ministry as chosen professions, and embraced urban life and the new professionalism. Why? The explanation seems to lie in his determination to preserve cultural values and promote civic virtue. To do this he tried to place himself at a critical intersection. He wanted to position himself astride the confluence of influence and morality.

Doing good was important not only for Jeremiah Evarts but for many other persons of his generation. Duty, piety, and benevolence were urged on Americans of his era in an ever-increasing cadence. Fear spread that a rapidly growing population, a startling increase in urbanization, and new and greater opportunities for wealth were eroding any sense of social responsibility among the population. Unity and vigilance were essential to curtail divisiveness as well as to detect and expunge vice. Should one "leave society to its natural inconsiderateness, the monster grows unseen, diffuses contagion, and enervates the body." The metaphor itself indicated a perception of disease and infection. Individuals were secondary to the larger society, Evarts believed, except insofar as they acted as agents for doing good within that society. Those who possessed influence, and this Evarts hoped to have himself, were to rouse the virtuous (healthy) part of the community, form associations, and do battle for the Lord.[39]

Lawyers seemed least apt to embody virtue, however, for if the legal profession often brought political influence and wealth to its practitioners, it did not engender a feeling of trust from the general public and by definition thrived on litigiousness. The fact that many young men decided to practice law only at the last minute, and often as a refuge from some other occupation, raised questions about respectability and opportunism. Even Evarts seems to have realized this, praying that "God preserve me from sin in this arduous undertaking" as he began study with Judge Chauncey.[40]

At twenty-three years of age Jeremiah Evarts fit the profile of those then entering the law. Late entry seems typical for many young men with professional aspirations in the early nineteenth century. As Joseph Kett has indicated, such a pattern appears to have been particularly prevalent among those persons whose fathers were not themselves professionals. This suggests a conflict, as in Evarts's case, between father and son (or between son and his conscience) over occupational choice. A commitment to attend college marked the beginning of this separation, at least for the student, but such a choice was difficult for New England farmers' sons, and indecision characterized their lives for several years. Many, like Evarts, finally admitted the obvious; they had no inclination to return to the farm. Jeremiah Evarts negotiated this wrenching collision of familial hopes and filial expectations. Although little correspondence survives to detail the psychic dimensions of the crisis, later letters revealed a lingering awareness of its disruptive character. The process encouraged these individuals, moreover, to move closer to their classmates and form personal networks outside the family circle—just as Evarts and his friends had united in a mutual covenant before their graduation from Yale.[41]

Evarts's search for "influence" also betrayed a desire for some upward mobility. His objections to becoming a farmer went beyond concern for his health and indicated a longing for a different lifestyle. Whatever its vices and irreligious influence, New Haven had whetted his appetite. He could not endure the isolation of farming, of a rural community, and of confinement to the company of family and a few friendly but less-educated neighbors. By becoming a lawyer he could regulate his work (thereby maintaining his health) and join a larger and more cosmopolitan community. In reaching this decision Evarts joined other young men of his generation to form an emerging professional class, one that became increasingly influential in social and political activities and eventually trained its sons for similar careers.[42]

Once he returned to New Haven the new law student immersed himself in his studies, declining the offer of a tutorship at his alma mater. In September 1804 he married Mehitabel Sherman Barnes, daughter of the influential Roger Sherman and widow of Daniel Barnes. The new Mrs. Evarts, who had one son from her first marriage, had received a sound education from a private female tutor.[43] While Evarts worked toward his master's degree at Yale, the couple took in college boarders to supplement their income. In 1805 Jeremiah Evarts received his degree and delivered a commencement oration on the vanity of pursuing fame. Published the next year, the address warned (in what was becoming typical Evarts fashion) that all youth seeking eminence looked forward to lasting fame. In many respects a personal exegesis, this commentary on fame cautioned against excessive ambition and the erosion of character. Women often sought fame or distinction, Evarts argued, by "the beauty and dress of their persons." Men pursued it through displays of wit and opulence or by trampling on their competitors.[44]

That quest, according to Evarts, was where the real dilemma began, for "success invariably brings with it perplexities unknown before." Pursuit of fame led to a lust for superiority. The more competitors one surpassed, the more one hungered to overtake those that remained. The quest was endless, and vanity precluded acknowledgment that success was unlikely. Since those persons defined happiness in terms of success, their personal enjoyment was fleeting. Too often their happiness was mere pretense, and to advance their fortunes they subordinated the public good to personal enhancement. Evarts argued that Christian benevolence should replace ambition, for it would promote obedience to parents, usefulness to country, gratitude to God, and more general good than anything else.[45] Such an attitude, of course, flew in the face of an increasingly effervescent individualism. It marked its proponent, moreover, as a throwback to older Puritan concepts of self-control and the public good. For someone about to enter that maelstrom of individual contentiousness which marked the legal profession, it was a striking statement.

This concern for individual commitment, public benevolence, and religious awakening increasingly dominated Evarts's consciousness and behavior. Writing in the *Connecticut Evangelical Magazine*, he insisted that only an early conversion could improve people's lives and advance society.[46] Other spokesmen echoed this position and reiterated the connections between religion, public virtue, and republican government. Preservation of republican government, argued one Thanksgiving speaker, required that the people be both well-informed and religious. "To neglect the promotion of useful and moral instruction is therefore to neglect our national interests."[47] Such utterances, moreover, came without reference to specific issues of the day. The concern seemed to be not so much any particular transgressions, but the general spirit of the people. "The foundation of our government," observed one Fourth of July orator, "is the virtue of the people, this virtue is made up of individual virtue." To neglect this weakened the government, for a virtuous nation would be a powerful one. Morality and true religion were the guarantors of political liberty, just as benevolence and wisdom were the bulwarks against poverty, ignorance, and idleness.[48]

Only a damping of the fires of personal ambition and strict adherence to Christian behavioral models would curb political discord and heal national divisions. Fast Day speakers and Fourth of July orators argued that only the true Christian was the true republican, for only by conforming to the golden rule did one rise above "party prejudice." Inattention to this virtue, they warned, would cause the United States to follow the path of Rome toward licentiousness and decay.[49] Only individuals, not the state, could check these dangerous tendencies, for in individuals and the societies they formed lay ultimate responsibility. For Evarts and others who held these convictions, therefore, every instance of religious awakening or missionary exertion signaled hope, progress, and the approaching millennium.[50]

On June 4, 1806, Jeremiah Evarts was admitted to the Connecticut bar and opened an office in New Haven. Although he had come to accept the necessity of defending "unjust" clients, he never completely resolved his misgivings about such practices. His judgments about a client's worthiness must have been well known, for although he was well-read and a good lawyer, he never became very popular. Strictly conscientious, Evarts lacked that all-consuming ambition for which the profession was notorious and about which he had warned. He drew his pleasure from reading the *Panoplist* and from his activities in the religious life of New Haven. Four years earlier, after all, he had formed a covenant with his classmates. Why couldn't persons in the larger society execute similar covenants with one another and join in common cause? This would remedy the prevailing neglect of piety and integrity. It would allow "civil rule" to be "built on the basis of morality." Justice, in his eyes, meant more than the legal renderings of courts and judges. It signaled correct behavior, republican principles, and "true patriotism."[51] Daniel Dana, pastor of a Presbyterian church in Newburyport, Massachusetts, provided a compelling rationale for the need of public officials to hold such beliefs, one that Evarts maintained for the rest of his life.

> In proportion as vice and irreligion prevail among a people, they become of course incapable of self-government. If a sense of moral obligation be relaxed; if licentiousness in principle and practice pervade all classes in the community . . . if the young grow up without instruction and without virtue—what is the inevitable consequence? The best men, wearied with a fruitless struggle against corruption, will retire from the public service in despair, or be violently thrust from office. Unprincipled, selfish, and ambitious spirits will seize the reins of power. . . . And the liberties of such a people . . . will finally fall a sacrifice to some ambitious chief, more successful, and probably more abandoned, than the rest.[52]

His reputation for honesty and diligence notwithstanding, Evarts's law business remained limited. Prospective clients were less interested in fusing morality with law to secure justice than in winning lawsuits. Evarts was either ahead of his time or out of step with his profession. Income barely met expenses, and only his practice of accepting boarders enabled him to meet family needs. Building a successful law practice took time, to be sure, but his conscience and his interests in benevolence diverted his energies elsewhere. He aspired to be a gentleman, to engage in philanthropic endeavors, but lacked the income that would permit this. Even so, he stretched his budget to contribute fifty dollars to a Vermont "evangelical society" for educating pious boys for the ministry. This quickly became another of his causes, an undertaking that would educate young men properly and increase the availability of ministers. It would also end up changing the composition of that profession and the nature of education.[53]

In 1806 he published an analysis of education and its relationship to social and political institutions. Education was important, he argued, but was difficult to acquire and perhaps not suitable for all men. Rejoicing that the myths of the French Revolution, which pronounced that all men "were speedily to become learned," were now dispelled, Evarts cautioned that more than "information alone was necessary to reform mankind."[54]

All knowledge, secular and religious, could bring enlightenment, but only to those who worked at true understanding. Education was not an ordinary transaction of life; all men were not competent to become teachers. The tendency to consider every man an oracle, which Evarts believed to be the product of the French Revolution and the 1790s, led only to mindless innovation and the demolition of carefully constructed systems of knowledge. Thankfully, he concluded all that was now changing—at least at colleges in New England. "Sound erudition" was returning, for "the severer studies have regained that ground, which a number of years since, they were forced to abandon to that light and frothy stuff, which, under a hundred names, our booksellers' shops were pouring upon the public."[55] Pursuit of romantic studies would give way, he hoped, as students returned to the study of languages, mathematics, and the classics.

What was this froth that Evarts bemoaned? It was to be found most frequently in popular novels, which corrupted the public taste and whose popularity testified to a growing concern with ephemeral matters. Serious mental reflection had given way to the pursuit of wealth and a corresponding increase in elegance and idleness. The apparent success of speculators, moreover, enticed others to gamble in hopes of attracting wealth and public attention. All this worldliness contradicted Evarts's ideal of a society whose inhabitants were devoted to serious study, hard work to avoid poverty, and a genuine concern for one's fellow man.[56]

In adhering to his ideals, the young lawyer was at once fighting the onrush of self-indulgent individualism and consigning himself to a lifetime of labor.

All these tendencies pointed, finally, to another unwelcome consequence—the "clamours of partisans." Even more troubling to Evarts than vanity and ambition was the struggle for public recognition through partisan huckstering. Persistence and a confident (if often ignorant) assertion of a position now seemed sufficient to gain public office. A new formula had emerged, Evarts lamented, one marked by electioneering and intrigue. "The candidate for distinction joins himself to a party, or, in more philosophical language, to a sect, and labours without hesitation and without respite, to make himself acceptable to the people, or the great men under whose banner he enlists."[57] By party Evarts meant any group that championed particular causes, regardless of its organizational structure. Men will now gain office, he complained, by bartering "conscience to the highest bidder." Party competition would arouse animosities, "drown the voice of wisdom," and prevent "worthy persons" from being elected. He feared that good men would retire to private life and that the public would be misled—unable to distinguish between meritorious public servants and the "most vociferous bawler."[58]

Such a possibility profoundly shocked and disturbed Evarts. That his world was losing its cohesion was bad enough; that it might also ignore morality and social responsibility portended disaster. But ever the optimist, the young lawyer argued that a competent judiciary was the "grand pillar by which the edifice of society is supported." Trained to advance justice to the exclusion of all else, lawyers were best fit to be rulers. In this statement, however, Evarts admitted that far too many in his profession chose popularity over integrity. For Evarts, justice meant morality, a legal opinion informed by religious principles.[59]

During the next four years, while he practiced law in New Haven, Jeremiah Evarts devoted increasing attention to religious affairs. He helped organize the Connecticut Religious Tract Society, served as its secretary while he remained in the city, and wrote many of its tracts. He and his wife also joined New Haven's First Church, then under the superintendance of the Reverend Moses Stuart. Both became active, and Jeremiah was chosen a deacon. Much of his time, however, he devoted to observing the state legislature and promoting the influence of religious principles in daily life. Typical was a letter to Leonard Worcester in Vermont which reported legislative efforts to repeal all support for religion and lamented that it was "greatly to be desired that people would learn that men of piety, virtue, public spirit, and patriotism, make the best rulers, and ought on *all* occasions to be preferred to those whose private lives are infamous."[60]

This connection between religion, politics, and the quality of American life fascinated Evarts, and under a variety of pseudonyms he contributed related articles to the *Panoplist*. He had by this time determined not to return to Vermont, regardless of his success in the law. This decision clearly upset his family, and his brother pleaded with him to take care of his property and his parents. His relatives needed him, his brother wrote, "especially Parents who took great pains to give you a liberal education expecting you to live in Georgie [Vermont] to be a comfort to them through life, but that is now decided you never mean to come. That is I think you do not. I wish you to have pity on your relations and move here to be a consolation to them though you will at your pleasure be it who will want you should come."[61]

Away from the farm and now professionally situated in New Haven, Jeremiah was not about to succumb to maudlin appeals or guilt and get behind the plow. His world was too different from that of rural Vermont, his objectives too large in scope and far-reaching in purpose to abandon. In addition, he had come to believe that his efforts *could* make a difference. Within a year after forming the Religious Tract Society, he wrote his sister that "the appearance of the town is greatly changing for the better." Attendance at religious meetings had risen, amusements had decreased in number, and many of the "young females" were meeting weekly for "reading and religious conversation."[62] This progress, or appearance of progress, sustained his commitment and confirmed his belief that everyone was capable of proper moral behavior with a little direction and encouragement.

In January of 1809, however, the struggling lawyer received an invitation to become assistant editor of the *Panoplist*. This would require him to leave his house on Chapel Street across from the college and move to the Boston area. It also presented Evarts with the opportunity to acquire that influence he so avidly desired and to find a setting compatible with his religious principles and moral scruples. The *Panoplist*, begun in 1805 by the Reverend Jedidiah Morse as a counterweight to the inroads of Unitarianism at Harvard, had by 1808 joined with the *Massachusetts Missionary Magazine* of the Reverend Leonard Woods to unite Hopkinsians and Old Calvinists as a bulwark against religious liberalism.[63]

Jedidiah Morse was twenty years older than Evarts. Like Evarts he had been reared on a farm, become sickly as a child, and acquired a fondness for books that paralleled his aversion to farm work. During his undergraduate years at Yale he had professed religion, in the face of ridicule from other students. He had been elected to Phi Beta Kappa and then following graduation taught school in New Haven. Later Morse studied divinity with Jonathan Edwards, Jr., wrote and published widely (and profitably) on geography, returned to Yale as a tutor, and received a license to preach throughout the state of Connecticut. In 1789 he had been installed in the pulpit of the Charlestown, Massachusetts, First Society. He was close to Boston, and the position carried with it a seat on the Harvard Board of Overseers.[64] This vantage point gave Morse a commanding view of the religious turmoil that accompanied the Second Great Awakening. With a career somewhat similar to date, Evarts would also find the new position uniquely suitable for his interests and activities.

Before accepting the assistantship, however, Evarts raised some questions about compensation. He was increasingly conscious of the need to provide his family with adequate support. In fact, so bleak were his financial prospects in New Haven as a lawyer that he had determined to go "eastward" at all events—if not to the *Panoplist*, then perhaps as a writer, bookseller, or even as a lawyer. That fall, traveling south to recover his health, Morse stopped in New Haven again to offer Evarts a position, this time as editor. Perhaps as a means of securing a larger salary, Evarts encouraged Morse but stopped short of acceptance. He later wrote a probing letter to Morse in South Carolina, noting that "if I could get established in literary pursuits, with a good provision for my family, I frankly confess I should prefer it to the practice of the law, tho' I would not have you suppose that I have an antipathy to my profession. But beyond all doubt it is best for me to remove as a *lawyer*. In two or three years it can be determined to which class of pursuits it is best to devote my whole strength."[65] Convinced that his talents were "better fitted for practice at the bar than for any other employment, *if I could only get business*," Evarts nonetheless accepted the editorship of the *Panoplist* in 1810.[66]

Jeremiah Evarts in February 1810 journeyed by himself to Charlestown, Massachusetts, to begin his duties. His family remained in New Haven to close its affairs, moving to Charlestown in May. In a manner characteristic of the slender, blue-eyed farmer's son, Evarts's letters to friends about his decision seemed designed more for personal reassurance than anything else. He had been guaranteed $1,000 a year, which seemed "competent support in Charlestown." Work on the *Panoplist* placed Evarts with the advance guard of moral reform, and he quietly confided that "the employment would be the means of doing much good."[67] Twenty-nine years of age, at last he had found work suited to his taste. By June he and his wife had joined the First Church in Charlestown and seemed to have found a community of friends mutually supportive of their interest in moral reform.

With his decision to join Jedidiah Morse in Charlestown, Evarts left a profession that was at once becoming influential and coming under attack from critics. But in many respects he was already out of step with many of his colleagues, who were more interested in monetary or political gain than in benevolence or in diffusing religious principles throughout society. The former held little attraction for Evarts. Instead he devoted himself to missionary work and to advancing efforts at moral reform—all in pursuit of a set of cultural values that recalled Puritan self-discipline while they also formed a foundation for a Christian republicanism.[68] The next two decades thrust unprecedented change upon Evarts's generation, and while some of it would be narrowly religious, or economic, or political, in sum it represented a sweeping cultural transformation.

CHAPTER TWO

More Than a Revival: The Second Great Awakening and New England Society

Jeremiah Evarts's decision to edit the *Panoplist* not only put him at the convergence of political and religious controversies and gave him a vehicle to articulate his Christian republicanism, but also it came at a fortuitous time for an advocate of benevolent reform. Much as the Yale revival had triggered a spate of conversions and increased membership in the Moral Society as it swept across the New Haven campus in 1802, so, too, did similar revivals of the Second Great Awakening revitalize and transform New England society. To understand the milieu of early nineteenth-century reform as well as the formative influences that shaped the character and ideology of Jeremiah Evarts, one must examine the awakening, where it came from, and what it spawned. For whether he was a leader or merely a participant in humanitarian reform, Evarts was never a solitary character. Just as he had made a compact with his Yale classmates, so he sought to create covenants with like-minded individuals whereby all might draw sustenance from a unity of spiritual purpose. The Second Great Awakening was a pivotal force in the cultivation of those covenanted communities and undergirded Evarts's search for the soul of America. The description of an early Connecticut revival published in the *Connecticut Evangelical Magazine* typified what followed. "This awakening was not, in a single instance, attended with outcry, or noise. The subjects of it appeared very solemn while attending public worship, and conferences. In conversation they complained of their ignorance and stupidity—they wondered that they had not before seen themselves on the brink of everlasting ruin; and expressed a strong desire to be instructed in the doctrines of the gospel, and to be dealt with in the plainest manner.... In those who appeared to become the subjects of saving grace, their first alarm was followed with a more full discovery of their moral pollution."[1]

Like hundreds of similar accounts published during the early years of the nineteenth century, this tale of religious revival elucidated themes of awakening, maturation, moral virtue, and, ultimately, revitalization—themes that characterized the Second Great Awakening. Whether begun by shopkeepers, middle-class women, children, the clergy, or pious laymen, the Second Great Awakening did more than form a chronological bridge between the American Revolution and the Age of Jackson. It marked America's coming of age and transformed the world of Jeremiah Evarts. If conversion was a rite of passage for the religious, the attempt to reconcile perceptions of moral decline with the visionary ideals of the revolution marked a similar pubescent stage for the nation. In addition, Americans had to adjust to the reality implicit in this metaphor; the nation was maturing. How could it retain the youthful vitality and innocence that in retrospect seemed so characteristic of the revolutionary years? Wasn't it the fate of all states, even republics, to become corrupt and to decay? As Thomas Jefferson had noted in 1781, "The spirit of the times may alter, will alter. Our rulers will become corrupt, our people careless.... From the conclusion of this war we shall be going down hill."[2]

The American Revolution changed more than the colonists' governments. It altered their behavioral patterns, their perceptions, and even their memories. What had once been a disparate array of individual colonies now, perforce, became a "nation." After acting together in the heat of protest and revolt, Americans often forgot that their unity was freshly forged, fragile, and perhaps even transitory. To patriots, the events and rhetoric of the revolt seemed etched forever, a vindication for their vigilance and virtue over the years. They ignored, in short, their own history; in the rush to create a new future, they remembered a different past. And once free from England, citizens and soldiers alike had to contend with the same blandishments of luxury, vice, and corruption that they had so valiantly opposed.

The revolutionary victory pleased Americans, of course, but it also made them wary and even a bit uncertain. Any deviation from the existing social or political situation they ascribed to corruption. Virtue assumed an almost religious aura and became at once the measure of behavior. The patriots, in sum, tried to maintain an equilibrium—to codify and perpetuate their expectations and visions in both behavioral and institutional terms. Yet in many respects there was no clear consensus about the nature of that equilibrium. Ideological, occupational, and geographical perceptions varied as did Americans. By the late 1790s almost every opinion had its opposite, and all claimed to represent virtue and consensus. Whether or not corruption *had* become more virulent by the 1790s, many Americans believed that it had and acted accordingly. Jeremiads issued forth from pulpit and lectern, seeking to arouse Americans against internal enemies—both of the spirit and of the flesh.[3]

As patriots saw in their revolution a model to be emulated by victims of tyranny elsewhere, so they conceived of a model citizen who would inculcate virtue and republican behavior at home. This they defined so as to embrace industry, frugality, morality, honesty, and the willingness to set aside self-interest to advance the public good.[4] They sought to seize a moment of unity and forge a republican future. That this agenda ignored basic divergences within American society they pushed aside; that the dream might become a nightmare they did not address. The revolution had created a hope, and although the reality that was America often transformed that hope into a myth, Americans themselves seldom lost sight of that hope nor ceased to believe in its ultimate realization.[5] Deviations from this model provoked alarms, including religious and secular jeremiads, and induced flurries of "reform" activities.

Americans saw the present as a portent of the future and believed that the increasing divisiveness of the 1790s forecast decay and decline. Revolutionary success had seemingly unleashed a dangerous heterogeneity. Ironically, as the very ideal of organic unity became more widespread, it also became less realistic.[6] Americans surely overemphasized the delicacy of a republic, but in doing so they signaled how closely they believed popular behavior and moral character to be linked. Speaking before the Humane Society of Massachusetts in 1808, Thomas Danforth enunciated these concerns. "Those virtues, which we flatter ourselves we all possess, we are too apt to neglect to cultivate. . . . If you permit the urbanity and duties of social intercourse, to be frequently undermined by the violence of party passion, or the malevolence of disappointed ambition, it may not be difficult to stain the character of free men with crimes."[7]

In many respects observers took the very successes of the revolutionary settlement—the growth, the prosperity, the realization of political liberty—to be indicators of decay. They feared what people would do with these, and their uneasiness led them to advocate behavioral controls. "National strength depends on national union," argued Joseph Lathrop, "and this depends either on internal virtue, or on external coercion."[8]

From a variety of perspectives, by the late 1790s the times also seemed ripe for a public religious awakening. Among Congregationalists, New Lights struggled with Old Lights for doctrinal supremacy. In other quarters the progress of Baptist and Methodist groups challenged the religious status quo, dividing parishes so that religious squabbles spilled over into politics and thereby heightening both the intensity of the debate and the impact of its resolution. Throughout all this period the clergy and other public figures publicly vented their concern about the state of society and asserted that a broad religious declension in the years since the revolution was to blame for any and all social ills. Whether or not this deterioration was true was irrelevant, for these advocates believed it to be true. They blamed the rise of avaricious, self-indulgent patterns of behavior on such a declension. What they were really doing (or so they later discovered) was placing themselves squarely in the path of an onrushing intellectual current, the liberalization of American society and of its individual and institutional relationships.[9] An increasingly naked individualism and self-seeking sprang from a cauldron of ambition and optimism in the American psyche and revealed that growing numbers of Americans seemed convinced that the millennium was secular and could be realized in their lifetime. Spokesmen like Timothy Dwight opposed this new liberalism and sounded the alarm. "One spirit actuates you all. From the success, or failure, of your exertions in the cause of virtue, we anticipate the freedom or slavery of our country. Even the new government of the United States, from which so many advantages are expected, will neither restore order, nor establish justice among us, unless it be accompanied and supported by morality, among all classes of people."[10]

Implementation of a national covenant, however, would prove difficult. The idea rested on shared assumptions and values. But here the harmonic memory of the revolution proved deceptive. Liberty could be both a goal and a vehicle for sociopolitical change, and many ardent supporters of the revolt had difficulty reconciling the two.[11] When Congregationalists recalled the revolution, for instance, they celebrated the triumph over tyranny and Anglicanism. But when Baptists and Methodists celebrated the same events, and then argued for *their* religious freedom, they alarmed Congregationalists. In other words, the majority of Americans believed that liberty and virtue were fundamental to republicanism, but they could not unite on a precise or common definition of just what those terms embraced. Those words, therefore, became themselves subject to debate. To assert unity proved far simpler than to forge it.[12]

New England ministers raised the specter of broad religious declension and linked it to moral decay. Led by the Congregational clergy, these alarmists mistook social differentiation and change for genuine religious decline. From their narrow perspective, however, they did have a point. Clerical dismissals and parish contentiousness rose, state tax support of religion came under attack, and religiously inspired law suits multiplied. But in other quarters, notably among Baptists and Methodists, church enrollments grew—and rapidly.[13] Those who pointed to a decline in religion, moreover, often really meant a diminished devotion to the clergy. But what they chronicled was change, not abandonment—a phenomenon that one observer aptly summarized: "as I shall shew presently, the attachment which the people have formerly had to their ministers, is by no means abated, although that servile awe, which, in a royal government, was felt both towards magistrates and ministers, may have been dissipated by the revolution."[14] This change reveals the waning of deference, not complete social or religious dissipation.

Behind all of this, furthermore, was an increasing fascination with power and authority throughout the country, often at the expense (or apparently at the expense) of religion. Election sermons still called for "good" government and wise rulers, but a new temperament seemed to be emerging in the face of secular change.[15] If the revolution was to have been in part a movement for moral reform, was its promise being fulfilled? The growing atomism of American society seemed to indicate that it was not, especially as this atomism was reflected in the growth of competing religious denominations. In short, disappointment had set in, and in some quarters this disappointment turned to alarm. "The decay of religion is a matter of real lamentation to many good men among us" insisted one critic.[16]

What emerged by the end of the 1790s, therefore, was a two-fold phenomenon; a response both to a perceived decline in religiosity and to an individualistic spirit in American society. The response sought to curb a growing selfishness; it tried to redefine liberty so as to include public benevolence and virtue and exclude political contentiousness and gross individualism. As one observer put the issue in 1799, "Private interest, or the good of the individual, farther than it may be considered as involved in the good of the whole, ought not to be, and cannot consistently be the object of the social compact. As the whole is greater than its parts, so the good of the community is greater than the private interest of any individual."[17]

These stimuli for the Second Great Awakening formed a continuum between the American Revolution and the political debates of the Jackson years. When Timothy Dwight argued in 1788 that "Liberty can exist only in the society of virtue," he was merely restating Benjamin Rush's earlier remark that "Liberty without virtue would be no blessing to us." But by 1800 optimism had given way to alarm, and this alarm led to activism.[18] In religious circles pastors talked about "declension"; elsewhere other spokesmen referred to a "crisis." Although the nature of this crisis was ambiguous, belief in its existence was not.[19] To combat this malaise and provide cathartic relief, two phenomena emerged: religious revivals and efforts at a general awakening.

❂

The Second Great Awakening usually refers to the wave of religious revivals that appeared in the United States from the late 1790s through the 1830s as well as to the emergence of voluntary societies along the trail of the revivals. There is no doubt that the awakening and the revivals emerged coincident with one another and that on occasion they were causally intertwined, but as a whole the two phenomena were independent of one another. That is, revivals were a response to a perception of religious decline, and even to interdenominational competition, while the awakening itself was a response to broader concerns about public morality and insufficient republican virtue. This sequence had been the experience of Jeremiah Evarts at Yale, for instance, where a moral society formed several years *before* a religious revival swept the college. To confuse the two impulses, or to merge one with the other, is to misjudge the thrust of both efforts. An upsurge of religiosity might well spark a concomitant increase of morality, and vice-versa, but obtaining a conversion was not the same as convincing someone to contribute fifty cents to join a moral society. As William McLoughlin has noted, revivals "alter the lives of individuals" while awakenings "alter the world view of a whole people or culture."[20] This difference is important, for it indicates the intent as well as the scope of early nineteenth-century moral reform.

The awakening and the revivals that contributed to it represented an effort not only to reinvigorate religion but to revitalize the entire culture as well. Leaders of the awakening feared that Americans had lost their moral underpinnings; leaders of the revival thought they had lost religious commitment and direction. The former seemed to be essential to preserve the meaning of the revolution, whereas the latter had a deeper personal meaning. Because both awakenings and revivals embrace notions of death and rebirth, they are stylistically similar. And because personnel instrumental in the two movements often overlapped, we tend to confuse the techniques and objectives of one with the other.[21] In the long run, of course, the two efforts complemented one another. Revivals would become a vehicle for the new moral ethos.

Revitalization efforts of various kinds sought to alleviate Americans' feelings of declension and to construct a more cohesive culture. "The physical existence of human beings," insisted Thomas Danforth, "is doubtless dependent on laws, which influence the rest of nature. The moral agent does not exist independent of the physical."[22] Violation of those laws led to "erroneous associations," which in turn eroded virtue. Linking religion, civil government, and national happiness, the Reverend Nathan Perkins carried this idea one step further—arguing that "piety and morality are the only CERTAIN MEANS of national happiness and prosperity."[23] Full revitalization, then, would effectively join religion, morality, industriousness, happiness, virtue, and prosperity to create a national culture. Behavioral patterns reflected values, and values had become cultural symbols, whether applied to the individual, the family, or the nation. The Reverend Edward Payson indicated just this sort of connective tissue when he noted the effects on Portland, Maine, of Jefferson's Embargo Act. "The embargo, humanly speaking, will be detrimental to the morals of the people here. They have now nothing to do but saunter about, and then, of course, they get in all manner of mischief; and I fear they will lose all habits of industry and sobriety. However, if I have any health, we shall endeavor to multiply meetings, and take up as much of their time as possible in that way."[24]

Although religious revivals had occurred sporadically throughout the years following the First Great Awakening, by the mid-1790s many churches and pastors began actively to encourage their appearance. Quarterly concerts of prayer, used fifty years earlier by Jonathan Edwards, reappeared in churches across New England, New York, and New Jersey. When revivals did occur, accounts of them were quickly printed in periodicals such as the *Connecticut Evangelical Magazine* and the *Panoplist*. These reports were also read at conferences and accorded notice at various gatherings.[25]

Religious revivals may be in part social phenomena that ultimately attempt to reshape society and advance particular cultural values. But initially they are fundamentally and intensely personal. When persons who have long been church members, or who perhaps have become adolescents or adults and entered a new phase of their lives, discover that their former feelings about religion are not very strong (and that their new feelings are), they undergo a *sudden* transformation. They discover a newfound zeal and embrace a new sense of piety and religious commitment. In the early nineteenth-century revivals these experiences were not only personal; they fostered a belief that the individual was in part responsible for his or her own salvation. This encouraged an active Christianity and made the religious revivals the instruments for a larger awakening. It gave the clergy and other advocates of religion and reform an almost limitless audience, for every person represented a heart to be converted and a mind to be awakened. In both instances advocates sought to reach the masses and believed their efforts to be central to the preservation of the republic.

Christianity and republicanism were both to be active faiths. For proponents of the revivals enlargement of the religious community promised to move the country toward realization of that near-mythic national community that the revolution had seemed to promise. The religious and the secular would then be one, and "the apparent moral change will be accomplished speedily and wonderfully."[26] Efforts to promote religious community through individualizing religious commitment and salvation, however, fell victim to some of the same problems that had made its supporters so critical of the growing individualism throughout American society.

How and why revivals appeared often mystified people. They usually followed a period when local attention to religion had sunk to new lows and as such carried with them the hope that perhaps they signaled more than individuals' concern for their own salvation. A millennial expectation accompanied these revivals, and various representatives were quick to enumerate the public benefits of such occurrences. Typical of those who did so was Nathan Strong, who linked individual salvation with public and political virtue.

> By this we do not wish to understand that civil government, either in the legislative or in the executive branches, shall be committed to the Church, in its ecclesiastical capacity, for Christ's kingdom never was and never will be

of this world. But the meaning of the prophecy [of the millennium] is that men shall generally be pious and sincere professors in the Church of Christ, and by the direction of providence and the choice of mankind, those will be raised to the highest places in civil trust who are eminent for their obedience to the truth. The state will encourage religion and the prevalence of religion will dispose the people to maintain government, order, subordination, and justice.[27]

The revivals advanced a theory of moral agency. The spread of individual salvation was necessary to the maintenance of public virtue, for "the government of our country is a government of opinion rather than force." Revivals embraced a doctrinal system that located moral accountability in individual responsibility but linked this moral ethos to the larger social environment. As Jeremiah Evarts had argued in his Yale graduation essay, sinners who violated moral laws committed a crime against national governments as well as against God's government. National vice led to national calamities, and New Divinity theologians sought to inculcate a sense of personal responsibility for one's moral condition. Regeneration, whether secular or religious, would lead individuals from selfishness to a disinterested benevolence. Effective moral agency betokened national salvation. Corrupt rulers could always be replaced, but only so long as the people avoided depravity, for "if the people themselves become corrupt, it is an evil without a remedy." Revivals were to put "the mind into active operation on the one hand, and to purify the fountains of moral conduct on the other." They were to be engines of great power.[28]

The doctrines implicit in the revivals advanced a thesis of revitalization. They sought not only to reawaken slumbering religious sentiments among the converted and the friends of religion but to reach beyond those individuals to the larger society. That is, although revivals used conversions as a measure of their success, they sought to reach beyond conversion to stir broader moral and religious sentiments. The age sector converted in these revivals, after all, does not demonstrate the demographics of religious conviction, only the demographics of religious conversion. It is only a partial profile of a segment of society not previously religious. Any expansion of church membership had to be drawn from the population at risk. Since revitalization assumed that politics could not be divorced from morality, and since proponents of the awakening insisted that morality sprang from the bosom of religious conviction, the doctrines of the revivals carried with them an activist impulse.

What were these doctrines? Historian Edward Lyrene succinctly enumerated them to include "(1) the sovereignty of God in the government of the world and in the dispensation of His grace, (2) the entire depravity of the human heart, (3) accountability to God, (4) necessity of regeneration by the special influences of the Holy Spirit, (5) justification by faith alone in the merits of Christ, (6) the nature of true repentance and faith, (7) the character of true obedience, (8) the place of good works in the Christian's life, and (9) the destruction of the neglectful."[29] This activist impulse found expression in the Hopkinsian definition of "disinterested benevolence." During the next two decades this concept emerged as a cornerstone not only of revivals but of the revitalization movement, for it sought to reconcile self-interest with true Christianity. For individuals like Jeremiah Evarts, drawing upon the legacy of Timothy Dwight, it became a foundation for an aggressive Christian republicanism.

Once under way, the revivals provided an opportunity to reassess the state of the nation and its inhabitants. This was, after all, in the best spirit of the revolution, and the public reassertion of a national covenant highlighted a sense that the earlier spirit had now been reborn. That the public had suddenly been religiously awakened seemed all the more providential where one could point to the absence of enthusiastic preaching or other measures considered dangerous. Timothy Dwight might seem strikingly alarmist, but men like Nathaniel Emmons did not. This difference was important, in part because religious conservatives feared a repetition of disorders that had accompanied the First Great Awakening, and in part because the steady spread of the revivals perhaps forecast the approach of the millennium. Concerned that the revivals' converts remain in the church after the revival itself passed, ministers were cautious in their acceptance of conversion narratives. Once convinced of their authenticity, however, they quickly moved to have them published so as to carry the revival's message to a wider audience. The *Connecticut Evangelical Magazine* and other publications emerged to broadcast this message and in so doing gave impetus not only to the revival but to the organizing impulse and the broader awakening that followed. In short time an organizational network emerged from a web of interrelationships among the clergy themselves, their college classmates now in other fields, a growing number of societies that aimed to advance particular causes, and a variety of journals that publicized these societies and causes.[30]

Revival narratives disseminated the meaning of this religious awakening to the broader public. While concerts for prayer and myriad sermons drew people's attention to the importance of religion, the printed narratives provided evidence of their personal impact and significance. In a response typical of others, a recent convert revealed his deepening commitment. "Then my mind turned on the cause of Zion. I longed to have it built up, and the present work go on. I thought of the poor heathen, and said, O that the angel with the everlasting gospel might fly through the earth! I could love my enemies; and confess to every one whom I had ignored."[31] Local pastors wrote long narratives describing their towns' encounters with this phenomenon, sketching the condition of religion before the onset of any religious excitement, the course of the revival, and its impact upon the religious condition of the community. The narratives became a literary form in themselves.[32]

In many respects conversion or participation in an orderly revival became a mark of respect, an outward sign of middle-class status. This is not to suggest that persons converted or professed conversion merely to acquire a toehold of respectability or to enhance their local reputation, for the conversion experience remained an intensely personal one. But when others quantified and publicized the progress of a revival and at the same time indicated a link between the numbers of converts and the manifestation of a national covenant, they openly sanctioned public acceptance of such a connection. In so doing they oversimplified a complex process, leading opponents of the revivals to charge that they were fabricated for partisan or professional purposes.[33] In substance the revivals and subsequent awakening responded to this by attempting to demonstrate that "doing good" was in an individual's self-interest. "I believe it my duty," wrote one such adherent, "to oppose every thing wrong in the world, in the churches, in ministers, and in myself."[34]

Four social institutions were the focus of particular concern throughout this process: schools, churches, the family, and civil government. For proponents of the awakening these represented the essential institutions, and changes (or perceptions of change) in any one of them prompted suspicions about their health or influence. On the other hand, they believed that full integration of these institutions into a cohesive social web would promote stability and quicken bourgeois values.[35] This attempt to revitalize the spirit and forge a middle-class respectability to accommodate social change and preserve "essential" values seems to have begun in small towns before invading the larger urban areas.

The small town became the early battleground of the awakening. As a community became more heterogeneous, leaders from its various sectors tried to assert a moral authority. To do so they turned to revivals and awakenings, hoping that these would counterbalance the egocentric and fragmenting tendencies of an expanding religious and political democracy and ameliorate an unease of the sort expressed by the Reverend Asa Packard. "I am going to Town Meeting with a heavy heart. The meanest—most vicious, ignorant, & contemptible democrat, will nullify my vote by depositing his own. This single circumstance, viz. the suffrage of the rabble, (always dupes to the awful demagogue) is a mortal, destructive germ in our constitution. But what remedy is possible?"[36] All voters might not enjoy a middle-class respectability, but an infusion of moral sensibility would presumably make them more sympathetic to republican virtues. If they were more aware of their own moral condition, perhaps they would be more attentive to their own behavior and that of others in the republic. It was a grand vision held together by a fragile hope.

Supporters of the revivals hoped to see multiplied a quiet introspection that would replace or subdue a turbulent secularism. One report of a Connecticut revival highlighted the values they most treasured. "The silence observable among those who were going to or returning from these meetings, was very impressive, and frequently noticed with surprise and pleasure. Little or no tumult or noise, and the appearances of most, much as if they had been going to, or more returning from the funeral of some near relative or friend. . . . Many were swift to hear, but all slow to speak."[37] But whom did the revivals most affect? What was their impact on the conduct of individuals within society? When the revivals faded, what remained?

Church membership clearly increased during the revivals. As the new religious fervor emphasized not only individual sin but individuals' free will and their moral ability to achieve salvation, it approached the larger individualistic ethos then so prevalent in this country. Instead of inducing a dichotomy between the secular and the religious, the awakening in some quarters produced a tension that sought to guide worldly endeavors by appeals to individual conscience. For many converts, especially those not yet fully engaged in the new patterns of behavior, the revivals had particular appeal. These persons, moreover, were the most vulnerable and susceptible to a moral uneasiness that the revivals sought to resolve. Young adults and women formed the two largest groups of converts.[38]

Much has been written about conversion and its meaning during the First and Second Great Awakenings. Whatever the instance, there does appear to be a connection between the timing of youthful conversions and maturity. That is, later ages of conversion reflect a delayed process of maturity. Although this delay may reveal something about individual personalities, it is far more important as a broad social indicator. When young persons (and at this time males in particular) entered or began to create their own distinctive life patterns—when they left home or started a career—they broke loose from the dictates of family. In so doing they not only ventured forth to seek their fortunes; they also ventured forth to seek themselves. The morphology of conversion—inquiry, awakening, special seriousness, anxiety, conviction, regeneration, and sanctification—closely paralleled the rhythms of life. Conversion became part of the maturing process, and many youths, like Jeremiah Evarts at Yale, then carried their new convictions into their life's work. For those few in the clergy, of course, it became their chosen occupation.[39] For the larger population, however, the onset of "seriousness" in religious or secular matters presaged entrance into the wider community. And the clergy (and parents) often used this connection as a lever, arguing that persons who would assume adult responsibilities should also shoulder their religious responsibilities. The two crises thus often became as one, and when the sweep of these revivals pushed the age of conversion even lower, then converts frequently considered themselves to be adults, whatever their age.

Youthful conversions carried with them other possibilities as well. They swelled the ranks of church members and gave greater impetus to the revivals, an impetus that conveyed an expectation that the next generation (as children of converted parents) would perpetuate and extend their accomplishments. With this extension through time they could bridge not only generations but two epochs of social, economic, and political change. If this was successful, then traditional values might live on under new conditions. If not, then fears abounded that dislocation would be permanent, a secular egocentrism predominant, and national decay certain. Only sustained religious activity could forestall these fears, supporters of the revivals argued, for then "Family religion is of consequence encouraged and increased, public worship is attended in places where it was not before observed, churches are established, and the settlements of ministers promoted. The morals of many individuals are reformed, and charity requires us to believe that not a few souls, that were perishing in unbelief, are recovered to the way of life."[40] That the majority of converts in these revivals were under the age of twenty-two undoubtedly excited the clergy, holding out as it did a promise for the future.

The other striking characteristic about the revivals' converts was that so many were women. Recent studies of New England revivals reveal that between 1795 and 1815 almost 70 percent of all revival converts were women, leading to what some scholars have called the "feminization" of American religion. If the next generation was to be pious and moral, then mothers' behavior and roles were crucial. "We look to you," Joseph Buckminster explained, "to guard and fortify those barriers which still exist in society, against the encroachments of impudence and licentiousness."[41] Other spokesmen echoed Buckminster's directive, arguing that women understood the needs of families better than did men and that they were more "patient, persevering, and thorough, in their investigations."[42] They allocated to women the characteristics of virtue and piety as the "cult of domesticity" increasingly defined women's role in society. A cult of female piety emerged, and in reconciling themselves to the preponderance of female over male converts, the clergy insisted that their effect would not be diminished. "The support of religion," the Reverend Joseph Lathrop argued, "depends greatly on the female sex." He went on to indicate just what this meant: "Men and women are appointed to act in different circles. The great transactions of society chiefly fall within the province of *men*. But *women*, in their more humble sphere, may contribute no less, and perhaps really more than the men, to the maintenance and transmission of religion in the world."[43] This divergence would be the pattern for the next several decades. Ministers welcomed adolescent males and females as converts and left to reformers the awakening of the general adult male population.

Cut off from the formal mechanisms of power in American society, women could nonetheless influence those who controlled those levers. In effect, this authority at once granted women a new and elevated status while at the same time ensured that they remained isolated from the real sources of power. Women became symbolic as the daughters of liberty, protectors of republican virtue, and guardians of a moral America. Set apart from the self-centered materialistic competition of early nineteenth-century America, they ironically symbolized as well the circumscribed influence of religion. This division of responsibilities threatened to legitimate a further bifurcation of male and female roles, in that it seemingly granted males greater freedom in the marketplace so long as women were at home instilling moral virtues in their sons and daughters. It concerned Jeremiah Evarts as he contemplated a career in the law, and it drew the attention of other spokesmen as well. "Mothers," said the Reverend William Lyman, "hold the reins of government and sway the ensigns of national prosperity and glory.... To them therefore our eyes are turned in this demoralizing age."[44]

In many respects this constituted a double standard in the strictest sense of the term: pious females seeking by influence and example to moderate the almost anarchistic behavior of materialistic and ambitious males, all the while granted by default custody of traditional social institutions and practices. In his analysis of the Rochester revivals of 1830–31, Paul Johnson found the same pattern but expressed it differently. "Finney's male converts were driven to religion because they had abdicated their roles as eighteenth-century heads of households. In the course of the revival, their wives helped to transform them into nineteenth-century husbands."[45]

The next step was for these women to form or join organizations to seek broad social reforms. Under most circumstances organization by women was not socially acceptable, but religious or moral reform groups were an exception. This outgrowth of the revivals expanded in subsequent years to become central to the larger moral awakening of the early nineteenth century. The spread of conversions among the female population provided a steady reservoir of support for these organizational efforts. Eventually an institutional setting emerged that replaced many of the functions formerly the province of the family. A larger institutional network, a network in which women exercised a significant influence, now advanced parental and familial values. In this manner the revivals legitimated a sphere of female activity outside the home, which in turn provided further impetus for a broader awakening. By the 1820s middle class women belonged to a vast array of ameliorative organizations.[46]

There was, of course, opposition to the revivals and to the new role of women. Assembling and exciting people in groups could only injure their health, according to one critic. Amariah Brigham, a doctor, argued that religious revivals more nearly resembled mass nervous disorders than outpourings of a divine spirit. They were momentary outbursts, not sustained conviction and true religious conversion. The excitement of any sustained mental excitement, moreover, injured the brain and nervous system and led eventually to insanity. Not many critics of the revivals focused on their medical aspects. But Brigham's complaint was part of a larger critique that encompassed all of American society. "Insanity," he observed, "is a disease that always prevails most in countries where the people enjoy civil and religious freedom, and where all are induced, or are at liberty, to engage in the strife for wealth, and for the highest honors and distinctions of society."[47] Such activity was injurious enough among men but far more threatening when encouraged in women and children.

Most critics of the revivals, however, objected to them on religious grounds. They asserted that evangelism produced a temporary excitement among the populace but that these "religious stirs" were neither lasting nor beneficial. Overlooking the "quiet" revivals of Nathaniel Emmons and others, these critics usually voiced one of several objections: that only the elect could truly experience conversion, that evangelical excitement produced false doctrines, that the revivals were engineered for effect and did not reflect actual religious conviction, or that they were simply too irrational to be effective. In short, they complained about the methodology of revivals and objected to a sort of democratic Arminianism that they believed to be pervasive.[48] These criticisms reflected a confusion apparent in the larger society. Were morality and religiosity to be measured by inner conviction (and conversion) or by external behavioral patterns? As the revivals deepened into the awakening, the latter seemed to supersede the former as the object of attention and reformation. In particular, an emphasis on moral behavior appeared to hold great promise as a way to offset the precarious nature of revivals and at the same time afforded a uniform public measure for private conviction. Some of its proponents would try to legislate the ideals of this public behavior when persuasion failed.

The revivals continued, despite critics and doubters, multiplying in number throughout New England and much of the nation. In addition, the religious and even the commercial press carried the message of the revivals to readers of all religious persuasions. Proponents sought to extend the moral values of the church to the larger society, hoping to realize the ideal of a national covenant, hoping to make religion at once an integrating and millennial force.[49] They argued that the entire national community would have to bear responsibility for individuals' sins and that only a general awakening to the importance of national virtue could forestall this moral disgrace.

But the nature of the conversion experience did not completely prepare later reformers for this process. Conversions meant climactic and dramatic change; reformation of public habits and behavior was slower and more developmental. In their efforts to effect this larger awakening, therefore, reformers constantly sought to create an atmosphere of crisis, one that paralleled the internal turmoil characteristic of individual conversions. The jeremiad became the election address, the speech at the formation of a moral reform society, or the Fourth of July lecture. We should keep in mind, therefore, that cries about moral decay do not mean that the nineteenth century was far more immoral than the eighteenth. The ethos changed; the revolution brought a new ideal against which to measure behavior, and broader political democracy brought new classes and new concerns under public scrutiny. All these changes stimulated an effort to effect decisive moral change and to remake American society. If a transforming crisis could reshape one's inner self and radically alter outward behavior, then why could not a similar transformation have the same regenerative influence on the larger society?[50] Americans like Jeremiah Evarts, who had long been sensitive to religion and had undergone a gradual awakening that culminated in conversion, also believed that such a transformation could and should occur. People like Evarts, however, were willing to be patient and seize opportunities as they developed. In the meantime organizational activity could fuse converted individuals in common cause, and during the second decade of the nineteenth century, Evarts and other reformers sought to do just that. This organizational thrust attempted to expand the revival into an awakening.[51]

Americans in the nineteenth century had an air of expectancy about them, an expectancy that they might in their lifetime realize their fondest material ambitions. Evangelicals and other persons anxious about morality and republican virtue shared this feeling. They did not retreat from the world in fits of asceticism but instead sought to infuse the material with the moral—wrapping both in a fervent embrace of material progress and national piety. Material prosperity indicated that the hand of God was on the land, but only if public behavior and public statutes reflected this presence could the nation approach redemption. For some evangelical reformers, this anxiety became a rationale for moral radicalism; for other Americans it represented something worth pursuing only if it did not compromise their material objectives. During the next several decades these two groups scuffled with one another for dominance, and the ebb and flow of this contest found expression in political as well as religious circles. The course of this struggle revealed how Arminianized the Calvinists had become, and that a lawyer like Evarts could represent and articulate the evangelical position indicated just how synthetic a movement had emerged. From his position in Boston as editor of the *Panoplist*, Evarts devoted the next decade of his life to mobilizing these forces so as to promote the universality of moral principles. In the process a model of the public voluntary society emerged as the cornerstone for a new model of citizenship.[52]

CHAPTER THREE

"If the Gangrene Strike the Vitals": Jeremiah Evarts, Benevolent Reform, and the Organizing Impulse

✧

"Beyond all question, a man ought to be devoted to this business in New England." With these thoughts, in 1810 Jeremiah Evarts moved from New Haven to Charlestown to become editor of the *Panoplist*, one of New England's leading religious periodicals. He believed that the times were dangerous, that foreign intrigues and partisan domestic conflict threatened to shatter the fragile republic.[1] Evarts's concern for the direction of New England and American society was rooted in a belief that too many members of the new generation sacrificed civic responsibility for private profit, that they seemed more inclined to raise merino sheep or invest in textile mills than to serve in government or provide public leadership.[2] This belief joined a determination that, once awakened to the problem, men would revitalize their society and recapture a sense of morality and virtue. Together these convictions had led Evarts to become editor of the *Panoplist*. Accepting this position enabled him to become perhaps the preeminent lay leader of the awakening.

The greatest dangers, from Evarts's perspective, came from the moral rather than the political sphere—dangers that were, in a sense, psychic. The concept of a virtuous republic was as much a set of mental images and ideals as it was a series of concrete institutions. The soul of a republic, its ultimate foundation, lay in the minds and hearts of the people. So long as they remained pure and undefiled, the institutional structure of the state reflected virtue. But when corruption seeped into the inner recesses of the spirit, then decay threatened to erode public institutions and the ligaments that connected their officials to the larger populace. "If the whole mass of society become contaminated, if the gangrene strike the vitals," one colleague warned, "the case is past remedy."[3]

For a while Evarts, like others of his generation, often mistook the mosaic of social and economic change for decay. And no wonder. The Charlestown to which he moved in 1810 was well on its way to becoming the third largest incorporated entity within Massachusetts, exceeded only by Boston and Salem. Its population tripled during the first three decades of the nineteenth century, as it became a thriving market town. The navy yard, which opened in 1800, added a strong federal presence as well. Within a decade of Evarts's arrival Charlestown boasted two dozen wharves, two breweries, seven meetinghouses, and a dozen schools. In addition, a library, an alms house, an insane asylum, the state prison, and a Catholic convent marked the townscape.[4]

Amid this atmosphere of change, Jeremiah Evarts and many of his young Federalist friends sought to recreate the conditions they deemed essential for the survival of a republican polity: public and private virtue, religious conviction, social harmony, the sacrifice of individual gain for the general welfare, avoidance of war, and a limited grant of power to any central authority.[5] They believed that although the people were not powerless, they had to be warned and awakened to the danger. This awakening became Evarts's personal mission. Prevented by his fragile health from becoming a missionary in the field, he worked tirelessly from a central office, going into the field whenever his health permitted or conditions demanded. Through the *Panoplist* he reached out to his larger audience, drawing on a jeremiad tradition familiar to his readers and tailored to his ability. "It becomes more & more obvious," wrote Edward Dorr Griffin, "that the existence of the Panoplist, under God, depends on you."[6]

As editor, Jeremiah Evarts labored to advance several specific causes during the next few years; taken together they reflect Evarts's organic vision of social behavior and moral reform. His letters and published essays focused on six issues that he considered central to a revitalized society: the nurture of children and the education of youth, the promotion of religion and an attack on Unitarianism, the problem of ministerial supply, Sabbatarianism, temperance, and the need to evangelize other peoples through foreign missions. These concerns undergirded his search for the soul of America. He took them to be the essential components in a concept of stewardship that advocated the use of both property and personal influence to persuade others to do good. "*Where there is no self-denial,*" he wrote, "*there can be no real virtue.*"[7]

To advance these themes, Evarts published several essays detailing the responsibilities of parental love and the education of children. The baptism of his first son, John Jay Evarts, in April 1813 undoubtedly increased his sensitivity on this matter, and he reminded parents that infants were helpless and completely under their control. The family was the linchpin to the social machinery, in Evarts's view, and he reiterated a traditional notion of reciprocity in propounding his theory of social relations. Parents must love their children and develop their character and piety, in return for filial obedience. The present times, he noted, were particularly difficult. "We of the present age," Evarts wrote, "who have lived thirty years, have seen greater changes within our own time, than could have been seen, at other periods of the world, in several centuries."[8] He was convinced that rapid change required more piety, greater discipline, widespread benevolent activity, support for schools and churches, and a spirit of self-denial. Heathenish families educated a heathenish posterity, argued Evarts in another essay. "The fireside is too seldom considered as the grand nursery of piety," he lamented, "in which plants of righteousness shall be reared, and fitted to flourish and blossom and bear fruit for ever."[9]

Women as well as men were central to this regeneration. Renewed emphasis on the family as *the* crucial training ground for future generations, coupled with a growing economic and occupational differentiation that altered eighteenth-century patterns of work, gave women a new and heightened domestic role.[10] Women were to rear the next generation, and to do so properly they must be moral and pious. Conversion statistics from the revivals revealed the apparent sensitivity of women to religion, and with the formation of new benevolent societies, they became increasingly active in reform activities. "How much good we might do," wrote Fanny Woodbury, "if we had but hearts. . . . And how we ought to seek out ways of doing good."[11]

Participation in charitable work brought both responsibility and respectability to women's activities in the larger world yet at the same time reinforced those prevailing tendencies that depicted women as more sensitive and vulnerable than men to vice and immorality. In the words of one male, "Women are happily formed for religion. Their sensibility, their vivacity, and sprightly imagination, their sympathy or tenderness toward distress and those in imminent danger of distress, as natural endowments, qualify them, with the grace of God added, to make christians of the first cast. Their affections are ardent and easily moved."[12] The dynamics of reform activity were to be left to men, but women could achieve a middle-class respectability by supporting those efforts through the formation of separate voluntary societies. For the most part the spheres of the two sexes were to remain separate from one another, with women consigned to a supportive role. With individual female reformers, however, this distinction was not always the case, for some found reform activity so vital as to absorb their full attention. In this way they became coworkers with God, not men, in their benevolent labors.[13]

Jeremiah Evarts welcomed the participation of women in the reform societies but remained more concerned about the role of men. Local revivals might awaken women to various causes, but Evarts feared that the excitement of these revivals would blind men to the promotion of "true" religion. In particular, he worried about a growing dichotomy in the popular sensibility between social intercourse and active piety. The revival experience seemed to suggest that part of the population, those persons who testified to a conversion experience or who attended religious services, was very different from everyone else. While in one sense that difference was probably true, what concerned Evarts was the encouragement it gave to the rest of society to believe that religion and worldly affairs were separate spheres. Advocates of the revivals, he advised, were too sensitive about charges of enthusiasm from critics. Behind these charges, he hinted, lay a fear that religious principles indeed possessed a latent power and would become more influential. Since this influence was the goal of the revivals, Evarts urged individuals with strong religious convictions to persevere and cultivate a disinterested benevolence. "No worship is acceptable to God unless it proceeds from a heart filled with benevolence to man," he insisted in words that echoed Timothy Dwight, "and no real benevolence to man exists in a heart destitute of love to God."[14] Charity work was to spring from religious conviction, not from a desire to acquire or advance a reputation. Commitment, not fame, was to be cultivated. In this way social intercourse and individual piety became a single active impulse: acknowledgment that the hand of God bestowed blessings on the living and would motivate individual sensibilities in times of prosperity as well as hardship.

Evarts's God was an optimistic God. Since love had supplanted vengeance, one ought to return this love and not abuse His blessings. To use this abundance to further sin or evil, to transform the grain harvest into ardent spirits, for example, was to pervert the natural world for the purpose of an immoral self-indulgence. "Let every man consider well the heinous sin of perverting, wasting, and abusing the bounties of Providence," he wrote. "Far from us be any disposition to gluttony, dissipation, riot, and drunkenness. While we enjoy the good things of life, without grudging, as is plainly our duty, let us not enjoy them without caution, prudence, and a constant sense of accountability to God."[15]

To support and augment this stewardship and self-denial, Evarts insisted that the churches should be unified and pure. He believed that the spread of Unitarianism threatened this purity and fought the diffusion of Latitudinarian opinions with strong attacks on Unitarianism. Unitarians controlled Harvard College after 1805, and this threat to orthodox clerical training alarmed Evarts. He tried to isolate the Unitarian menace and expose its errors. "A loose Theology," he argued in one public appeal, "always leads to a correspondent relaxation in the duties of morality."[16] Evarts soon injected himself into one of those persistent factional divisions between pastor and parishioners that had become such a common phenomenon in early nineteenth-century New England. Part of a larger dispute between religious liberals and conservatives, these divisions raised legal as well as theological questions.

The Dorchester, Massachusetts, church fell victim to this factionalism in 1814, when parishioners charged that the minister, the Reverend John Codman, had refused a frequent exchange of pulpits with Boston ministers. The real issue, however, was Unitarianism. Unitarians brought the charges, and it was with Unitarian clergy that they wanted Codman to exchange pulpits. Like so many other disputes of this type, the conflict was basically between members of the church (who favored Codman) and residents of the parish (who did not). Evarts reviewed the controversy at length in the *Panoplist*, pointing out the similarity of this controversy to others throughout the region and reviewing the causes and arguments as a way of instructing his readers and preventing further dissension. Evarts himself served as a delegate (pro-Codman, of course) to the council called to mediate the charges and generally supported the majority's conclusion that although the charges were unfounded, the Reverend Codman should provide more frequent exchanges with other ministers.[17] Evarts would have lengthier confrontations with Unitarians in the postwar years.

To discourage such deviations, however, Evarts joined others to form the New England Religious Tract Society and became its treasurer following the organizational meeting in Boston on May 23, 1814. Known more commonly as the New England Tract Society, the organization was the brainchild of five men: Ebenezer Porter, Moses Stuart and Leonard Woods (professors at Andover Theological Seminary), Jedidiah Morse, and Evarts. They hoped to circulate cheap tracts through the already-established network of town and village societies. The new society would, in essence, centralize the publication of tracts, thereby sounding a single message throughout the region.[18]

This efficient uniformity did not materialize. Poor business management and a slackening of the earlier revivals left the society in serious financial difficulty by 1819. The resignation of Jedidiah Morse and the emergence of the Reverend Justin Edwards as the new administrator eventually improved the society's prospects. In 1823 it joined forces with the New York society to form the American Tract Society. With Presbyterians, Congregationalists, Baptists, and Episcopalians joining hands, the ATS formed more than 2,600 associated branches and distributed nearly six million tracts annually by the close of the decade.[19]

The third cause that Evarts embraced, intimately related to the first two, was the matter of ministerial supply. Perhaps remembering his own childhood among the irreligious farmers of Vermont, or perhaps looking ahead to what the recruitment of hundreds of missionaries could mean to New England's churches, Evarts highlighted the need to increase the supply of ministers throughout the country. In New England alone there were too many pulpit vacancies, he argued, and the spread of population to the west as well as a growing denominationalism exerted tremendous pressure for more ministers. Continuing popular attention to secular instead of religious matters, moreover, threatened to halt the revivals and forestall a general awakening. "The people feel about nothing but money," the Reverend John Rice wrote from Virginia. "As to religion, the very stillness of death reigns amongst us."[20] The religious ramparts had to be manned to guard against the spread of corruption and the atomistic tendencies of society. In the words of one proponent: "Indeed, the religious, moral, and political principles, and habits, of a free people, are their only barrier against anarchy, revolution, and despotism. And when once those principles and habits are corrupted, and broken down, the civil authority and laws become odious restraints; and are soon prostrate at the feet of ungovernable licentiousness."[21]

The solution Evarts advanced was to educate and train pious young men for a career in the ministry. There was a vast reservoir of interest and talent available to meet the needs of parishes and churches, but many who might otherwise follow this calling were too impoverished to do so. What Evarts had in mind was not some benevolent scheme to defray the expenses of theological training so that more college graduates would consider the ministry as a profession. He had in mind a plan far more sweeping, a plan designed to assist "promising youths, as soon as they have left the state of childhood, and carrying them through a regular course of education, till they are fit to enter upon the evangelical and pastoral office."[22]

Throughout New England several circumstances recommended Evarts's proposal. First, the revivals themselves had nourished religious convictions and brought forth evidence of youthful piety. From this cluster of young converts the most talented could be selected and their further education supported. Second, numerous grammar schools and academies (such as the one Evarts had once taught in at Peacham, Vermont) already existed in towns scattered across the region. They provided a means to educate these youths at minimal expense. In addition, academies such as Andover and Exeter currently accepted students who were unable to pay their own expenses. "As these schools were founded for the purpose of promoting piety and virtue, as well as learning," Evarts noted, "the pious, other things being equal, will obviously be entitled to a preference."[23]

At another level there also existed colleges whose primary concern was to promote religion. Although these institutions were expensive, Evarts was convinced that wealthy individuals could and would support particular students if the cause was right. Finally, building on the Andover model, the student who made it that far would have to attend a theological seminary so as to ensure a learned ministry. Again Evarts asserted that men of wealth who appreciated "the value of religious instruction, and the worth of immortal souls" would donate the necessary funds. All this training was necessary to maintain religion as the bulwark of a free and moral society. Uneducated ministers, complained Evarts, had damaged the cause of religion, "especially in the new settlements."[24]

The western tour of John F. Schermerhorn and Samuel J. Mills in 1812 reinforced Evarts's fears. Their report, published in 1814, revealed not only the growing strength of Baptists and Methodists in the region west of the Alleghenies but also the scant number of churches and clergy. The report, indeed, went beyond its focus on religion and morals to argue for the importance of that region to the future of the nation. This new line of settlement, it insisted, carried with it the hopes of future generations. Vacant pulpits must be filled, and tracts and Bibles disseminated, if the religious and moral foundations of the nation were to advance with its settlement. Within a year, Evarts joined fund-raising efforts to help the attempts of men like Lyman Beecher to recruit and train ministers for those pulpits. Formally launched in 1814 with Beecher's *Address of the Charitable Society for the Education of Indigent Pious Young Men for the Ministry of the Gospel*, this endeavor sought to provide "a Bible for every family, a school for every district, and a pastor for every 1000 souls." In 1815 Evarts helped prompt the Massachusetts Missionary Society to sponsor Mills and Daniel Smith on another western tour. They reported that "*half a million of Bibles*" were needed west of the Alleghenies.[25]

Evarts's larger scheme, however, embodied numerous implications. On the one hand support for ministerial candidates at a few theological seminaries promised to accelerate a centralization and conformity already under way. A narrow range of institutions would provide new ministers a common education from a select faculty. This would curtail the eighteenth-century practice, then still popular, whereby each candidate studied under some local minister. Loyalties would be more uniform, and perhaps theological divisions within denominations might become less intense. Cooperation would mark the future, and discussion of theological doctrine would give way to the organization of benevolent societies.[26] At the same time, financial support for "poor but pious youth" would alter the character of the profession. Piety, not family connections, would be the requisite measure for the clergy. Unlike the legal profession, which set tutorial charges so as to exclude the poor and prevent democratization, the clergy moved in the opposite direction. That led in 1815 to the formation of the American Education Society.[27]

The fourth cause that Evarts believed vital to the soul of the republic was that of Sabbatarianism. The education of children, the promotion of religion, and provisions for an adequate supply of ministers, Bibles, and tracts would fail to revitalize society if the Sabbath was not retained as a day of worship. Passage of a law in 1810 requiring every post office to be open one hour on Sundays for the sorting and pickup of mail aroused Evarts's concern.[28] With its enactment of this law, Congress ventured into the maelstrom of church-state relations at the very moment when the states were backing out. To Evarts, this federal legislation seemed another step toward the secularization of American society and prompted petitions opposing Sunday mail deliveries. Still willing to be flexible, the next year Postmaster Gideon Granger admitted that this one-hour provision might cause problems. "Although in cases of extreme anxiety or national calamity, it may be proper for Postmasters to open their offices for the reception and delivery of letters on the Sabbath, and particularly to the officers of Government, still it is believed that the good sense of the officers is a sufficient safeguard for the delivery of letters under all such circumstances; and that compelling Postmasters to attend to the duties of the office on the Sabbath, is on them a hardship, as well as in itself tending to bring into disuse and disrepute the institution of that holy day."[29]

Along with his Congregational and Presbyterian colleagues, Jeremiah Evarts attacked this erosion of the sanctity of the Sabbath. Such laws, he insisted, threatened to transform Sundays into regular days of business. Merchants would receive letters, and, so as not to sacrifice any temporal advantage, they would write other letters in reply. Secularization of the Sabbath would undermine the maintenance of morals and thereby threaten the republic.[30] The legislation redirected public attention back toward the legislative process as a device for effecting moral reform at the very moment that voluntarism seemed to be taking hold. It appeared to suggest that voluntary societies and techniques of persuasion would be insufficient to safeguard republic virtue and public morality. "We have always viewed it as a national evil of great magnitude, and one which calls for national repentance and reformation," Evarts wrote, "that the mails are carried, and the post-offices kept open, on that holy day, in every part of our Country."[31]

The danger, in his opinion, was not only that Sunday mail delivery symbolized a deterioration of religious feeling, but that the *nation* itself—which had received God's favor in abundance—courted disaster. The civil authorities were to preserve the Sabbath and promote sound morality; instead, he warned, they "have been engrossed either with great political questions, or with the applications of individuals for favors of a private nature."[32] Evarts maintained a strong belief that elected leaders should govern in the interests of the nation and avoid party factionalism. When they failed to do so, then the public or segments of the public should seek to correct their negligence.

Such a theory of politics was, of course, romantic and largely outmoded by 1815. Nonetheless, Evarts and other benevolent reformers still believed such a governance structure to be possible. Not until the late 1820s, with the election of Andrew Jackson, did they lose their faith that the elected leaders were virtuous. In the meantime, men like Jeremiah Evarts and Lyman Beecher organized a petition campaign on the Sabbath issue. For more than a decade they wrote circulars and petitions, published pamphlets, and sought to enlist members of Congress and other influential persons in this cause. Their immediate target was the 1810 law that required post offices to remain open for the distribution of any mail that arrived on Sunday.[33]

The Sabbatarian campaign produced hundreds of petitions to Congress, all insisting that civil institutions were grounded in a public morality and that violation of the Sabbath threatened both. In reply, Postmaster Return J. Meigs, Jr., testified that the exigencies of the times required Sunday travel and mail deliveries. He agreed that "public policy, pure morality, and undefiled religion" favored observance of the Sabbath and indicated that when wartime conditions ended "it will be at all times a pleasure to this Department to prevent any profanation of the Sabbath." More determined opposition to the petitions came from the business community, labor groups, and even from other religious denominations. Although each group opposed this strict Sabbatarianism for different reasons, their opposition revealed a broad heterogeneity that challenged that tightly knit organic unity characteristic of the Sabbatarians' beliefs.[34]

As central as the Sabbatarian effort was to the public promotion of religion, the temperance crusade embraced even more dramatic images of a moral order gone awry. In October 1810 Jeremiah Evarts joined the outcry against intemperance, publishing a short essay on "Arithmetic Applied to Moral Purposes" in the *Panoplist*. Evarts's perspective and argument revealed the symbolic importance of the temperance crusade, and so long as he edited the *Panoplist*, its pages were open to the enemies of liquor. This reform was to be thoroughly middle-class, equating intoxication with a release of inhibitions which accompanied a loss of self-control. The besotted were dangerous—to themselves, their families, and the larger society. As his title indicated, one could calculate how much was spent daily on drink and then save that amount and give it to some benevolent cause.[35]

This latter suggestion revealed the organic harmony that Evarts hoped to nurture in society. Everything was interrelated in a sort of dynamic tension. Money not frittered away on alcohol could support libraries, schools, roads, bridges, poor relief, or other benevolent activity. With temperance as with other reforms, moreover, Evarts focused attention on the more subtle corruptions rather than on the obvious. "It is not the abuse of ardent spirits by habitual drunkards, which is here principally referred to," he insisted, "but that immoderate consumption of them to which many of our farmers, mechanics, day-laborers, and others, are addicted."[36]

Two years later Jeremiah Evarts joined with prominent men from the General Association of Massachusetts, such as his colleague Jedidiah Morse, Samuel Worcester of the American Board of Commissioners for Foreign Missions, the Reverend Abiel Abbot, and others, to form the Massachusetts Society for the Suppression of Intemperance. He published articles on the liquor problem, emphasizing its deleterious social and personal effects and arguing that the problem was essentially one of self-discipline. The erosion of self-discipline, he believed, had political, economic, and even national implications, in addition to the debilitating effects on the individual. Not only did intemperance increase demands on public charity, but it was like a cancer that attacked the body and weakened the spirit. Hard drinking forced families onto public charity, caused sickness, produced poverty, and eroded that industrious virtue so essential to society. In the words of the Reverend Nathan Strong: "Industry is an excellent quality of character. The diligent use of time, for some good purpose is a christian duty. The indolent person cannot be a practical christian. The sinful may be industrious from motives of shameful parsimony; but christians have never a right to be indolent and misuse time."[37] To revitalize those values, a committee of the MSSI endorsed a publicity campaign to demonstrate the magnitude of the problem, greater activity by the clergy on the subject, the circulation of cheap tracts outlining the evils of intemperance, enforcement of state laws against insobriety, the use of spirits for medicinal purposes only, and the formation of voluntary associations to promote temperance.[38]

The Congregational clergy enlisted immediately. The Reverend Ebenezer Porter typified their approach when he observed that prosperity often encouraged sloth. "The richest soil bears the rankest weeds," he noted, and "the vices of men flourish most in the midst of fertility and plenty."[39] Intemperance was such a vice; it lured young men to "infamy and the grave." A growing army of sots, he warned, threatened "destruction of our morals, and to our precious and venerable institutions." *The Student's Companion* highlighted the web of decay that intemperance harbored. "Poverty is the fruit of idleness. Idleness is the parent of vice and misery. The chief misfortunes that befall us in this life, can be traced to some vices or follies which we have committed. Were we to survey the chambers of sickness and distress, we should find them peopled with the victims of intemperance and sensuality, and with the children of vicious indolence and sloth." All contributors to this benevolence would be rewarded, other clergymen insisted, even "to giving of a cup of cold water!"[40]

As a founder of the temperance movement in the United States, Jeremiah Evarts sought to mobilize an interdenominational force to combat the evils of alcohol. Such broad agreement was possible for two reasons. First, the notion that relationships existed between insobriety, poor health, domestic troubles, and poverty was itself widespread. Second, not only did it offer an explanation for many prevailing social disorders; this conviction also placed the blame for deviance on the individual. The individual, reformers believed, was susceptible to reform through voluntarism and persuasion. In the words of an 1813 circular: "The duty of temperance in the use of ardent spirits, demands the attention of every friend to his country. The evils arising from the opposite vice are vast beyond all calculation. Need we refer you to the enormous expense, which it occasions; to its destructive influence on the health; to the disorders, which it produces in the family and in society; or to the idleness, the poverty, the disgrace, the remorse, and the final ruin, which follow in its train?"[41] Only later, when temperance turned to prohibition and an awareness of broader social or institutional causes for insobriety emerged, did reformers turn to politics and legislation to achieve their objectives.

In Massachusetts, Jeremiah Evarts became a counselor for the Society for the Suppression of Intemperance. His earlier opposition to Unitarianism did not prevent him from cooperating with Unitarians in the temperance crusade, although the extent of interdenominational cooperation remains unclear. Few studies of local temperance societies exist, and most analyses of benevolent societies have focused more on class than on religious affiliation. Membership in these societies points toward the upper and middle classes as the progenitors of reform, with the national leadership drawn from a cadre of leading public figures or wealthy individuals. A quick glimpse at the MSSI auxiliary in Concord, Massachusetts, reveals the nature of the temperance effort. Attractive to the town's church members, the Concord society drew broad support from the unchurched as well. In addition, drinkers and nondrinkers joined in almost equal numbers, in part a reflection of the parent body's condemnation of intoxication and not of alcohol in general. What seems more important here is the idea of respectability and moral character. Neither group tolerated the spectacle of sots lolling about neighborhood streets. This stigma meant, of course, that those individuals who wished to guzzle had to do so in private. In addition, the vast majority of the auxiliary's members did *not* belong to the local church. Hence, while membership in voluntary societies might be growing, it masked a contrary trend among the churches. Perhaps by default the expanding network of these societies came to embody the hope for a moral rebirth.[42]

Membership statistics aside, there is no doubt that Americans imbibed enormous quantities of liquor in the early nineteenth century. The 1810 federal census revealed that Americans produced more than twenty-five *million* gallons of these "ardent spirits" in that year alone and imported several million additional gallons. Not only did they produce the liquor, they consumed it as well. Per capita consumption of hard liquor reached 4.12 gallons in 1809 and 1810, an increase of 145 percent in just fourteen years. Critics warned that we were producing a generation of sots, a generation so saturated with alcohol that it lacked the self-discipline and restraint characteristic of orderly societies. For many temperance became a scapegoat for "numerous and threatening mischiefs," including crime, Sabbath-breaking, poverty, and virtually every other deviant behavior.[43]

The men at the helm of the MSSI reflected these tendencies. Most were either clergymen or lawyers—men like Samuel Worcester and Jeremiah Evarts from the reform community, Nathan Dan (lawyer), Timothy Bigelow (lawyer and former speaker of the Massachusetts General Court), the Reverend John Kirkland (president of Harvard College), the Reverend Abiel Abbot, or Samuel Dexter (lawyer, secretary of war and treasury in the Adams administration).[44] More restrictive than most of the voluntary societies, the MSSI required nomination from an existing member and payment of a two-dollar fee for membership. These requirements ensured a homogeneity not found in society as a whole and probably guaranteed that members would ascribe excessive drinking to a lower-class mentality. They also limited the society's appeal, and for more than a decade, while temperance rhetoric echoed across the New England landscape, the MSSI made little headway. Deferential habits had waned, and the notion that the hoi polloi would imitate the elite was no longer a valid theory of social relations.[45] What made this effort important, however, was the attempt to persuade the public en masse to alter its habitual practices. Because the emphasis was on the individual, and because the issue had overtones of religion, class, and ethnicity, when persuasion turned to legislation temperance became a volatile political issue.

The final cause that Evarts embraced, the one that remained closest to his heart until he died, was the foreign missionary enterprise under the auspices of the American Board of Commissioners for Foreign Missions (ABCFM). Founded on September 16, 1810, the ABCFM sprang from impulses unleashed by the Second Great Awakening and Samuel Hopkins's doctrine of disinterested benevolence. As such it represented the potential of the revivals to stimulate a larger awakening that was at once broader in scope and purpose than the emphasis on individual conversion. During the June 1810 meeting of the General Association of Massachusetts (an organization of clergymen), Evarts took an active part in discussions that led to the formation of the American Board, although he was not a clergyman and hence not a member of the association. At that time, the association approved the request of four students from Andover Theological Seminary—Adoniram Judson, Samuel Nott, Samuel Newell, and Samuel J. Mills, Jr.—to become foreign missionaries. As an avid supporter of the idea, and in his role as editor of the *Panoplist*, Evarts placed the plan before the public. He promoted the use of paid agents and the formation of local auxiliary societies throughout the country to raise money for the board and in so doing spearheaded a broad organizing impulse that came to typify the revitalization effort that sprang from the revivals.[46]

The broader organizational structure of the ABCFM—those local societies and auxiliaries beyond the commissioners and the Prudential Committee (who decided policy)—reflected not only an organizing impulse inherent in the awakening but what Evarts and his colleagues considered a model of the ideal social structure. The American Board was a rather monolithic structure that sought to provide some cohesive bonds to unite society. Anyone could contribute, and everyone was encouraged to give *something*. The commissioners hoped that this public solicitation would establish a lasting commitment as well as reflect a harmony of interest. Not every contributor, however, could vote; that privilege was reserved for the commissioners. In addition, another group of honorary members—the wealthy, the famous, the well placed—could attend the annual meetings and participate in discussions, although they could not vote. Representing the American Board in local communities were the auxiliaries. Formed by men and women (separately), these local branches held meetings, raised money, circulated the board's publications, and enabled the ABCFM to reach into every community from its office in Boston. What emerged was a marvelous communications network that was probably unrivaled on a national scale in its day. The *Panoplist* (later the *Missionary Herald*) was the mouthpiece for this network.[47]

Foreign missions quickly developed into a major undertaking, as Evarts and other organizers urged young men to "go into the destitute regions of the earth and spend your days in winning souls from pagan darkness to your dear Savior."[48] Missionary ventures comprised part of a larger plan in the minds of ABCFM organizers. What was important, they argued, was doing good. With their commitment to foreign missions, they had enlarged the scope of their effort, seeking now a virtuous world as well as a virtuous nation. Millennial expectations were rampant; all the world could be America. But harnessing these energies and developing a permanently supportive organizational structure took time.[49] Evarts believed support for foreign missions to be inseparable from support for religion in general. "The time has arrived," he insisted, "for prosecuting this business with more zeal, more extensive means, and more assurance than ever. . . . the approach of the Millennium, may be in great measure dependent on the course pursued by the present generation." "Let us cultivate national virtue," echoed another spokesman; "it is the palladium of our republic, it is the aegis of our independence."[50]

Elected treasurer of the ABCFM in 1811, by the next year Evarts had become a member of the board itself and of the Prudential Committee. His election and increased involvement in the operation of the American Board signaled a gradual shift in fund-raising techniques and organizational philosophy of that organization. Until then the board had directed its energies toward wealthy *individuals*, hoping to solicit large donations from a few influential people to underwrite the enterprise. Contributions from other sources were accepted, of course, but the general public remained largely outside the Prudential Committee's range of vision. Everyone hoped, or perhaps assumed, that once the ABCFM was firmly established, the generosity of a few would influence the larger populace. But no plan existed to advance that purpose, and the economic embarrassments flowing from the Embargo Act and subsequent disruption of business and trade made mere hope a slender reed on which to lean. At the same time, however, they provided a stimulus to extend the base of support for the ABCFM.[51]

Evarts initiated a plan to broaden support and increase ABCFM influence. He encouraged the formation of local auxiliaries to the American Board as well as benevolent societies of all types. This had the effect of partially democratizing the missionary impulse. Although an elite still directed the local as well as the national societies, wider popular participation and public recognition was now possible and welcome. All could (and should) contribute their mite and then by purchasing the *Panoplist* see their donations credited in print. Of course, they could not control any society's activities, but this heightened sense of participation increased public attachment to the cause. Acquisition of more extensive support, regardless of the depth of commitment, gave the missionary cause momentum as well as greater visibility and influence. This latter point was a sensitive one, for Evarts and his colleagues sought above all to impel individuals to seek what was right. At some point, however, this inner conviction had to bear public fruit. Private visions must influence public behavior, and the patterns of the latter should follow the dictates of conscience and not the weight of public opinion.[52]

By the close of the year (1811), however, the *Panoplist* was in financial difficulty. Circulation had remained small, and many subscribers were behind in their payments. In a public plea for help, Evarts warned that unless those circumstances changed, "it is very doubtful whether this work will be continued longer than to the close of the current volume." The Reverend Samuel Worcester, corresponding secretary of the ABCFM, proposed a plan to save both Evarts and the *Panoplist*. "It is this, that the Panoplist should be held so connected with the great missionary interest as to have security for its support in missionary funds. In this case, the editor must be assured of a stipend to a certain amount, say 1300 dollars; the profits of the work to be applied as far as they will go, & the deficit to be made up from the funds. If the profits of the work shall exceed the specified stipend, either a certain part of the surplus shall accrue to the editor & the remainder to the funds; or else the editor shall be entitled to the whole until the surplus rise to a certain point, & the funds to all beyond this point."[53]

To support his plan, Worcester argued that religious periodicals had always found support tenuous, and those that stood alone usually did not stand long. The *Panoplist*, he insisted, was too important to wither in isolation. Should the journal be connected intimately to the missionary cause, it would not only increase its circulation but also help bring additional monies into the board's treasury. At the same time, it would serve as a communications conduit from the American Board to the general population. Within a short time, he insisted, the journal would become profitable as the growing popularity of the missionary cause expanded its circulation. This income would then provide adequate support for Evarts as editor. The scenario outlined by Worcester did in fact occur. Within a year the journal's title had changed to the *Missionary Herald*, and Jeremiah Evarts drew nearly $2,000 in annual salary. This was, indeed, a comfortable salary—in a time when urban Baptist pastors received about $1,000 per year, Presbyterian ministers less than $2,000, and Methodist preachers about $80.[54]

Until that increase occurred, however, Evarts retained his connections to the legal community. In January 1812 he was admitted to the bar of Franklin County, Vermont. If Worcester's plan did not succeed he could return to Vermont to live with his brothers and parents, an eventuality he discussed when he visited them in the winter of 1812. His father once again urged him to return, and Mehitabel was agreeable.[55] But Jeremiah was unwilling to quit just yet. Motivated by a commitment to benevolent work as well as by the fear of failure, and perhaps haunted by the specter of returning to rural Vermont, Evarts plunged headlong into his literary and missionary work after his return to Charlestown. In February the American Board's first foreign mission embarked for India, an event that fired the public's imagination while it gave an aura of permanence and respectability to the board itself. "The Foreign Mission," reported the Reverend Ebenezer Porter from Andover, "has had an electric influence on Christians in this region. It promises to become the grave of their jealousies, and the central point of their efforts."[56]

Only months after the departure of the mission to India, war broke out between the United States and England. Although the American Board and the London Missionary Society urged their respective governments to permit continued cooperation (and with some success), the onset of war nonetheless forced the ABCFM's Prudential Committee to increase its public appeals for funds. As a member of the Prudential Committee, treasurer of the ABCFM, editor of the *Panoplist*, and treasurer of the local Foreign Mission Society of Boston and the Vicinity, Jeremiah Evarts was in the forefront of this effort. In March 1812 he published an essay noting the practicality of foreign missions and providing examples of missionary activity. A series of articles, "Evangelical Exertions in Asia," informed the public about the natives, history, and customs of that region. Editorial commentary in the *Panoplist*, furthermore, reminded readers that all profits "*are devoted to Foreign Missions.*"[57]

Ministers supportive of the cause added their own contributions from lectern and pulpit. Ministers must evangelize the heathen, the Reverend Leonard Woods told an excited crowd gathered in Salem, Massachusetts, to witness the ordination of the American Board's first foreign missionaries, and "the Christian world *must support them*."[58] Speaking at the formation of a local auxiliary in the western part of the state, the Reverend Joseph Lathrop bemoaned the calamities brought on by the war but reminded his listeners that money was still needed; "the urgency of the call is not abated." A new age had dawned, the Reverend Thomas Baldwin exclaimed at a meeting of the Massachusetts Bible Society, and a period of great reformation was about to begin.[59]

In "Address to the Christian Public," published that fall in the *Panoplist*, the American Board of Commissioners implemented and sought to extend its plans first announced two years earlier. Auxiliary societies were to be formed in each major town to rally public interest and raise funds. The emphasis, however, was on fund-raising, and the board appointed agents to "open durable sources of supply to the treasury."[60] Once in place, these local societies would form a web of influence, creating lines of communication with the board's offices in Boston as well as within the communities themselves. Along those lines traveled the message that although times were perilous, people should still give what they could to missions. That this effort required enormous labor was just as the ABCFM planned; as more volunteers appeared to build these webs, then more people became connected to the missionary enterprise, and the more extensive the connections, the greater their influence. "The genuine patriot," the committee argued, "and the genuine philanthropist, must labor, so far as they value the prosperity of their country and the happiness of the human race, to diffuse the knowledge and the influence of Christianity, at home and abroad."[61]

Behind these organizing efforts, and behind the missionary efforts of the ABCFM, lay a general missionary theology. That theology, which sprang largely from the religious transmutations of the Second Great Awakening, embodied four essential elements: a belief in the millennium, the concept of disinterested benevolence, a commitment to Christ's last command ("Go ye unto the world"), and a determination that those who remained mired in their indigenous cultures were "perishing heathen" in need of salvation. It was to those themes that Jeremiah Evarts spoke in the pages of the *Panoplist*, and it was those themes that drew men and women to the missionary cause.[62]

During the war years, however, numerous factors retarded the growth of the foreign missionary enterprise. The failure of subscriptions to the *Panoplist* to materialize as fast as Evarts had hoped prevented him from immediately enlarging the periodical to boost foreign missions. War disrupted transportation routes and siphoned energy and money that might otherwise have gone to benevolent causes. The Massachusetts Missionary Society experienced a drop in the level of its contributions, and as the society's treasurer Evarts admonished the public not to "grow cold in their charity, languid in their zeal, or weary in their well doing."[63] To reverse these tendencies, after the annual meeting of the American Board in Boston in the fall of 1813, Samuel Worcester, Jedidiah Morse, and Evarts drafted another appeal to the public. They tried to be optimistic, but Morse's tendency to focus on the specter of threats to foreign missions seemed to have prevailed in many instances. More support and greater effort emerged as the twin themes of the address, and its authors used the American Board's recent mission to India as a reminder of what could be done. To evangelize all nations, they reminded readers, would take time. Not only did missionaries have to be recruited and funds raised, but the missionaries had to learn new languages and then translate the Bible. The general public, however, displayed a dismaying tendency to expect quick results and rapid transformations.[64]

To counter this expectation, Evarts, Worcester, and Morse pointed out that although the American Board's sole object was to promote Christianity abroad, support for that goal accrued additional benefits. Without doubt, they insisted, *"the readiest and most efficacious method of promoting religion at home, is for Christians to exert themselves to send it abroad."*[65] The British had supported foreign missions and soon thereafter had experienced a twenty-fold increase in the number of evangelical preachers throughout their country. Foreign missions were not, therefore, a separate enterprise. They were intimately connected to the twin beacons of piety and nationalism. Christians should support the cause, and each individual's level of financial commitment should represent a personal sacrifice. These men hoped that this Christian communalism would supplant an increasingly prevalent autonomous, secular individualism. After all, the authors reminded their audience, this "decision is to be re-examined at the *judgment-seat of Christ.*"[66]

No sooner had the ink dried on that appeal than they published another one, calling in January 1814 for more money and tighter organization. Already planning another mission to India and Ceylon, the

Prudential Committee refused to consider wartime exigencies a sufficient excuse for inactivity. Led by the pen of Evarts, it admonished that "numerous societies must be formed, sermons must be preached, tracts must be distributed, till the community shall be thoroughly apprised of their danger and their duties; till the virtuous shall raise their courage and activity, in some good proportion to the excellence of their cause, and the vicious shall be confounded and dismayed."[67] This was not the time, preached James Richards, for any person to sit still; the millennial day was dawning.[68]

Despite a surface similarity to jeremiads of decline and decay, beneath these warnings lay a barely concealed optimism. Americans possessed sufficient resources to support a vast network of mission stations. Economic progress and advances in international commerce had created opportunities to reach all areas of the globe. In the words of the Reverend Evan Johns, "Divine Providence calls on us, solemnly, to awake from our lethargy, and use our utmost efforts to dissipate the gross darkness which has, for ages, covered so large a portion of the human race."[69]

Evarts and Johns had pinpointed the challenge to the moral reformers, but could they persuade their countrymen to rein in personal ambition and curb their gluttonous appetites in order to evangelize others? Would Americans, in fact, stop even to care for their own spiritual welfare? Quite obviously the answer was mixed; the signs pointed in both directions. But Evarts assumed the best and outlined a truly monumental plan that would not only realize his goal but reorder the planet. It was at once compelling and frightening.

> In aid of the great scheme of evangelizing the world, numerous colonies could be formed, and placed at moderate distances from each other, on the skirts of every uncivilized and heathen country. Each one of these should contain husbandmen, one faithful Gospel minister, and one or two good schoolmasters, and a handicraftsman of every useful trade. All should be industrious; all should have the fear of God in their hearts, and exhibit proofs of·uprightness and benevolence in their conduct. In the commencement of these colonies, the outfit of the missionaries, and the transportation of all their goods, the remaining millions would be expended; as the extent of the colonies could be regulated according as the money should hold out.[70]

Faithful farmers and skilled handicraftsmen, their minds and consciences guided by education and religion and their causes funded from the fruits of their labor, would undertake to transform the world.

Evarts believed that this plan could be put into effect just as soon as monies needed to prosecute the war could be shifted to benevolent causes. He expressed publicly his hope that Christians would be as diligent in raising money for benevolence as they were for warfare, but his scheme revealed far more than that. It betrayed in part his ideal for the perfect society: orderly, balanced, religious, and largely middle class. Leadership would rest with the educated, who would exercise a benevolent superintendence over community life. In short, it reflected his search to define and animate the soul of America. People should work hard, improve themselves, obey directions from their superiors, and let religious principles guide their actions. The sobering reality, as Evarts noted, was the expense involved. Yet here the slender reformer revealed his biggest dilemma; success seemed to reside more in the wallets of the benevolent than in the hearts of the converted. However farfetched this scheme might appear, it is precisely the plan that the ABCFM implemented with its missions to the Indians of North America and to other peoples throughout the world.

Underlying this plan was an assumption that all mankind was somehow interconnected; those who could afford to do so should contribute to the common good. Expressed in essays and sermons, this theme drew criticism both for its scope and its expense. Solicitors from all kinds of benevolent and charitable causes canvassed the populace asking for money, and critics questioned the wisdom of it all. Why should people send money into the wilderness or to foreign lands, one "non-donor" asked Evarts, when the needs at home remained so great? Did not charity begin at home? "Leave us to do what is right in our own eyes," he pleaded.[71] While some persons in the missionary effort, such as Elias Cornelius, did favor North American Indian missions to the more costly expeditions to Hindustan and elsewhere, this complaint focused on a more fundamental gripe. It asserted an individualism and self-determination that, to Evarts and his colleagues, symbolized those centrifugal forces that were eroding a sense of community and commitment. Clerical warnings that to oppose missionary and Bible societies was "to rebel against God" would not heal the breach. It was an issue that Evarts sought to avoid.[72]

Jeremiah Evarts's commitment to these six causes led him to publish widely. Within four years after becoming editor of the *Panoplist*, he had published more than two hundred essays. They ranged across a variety of topics but focused on benevolence, charitable efforts, and the organic connection between the private person, public character, and the well-being of society. His essay "On Human Depravity" typified his approach. Inattention to religion, he lamented, afflicted mankind. That inattention led to profaneness, which he feared would influence the character of the nation. He saw proof of its influence all around him: in a decreasing observance of the Sabbath, in the eager pursuit of wealth (which was really a gift from God), in individuals' eagerness to secure the approval of their fellow man. What was missing, Evarts observed, was the influence of religion and religious principles on everyday behavior. A narrow pursuit of immediate and tangible rewards had stilled the internal divine voice.[73]

The War of 1812 had brought other problems, but it was also an occasion for "immediate and vigorous efforts." At a time of conflict, Evarts spoke out for unity and harmony, for a foundation of values that joined the various segments of society. In a Fourth of July speech to the citizens of Charlestown, he avoided any references to specific party animosities and emphasized the value of republican institutions. Refusing to become directly embroiled in Federalist opposition to the war, to the Jeffersonians, to the South, or to the drift of national policy and political development, Evarts instead returned to interpret the principles of the revolution. The *character* of the people was the essential bulwark for a free society and just civil institutions. "At all times," he warned, "it behooves us to have an especial regard to the internal administration of justice, the purity of our elections, and the preservation of our civil rights from domestic tyranny."[74]

Oppression and tyranny were the nation's real enemies, and he urged his audience not to forget that only the wisdom and ability of "the first settlers of this country" gave us republican government. Their concern for education, constitution-making, virtue, justice, temperance, industry, and the election of Christian rulers enabled the country to grow and prosper. In addition, "they wrought subordination into a habit."[75] This last reference betrayed Evarts's Federalist politics but was as close to a statement of political ideology as he would ever utter.

Evarts warned that, despite this national heritage, the country now faced several evils that might erase the accomplishments of the past and dash hopes for the future. Three dangers, all interrelated, posed the most immediate threat: the press, party intrigue, and the character of national leaders. The press, driven by the demands of partisanship and acting as an agent for party mischief, propagated falsehood in the name of electoral victory. "These engines of mischief," cautioned Evarts, "will destroy the distinction between truth and falsehood." Their goal was party victory, and editors printed any lie to reach that objective. When they persisted, he warned, the press abdicated its responsibility to inform, the public adopted falsehood as truth, and a cornerstone of American liberty fell victim to factional interests.[76]

His contempt for "hireling scribblers" was surpassed only by his alarm at the "unprincipled ambition" of office seekers. Parties supported as candidates for public office men "to whom the individuals of the same party, in their private capacity, would not have entrusted any private concern whatever." If American liberties rested on the character of the people, then the want of integrity of the men standing for office revealed that "*all is not well.*" He called for more experienced national leaders, noting that "more skilful [sic] pilots are needed to manage the vessel of state at this stormy period."[77]

Finally, the one evil that promoted these other malignancies was that of party spirit. Evarts argued that this menaced all republican institutions "by producing a surrender of all personal and political independence into the hands of ambitious, and often unprincipled leaders." Differences of opinion could exist without narrow partisan feelings, he pointed out, for that had been the case during the revolution. But that Revolutionary ideal had faded, and the prevalence of malignant passions reflected an erosion of community spirit. "Party spirit," Evarts concluded, "is to be defined only by a reference to the object in view, which is always the aggrandizement of a part at the expense of the whole." It has, said another spokesman, "usurped the place and assumed the name of patriotism."[78]

Evarts's community was the nation, his spirit a benevolent one. He had become increasingly uneasy at the individualistic and entrepreneurial energies being loosed in the nation. The War of 1812, the party passions it inflamed, and the economic tendencies that followed in its wake were not congenial to his vision of a Christian American republic of virtuous citizens with high-minded leaders. Evarts counseled restraint, but Americans chafed to be unleashed; he looked inward to the heart, but their vision was outward to the marketplace.

The vicissitudes of war clarified these alternatives and to Evarts posed a choice for Americans between selfish passion and national regeneration. The war revealed just how much money could be raised; if taxes could support war then why couldn't they improve the schools, help the poor, and advance foreign missions in its stead? Evarts calculated that in one year such a fund (invested at 6 percent!) would amount to $194,100,000. "It is time," he wrote, "that men had found out that war is not the way to happiness; let them pursue a different plan; let them become faithful subjects of the Prince of peace, and use all their efforts to extend his dominion." Neither war nor party politics could carry one to heaven, for "this preference of politics to Religion is not of the Father, but of the world."[79] Christians were all of one family, he insisted, the family of man. They had a duty to one another and should supply each other's spiritual wants. In the same vein, he implied that those who promoted party views and social divisions were perhaps not Christians. The test, according to Evarts, was "whether they keep the common interest in view, or lose sight of this elevated object in a miserable scuffle for some trifling personal or party triumph."[80]

These pronouncements reflected two underlying principles that Evarts had embraced. He believed that the application of Christian principles through benevolent activities ensured republican virtue and hastened the millenium, and he was convinced that failure to imbue public actions with principle and piety threatened to create an atomistic society based on greed and ambition—which ultimately invited national disgrace and ruin. What he had not admitted, however, was that his own impassioned discourse was itself political. Evarts sought to build a consensual community as much as did politicians on both sides of the aisle. But until well after the War of 1812 he never seems to have realized that fact. Indeed, almost until his death in 1831 he counseled friends and readers alike in much the same vein that he wrote Jedidiah Morse's son Samuel in 1812: "I am happy that you are so industriously and prosperously engaged in the prosecution of your profession. I hope you will let politics entirely alone for many reasons, not the least of which is a regard to the internal tranquillity of your own mind. I never yet knew a man made happy by studying politics; nor useful, unless he has great duties to perform as a citizen. You will receive this advice, I know, with your accustomed good nature."[81]

Despite the war, Evarts's personal commitment never wavered. In the spring of 1813 he helped organize the Charlestown Association for the Reformation of Morals. Reflecting his conviction that no one remedy would suffice to effect the desired moral reformation, the Charlestown society launched a sweeping attack on idleness, intemperance, gambling, Sabbath-breaking, profanity, and children's disobedience of their parents. In an address before the society, Jedidiah Morse explained the necessity for its formation and advanced what amounted to a paradigm of the moral reformer's perspective. "In the corrupt moral atmosphere of this world," he said, "the tendency in all communities, is to pollution and guilt. If this tendency to corruption, which exists wherever man exists, be left to operate unchecked, in any community, strengthening with surprising increase, as it proceeds, it soon becomes formidable and bids defiance to all opposition, and the utter ruin of that community, of course, becomes inevitable."[82]

Morse's statement and others like it bespoke the anxiety of a person uncomfortable with the world around him and uncertain about the future. People and events seemed to be running out of control. But what critics perceived as a weakening of the bonds of society often reflected their growing inability to find and influence the mechanisms that drove that society. Jesse Appleton, president of Bowdoin College, revealed this frustration in a more positive manner when he observed that "civil society is . . . a union, by which the good are enabled to act, with system and efficacy, against the disturbers and invaders of human peace."[83] The purpose of the organizing impulse was to overcome that problem. New institutions might marshal sufficient resources and exert the pressure required to encourage morality. The Reverend Peter Eaton explained their objectives: "It is because we love religion, liberty, order, good government, and good morals, that we associate. We only oppose vice, disorder, confusion. We wish to combine, and actively engage the virtue of the community, in the preservation of those institutions and habits, which experience has taught us are highly salutary, and transmit them to our children."[84]

The prewar and wartime campaigns for reform, despite their particular objectives, sprang in large part from a sense of cognitive dissonance. Whether or not New England, or even the country as a whole, was in the throes of a declension and decay inimical to Christian and republican values explains not nearly so much as does the fact that men like Jeremiah Evarts believed this decline to be the case. Whether they resided in small towns which saw young men leaving steadily in search of opportunity, or lived in expanding market communities whose very growth marked their secular success, these individuals had come to understand that a new age was dawning that promised to transform their cultural landscape. Men like Evarts sought not so much to resist the changes that enveloped them as to arm the individual conscience so that it might preserve an underlying moral ethos in the face of secular seductions emanating from the marketplace. They did not court the past to hold back the future; indeed, they more often saw the transformation of their world as symbolic of

God's favor and a sign of the approaching millennium. In the words of Evarts's former teacher, Timothy Dwight: "the Millenium is not to come all at once, but to alleviate the evils of mankind by degrees. It is not to burst upon us like the morning, but creep upon us like the twilight. I think then there is no reason to go back: but, on the contrary, constantly forward. Improvements are making on so large a scale, as to outrun every thing which has been known before. I do not think that Providence is doing all of this to no purpose."[85]

Jeremiah Evarts saw the arrival of peace as the herald of millennial expectations, and his hopes quickened. By 1815 he was not only a Charlestown selectman, treasurer of the American Board, and editor of the *Panoplist*, but also active in the New England Tract Society, the Massachusetts Missionary Society, the Massachusetts Bible Society, the Middlesex Bible Society, the Foreign Mission Society of Boston and Vicinity, the Charlestown Society for the Reformation of Morals, and several other local and national benevolent causes.[86] This activity exhilarated the slender reformer. The nation had survived the threat of disunion and the wrath of Great Britain; now it should turn to its own salvation and the salvation of other peoples around the world.[87]

CHAPTER FOUR

Apocalyptic Visions: Jeremiah Evarts and Postwar Reform, 1815–1821

☼

Peace arrived in 1815 and with it the promise of change. But the nature and direction of that change was uncertain. "When or where or what the change will be," wrote Daniel Webster, "is known only to the all-seeing eye of heaven."[1] A shifting economic base, rapidly expanding urban centers, the transformation of rural towns into factory centers, and demographic instability characterized the region. All signs seemed to indicate a profound alteration, a tension between the promise of change and an attachment to old habits. Daniel Webster said it most succinctly: "If New England *reforms her morals*, & maintains her religious, literary, & social institutions, she will have the best Securities for her prosperity, which the case admits. These constitute her real strength. With these, if she should be compelled *to take care of herself*, she will have nothing to fear."[2]

Herein lies the story of the postwar years, as an increasingly boundless belief in economic and political expansion wrestled with a longing for old values to form a new order. For a decade or more following the peace at Ghent, these two forces swayed back and forth, until the election of Andrew Jackson announced that the public wished to reconcile the conflict. By that time, however, a new order had emerged; the face of America had changed, or at least the forces of that change had been set irrevocably in motion.

The revivals of the Second Great Awakening had spawned a variety of apocalyptic visions and organizing impulses. Reformers believed the years following the War of 1812 to be critical to their causes. Building on the organizational energies of the awakening, they tried to alter the public order fundamentally by divorcing character from class to transform society horizontally rather than vertically. They pursued reformatory measures not only to halt the spread of particular evils but to develop humane principles and correct behavioral patterns. Restraint became a watchword. Moral treatment became a curative system, righteousness an antidote for evil. The Board of Visitors of the Massachusetts State Prison summarized an ideal reformation: "It should be as severe as the principles of humanity will possibly permit. . . . Whenever a prisoner transgresses, he should be punished until his mind is conquered. Convicts ought to be brought to the situation of clay in the hands of the potter. The guards should consider the prisoner as a volcano, containing lava, which if not kept in subjection, will destroy friends and foe."[3]

The prescription revealed more than a cure; it laid bare a paradigm for reform embraced by men like Jeremiah Evarts, men who feared that a resurgent individualism and rationalism might unleash an unrestrained pursuit of private interests and who sought a community consensus to mold individuals' behavior. Historian Joyce Appleby has argued that politics imposed power structures which led to stability, and economics developed exchange networks through voluntary participation. Both forces thereby ordered society while providing opportunities for individual freedom. What concerned Jeremiah Evarts, however, was not so much the external influences upon individual behavior as the very wellsprings of that behavior itself.[4]

For Evarts the war had an urgent message. He insisted that national sins had been the underlying cause of the war; political dissension had been only a surface manifestation of those evils. As he contemplated the future of peacetime America, he saw "no sure indications of returning prosperity, without national repentance and reformation."[5] Herein, Evarts believed, lay the real change that the war signified. The association of piety and virtue with secular prosperity was no longer second nature to many Americans. The shift, of course, had been in process for some time, but evidence now mounted that the religious revivals of the Second Great Awakening had not reversed that process. Religion remained important in the lives of most Americans, but it had become largely a concern of the individual and not a framework for the institutional structure of society. To Evarts, the underlying ethos—the soul of America—was becoming too secular and materialistic. He called once again for a renewed emphasis on disinterested benevolence.

After the war Evarts remained active in local, state, and national Bible, missionary and tract societies. His wife, Mehitabel, also became active in the Boston Female Bible Society. Like a growing number of upper- and middle-class women, she found that benevolent work provided a rewarding outlet for her creative and moral energies. Domestic cares still consumed much of her time, however, for she had to care for four children under the age of ten.[6] Family cares took precedence over other concerns, she believed, for she accepted the dictum that "families are emphatically, the nurseries of the church and the state." In the words of her husband's mentor, Timothy Dwight:

> Confinement, censure, find their place.
> Convince, ere you correct, and prove
> You punish, not from rage, but love;
> And teach them, with persuasion mild,
> You hate the fault, but love the child.[7]

During 1815 the Evarts household underwent some changes, with the birth of Sarah in February and the arrival of a nephew, John Todd, in the fall. In 1815 Jeremiah's East Guilford relatives decided that John could find better schooling in Massachusetts than in Connecticut and accepted Jeremiah's offer to take the boy as a boarder. The addition of a fifteen-year-old boy to the family of three girls (ages nine, six, and six months) and one boy (age two and a half) provided a welcome relief from menial chores for both parents. John was expected to draw water, run errands, chop wood, and help out in other ways. The Evartses also had another boarder, an older woman of moderate wealth, who called on the boy for additional errands. After a few months of incessant after-school chores that must have tested his patience and affability, John went to work for his uncle at the ABCFM offices in Boston, binding pamphlets to be sent to benevolent societies throughout the country.[8]

Religious divisions among Congregationalists reached the Charlestown church, meanwhile, and a second Congregational society formed. Although the Evarts family remained with the majority in the First Church, this divisiveness exemplified the growing fragmentation that confronted Jeremiah Evarts throughout the next few years. Not surprisingly, during this same period his health problems returned. Until his death in 1831 his health remained more precarious than robust, and the thin-lipped, slender reformer was consumed almost as much by disease as by his causes.[9] But his periodic physical setbacks rarely forced him to break stride or curtail his voluminous correspondence.

Institutional complexity and economic diversity increasingly characterized the postwar years, and many Americans seemed more concerned with "the most appropriate means of national development . . . not the very meaning of America itself." An expanding market economy enlarged the sphere of political as well as economic intercourse, and as the revisions of state constitutions extended the franchise, Americans increasingly turned to politics to resolve not only political and economic issues but also the social concerns that accompanied them. The youth and promise of the revolutionary generation seemed to have passed, and issues such as intemperance, Indian removal, banking, internal improvements, and slavery increasingly divided Americans.[10]

In speech after speech following the war, ministers lashed out at party spirit as an organizing principle. "Political considerations have more weight with the great mass of people, than religious ones," the Reverend James Tucker of Rowley, Massachusetts, lamented, and "men are more anxious to hear of the advances of their party, than of the triumphs of their Redeemer."[11] Party names should be set aside with the coming of peace, urged the Reverend Abel Flint, for "they are totally inconsistent with that spirit of accommodation, which we ought now to cultivate."[12] "Man is at war even with himself," exclaimed the Reverend Daniel Sanders, and these kinds of passionate conflicts should cease with the onset of international peace.[13] Unless these differences could be resolved, concluded another observer, the country was headed for civil war and the ruin of liberty. Party affiliation had come to bespeak a larger meaning than voting propensities and now seemed to indicate one's character and patriotism as well. Indeed, concluded one observer, the "word republican had acquired a magic, a resistless charm."[14]

The end of the war had brought peace, not reformation. In his annual address as editor of the *Panoplist* in 1816, Jeremiah Evarts asked readers to devote more time to God and the reformation of public morals. He also urged religious periodicals to publish lists of donors so as to encourage additional financial contributions. "All benevolent institutions," wrote one advocate, "may be regarded as so many sisters, each having a distinct branch of duty to perform for the general good of the family." What emerged was a renewed patriotic perspective that sought to join morality and politics in a holy cause. "What is morally wrong," argued the Reverend Abel Flint in an election sermon, "can never be politically right." Evarts added: "It is a notorious truth . . . that there is not in Massachusetts a single man capable of leading the moral exertions of the friends of religion and morality."[15] But there was such a man; his name was Jeremiah Evarts, and by publishing the names of donors he was willing to join economics to benevolence to advance the cause.

His religious recipe was to evangelize the irreligious at home and abroad. Individual conversions promoted the cause (and his nephew underwent conversion during a revival in Charlestown in 1816), but thousands were in need of ministers, Bibles, and general religious awakening. More ministers were required, and reformers sought pious youths to educate for the task. "By sending bibles and instructors" to the West, the Reverend Ward Cotton told a women's foreign mission society auxiliary, "we send them to our own children." Making people better Christians, he argued, made them better citizens: "it may be the means not only of the salvation of their souls, but also of the political salvation of our country." Evarts added that there "is no fear that Socinianism will spread among a people who are inquiring earnestly what they shall do to be saved."[16]

Yet Evarts himself became deeply embroiled in sectarian controversy in 1816, when he reviewed the pamphlet *American Unitarianism*. The pamphlet, printed in England but circulated in the United States, sparked a controversy between religious liberals and conservatives that had its most recent origin in the Codman affair and in a debate between William Ellery Channing and Samuel Worcester. Channing denied that New England religious liberals were Unitarians in the British sense; they were, instead, Socinians who considered Christ only as a moral instructor to mankind. This was, he insisted, neither heresy nor hypocrisy. Difficult questions, like the Trinity, were not central to the message of the Bible; individual actions and not dogma were the true indicators of Christianity. Worcester disagreed, arguing that liberals failed to preach the true gospel precisely because they ignored Christ as the divine savior. This, he insisted, was the essence of Christianity.[17]

At this point Evarts jumped into the fray, arguing that religious controversy was at times essential. One must defend the true Gospel, he insisted, even if such controversy was generally undesirable. "The time will come," he predicted, "when controversy shall cease; but this time will not be hastened by the timid counsels of those, who would suffer the abettors of false doctrine to repeat their assertions and their sophistry without examination and without an answer." There must be, he argued, a "universal reception of the truth." Only Christianity developed the moral restraints of mankind, and in so doing advanced the community. But true Christianity rested on a set of shared doctrines, beliefs so basic that their rejection necessitated a rejection of Christianity itself. "We are sincere believers in the great doctrines of the Reformation," Evarts wrote, "in the inspiration of the Holy Scriptures; in the unity and perfection of the Godhead; in the Supreme divinity of the Son and Spirit; in the atonement and intercession of Christ; in the native and total depravity of the unregenerate; and in the reality and necessity of special divine grace to renew and sanctify the souls of men, that they may be capable of participating in the holy enjoyments of the whole of our creed, but they are among the prominent and fundamental articles of it; they are points in which we differ essentially from Unitarians."[18]

Since Unitarians rejected these truths, Evarts insisted that they were not Christians, and he bemoaned their presence in New England. They perverted their talents, misapplied their erudition, and exerted a baneful influence over Harvard College. Worse, they conspired to promote their beliefs and extend their influence. Religious liberals, he charged, deliberately concealed their religious beliefs in an effort to gain settlement over orthodox churches. Then they praised one another, what Evarts called the "nauseating" practice of "universally bedaubing each other" with adulation. "Let a man only turn Unitarian, and he becomes at once a man of talents, and consideration. The newspapers puff his performances. He is flattered while he lives; and canonized when he is dead. . . . The Editors of papers are not at the bottom of this. It lies in the taste of the Unitarian public."[19]

Unitarians did not tolerate the orthodox, Evarts argued, and this intolerance should be reciprocated. Massachusetts should follow the lead of other states and withhold communion from Unitarians. Orthodox ministers should profess their beliefs and preach against the Unitarian menace. They must assert the true religion or else the liberals might carry the day. Fundamental principles were at stake. "There are others, too, who are too *modest* and *unassuming* to preach or act decisively, because forsooth, they are not *satisfied* about certain controverted points. Let such persons abandon the office of teaching, and return to their studies until they *are* satisfied. What right have they to teach religion, when they themselves are not satisfied about its fundamental principles?"[20]

Jeremiah Evarts's review of American Unitarianism represented more than an attack on Unitarian beliefs and influence; it marked a new aggressiveness on the part of conservatives to define the parameters of respectability and moral character. The pursuit of moral character became a hallmark of reform efforts, and benevolent societies adopted strict rules to quarantine their membership from deviancy. The rules of the Female Missionary Society of Rindge, New Hampshire, reflected that concern: "We promise to be watchful over one another in sisterly love, tenderness, and kindness, and not *to expose* one another's infirmities. If our members shall prove disorderly or scandalous in her daily walk, or fall into dangerous errors, and if after some private means of reformation be used, they do not succeed, and should our united efforts and prayers and admonitions prove ineffectual to reform the offender, she shall be excluded from the society."[21] For his part, Jeremiah Evarts became a manager of the American Bible Society, formed in 1816; subscribed to the Massachusetts Bible Society; and assisted with the early work of Sunday Schools in Charlestown from their formation in 1816.[22]

Evarts's view of the world was both macrocosmic, the nation as the arm of God, and microcosmic, a concern for vice and immorality at the level of individual behavior. Economic man and political man were not merely incomplete in his view; they were positively destructive of order and communitas. The individual was not autonomous, for civilization was a social contract. This was the spirit of the awakening as he understood it. It was to reach out, not only to the less fortunate or the fallen, but also to those who might not be sensible of their condition. He urged the development of a moral science, a science of doing good, which would incorporate religion with morality to invigorate virtue. Evarts's cosmic views led him to be an optimist but not to believe that mechanistic social or political principles would bring the millennium. Moral corruption destroyed republics; only moral virtue preserved them.[23]

Jeremiah Evarts repeatedly addressed this theme in articles in the postwar years, publishing "On Atheism," "On the Duty of Praying for the Salvation of Relatives and Friends," on "President [Jonathan] Edwards' First Resolution," and "On the Intercourse of Christians with the World." His message was virtually the same in each essay: a plea for wisdom, piety, humility, and morality to advance the good of mankind and evangelize the world. True Christians had an obligation to do good, to set an example for the great mass of people who had not acquired true religion. Religious persons had an obligation to confront difficult subjects, to "lead the minds of their people." Christians should not act like other men and women, or be agreeable for the sake of social harmony, but should set the tone for the larger society and impregnate social intercourse with religion. All should give what they could, when they could; promises for the future only postponed the millennium.[24]

The message and the intent were revolutionary. "We live in a remarkable period of the world," wrote Samuel Etheridge. Heathen customs and moral darkness were fading. "Such a radical change in the feelings of men, requires . . . a corresponding change in the institutions of society." The Reverend Heman Humphrey was even more direct: "we must take men as they *are*, and try to make them what they *should be*." Moral and intellectual improvement, insisted another speaker, required mutual cooperation and exertion. All men "have essentially the same wants, infirmities and dependency." It was immoral, therefore, for "a man to regulate his conduct upon the selfish principle of individuality." Only a disinterested benevolence could produce this happy state; only the Christian religion coupled with moral societies and institutions could subdue men's passions and develop a sense of moral obligation.[25]

These societies and admonitions had a synergistic effect. Evarts and other evangelicals looked to the rising glory of America as a herald of the millennium, insisting that New England must be the "irradiating point" for future progress. Joshua Bates, president of Middlebury College, captured their underlying message: "Without religious principles and religious hopes, no man can be really and permanently happy; and, without a general prevalence of these principles and hopes, no society can long enjoy peace and prosperity." Beyond that, warned the Reverend Daniel Dana, "Remove all restraints" that a deep religious conviction cultivates, "and you unhinge human society.[26]

Divisiveness, faction, a lust for power, the failure of religious principles, geographic dispersion, and a concern for worldly advancement were among the primary threats to republican virtue and behavioral propriety, according to Evarts and his colleagues. What could be done to thwart and even reverse their progress? Reformers advanced three remedies. First, as noted above, they believed that the acquisition and practice of certain behavioral principles by the general populace were essential. These principles would insulate the United States from that decay historically associated with republics. "Rome fell," warned Benjamin Oliver, "because virtue in her did not keep pace with knowledge." The Reverend Heman Humphrey was even more specific, sketching an image of popular behavior that depicted human nature as undisciplined and threatening. "Man, by the fall, lost the image of his Maker. He is totally depraved. Reason and conscience are dethroned and enslaved by passion and appetite. Restless as he is, labour and business are extremely irksome. Indolence and vice are his favourite elements. If he can gain a subsistence, however scanty and precarious, without the sweat of his brow, he will not work."[27]

The second remedy was to emphasize the central role of women as incubators of virtue and to encourage their participation in religious awakenings and reform activities. Female reform societies organized, and female auxiliaries to almost every national reform cause became commonplace. Jeremiah Evarts had argued earlier, as a student at Yale, that although women and men operated in separate spheres, women should play an important role in society. By the second decade of the nineteenth century this expectation had become almost a maxim. As officials of the New Hampshire Missionary Society concluded, "Though a wise Providence has much circumscribed for females their sphere of public action; yet the same wise Providence has permitted their influence in society to be very great and powerful." By joining their male counterparts in benevolent societies and reform crusades, therefore, women placed themselves at what many people considered the touchstone of national survival. As sixteen-year-old Susannah Tucker wrote, "When I meditate on the . . . deplorable condition of the heathen, and the usefulness of a female missionary among them, I feel impatient to go and labor in their behalf." Women eventually populated the domestic and foreign missionary fields in considerable numbers.[28]

A third remedy advanced was to urge all Americans to embrace benevolence as a general principle, to reform society by attacking specific ills. This hoped to meliorate what Michael Zuckerman has called the conflict between public virtue and self-interest or between eighteenth-century republicanism and a nineteenth-century liberalism. The agent for this reformation was to be the voluntary society. The acceptance of voluntarism by the likes of Timothy Dwight, Lyman Beecher, and Jeremiah Evarts was a tacit admission that individual autonomy had supplanted community coercion. Benevolent reform had embraced the entrepreneurial spirit. By the postwar years these voluntary societies had become numerous and their causes diverse. Jeremiah Evarts had attached himself to several of these efforts, among them societies that advanced the Bible and the Sabbath. In 1817 the American Bible Society petitioned Congress, requesting free postage and an exemption from the duty on paper used to print Bibles. Although Congress refused to act on the request, it was the forerunner of other requests seeking to enlist the federal government in the process of evangelical reform. The problem, according to the *Panoplist*, was that "The tendency of the American character is then to degenerate rapidly; and that not from any peculiar vice in the American people, but from the very nature of a spreading population. The population of the country is out-growing its institutions."[29]

From his vantage point at the ABCFM offices in Boston, Jeremiah Evarts had seen these changes sweeping across the land. As his attack on Unitarianism demonstrated, his own inner convictions not only remained strong but took on new life in the postwar years. He stayed active in various societies, including the Foreign Mission Society of Boston, the Massachusetts Peace Society, and the Massachusetts Missionary Society. These exertions took their toll on his health, however, and to escape the pressures of his duties in June 1816 he visited lower Canada and western New York as well as his relatives in Georgia, Vermont. His travels reaffirmed his conviction that something had to be done to restore "the sanctity of the Sabbath" and elevate the tone of public morals.[30]

Reformers linked observance of the Sabbath to the progress of civilization. "He who never raises his mind above the world . . . and the pursuits of this world," the Reverend Zephaniah Moore told Massachusetts legislators, "debases his intellectual nature, and rises little above the brutes." Public worship preserved a sense of accountability, which Moore saw as the basis for all society. Reformers viewed the Sabbath, Sunday schools, and the Bible as links in the chain of civilization and once again petitioned Congress to halt the delivery of mail on Sundays. When the postmaster general opposed this halt in 1817, noting that it would disrupt the chain of communications and the conduct of commercial enterprise throughout the country, he allied himself with the forces of liberal capitalism. On the other side, Jeremiah Evarts argued that strict observance of the Sabbath promoted physical and spiritual wealth and that it was the duty of the government "to punish Sabbath-breaking" as "violations of the divine law, and at war with the welfare of the community."[31]

A third theme in which Evarts's interest persisted after the war was that of temperance. As the Massachusetts Society for the Suppression of Intemperance had demonstrated earlier, Americans guzzled enormous quantities of alcohol, drinking to each other's health so frequently that they threatened it. Evarts was concerned about issues of health, of course, but worried more about the impact of intemperance upon the moral character of the nation and its citizens. Reformers urged voters to shun candidates for public office who were intemperate, for, as one speaker asserted, "Vice and immorality usually accompany each other; and they totally disqualify a man for usefulness in society." Others linked intemperance to poverty. Drunkenness led to debauchery, argued selectmen in nearby Cambridge, Massachusetts, and led one down the road to profligacy, licentiousness, and the work house or prison. While the poor should receive aid, only the "virtuous poor" were worthy of public or private support.[32] In the words of an 1820 temperance song:

> It makes the eyes like furnace blaze,
> And puts our senses in maze,
> Calls poverty with all her train.
> Horror and darkness round us reign.
>
> When in the tyrant's chair it rules,
> Makes kings and beggars perfect fools;
> It has no power at all to save
> The drunkard from his hopeless grave.
>
> Turn from the charmer in the glass—
> With her enchantments bid her pass,
> Resist the tyrant's beastly sway,
> Nor longer tribute to him pay.
>
> Come, break at once the fatal chain
> That binds thee to that deathly train.
> Cast off thy shackles—be a man
> Once more, while yet you can.[33]

What Evarts and other reformers hoped was that by defining more clearly what was virtuous and moral, they might stigmatize deviance and thereby exert a powerful public influence. "If we are to be the instruments of doing anything worth mention for the church of God and the poor heathen," Evarts warned, "we must exhibit some of that enterprise which is observable in the conduct of worldly men."[34]

Despite his active participation in numerous benevolent causes after the war, Evarts increasingly focused his energies on foreign missions. His duties as treasurer of the ABCFM increased; contributions had declined, and he now directed fund-raising efforts whose canvass reached well beyond the limits of New England. Although members of the Prudential Committee still came largely from Massachusetts, residents of New York, Pennsylvania, and New Jersey received election to board membership.

Aided by quarterly circulars, financial legacies, religious newspapers like the *Boston Recorder*, and more efficient organizational structure, under Evarts's leadership the ABCFM rose to dominate the foreign mission field in the postwar period.[35]

During this time, the American Board took up the challenge of missions to the North American Indians. Samuel Worcester, corresponding secretary of the ABCFM, had long been interested in the study of Indian languages, and in an 1815 letter to Evarts he outlined a plan for the establishment of missionary stations among them. To begin with one tribe and then expand to others, the plan was to teach Indian children the English language and the principles of Christianity.[36] Worcester was convinced that the Indian nations were doomed to extinction and believed that any perpetuation of their own languages or religions would only hasten that extinction. He proposed to destroy the culture to save the people.

What began as a private letter to a close colleague became, within little more than a decade, a flourishing concern and a controversial political issue. Worcester's timing, whether accidental or not, was nonetheless impeccable. Following the War of 1812 the federal government initiated a new Indian policy, a policy shaped by men like Andrew Jackson and Lewis Cass, to dominate and manipulate the tribes. Agencies and subagencies were established; presents and provisions flowed to the tribes. These increased the native Americans' dependence on whites and eroded native ways. At the same time, the government promoted agriculture and domestic manufactures "to lead them from a state of hunters to that of herdsmen and cultivators."[37]

Several divergent impulses converged and together drove government policy toward the destruction of the Indian culture: the movement of population westward, a nationalistic feeling of self-confidence and even arrogance, a rapacious lust for "development" on the part of states and territories, the rage for internal improvements, and a recognition that military power had irrevocably shifted from the red man to the white. The American Board's decision to "civilize" the Indians through missionary activity placed it squarely in the middle of this developing conflict. Establishment of a Foreign Mission School at Cornwall, Connecticut, in 1816, and the initiation of a mission to the Cherokees that same year, were but a beginning.[38]

The *Second Quarterly Circular* of the American Board of Commissioners for Foreign Missions, issued in April 1816, argued for the establishment of educational facilities for "heathen" youth modeled on the Lancastrian system. Its inspiration sprang from missionary schools in India as well as the work of the Reverend Gideon Blackburn among the North American Indians. James Morris, Charles Prentice, and the Reverend Joseph Harvey were appointed a Board of Trust, and at its October meeting the Prudential Committee approved procedures to establish the institution. It also approved the appointment of Elias Cornelius to solicit funds for the education of "heathen" children and ordered the Reverend Cyrus Kingsbury into Cherokee country to construct a mission station. This far-ranging program sought a cultural as well as religious transformation. Students at the Foreign Mission School were to receive instruction in the mechanic arts, agriculture, and commerce as well as in religion and "civilization." They would then return to their native societies and assist missionaries. The institution was to be a model for the transformation of the "perishing heathen."

> Such an institution in our country would probably exert a powerful influence on the Christian public in favour of missions. It would bring heathen into contact with Christians, and exhibit heathen manners, as a living and impressive spectacle. It would afford a constant fund of interesting facts rendered weighty by their proximity, by which we may rouse the attention and call forth the resources of our country in the cause of missions. . . . It would not only furnish them [missionaries] with companions, acquainted with both languages, and prepared to introduce them to immediate usefulness, but by being conversant with this school, and perhaps spending some time in it as assistant teachers previous to their departure, the Missionaries might learn something of the language of the country to which they are going.[39]

The school opened in May 1817.

The selection of Cornwall, Connecticut, illustrated some of the problems facing prospective missionaries and moral reformers. Most striking about the town, aside from its willingness to donate land and buildings to the undertaking, were its isolation from the winds of change then sweeping the region and the strong religious convictions of its residents. Instructive as well was its physical and social structure. Cornwall remained a predominantly rural community, populated with a variety of craftsmen and farmers, and the board was able to overlook its most important articles of manufacture, gin and cider brandy. In every aspect except the last, therefore, it fit the benevolent reformers' recipe for the ideal society. In the words of the Prudential Committee, "It is necessary to a well ordered and harmonious state of society, that the members should converse and act together; that they should feel their common interests, and be moved, as by a common impulse, to the promotion of a common end."[40]

This was a far cry from what the American Board was about to discover in the South and West as it began to establish missions to the North American Indian tribes. In 1816 and 1818 the ABCFM opened missions among the Cherokees and the Choctaws, and in 1820 it began a mission among the Cherokees then living in Arkansas. By 1826 the board had numerous mission stations throughout the Choctaws in Mississippi as well as the Cherokees in Tennessee, Alabama, and Georgia. Although their focus was on the instruction of children, Evarts and the board considered their mission to be a civilizing one in the broadest sense of the term.

The missionaries who ventured out to maintain these stations often faced opposition from state or territorial officials as well as the enmity of settlers and land speculators who hoped to eliminate the natives and secure their lands, although they had the blessing, and occasionally the aid, of the federal government. The years following the War of 1812 brought demands for Indian land cessions and opportunities for self-enrichment. Men like John Coffee and Andrew Jackson sought to use their influence and expertise to speculate in western lands. While some government officials dutifully warned that the intrusion of whites onto Indian lands violated both the law and government policy, local officials were loathe to take any action.[41]

Among the factors complicating the issue of Indian relations and policy were the differing perceptions of the problem among settlers and missionaries. A series of articles in the *Panoplist* outlined those differences and argued that the missionary should be the advance agent of civilization. "One Christian missionary, with the weapons of his holy warfare, will do more to give security to our frontier settlements, than whole armies with their instruments of death." Only when the Indians were "assimilated to us in language, manners and religion" would the threat of warfare and revenge abate. There were two options available: One could remove Indian youths and educate them in white schools, whereupon they could return to the tribe and instruct their brethren; or missionary schools could be established among the tribes and the natives instructed in English. The first option would subject the youths to a discipline and confinement unfamiliar to them as well as bring them into contact with some unsavory elements in the white population. The second option was more appealing, for it would "raise them, gradually from one stage of improvement to another, without subjecting them to a discipline, that would be at once irksome and unprofitable."[42] The ABCFM embraced the first option with its establishment of the Cornwall School, but after 1819 the board changed and, together with the federal government, promoted the second alternative.

Yet while religious reformers advanced a policy of Christian benevolence, men like Andrew Jackson admonished treaty negotiators to address the prevailing passions among the tribes—avarice and fear. Even those officials who appeared to profess a benevolent intent, like Secretary of War William Crawford, advocated essentially the same purpose even if they urged different procedures. Crawford emphasized civilization of the tribes over expropriation of lands but insisted that the civilizing process required disruption of the tribes' cultural integrity and the promotion of individual property ownership or even intermarriage. In March of 1816 Crawford framed the issue as he understood it, writing that

> it is the true policy and earnest desire of the Government to draw its savage neighbors within the pale of civilization. If I am mistaken in this point— if the primary object of the Government is to extinguish the Indian title, and settle their lands as rapidly as possible, then commerce with them ought to be entirely abandoned to individual enterprise, and without regulation. The result would be continual warfare, attended by the extermination or expulsion of the aboriginal inhabitants of the country to more distant and less hospitable regions. The correctness of this policy cannot for a moment be admitted. The utter extinction of the Indian race must be abhorrent to the feelings of an enlightened and benevolent nation. The idea is directly opposed to every act of the Government, from the declaration of independence to the present day.[43]

During the next several years government officials vacillated between a desire for profits from the Indian trade, reformers' insistence that civilization of the Indians should be the paramount objective for all policies and measures, and growing demands from whites that the tribes be removed by the most efficient means available and their lands opened to settlement.

Even among friends of the natives, concern focused on preservation of the race and not the integrity of the culture. Cyrus Kingsbury, writing from the newly opened Chickamauga (later Brainerd) Mission in Cherokee country, expressed not only his personal observations but what was in effect the policy of the ABCFM. "Considering therefore the relation in which we stand to these people, it has appeared no less an act of justice than a dictate of humanity & a duty enjoined by the gospel, to extend to them as far as practicable the distinguished advantages which we enjoy. This duty is incumbent on individuals & on societies, as well as on the government."[44]

Southern demands for expansion and land, however, challenged this policy almost from the outset. As Andrew Jackson wrote from Tennessee, "the people of the west will never suffer any Indian to inhabit this country again." Only government coercion could keep whites off tribal lands, and that might mean civil war. Further to the north, Lewis Cass faced a different set of circumstances as governor of Michigan. Tribes were less powerful and more scattered, land for settlement was plentiful, and Cass could wax eloquent about the need to ameliorate the conditions of the natives and not hurl thunderbolts at the federal government. "We can," Cass insisted, "reclaim them from the pursuits of the chase to the labours of agriculture, and render them useful to themselves without being dangerous to us." But the discovery of mineral resources, as well as a surging interest in the development of a network of roads and canals, soon led officials away from benevolence and toward expropriation in the North as well.[45] In a letter to the Indian commissioners, Secretary of War Crawford outlined both the government's policy and its dilemma. "The determination to purchase land only when demanded for settlement, will form the settled policy of the government. Experience has sufficiently proven that our population will spread over any cession, however extensive, before it can be brought into the market, and before there is any regular and steady demand for settlement, thereby increasing the difficulty of protection, embarrassing the government by broils with the natives, and rendering the execution of the laws regulating intercourse with the Indian tribes utterly impracticable."[46]

The missionary community, essentially an outside force in all these instances, pursued a course that threatened to alienate every one of these interests. Missionaries sought to establish schools; educate the natives in language, religion, and husbandry; and thereby close the "civilization gap" between natives and settlers. These efforts, in essence, pointed toward a policy of assimilation and would make the natives more resistant to removal attempts. The ABCFM missionaries, moreover, did not share the fear and hostility to Indians so prevalent along the frontier. Their presence after 1816 frequently became a divisive one and, as William McLoughlin has noted, it further politicized an already politically divisive situation. The opening of the Chickamauga Mission (later Brainerd) in 1816 began a period of missionary expansion which soon led to the formation of other stations at Carmel, Creek Path, Hightower, Willstown, Haweis, Candy's Creek, New Echota, Ahmohee, Red Clay, and Running Water.[47]

As the American Board opened these stations and as federal Indian policy became more controversial, Jeremiah Evarts immersed himself in these affairs. In late 1817 his physician advised him to visit a milder climate and relax from business. In January 1818 Evarts left for Savannah, Georgia. The trip, designed to restore his health, opened his eyes to new moral crises and opportunities for melioration. Never able to divorce professional from personal activities, he went south as an agent of the board and toured its newly established Indian missions. Evarts's immersion in professional activities once again left his wife and family alone in Boston. (This would be a pattern for the rest of his life.) He eventually traveled through South Carolina, Georgia, Tennessee, Kentucky, Ohio, Pennsylvania, and Virginia before heading back to Boston. His exertions were vigorous, and it is difficult to see how the trip was bound to improve his precarious physical condition. Evarts himself must have realized this risk at the outset, because before his departure he sent his wife an itemized statement of his worth. Overall his financial affairs were in good shape, but more significant was the act of accounting itself. Perhaps he did not expect to survive the journey.[48]

Throughout the trip he documented his travels and observations with a steady stream of letters to Samuel Worcester at the ABCFM and maintained a journal. Aside from particular commentaries on board activities, these records reveal his humanitarian sensibilities. At Savannah, for instance, he attended a slave auction to get a first-hand view of the institution. "It was a humiliating spectacle," he wrote, "to see a human being put up with damaged cheese, shoes, etc., to be disposed of for life to any man who might purchase him."[49]

He also wrote occasional letters to his wife. These were never very intimate and revealed a personality that seems formal even for its day (when writers rarely assumed that such letters would ever be read by anyone other than their intended recipient). Most of these letters document the state of his health, which gradually improved despite the rigors of his travels. They also revealed that behind Evarts's formal exterior and professional drive lay a deep concern for his family. In March he recorded that he was "extremely happy, after being disappointed a long time, to receive letters from home. One of them informs me of the birth of a son. For this signal favor of divine providence, I hope to be thankful." He quickly wrote to his wife, suggesting the name "William Maxwell" for "the little stranger," but left the final choice up to her. (She concurred.) He also reflected on the whims of humanity: "I could not but think how differently the destinies of men are disposed of in this world. My children might be taken and sold with as much justice and propriety as the immense multitude of native Africans."[50]

The birth of a son, his persistent health problems, and the long absence from his family led Evarts to be somewhat introspective. Expecting to be away at least six months, he urged his wife to be a moral guide to the children: "a Christian example, & continual religious instruction . . . should conspire to promote their salvation." To his wife he confided fears of an early death. Although he was only thirty-seven years old, he was not sure that he would survive his children's youth. He clung to his religious and millennial hopes: "death will separate us with a few years at the longest. . . . we may meet in a world where sin & danger & anxiety & inquietude shall be forever unknown."[51]

Before that time came, however, Evarts determined to promote the American Board's objectives. He traveled extensively throughout South Carolina and Georgia to rally public sentiment and gather donations for the missionary cause before heading west to inspect the board's Cherokee missions. Much of his favorable reception probably stemmed from the fact that he was the first agent of the ABCFM to visit the churches of that area. He rejoiced when he found an occasional missionary box in a local tavern and found it easier to silence critics than to convert them, but concluded nonetheless that cities like Charleston were fertile ground for missionary solicitations. What was needed was a plan.

> I have thought much of a circular letter . . . one adapted to make each individual addressed feel that the appeal is made to him particularly, and aimed directly and boldly at his heart. We have conversed together about a letter for very rich men. This is wanted, and will do good. We want at least two others . . . one designed for persons possessed of a competency, who maintain the character of exemplary Christians, calculated to induce them to make regular, unsolicited, and punctual remittances for our objects. The other should be addressed to persons of whom less can be hoped in a systematic way, but who would do something handsome, if the subject were brought powerfully to their minds by a concise abstract of facts and arguments.[52]

To advance those ideas he distributed copies of missionary reports and the *Missionary Herald* throughout his travels.

In early spring Evarts braved mud and bad weather to visit the ABCFM mission at Chickamauga (its name was changed to Brainerd with this visit). He spent almost two weeks there, talking with Indians and ABCFM missionaries, and visited with Moravian missionary John Gambold along the way. His journal entries and letters home reveal that the order and decorum of the Indian children captivated his attention and led him to ponder how best to dramatize their conversion from heathenism so as to fire the imagination of the Christian public. The behavior of the children also impressed the governor of Tennessee, who stopped by the mission and watched them sing several hymns. Later, with the arrival of missionary Elias Cornelius at Brainerd, Evarts planned the establishment of a mission among the Choctaws. When Evarts and Cornelius left Brainerd to begin the journey back to New England, they took with them three Cherokee youths for the Foreign Mission School. The board still believed that cultural transformations were most effective when young people were trained outside their native culture, even though Evarts candidly admitted that it would be a very expensive task.[53] Nonetheless, he left Brainerd full of optimism about the future of Indian missions, convinced that his trip was necessary if "I am to have any influence hereafter in directing Indian missions." He urged the American Board to establish a mission among those Cherokees who had already emigrated west across the Arkansas River, indicating that the natives themselves sought the station.[54]

Throughout his journey Evarts seized every opportunity to address the public on the subject of missions and published tales of his travels in the *Panoplist* to reach audiences beyond the sound of his voice. He also lobbied the federal government, writing to the superintendent of the Indian trade, Thomas McKenney, in November 1818: "Cannot something effectual be done for the benefit of the Indians during the present session of Congress? What is the character of the Committee on Indian affairs? Can anything be done by the people here to promote the success of good & wise measures in Congress, on the subject?"[55] Along with Elias Cornelius he engaged the secretary of war in similar conversations but found the government more willing to accede to the removal views of western politicians than to support efforts of the ABCFM east of the Mississippi. While Evarts supported Indian claims to their ancestral tribal lands, for the moment he was more concerned about organizing Indian missions than in opposing an emerging governmental policy of removal. Convinced that the board was in the right, and hopeful that Indian youth educated at the Foreign Mission School would open natives' souls to Christian conversion, Evarts urged the ABCFM to mount an aggressive campaign to develop missionary fields.[56]

His contacts with the federal government came none too late. Americans were wrestling, not only with who was an American, as historian William McLoughlin has noted, but with a collision between the forces of liberal capitalism and those of republican idealism. At the same time, the various tribes which had often seemed to circumscribe the American future no longer represented a military threat that challenged the ideology of expansionism.[57]

Pres. James Monroe, in his first inaugural address, said only that the federal government should promote civilization among the tribes. But officials like Andrew Jackson urged Monroe to regulate the tribes, not negotiate with them. "I have long viewed treaties with the Indians," wrote Jackson, "an absurdity not to be reconciled to the principles of our Government." They were subjects, not sovereigns. Accordingly, Congress had the "right to prescribe their bounds at pleasure." He urged Monroe to authorize surveys of Indian lands and then to bring those lands onto the market.[58]

Federal authorities were not quite ready to swallow Jackson's advice, however, and in an 1817 treaty with the Cherokees granted land to about three hundred heads of households and made them citizens. This effort, an experiment to test a civilization program that would integrate the Indian population into the United States, was an important failure, and its ramifications set the stage for the alternative solutions that emerged during the ensuing decade. States and territories voiced their opposition and became more insistent about removal. White Americans recoiled from the idea that tribesmen were their equals. And the Cherokees themselves discovered that denationalization meant cultural extermination. All of these reactions hardened opposition to civilization programs, whether federal or private, and made the task of the government and the American Board more difficult in the years ahead.[59]

A letter from Monroe to Andrew Jackson in 1817 revealed that the president was rethinking Indian policy and seemed to promise a new policy compatible with westerners' views.

> The hunter or savage state, requires, a greater extent of territory to sustain it, than is compatible with the progress and just claims of civilized life, and must yield to it. Nothing is more certain, than, if the Indian tribes do not abandon that state, and become civilized, that they will decline, and become extinct.... It has become customary to purchase the title of the Indian tribes, for a valuable consideration, tho' in general that of each tribe, has been vague and undefined. A compulsory process seems to be necessary, to break their habits, and to civilize them, and there is much cause to believe, that it must be resorted to, to preserve them.[60]

This new attitude prompted some, like Jackson, to envision rapid removal. Requests from federal authorities to territorial governors William Clark and Ninian Edwards that they negotiate land cessions from various tribes encouraged this perception. President Monroe's annual message in December 1817 further heightened expectations. Monroe argued that "the earth was given to mankind to support the greatest number of which it is capable, and no tribe or people have a right to withhold from the wants of others more than is necessary for their own support and comfort." In addition, the War Department agreed to remove interpreters who opposed tribal cessions, and in 1818 Secretary of War John Calhoun supported withholding supplies and arms from Cherokees who refused to move to lands along the Arkansas River. Calhoun also elaborated the president's policy, arguing that the tribes were not the proper judges of their own interest: "I do not see what an intelligent Cherokee has to hope, situated as his nation is, except in emigrating to the West, or taking reservations, and settling down under the fostering protection of our laws. As our population grows dense around them it will be out of the power of the government itself to protect them in their present condition."[61]

This was not the only perception of what future United States Indian policy should be, however. The American Board now sought to extend its system of Indian schools and embraced civilization rather than removal as the key to tribal survival. Civilization and salvation went hand in hand in its view, although both represented long-term responses and might be difficult to effect in the face of growing demands for immediate solutions. Advocates at the ABCFM found a willing collaborator in the person of Thomas McKenney in the War Department, and McKenney forwarded letters from persons seeking to work with the tribes to Jeremiah Evarts at board headquarters in Boston. The tribes themselves were somewhat receptive and supported the establishment of schools. They did not, however, embrace the idea of cultural transformation inherent in the missionaries' approach. Acceptance of missionary stations, nonetheless, accelerated the tribes' dependency on white institutions as well as internal tribal divisions over future responses to outside pressures. It deepened their vulnerability to cultural forces beyond their control.[62]

The entrance of an outside agent, like the ABCFM, upset local officials and quickly led to conflicts. Tennessee governor Joseph McMinn attacked the missionaries' motives, complaining to Calhoun that ABCFM agents such as Elias Cornelius were urging the tribes not to sell their lands or to remove west of the Mississippi River. Samuel Worcester, corresponding secretary of the American Board, argued forcefully that missionaries had been advised not to interfere with treaty negotiations and urged Calhoun to quash the controversy. Calhoun did so immediately, admitting that Cornelius was blameless but warning that the government expected from missionaries "a proper support of all its measures." Even Indian agent Return Meigs concluded that establishing missionary schools at Brainerd would not "retard the emigration to Arkansas."[63]

What President Monroe embraced that fall, however, was the elimination of tribal independence through "civilization." "To civilize them, and even to prevent their extinction," wrote Monroe, "it seems to be indispensable that their independence as communities should cease and that the control of the United States over them should be complete and undisputed." This was not what the tribes expected, however, and missionaries' visions of what might emerge differed from those of the president. "These people," wrote one missionary at Brainerd, "consider the offer of taking reserves, and becoming citizens of the United States as of no service to them." ABCFM missionary Moody Hall wrote Evarts to urge "the pious of N.E." to pray directly for the tribes. "Have not the aborigines of America, been long enough trampled upon & trodden underfoot!"[64]

All of these considerations came to a head in 1819, a year that proved to be a turning point in the development of the American nation. A severe panic punctured the country's economic fabric, and its course not only led Americans to reevaluate their relationship to world markets but strained domestic resources as well. It undermined the resources of benevolent organizations and threatened to curtail their vision of moral progress. The Transcontinental Treaty with Spain enabled the United States to annex Florida and extended American territorial claims to the Pacific. In so doing it kept alive Americans' vision of westward expansion and change across space rather than through time. The eruption of the Missouri debates threatened to fracture the political system, aroused public opinion, raised the specter of slavery, and portended a realignment of parties along sectional lines. In addition, the ABCFM sent missionaries to the Sandwich Islands, and Congress created the Indian Civilization Fund.[65]

The Indian Civilization Fund stemmed directly from President Monroe's 1818 annual message and the report of the House Committee on Indian Affairs for the same year. Both argued that the choice for the tribes was between civilization and extinction. Two years earlier missionary Cyrus Kingsbury had urged the creation of such a fund, and for more than a year Secretary of War Calhoun had been providing monies to missionary societies to build schools and pay teachers. The intent of this fund, as Michael Green has argued, was to "educate Native people off their land." Since 1817 the ABCFM had spent $10,000 a year for missions among the Cherokees.[66]

To investigate reports of government removal plans, the ABCFM sent Samuel Worcester to Washington. Worcester was alarmed at the prospect that the Cherokees would cede all their eastern lands and be removed to lands along the Arkansas River. He did not believe that they would be any better protected there than in the east and worried that future administrations would lack the zeal to prevent white intrusions on their lands. "If the government are now disposed to do them justice," Evarts warned him, "they can do it more easily by quieting them in their present possessions, than in any other way." The government eventually agreed to allow the Cherokees to remain on their ancestral lands, and a visit by President Monroe to the board's Brainerd mission that May helped convince him to support a formal government appropriation to advance Indian civilization and education. This, in turn, led the American Board to enlarge its plans for missions among the Cherokees, Choctaws, and Chickasaws, on the assumption that these appropriations would be permanent.[67]

But the crisis had not passed. Jeremiah Evarts warned that "the present is an eventful crisis with the Cherokees, with our own establishment of course, & with all the Indian tribes." Cherokee agent Return J. Meigs argued strongly that now was the time to change the government's relationship with the Cherokees and urged Calhoun to let Georgia and Tennessee extend their laws over that part of the tribe that refused to remove. "It is time that their present customs . . . should be abolished." Cultural change or removal was essential to prevent further white pressure and "perpetuate their national existence." The Cherokees must listen to the government, Meigs insisted, for *"their safety depends on their dependence,* but it is difficult to make them comprehend this." In a talk to the Cherokee delegation, Calhoun emphasized that they were "now becoming like the white people" and must therefore abandon the hunt as well as their large landholdings. "You see that the Great Spirit has made our form of society stronger than yours—and you must submit to adopt ours." A Cherokee cession in 1819 quickly took on two meanings: for whites it represented the first of several such arrangements that must necessarily follow; for the tribe it represented a definitive settlement regardless of subsequent emigration.[68]

Following the treaty, Evarts wrote that he feared future administrations would not protect the tribes and that perhaps they ought to remain where they were. This was not yet his settled conviction, and Samuel Worcester replied that he believed the government would now abandon efforts to remove all of them. John Calhoun, however, insisted that "our system in relation to the Indians ought to undergo an entire and radical change." "To effect this great change," Calhoun told a delegation of Creeks, "you must establish schools, learn to spin and weave and cultivate the ground. We are willing to give you aid, if you will but adopt our advice." Calhoun had assimilation in mind, but others had different objectives. Andrew Jackson warned that the "Treachery of the Indian character will never justify the reposing of confidence in their professions."[69]

Passage of the Indian Civilization Fund and the subsequent appropriation of $10,000 by Congress closed one phase of the debate over Indian removal and initiated another phase. Indecision about the government's objective ended with the commitment to education and civilization. As the Massachusetts Peace Society reported in 1819: "They afford ground of hope, that a humane policy will be pursued, by which our nation will be saved from the guilt and reproach of exterminating the residue of these unfortunate tribes. Should similar schools also be established among the white people in the vicinity of Indian settlements, still greater benefits might result. For the savage character is not peculiar to red men."[70] But as groups who favored removal thought about the implications of the civilization plan, Indian policy increasingly became a highly charged and divisive political issue.

Mixed with these extremes was another view, or hope: that the tribes would abandon their traditional cultures and become "a stationary, industrious and farming people." This reflected not only the conviction of men like Lewis Cass that red and white cultures could not coexist but also the perpetual optimism of the missionaries. They did not seem to comprehend the difficulties in effecting a wholesale cultural revolution among peoples who were simultaneously beset by their own internal conflicts as well as by constant subversive pressures from whites who wanted their land and loathed their very presence. ABCFM missionaries hoped to change the Indians' language, customs, dress, religion—indeed, their very culture. At the same time land speculation soared, land sales boomed, and visions of a continental manifest destiny danced in the heads of politicians from East to West. Promulgation of a formal civilization policy crystallized political discontent in ways that the previous governmental ambivalence had not. On the other hand, publication of *Catharine Brown, The Converted Cherokee: A Missionary Drama* in 1819 highlighted what the missionaries hoped to achieve. "When she came here [Brainerd Mission Station], she was gay, ignorant and vain. She can now knit, sew, and spin; can read well, and writes a decent hand—and her deportment, is such as I think, will highly interest you."[71]

What was the problem? Proponents of removal feared that the promotion of civilization and a settled agriculture might be successful and would encourage the tribes to remain where they were. Opponents of removal feared that concentration on nations bordering white settlements indicated an intent to threaten those tribes with the option of cultural annihilation or removal west of the Mississippi. For the moment, Jeremiah Evarts and the American Board remained optimistic that the tribes could be civilized on their ancestral lands. The recent Cherokee treaty seemed proof enough. The Cherokees had asked that a member of the ABCFM Prudential Committee accompany them in the negotiations, and Samuel Worcester had gone to Washington. In its annual report, the Prudential Committee reported his success. The tribe could now pursue the arts of civilization and not be cast into a "boundless wilderness" where they would revert to a savage life. This marks, the committee concluded, "a new and propitious era."[72]

Proponents of civilizing the heathen found that 1819 marked a new era in another respect as well. That October the ABCFM outfitted and dispatched four new mission companies to foreign lands. ABCFM missionaries had previously gone to India (1812, 1815, 1817) and Ceylon (1815), but those missions had been closely connected to British efforts and had evoked more curiosity than support from the American public. Now, in 1819, the board sent missionaries again to India and Ceylon but also to Palestine and the Sandwich Islands (Hawaii). This latter mission captivated the religious and romantic imagination of the American public. The intent was little different from that of missions to the North American Indian tribes: "to promote improvement and civilization; to introduce husbandry and manufactures; to inculcate conjugal fidelity and domestic attachment, parental care and filial obedience, with all the duties and charities of life; to educate the rising generation; to meliorate the condition of the female sex; and to diffuse the blessings of knowledge among those who now divide their time between that small degree of labour which is necessary for their bare sustenance and those animal enjoyments which are common to them with the brutes."[73]

Why did the Sandwich Islands mission attract public attention, sympathy, and support to a larger extent than missions to other countries? Pinpointing one answer is difficult, but several perspectives seem central to any explanation. First, descriptions of the Pacific Islands' natives paralleled those of American Indian tribes. The *Panoplist* and other publications reported them to be warlike at times but also possessed of a fascinating romantic character that seemed malleable and susceptible to civilizing tendencies. Second, children from both cultures had spent some time at the Foreign Mission School and were therefore familiar to New Englanders. Many had even been renamed in honor of donors to the cause, carrying names such as "Jeremiah Evarts." Books like *Narrative of Five Youths from the Sandwich Islands* and press promotion of the lives of island natives such as Henry Obookiah stirred public interest. Obookiah had arrived in New Haven from Owhyhee (Hawaii) in 1809, lived with Timothy Dwight, president of Yale, and traveled throughout New England. In the process he met (and seemed to inspire) most of the men who were instrumental in founding the Foreign Mission School. Obookiah's sudden death in 1818 sparked the idea of a mission to the Sandwich Islands.

In addition, American (particularly New England) commerce with the islands had been extensive, profitable, and growing. There was, therefore, an economic as well as an evangelical interest in the islands' future. Fourth, this was an *American* venture. It played to a nascent nationalism and separated the ABCFM in the public mind from the London Missionary Society. Fifth, the ABCFM and its constituent auxiliaries spared no effort to publicize the Sandwich Islands mission and to cultivate support for it prior to its departure. Tales of exotic religious and national customs sent back by missionaries to India and Ceylon had fascinated readers of the *Panoplist*, but tales such as this appeared in the religious press even before Asa Thurston, Hiram Bingham, and their colleagues had left port. There was, in short, a sense of anticipation about this mission that did not surround other missionary endeavors. As the *Boston Recorder* observed, "We know of no Mission that has hitherto left this country, which has excited such general interest and prompted so many prayers as that to the Sandwich Islands."[74]

Finally, when the missionaries arrived off Oahu they learned that a revolution had just occurred. King Kamehameha was dead; the ancient "tabus" had been abolished. The path was now open for Christian practices to supersede native customs. The news electrified not only the missionaries but also readers of the religious press at home. It seemed a sign that the mission was blessed. As Heman Humphrey had told Bingham and Thurston at their ordination: "The ultimate conquest and possession of all the heathen lands is certain. The heathen themselves may rage—Satan may come down with great wrath, and in his convulsive struggles for empire, may yet shake the foundations of the earth; but the promise cannot fail."[75]

If the Indian Civilization Bill and the Sandwich Islands mission promised success in 1819, the eruption of the Missouri Crisis challenged the evangelical ethos. Sparks generated by debates over the admission of Missouri to the union prompted Jeremiah Evarts to write several essays on slavery, morality, and republican government. Evarts was no abolitionist and counted many slaveholders among his personal friends, but the slave auction blocks he had seen on visits to Washington horrified him, for he considered slavery to be the "greatest question which will probably come before the assembled council of our nation during the present century."[76] He quickly cast the question as one of national morality, embracing not only the good of the union but the security of southerners and improvements in the condition of the black population.

To Evarts and other moral reformers the Missouri question posed numerous challenges. First there was the issue of slavery, which they considered "*an inherent vice* in any community, where it exists." A second fear was that divisions over Missouri would subvert efforts to create a sense of community in the country. Moral crusaders believed that the revivals of the Second Great Awakening had given impetus to these efforts and feared that a resurgent sectionalism would frustrate their work. As an essay in the *North American Review* cautioned, "You do not care enough about people two thousand or one thousand miles off, to wage a speculative war with them, upon an interest in which you have only a limited community."[77] Politicians like Daniel Webster insisted that the central issue in Missouri was the geography of political power, one which affected the North's right *"to an equal weight in the political power of the Government,"* and predicted a realignment of parties along sectional lines.[78] A final concern was a fear of the future. Many observers believed that the Missouri question teemed "with unknown and unimagined issues" that threatened the happiness of the Republic, issues that would be so dominant as to excite local prejudices and become the touchstone of all future political discourse.[79]

So central was the Missouri question and the issues it raised that Jeremiah Evarts undertook to write an extended editorial on the matter for readers of the *Panoplist*. Evarts argued from the outset that the crucial concern for evangelicals was the issue of national morality, "on which our character as a just, magnanimous, humane, and Christian people, will much depend." There were, according to Evarts, several related matters. First was the need to retain the Union. Second was the question of slavery, which perpetuated vice and should be condemned. A third factor was the constitutional one, and here he insisted that Congress had clear authority to make laws for the territories. In addition, the Constitutional clause that guaranteed each state a republican form of government made it imperative that Congress act to prevent slavery in Missouri. Perhaps even more decisive was the precedent that a decision on Missouri would set for the remaining western territories. Evarts's moral hackles bristled at the prospect that "If slavery is admitted here, it will be admitted into the whole country west of the Mississippi. The shrieks of bondage will reverberate among the cliffs of the rocky mountains, and the groans of oppression be heard along the shores of the gulf of Mexico. The forests will be felled, and the cornfields ploughed, the cotton plantations tilled, and the sugar manufactured, by the hands of slaves."[80]

The Missouri Crisis galvanized Evarts's moral conscience, but the prospects for its resolution paralyzed him. He had little to offer. He did suggest colonization of blacks elsewhere, but almost in passing. He worried more that the free and slave balance in the Union would be upset and interpreted this imbalance as part of a pattern that promoted national immorality. Finally, after tracing the history of slavery in the United States and lamenting the failure of the framers to settle the question in the Constitutional debates, he could only offer delay as a corrective measure. Postpone statehood, Evarts suggested, and continue territorial status for

Missouri and other western areas for a few more years. Perhaps then, with Congress prohibiting the importation of slaves into the territories, the question could be resolved.[81]

As a representative for an organization (the ABCFM) that considered itself a national body, and particularly one which was developing extensive operations in the South, his publication of this lengthy editorial was remarkable. Why did he do it? Clearly his concern for national morality is central to any explanation, and throughout his essays Evarts tried to tread carefully along a narrow path—condemning slavery but not the South. He took pains to announce that many slaveholders were humane and benevolent but then asked if "our southern brethren wish to be slaves themselves, even to the kindest and most benevolent masters within their knowledge?" Man's natural depravity, he insisted, led him to abuse the sort of unrestrained power found in the slave relationship.[82]

Evarts also believed that the time had come to do something about slavery, and following his Missouri editorials he launched another series of essays, "On the Condition of Blacks." The timing was not coincidental; Evarts believed that slavery threatened to erode national efforts of the benevolent crusade by provoking sectional tensions. The South might become indignant about a discussion of slavery by the North, but it had failed to do anything about the evils of the institution. He highlighted the moral certainty which undergirded the evangelical effort:

> What then is to be done? Let the people be informed of the nature and extent of the evil, without exaggeration and without concealment. Let the truth be kindly, though fearlessly, told. Let the plans of the benevolent be submitted for consideration. Let the friends of Africa and her sons be active and vigilant. Let there be a rallying point in every slave-holding state, at which the friends of liberty and of equal rights shall meet, for the expression of their opinions, and the promotion of the good cause. No doubt this process will excite much opposition on the part of the interested, and the violent. But opposition must not deter from duty. . . . The friends of truth and righteousness never yet achieved any great victory without a great struggle.[83]

He was convinced that the South had mistaken its own interests in the heat of debate, that reformation was more important than economics. He tried to convince southerners that their continued embrace of slavery was criminal without at the same time branding them national sinners. Ever the optimist, Evarts believed that once they digested his sermonizing and awakened to the moral imperatives, they would move to improve the condition of blacks and restrict the spread of slavery. As evidence of the moral decay inherent in such a system, he cited the recently enacted laws of Virginia regarding slavery. The Virginia legislature had prohibited meetings of slaves, which had the effect of driving black children out of Sabbath schools, making religious worship difficult for all blacks, preventing slaves from learning to read and write, and restricting the teaching of the gospel. Support for these measures meant that slaveholders were fighting against God; all were contrary to the promotion of public morality.[84]

But all these arguments only revealed Evarts's underlying dilemma and exposed a weakness of the moral crusade. Corrective action, in his view, rested on an awakening of the individual conscience which would then lead citizens to do the "right thing" and advance a Christian republicanism. Yet while some slaveholders might be willing to lament the institution's existence, they were not willing to act against it. Economic and social considerations took precedence over matters of conscience. If there was an underlying moral ethos that comprised the ligaments of American society, it had lost its connective power. The soul of America seemed to have lost its humanitarian sensibility. There was an alternative, of course. Reformers could insist on the morality of their cause and push ahead at all costs. But this action would create deeper and wider divisions, whereas they sought to heal. In 1819 the disinterested benevolence of men like Jeremiah Evarts still embraced moral suasion rather than political coercion.

Not surprisingly, however, Evarts received a considerable volume of mail sharply critical of his essays. It came chiefly from southerners, who complained that, like most northerners, he had looked only at the dark side of slavery. "I really fear," wrote one South Carolinian, "that such publications . . . will defeat the professed benevolent design of their authors, and paralyze the exertions of the pious of these states." In a subsequent installment, Evarts admitted the complaints but insisted that he was right and that the subject had to be discussed. Southerners, he warned, should read his editorial comments cooly or throw the pages away! If southerners refused to discuss the subject, how could measures to improve the condition of blacks be adopted? "The time must come," he insisted, "when this subject shall be boldly discussed, no matter how wisely and temperately, but still boldly, even in the southern states, or the time of deliverance to the slave-holding country will never come. It would be better undoubtedly, that the southern people should take the lead in this discussion; but if they persevere in silence, is all the rest of the world bound to be silent also?"[85]

In his own mind, no doubt, Jeremiah Evarts was being the model of the Christian statesman. But southerners did not view his remarks from the same perspective and resented outside interference in their affairs. Few persons, especially those convinced of their course, enjoy being told they are sinners. Southerners were no exception. They found themselves being called to a moral awakening yet could not agree that they lay mired in immorality. In this respect his remarks forecast a conflict that deepened with time. Evangelical that he was, Jeremiah Evarts could not accept enslavement of human beings as a permanent feature of the American landscape. He advocated caution but also confrontation: "the fundamental principles of freedom should never be abandoned; the great and paramount and spiritual interests of immortal beings should never be deserted."[86]

Evarts's belief that moral reformation could occur only if people confronted sin directly betrayed the driving optimism that energized the moral reform effort in the postwar years. His moral prescriptions also pitted him against the tendencies rapidly becoming ascendant in American society and politics, for they opposed the logic and practice of liberal capitalism and a reliance on market forces to shape the future. Whether slavery would be economically viable or politically possible in the western territories was irrelevant to him; it was morally wrong and that itself dictated the need for reform. Throughout his efforts Evarts himself did not seek power. He was, instead, a proxy for larger forces which he believed would determine American destiny, forces in which republicanism had joined with morality to birth a new ethos. Slavery was symptomatic of the dangers and temptations that lay about. A state with slavery, concluded an essay in the *North American Review*, "possesses within itself sources of corruption, weakness, and degeneracy, which must endanger its safety and finally accelerate its ruin. The employment of slaves has an obvious tendency to banish that steady, cheerful, and active industry, which is among the chief causes of national wealth and strength."[87]

All these controversies kept Evarts busy with his duties for the American Board. By 1820, however, when the American Board decided to abandon the *Panoplist* for the *Missionary Herald*, his increased labors forced Evarts to resign as editor.[88] Family crises also influenced his decision. His sister Sarah lost a young child that spring, and with typical evangelical fervor Jeremiah sent his condolences: "I mourn with you the untimely & unexpected death of your little babe. It has been no doubt a severe trial to you; but it may teach you a salutory lesson. You committed that child to the disposal of Him, who has a right to do what he will with his own; and he saw fit to remove it from your sight."[89] In addition, his father suffered from declining health and was in financial straits. Jeremiah urged him to sell off some land to pay debts but warned him that while he could send some money his own financial situation remained precarious. All this advice he gave from afar; the son was too committed to his own professional career to consider returning to Georgia, Vermont.[90]

Aside from his personal crises, Evarts faced another problem at the American Board. By the spring of 1820 the board's treasury was woefully short of money, and expenses averaged $190 for every weekday of the year. Letters to ABCFM agents cautioned against accepting too many donations of clothing in lieu of money, and the Prudential Committee pointedly asked supporters "whether there is in this country Christian benevolence enough" to evangelize the heathen. The committee warned that either foreign missions must be supported or they would fail; missionaries could not be sent out and then called back because of temporary shortages of funds. Not until 1821, when news of the missionary successes in the Sandwich Islands reached subscribers of the *Missionary Herald*, did the board's fortunes improve.[91]

Despite personal crises, missionary success at the Sandwich Islands, or the Missouri debates, the attention of Evarts and the ABCFM increasingly focused on the maturation of the government's policy toward the Indian tribes. Passage of the Indian Civilization Bill beckoned societies like the ABCFM to apply for government funds. Despite the board's financial difficulties, however, money was not the attraction; more important was the apparent encouragement of evangelical objectives. This led Evarts to cultivate the interest and support of federal officials for the American Board's policies. During the next few years proponents on each side became increasingly intense about their respective commitments. With the support of the Civilization Bill, however, the missionary side captured the romantic imagination of Americans who lived near neither the frontier nor the tribes.

The atmosphere within which the American Board of Commissioners and other missionary societies had to work, therefore, steadily changed. The federal government was trying to move away from an ad hoc arrangement of treaties with the various tribes and toward a systematic civilization policy to convert Indians into farmers and mechanics, condense their population, grant land titles in severalty, and take other measures to prepare them for citizenship. President James Monroe's second inaugural address in March 1821 outlined a plan to end all recognition of them as independent nations and proposed a fundamental transformation: "Their sovereignty over vast territories should cease, in lieu of which the right of soil should be secured to each individual and his posterity in competent portions; and for the territory thus ceded by each tribe some reasonable equivalent should be granted, to be vested in permanent funds for the support of civil government over them and for the education of their children, for their instruction in the arts of husbandry, and to provide sustenance for them until they could provide it for themselves."[92]

At the same time, however, Indian nationalism expanded, and tribal leaders began to embrace the evangelicals' civilization program not as a prelude to integration with white society but as a bulwark against it. The states, meanwhile, increasingly insisted on their rights to remove the tribes as they saw fit and belligerently demanded that the federal government assist them. Thus were the conditions for future conflict assured.

In their pursuit of disinterested benevolence and their search for the soul of America, these reformers argued for a gospel of restraint. Restraint, or self-discipline, would bank the fires of self-interest. Partisan or other divisions (such as the Missouri Crisis) might rock the country from time to time, but "so long as the broad basis of public virtue remains, it will receive additional strength from every shock."[93] Jeremiah Evarts feared that Americans were no longer ready to sacrifice personal gain for the common good. He saw the Panic of 1819 as just one sign that a rampant immorality had unleashed God's disfavor. At the same time, of course, his message remained essentially ambivalent. For as he endorsed restraint on the one hand, on the other he counseled an ethic of hard work and productivity. Evarts believed, moreover, that the visible reflected the invisible. Behavioral impropriety and excess—whether it be individual tippling, public inattention to religion, or interpersonal relations—reflected the state of individuals' consciences and their commitment to an underlying moral ethos. Vital sustenance, he insisted, was still to be found in the converted soul rather than in the marketplace.[94]

CHAPTER FIVE

Taking Control, 1821–1825

In 1821 Jeremiah Evarts took firm control of the missionary activities of the American Board of Commissioners for Foreign Missions. Samuel Worcester, traveling south for his health, had died in June 1821 at the Brainerd Station in the Cherokee Nation. Evarts assumed the duties and responsibilities of clerk for the board's Prudential Committee and became corresponding secretary of the ABCFM in Worcester's absence. He retained these duties after Worcester's death and then was formally elected to the position at the September 1822 meeting of the American Board. Evarts remained at the helm of the ABCFM until his own death in 1831.

The additional duties quickly exacerbated Evarts's own physical problems. During the winter and spring of 1823 he frequently hovered near death, working from his bed while he struggled to breathe through defective lungs. Family problems added further pressure. He had to respond to pleas from his Vermont relatives to intervene and settle debts contracted by his father, who became increasingly impecunious as his own infirmities increased. Jeremiah also purchased additional land in Georgia, Vermont, and convinced his father to give him a quitclaim to his land. This property served as security for his father's debts, which were over $3,000.[1] Throughout 1823 Jeremiah tried as best he could to take care of his relatives from afar, insisting all the while that he would not leave his work in Boston and move to Vermont. He acquired additional deeds to land, usually as security against loans to relatives (for which he computed interest he did not expect to receive), and tried to preserve some property for his father during his lifetime "so that he could not be driven from the old place of his residence."[2]

The proliferation of reform efforts and the continuation of religious revivals, meanwhile, fueled his optimism that "a great and general revolution is about to break upon the moral world." But Evarts had long believed in that, and while he remained enthusiastic about the "signs of the times," he insisted that strenuous efforts were needed to effect the desired changes, arguing that "the great ends of government must fail in every nation, without national morality." And not enough had been done. The characteristics of a proper Christian society, said one speaker, included independence, universal charity, mutual beneficence, seriousness, and purity. Evarts agreed, believing that personal virtue and national morality were inextricably linked.[3]

Missionary enterprises emerged as experimental models to advance the new ethos. Evarts wanted to create model societies so as to demonstrate paradigmatic processes which he hoped would take root in the larger society. He seemed happiest when serving others. This service often brought him power, but he sought this power not for selfish reasons so much as to advance the ideals of disinterested benevolence.[4] Politics, for Evarts, was a moral exercise. Sin, argued Methodist Timothy Merritt, was no longer a private matter, no longer a private issue between the sinner and God. Now a third interest, "that of society," entered the relationship. Patriotism and philanthropy joined in a just society. The founders of New England, claimed one speaker, "believed that the temporal prosperity of towns, is intimately connected with their moral and religious welfare."[5]

American culture celebrated a democratic and economic individualism, believed that competition led to progress, and assumed that its citizens embraced a common set of cultural parameters which mediated divisive social, economic, or political tendencies. In many respects evangelical reform sprang from a conviction that these assumptions were false and that the forces at work had become centrifugal rather than centripetal. "There is one danger against which we cannot be too watchful," warned one Fourth of July speaker. "You hardly need be told that I allude to geographical distinctions and sectional interests."[6] Proto-Victorians like Jeremiah Evarts hoped to substitute self-restraint for unrestrained passion, and in so doing they began the cultural trek from evangelical reform to Victorian orthodoxy. They believed that a selfish individualism degraded "the character of the freeman, into that of a pimping, fawning retainer of some aspiring demagogue." To ignore the public good, to emphasize professional and personal development at the expense of the moral faculties, was to fragment life and culture into a series of material commodities. By asserting a set of ideals which differed from those of an emerging bourgeois culture, they injected a new set of tensions into early nineteenth-century American culture.[7]

Tensions between the ideals of religious commonwealths and the realities of life in the material world were never more evident than in the foreign missionary ventures to distant lands. They were, as historian William Hutchison has observed, nineteenth-century "errands into the wilderness." As corresponding secretary, Jeremiah Evarts superintended these efforts from ABCFM headquarters in Boston, seeking to spread evangelical as well as American influence throughout the world. In the words of a missionary catechism used at Yale, foreign missions demonstrate to other peoples "the folly of their cruel and costly sacrifices, their self-torture, and idol worship; promotes knowledge, order and industry in society, and tends to make them love each other; to support them under affliction, and to inspire them with the hope of eternal life."[8] Jeremiah Evarts became the preeminent advocate of missions as a civilizing tool.

These peoples were to be transformed, culturally as well as religiously. They should, the Yale Missionary Catechism instructed, be taught to trade their nomadic savage life for that of the settled husbandman, to cultivate the soil and educate their children in lieu of idleness and wanton dissipation. Missionary societies were millennial to the core, harbingers of a romantic vision that saw religious benevolence suffusing the globe and reforming the moral landscape. As students at the Princeton University Society of Inquiry wrote to Sandwich Island missionary Hiram Bingham: "Then perhaps the empire of China will be pouring its bibles over the unhospitable regions of the North. There will then be but one caste in India, and not an idol. The native missionaries from Bombay will have met those from Judea. Our Western Indians will be exploring the coasts of the Northern Ocean to see, if per-chance, there should remain any wandering brother who had not heard of Jesus. Our sable preachers will have gone from sea to sea. Mecca will be abandoned. The Jews' Messiah will have come; Babylon, the great, have fallen." China, Bombay, Ceylon, or Palestine might lie at great geographic distances from New England, but the spiritual world was small, and "every man is our *neighbor* to whom we can possibly do good."[9]

During the early 1820s the problem was money, not distance. ABCFM resources lagged behind its ambitions, troubled by economic problems at home as well as by a need to demonstrate success abroad. "Pray," Evarts wrote missionaries Levi Parsons and Pliny Fisk in Palestine, "pray earnestly for an increase of the spirit of self-denial in your native country."[10] For their own part, Evarts and his colleagues used the religious press to keep the cause and its needs before the public. "It is chilling," editorialized the *Boston Recorder*, "to see the evident reluctance with which some men *professing godliness*, and possessing some thousands of dollars, drag out a single dollar . . . even after a great deal of persuasion."[11]

Success at the Sandwich Islands by 1821 buoyed their hopes. Hiram Bingham wrote from the islands that "the Idols and Moreahs of these Islands are burned with fire, the priesthood of superstition is abolished, & the religious taboos are at an end." One woman, after reading Bingham's report in the *Missionary Herald*, confided to her diary that "The reception of those at the Sandwich Islands surely is enough to excite the grateful song and joyful tear; while the embarrassments of others, and particularly of the Board, the source of their subsistence, must in turn excite the tear of sorrow. . . . The heathen have claims upon us. More than we absolutely need to supply our wants, is not ours."[12] Support for the Sandwich Islands mission became popular, and hopes soared that the "perishing heathen" would overturn their pagan idols throughout the world. Congregational clergy used their pulpits to celebrate success in Hawaii and to argue that the "career of degeneracy" had ended, to be replaced by "the happiest forms of civil polity." Contributions to the American Board increased, more prospective missionaries volunteered their services, and additional agents scoured New England to solicit support for the ABCFM. In December Evarts reported that sufficient numbers of young men and women had volunteered for missionary service to allow the board to reinforce its missions in India, Ceylon, Palestine, and the Sandwich Islands, as well as to establish new stations in other countries. Missionary successes had also brought forth new candidates to fill ministerial needs at home. "The attempt to send salvation to remote pagans," concluded Evarts, "has proved as life from the dead to many slumbering churches."[13] Now was the time to press forward.

Letters of application from aspiring missionaries, as well as from his counterparts in the London Missionary Society, filled Evarts's correspondence. Applicants emphasized their commitment and self-denial, but many were in debt and hoped that the ABCFM would help settle their accounts before departure. Cynics questioned the sincerity of such applicants, especially since many of them collected funds not only to help the board but to pay off their own debts in the process. Yet to become a foreign missionary was not an easy way to elude a few hundred dollars of debt, and few could really doubt the commitment of these young men and women. James Douglas's book, *Hints on Missions*, popular in England and reprinted in the United States, argued that "Bodies of Christians who make no efforts to Christianize others, are Christians but in name." Religious commitment and not personal poverty motivated prospective ABCFM missionaries to volunteer for foreign missions.[14]

Recruitment of missionaries, publicity for existing missions, the search for funds to support the board's activities, and superintendence of existing missions demanded Evarts's attention. Between 1823 and 1825 the American Board sent out more than twenty missionaries to stations around the world. As corresponding secretary of the American Board, Evarts had not only to keep in touch with these stations and publicize their activities; he had to prepare copy for the *Missionary Herald* and handle the day-to-day administration necessary to support these endeavors. He urged missionaries in Ceylon, for instance, to set up a printing press. But the ABCFM could supply neither a press nor sufficient funds. To gather additional support, Evarts contacted officials of the London Missionary Society and solicited the British East India Company as well as the British Parliament. They, in turn, promised to contact the governor, judge, and other influential British residents at the Bombay mission and throughout India. Such was the network necessary to sustain these ventures. As Evarts cautioned his Ceylon brethren, "Missionaries seem often to think that men enough of the right character can be had at a moment's warning. This is altogether a mistake."[15]

Evarts was also cautious about his approach to the general public. He knew that its support was critical to missionary success, but he also was aware that secular attractions were often more alluring than religious convictions. While he fervently hoped that the moral reform crusade would be effective, Evarts was enough of a realist to understand that attacks on the public conscience were likely to be more effective than direct accusations against individual inaction. "However just the language of crimination may be," he warned, "and however necessary that professed Christians should be made to feel their guilt in this matter, it is not best that a formal accusation should be preferred by a missionary." Instead, missionaries should express gratitude for any support received, encourage greater commitment, and convey their personal commitment to the task before them. When Evarts visited various foreign mission societies and their auxiliaries, he read aloud letters from missionaries and challenged the audience to support their efforts. These men and women, he argued, were "soldiers of the cross," "ambassadors to negotiate a peace between the King of heaven and his revolted subjects." They deserved support.[16]

To elicit that support, Evarts met with other ABCFM officials in 1823 to design a sweeping plan of organization to systematize the auxiliaries and channel support to ABCFM enterprises. Greater organization was needed, he insisted, to make better use of evangelical and benevolent energies. At the moment, "every man comes when he pleases, and goes when he pleases; and there is little calculation to be made as to the achievement in future campaigns. This damps the spirit of enterprise."[17] Evarts proposed a general plan anchored by two types of societies. One would be a large society designed for urban areas, or organized on a county-wide basis, auxiliary to the ABCFM. A second tier, small town, parish, or school district organizations, would be subsidiary to the larger societies and be formally known as associations. Separate male and female associations perpetuated sexual segregation, but the plan was designed both to speed the flow of funds to the American Board and to serve as a line of communication from the board to its constituents and supporters. "Such Associations," he wrote, "as to the spirit with which they are conducted, may be compared to a watch or a clock, which is always running down, except when some external force is applied. Hence their frequent dissolution. Few, which arose twelve years ago in aid of this Board, are now in existence."[18]

Jeremiah Evarts did not labor alone in these efforts; many others supported his ideas and worked to develop a system of benevolence. The board itself publicized the new scheme and presented a rationale for it. Agents roamed the countryside, searching for donations but also carrying the missionary message that Christian benevolence could redress "pagan" practices. In a sense, the American Board of Commissioners had determined that general solicitations or Christian goodwill were no longer sufficient to sustain the missionary enterprise. While public support had launched foreign and domestic missions, the expected groundswell of sustained public donations had not materialized, despite exhortations from pulpits across the region and the publication of appeals in periodicals like the *Missionary Herald*. A more systematic attack was needed, and Evarts launched one. The ABCFM urged community leaders, secular as well as religious, to lead fundraising efforts: "If gentlemen somewhat accustomed to business, and having a full comprehension of the plan now proposed, and a clear view of its operation, could accompany an agent, introduce him into their respective circles, and second his proposals with a hearty concurrence, it would have the best effects."[19]

Evarts envisioned a sprawling missionary enterprise under the auspices of the American Board. The ABCFM had already sent missionaries to the Sandwich Islands, Ceylon, India, Palestine, and elsewhere, and now he wanted to include China in that enterprise. "China is an empire, which is not to be abandoned as ultimately to be under the power of Satan," he wrote to Henry Hill in Philadelphia. "Let America step forward & do something for this important portion of the human family." Although critics attacked his "handsome" salary, Evarts labored constantly to advance these causes. In September 1824 alone he traveled to attend a special meeting of the Hartford County (Connecticut) Foreign Mission Society on Monday, September 20, then to the annual meeting of the Farmington, Connecticut, auxiliary on Tuesday, September 21. On Wednesday he was in Middletown for the annual meeting of the Auxiliary Foreign Mission Society of Middletown and the Vicinity, and the next day he was in Saybrook for the annual meeting of the Auxiliary Foreign Mission Society of the Middlesex (Clerical) Association. On the following Tuesday he traveled to Hebron, Connecticut, to attend the annual meeting of the Foreign Mission Society of Tolland County. At each meeting Evarts spoke about the needs and opportunities of the missionary cause, trying to inculcate a moral ethos that would remain after his departure.[20]

While the overseas mission was a major vehicle for the extension of American culture abroad, missions to the Indian tribes of North America unleashed powerful acculturating forces of their own. And during the early 1820s Jeremiah Evarts became increasingly concerned both with the status of ABCFM missions to the Indian tribes and with the condition of the tribes themselves. In the spring of 1822, suffering again from poor health, he visited Indian missions in Georgia and then returned to Boston through eastern Tennessee and Virginia. In December 1823, this time as a formal agent for the American Board, Evarts followed visits to New York, Philadelphia, Princeton, and Washington with another visit to various Cherokee mission stations as well as to Choctaw missions in Mississippi. He made additional visits in the late 1820s. On each of these tours Evarts's object was to assess the operation of the missionary stations and gauge the board's progress, although he also went predetermined to document the progress of civilization and Christianization among the tribes so as to generate public support for the board's endeavors. The ABCFM received the lion's share of the government's Civilization Fund, but Evarts knew that these monies were insufficient to sustain the missionary enterprise. At the same time, the expansionist energies of white settlers and a developing sense of self-conscious independence among the tribes (especially among the Cherokees) were sharpening tensions and threatening missionary objectives. Evarts was beginning to discover that he had to rally public support as well as raise funds.[21]

In fact the rapid expansion of Indian mission stations since 1821, coupled with a growing controversy over federal Indian policy, forced Evarts to devote more and more of his attention to this matter. A revolution of sorts had occurred in whites' perception of their Indian neighbors, especially east of the Mississippi where settlement had leapfrogged tribal lands. This revolution led frontier whites to clash with their countrymen living further east and at a greater distance from the tribes. While frontiersmen greedily eyed Indian lands, their eastern counterparts developed a paternalistic pity toward the occupants of those lands. As Samuel Jarvis told members of the New-York Historical Society: "As long as they were formidable, curiosity was overpowered by terror; and there was neither leisure, nor inclination, to contemplate their character as a portion of the human family, while the glare of conflagration reddened the mid-night sky, and the yells of the savage, mingling with the shrieks of butchered victims, rode, as portentous messengers, upon every gale. But that state of things has long ceased to exist. The white men of America have become too numerous, to fear any longer the effects of savage barbarity.... In the room of fear, should now arise a sentiment of pity."[22]

From the West two sources of protest surfaced which opposed the federal government's policy of civilizing the Indians in situ. One came from settlers or potential settlers and found ready adherents among politicians and politicians-to-be. Andrew Jackson proved to be the archetype here. A letter to Secretary of War John Calhoun in 1821 summarized Jackson's position that the government extinguish all Indian titles to lands east of the Mississippi: "This is a precedent much wanted; that the absurdity in politics may cease, of an independent sovereign nation holding treaties with people living within its territorial limits, acknowledging its sovereignty and laws, and who, although not citizens, cannot be viewed as aliens, but as the real subjects of the United States." The other spur to protest was statehood. As western territories became states they immediately petitioned the federal government to extinguish all Indian land titles within the state and frequently requested that no additional Indians be removed into the state from other areas. Extinguishment and removal became the watchwords of western politics.[23]

For members and agents of the American Board of Commissioners, on the other hand, their embrace of a providential paternalism required funds to effect Christianization and acculturation. And funds were short in the early 1820s. "Providence has restrained our means," Evarts lamented to missionary Cyrus Kingsbury; "if the Indians should be disappointed and discouraged, the evil seems inevitable." To Ard Hoyt at Brainerd, Evarts complained that the ABCFM could not afford to send additional missionaries: "we have not the money—we have not time to select suitable persons—and our feeble powers must be directed to save from sinking the missions already in existence and the missionaries already on the ground." The fiscal crisis forced Evarts to do so much writing that it endangered his always precarious health. Expenses exceeded receipts by more than $10,000; half the board's permanent fund was exhausted. Further disbursements were impossible, and Evarts insisted that the only alternatives were to suspend all new mission stations, dismiss all hired help, and close the schools.[24]

The American Board of Commissioners had paid a price for its postwar optimism. Its missionary stations were overextended; success in the field had been insufficient to stimulate adequate contributions from the public. Evarts's cure for the crisis, retrenchment, also tried to clarify another matter—whether the board's primary concern was to Christianize the tribes or to civilize them. Many persons, of course, drew no such distinction. But the original support for missions had emanated from the Second Great Awakening and was inherently religious in nature. Conversions rather than cultivation were to be the measure of progress. Evarts's letter to Worcester and to missionaries in the field made clear his conviction that civilization followed Christianization; nonetheless, the priorities became confused both at home and abroad. Revitalization was coming to mean more than a religious awakening. The policy and priorities of the federal government, moreover, clearly placed cultivation ahead of Christianization. In the words of Thomas McKenney, superintendent of the Indian Trade: "I will also send you some wheat for seed, that the Indians may be encouraged in the growth of this article. This is the way that you will most effectually promote the *great object of the Govt* towards these unenlightened people—Invite their attention to agriculture and the arts, and help them, for they are helpless. Our object is not to keep these Indians hunters eternally. We want to make citizens out of them, and they must first be anchored in the soil, else they will be flying about whilst there is any room in the wilderness or an animal to be trapped."[25]

As Jeremiah Evarts's concern about the state of the American Board's Indian missions mounted, he found himself increasingly drawn into the complexities of federal Indian policy. For Evarts this was more problematic than providential. New pressures, old pressures reborn, economic and political change, an emerging romantic racism, continued expansion, and the influence of several vibrant and destabilizing personalities led to one crisis after another in Indian affairs. At stake was not only land, economic growth, or political supremacy, but also national honor and the future of the new moral ethos. Evangelical operations clashed with individual and sectional greed. Millennial expectations wrestled with market forces in a struggle to shape the American future.

War and impatience triggered the conflict. Up and down the Appalachians, the War of 1812 had thrown open gateways to the west by removing British and Indian harassment of white settlers. In addition, early missionary activities had failed to transform the tribes quickly. Now, at the very moment that the government supported civilizing programs, earlier white hopes that such efforts might succeed turned to a fear that they might not fail. For to the extent that civilization programs did succeed and the tribes became more like whites, the more difficult it became to remove them from their lands and open areas for development by whites. This reservoir of greed and fear was what sustained support for men like Andrew Jackson. Jackson, more successful than most of his counterparts, used the language of market forces and paternalism to mask a speculative ambition that knew no bounds. Under these pressures, from 1821 to 1830 federal Indian policy moved from civilization to voluntary removal to removal under any circumstances. Even a protective veneer of paternalism could not hide a fundamental transformation.[26]

Efforts in 1821 and 1822 by the state of Georgia to force the federal government to implement its understanding of the Compact of 1802 did much to precipitate this shift. In 1802 the federal government had agreed to open for settlement all tribal lands in Georgia as soon as it could convince the Indians to remove west. Removal was to be voluntary, but the government was to initiate the removal. Now Georgians were insisting on immediate removal, whether voluntary or involuntary, and the matter became a political test within the state. Georgia's efforts to enlist the support of its neighbors, however, failed. Tennessee, where tribal lands encompassed millions of acres, refused to help. Removal might be beneficial to the tribes, a report of a joint select committee of the Tennessee legislature concluded, but the country's fiscal condition was too poor to afford those funds necessary to effect a successful treaty, and land acquisitions following the War of 1812 still glutted the market. Alabama was more receptive but was content to offer modest financial support and observe that at least the Creeks would not favor such an effort. President Monroe was evasive, promising Georgia's governor, John Clark, that he would push for removal if and when the Congress appropriated funds for that purpose. Cherokee Chief Charles Hicks was more direct, telling Clark that "I wish you Sir to understand distinctly that we are unwilling to sell one foot more of our circumscribed country, although we are reduced to a handful and you are becoming as the trees of the forest."[27]

Within the government, meanwhile, receipt of ABCFM missionary Cyrus Kingsbury's annual report stimulated a reconsideration of federal policy. Kingsbury wrote that "The wretchedness of this people is daily becoming more manifest; as is also the importance of extending as speedily as possible to the rising generation, the salutary influence of civilized & Christian education."[28] After receiving Kingsbury's report, Secretary of War Calhoun drafted a long letter to President Monroe, arguing that it was still too soon to judge the effectiveness of the civilization policy. "The present generation, which cannot be greatly affected by it, must pass away, and those who have been reared under the present system of education must succeed them, before its effects can be fully tested." The tribes clearly wanted education, Calhoun observed, but "whether such an education would lead them to that state of morality, civilization, and happiness, to which it is the desire of the Government to bring them" remained an open question. He recommended a change in the relationship between the tribes and the federal government; government treatment of the tribes as independent entities should cease. "It has not one of the advantages of real independence, while it has nearly all the disadvantages of a state of real subjugation." He blamed most of the tribes' continuing ills on this system and argued that unless the extension of governmental authority accompanied the spread of education, federal policy would ultimately fail. "Depressed in spirit, and debauched in morals, they dwindle away through a wretched existence, a nuisance to the surrounding country." When the Congress requested a summary of the condition of the Indian tribes, Monroe forwarded Calhoun's analysis to Capitol Hill. From the field, meanwhile, Cherokee agent Return J. Meigs urged Calhoun to break down tribal government and reserve tribal lands in severalty.[29]

The policy of the American Board of Commissioners for Foreign Missions, however, did not change. Evarts became a special correspondent for a new (and short-lived) society, the American Society for Promoting the Civilization and General Improvement of the Indian Tribes Within the United States. Directed by Evarts's friend Jedidiah Morse, the society dissolved within two years from lack of financial support. Its coming— and going—however, revealed the shifting relationship between the benevolent community and Indian affairs. The deepening controversy over removal and civilization eclipsed earlier emphasis on revivals and Christianization. As this shift continued Jeremiah Evarts and the ABCFM were drawn more firmly into the politics of Indian removal. Millennial expectations gave way to political maneuvering.[30]

Evarts's exertions eroded his health. "It is distressing that a man occupying a station more important perhaps, than any other layman in the United States, should be thus prematurely broken down," wrote the Reverend Ebenezer Porter after a visit with him. Evarts told Porter that he hoped to recover, but for the moment "I must make my letters short, as my physician forbids much writing and much talking." Riding horseback through the Georgia backcountry and visiting primitive ABCFM mission stations, however, infused Evarts with optimism. And as his spirits soared his health improved. Everywhere he went he laid plans for expanding mission stations and sought to inspire a new spirit of cooperation and dedication. "There is much good here," Evarts reported from the Brainerd mission. He prescribed additional missionaries and closer administrative control, for "No man can tell how great a change it makes when the pressure of civil society, and especially of Christian character, is taken off."[31]

However much Evarts found himself drawn to the political implications of missionary activity among the Indians, his travels through the South repeatedly brought him face to face with evidence that the strictures of benevolent reform and the new moral ethos had to be promoted. The condition of slaves in particular touched Evarts deeply. As with Indian missions, Evarts looked at the slaves with a paternalistic vision: "Their poor bodies appear to be worn out by hard service and scanty fare, while their minds are in perpetual infancy—not having advanced towards enlarged thought, or made the least progress as immortal beings." He believed that, with slaves as with Indians, education and Christianization held the key to revitalization. "I am fully convinced," he concluded, "that there are no difficulties but moral ones, in the way of a thorough renovation of this whole southern country."[32] The paradigm he sought to fulfill was the one familiar to him from the foreign mission enterprise, as his diary reveals.

> But every scheme of meliorating the condition of the slaveholding country without the aid of the Gospel, must be chimerical. The first step in the progress is, to get a competent number of religious teachers, who will cheerfully and heartily devote themselves to the work; and this number must be much greater than has ever been estimated. . . . It is greatly to be desired that as many pious young men, natives of the southern states, as God shall endue with the requisite qualifications, may be employed as spiritual teachers of their countrymen. They have many advantages over northern young men; as they are able to bear the climate, and there are fewer prejudices against their efforts.[33]

Religious instruction, the creation of missionary stations, the use of people native to the region and culture to be transformed, and a concerted effort to capture the hearts and minds as well as the souls of the "afflicted" had come to constitute the missionary model for a revitalization effort.

The other ingredient of this paradigm was public optimism. To secure public support and prove the cause worthy of continued financial support, the ABCFM publicized the progress it had made. In so doing the board found that it had to walk a narrow tightrope between an exuberant optimism, which would be clearly false and might lead contributors to believe that the missionary task was an easy one, and a presentation of vivid despair, which might doom its hopes by making the obstacles to success seem insurmountable. Evarts asked missionaries to be candid in their remarks to the Prudential Committee but circumspect in what they published from their diaries or letters. Evarts himself followed the same rule, reporting great progress among those who had converted but recognizing that most individuals remained outside the flock:

> it is not to be disguised, that many things still remaining among the Cherokees, are greatly to be deplored. Much poverty and wretchedness, several gross vices, particularly drunkenness, and an almost total ignorance of God, his law, and the plan of salvation, need to be chased away, before the people generally can reach the proper standard of rational and immortal beings.

> What has been already done in the way of communicating evangelical instruction, though of inestimable value to such individuals as have received spiritual benefit, and as an experiment of what may be done, is yet a mere specimen of the benevolent agency which needs to be extended, not only to every part of the Cherokee country, but to all the Indian tribes of North America, and to all the heathens on the globe.[34]

This was a formula for an expansionist empire based on benevolent reform.

It was, for Evarts, also a formula to save the Indians. His travels throughout the South reinforced his conviction that efforts at removal were moving fast. "The present state of things cannot continue long," he wrote the board. "The Cherokees, the Choctaws, and the other tribes, must either rise to the rank of intelligent men and well instructed Christians, or they must melt away, destroyed by vices copied from unprincipled whites, having sold their birthright for a *mess of pottage*, and being left, in the land of their fathers, without property, without a home, and without a friend."[35] Evarts still believed that removal was a secondary problem, that if the tribes could exhibit the characteristics of "civilized" people they would find acceptance on their ancestral lands and among the white population.

This belief sprang from his conviction that moral reformation led individuals, regardless of culture or race, to recognize, appreciate, and accept a common set of behavioral characteristics which bestowed on those persons a moral equality. This moral equality rested on a set of cultural assumptions and values that a close examination of Evarts's letters makes evident. Central to the process of reformation or revitalization was that there was only one central moral ethos—one that stemmed from the progress of the Second Great Awakening among white society. The reasoning behind this process was essentially circular, for this ethos equated progress and intelligence with an acceptance of the ethos itself. Hence, the "best informed and more intelligent Cherokees" were those who supported the American Board's missionary activities. It was also an ethos which rested on a moral elitism. The converted, by the very fact of their conversion, were to lead; the unconverted, to struggle toward moral equality by reforming their behavior (for example, eliminating drunkenness) and searching for a conversion experience. In addition to individual reformation, the truly moral society embraced several other parameters as well. These included the organization of civil government, a recognition of the rule of law, a commitment to steady work habits, the opening of village schools, and an attachment to education among the younger generation. They would lead, in the words of the secretary of the United Foreign Missionary Society, to a time "when . . . the red man and the white man shall every where be found, mingling in the same pursuits, cherishing the same benevolent and friendly views, fellow-citizens of the same civil and religious community, and fellow-heirs to an eternal inheritance in the kingdom of glory."[36]

The dream of integration, so strong in the missionary world, found little acceptance elsewhere. Led by Georgia, the southern states pressed the government to remove the tribes. Calhoun and Monroe agreed that removal was desirable but also insisted that it could be effected only with tribal consent. Spokesmen from all sides—missionaries, federal officials, and state authorities—purported to speak for the best interests of the Indians. At the same time, all sought to safeguard their own interests. Not one of them, whether an integrationist like Jeremiah Evarts or an amalgamationist like William H. Crawford ("The idea of civilizing the Indians by amalgamation with the whites . . . is I believe now admitted at length to be the most practicable mode"), seriously considered the tribal perspectives in this matter.[37]

Tribal leaders like John Ross, meanwhile, continued to believe that philanthropic whites were right, that the missionary experiment truly sprang from benevolent motives, and that the federal government—"when the Indians are themselves seen to manifest a thirst to reach after the blessings and happiness derivable from civilized life"—would not move them off their ancestral lands to an unknown wilderness. Despite a growing concern about the pace and direction of acculturation within the tribe, this hope persisted. To support their refusal to sign new treaties and grant new land cessions, Cherokee leaders appealed to previous treaties and the centrality of the rule of law within the constitutional system. As they did so, they fostered a belief that they were an independent people, a sovereign government. During the next few years this assertion gradually shifted the focus of the debate from benevolent reform to legal and political rights. One effect was to expose the Cherokees to the vagaries of an emerging Jacksonian political system, a system steadily more preoccupied with the satisfaction of regional or sectional interests than with benevolent reform.[38]

Evarts's answer to these changes was expansion—expand the number of schools throughout the Choctaw and Cherokee nations by creating small stations through singular effort, hard work, and prayer. He supported the recommendations of his former colleague, Jedidiah Morse, that the American people and their government had a duty to civilize the tribes to save them from destruction. Morse had visited tribes throughout the United States and hoped to use his lengthy report to the War Department as a mechanism to lobby for this cause. He even formed a society, the American Society for Promoting the Civilization of the Indians, to further this work. But despite the presence of Evarts and the warning of Congressman Stephen Van Rensselaer that people in Washington considered Indians to be "more like wild Beasts than human beings," the society failed almost immediately. Morse discovered that the American public was more willing to support efforts to christianize "heathen" peoples than to endow them with social, economic, or political rights. It was a lesson that many of his colleagues learned repeatedly during the remainder of the decade.[39]

The growing reluctance of the Cherokees to negotiate additional treaties and cede more land to the states, meanwhile, created repercussions for missionaries active in the Cherokee Nation. Since pleas from southern states to the federal government had no effect so long as the government was unwilling to coerce the tribes, officials and citizens of those states turned their efforts to attack what they saw as a cause of that resistance. At least one Georgia commissioner, wrote Moody Hall to Jeremiah Evarts, "has resolved to use his influence to have them [missionaries] expelled from the nation." This new determination was more apparent to the missionaries than to the Indians, however, for Elias Boudinot wrote Franklin Gold of Cornwall, Connecticut, that "We are progressing rapidly in civilization—a little more exertion will make us respectable among Nations—at least among our neighbors, to whom formerly, we have been detestible." Among missionaries the old integrationist hopes remained strong and the old cultural ideals vibrant. The board of managers of the United Foreign Missionary Society best summarized these hopes: "you may look forward to the period when the savage shall be converted into the citizen; when the hunter shall be transformed into the mechanic; when the farm, the workshop, the School-House, and the Church shall adorn every Indian village; when the fruits of Industry, good order, and sound morals, shall bless every Indian dwelling; and when . . . the red man and the white man shall everywhere be found, mingling in the same benevolent and friendly feelings."[40]

Not all missionaries still agreed with that prescription, however, and in 1823 Isaac McCoy of the Baptists outlined a plan to remove the Indians to lands west of the Mississippi. McCoy had worked as a missionary among several tribes for years and was convinced that civilization was coming too slowly to guarantee their survival. Only their removal beyond the reach of white settlement could prevent their extinction. "Indians, however improved," he argued, "do not thrive among the whites. . . . they often become profligate & wretched, or wander back into the forest, and mingle with their barbarous kindred." McCoy compared this plan with the one to colonize "negroes" in Africa and insisted that in each case colonization represented the "only hope of deliverance." Missionaries would accompany the tribes, in McCoy's scheme, to establish farms and encourage the creation of civil communities which would lead them to eventual citizenship. In 1823 McCoy's plan was significant not so much for its particulars but for its dramatization of a split in the benevolent community that politicians could exploit for their own purposes.[41]

In December 1823 Jeremiah Evarts began another tour of the American Board's Indian missions. His decision to travel extensively may have stemmed from this new crisis in Indian relations, for this time health problems do not seem to have been a catalyst for travel. He sought firsthand proof to refute southern claims that Indians could never be more than hunters. He also hoped to implement ideas outlined earlier to Cyrus Kingsbury, that larger stations should be reduced and smaller stations multiplied. Smaller stations meant labor difficulties, however, and Evarts gave Indian missionaries permission to hire slave labor, but only if the slave agreed to the conditions of employment. That is, in all except legal status the slave would be regarded as free. Evarts's personal letters and published work indicate that he favored the peaceful removal of slavery, but he refused to embrace abolition as a moral imperative. He took a similar position when he accepted the black slave Betsey Stockton as a member of the first reinforcement to the Sandwich Islands mission.[42]

First, however, Evarts hurried to Washington. Congress was in session; Indian affairs were on the agenda. "The time must come," said a memorial from the Georgia legislature, "when the soil of Georgia shall no longer be imprinted with the footstep of the savage." Even Calhoun seemed inclined to change federal policy. "I am apprehensive," he wrote Cherokee agent Joseph McMinn, "that this nation is becoming disposed to be troublesome."[43]

As he headed for the nation's capital to watch out for the political interests of Indian missions, Evarts attended to other ABCFM concerns as well. In 1822 the board had sent Rufus Anderson on a missionary tour of Greece, a tour sparked largely by an intense American interest in Greece and a desire to educate Greek youths in the United States. Evarts now urged the ABCFM to establish a mission there. He also spoke with men involved in the China trade and sent an outline for an ABCFM mission to China back to board headquarters in Boston. As he traveled to Washington, Evarts discovered that political pressures related to the 1824 presidential canvass were building. Mahlon Dickerson of New Jersey put it most succinctly: "Do we flatter ourselves that party violence is at an end; that we are permanently to remain all Republicans, all Federalists? If we do we deceive ourselves. The same array of parties which for many years distracted our country may not again take place; but if not the same certainly a different one, probably more violent, more sectional, more geographical, more clannish, more inveterate, more dangerous."[44] Henry Clay, John Calhoun, John Quincy Adams, William Crawford, and Andrew Jackson were the names most frequently mentioned. All had more than a passing relationship with Indian affairs.

But Jeremiah Evarts was more interested in American Board missions than in presidential politics. Thomas Jefferson's refusal to accept the presidency of the American Society for Promoting the Civilization and General Improvement of the Indian Tribes in the United States, for fear that the society's goals were at odds with those of the government, led Evarts to worry about a coming collision between ABCFM objectives and federal policy. Evarts forged ahead, nonetheless, preparing a memorial to Congress for additional funds to civilize the tribes. Warning that "wicked and unprincipled white people" wished to terminate the board's influence, he insisted that the work must go forward because "the civilized is preferable to the savage state." The pressures of white population on tribal hunting grounds were unremitting; Indian tribes were "compelled to obtain their support in the manner we do ours." Although the report admitted that most of the tribes did not endorse a complete extermination of their traditional way of life, it insisted that they must soon recognize that fact: "There is not place on the earth to which they can migrate and live in the savage and hunter state. The Indian tribes must, therefore, be *progressively civilized*, or *successively perish*."[45]

Evarts's notes from his 1824 visit to the American Board's Indian missions reveal a preoccupation with three concerns: the need to rely on religion for "the renovation of the heathen"; an awareness of how "vast a work is before us"; and a worry about "what encouragement is there to persevere?" He still believed that a broad civilization program remained essential to advance the board's objectives. The "heathen" had to hear more than the preaching of the gospel; they had to witness the practical effects of religion on everyday life. Increased federal appropriations were the antidote to southern efforts to repeal the Civilization Fund. But Indian affairs had already become more than a struggle between northern benevolent societies and southerners anxious to acquire new land. Western influences had become increasingly important, along with other political issues such as internal improvements and the expansion of slavery. As northerners divided in different proportions on each of these questions, forging any sense of unity on Indian affairs became more difficult. Southerners and westerners, meanwhile, found common cause in their desire for more land and Indian removal. Subsequent debates turned more on political objectives than on humanitarian concerns.[46]

The efforts of Jeremiah Evarts in Washington were successful to the extent that Congress rejected a bill to repeal the Civilization Fund. At the same time, however, he failed to obtain additional funds for the American Board's program. He continued to hope that a broad religious humanitarianism and the revivals of the Second Great Awakening would stimulate a new moral ethos among the general public. As he advised David Brown, a Cherokee, "The prevalence of the Christian religion among your people is the only thing that will secure the public opinion of this country strongly in their favor; and if public opinion is strongly in their favor, our national government will treat you all with kindness & attention." To secure that favorable public opinion, Evarts warned friends and colleagues to be cautious about the "reasonings and motives presented to the Christian public." Missionary standards had to be maintained, and no one offended, for the cause to prosper.[47] His concern for caution, however, betrayed Evarts's awareness that no new moral ethos had yet seized the general public.

Events in 1824 heightened Evarts's concern. In mid-January a delegation of Cherokees informed President Monroe that they would not negotiate another cession of lands. "It is a gratifying truth," they announced, "that the Cherokees are rapidly increasing in population; therefore, it is an incumbent duty on the nation to preserve, unimpaired, the rights of posterity to the lands of their ancestors." Here lay the kernel of conflict; here lay a dramatic declaration that the integrationist policies of the past no longer retained their luster. At the very moment that southerners were trying to end federal support for Indian civilization and argue that the Indians were dependent residents of the individual states, the

Cherokees announced that they intended to move in the opposite direction, toward greater independence. Secretary of War John Calhoun told them bluntly, "Surrounded, as you are . . . you must either cease to be a distinct community, and become . . . a part of the State within whose limits you are, or remove beyond the limits of any State."[48]

Jeremiah Evarts, who was in Washington during the visit of the Cherokee delegation, discovered the depths of this conflict while lobbying for the board's civilization programs. Evarts conferred daily with leading congressmen and administration officials and, while he found support for the Cherokee position, he also encountered growing support for the views of Georgia and other states that the Indians be removed. Several long discussions with Calhoun elicited the hope (from Calhoun) that Congress would purchase the Indians' right of the soil from Georgia so that they could remain where they were, but other officials insisted that the Indians could never be civilized and urged that the money be spent on other projects to promote the national interest. Evarts emerged from these encounters very depressed, writing Cyrus Kingsbury that "it seems to me that the prospects of the Indians, so far as their connexion with the government of the United States is to be regarded, are very dark and discouraging." He urged Kingsbury and the other missionaries to do what they could but admitted that he could "think of no relief for them as a people, unless our whole American community were to become just and benevolent, which is not to be expected." The best he dared hope was that the public would not endorse forcible removal.[49]

Georgia officials quickly attacked the Cherokee refusal to negotiate, blaming white missionaries as well as tribal leaders for this "effrontery." Their refusal, Georgia's Governor Troup insisted, was "not the spontaneous offspring of Indian feeling and sentiment, but a word put into his mouth by white men," by missionaries "nourished and protected by the power of the United States." The government should remove forcibly those Indians who refused to remove voluntarily. Georgia's bitter attack did not surprise Evarts, but it did sting Monroe, who repeatedly discussed the matter with his cabinet that spring. Both Calhoun and Adams insisted that Georgia's demands were unreasonable and a violation of existing agreements with the Cherokees. But other states, Indiana and Mississippi, joined in, not always so shrilly, and petitioned the government to extinguish the Indian title to lands within their boundaries.[50]

Evarts's letters to the board, which were usually printed in the *Missionary Herald*, advanced a public optimism that carefully concealed his private skepticism. From station after station he reported that the Indians desired religious instruction but needed more interpreters and missionaries. "It is certainly no easy matter to reclaim an ignorant, and a savage people," he told readers, but "it can be accomplished." Yet to the extent that it was accomplished, to the extent that the tribes embraced the white man's view of civilization, that much more difficult it became to depict them as mere savages and hunters, to secure land cessions from them, and to argue for their forcible removal. Pres. James Monroe conceded this much in a special message to Congress in March 1824 when he observed that while the Cherokees' own self-interest should impel them to remove west of the Mississippi, the government could not force them to do so, the Compact of 1802 notwithstanding. Yet at the same time, reports in the *Missionary Herald* revealed that Indian missions were carrying more than Christianity to the tribes. Extracts from a journal of the Chickasaw mission demonstrated the missionaries' discovery of a compelling connection between religion, capitalism, and the civilizing process. It is worth quoting at length.

> We have adopted a plan which has a very happy influence on the conduct of the children both in and out of school. We have tickets (which are nothing more than scraps of paper, marked No. 1, 2, 3, and 4,) with which we reward them on every Monday morning for the preceding week's performance, taking their conduct on the Sabbath into consideration. These are valued at six and a fourth cents per No. and pass as current money among them. The highest No. is given for a week's good attention to business. When any have been idle and inattentive, we present them with a No. 0, which is truly mortifying. In order to avoid imposition we keep an account book in which the sum due to each one for tickets is recorded; and when any one has earned the amount of a garment of clothing which he needs, he receives it in exchange for his tickets. In this way they clothe themselves, after receiving a change of raiment when they first enter the school. . . . The same plan is pursued in the school; we reward them according to their performance. With their school tickets they buy spelling books, Sunday-school hymn books, and small cheap books. These arrangements entirely preclude the necessity of using the rod.[51]

By mid-summer Evarts had returned to ABCFM headquarters in Boston. His visit to Washington and his lengthy tour through the board's Indian missions had left several impressions in his mind. He was now more aware than ever that whites in the South and West were determined to wrest Indian lands from the tribes and subjugate or remove the occupants. He was also convinced that these missions were having a positive effect on the Indians, but progress was slow and not likely to accelerate in the immediate future. Those two considerations were on a collision course. As Congressman John Forsyth of Georgia told the House of Representatives, "the United States may be under the fatal necessity of seeing the Cherokees annihilated, or of defending them against their own citizens." Time was of the essence, but time was running out. To make matters worse, support for Indian removal was a sure-fire path to political success in the affected states; the presidential election of 1824 could only inflame the issue further. The real significance of these latter two developments was not so much the appearance of a candidate like Andrew Jackson, a candidate determined and outspoken in favor of immediate removal, but instead the opportunity to transform the problem from a religious or moral question into a political issue.[52]

Perhaps the most important conviction that Evarts brought back with him to Boston, however, was that the alternatives available to the tribes (and by inference to the American Board) had polarized. White Americans were increasingly disinclined to invest in Indian missions those long-term hopes for Christianization and civilization they had brought to other foreign missions. Although they appeared to agree that civilization, integration (if not amalgamation), and citizenship on the one hand, or removal west of the Mississippi on the other, were the acceptable alternatives, in fact their growing insistence that the transformation of tribal residents into citizens be immediate essentially guaranteed that removal was the likely outcome. Letters on Indian affairs written in 1824 and after, with the exception of those drafted by the missionaries themselves, omitted reference to the original purpose of those missions. As Jeremiah Evarts reminded the Reverend Cephas Washburn: "Missions to the heathen are established with a view to the salvation of perishing souls. The object is altogether a religious one, and it should be held continually in view."[53]

Yet by 1824 the battle was not over. Indeed, it was just beginning. The forces of benevolence still believed their cause to be just, still insisted that their efforts would be successful. Some government officials agreed, noting that "patience, and zeal, will effect all that was ever anticipated." Jeremiah Evarts was more direct in the evaluation of Indian missions he sent to Secretary of War John Calhoun: "On the whole, I think that you will never have occasion to regret the benevolent part you have taken, as an organ of the government, in the great & good work of improving the condition of these children of the forest."[54]

In fact, although change was in the air, the government had not altered its policy. It still supported the efforts of the American Board and other missionary organizations; it still urged the Indians to "cultivate the ground, and be industrious and sober, and honest, and you will do well." Thomas McKenney directed all Indian agents to sanction and support existing plans for the civilization of the tribes and to cooperate with the missionaries. Disbursements from the Civilization Fund supported missionary efforts, but the demands for rapid success and the scope of the enterprise taxed even the resources of the American Board of Commissioners. The civilizing process, Evarts admitted to Calhoun, was an expensive one. It was a process, however, which remained a transformative one, at least in the eyes of southerners and westerners. In the words of Governor Troup of Georgia, "If the millennium is to come, American institutions . . . will bring it to pass."[55]

Whether or not the American Board and other missionary organizations filled the forests with "sylvan seminaries," the Indian question had become a matter for debate and rancor. Gone were the fears of the immediate postwar years. Economic growth and prosperity fed dreams of geographic expansion. Republican fears dating to the revolution or postrevolutionary years had dissipated amid a newborn feeling of nationalism and independence. To the generation coming into power in the 1820s, independence meant possibilities, a feeling of being set free, unleashed. The question, in many respects, was whether the nation as a collective entity had been set free or whether an aggregate of individuals within that nation had merely been unleashed. To be sure, individuals like Jeremiah Evarts remained concerned about maintaining the old republican virtues. Yet even Evarts realized the importance of the moment, as he admitted to Cyrus Kingsbury: "The concerns of the Indian missions lie with great weight upon my mind. Their situation is very critical. I do not apprehend them in immediate danger of extinction, but, unless I mistake, they are in great danger of coming far short of our hopes & of what might be deemed our reasonable expectation. I mean the reasonable expectations of the Christian public."[56] The question for the next several years would be to determine the boundaries of this romantic nationalism and its relationship to Christian republicanism.

The fact was, however, that by the mid-1820s the benevolent empire had grown to the point that its ambitions constantly threatened to outrun its resources. As the *New York Observer*, a pro-missionary paper, noted, "The present state of benevolent feeling in our country is such, that if there were not special exertions made to keep it alive, and to increase it, it would soon become extinct." A case in point was the American Board's desire to establish a mission in Africa and to bring "negroes" to the Foreign Mission School to be trained for such a mission. A shortage of funds forestalled these efforts, however. As corresponding secretary, Jeremiah Evarts appealed for additional monies but admitted that the poor seemed to be more active than the rich. Whether true or not, his comment reflected the ABCFM's constant need for money and his own determination to promote disinterested benevolence. "The fact is unquestionable," he argued, "that a habit of earning and saving money for religious charity is a most prolific source of enjoyment." At the same time, however, he admitted that it had been six months since he had been able to send anything to mission stations at Bombay or Ceylon, "& we are still considerably in debt." To the Ceylon missionaries, Evarts held out hope that the board's resources would increase but acknowledged that "my belief is founded on the general aspects of the times, and on the promises of the Bible which relate to the future enlargement of Zion; but not at all on our own skill or wisdom, or on the hold that we have upon the Christian public, or the interest that the public take in missionary concerns, or the reasonableness of the missionary cause, or the ingratitude and folly of deserting it."[57]

To overcome this inertia Evarts toured New England and encouraged the formation of additional benevolent associations. The ABCFM hired George Cowles to organize a system of collectors in each county and used popular celebrities (such as Samuel Frey, a Jew who had converted to Christianity) as agents. Evarts and the American Board also launched another public relations campaign designed to convince readers of religious periodicals that public benevolence was widespread and that the arrival of a "Missionary Republic" was near. The campaign, actually underway since 1823, was modestly successful. More than thirty auxiliary societies and six hundred local associations formed or reorganized. Each hoped to shape the character of the people, a hope that reflected not so much a fear of change as a fear that the scope of change would upset the moral gyroscope that guided individual behavior. Timothy Flint, writing from Cincinnati in September 1825, defined the problem succinctly: "Have we not to fear, that this rage for travelling, this manufacturing and money-getting impulse, and the new modes of reasoning and acting, will overturn your puritan institutions? New England founded her empire of industry and opinion, not in natural, but moral resources, in her ancient habits, and her ancient strictures, her schools, her economy and industry, her stable and perennial habits of worship. Should these be changed, as I much fear this new order of things is changing them, it will then be written upon the tablet of her forsaken temples, 'the glory is departed.' "[58]

During the fall of 1825 Evarts attended the annual meetings of various auxiliary societies throughout New England, making a plea at each one for financial support and exuding optimism that benevolent and missionary enterprises were winning converts and reshaping the moral climate. Indicative of this expansive mood was the decision by the American Board, at its September 1825 meeting, to accept the offer of a merger from the United Foreign Missionary Society. In addition, the board authorized the acceptance of Africans at the Foreign Mission School and appointed John Hooker, Calvin Chapin, and Evarts to a committee to look into the continuation of the school. "The various benevolent institutions," the Reverend Warren Fay told members of the Boston Foreign Mission Society, "are component and intimately connected parts of one great system."[59]

To advance that system, and to relieve his persistent consumption, Jeremiah Evarts left Boston in early 1826 for Charleston, South Carolina, and another tour of Indian missions in Georgia, Tennessee, Alabama, and Mississippi. By the time he returned to Boston in June, ABCFM finances had stabilized, and the board's enterprises had acquired an air of permanence. The sense of permanence stemmed not only from a stronger financial base but from an admission that the world would not be converted overnight. Expectations became more reasonable, and the board publicly admitted that its task was difficult. Only hard work, not the kind of "miracles" witnessed by missionaries on their arrival at the Sandwich Islands, would generate results. In a long discussion of the Palestine Mission, Evarts invited its "friends and patrons" to "consider the *nature of the enterprise*, and to gird up their minds for a long, and arduous, but glorious struggle."[60]

Gone now was the innocence of earlier years. Evarts's admission that missionary success in Palestine might take five years or more even to become apparent perhaps marked a turning point in the missionary enterprises of the American Board. He still believed that piety and morality went hand in hand, however. And as political democracy spread and gave greater weight to public opinion, he believed that the cultivation of individual morality was a responsibility of citizenship. The 1826 constitution of the American Home Missionary Society said it best: "If . . . we would guard the administration of our government from abuse, and our political institutions from ruin, we must purify the twelve million sources of political power and public influence which are to be found in the sentiments and manners of the individuals who compose the nation."[61]

Much had changed since Jeremiah Evarts replaced Samuel Worcester as the corresponding secretary for the American Board of Commissioners for Foreign Missions in 1821. The breadth of the missionary enterprise had expanded significantly, the duties of the corresponding secretary had multiplied impressively, and the immediate focus of ABCFM efforts had shifted from overseas missions to its missions among the North American Indians. Perhaps most important, however, was the increased controversy with respect to the board's operations. In part a recognition of their importance, and in part a measure of their success, by the mid-1820s the swirl of controversy threatened to becloud the future.

CHAPTER SIX

Clouds on the Horizon, 1825–1829

Jeremiah Evarts's first four years as corresponding secretary of the American Board of Commissioners for Foreign Missions had been years of growth and optimism. During the next four years, however, several incidents arose to challenge both the growth and the optimism. These incidents appeared as clouds on the horizon; they were not completely unannounced, but neither were they expected. Taken together they brought Evarts and the American Board face to face with some of the unpleasant social and political realities of early nineteenth-century America. The most pressing challenges arose at the Foreign Mission School and in debates over the future direction of American Indian policy. Both instances forced the ABCFM to become more political in its public persona. Their emergence led Jeremiah Evarts's Christian republicanism to become as much a political force as a moral ethos. Innocence gave way to intrigue.

Symptomatic of this loss of innocence was the uproar at the Board's Foreign Mission School in Cornwall, Connecticut. Founded in 1816 to instruct students from "heathen" societies in agriculture, the mechanic arts, commerce, religion, and "civilization," the school erupted in controversy in 1825 and 1826 when Harriet Gold, the nineteen-year-old daughter of Benjamin and Eleanor Gold, asked permission to marry Elias Boudinot, a Cherokee Indian and a student at the school. Two years earlier, in the winter of 1823–24, school trustee John Northrup had seen his daughter, Sarah, marry John Ridge, also a Cherokee. After a brief editorial furor in the local Litchfield *Eagle*, however, opposition to the earlier marriage subsided. Sarah and John had been courting for some time, and the couple rode off, driven by a black coachman in livery, in a large coach pulled by four white horses. In 1825–26, however, the furor did not subside quickly, even though Benjamin Gold had defended the earlier Northrup-Ridge marriage.[1]

Community residents led the opposition, but agents of the Foreign Mission School (Lyman Beecher, Timothy Stone, Joseph Harvey, and Philo Swift) quickly joined the chorus of criticism. Which group outdid the other is difficult to determine. The agents not only criticized the secrecy of the marriage arrangements but voiced their opposition to all such marriages as well and labeled the bride and groom's conduct "criminal." They complained that such marriages were an affront to community sensibilities and violated guidelines of proper decorum. They urged the community not to blame the Foreign Mission School and promised to adopt "additional restrictions" to prevent yet another recurrence. This did little to mollify Harriet's family, who were "as white as sheets."[2]

The affair traumatized the town. Harriet Gold herself described the excitement about a second interracial marriage in the community in a passage best quoted in full.

> It being thought unsafe for me to stay at home, I left the night before and was kept in a chamber at Capt. Clark's where I had a full prospect of the solemn transactions in our valley. In the evening our respectable young people, ladies and gentlemen, convened on the plain to witness and approve the scene and express their indignation. A painting had before been prepared representing a beautiful young lady and an Indian, also on the same, a woman as an instigator of Indian marriages. Evening came on. The church bell began to toll, one would certainly conclude speaking the departure of a soul. Mr. John C. Lewis and Mr. Rufus Payne carried the corpse and Brother Stephen [Gold] set fire to the barrel of tar, or rather the funeral pile, the flames rose high and the smoke ascended, some said it reminded them of the smoke of their torment which they feared would ascend forever. My heart truly sung with anguish at the dreadful scene. The bell continued to toll till 10 or 11 o'clock. ——There is a great division of feeling among many, but especially in our family. It appears as though a house divided against itself could not stand. Ma is almost worn out, she feels as though her children had no tenderness for her, and instead of comforting her, were to fill up her cup of affliction till it is more than running over. I attended meeting today as usual. As I had been requested to leave the singers' seat that I need not disgrace the rest of the girls, I took our pew. . . . The few friends I now have are dearer to me than ever—many delight in showing disrespect, others take uncommon pains to notice and respect me. I feel as

though I had wronged no one. I have done nothing but what I had a perfect and lawful right to do.[3]

To seek solace and find support, Harriet carried on an extensive correspondence with her brother-in-law, the Reverend Herman Vaill. Vaill had taught at the Foreign Mission School before marrying Flora Gold and moving to Millington, Connecticut. But Vaill offered scant solace. He reminded Harriet of her desire to be a missionary to the Indians but wondered if she had confused love of a particular person with love of Christ. Vaill also warned that the marriage could hinder Indian missions and predicted that *"another such event would annihilate"* the Foreign Mission School. Her marriage to an Indian, he concluded, was a betrayal to the cause. Vaill was agitated about the racial angle, as were the townspeople.[4]

Race had become a controversial factor in plans to civilize the Indians. Only a year before [1824] Thomas Cooper had published an attack against William H. Crawford's proposal to resolve the Indian problem in the United States through the intermarriage of whites with Indians. Cooper warned that such a scheme eviscerated the "purity and permanence of our Republican Institutions" and vilified Crawford's character for even suggesting it. The idea, said Cooper, of encouraging Americans to "enter into the tender connexion of matrimonial union with the neighbouring savages, in order to extend the empire of civil liberty and social happiness" was reprehensible. How could the young men and women of the frontier, "blooming, healthy, hardy, active and enterprising," be allowed to "prostitute their persons, to the dirty, draggle-tailed, blanketted, halfhuman squaws, or the filthy ferocious half naked savages, bedecked, indeed, with pewter pendants in their ears, lips and noses." Such a "motley intercourse," Cooper ranted, is as bad as "intermarrying with the stinking negroes for the same benevolent purpose."[5]

Although the American Board had, on occasion, referred to racial characteristics in describing its civilizing efforts among the tribes, the reaction to the Gold-Boudinot marriage horrified Jeremiah Evarts. "Can it be pretended at this age of the world," he wrote, "that a small variance of complexion is to present an insuperable barrier to matrimonial connexions, or that the different tribes of men are to be kept forever & entirely distinct?" He urged his colleagues to pay little attention to public outcries, insisting that "the public have nothing to do with the matter, so long as public morals are not violated." Evarts's chief concern was that the furor not damage ABCFM Indian missions. Only a year earlier Daniel Butrick had advised Evarts that John Ridge had been upset by his treatment in the North after his marriage to Sarah Northrup. Christian cruelty, concluded Evarts, made him feel very anxious about the future of missions to the Indians.[6]

The Gold-Boudinot affair not only stirred the "retired romantic valley" in Connecticut; it dealt a rude shock to Jeremiah Evarts's broad humanitarian vision. It also presented reformers with a dilemma. Were they interested in encouraging a new moral ethos primarily to promote public decorum, or was this an effort to challenge and reform the structure of American society? Evarts defended the marriage, lamented the public's racial attitudes, but also admitted that the affair would "produce disastrous effects upon the Cherokee mission" and called for an investigation of the Foreign Mission School. That August, prior to the American Board's investigation, Evarts privately attacked the report of the school's executive committee. That report, which had been published, voiced strong opposition to the marriage and blamed the individuals involved and not the school. Would not such views, Evarts asked one member of that executive committee, "strike their [Cherokee] minds as equivalent to a declaration that they & their people are doomed to perpetual inferiority; and that every attempt to rise to an equality with the whites is imprudent & criminal?"[7]

Evarts clearly thought this to be the case and quickly wrote missionaries Cyrus Kingsbury at Mayhew and William Chamberlain at Willstown to give them details of the affair and ask that they not send any more Indian youths to the school for the moment. He also wrote missionary David Butrick and Chief John Ross, asking both of them to talk with Boudinot and encourage him to persevere as a Christian. Converted Cherokee David Brown added to Evarts's embarrassment when he wrote that the affair puzzled his tribesmen; it contradicted what the missionaries had told them about New England and its principles. Butrick replied, somewhat sarcastically, that "even the *heathen* world blushes, and humanity sickens at the thought." By the time of its annual meeting, the Prudential Committee admitted the obvious: "There are serious difficulties in conducting an institution, composed of young men brought from the wilderness, or from distant pagan countries, and formed into a little community by themselves, while they are more or less exposed to various influences from the surrounding population."[8] It was an ironic admission. An institution established to teach the values of a Christian society and to inculcate its moral principles found its major threat to emanate from that very society.

Although the board tried to minimize the impact of race in the affair, it had to admit that "the differences of complexion" as well as traditional white hatred for Indians lay behind the uproar in Cornwall. Nonetheless, it blamed "inquisitive curiosity" mixed with a "Christian benevolence" as well as "established prejudices" for the outcry. By the fall of 1826, after waiting more than a year, the Prudential Committee voted to discontinue the Foreign Mission School. Insisting that its objectives remained intact, but that missionary schools among the tribes were a better alternative, the ABCFM refused to admit that it had caved in to local prejudices.

In fact, even though many persons connected with the school argued for its continuation, the Prudential Committee had decided only months after the affair to close the school. It had no intention of offending New Englanders. The committee's response was more than mere decorum, however. Committee members truly believed that the continued presence of native youth in the midst of white society courted further difficulties. Its ends, Evarts argued, could be "secured in other ways at less expense & with less hazzard than has attended the experiment."[9]

The Foreign Mission School controversy revealed a serious dilemma for the philosophy and operations of the American Board's missions. On the one hand, if the ABCFM had been at all successful during the past ten years, it should now be able to educate native youth at mission stations in their own lands. In that case such an institution was superfluous. On the other hand, however, if white society—even New England society— remained so militantly hostile to native cultures and their practitioners, then was there any point at which white society considered other peoples to be "civilized"? Were whites willing and able to practice humanitarianism only at a distance? How much "difference" was American society willing to tolerate?

For Jeremiah Evarts those questions took on a new urgency after 1825, especially as they related to Indian affairs. The Foreign Mission School controversy revealed only one side of the problem, for although the ABCFM missionary stations among the tribes seemed to be prospering, opposition to missionary preaching was growing among the tribes themselves at the same time that state-federal conflict over the future direction of Indian affairs escalated. Evarts warned missionary Cyrus Kingsbury in March 1825 that "You will see by the papers that the circumstances of the Indians are daily becoming more critical. . . . The subject is daily becoming more difficult for us, as the government are determined to remove all the natives to the westward of the Mississippi. We must be cautious what we say & what we do in this matter."[10]

Evarts's concern was well founded. By the mid-1820s four parties interested in Indian affairs were on a collision course: the federal government, state governments, missionary societies, and the tribes themselves. Each of them had changed their perception of the problems and possibilities embedded in relations between the federal government and the tribes, and each either had formulated or was in the process of formulating new policies to accommodate those changes. Some of the stimulus for this increased conflict lay in Pres. James Monroe's special message to Congress in January 1825. Coming on the heels of a treaty with the Choctaws for five million acres of land in Arkansas Territory, and drawn in part from a survey on the status of tribes east of the Mississippi by Secretary of War Calhoun, Monroe's message stated that "in their present state, it is impossible to incorporate them . . . into our system" but held out the promise of removal only "whenever it may be done peaceably and on reasonable conditions." Although Monroe implied that removal could occur only with Indian consent, his phrase "reasonable conditions" left unclear who would determine those conditions. In the eyes of southerners and westerners, however, there was no doubt. One day after the message Missouri's Sen. Thomas Hart Benton of the Indian Affairs Committee wrote Calhoun to announce that the committee had just adopted unanimously a plan to promote emigration.[11]

Two weeks later Director of Indian Affairs Thomas McKenney secretly wrote Evarts to solicit his reaction and ask if he would be an Indian commissioner. Evarts replied that Monroe, Calhoun, and McKenney seemed to have benevolent intentions but confessed that "I have many fears as to the expected efficacy of the measure." Four major obstacles presented themselves to Evarts. First, the government would have difficulty finding land in the west which the tribes would consider equal to that they were leaving. Second, there would be "the difficulty of persuading them, that it is for their interest to remove." Unless entire tribes removed, the "more intelligent and industrious" would stay behind. Third, there would be many problems in the establishment of a government over the emigrants so as to ensure the peace. Finally, Evarts was convinced that any habitable region to which the tribes removed would again be surrounded by whites clamoring for land. Removal would not really aid the tribes, therefore, but merely prolong their agony. Despite these reservations, and even though he freely admitted that his Boston friends opposed his decision, Evarts confessed that "I should delight to be an agent of some kind among the Indians so that I could labor in the wilderness, with a prospect of success, for their benefit."[12]

Two other obstacles quickly surfaced to agitate the controversy over removal, presenting Evarts with problems more important than his eventual failure to secure an appointment. First, election contests in Georgia focused on Indian removal, as various political factions sought to curry favor with voters. Although both houses of the Georgia legislature supported a controversial 1825 treaty with the Creeks, the gubernatorial election that year turned on which of the two candidates was the more militant supporter of states' rights. George Troup defeated John Clark by 683 votes chiefly because he adopted a more radical position, successfully attacking Clark's view that harmony between the state and the federal government was necessary to carry out removal. Troup insisted that the state of Georgia could do whatever it wished within its boundaries, and announced his intention to follow that line wherever it led. His fiery correspondence with the Creeks and the federal government throughout the campaign kept his views before the public, and the fact that 1825 was the first popular election of the governor in Georgia further excited the populace. Since the Clark faction supported Andrew Jackson, and since virtually every white citizen of the state favored the immediate removal of the Indians, who won the election was not as important as the passions inflamed by the issue itself. That ardor outlived the campaign and became a fixture in state-federal politics for the next five years.[13]

The second obstacle lay with the tribes themselves. By the mid-1820s many tribes had begun to adopt a hostile posture toward both the missionaries and the government. Led by the Cherokees, they sought to develop a third alternative to those of integration or removal. That alternative was nationalism. Adaptation to the white man's presence or the adoption of particular "civilizing" tendencies did not necessarily mean a willingness to abandon all tribal customs and an autonomous culture. To put their opposition to removal in sharp relief, in 1825 the Cherokee General Council passed a law decreeing the death penalty for those who sold any more land to whites. Although most of the Cherokee leaders still supported the policy of integration, they were coming to realize that this meant cultural annihilation and began to probe its psychological consequences. The result, ironically, was that the emergence of romantic nationalism among the white population coincided with the emergence of a similar feeling among the native population. The logic of these nationalistic impulses led both groups, separately, to conclude that their fulfillment required both an end to the vision of integration and support for their own cultural hegemony within a separate sphere.[14]

Led by Governor Troup of Georgia, however, state officials tried to inject themselves into these relationships as well as to seize the initiative to promote Indian removal. The various parties collided with one another. Secretary of War Calhoun sought to persuade tribes to exchange lands in the East for territory west of the Mississippi. ABCFM missionaries preached the gospel and urged the tribes to remain where they were and become "civilized" in the white man's image. State officials pressured the federal government to remove the tribes by any means possible and approached selected tribal leaders themselves to cajole, threaten, and deal. They came to believe that their success was inversely proportional to that of the missionaries, blaming on missionary interference the growing reluctance of tribal chiefs to succumb to threats and promises. This mistaken perception, of course, gave no credit to the intelligence of the chiefs. The statement of a delegation of Arkansas Cherokees to John Calhoun defined the new reality: "A removal of our eastern boundary, would drag with it, the white population:—and we are fully convinced, that we can never get out of their reach—therefore it would be folly in us, to try, by removing from place to place, under these circumstances—And for the reasons we have given—We explicitly say that we cannot consent to *remove* our eastern boundary, as recommended."[15]

An article in the *Christian Advocate* highlighted these conflicts and expressed the concern of benevolent reformers. Indian affairs, the editors stated, had become their preeminent moral concern, and the "unhappy Aborigines" were in a "predicament that is little short of a dilemma." To remain where they were meant extinction. To remove elsewhere would not only sunder traditional tribal ties but place them "in a region less favourable to their immediate civilization and to the benign influence of the gospel." Although the editors still trusted the national government to act benevolently toward the Indians, they did not believe this attitude to be true of all the state governments, especially those which bordered on tribal lands. Prejudice and cupidity, moreover, guaranteed that nothing the federal government did would satisfy everyone. To send Christianized Indians to a "howling wilderness" was unconscionable. They urged the federal government to resist this course but admitted that many states would never extend the privileges of citizenship to Indians regardless of their education, religious conviction, or conduct.[16]

Secretary of War James Barbour's 1825 plan voluntarily to remove the Indians to a separate territory and then use the federal government to protect them from whites further sharpened the debate. States anxious to secure Indian lands through removal insisted that such was their inherent right as states; missionaries and the more educated tribesmen argued that what was at stake was not only tribal lands and the treaty authority of the federal government but the very character of a people. This felicitious phrase, embedded in republican discourse, infused the opposition to removal. It was the basis for pleas from Cherokee chiefs John Ross, George Lowrey, and Elijah Hicks, who insisted that "tribes who are now successfully embracing the habits of civilized man within their own limits" should never be removed. "The arts of civilized life have been successfully introduced among them," the chiefs observed, so changing their character that "no inducement can ever prompt them to abandon their habitations for a distant, wild, and strange clime."[17]

Regardless of tribal feelings, and sometimes because of them, the debate over Indian removal quickened. Federal officials did their best to convince tribes to remove voluntarily, warning them frankly that removal was in their best interests but promising that the federal government would never use force to "fall on a poor, helpless, red child and kill it, because it is weak." Even some ABCFM missionaries, such as Cyrus Kingsbury, relaxed their objections to removal, "provided it is done on any thing like fair & equitable terms." Kingsbury warned Evarts that "Evils must attend the Indians, whereever they are, for many years to come," and that they probably could not stay where they were long enough to be civilized.[18]

The rantings of Georgia's Governor Troup, or the quiet but firm insistance of Gov. Israel Pickens of Alabama, had convinced Kingsbury that missions to the Indians were unlike other foreign missions of the American Board. Historian William Hutchison has observed that missionaries in distant lands became the primary interpreters of "remote cultures" for Americans at home and through their reports were able to shape public attitudes and expectations toward their enterprise. The situation with the missions to North American Indian tribes differed enormously, however, for enough of the public had acquired some experience or folklore about the tribes and was either able or willing to make their own independent judgments on grounds that had little to do with the progress of Christianity at the mission stations. In controversies such as that over Indian removal, or the one at the Foreign Mission School, independent actions by the populace at large took the initiative away from the missionaries.

Jeremiah Evarts was aware of these developments and worried lest the American Board become entangled in the growing political wrangles in the states as well as within the tribes. He instructed missionary Samuel A. Worcester (son of the American Board's former corresponding secretary) on his departure for the Cherokees to "carefully abstain from interfering, by advice, or in any other way, with their transactions of a political nature." This abstinence proved difficult, for the very definition of their task led missionaries to grapple with political matters. They were, after all, not only to preach the gospel but to create a Christian civilization. Civilization for "heathens," from the missionary perspective, required that the institutional and behavioral foundations of the culture be transformed. Moral behavior required Christian legislation, and this in turn rested on the election of converted leaders as well as the inculcation of a moral ethos. Keeping missionaries aloof from politics proved unlikely and impossible.[19]

The determination of the Adams administration that any removal would occur *only* with the tribes' consent infuriated states like Georgia. At the same time, it excited fears among the Indians and aroused concern at the American Board. Independent actions of impetuous men like Troup of Georgia, moreover, fanned the fires of discontent on all sides. In 1825 Troup had gone so far as to bribe his cousin, Creek Chief William McIntosh, and negotiate the fraudulent Treaty of Indian Springs. After first accepting the treaty, President Adams learned of the corruption and of the treaty's rejection by the Creek Nation and reopened negotiations. This reexamination led to the 1826 Treaty of Washington.[20]

It also led to some searching discussions within the administration about the feasibility and implications of the treaty and removal process. Thomas McKenney wrote Secretary of War Barbour to push for removal, arguing that the tribes would soon become extinct unless they were removed and separated from the white population in their own permanent territory. Barbour, on the other hand, urged Adams to incorporate the Indians within the states, to cease making treaties with them and change the character of Indian relations by bringing them under federal laws. Secretary of State Henry Clay, although nominally a friend of benevolent causes, opposed such a course with language that contradicted both Barbour and Adams. The president recorded it in his memoirs: "Mr. Clay said . . . that it was impossible to civilize Indians; that there never was a full-blooded Indian who took to civilization. It was not in their nature. He believed they were destined to extinction, and, although he would never use or countenance inhumanity towards them, he did not think them, as a race, worth preserving. He considered them as essentially inferior to the Anglo-Saxon race, which were now taking their place on this continent. They were not an improvable breed, and their disappearance from the human family will be no great loss to the world."[21]

In the end this debate turned on character and politics. Barbour's proposed response to Georgia over the McIntosh affair suggested that since Clay might be correct, "and the Indians were going to inevitable destruction," the administration should yield to Georgia's claims that the Treaty of Indian Springs was valid. Why seek a conflict in which "Georgia would necessarily be driven to support General Jackson"? Adams refused. Clay's remarks, he wrote in his memoirs, were only a general observation on the current course of events. They should not shape policy, which should continue to rest on the benevolent character of the American people as Adams understood it. To yield to Georgia would be a "gross injustice," and the president maintained that he "felt little concern or care" about Georgia's supporting Andrew Jackson, admitting that he "had no more confidence in one party there than in the other."[22]

The benevolent community supported Adams's stand and also emphasized the conjunction of morality and character. A report on the Georgia-Creek controversy, first published in the *New York Review*, set the tone. What was at stake, the authors insisted, was the "character of the Confederacy of the United States." The power of this confederacy was essentially moral, not physical, and "consists in a national character, unsullied by injustice and oppression. . . . it cannot shape its course according to the dictates of a temporizing, prevaricating policy." Delegates at the annual meeting of the American Board of Commissioners in 1825 heard much the same message. "Nothing like civil liberty, united with social order and security," said Joshua Bates, president of Middlebury College, "now exists in any country beyond the limits of Christian influence." Missionaries had to venture forth to spread the gospel and extend the sphere of civilization; this enterprise was the essence of the progressive vision. But how would it comport with the emerging vision of liberal capitalism and its demand for a liberal polity? Leonard Bacon told a Boston audience that, under a panoply of Christian principles, they would fit together very nicely. "You love your country. You exult in the anticipation of its ever growing prosperity and its enduring renown. Cherish the sentiment if you will. It is a high and manly feeling. . . . Look far away to the south, and far, far to the west, and you may see an empire rising into being, to which the shores and cities of New England will be only as the hem of the garment. Every day the growing tide of population rolls farther and farther,—the wilderness falls and vanishes before it,—and rich plantations, and smiling villages, and crowded cities, come out upon our vision like the stars at evening."[23]

Under the leadership of Jeremiah Evarts, the American Board and its auxiliary societies broadcast this expansive vision, linking the missionary enterprise to secular as well as religious prosperity. They needed to look outward, announced one missionary paper; "we need safety valves to let out our superfluous abundance." The authors concluded that "national improvements, and missionary efforts to evangelize the world, are the merciful provisions of providence for this end." As Lyman Beecher told listeners in Essex County, Massachusetts, nations have "perished always by plethora, never by depletion." Prosperity carried its own perils, foremost of which was a corrupting influence on the human character.[24]

Critics of the ABCFM took up this same theme and attacked the board's constant solicitation of funds as well as the salary of its corresponding secretary, Jeremiah Evarts. By 1825 Evarts received $2,000 annually from the ABCFM. He lived comfortably but spent most of his salary to support his immediate family as well as various Vermont relatives. Although recurring health problems and his attention to the affairs of the American Board kept his visits to Vermont infrequent, perhaps he also felt a twinge of guilt. He had no intention of trading his cosmopolitan Boston surroundings for the life of a Vermont farmer. As he wrote his wife from Charleston, South Carolina: "I hope to have grace to do my duty; but I should be very glad to be excused from visiting Vermont." To compensate for his absence, and perhaps to acknowledge that he was better off financially than the rest of his family, Evarts spent his own money to manage his father's estate. He floated loans from his personal funds (expecting to recover principal as well as interest when the lands were sold) and sent a steady stream of advice to his brothers about money management. In July 1825 he finally went to Georgia, Vermont, wrote some disparaging letters about the state of religion back to the ABCFM offices, and sold his father's homestead to his brother Jonathan Todd Evarts. Even after that sale, however, Jeremiah still owned six large lots (about a hundred acres) in the town. He also owned some land in Illinois.[25]

Jeremiah Evarts's cash books for 1826 reveal that he spent much of his salary on charity and his own home. He made constant contributions to a wide range of charities and purchased an assortment of tracts, sermons, and Bibles. For his home he purchased carpeting and furniture. His constant travels to relieve his consumption were also expensive, although the American Board paid some of those expenses when he traveled on official business. The cash books appear to indicate that his wife handled virtually all of the family's needs, and when he was away from home for an extended period of time, he had his salary paid directly to her. What emerges from these books is a picture of a man who was away from his family as much as he was home, who drank ale, beer, or cider on occasion, who wore silk socks and leather pants, a hat and gloves, and who kept scrupulous accounts. He even noted the thirteen cents lost by his son! He was also a man who loaned his money to friends, relatives, and causes he supported. The books show, for example, a six-hundred-dollar loan to Park Street Church and payment of principal and interest on a note of his sister's (four hundred dollars). He also advanced money to various mission stations as he visited them and acted as an agent for the American Board throughout his travels.[26]

These travels probably caused more difficulty for his family than any of his other duties. Even though he often undertook them to recover his health, they kept him away from home for extended periods of time, placed additional burdens on his wife, and separated him from the natural rhythms of family life. Jeremiah, and apparently Mehitabel as well, took all of this in stride—although he lamented "how much more pleasant it is to remain at home . . . than to be absent on any business, or in any pursuit whatever." But evangelical commitment required sacrifices, and his letters reveal that he was willing to accept whatever was his due. In May 1825, for instance, he arrived in Charleston, South Carolina, to discover that his daughter Sarah had died unexpectedly. His letter to Mehitabel reveals not only a sense of loss, but a conviction that God's will governed all human affairs. "It would have been a gratification, if I had been at home," he wrote, "and could have attended the poor child in her illness; but, for good and wise reasons, this gratification has been denied me." His presence would not have changed the outcome, he insisted, "and I pray that the survivors may duly consider the meaning of this Providence. . . . They are strikingly reminded of the uncertainty of life, and of the suddenness of the call into eternity." To his wife, he urged that they both rededicate themselves to the salvation of their remaining children—"to be more faithful to our remaining children and to each other, in regard to the things of religion, than we have ever yet been."[27]

In 1826 Jeremiah was off again—to recover his health and to visit ABCFM missions in a six-month tour extending from January to June. He visited the Cherokees, Chickasaws, and Choctaws to study progress in the field so as better to direct missionary labors and "promote vigor and economy." Evarts felt the press of government policy and public opinion for removal and was wary about the gathering clouds of controversy. Visions of progress and prosperity danced in the heads of state officials, visions they believed realizable only with Indian removal. To offset their influence, Evarts sought to educate public opinion to support the tribes. In South Carolina, for instance, he spearheaded formation of an interdenominational Charleston Society in Aid of Missions to the Heathen during his 1826 visit. Its purpose was to support missionary work and establish a printing press in the Cherokee Nation.[28]

While Evarts traveled, others wrote. Lewis Cass published a long study, "Indians of North America," in the *North American Review* that January. Cass, governor of Michigan Territory, argued that Americans knew little about the Indians' moral character or mental discipline. Most adult tribesmen, he insisted, had long been corrupted by contact with white society and were poor examples. "Our hopes must rest," he concluded, "upon the rising generation," and he praised missionary efforts to educate and Christianize the young. Cass had not yet cast his fortunes with the forces of removal gathering around Andrew Jackson, and in 1826 he urged the government to do little lest it increase the misery of the tribes. More money should be appropriated to the Indian Civilization Fund, whiskey kept off Indian lands, the intercourse laws enforced, hunters and trappers excluded from their territory, and tribesmen encouraged to hold private property—but "after all this, we should leave their fate to the common God of the white man and the Indian." At the same time that Cass defended the integrity of Indian lands, however, he purchased $20,000 worth of Ohio bonds to further canal construction in the Northwest.[29]

Evarts and supporters of missionary activity favored a much more activist approach to the tribes. They urged the tribes to become settled farmers and expected that the infusion of missionaries together with moral farmers would accomplish the work of civilization. Isaac Darneille urged the government to grant each tribe a permanent residence and in return advised the tribes to abandon the chase. "They have," Darneille wrote, "neither cornfields, domestic animals, nor decent nor comfortable clothing, nor houses, nor homes; nor do they seem to know that these things are essential to their happiness—nor that the care and culture of them would produce greater facilities in the acquisition of supplies than the chase." But so long as the federal government held out the promise of treaties, to the states or to the tribes, then so long the situation remained uncertain and unstable.[30]

Evarts's tour prepared the foundation for an end to this instability. Formation of the society in Charleston was one step, for its monies would support a Cherokee academy and printing press. These efforts also left Evarts in a dilemma. As he wrote Henry Hill in the ABCFM Boston offices, success would withdraw more funds from the board, and failure would discourage supporters of Indian missions. What he did not say was that success would also likely force a crisis in Indian-white relations. The more permanent tribal society appeared, the more white demands for immediate removal escalated. Evarts confided, however, that "I have no confidence that the Cherokees alone will have skill and energy enough to carry these designs into execution, in even a tolerable manner, without extraneous aid."[31]

Coincident with this initiative came the announcement of a Cherokee syllabary. The American Board opposed this, arguing in the *Missionary Herald* that its use would effectively cut them off from discourse with other nations. Few outside the Cherokee people would learn the syllabary, expenses would soar, and printing would be difficult. Its use, in short, might actually retard the progress of civilization and deprive the Cherokees "of an acquaintance with the many excellent works, in the English language, on religion and general science." Federal officials also expressed concern. Thomas McKenney wrote missionary Cyrus Kingsbury: "I believe the less of it [their language] that is taught, or spoken, the better for the Indians. Their whole character, inside and out; language, and morals, must be changed." Nonetheless, development of the syllabary heightened the sense of nationalism among the Cherokees, impressed whites with their progress toward civilization, and frightened land-hungry settlers to fear that they might become more stubborn about ceding their lands and removing to the west.[32]

This last sentiment became strikingly apparent to Evarts as he traveled through the South and especially through Georgia. Residents of Georgia were united in support of removal, and even neutral observers expected the state government to seize Creek lands within its borders by fall. Evarts warned Henry Hill that Georgians would "volunteer *en masse* to defend *state rights*, as they express it." Georgians, of course, were not alone. Governor Brandon of Mississippi alerted state legislators that the longer Indian tribes remained in the state, the more difficult it would be to remove them. "For the United States to suffer them to continue, without an effort to extinguish their title is depriving us of that territory we had a right to expect when we were admitted to the Union." A select joint committee of Congress warned, "We are rapidly approaching a crisis in our affairs with a portion of the natives of the country." They recommended a new system of relations with the tribes.[33]

James Barbour's plan represented just such a system, but one destined to be unworkable from the outset. Although he modified it, giving up the idea of incorporating the tribes into the states where they lived, even Pres. John Quincy Adams doubted that it would work. Perhaps the most significant portion of Barbour's report was his understanding of how current policy affected the tribes. How can you persuade Indians to give up the chase and engage in settled agriculture, present them with gifts of tools and domestic animals, and express an interest in their well-being, he argued, and then send government agents out to negotiate treaties for land cessions and convince them to move to unsettled lands west of the Mississippi without arousing an "unmixed indignation of what seems to them our ruthless purpose of expelling them from their country?" Whatever else the federal government does, Barbour concluded it must either "let him remain and enjoy his home, or, if he is to be driven from it, abstain from cherishing illusions we mean to disappoint."[34]

Evarts backed Barbour's plan in the hopes that establishment of an Indian territory in the West would guarantee that they never again had to move. During the next two years, however, as he listened to Congress debate the Indian question, Evarts changed his mind, perhaps realizing that Congress would never approve such a plan. What apparently helped change his mind was a greater militancy on the part of those who favored removal under any circumstances. In letters and speeches congressmen, government bureaucrats, governors, and other public officials made clear during the spring and summer of 1826 that removal *would* only be voluntary under Barbour's plan. Thomas McKenney was most direct, writing to David Folsom that *"you will never be pushed off your land. If you go, it will be by your own consent, and free will. Therefore do not be uneasy. You know me. I will never deceive you. Therefore mind my words. Tell your people this. It is true the Government think it best* for you to be altogether—and on lands that will be forever your own;—But you will not be forced."[35] The more unequivocal the statement that removal would be voluntary, the more feverish state opposition to this policy became.

Throughout his travels, Evarts tried to gauge the prospects for further missionary efforts. After visiting eighteen mission stations, he concluded that education was the gateway to evangelical success and that all missionaries and teachers should learn "the language of the people where they labor." He believed that civilization advanced only so far as white influence spread among the natives. But that white influence should be selective and carefully regulated. Intermixing white settlers with the Indians would, he insisted, be disastrous. Only missionaries and selected mechanics possessed the proper character to yield the desired results. In the same manner, the uproar at the Foreign Mission School and the reaction to it among the tribes led him to conclude that "it would not be well for any great number of youths to be brought thence for education among the whites." Teach them among their own people, Evarts concluded, and they "will not lose their standing & influence with the chiefs & people; but will gradually become the persons of most consequence." Visits with the Reverend Gideon Blackburn among the Cherokees deepened his convictions, and on his way back to Boston he stopped in New York and other northern cities to raise funds to advance these prospects.[36]

By 1826, however, demands for immediate removal from the southern states increasingly threatened Evarts's vision and timetable for this civilizing process. Georgia's Governor Troup adopted the most dangerous position, arguing that since Indian tribes resided *within* the states the matter was one for the states themselves to decide. This put him on a collision course with the federal government; only the hope of a policy change after the 1828 election stayed his hand. For the moment Troup remained content to protest government policy, especially as he realized that Barbour's proposal embraced only voluntary removal. Despite Georgia's dismay, however, federal agents really were doing their best to convince the tribes to remove. Their arguments even became somewhat novel, as in the case of John Coffee's approach to the Chickasaws: "The only advantage the Government derives from its red children is, to get occasionally some of their lands at a fair and reasonable price. By refusing to sell us lands, you withhold the only means in your power of contributing to the support and prosperity of the Government of the United States."[37]

Progress meant development, and development meant Indian removal. Governor James Ray of Indiana wrote Henry Clay that prompt acquisition of Indian lands in that state was essential. Ray warned that *"the rough appearances of nature must be overcome and made to yield to human enterprise. Our waters must be imprisoned in new channels, and made to subserve the essential purposes of commerce."*[38] Indian Affairs director McKenney counseled Barbour that voluntary removal was still feasible; only the approach had to be changed. Influential chiefs should be approached individually and offered special parcels of land. Indians educated at the mission schools should be used as intermediaries between the whites and the chiefs. Missionaries should be advised that they would be needed more than ever west of the Mississippi, and the government should reimburse the missionary societies for monies expended in constructing existing mission stations. Encourage the missionaries to move, McKenney advised, and they would take the Indians under their charge with them.

McKenney found one convert in Baptist missionary Isaac McCoy, then engaged in a dispute with his Baptist board about missionary policy and the importance of Indian missions. He made less headway with ABCFM missionaries, however, although they had come to recognize their dilemma. Daniel Butrick summarized the problem in a letter to John Ridge and Elias Boudinot. "As we do not wish to prevent the Cherokees from emigrating, so, on the other hand we do not wish to urge their removal, lest they should say, as some do already, that our object in coming among them was to get them away; but to dismiss our schools and to go to the west before the people are ready to go, would be as much as telling them they must go or not enjoy the benefit of our labors, which would be taking a political stand altogether inconsistent with the mission character."[39]

For Jeremiah Evarts and the American Board of Commissioners, this concern became pressing during the next two years. McKenney believed that his proposal would further the civilization program; removal would quiet the states and separate the Indians from the whites, thereby guaranteeing their survival. This could best be done west of the Mississippi; perhaps it could *only* be done west of the Mississippi. Evarts and the missionaries, on the other hand, worried about the plans and pleas of the government. State demands and political pressures, they believed, would palsy the government's hand. Clear divisions had begun to emerge in Congress, and Indian affairs had become one of the determinants of political alignment. Coalitions had not yet become institutionalized parties, but lines were being drawn. As they were, drawing public attention to the question of national character and away from particular issues as an end in themselves became increasingly difficult.[40]

Amid the clouds of controversy, the heroic image of Andrew Jackson—Indian fighter, victor over the British at New Orleans, a man who appeared direct in word and deed—betokened a new romantic impulse. It was a difficult image to counteract, for the moral ethos promoted by Evarts was grounded in self-restraint and the uncertainty of the future. The romantic ideal, on the other hand, envisioned an ethos of opportunism—a world restrained only by the limits of human endeavor and governed by an unshakable confidence in the future. In short, opportunism beckoned and morality restrained. That Jacksonianism had become a haven for a variety of diametrically opposing visions for the future was of little consequence for the moment. That both sides claimed to represent a moral ethos was more central to public discourse. As historian Richard Latner has argued, the Democrats insisted that individual morality bound society. But their moral concerns differed from those of reformers like Evarts. Morality for Andrew Jackson meant the sanctity of debts, political democracy, rotation in office, economy in government, states' rights (on some issues), the union (above all), and individual freedom. For Jeremiah Evarts, on the other hand, morality included the observance of national commitments, stimulation of a community ethos, religious conviction, and individual restraint and self-control.[41]

More than any other issue, the question of Indian removal came to delimit the boundaries between the contending definitions of morality. In effect, Indian removal in the late 1820s represented a clash between liberal and republican visions of the future. And for those persons attracted to the respective positions of Jackson and Evarts, the last two years of the Adams administration proved critical. In those years the assertions of the former confronted head-on the warnings of the latter. Removal was the issue; Georgia was the locale. Complicating the process was the maturity of a morally strong third force: the Cherokee Nation.

By the winter and spring of 1827, Indian removal had become a political problem for President John Quincy Adams. When he had taken office two years earlier, he had tried to assure the South that he stood for the removal of all eastern tribes. But advocates of removal had quickly learned that, for Adams, all removal had to be voluntary. By 1827 when southerners realized that the tribes would not remove voluntarily, they demanded sterner measures. The approach of the 1828 presidential election and the candidacy of Andrew Jackson gave them an opportunity for leverage, and southern demands for immediate removal steadily became more insistent. At the same time, government officials such as Thomas McKenney made clear their belief that defects in native character as well as particular racial attributes made them perpetual children and required a governmental paternalism to define and promote their best interests. McKenney was convinced that removal was essential to their continued survival as a people. Other politicians like Lewis Cass agreed, arguing that despite the efforts of the American Board of Commissioners and other missionary societies, despite government appropriations under the Indian Civilization Fund, the Indians remained uncivilized. Perhaps removal would change them.[42]

Jeremiah Evarts noted another consideration: Indian lands. "The prospects of the aborigines of this country are, indeed dark, as you observe," he wrote, "and where their wrongs are to terminate, or what is to be the result of the eagerness of the whites to obtain possession of their lands, it is not in our power to foresee." Georgia officials initiated a series of independent actions to force the government's hand. Governor Troup pressured the administration to allow all Creek lands in the state to be surveyed. Internal state politics complicated matters for the president. Support for removal was so popular in Georgia that its state representatives scrambled to devise measures for which they could claim credit. When demands for land, hopes to exploit and develop those lands, and an ingrained racial hostility toward the Indians mixed, the atmosphere became highly volatile.[43]

Then there was that other issue: Indian sovereignty. Government officials made no effort to conceal their contempt for Indian claims to intellectual and political independence. Even many of the missionaries made clear their paternalistic beliefs, although their letters imply that they tried to conceal those attitudes from the Indians. As Evarts wrote Cyrus Kingsbury: "The very attempt to instruct the Choctaws goes upon the presumption that they are not able to judge in regard to their true interests. Still, I would avoid collision of opinion with them, as far as practicable." That their efforts at concealment succeeded is doubtful. Nonetheless, government treaty negotiations traditionally had supported at least the illusion that the tribes were independent, sovereign entities.[44]

Congress debated Indian matters in the spring of 1827, and Jeremiah Evarts went to Washington to monitor those debates. While he stopped in numerous towns and cities along the way to organize or encourage missionary societies, the chief purpose of the trip was to evaluate the government's handling of the fraudulent 1825 Treaty of Indian Springs. Governor Troup claimed that this treaty gave Georgia the right to survey Creek lands. President Adams disagreed, and in March 1827 a select committee (stacked in favor of Georgia) reported to the Senate and exonerated Georgia. At this point Evarts still supported the administration's position, favoring removal so long as it was voluntary. In Washington Evarts dined with Samuel Lorenzo Knapp, the new editor of the *Daily National Journal*. He argued that the subject of Indian affairs needed to be placed "in proper light before the American people," and Knapp agreed to publish anything Evarts sent him on the subject. All this activity, ironically, further politicized the controversy and seemed to support Georgia's specious claim that Indian missionaries were northern political agents.[45]

Evarts maintained a busy Washington schedule, dining repeatedly with Thomas McKenney and other officials, meeting congressmen, and even engaging President Adams in discussions about Indian missions and removal. Although he promoted American Board missions, Evarts had become discouraged with the lack of progress and the failure to ease the many irritants that afflicted Indian-white relations. In early March he wrote Rufus Anderson at ABCFM headquarters that "These reasons would weigh powerfully in favor of a removal of the Indians, if it were possible to get them out of the reach of vicious white men. As the case now is, I think their prospects very gloomy. . . . The history of savage nations, however, coming into close contact with civilized nations, gives us little reason to make very sanguine conclusions, as to the preservation of the former in their national capacity."[46] Evarts's admission that cataclysmic cultural change would overpower native societies was not really very remarkable; that, after all, was the intent of the missionary endeavor. But it revealed that this change would obliterate not only the culture but the separate identity of native peoples. ABCFM efforts to organize model commonwealths now seemed doomed.

A subsequent letter to Anderson outlined additional problems for the ABCFM and the tribes. Secretary of War James Barbour had told Evarts that the "cupidity" of the southern states would overwhelm the federal government and that "If in the election of President, the vote of Georgia should be necessary to a choice . . . that men might possibly be found, who would engage to do whatever Georgia should require." These were, Evarts wrote Anderson, "pretty humiliating facts." To Cephas Washburn at the Dwight Mission, Evarts lamented that "if the present exertions should fail, I know not how we could induce the Christians of our country to try another experiment."[47]

In a letter marked "private," Thomas McKenney urged Evarts to find some way to elevate the debate above merely political considerations, to arouse the public by focusing on the moral principles central to the issue. The clarion call came from an unlikely source.

> You are aware of the crisis which has arrived in regard to our Indians. You see as well as I do that without the intervention of some power that shall rouse the Congress of the U.S., into a due consideration of the real condition of these people the stigma will be fixed upon our country, and with it the crime, of abandoning them to destruction, and that too in the face of the civilized world, and in direct opposition to all those just and generous feelings by which it is understood to be governed. We first invaded their rights, then dissolved their power, and then, unless something is speedily done, it will have to be added, persecuted them out of existence.[48]

McKenney's plea roused Evarts to ask that all Christians petition Congress in support of the Indians. In a letter to ABCFM headquarters, he urged that the petitions should differ from one another so they would "not appear to emanate from one source." Evarts had become politically sensitive. He also remained sensitive to the politics of religion, warning Rufus Anderson that unless Congregationalists worked hard they would be overshadowed by the Baptists and Methodists, whose greater numbers gave them more votes and probably more influence with Congress.[49]

But McKenney's warning, coupled with Georgia's intransigence and his own reading of congressional opinion, led him to support Barbour's and McKenney's plans for Indian removal. They supported removal, Evarts pointed out, only to prevent the Indians from being trampled and "hunted down like wild beasts," and only under certain conditions. Five restrictions defined Evarts's support for removal: (1) the Indians had to be satisfied with their new country; (2) that country had to be secured to them; (3) the government must protect them from white intrusion; (4) good government and schools must be secured to them (meaning that the missionary stations would remove with them); and (5) removal must be slow and deliberate so as to avoid suffering. American Board missionaries, he wrote Cyrus Kingsbury, must avoid interference in tribal political matters and should support voluntary removal.[50] These conditions proved easier said than done, for proponents of removal in Georgia and elsewhere viewed missionary support for voluntary removal itself as political interference. The problem, of course, was that whites who desired Indian lands viewed *all* efforts to help the Indians improve themselves—spiritually, economically, or politically—as inimical to removal.[51]

After Evarts returned to Boston in late April, a resurgence of nationalism among the Cherokees compounded the controversy—a controversy, historian William McLoughlin has perceptively observed, that defined what it was to be white as well as Indian in nineteenth-century America. Cherokee nationalism was not new, but its previous manifestations had not occurred at a time of such convergence in Indian-white relations. In 1827, presidential politics, states' rights assertions, a mania for development and expansion, and a realization among whites that voluntary removal had apparently reached its limits all converged. Reformers such as Jeremiah Evarts sought to shackle these developments to a moral ethos, but exhortations about national morality were slender threads with which to restrain such powerful centrifugal forces.[52]

The outbreak of White Path's Rebellion in 1827 divided the Cherokee community, as tribal traditionalists resisted the movement toward acculturation. At issue were not only missionary activity and its objectives among the Cherokees, but the very structure of the Cherokee Nation itself. Anti-mission sentiment had been building for at least six years, and in 1827 it burst forth to oppose further acculturation. Similar in many respects to a rebellion in the Sandwich Islands by George P. Tamoree and to anti-mission sentiment that troubled the Sandwich Islands Mission in the mid-1820s, White Path's Rebellion came after the Cherokee Council passed a series of laws to encourage that moral ethos so ardently advanced by Evarts.[53] Traditionalists focused their energies to oppose adoption of the Cherokee Constitution, formulated in 1826 and deliberately modeled on that of the United States. Because the rebellion contained religious as well as political impulses, it concerned the ABCFM missionaries. But it was not violent, and by midsummer the factions had met and reconciled their differences. Or at least they appeared to. New threats from Georgia obscured the degree of voluntary reconciliation that took place among tribal members.[54]

The Cherokee adoption of a constitution in 1827 enraged Georgia officials. John Forsyth sent a copy to President Adams, along with citations from the United States Constitution, to argue that the Cherokees had illegally established a state within a state. Adams rejected the argument and observed that the Cherokee Constitution did not alter relations between that nation and the United States. Cherokee chiefs Ross and Ridge agreed. But the appearance of the constitution led Georgia officials to conclude that resistance to removal had quickened. Whatever the basis for this conclusion, and Georgians always suspected the presence of anti-removal sentiment, it was correct. Missionary Elizur Butler wrote Evarts in early August that the Cherokees now were convinced that removal was to their disadvantage and would not remove voluntarily.[55]

Back in Boston, meanwhile, Evarts admitted that Indian relations had deteriorated and that the success of Indian missions had not been commensurate to the expense. Still, he insisted, the experiment remained valuable. The Reverend Benton Pixley reported to Evarts from the Osage Mission that "vice reigns everywhere." Idleness, improvidence, lying, and thievery eroded missionary efforts, Pixley reported. But in 1827 the Cherokee, not the Osage, was the model Indian nation for the ABCFM, and the Cherokee adoption of a constitution stirred Evarts's optimism. The ABCFM made a renewed plea for public financial support. "The transforming efficacy of the Christian religion, both upon individuals and upon neighborhoods," Evarts wrote, "is now seen in different parts of the Cherokee nation.... Still there are powerful counteracting causes." But the new constitution heralded progress.[56]

Evarts hoped to expand the American Board's missionary enterprises and influence. In November 1827 he approved new Indian missions but warned Cephas Washburn to watch expenses and keep future stations small. Not only did Evarts want to extend the board's influence throughout the West; he also watched closely the growing enthusiasm of the Baptists for Indian missions. Directed by the Reverend Lucius Bolles, corresponding secretary of the Baptist General Convention for Foreign Missions, and supported by men like Heman Lincoln, a Boston lumber merchant, Baptist Indian missions had expanded, and the society lobbied Congress for federal funds. The Reverend Isaac McCoy, although he often disagreed with the Baptist Board about mission policy, had established close contacts with the government as well as with Georgia officials and sought to play a central role in federal Indian policy as it evolved. As the ABCFM became identified with the anti-removal forces, McCoy adopted an increasingly strident pro-removal stance. By late 1827 government Indian officials began to shift toward the Baptist position.

This shift became strikingly evident after the Cherokees adopted a constitution. Thomas McKenney, following a tour of the major southern tribes (excluding the Cherokees), reported his conviction that *"they ought not to be encouraged in forming a Constitution and Government within a state of the Republic, to exist and operate independently of our laws.*" Although publications such as *Niles' Weekly Register* praised the Cherokee constitution and Cherokee plans to publish a newspaper, McKenney insisted that neither the federal government nor the Indians themselves could preserve tribal integrity where they now lived. He wrote Secretary of War James Barbour: "I hold their recovery from it, and from its long train of miseries, *whilst they retain their present relation to the States, to be hopeless.* No human agency can reform them, as a people. It is vain to try. They are a devoted people, and destruction lies just before them. Humanity and justice unite in calling loudly upon the Government, as a parent, promptly to interfere and save them."[57]

In effect, the difference between the position articulated by Evarts and that supported by McCoy and now McKenney was one of methodology as well as politics. McCoy did not believe that missionary activity possessed sufficient transforming power in the face of political opposition. Legislative action alone, he believed, could remedy the situation. While McCoy developed plans to colonize Indians on lands west of the Mississippi, he also seemed oblivious to the fact that much of his political support came from those areas most interested in acquiring tribal lands. What he took to be humanitarianism was all too often simple greed. Evarts, on the other hand, supported voluntary removal and remained suspicious about state motives. He also wanted to avoid casting the American Board in an adversarial role with respect to federal policy. Above all else, Evarts believed in the missionary enterprise and the transforming power of Christian benevolence. He advocated a continued missionary presence *either* east or west of the Mississippi. During the next two years both McCoy and Evarts spent much of their time in Washington lobbying for their respective views. Their differing visions, as Lucius Bolles told McCoy, often frustrated efforts to coordinate their energies. "I hope Col. McKenny [sic] of the Government, may be satisfied of the coincidence of our views with theirs," he wrote. "We have taken the course we have from necessity. Mr. Everts [sic] on whom I called twice upon the subject, thought we were not prepared to petition the Congress, & objected specially, to the various religious bodies, subscribing to & the same Memorial. . . . The Col interests himself kindly in behalf of our Missions & we feel obliged by it, & for all the favor he shows to you."[58]

Jeremiah Evarts's concern for Indian missions and Indian affairs, strong in 1827, became a virtual preoccupation by 1828. The papers of the American Board of Commissioners for 1828 reflect this focus, for correspondence with Indian missions rather than with overseas missions predominates. The reason is clear. In early 1828 McKenney stepped up both his efforts and his rhetoric to promote removal among the missionaries as well as among the tribes. Typical was a letter to the Reverend Lee Compere. In it McKenney insisted that *only* removal would save the tribes. Opposition from the chiefs was natural, he told Compere, but "it is selfish, and will be broke down." He also promised to support missionary activities in the western lands and urged Congress to pay all costs associated with the proposed removal. From Creek Path station William Potter warned Evarts that while he hoped the Cherokees would not lose their lands, "we ought to stand prepared for such an event."[59]

Two events made this possibility more likely. The first challenge came from the Georgia legislature. In December 1827 it passed a series of resolutions to take control of Indian lands within the state's borders. The resolutions asserted the primacy of Georgia law within its borders and insisted that the Cherokees had no legitimate claims to lands within the state. Georgia demanded that the federal government honor its interpretation of the Compact of 1802 and negotiate for the immediate cession of Cherokee lands. The state promised to grant lands to individual Indians who wished to remain but refused to extend any legal or political rights to them. Warning that the Cherokees must cooperate, the legislature threatened to exercise its sovereign power and seize the lands if resistance persisted.[60]

These resolutions threw the Cherokees into confusion and led Jeremiah Evarts to despair. He wrote Cyrus Kingsbury that it would "be more & more difficult for Indians to live in the old states." Their hearts remained depraved, Evarts lamented, and this retarded the progress of civilization. He saw little hope for them unless the American Board's missions succeeded. "If they would all receive the Gospel, renounce all wickedness, become industrious & exemplary," he wrote, "they would be safe, notwithstanding all the cupidity & injustice of the whites." At the same time, he insisted, if the whites practiced true benevolence, the Indians would have a chance under any circumstances. This was, as President Adams admitted, unlikely: "We have talked of benevolence and humanity, and preached them into civilization, but none of this benevolence is felt where the right of the Indian comes in collision with the interest of the white man."[61]

Although John Quincy Adams did not believe that the Indians held permanent rights to their lands, his was a voice of moderation in contrast to demands from Georgia and its representatives. In February Wilson Lumpkin took the floor of the House to call for removal. He denounced the current policy as "imbecile" and attacked "Northern fanatics, male and female," who had sent petitions to Congress "protesting against the removal of the poor dear Indians." Lumpkin's tirade was the opening salvo in Georgia's renewed campaign for removal, but Lumpkin also believed that time was on the side of the Georgians. Andrew Jackson, he believed, would be the next president. And Andrew Jackson supported states' rights and Indian removal.

Almost as Lumpkin spoke, a new voice was heard in opposition to Georgia's claims. In February 1828 the *Cherokee Phoenix* began publication. While it provided anti-removal forces with evidence of civilized progress, its appearance, along with the ratification of the Cherokee Constitution, convinced pro-removal forces that the Cherokees would not go voluntarily.[62]

These activities once again sent Evarts scurrying off to Washington to lobby for the Cherokees. He now believed that Congress was unwilling to adopt a definite emigration plan with guarantees for the tribes in advance. Under those circumstances, Evarts concluded, removal should not take place at all. In mid-March he opposed an appropriation for exploring the western country to locate sites for removal, placing himself in direct opposition to the efforts of McCoy. Editorials in the *Cherokee Phoenix* supported Evarts's position, arguing the absurdity of removing the tribes "from a land of civil and religious means, to a perfect wilderness, *in order to be civilized.*" Such an experiment, the paper editorialized, was like "building castles in the air."[63] McCoy *and* Evarts, on the other hand, agreed that the Indians needed a permanent home if missionary efforts were to be successful. Isaac McCoy posed the issue most succinctly in his journal: "Why should we spend money and wear out our lives in the wilderness, to rear Indian youths to maturity, merely to mingle with their hopeless relatives, and with them to perish?" Evarts agreed with this assessment and insisted that missionaries had to make the "remnant" of the tribes that might become civilized as large as possible.[64]

Despite his opposition to removal, Evarts understood the political realities and hedged his bets. In late March he wrote Cephas Washburn at the Dwight Mission in Arkansas Territory to inquire about the land and the character of the white population west of the Mississippi. To Washburn he posed a series of questions about the ability to remove tribes beyond the influence of whites, the likelihood of those lands being intersected by roads and thereby opened to the influence of whites, and the political arrangements necessary to maintain this protection. Evarts also raised the issue of money. Would additional western missions be expensive? The ABCFM was more than $40,000 in debt, and "half our time and care and anxiety at the Rooms is expended upon raising funds." Perhaps more important, Evarts realized that public land prices were inflated. In Ohio, Illinois, Missouri, and elsewhere millions of acres of public lands remained on the market, available to settlers. And in Congress men like Richard Johnson of Kentucky were urging that land prices be decreased so as to encourage settlers to move west. A simultaneous movement of white settlers and Indian tribes into the West would defeat missionary purposes. Washburn agreed and told Evarts that to drive the Indians onto the dry prairies of the West was "chimerical & unwise." "It would be equally, if not more, humane, to drive all the aborigines down to some vast *slaughter house & butcher them at once*, as to remove them all to the region contemplated."[65]

The second challenge to Indian missions came in June 1828 when President Adams named Peter B. Porter to replace James Barbour as secretary of war. Barbour had tried to promote removal and resolve the conflict with Georgia through persuasion and negotiation. Porter, on the other hand, a former war hawk and Indian fighter, advocated removal much more vigorously. As historian William McLoughlin has observed, his appointment was probably an attempt to convince southern and western states that Adams meant to support plans for immediate removal. Perhaps it was also undertaken with an eye to the upcoming presidential election. Whatever the case, Porter quickly attacked the missionaries and their schools and endorsed the view that earlier efforts at civilization and integration had failed.[66]

He found support for these views in Congress. Despite the lobbying efforts of Jeremiah Evarts, Congress approved legislation to fund an expedition to explore the West. Among its leaders was Isaac McCoy. Its purpose was to locate suitable lands west of the Mississippi for the removal of the eastern tribes. While Congress hoped that they would find suitable lands south of the Missouri Compromise line of 1820 (some of the tribes owned slaves), the Indian Affairs office paid secret agents to convince them to emigrate. The *Cherokee Phoenix* voiced its strong opposition, insisting that "those inducements will not procure a single emigrant." Civilization had proceeded too far, and the old way of life had deteriorated too much, the paper editorialized, so that as a "blanket has lost its former value with us, so has the rifle and the kettle."[67]

These last remarks highlighted one of Porter's primary problems. Conditions among the tribes varied widely: some, like the Cherokees, were led by men who had embraced much of the Anglo culture; others, however, practiced more traditional pursuits. The government, almost without exception, officially treated all the tribes alike in its negotiations. They were, in official language, children of the forest, primitive in habits and thought, whose culture and very physical presence would disappear unless they removed beyond the reach of white settlement. Treaty negotiators, who were after all official representatives of the federal government, offered as inducements for removal unsettled lands, goods which reflected primitive needs, and the promise (often implied) that they could continue their traditional lifestyle.

While these proposals reflect a desire to remove the tribes from their proximity to whites and open tribal lands to development, they also reflect a belief that the missionizing and civilizing efforts of the previous decade had failed. To be sure, success in civilizing the tribes now seemed more of a threat than a promise—the Cherokee situation attests to that—but this rejection of missionary efforts is indicative of something else as well. The pace of change in the United States had quickened, and the horizons of negotiators and missionaries differed. Government officials wanted a rapid transformation. They were, they believed, in the process of reshaping the landscape through expansion, settlement, roads, canals, and the like. Removal was preparatory to those efforts, and they had little patience to cultivate the kind of revitalization sought by missionaries. Missionaries, on the other hand, remained optimistic even while they lamented a lack of progress. Typical is William Requa's description to Jeremiah Evarts of the Hopefield Village mission: "Nothing very encouraging can be said in relation to the moral condition of this people.... As a general thing in all our religious meetings the Indians have given a respectful attention yet they appear to be but little interested in them. There is no doubt but they are gradually becoming more & more enlightened, & there is no doubt, when the doctrines of the gospel shall be fully & clearly communicated to them but that they will be impressed with them & that they will have the same happy effect upon them as individuals & as a nation as upon any other people. We have no real cause for discouragement."[69]

Government officials seized on descriptions like this to support their call for removal. The presence of Porter, the approach of a presidential election, the candidacy of Andrew Jackson, escalating demands from Georgia, growing evidence of "civilization" on the part of the Cherokees, and the increased resistance to treaty negotiators by most of the tribes dramatized the issue and brought the American Board of Commissioners deeper into the politics of Indian removal. "It will be difficult," Evarts wrote one correspondent, "to find a place for them any where within the limits of the United States. . . . These schemes [for removal] are supported by many real friends of the Indians, but I have always feared for the result."[70]

During the summer of 1828 Porter used the resolutions passed by the Georgia legislature the previous December to induce removal. In so doing, he sent a clear message that the federal government had abandoned its policy of integration. The government sent troops into the area, ostensibly to prevent Indians from crossing over into Georgia but also to protect those tribesmen who accepted its offer to emigrate. Removal was still on a voluntary basis, but, as Evarts had noted, the tone was different. "It is highly important," Porter instructed an agent, "in order to ensure success that you impress upon the Creeks their deplorable condition; and the better prospects that await them at the west." Similar efforts among the Cherokees brought a protest from the *Phoenix* that the Cherokees were not degraded like the Creeks, that this "misrepresentation" was "intended merely to *electioneer* us out of our present homes."[71]

Porter's energetic commitment to removal brought protest and action from Jeremiah Evarts. He complained to Cephas Washburn that the government was now abetting the "unjust & covetous spirit of our countrymen," and he warned that time was running out for the Indians. As in the past, Evarts did not so much fear removal as worry that it would be carried out in haste or with violence. He had already decided that the ABCFM missions should accompany the tribes west of the Mississippi, and remarks published in the *Missionary Herald* admitted that Indian missions were still experimental—"the problem to be solved has been, and is, *how the greatest and best influence can be exerted, with the least expense of men, and time, and money.*"[72]

Evarts's concern about the Indians' future was well placed, but government efforts to effect a prompt removal in 1828 were no more successful than its earlier attempts. By mid-October only four Indians had enrolled to emigrate. The *Cherokee Phoenix* published letters opposing emigration. One, by a "Young Beaver," pointed out the ironic contradiction in government policy. For years, the writer observed, the government had tried to wean the tribes from their traditional hunting culture and inculcate an acceptance of settled agriculture. Now, after this policy had largely succeeded, "we are led into the deep forest where game is plenty, by the hands of those who would once have had us abandon the chase. Admirably consistent."[73] Chief Justice John Marshall joined in opposition to removal, although for the moment he confined his thoughts to private correspondence. In a letter to Joseph Story he argued that the time had arrived for the white population to give "full indulgence" to "principles of humanity and justice."[74]

Thomas McKenney, meanwhile, sought to tie the government's removal policy to humanitarianism, insisting that humanity and justice necessitated removal as soon as possible. McKenney's actions, however, belied his intentions. He sent instructions to Cherokee agents, for instance, that they withhold government rations and transportation and throw the Indians "as much as possible upon their own resources." A paternalistic conviction that removal was necessary too often became a justification for all measures required to effect that removal. Political conflicts complicated the matter, for, as Henry Schoolcraft confided to his diary, "The whole Indian race is not . . . worth one white man's vote." Despite his actions, McKenney professed strong attachment to the civilization program and insisted that removal would advance its progress. This became the foundation for his pro-removal position. Only in the West, away from the white population, he concluded, could this work continue. But McKenney had misjudged the motives driving removal. First, the benevolent community did not agree wholeheartedly that removal was better than the alternative. Second, while McKenney intended that the Civilization Fund be increased after removal to speed the civilizing process, this notion found no support in political circles. The firmest advocates of removal embraced the "out of sight, out of mind" principle; removal was the way to dispense with, not relocate, the Indian question.[75]

By late December 1828 the removal issue seemed to be coming to a head. As Evarts wrote missionary William Vaill, "The intercourse between them [Indians] & the government is becoming more complicated; and probably the officers of the government are becoming more & more perplexed with it, & more tired of it; & the aspect of things now is, that some general, decisive plan is to be devised if possible, by which the government, may rid themselves of the complaints of the interested states, & of the trouble of taking care of the Indians."[76]

Two matters troubled Evarts. The first was a charge, made directly to Secretary of War Porter, that ABCFM missionaries and not the Cherokees were the actual editors of the *Cherokee Phoenix*. Elias Boudinot, informants insisted, was only the nominal editor; missionary Samuel Worcester was the real editor. If true, this charge meant that the missionaries were meddling in political matters. McKenney told Evarts about it, and Evarts hastily wrote a letter of denial to Porter. Worcester, he said, was not the editor, had not written any articles for the paper on political matters, and had not given any advice on such articles. Evarts also wrote Worcester, instructing him to continue to work closely with Boudinot on the publication of tracts and admonishing him, "Do what is right, & you need not fear."[77]

The other concern was a broader one, an issue that Evarts had raised in his letter to Vaill—the question of a definitive removal plan. On December 20, 1828, Georgia's Governor John Forsyth signed into law an act that extended the laws of Georgia over the Indians within its boundaries. Designed to assert the state's rights and to force the hand of the Adams administration, it was not only a recognition that only 122 Indians had agreed to emigrate, but also a sign that Georgia foresaw a change in Indian policy and believed that it could shape its direction under a new president. The act stated that, beginning June 1, 1830, all Indians within the boundaries of Georgia would be subject to state jurisdiction and that all Cherokee laws would be null and void. It also prohibited any "Indian, or descendant of Indian," from testifying in any suit to which "a white man may be a party." Few observers expected anxious Georgians actually to wait eighteen months before acting under the new ordinance.[78]

These two developments convinced the American Board's Prudential Committee that the tone of Indian affairs had indeed changed, and it commissioned Evarts to go to Washington as soon as possible. Forcible removal seemed likely, and the committee wanted him to represent the rights of the Indians and to protest the recent act of the Georgia legislature. To rally support, Evarts wrote Baptist leader Heman Lincoln, then in Washington, and urged him to emphasize the need for caution in Indian affairs. He also wrote President Francis Wayland of Brown (an influential Baptist) to ask that he write an article on Indian affairs for the *Journal of Commerce*. Finally, in a letter to the Reverend Thomas Stuart at the Monroe Mission among the Chickasaws, Evarts predicted that "the present winter may be a very eventful one to the Indians. Our rulers have the general subject of removal before them, and strong exertions will be made to adopt some principles, which will operate very unequally upon different tribes, and very oppressively upon some of them."[79] With that, Evarts departed for Washington to lobby Congress and rally the benevolent community.

Thus began an almost unremitting effort by Evarts for the Indian cause. In the past his lobbying had sought specific and limited objectives, turning to politics to secure funds or shape particular policies. Now Evarts believed that new political patterns threatened the moral ethos he firmly embraced. But as he devoted himself almost completely to the Indians' cause, what did he leave behind? What happened to the other affairs of the American Board in his absence?

As corresponding secretary of the American Board of Commissioners for Foreign Missions, Jeremiah Evarts supervised all the board's missionary operations. By 1828 these operations were extensive, but they were also self-operating, and there was little that board headquarters could do on a day-to-day basis, aside from keeping up with the correspondence. Rufus Anderson and David Greene, his assistants, handled most of that, leaving him free to supervise the board's network of agents and societies, to promote the *Missionary Herald*, and to devote his energies to other problems which demanded his immediate attention.

ABCFM records reveal Evarts's constant attention to board matters. On his many trips to Washington he had not only pleaded the cause of Indian missions, but met with officials (usually those of the State or War departments) on issues related to the board's overseas missions as well. He did not hesitate, for instance, to discuss with the State Department the appointment of a consul for the Sandwich Islands or defend missionaries in their long-running battle with merchants trading in the islands. He also seemed to be constantly raising money. Throughout the late 1820s the board's missions were somewhat overextended, and funds were always insufficient to support them. The Prudential Committee repeatedly told the public that it had always "acted with the expectation, that the missions, the stations, the schools, the printing presses, the expenditures, were to be increased from year to year." Appeals for funds became a permanent part of Evarts' public life.[80]

Evarts also supervised the formal closing of the Foreign Mission School. Wracked by controversy for two years, the school closed in 1827. He had not only to wrap up the institution's affairs but also to explain to the public why it was closing. To do so he published a long article in the *Missionary Herald*, in which he blamed the closing primarily on two factors: the board's decision that native youths could now be better educated at the missionary stations among their own peoples, and the difficulties of bringing "heathen" youths from "pagan" cultures to their own community within an alien society. Pressures from the surrounding population led them to feel inferior, and the policy of isolation rather than integration denied them the benefits of a Christian country. Evarts admitted that this stemmed "not merely from the difference of complexion, but from the hereditary feelings of our people in regard to the Indians."[81]

While his argument that the spread of missions now made instruction among indigenous cultures possible was correct, it artfully masked the dilemma the American Board faced but did not admit. That is, if missionaries were to Christianize and civilize native peoples, what would happen to those peoples if the missionaries succeeded? Would white society accept them as equals in religion, morality, and civilization? Was integration, in short, a feasible objective under any circumstances? Although the events which led to the closing of the Foreign Mission School indicated that it was not, neither Jeremiah Evarts nor any other member of the ABCFM community seemed to recognize its implications for the objectives of its missionary enterprise. Even in 1828, as Evarts came face to face with strong pro-removal sentiment in Washington and elsewhere, he ascribed that sentiment to sectionalism, political considerations, land hunger, or anti-Indian prejudice. He failed to recognize the truths buried in the convictions of men like Thomas McKenney, who, despite his often self-serving political sycophancy, saw removal as a help and not a hindrance to the tribes.

Jeremiah Evarts's other major objective and responsibility was to stimulate and maintain public enthusiasm and support for foreign missions. To that end he used the *Missionary Herald* not only to solicit funds but to promote the American Board's ambitions. Oregon, Greece, and China were just a few of the locales projected for missionary activity. Evarts traveled to the meetings of the many auxiliary foreign mission societies and actively recruited missionaries as well as monies. To reach beyond the religious community and to counter criticism from opponents of foreign missions, he prepared articles highlighting ABCFM successes around the globe. As corresponding secretary, he found his life divided into active and passive phases. He actively sought to establish missions, but once he had done so he passively had to await news from the missionaries about obstacles or progress. When this news reached his desk, Evarts swung into action, publicizing successes and trying to comfort missionaries that failures were to be expected in such a difficult endeavor. Throughout it all he maintained a public face that radiated optimism. Typical was his 1827 appeal to the churches, an effort to raise $100,000 from public donations:

> In a new and growing country, already containing great resources, and making rapid progress in the acquisition of greater;—a country, in which a singular impulse has been given to the human faculties by the great events in our political history, and by the prospect of improving his condition, which is held out to every individual;—a country, maintaining a constant intercourse with all parts of the world, and exhibiting a commercial enterprise never surpassed; and, above all, a country upon which spiritual influences, in the form of revivals of religion have descended with most benign efficacy for the last thirty years:—in such a country, with such resources and such prospects, what may not be accomplished for Christ?[82]

Despite this optimism, Evarts admitted that the missionary cause was an arduous one. "There is no safe course for a missionary," he told readers of the *Missionary Herald*. There also seemed no end of work for Evarts. In 1828 he helped organize a new religious periodical, the *Spirit of the Pilgrims*, to detail religious issues in the United States as the *Panoplist* had once done. His involvement in this new venture reflected his continuing belief that individual religious conviction lay at the heart of any civilized society. Despite an obvious preoccupation with foreign missions, he had never lost the faith in moral virtue that had sustained him since his conversion as a student at Yale. His instructions to Rufus Anderson, sent by the Prudential Committee as a special agent to the Mediterranean in 1828, reveal this passion: "What is the state of morals among the people? How far truth and integrity prevail? What is the state of things, in regard to industry, temperance, chastity? How the female sex is treated? What is the state of morals among women? Whether the people are desirous of having their daughters well educated? . . . How far there is such a thing as moral integrity among eminent merchants? What is thought by the people of such vices as lying, cheating, lewdness, and drunkenness?"[83]

Above and beyond all this activity, of course, Evarts had a personal life. Or did he? While that may seem to be a facetious remark, there is little evidence that Evarts took much time from his work for his family.

Few letters to his wife or children survive, and the demands of his job, his frequent travels, and ill health, as well as the daily volume of his correspondence, must have left little time for family activities. Indeed, Jeremiah Evarts's public life seems to have been his private one as well. He was clearly the most successful man in his family, and his family papers document his efforts to find jobs for needy relatives. But his world was a cosmopolitan one, a far cry from the agrarian communities of northern Vermont. Despite that, as he told one ABCFM agent, his home life was simple. "As to our family expenses, we eat plain food, drink neither wine nor spirits nor beer nor cider (except very little of the latter a few times of the year when visited by strangers), make no expensive entertainments, possess no expensive furniture, employ very little hired help, cannot afford to keep either a horse nor cow & endeavor to manage our affairs with discretion."[84]

By the winter of 1828–29, however, he riveted his attention on the plight of the Indians. After the election of Andrew Jackson that fall, and as Congress opened debate on Indian affairs once more, Jeremiah Evarts again left his family in Boston and headed to Washington. This time there was an air of expectancy missing from earlier debates. John Quincy Adams's defeat seemed to symbolize not only the rejection of a sitting president but the rejection of a form of republicanism dear to Evarts and his associates. Restraint and self-control appeared ready to give way to a boundless spirit of unbridled opportunism. A new president seemed determined to encourage and foster that new liberal spirit; Jeremiah Evarts was equally determined to harness it to a moral ethos based on a gospel of restraint and individual moral responsibility.

CHAPTER SEVEN

The General and the Missionary

The election of 1828 ratified a shift in power that had been underway in the United States for several years. The arrival of Andrew Jackson and the new importance of men like John Eaton, John Berrien, Wilson Lumpkin, and Richard Johnson marked the ascent of the South and West to political power. With that change, republicanism and liberalism were transformed; a sense of unfettered boundlessness seized center stage. The differences were not only political, but conceptual.

Andrew Jackson and Jeremiah Evarts, the general and the missionary, knew each other only by reputation in early 1829, but they represented opposite sides of a conceptual chasm. By the spring and summer of 1829, their conflicting visions of the American future were locked in mortal combat. For each of them the stakes were high. The issue was Indian removal.

Andrew Jackson cut a striking figure. Over six feet tall, his angular frame carried a scant 140 pounds and was topped by a shock of white hair that revealed his years. In 1829 Jackson was sixty-two years old, the oldest man ever elected to the presidency. He was also sick, the result of a turbulent frontier upbringing, innumerable duels, a combative military career, and the primitive medical practices of the early nineteenth century. As one White House visitor remarked, "The hero looks old and his hair which is grey and stiff stands up all over his head as if it were Electrified and struggling to disengage itself from its parent."[1]

But while his health was frail, his will and his passion were not. He had spent much of his life chasing, fighting, and subduing Indians—seeking to open lands and create a safe environment for white settlers to exploit

Andrew Jackson and Indian Affairs. Undated lithograph from unknown artist. (Courtesy William L. Clements Library, University of Michigan)

the wealth of the continent. As president he intended to complete the task, to remove the Indian as an issue in American political life. Residents of the South and West, in turn, expected no less of him. A Jackson presidency, they believed, would unlock the doors of opportunity and create an environment conducive to material gain without limitation or control. Their expectations, in short, were as high as his; both were determined to proceed and succeed. Jackson was also a man possessed of unshakable moral certainties. His morality was a secular one, grounded in a commitment to virtue—be it feminine, economic, or political. He defended women, distrusted banks and bankers, and believed that the use of the state by special interests endangered political virtue.[2]

Jeremiah Evarts represented a different world, a contrasting conceptual universe, and pursued different objectives. But in several respects he was very much like Jackson. Evarts's health had never been robust, and through the years ill health had forced him to take several trips from Boston to Charleston to seek relief. Evarts was also angular, although he was neither as tall and striking nor as old as his counterpart. He was also strong willed but tempered that determination with a humanitarian sensibility. The world that Jeremiah Evarts sought to advance was a world governed by self-control, not by a boundless individualism. His was a republican comity marked by a community ethos and dedication to a morality that governed the commonwealth as well as the individual. To Evarts, republican virtue and moral vision defined the parameters of liberalism and opportunism. Morality lay inside the individual like an internal gyroscope. Unlike Jackson, therefore, Evarts was not concerned so much about the morality or immorality of a particular problem but about the basic moral structure of the nation, the individuals who comprised it, and the laws they formulated.

The renewed campaign against Sunday mail delivery in 1829 epitomized Evarts's conceptual universe and the travails of Christian republicanism in the late 1820s. The issue was clear. In early January 1829 Congress again debated a proposal to allow delivery of mail on Sunday. Various religious groups asked Evarts to go to Washington and lobby against the measure. He had already planned a trip to defend the board's Indian policy, but now he advanced his timetable. At the same time, religious organizations throughout the northeast mounted a petition campaign against Sunday mail delivery.

In mid-January, the Senate received Richard Johnson's report on the Sunday mails, and the issue was joined. The report argued that while a day of rest each week was a good idea, the purpose of government was not to determine what day that should be. Government was to protect the rights of all citizens and should strictly separate church and state. Transportation of the mail on Sunday did not interfere with anyone's rights of conscience. Although the report was prepared by a Baptist minister (who was also chief clerk of the Post Office Department), its major significance was not just this strict separation between the religious and the secular. Also central to the Sunday mail argument were the new demands of a liberal society: "The commercial, manufacturing, and agricultural interests of our country are so intimately connected as to require a constant and the most expeditious correspondence betwixt all our seaports, and between them and the most interior settlements."[3]

Most of the religious community, especially in the northeast, attacked both the report and Senator Johnson's claim that opposition to it represented "the entering wedge of a scheme to make this government a religious instead of a social and political institution." Protagonists on both sides focused largely on separate and often unrelated arguments. The religious community emphasized that mail delivery simply should not occur on a Sunday; the government should not force individuals to violate the Sabbath. Supporters of the legislation, on the other hand, largely ignored this objection. They asserted that the law forced no people to violate their consciences and was religiously neutral, but that it emphasized chiefly the financial and commercial aspects of the issue. The volume of mail had so increased, the report concluded, that daily deliveries were essential to prevent private express companies from taking over the task as well as to "afford the utmost facilities to all commerical transactions." The report warned that "in some of our large cities a failure of the mail, or the delay of a few hours in its delivery, has been of serious consequence to persons extensively engaged in commercial operations."[4]

Jeremiah Evarts penned a reply, *The Logic and the Law of Col. Johnson's Report to the Senate, on Sabbath Mails*. Insisting that the issue was significant because "it involves one of the most momentous points in the whole affair of government," Evarts actually supported many of Johnson's conclusions. He agreed that church and state should be separate, that no one should be forced to go against conscience, and that works of necessity were permitted on the Sabbath. He argued that Johnson seemed to consider sound moral principles to be essential for the nation's welfare. But then he broke with the report and its sponsor, insisting that it was wrong to insist that petitions and other efforts to stop Sunday mail deliveries were unconstitutional. Describing the Sabbatarians (including himself) as "old fashioned republicans," Evarts argued that by ceasing its other activities the federal government recognized the Sabbath. The government of the United States, Evarts concluded, is a Christian government—a fact reflected in the various oaths administered and the use of prayers to open Congress.[5]

The central theme of Evarts's argument, however, concerned morality and virtue more than religion. He maintained that the *character* of the government under which a citizen lived was more important than whatever particular attention it gave to religion, although he observed that a moral government encouraged religion among its citizens. But while Evarts emphasized character and national morality, almost all the petitions rested their arguments on religion and biblical pronouncements. They assumed implicitly that moral character and attention to religion were one and the same. As Evarts discovered in his Washington lobbying, this assumption was not safe. Opposition to the petition campaign, he wrote ABCFM officials in Boston, "originates in the dislike of religion, and the fear that religion is likely to gain too much influence." The answer, Evarts concluded, was to expand and intensify the petition campaign throughout the spring and summer to include all denominations and all sections of the country.[6]

An article in the *Spirit of the Pilgrims*, influenced if not written by Evarts, was more apocalyptic. Maintaining that the Sabbath was the "mainspring of our republican institutions," the author cast the issue as between protecting or abolishing the Sabbath. "Between the cradle and the grave of liberty," he exclaimed, "we take our stand; and to the nation, and to heaven, we here pledge ourselves, never to abandon our post, or to keep silence, till the Sabbath, the palladium of our hopes, is rescued, or the grave has closed upon our country's glory." Sunday mail delivery, he concluded, was "like the letting out of waters,—first the drop—next the stream." Permanent damage to the moral fiber of the country would quickly offset whatever temporary, commercial gains Sunday mail deliveries achieved. Christian republicanism would disappear unless the nation's moral energies were harnessed to the Sabbatarian cause, the author insisted. Yet he was sufficiently perceptive to recognize that coercive legislation could not preserve the national character; only a spontaneous public awakening could curtail the "temptations of the seaboard, and steamboats, and canals."[7]

During the spring and summer Jeremiah Evarts visited local societies, wrote speeches, and solicited petitions and memorials to support the Sabbatarian campaign. Yet his journals and correspondence never once reveal that he recognized what the need for these labors meant. For three decades religious revivals, moral reform crusades, and a multitude of organizational efforts (the latter spearheaded by Evarts) had struggled to revitalize American society and its constituent elements. What had they accomplished? Why, in 1829, did the idea of Christian republicanism not possess a transforming energy capable of shaping the secular culture? One answer, an answer that Evarts had come to recognize, was that just as Arminian influences and denominational competition had liberalized religious practices, so, too, had economic and political liberalism transformed the secular landscape. For the moment Evarts sought to stem that tide through a massive petition campaign which he hoped would reveal a continuing and underlying commitment to a national moral ethos.[8]

Sabbatarians in some towns did more than petition, however. The *Philadelphia Gazette* reported that Princeton, New Jersey, residents forcibly stopped the driver of a mail coach and kept him prisoner until Monday morning, "all out of piety." Their justification for such an action stemmed from their belief that this was a Christian nation and that Sabbath-breaking was therefore a national sin. They were, in their own eyes, both patriots and Christians. Evarts, however, preferred quieter methods and wrote friends and colleagues to urge their participation in the petition campaign. There was, he said, "a great advantage in having petitions written with care; not that they will, as a matter of course, have any effect upon Congress." What, then, was his purpose? Evarts hoped that publication of the petitions, as well as the appearance of articles and letters in newspapers supporting the Sabbatarian cause, would have the same effect that publication of revival notices had had earlier. That is, they would themselves serve as instruments of revitalization to promote a national moral ethos.[9]

In a September 1829 circular, Evarts prescribed a formula and method for the petitions to Congress. Petitions should be "handsome" in appearance, and the most respected men of the community should be invited to sign first. In addition, signatories should be solicited from as many different denominations as possible, and each town should submit a separate petition. Finally, a word of caution: "public meetings should be avoided in any case where contention might be expected." Sabbatarians hoped to present the appearance if not the fact of harmony and wanted the petitions to demonstrate the existence of a broad consensus on a national moral ethos. To enhance this effect they published *An Account of Memorials Presented to Congress During its Last Session, By Numerous Friends of Their Country and its Institutions; Praying that the Mails may not be Transported, nor Post-Offices kept open, on the Sabbath.* Assembled by Jeremiah Evarts, this pamphlet reprinted excerpts from various petitions and listed the towns and states which had drafted them. Preservation of the Sabbath, the author concluded, was the key to national greatness. Ever since the War of 1812 ended, Evarts warned, "the multiplied evils of Sabbath-breaking have become more and more apparent; and the apprehension has been extensively felt, that an irresistible flood of business and pleasure will roll over the sacred institutions of religion, and leave our beloved land a moral desolation."[10]

More than 440 petitions flooded Congress. But, as John Jentz has demonstrated, while local elites circulated the petitions, the bulk of those who signed were artisans and shopkeepers. Artisan moralism meshed with elite efforts to define a moral ethos, but in the process a subtle change occurred in the American moral and political landscape. Most earlier efforts to revitalize society had attacked the individual conscience and operated through voluntary associations outside the formal political process. But now, with the Sabbatarian crusade and growing antislavery efforts in the late 1820s, the two came together. This union went far beyond former instances, such as Fast Day sermons and election addresses by invited clergy. The organizing efforts of the petition campaigns brought with them a sense of immediacy, a sense of imminent crisis that only demonstrative action would ameliorate. "Can a man take live coals in his bosom," asked one speaker, "and his flesh not be burnt?"[11]

There was, of course, another side to all of this effort, and various newspapers announced their opposition to the Sabbatarian campaign. Most followed a common theme: Sabbatarianism demonstrated the dangerous tendency of religious zealots and pious politicians to promote ecclesiastical establishments; government should be a secular operation. Sabbatarians, one editor argued, sought to destroy religious liberty and invade the rights of individual conscience. They threatened both the country and the cause of true Christianity. Yet opponents of the petition effort admitted the power that a "moral politics" portended, even as they decried it. "It is not difficult to perceive," said another editor, "that a crisis is approaching in this country, such as has not been witnessed since we became a nation." True religion, they contended, did not need such legislation.[12] But as Jeremiah Evarts lobbied to repeal laws providing for the delivery of mail on Sunday and sought to stimulate a groundswell of support for his visions of a society governed by a national moral ethos, another issue seized his attention. Andrew Jackson arrived in Washington, and Indian removal became the order of the day.

Over the years historians have concentrated on the banking controversy as the one issue that most clearly defined Jacksonian Democracy, using it not only to explain national economic issues but also to approach such related topics as workingmen or Anti-masons. While various monographs have analyzed Andrew Jackson's Indian policy, rarely have they placed it at the center of politics during Jackson's first term. Yet while few issues are more complex, few reveal more thoroughly the Jacksonian vision of the American future. More than any other topic, Indian policy delineated the emergence of a new era, of a new set of parameters to govern individual behavior and shape political policy. As republicanism became liberalism, it demanded the removal of the Indians. Here, more sharply than anywhere else, the community and moral ethos of Jeremiah Evarts gave way to the boundless individualism and liberal opportunism of Andrew Jackson.[13]

It also marked, more distinctly than either the War of 1812 or the Hartford Convention, the passing of New England's political dominance and the ascent of the South and West in the national political equation. Indian removal was Jacksonian Democracy's first great crusade. It became a key to understanding a concomitant change in American culture; men like Jeremiah Evarts now demanded that the state support and defend a moral ethos rather than any formal religious structures. They feared that "democracy" and "opportunity" only masked an unquenched appetite to barbecue moral values. That fear led them to defend a republican social and cultural paradigm in an increasingly liberal economic and political climate. Men like Evarts were more concerned with morality than with growth. They were unwilling to accede to acquisitive forces and hope that those same forces would have sufficient charity to take care of the rest. In the years to come, the Indian issue appeared to demonstrate that Americans had lost their moral bearings, that they had lost sight of the larger social relationships that accompany and help define civilization and were only interested in development and individual gain.

The crisis began even before Jackson arrived. When Jeremiah Evarts went to Washington in the winter of 1829, he did so primarily because the tone of Indian affairs had changed and the American Board of Commissioners wanted him to monitor Congressional debate. The board, and

Evarts, feared that Congress might now remove the Indians without their consent. They believed that such a measure would not only violate legal and moral commitments to the tribes but endanger ABCFM missions as well.[14]

By 1829 those missions had come face to face with the allure of manifest destiny. White Americans who looked west demanded instant gratification and short-term results. They rejected the admonitions of missionary spokesmen, who observed that while progress had been slow, perseverance would "contribute to the salvation and civilization of men." They embraced, instead, the views of men like Caleb Atwater, who toured the upper Midwest in 1829 and penned a compelling vision of the American future in the West. The interior of North America, he told readers, was filled with wonders and riches waiting to be exploited: mountains, bays, minerals—all connected by rivers, the arteries of the body politic which would circulate wealth and commerce. Only the Indians marred this paradise: primitive, able to speak only in guttural sounds, fickle, polygamous, superstitious. They would and must, Atwater argued, "recede farther and farther west until they reach the Pacific Ocean, and finally become extinct, as a people." Only congressional efforts could delay their doom, unless, of course, a civilizing process revolutionized their habits and culture.[15]

Atwater eventually concluded that the Indians could be civilized, but only through private benevolence rather than government intervention. Continued federal intervention in Indian affairs, he warned, led only to corruption and hastened their destruction. With this observation, Atwater joined an increasingly divisive debate over the future of Indian affairs. A year earlier Michigan governor and Jacksonian politician Lewis Cass had insisted that the tribes were content with their present culture but that they would become extinct unless they changed. They clung, Cass concluded, with "a death-grasp to their own institutions," but no *"fulcrum"* existed to effect a radical change in their condition. Baptist missionaries, led by Isaac McCoy, had concluded that so little progress had been made in the past three years that removal of the tribes to lands west of the Mississippi was the only hope for their preservation. McCoy's disagreement with the policies of Jeremiah Evarts and the American Board, detailed in his *Remarks on the Practicability of Indian Reform, Embracing Their Colonization*, enhanced his political influence by giving proponents of removal a friend in the religious community. Particularly useful was his assertion that, despite years of earnest missionary efforts and several individual conversions, the condition of the tribes themselves had worsened rather than improved. Missionary work, McCoy concluded, was a work of time; the Indians needed a country of their own beyond white settlement to gain this time.[16]

In 1829, this idea was not new. Government officials since Secretary of War Henry Knox in Washington's administration had insisted that civilization meant radical cultural change. But to Jeremiah Evarts, radical cultural change did not necessarily mean removal. The American Board, after all, had been formed primarily to engage in radical cultural change. Missionary endeavors embraced revitalization as well as revivals, cultural transformation as well as religious conversion. What was different in 1829 was the influence of Andrew Jackson, a man who apparently did not share the same moral values as the "Christian public." And it was to that public that Evarts turned, inserting articles in the *Missionary Herald* that would "interest the people in this part of the country in the Indians, at this critical time." In the waning months of the Adams administration, Secretary of War Peter Porter had embraced Indian removal; he carried on an extensive correspondence with southern officials favorable to his cause. Evarts and his colleagues believed that the hand of John Quincy Adams would stay Porter's efforts, and within the Office of Indian Affairs, Thomas McKenney continued to operate as if any removal would be voluntary. But opponents of removal feared that this restraint would vanish once Jackson arrived, decimating the tribes and retarding the board's missionary efforts.[17]

Evarts's arguments for continued missionary exertions, as outlined in the *Herald*, rested primarily on the assertion that, while many Indians had made little progress toward civilization, those living near missionary stations demonstrated considerable progress. This, in effect, argued for more missionary stations and credited the American Board with having a transforming influence. The problem for Evarts, in short, was insufficient missionary contact rather than the ineradicable depravity of tribesmen or the proximity of settlers. "Eight missionary stations," he insisted, "cannot exert a powerful influence directly over a population scattered through a territory, as large as the State of Massachusetts."[18]

Evarts arrived in Washington February 11, 1829, and immediately initiated meetings with the various parties to the controversy. While he pushed the Sabbatarian cause at the same time, his letters reveal that Indian matters remained primary. He stayed at the same boarding house as Andrew Jackson and found several opportunities for discussions with the president-elect about Indian affairs. He also cultivated a friendship with Thomas McKenney, with whom he had had previous contact. Baptist leader Heman Lincoln, however, also tried to enlist McKenney's support for his denomination's Indian policy. Meanwhile, the government of Georgia secretly sent emissaries into the Creek Nation to solicit lands and agreements. This mission threatened to undermine federal policy, enraged McKenney, and worried Evarts. Evarts feared that similar actions among the Cherokees would lead to conflict; they would prefer "death to subjugation or exile."[19]

Evarts's discussions with Jackson alarmed him further. Jackson made clear both his refusal to defend the Cherokees from Georgia and his fear of a collision between federal and state authorities. Evarts pressed his points but admitted to other ABCFM officials that "it is very difficult to be faithful & sufficiently respectful." The prospect that John Eaton would become secretary of war worried him as well, for he considered Eaton to be militantly anti-Indian. But Evarts's only hope appeared to be opposition to Eaton from the "Washington ladies," who he ardently wished would compel "the General to send Eaton off to Mexico, (where he could not do so much hurt)." Evarts's candidate for the War Department was McLean, not because he agreed with him but because he was candid and principled. Eaton, he argued, was neither.[20]

While rumors of cabinet appointments stirred Washington's political environment, Evarts threw himself firmly and openly behind the Cherokee cause, organizing petitions and consulting with tribal chiefs visiting the capital, while at the same time disclaiming any notion that he was their agent. Led by Chief John Ross, the Cherokees petitioned the Congress in February to block any removal efforts. But only weeks later John Quincy Adams and Peter Porter relinquished their offices to Andrew Jackson and John Eaton, and pressure on the Cherokees mounted. Whereas Adams had largely ignored state efforts to extend their laws over the tribes within their boundaries, Jackson not only recognized such efforts but encouraged them. The appointment of Georgian John Berrien as attorney general further revealed Jackson's determination to permit the states to control their own Indian affairs. Evarts reported to ABCFM officials that most Washington officials believed the Indians' cause to be hopeless. "I have not seen a single man, of any party," he wrote, "who thinks that anything effectual can be done to protect our weak red men of the forest." Two possibilities appeared likely: that the government would do nothing to prevent white politicians and settlers from trampling and destroying the Indians or that the government would openly align itself with whites against the Indians.²¹

In some despair after his discussions with Jackson and his assessment of the cabinet, Evarts turned to the press to secure relief for the tribes. He hoped that a public campaign based on law and morality, twin themes of his own career, would influence Congress before the next session in December. To advance that influence, he met regularly with individual congressmen on both sides of the issue. As his meeting with Georgian Wilson Lumpkin revealed, Evarts was not committed to resist removal at all costs. He admitted (as did Lumpkin) that all Indians east of the Mississippi would eventually have to remove. He even agreed with Lumpkin that the tribes should not be forced to remove. Where they disagreed, however, was over the issues of law and morality. Lumpkin insisted that the southern states had a right to extend their laws over the Indians within their jurisdiction; Evarts believed that extension to be legally and morally wrong. To support these views, Evarts prepared a document on the rights of the Cherokees to submit to Congress. This not only argued the Cherokees' cause; it outlined the American Board's strong opposition to a coerced removal. Evarts never finished his presentation, deciding instead that a broader public appeal would be more effective.²²

In April an article in the *North American Review* questioned the efficacy of Indian missions but admitted that Christianization and civilization were the tribes' only hope. These goals could not be accomplished, however, "while they remain hunters and warriors." To remove them west of the Mississippi, therefore, would retard their progress and inhibit missionary success. To Evarts these alternatives presented a dilemma. Change had been and would likely continue to be slow; yet demands for tribal lands and whites' hopes for evangelical success insisted on immediate gratification. Reports of the revivals during the Second Great Awakening had often emphasized that such transforming change was swift and widespread, not slow and partial. Here, perhaps, the missionaries were victims of their own propaganda. Reports of the revivals had appeared *after* the fact; reports from missionary stations began with first contact. Yet the implication often was that change would quickly be forthcoming, even though there was no evidence to support such optimism.²³

Evarts left Washington in early April, discouraged about the Cherokees' prospects. The president was hostile; Congress seemed apathetic. Discussions with John Eaton, and then with John Berrien on the steamboat to Baltimore, reinforced his pessimism and determination. Both men strenuously defended Jackson's views, and Evarts realized that the entire administration would be hostile to any intervention on the side of the Cherokees. The course he was setting, therefore, was politicial dynamite; he admonished David Greene not to mention those matters outside the missionary rooms. The course of the administration, in fact, had already alarmed him. Less than a week after taking office, Secretary of War Eaton had advised all Indian offices that they had to reduce expenditures to the lowest possible levels. Even though Thomas McKenney insisted that some funds had been illegally diverted and quickly demonstrated to Eaton where the monies were to be found, Eaton persisted. This persistence threatened the missionary operations of the American Board, which received more than $4,000 from the Civilization Fund. McKenney had to notify Evarts that these disbursements would be delayed. Evarts was suspicious.[24]

Evarts believed that publicity would help the Indians: "if the Indians are firm & quiet, it will be very difficult for the government to remove them." From his vantage point in Washington, however, McKenney was not so confident. In early April he wrote Bishop Hobart of New York to urge that a New York Indian Board be formed to support removal and protect the tribes. Efforts of the American Board and similar groups, McKenney argued, were diffused between foreign and domestic missions; and in light of congressional opposition to missions and presidential insistence for removal, the schemes of these religious organizations were too visionary. Removal, he concluded, was a "political & Christian" duty. At the same time, McKenney concealed these convictions from the Cherokees through a maze of disingenuous remarks. He told the Cherokee delegation that April that Eaton "is not now prepared" to decide if Georgia's position was proper. McKenney knew full well, of course, that Eaton as well as Jackson supported state intervention; even Evarts admitted that both men had arrived in Washington with such a conviction.[25]

A week later Eaton informed the Cherokees that he did not believe they had any claim to sovereignty and that he could not and would not contest Georgia's own claims of sovereignty over the tribes within her boundaries. Conversations with the secretary, however, left the Cherokees convinced that they would nonetheless be protected on their lands. In addition, Chief John Ross made clear that Cherokees would resist white aggression. The issue was joined. In the words of Thomas McKenney, "The *crisis* has arrived."[26]

The Jackson administration had created the crisis but lacked confidence in its ability to control it and effect the desired outcome. Despite support from southern and western states, vocal and even physical assistance from speculators and would-be settlers, demonstrated backing in Congress, and a cabinet created with this issue in mind and firmly aligned behind the president, Jacksonians feared the power of the American Board of Commissioners and the effectiveness of Jeremiah Evarts to mobilize residual religious support throughout the country to defend the Indians' legal and moral claims. The impulses of individualism and liberal capitalism which helped sweep Jacksonians into power were formative developments that revealed a shifting American culture. But much of the old remained; liberalism had not yet completely superseded republicanism. It was in this context that Jacksonians supported Thomas McKenney's efforts to organize the New York Indian Board.

The New York Indian Board, formally the New York Board for the Emigration, Preservation, and Improvement of the Aborigines of North America, formed in July 1829. Led by the board of managers of the Mission Society of the Reformed Dutch Church, but initiated by Andrew Jackson and Thomas McKenney, the New York Board sought to generate support among the religious community for the government's removal policy. Its organization stemmed, in part, from McKenney's failure in 1828 to convince Jeremiah Evarts and the American Board to support removal. By 1829, his job in jeopardy, McKenney supported Jackson's Indian policies and solicited support from the public. But the New York Board was solely an engine for propaganda; it had no significant treasury, failed to develop an extensive organization, and recruited no missionaries. The War Department picked up the tab for printing its pamphlet supporting removal. In the struggle over Indian removal in 1829 and 1830, however, the New York Board proved ineffectual. Most of the religious community supported either the ABCFM and Jeremiah Evarts or the Baptists and Isaac McCoy. The contending forces of political power and a humanitarian sensibility were too powerful to be diverted by a contrived propaganda drive.[27]

Other forces thickened the clouds of crisis, especially the determination of Georgia to exercise sovereignty and the efforts of the administration to encourage other states to follow her lead. In late May 1829 John Eaton circulated copies of Jackson's remarks on Indian affairs to the governors of Tennessee, Mississippi, and Alabama. While Eaton and Jackson increasingly expressed concern that "A crisis in our Indian Affairs has arrived," it was a crisis which they had actively encouraged. Jackson had, in effect, revealed his hand and was now in the process of allowing it to be "forced." And as the states became more insistent in their support for immediate removal, Jackson and Eaton argued that humanitarianism and the preservation of the tribes required removal. At the same time, the administration sent secret agents throughout the Indian nations to induce removal.[28]

Secret agents, bribery, avarice, propaganda agencies—all reveal the weakness and uncertainty of the Jackson administration that it could effect removal on its terms, as well as its determination to do just that. But they also aroused opposition, an opposition that mixed the political with the humanitarian. As the *Cherokee Phoenix* editorialized: "We feel indignant at such arbitrary measures.—We often ask ourselves are we in the United States, the refuge of the oppressed—the land of christian light and liberty?—Where is the superior excellence of republicanism?"[29] Officials and missionaries of the American Board asked the same question. Jeremiah Evarts solicited missionaries' views on removal and its impact on the tribes. From New Echota in Georgia, missionary Samuel Worcester in turn told Evarts that tribal factionalism had grown as the government's policy had hardened.[30]

By the summer of 1829 the differences between the policies of the administration and those of the American Board, between the general and the missionary, were manifest. On the surface, they seemed to agree on the problem and to disagree about the solution. Judging by their rhetoric, each wanted to preserve the Indians but disagreed on the best means by which to do so. But if that had been the only difficulty, then emotions would not have run so high on both sides. More pertinent, therefore, and more difficult to ascertain with any concreteness, were the motives upon which these policies rested. Here each was suspicious of the other. Jacksonians believed that a narrow religious and elitist leadership conspired to shape the country in its image, an image contrary to majoritarian democracy and the spirit of liberal capitalism. Reformers like Evarts, on the other hand, feared that an avaricious political cadre wanted to use the powers of government to promote an unchecked individualism and secure political power. To do so they would discard not only religion but basic moral values and responsibilities; a licentious individualism hostile to any underlying moral ethos would shape legislation. The substitution of involuntary for voluntary removal epitomized the difference. But to complicate matters further, and despite its opposition to Jackson's policies, the American Board also wanted government support for Indian missions west of the Mississippi River if removal occurred.[31]

The tribes themselves were divided. Treaties supposedly secured their ancestral lands, or at least the portions they had been able to protect. Several of the tribes, most notably the Cherokees, had adopted many of the white man's ways. In the words of one Cherokee, "The chase we despise—the kettle, gun, and steel-trap are no inducements for us—we delight in cultivating the soil." But even the most acculturated Indian had to be wary of whites' intentions and skeptical about their own future prospects. If the lands were good, if the missionaries provided schools, if the government protected them from the encroachment of whites, and if the government respected *this* treaty and left them alone—if all this came to pass, then removal had much to recommend it. And for those tribal members who had failed to accept acculturation, or who rejected it outright, removal offered additional attractions, particularly the preservation of traditional mores. Whatever their inclination, the decision was not likely to be theirs to make.[32]

During the summer Jeremiah Evarts outlined the American Board's policy and energized anti-removal forces. In late July Cyrus Kingsbury wrote Evarts from the Mayhew mission to oppose Jackson's policy; in passing he observed that "the public & our legislators are certainly in great need of correct information on Indian affairs." Little did he realize that Evarts was already busy preparing a series of essays opposing removal. These essays, published in various newspapers and eventually in pamphlet form, became the only sustained defense of Indian rights, and as such they formed the foundation for the anti-removal crusade. Known as the "William Penn" essays from the pseudonym Evarts used, they not only defended the rights of Indian tribes but articulated a vision of the United States as a just republican country whose institutions and habits rested on a foundation of law and morality.[33]

In his essays Evarts opposed the government's use of the parent-child metaphor in its interaction with Indians and argued that its treaties stemmed from negotiations between independent societies. The balance of power had since shifted, but those treaties represented good-faith efforts and were the law of the land. They should be honored. The law, Evarts insisted, provided for harmony in a diverse society. Following this tone throughout the twenty-four essays, Evarts sought to arouse what he believed was a moral majority and at the same time educate it about the nature of federal Indian policy. He particularly hoped to reach influential individuals and for this reason first published the essays in the *National Intelligencer*, probably the country's leading political newspaper. To recognize Evarts's motives, of course, is also to recognize that these essays were essentially political in nature. They sought not only to encourage memorials and petitions but to influence Congressmen and line up votes against removal. More than forty other newspapers reprinted the essays, which were also collected and published in pamphlet form. Evarts himself was candid about his mission: "In regard to the condition of our Indians, it would seem to me that no relief can be hoped, except through the influence of the press. This may operate upon the members of Congress, or some of them by the next session."[34]

While the essays discussed the "present crisis in the condition of the American Indians," Evarts established his central theme at the outset. The essential problem, he insisted, was a moral one; the character of the United States was at stake, not just the physical location of various Indian tribes. "Most certainly an indelible stigma will be fixed upon us," he maintained, "if, in the plenitude of our power, and in the pride of our superiority, we shall be guilty of manifest injustice to our weak and defenceless neighbours." The United States had land and wealth, Evarts observed, but true national prosperity was more than material possessions. "It may be truly said," he warned, "that the character which a nation sustains, in its intercourse with the great community of nations, is of more value than any other of its public possessions." Amid the political rubble of the late 1820s, Jeremiah Evarts was searching for the Christian republic he had so long envisioned.[35]

When Evarts explored the rights of the Cherokees to their lands, he skirted the assumption that people should "improve" their land or lose it. Instead, he emphasized that the Cherokees had always held their lands, that whites had never possessed them except through purchase from the Indians, and that the Cherokees were primarily an agricultural people. That is, they were no different from anyone else attempting to farm and improve their land. In so doing, he challenged the administration's argument that at heart the Indians remained hunters unconcerned with settled agriculture and improvements. In fact, of course, the administration had long since contradicted its own arguments when it offered to pay emigrating Indians the value of their improvements. But such contradictions rarely trouble the committed, and there is no evidence that they troubled advocates of removal. Evarts also advanced two other arguments related to land: a declaration of sovereignty was not the same as actual sovereignty, and large tracts of lands were necessary to separate Indians from whites so they might create their own community and their own "national character."[36]

After outlining the framework within which American Indian policy should be considered, Evarts devoted the next several essays to a history of that policy since Washington's administration. Emphasizing that these treaties were now the law of the land, he detailed many of their key provisions and stressed the legal relationships they created between the government and the tribes. Most readers were undoubtedly seeing these treaty provisions for the first time, and Evarts carefully delineated the legal as well as the moral parameters of each one. The United States, he observed, did not enter into any of these treaty arrangements casually; each one gave us something we wanted at the time. The Senate had ratified the treaties. They were legal documents, not merely "a jumble of words."[37]

In his essays, Evarts continually tried to elevate the argument to one of law and morality. Proponents of removal argued that these treaties were merely convenient arrangements with a savage people and that the Cherokees remained a savage people despite the accomplishments of a few leaders with mixed blood. Evarts's response, aside from a contempt for those who used sophistry to skirt the law, was to insist on the one hand that the Cherokees were no longer savages, but to argue on the other that even if they were, they had rights recognized through treaty negotiation. "Has not God endowed every community with some rights?" he asked, "and are not these rights to be regarded by every honest man and by every fair-minded and honorable ruler?"[38] Central among those rights guaranteed by treaty was the commitment by the United States to protect Indian lands not ceded by treaty, and Evarts attacked the Jackson administration directly for deviously trying to renege on this agreement:

> The seventh article [of the Treaty of Holston, 1791] is short, and will bear repeating.—It reads thus: "The United States SOLEMNLY GUARANTY to the Cherokee Nation ALL THEIR LANDS not hereby ceded." This seems to be, upon the face of it, a plain sentence. A man of moderate information would at least suppose himself to understand it. He would not suspect that there was a secret, recondite meaning, altogether incompatible with the apparent one. But it seems that there *was* such a meaning. How it was discovered, or by whom, the public are not informed. The present

Secretary of War, however, has lately adopted it, and urged it upon the Cherokees as decisive of the whole question at issue.[39]

Exploring the language of the treaty further, Evarts concluded that there was no secret meaning; we meant what we said and got what we wanted.

His next several essays presented the history of treaty-making between the government of the United States and various Indian tribes. Evarts carefully explored the language of those treaties, especially as it concerned rights and guarantees. In Essay IX he returned to the parent-child metaphor. Noting that it was the United States who "obtruded the word" "Father" upon the Indians, he argued that we did so not only as an expression of our paternal concern for the tribes but to indicate that the President of the United States would be "their protector from aggression." This extended the sphere of the federal government beyond its constitutionally mandated one to control Indian affairs to that of providing protection and justice. The government became a guarantor as well as a negotiator. A Christian father, Evarts warned, did not tell lies to his children or break his promises to them.[40]

But the issue was not just that of Indian relations or Cherokee removal. It was that of national morality. Evarts warned of the consequences should the Cherokees lose their case: "it will be necessary that foreign nations should be well aware, that the People of the United States are ready to take the ground of fulfilling their contracts so long only, as they can be overawed by physical force; that we as a nation, are ready to avow, that we can be restrained from injustice *by fear alone*; not the fear of God, which is a most ennobling and purifying principle; not the fear of sacrificing national character, in the estimation of good and wise men in every country, and through all future time; not the fear of present shame and public scorn; but simply, and only, the fear of bayonets and cannon."[41] Law mixed with morality, in Evarts's mind, to form a series of first principles that were binding on peoples and nations and that ennobled and protected. Georgia would throw them all away in her greed for Cherokee lands.

With Essay XIV Evarts concluded his discussion of treaties and turned to an analysis of the present controversy and crisis. His earlier thirteen essays detailing legal and diplomatic issues indicated his intent to appeal to the educated and influential; now he addressed the political issues and ramifications inherent in the dispute. In doing so he castigated the state of Georgia for its course of action, its willful misinterpretation of earlier treaties, and its lack of scruples and concoction of disingenuous arguments in pressing its case. Reminding readers that Georgia's claims were of recent origin, he tried to transform the issue into one of nationalism versus states' rights. In the process he raised the question of executive usurpation and its danger to republicanism. "Let me ask here," he wrote, "whence did the Secretary of War derive the power of repealing an act of Congress? This is a plain question; and the people of the United States would like to receive a plain answer. Whence did he derive the power to set aside existing treaties? ... Is he not aware of all this? or does he really think he has the power to annul treaties and repeal laws, according to his sense of convenience and propriety?"[42]

In reply, Evarts returned to his discussion of the legal and moral implications of treaty obligations. He observed that Georgia had consistently recognized Indian sovereignty in her negotiations with the tribes within the state's boundaries, at least until her 1802 compact with the federal government. So her arguments for removal were of recent origin. Evarts asserted that they were also visionary. There was no experiential evidence to support her claims that removal would be beneficial to the tribes. State claims that the United States government could not cede state territory through treaties was a mere sophism, Evarts warned. The United States never ceded Georgia lands to tribes; it only guaranteed already-existing tribal lands within that state. In addition, the national government *did* possess such power of cession should it choose to exercise it. It had adjusted state boundaries in various treaties.[43]

Evarts's remaining essays elaborated the problems inherent in the powers claimed by the state of Georgia over Indian affairs within its boundaries. These claims not only challenged, perhaps abrogated, nationalism; they contradicted the very experience and demands of Georgia until the arrival of the Jackson administration. Although he never used the words, Evarts clearly indicated his belief that Georgia's claims were not only illegal and immoral but basely opportunistic. Her attempt to extend state laws over the Cherokees threatened to degrade the Indians and reduce them to virtual servitude. "As soon as the net of Georgia legislation is sprung over him," Evarts warned, "he is equally and instantly exposed to public persecution and private indignity." Yet these individuals were not ignorant and degraded savages; they were "civilized and educated men;—these orderly members of a society, raised in part by the fostering care of our national government ... these laborious farmers, and practical republicans."[44] Georgia's actions threatened to subvert law, order, and morality.

Finally, Evarts closed with a dissertation on the morality of law. In words that often echoed his senior essay, "On the Execution of the Laws," he tied moral principles to legal strictures. Christianity, he argued, was the "basis of the present law of nations." He reminded judges and legislators that the spirit of Christianity, particularly that of the golden rule, should regulate legislation as well as behavior. The plan to remove the Indians to lands beyond the Mississippi violated that spirit. First, it represented an attempt to benefit whites and not Indians. Removal would open Indian lands to white settlers and gratify whites; this would destroy rather than save the Indians. Second, advocates of removal ignored the legal and moral dimensions of existing obligations and spoke only of visionary schemes that might improve the tribes in the future. Evarts's third objection was that the plan itself was visionary. There was no experiential evidence to support it. Indeed, the idea of throwing together various tribes with diverse languages and customs in one Indian state was "chimerical." Finally, the tribes themselves objected strenuously to the proposal. They were not only unwilling to remove; they believed that insufficient good land existed in the proposed western country and that the government could not fulfill its promises to emigrating Indians. Claims of "moral necessity" should not be used to subvert law and order. The moral integrity of the country was at stake.[45]

The "William Penn" essays became almost instantaneously influential. Roberts Vaux wrote from Philadelphia to congratulate Evarts for his effort and to urge that copies be sent to all congressmen. The essays "must have an effect," Vaux argued, and had already excited public sympathy for the Indians. To extend that influence, and to popularize the message of the essays (which were a bit learned and lengthy for popular consumption), Evarts drew up *A Brief View of the Present Relations Between the Government and People of the United States and the Indians Within our National Limits*.[46]

At the outset of the pamphlet Evarts summarized the major arguments of his earlier essays, listing them as firmly established positions familiar to "a large portion of the intelligent and reflecting men in the community." He then proceeded to state his four broad principles: that "the removal of any nation of Indians from their country by force would be an instance of gross and cruel oppression"; that efforts to accomplish such a removal by bribery or fraud were also acts of oppression; that treaty obligations bound the United States to protect the Indians "from force and encroachments on the part of a State"; and that the Cherokees had the solemn guarantee of the United States to keep all intruders away from their lands. To reinforce his position, Evarts then discussed Georgia's claims. In the process he dismissed the issue of *imperium in imperio*, the existence of a state within a state, which seemed to be a cornerstone of Georgia's argument. "When the case is accurately examined, however, all the fog clears away, and nothing appears in the prospect but a little tract of country full of civilized Indians, engaged in their lawful pursuits, neither molesting their neighbours, nor interrupting the general peace and prosperity."[47]

Evarts's defense of the Cherokees reflected his own convictions as well. On the one hand he strongly believed in the combination of law and morality articulated in his essays. It had been the basis of his own life since college, and his multitude of writings since then had reflected that theme. It also mirrored his belief in a Christian republicanism as an operative philosophy of government and citizenship. From another perspective, such an argument was essential to a man who, like Evarts, had been a leader of the benevolent cause. His portrayal of the Cherokees as a mildly progressive people, adapting to civilization and embracing Christianity, reflected his commitment to the missionary enterprise. If in 1829 the Cherokees could not demonstrate progress toward civilization, then what had the American Board been doing for the past ten years? How could they have been more successful in the Sandwich Islands than in the American forest? With so many other causes, secular as well as religious, contending for public support, Evarts believed that ABCFM missions must demonstrate some signs of success. Even though he continually warned that conversion and revitalization were a long, slow process and that the public should not expect any instantaneous transformation of "heathen" natives, he nonetheless recognized that signs of progress were crucial to maintaining support for the cause.

Evarts essentially avoided, finally, the question of whether or not the Indians would be better off somewhere else. After stating this argument directly, he addressed his answer not to the question itself but to the issue of law and morality. Cannot the United States, he asked, "in the very prime and vigour of our republican government," enforce its own laws and treaties? He was reluctant to admit that the American Board would go west if the Cherokees did, that removal would not mean the end of missionary efforts, lest the public fail to understand the underlying issues of the removal controversy. To reinforce his position, and probably to undercut the arguments of removal advocates that in fact morality dictated such a policy, Evarts concluded his *Brief View* with an enumeration of the physical and moral problems inherent in removal. It would destroy the Indian community, he insisted, create widespread suffering, break up families, and mix different tribes indiscriminately in an undesirable country which the government could not secure against the cupidity of whites for long. Removal, in short, was a visionary scheme destructive in nature and able to be implemented only through force.[48]

The purpose of *A Brief View* was to reach the general public and convince them to sign petitions. The structure of the pamphlet reflected the purpose. Evarts avoided all the legal and technical references that dotted his "William Penn" essays. Instead he cast the pamphlet's language in a popular tone, using and drawing upon images both dear and familiar to the benevolent community and the public that supported it. He used words—family, community, suffering—to stir the passions and generate outrage against the inhumanity of removal. Missing completely was any discussion about the impact of removal on the board's missionary enterprises and objectives. Evarts sought to keep alive the romantic and Christian impulses that had fed the missionary movement through an appeal to traditional values, legal obligations, and moral purpose. The growth of anti-removal sentiment during the latter months of 1829 and in 1830 reflected the success of his efforts.

During the remainder of the year additional pamphlets and essays appeared to advance the anti-removal cause. In one pamphlet, *Examination of the Relations Between the Cherokees and the Government of the United States*, the author (probably either Evarts or Samuel Worcester) asserted that white Americans had a moral obligation to do more than avoid injustice in their relations with the Indians. The act of settlement, he argued, vested them with the responsibility of educating and civilizing the tribes. The American Board's missions had partially succeeded in doing this; removal now threatened that success. The author urged the Cherokees to resist and the benevolent community to support them.[49]

In a speech on Indian rights, Heman Humphrey spoke of the motives that should energize Christians to defend the Cherokees. In an interesting twist to Georgia's argument, Humphrey observed that the Indians had helped the early colonists settle the land and had not subsequently come and asked for their houses and agricultural improvements on the basis that the whites were "mere tenants at will." "They allowed us to abide by our own council fires," he said, "and to govern ourselves as we chose, when they could either have dispossessed, or subjugated us at pleasure." Purchase, conquest, and disease then swept away most of the aboriginal population and sovereignty, but recent missionary efforts held out the promise of a new future for them. "The truth is," Humphrey wrote, "that a mighty change is taking place in the character, and condition, of the southern Indians. Under the influence of industrious habits, of education, of religion, and of efficient laws, they are waking up to a new existence. . . . Having abandoned the chase, multitudes of them are living in the enjoyment of independence and plenty, in comfortable houses, and upon their own well cultivated farms. They wear their own domestic fabricks."[50]

But how could any one individual make a difference? This dilemma was at the heart of Humphrey's message, and he urged listeners (and readers of the subsequent pamphlet): "I have a right to petition, to remonstrate, to implore, and God forbid that I should be silent." Justice and humanity should propel individuals to action; "thus we may hope, that there will be a general and simultaneous movement of the people towards Washington."[51]

As anti-removal advocates became more vocal, certain central themes emerged time and again in their petitions, memorials, and speeches. Jeremiah Evarts had articulated many of these in his *Brief View*, and Heman Humphrey added others in his defense of Indian rights. But the language of the Indians themselves was perhaps most revealing about the proclivities of the moral reform community. In various addresses to federal officials, in the columns of the *Cherokee Phoenix*, and in letters to Evarts and other supporters, Indian spokesmen consciously drew upon and developed images which tugged at the emotions as well as the moral conscience. Heman Humphrey quoted from one such appeal: "Colonel Ward knows, that we have just begun to build new houses, and make new fields, and purchase iron. We have begun to make axes, hoes, and ploughs. We have some schools. We have begun to learn, and we have also begun to embrace the gospel."[52] Home, family, religion, community, industriousness, education—in short, progress—became (with moral and legal arguments) the defining themes of the effort to block removal.

But while the campaign against removal gathered support, advocates of removal in Georgia and in Washington pressed their cause with equal fervor. Certain that the president supported their position, Georgia surveyed Indian lands and circulated agents among the tribes to persuade them to sell their lands and remove. The Cherokees protested the government's failure to fulfill its promise to remove intruders from their lands, a failure which enraged the Indians and encouraged settlers and speculators. But their haste to effect removal, and their confidence that Andrew Jackson supported them, led Georgians to become arrogant. Seeing only their own objectives, they became oblivious to public opinion and the potential of anti-removal forces to rally the moral and political communities. Jackson, however, remained very much aware of this opposition and had John Eaton counsel Georgia governor John Forsyth to go slow, to avoid even the appearance of compulsory removal. Jackson and Eaton hoped that the New York Indian Board would rally sufficient support in the moral reform community to counteract the influence of the "William Penn" essays among both the public and the Congress. "It is all important, with a view to success," Eaton wrote Forsyth, "that nothing of excitement should arise, if practicable to be avoided, but that every thing should remain quiet and peaceful."[53]

But the essays of Evarts had an effect, and public opposition to removal became more apparent through petition campaigns and memorials. David Greene wrote Cherokee missionary Samuel Worcester from ABCFM headquarters that the board had expected apathy but now believed that influential congressmen would be able to block removal. Greene warned Worcester, however, that the firmest opposition must come from the Indians themselves; they must continue to act as if "every thing depended on themselves." The board expected Worcester, who was at the mission station in New Echota, to convey this message to the Cherokees. Should Congress fail to protect them, Greene concluded, the Cherokees should appeal to the United States Supreme Court. Greene, who was Evarts's son-in-law, clearly expressed the advice and expectations of the corresponding secretary. The import of this advice was clear: legal and moral commitments obliged the government to protect the Indians where they lived, and the tribes should demand no less.[54]

Almost lost in this debate was perhaps the paramount issue: what was the best course for the Indians themselves? Evarts's long defense of the Indians in the "William Penn" essays had articulated the government's legal and moral obligations but said little about the welfare of the tribes themselves. He assumed that they would be best served by remaining where they were but admitted that this course also entailed a willingness by the government to protect them from intrusions by individuals and states. Since Jackson did not appear willing to do that, what was next?

Speaking for the government, Thomas McKenney argued that the real issue was "the welfare of the Indians, and the prosperity and happiness of their race." Like most whites, McKenney did not consider the Indians themselves to be the proper arbiters of their own fate and refused to admit that the underlying factor in Indian-white relations was race. As the concept of racial uniqueness became popular in the second quarter of the nineteenth century, it sharpened the complexity of the missionary impulse. It argued, on the one hand, that certain peoples were savage by nature rather than by circumstances. Hence, their removal from proximity to whites and all the civilizing and missionary efforts in the world would not change their nature. On the other hand, as civilization progressed it would eradicate not only the traces of savagery but the entire culture. The more the culture disappeared, the more nineteenth-century romantics heroized it as a counterpoint to the material and spiritual baseness of civilization itself. To talk about Indian rights, therefore, was to miss the point. Indians, in the eyes of McKenney, remained mere children in need of protection: "let all . . . put the question each to himself, what is best to be done to save this hapless race from the necessary and *fatal consequences* of anomalous relations to us?"[55]

Experiments were vain, McKenney insisted, until these relations were resolved. And he believed that removal was the only action that could provide that resolution. "These people are far gone in their delusion," he wrote. "I tremble for their destiny. Their advisers, will I fear, ruin them! Nothing but the intervention of God's providence can save them. I feel for the Indians; and sincerely desire their prosperity and happiness. But it seems they are taught to look upon that man as their *enemy*, who shall not see their condition thro' the medium in which their opposite advisers have, unhappily for them, as I believe, taught them to see it."[56] Whether for personal or political reasons, McKenney believed that the American Board was mistaken to assume that the president would forcibly remove the tribes. But while McKenney's long familiarity with Indian affairs led him to question the progress achieved after a decade of extensive missionary efforts under the Indian Civilization Fund, it also made him sensitive to the shifting politics of Indian affairs. And in the fall of 1829, with Andrew Jackson in the White House, those politics shifted sharply.

The Cherokees moved first. In late October the Cherokee National Council passed a law that any citizen who emigrated or agreed to emigrate would "forfeit all rights and privileges they have enjoyed as citizens of this Nation." In addition, those who sold their improved property to anyone enrolled to emigrate would be fined "not less than one thousand dollars, and be punished with one hundred lashes." The Cherokee National Council also protested the suspension of the government's commitment to remove intruders. Appealing to justice and the "promises of the Presidents," the council asked for immediate relief.[57]

But while the council protested and the *Phoenix* editorialized against the new government policies, the benevolent community divided over its next step. Evarts pushed for memorials to Congress and urged supporters in Boston, Philadelphia, and New York to call public meetings on the issue. But his correspondents in those cities held back, warning him that public meetings would arouse opposition and excite "a political ferment." Evarts's essays were still appearing in the press, and Andrew Jackson had yet to outline his Indian policy clearly. Newspapers like *Niles' Weekly Register* commented approvingly on the appointment of Generals John Coffee and William Carroll as commissioners to the Cherokees but did not realize that their missions were originally secret. "Professional" reformers like Evarts or Catharine Beecher were sensitive to the issues, but the larger public had yet to be awakened.[58]

Then the general answered the missionary. While Jeremiah Evarts labored to stir public support for the Cherokees, and while even the Reformed Dutch Church (backers of the abortive New York Indian Board) opposed the claims of Georgia, Andrew Jackson's first annual message in early December 1829 sharply joined the issue. The president summarized the government's Indian policy over the years, noting that it embraced two incompatible objectives. First, it sought to civilize the Indians "in the hope of gradually reclaiming them from a wandering life." But at the same time, it also sought to purchase their lands and remove them into the western wilderness, thereby keeping them "in a wandering state." The government thus defeated its own policy, and the Indians "retained their savage habits." Those few tribes who had successfully embraced civilization had subsequently attempted to establish independent states within the boundaries of existing states. The latter, in turn, had resisted these efforts and extended their laws over those tribes. Jackson made clear his determination to support states like Georgia and Alabama in these conflicts and advised the Indians to emigrate.

The central theme of his discussion of Indian affairs, however, was not a summary of government policy but his characterization of the protagonists as well as the policy. Much like Jeremiah Evarts, ironically, Jackson argued that "our conduct toward these people is deeply interesting to our national character." But then he continued, arguing that should the Choctaws, the Cherokees, and the Creeks remain on their ancestral lands, the white population would engulf them and destroy them. "Humanity and national honor," according to Jackson as well as Evarts, demanded that something be done. Jackson's solution, however, unlike that of Evarts, was to remove those tribes to lands west of the Mississippi. He sought, moreover, to treat them as individuals and not as tribes and insisted that the states would proceed in a similar fashion for those who refused to emigrate. As for tribal claims to their ancestral lands, Jackson endorsed the view that those lands should be granted to individuals who would develop their productive capacities. "It seems to me visionary," he concluded, "to suppose that in this state of things claims can be allowed on tracts of country on which they have neither dwelt nor made improvements, merely because they have seen them from the mountain or passed them in the chase."[59]

A desire for land, a need to settle a growing conflict between the federal government and the states, a conviction that Indians must be removed from any proximity to whites, a determination to open the southwest to expansion and development, racial biases, and perhaps even a conviction that this policy was more humane than any alternative—all these motivated Jackson. What was missing in his analysis was any consideration of legal treaty commitments or an empathetic understanding of other points of view. But those had never been Andrew Jackson's strong points. While Jeremiah Evarts (and "William Penn") articulated alternative considerations, it remained for an aged Indian to set forth a more complete alternative to Jackson's history.

> Brother! The red people were very numerous. They covered the land like the trees of the forest, from the big waters of the east to the great sea, where rests the setting sun. The white people come—they drove them from forest to forest, from river to river—the bones of our fathers strewed the path of their wandering. Brother, you are now strong: we melt away like the snow of spring before the rising sun. Whither must we now go? Must we leave the home of our fathers, and go to a strange land beyond the great river of the West? That land is dark and desolate—we shall have no pleasure in it. Pleasant are the fields of our youth—We love the woods where our fathers led us to the chase—Their bones lie by the running stream, where we sported in the days of our childhood—When we are gone, strangers will dig them up—The Great Spirit made us all—you have land enough—Leave us then the

fields of our youth, and the woods where our fathers led us to the chase—Permit us to remain in peace under the shade of our own trees—Let us watch over the graves of our fathers, by the streams of our childhood.[60]

Jackson's policy distressed the missionaries, and Cephas Washburn wrote Evarts that the prospect of Indians remaining east of the Mississippi was now "*utterly hopeless*" unless they agreed to submit to state laws. Gov. George Gilmer of Georgia, on the other hand, was so buoyed by Jackson's message that he told the legislature to take "the most liberal and forbearing course" with respect to Indian lands within the state. He warned that Georgia must avoid "the very appearance of violating rights" so as to soothe the public; Indian lands were certain to revert to the state with Jackson in the White House. Gilmer wrote Jackson to endorse the president's policy. He did so in language certain to excite Jackson's support and arouse his suspicions about the opposition. The people of Georgia, Gilmer wrote, know that Jackson "will be opposed by the prejudices, the ignorance, and the feigned sensibility of affected philanthropists, and still more by the party seeking to succeed him in office." No words could have been better suited to alert the political antennae of Andrew Jackson.[61]

When news of Jackson's message reached Evarts's colleagues in New York, they agreed that the time for public meetings had arrived. The prospect of coerced removal was no longer a vague fear, but a certain policy. The general had succeeded where the missionary had not. As the House Committee on Indian Affairs formulated a removal policy, religious publications throughout the North sounded the alarm and sought to arouse public opposition. Evarts seemed almost relieved that the battle had been joined. He wrote Eleazar Lord in New York that the prospect of public meetings encouraged him, and he immediately initiated a swirl of activity designed to publicize their efforts. He also warned that the Indians might be "frightened out of their rights before Congress and the Supreme Court can interfere in their behalf." The Indians believe the president, Evarts warned, and believe that they must obey. "Numbers, from this apprehension, begin to remove, or to make preparations for a removal. This is represented by the government as proof that the Indians are willing to remove. And thus one result of oppression is made a plausible excuse for continuing the oppression." A letter-writing campaign began to encourage memorials to Congress from New York, Philadelphia, Boston, and a variety of other cities.[62]

Despite Governor Gilmer's earlier pleas that the legislature refrain from restrictive laws that might arouse broad opposition to the president's plan, legislators could not restrain themselves. The Georgia legislature passed a series of laws further circumscribing the rights of Indians within that state. They prohibited anyone from trying to prevent Indians from enrolling as emigrants or from emigrating; nor could they try to deter Indians from selling their lands or negotiating with treaty commissioners for the sale of Indian lands. Their actions aroused public excitement which, in turn, encouraged opponents of removal to believe that public opposition could influence Congress and stay the hand of the president. Evarts set in motion the network of benevolent and missionary societies so painstakingly constructed during the past two decades. One correspondent commented on its effect: "The circular addressed to the Ladies of our Country to call forth their sympathies & efforts for the oppressed and distressed Indians has awakened our deepest sensibilities and prepared us to exert all our influence to avert the calamities which threaten them. And reasonably to do all that is proper & becoming Women to do in bearing testimony against oppression & injustice."[63]

As the year closed and Congress prepared to take up the issue of Indian removal, Georgia governor Gilmer wrote President Jackson almost daily to support his policy and to discredit his opposition. Evarts, meanwhile, prepared to do battle on all sides—against Jackson's policy, against the predatory demands of Georgia, in support of the American Board's Indian missions, on the legal front through appeals to treaties and the Supreme Court if necessary, and by a broad humanitarian appeal about the need to preserve the national character through an effective moral ethos. In a letter to fellow combatant Eleazar Lord, he expressed optimism that Jackson's policy would fail and that the public could influence Congress. He appeared convinced that the national character would be preserved, a moral ethos sustained, and the Indians saved. The battle now became one between the benevolent community and the president; the battleground, the committee rooms and floor of the United States Congress.[64]

CHAPTER EIGHT

"The Torches Are at Hand": The Removal Battle in Washington

❧

Andrew Jackson's first annual message forced the hand of Jeremiah Evarts and the American Board. Evarts and other ABCFM officials had long argued that missionary efforts advanced a progressive view of history—that the conversion of heathen natives and their subsequent acceptance of evangelical truths advanced them from a semi-nomadic hunting society rooted in pagan superstition to a culture based on Christian teachings and practices and grounded in settled agricultural villages. To Evarts, spiritual progress promoted national stability; Christian republicanism promoted civic virtue. It seemed to be true, as historian William McLoughlin has noted, that "to be a good American one had to cease to be a good Indian."[1]

The renewed debate over Indian removal challenged missionaries to defend both the premises and the effects of their efforts. The "progress" of the Cherokees appeared to support Evarts's view of history. Between 1817 and 1827 the Cherokee Council had enacted more than a hundred laws, and in 1828 it passed a constitution which resembled that of the United States. The Cherokees, in short, became a nation rather than a collection of loosely governing entities. Emulation may be flattery, and few could deny (although many disliked) Cherokee progress in the governmental arts. Their acceptance and practice of Christianity, however, was another story. By 1830 fewer than two hundred Cherokees had become church members, and most of those were mixed bloods. Although the council's laws often had a Christian tone to them, Christianity's penetration of native life was slow and often inflammatory. After the mid-

1820s anti-mission sentiment became more pronounced among the tribe, as even the limited success of missionary exertions reinvigorated the traditional Cherokee religion. "Traditionalists" clashed with "progressives"; the pages of the *Cherokee Phoenix* dramatized this split, with columns in English nestling next to those in Cherokee.[2]

This split, coupled with Jackson's removal policy and Evarts's Christian republicanism, led to several dilemmas. How were missionaries and government officials to deal with the divisions among the Cherokees? The leaders, who embraced the literate and rational culture of Anglo-America, had become estranged from their countrymen who remained enmeshed in the Amerindians' traditional mythic structures. As a result, they were often closer to whites than to their own countrymen. For traditionalists, going west meant the preservation of these mythic structures even while it meant leaving the lands of their ancestors, who were often central to those very structures. But whether they removed west or remained east of the Mississippi, settlers and missionaries alike threatened traditionalists and their culture. The real question, therefore, was which was the true path to preservation? Was the annihilation of those mythic structures worth trading for preservation? Closer examination of the debate and its assumptions, however, reveals that even these questions were largely specious. Traditionalists were doomed; the parameters of the debate did not include their worldview. Cherokee representations to the federal government, like those of the missionaries, framed their arguments in an Anglo-American rather than an Amerindian context. They spoke of treaties, water rights, and progress toward civilization, not of spirits or of practices indigenous to their culture. They had lost the debate over culture before the debate over removal began.[3]

Behind the debates over Indian removal, moreover, lay the issues of motive and character, not culture. The missionaries had never really accepted the idea of cultural pluralism, and Evarts's "William Penn" essays had emphasized legal obligations and national character rather than cultural preservation. Concentration on these issues, together with Jackson's determination to resolve the matter, also made the question a political one. This development was ambiguous for the American Board. Its missions were expensive; their results, disappointing. Missionary arguments that removal would jeopardize existing missions often obscured these problems. At the same time, the decision to resolve the question in the political arena created a test case for the power of Christian republicanism to shape the behavior of the state. On the other hand, as the issue became more politically charged, it took on a life and purpose of its own. In so doing questions of missionary activity as well as decisions about Indian policy moved beyond the control of Evarts and the American Board of Commissioners and into the public arena. As issues of character, motive, and behavioral propriety became part of the political agenda, Indian affairs became just one more issue in the vituperative language of Jacksonian politics. The biting words of one Vermont politician captured the rhetorical tone of the period.

> A Democrat's picture is easy to draw.
> He can't bear to obey, but will govern the law;
> His manners unsocial, his temper unkind,
> He's a rebel in conduct a Tyrant in mind.
> He is envious of those who have riches and power;
> Discontented, malignant implacable sour;
> Never happy himself he would wish to destroy
> The comforts and blessings which others enjoy.[4]

The conjunction of several issues and debates in early 1830 further roiled the mixture of character and politics. The first of these focused on the debate between Daniel Webster and Robert Y. Hayne over the Foot Resolution. Introduced on December 30, 1829, the resolution proposed an inquiry into the "expediency of limiting for a certain period the sales of the public lands" and into the effect of abolishing the office of surveyor general. Congressional debates quickly separated east from west. Missouri senator Thomas Hart Benton attacked the resolution for fomenting a crisis. Ignoring the fact that it proposed only an inquiry and not definitive action, he warned that it would curtail American expansion and development by preserving "the vast and magnificent valley of the Mississippi for the haunts of beasts and savages, instead of making it the abode of liberty and civilization."[5]

But it was Robert Hayne, rising in defense of Benton's position, who framed the matter in terms of larger issues. Hayne's attack on the resolution moved beyond its specific parameters to a larger framework. Land sales, westward expansion, internal improvements, banking, the distribution and exercise of political power, the sovereignty of individual states, the power of the executive—all became components of this comprehensive vision. "It is bad enough that Government should presume to regulate the industry of man," he warned; "it is sufficiently monstrous that they should attempt, by arbitrary legislation, artificially to adjust and balance the various pursuits of society."[6]

After Foot modified his proposal, tying future land sales to the amount of land still available on the market, Daniel Webster rose to deliver his reply. Insisting that the public lands belonged to the people of the United States and not to the individual states, Webster also linked land sales to banking, internal improvements, states' rights, and national prosperity. While Webster's reply articulated a broad nationalism, his line of argument did not differ significantly from that of Hayne. It, too, emphasized the separate nature of the various regions of the country—differing chiefly in its assertion that national interests should retain their primacy. He missed much of the thrust of Hayne's critique.[7]

In late January Hayne sharpened his argument, directly attacking the spirit of the times rather than any particular legislative issue. Now the underlying discontents surfaced, discontents that were as much cultural as they were political. Hayne launched a broadside against "the spirit of false philanthropy." This spirit, he warned, was an evil spirit that stalked the land, "lighting up the torches of discord throughout the community." What was it? According to Hayne, it was the willingness of some to "regulate the affairs and the duties of others." He singled out New England, the region's missionary spirit in particular. Missionary zeal, he said, was dangerous. When it mixed with politics it became deadly. "When this [missionary] spirit infuses itself into the bosom of a statesman, (if one so possessed can be called a statesman) it converts him at once into a visionary enthusiast. Then it is that he indulges in golden dreams of national greatness and prosperity.... It is a spirit which has long been busy with the slaves of the South, and is even now displaying itself in vain efforts to drive the Government from its wise policy in relation to the Indians. It is this spirit which has filled the land with thousands of wild and visionary projects, which can have no effect but to waste the energies and dissipate the resources of the country."[8]

When Webster rose to reply to Hayne a second time, he did not miss the import of these remarks. He observed that Hayne had talked about everything but the public lands and couched his own reply in similar fashion. But although Webster's argument articulated a broad nationalism, it focused on legal and constitutional issues that defined the nature of the union. Webster outlined the dangers of states' rights and disunion but failed to address the specific issues and attitudes then prevalent which had prompted Hayne's outburst. Hayne, and Benton as well, linked the moral reform crusades for Indians, anti-slavery, and Sunday mails to political conduct and combinations against the South and West. Benton drew the connections explicitly:

> Now, I can have a vision also, and of a banner with inscriptions upon it, floating over the head of the Senator from Massachusetts, while he was speaking: the words "Missouri Question, Colonization Society, Anti-Slavery, Georgia Indians, Western Lands, More Tariff, Internal Improvement, Anti-Sunday Mails, Anti-Masonry." A cavalcade under the banner—a motley group—a most miscellaneous concourse, the speckled progeny of many conjunctions—veteran Federalists—benevolent females—politicians who have lost their caste—National Republicans—all marching on to the next Presidential election, and chanting the words on the banner, and repeating, "under these signs we conquer."[9]

Senator Barton, Benton's Missouri colleague, aptly characterized the "latitude and liberty of this debate" as "a kind of Saturnalia in the Senate."[10]

The debate over the Foot Resolution revealed the depth of tensions and the breadth of issues that would dominate the first Jacksonian Congress. It also demonstrated that these tensions and issues would spill over, one to the other, as both sides sought to articulate a political cosmology. Congressional discussion of the Foot Resolution was not so much a debate as it was a venting of spleens on topics that had bothered people for more than a decade. They came to a head in the winter of 1830, seeking to set the agenda for the next decade. Indian removal lay at the center of that agenda, largely because it touched so many related issues. But it was not alone.

The Sunday mail issue reappeared in 1830, and like Indian removal the matter of delivering the mail on Sunday called into question the boundaries of American society and who was to establish those boundaries. With Indian removal the boundaries were geographic and legal as well as moral; with Sunday mails they were primarily economic and moral. In both instances a central issue was not only the determination of boundaries but the respective roles of the state and the individual in fixing them.

The campaign against Sunday mails in 1830 was really an extension of the 1829 effort. During the winter petitions again flooded Congress, in response to Evarts's pleas the previous fall. The issue for Evarts remained that of morality and virtue, and he worked closely with congressional leaders like Sen. Theodore Frelinghuysen of New Jersey to prevent Sunday mail deliveries. But the opposition to change had coalesced, and many localities and states instructed their representatives to maintain Sunday mail delivery. Baptists and Universalists alike opposed Evarts's efforts. Ironically, few of the Sunday routes were in New England, source of greatest opposition, while most were in the South or West. Sectional interests, as in the Foot Resolution, found common cause.[11]

Central to the debate as well was the issue of the economic, political, and moral boundaries of American life. That is, to what extent should governmental bodies institute or enforce boundaries? To what extent should they attempt to control or direct the people? Senator Johnson's report to Congress as well as the debate over that report focused on whether the government should sanction or designate time for religious worship. While critics of the report often tried to shift the debate to one of patriotism, they linked patriotism with Christianity. Supporters of the report, on the other hand, emphasized the need for personal autonomy. But evangelicals worried about personal autonomy in a society that was busy casting off externally imposed behavioral restraints. Religious revivals and individual conversions might supplant those external controls with internal ones, but what about the larger populace that remained unconverted? Who was to define and superintend the society's behavioral ethos? While the committee's minority report argued that a desire for "commercial convenience" motivated the majority, they really meant that capitalism rather than morality defined the behavioral boundaries of American society.

Writing in opposition to the majority report, Alexander Hill Everett, editor of the *North American Review*, voiced another concern. He attacked the growing influence of party to decide such issues and insisted that the "only sure way of rising above the influence of proper motives, whether absolutely vicious, or only narrow, is to give no weight to any considerations but those of duty, or in other words, religious principle."[12]

By the spring of 1830, however, despite Evarts's lobbying and cries about Christian obligations, the Sabbatarian campaign had failed. Evarts blamed the failure on the inability of the religious community to exert sufficient pressure and the triumph of political considerations over religious motives. He might also have observed, however, that Congress heard only two speeches on the issue—one from each side—before voting to table the matter in early May. Evarts's comments in his personal journal are sparse, unlike those on other matters, perhaps revealing an awareness that religion had now become a private rather than a public matter. He worried about that change, of course, concerned that a commercial spirit unrestrained by moral boundaries had seized the soul of America. But at the same time he was embroiled in a larger struggle, a struggle that he also believed would shape and reflect the soul of America. This was his opposition to Andrew Jackson's policy of Indian removal.[13]

If Jackson's first annual message had been a call to battle, Jeremiah Evarts and the American Board were quick to respond. Within weeks after Jackson's remarks, Evarts had mobilized a vast network of societies to send a steady stream of memorials and petitions to Washington. Circular letters addressed to these constituencies flooded the mails, outlining the historical roots of the crisis, demonstrating missionary progress during the past decade, and warning that removal would retard the civilizing process and coerce the tribes into surrendering their national character and rights. "It appears," warned one circular, "that measures are fast ripening, which, if put in execution, are to exterminate the Indians." Public meetings in New York, Boston, Hartford, and elsewhere sounded similar alarms and urged listeners to petition Congress against such an outrage.[14]

In their efforts, Jeremiah Evarts and his colleagues argued that more than the fate of the Indians was at stake. National honor, morality, adherence to the tradition of law—indeed, the very essence of America was at issue. The report of a Philadelphia town meeting on the issue warned, "But shall a government founded on that celebrated exposition of the rights of man, which accompanied our declaration of independence, grossly violate those rights in others, for which they then contended?" Americans' "unprincipled cupidity" threatened the very character of their institutions. Not only did treaty guarantees have to be honored; the United States and its people had to restrain their sense of expansive autonomy to recognize basic human rights as well. "If such be the irrepressible, and insatiable covetousness of the people of the United States, and such the feebleness and ill faith of their government, what have the Cherokees to expect? Is it not first to be chased beyond the Mississippi, next beyond the Rocky Mountains, and finally to be driven into the Pacific? Is there any permanent asylum for them on this side the grave?"[15] Citizens of Hartford, Connecticut, argued that the issue was one of national honor, not solely a matter of sectionalism or party. Removal would violate morality and Christian republicanism. A large meeting of New Haven citizens concurred and sent their own memorial to Congress.[16]

In reply to these concerns, and particularly to the longer exposition of them in the "William Penn" letters, Lewis Cass wrote a long essay on the present state of Indian affairs for the *North American Review*. Cass, the governor of Michigan Territory and long a major figure in Indian affairs, traced the decline of Indian societies across North America in the face of white settlement. We might wish, Cass noted, that this "progress" had been achieved at a "smaller sacrifice," but such a wish was "vain." "A barbarous people, depending for subsistence upon the scanty and precarious supplies furnished by the chase, cannot live in contact with a civilized community." He warned that only their immediate removal from the influence of white civilization could save them from "utter extinction."[17]

Relying heavily on Isaac McCoy's "Remarks on Indian Reform," Cass insisted that missionary efforts to christianize and civilize the tribes had been unsuccessful and unproductive. He blamed the Indians, not the missionaries, for that failure—"there seems to be some insurmountable obstacle in the habits or temperament of the Indians, which has heretofore prevented, and yet prevents, the success of these labors." Only a few half-breeds had prospered; the remainder were in "a state of helpless and hopeless poverty." Using terms such as "wretched," "disgusting," "degrading," and "habitual indolence" to describe the Indians of North America, Cass traced their failures to something in the "institutions, character, and condition of the Indians themselves." In short, missionaries were not to blame; they had done their best to bring civilization to the tribes. But they had failed, and Cass carefully punctured the prevailing romantic descriptions of the Indian character as unrealistic and visionary.[18]

In the face of such failure, what could be done? Cass believed that removal was the only solution. The condition of the Indians was fast becoming hopeless; extinction was likely. Cass concluded that since the purpose of American settlement was to redeem the continent from a state of nature, a purpose endowed by the Creator and cultivated by settlers, only Indian removal would advance that cause. This was, he observed, removal and not dispossession, for the tribes had traversed rather than occupied the land. Earlier treaties of cession had been an error. "In the ardor of a mistaken benevolence, they have elevated these little Indian communities to an equality with the civilized governments under whose protection they live." The time had arrived when change was necessary.

The government's authority in the matter was unlimited; only the choice of means remained.[19]

Cass, who had supported federal Indian policy for more than a decade, aroused a furious storm of protest with his essay. Its publication in the *North American Review*, which had strong Federalist and Whiggish connections throughout the Northeast and in the benevolent community, added to this furor. At the same time, it touched a nerve. In blaming the failure of missionary efforts on the Indians' character, he spoke to the growing chauvinistic and racial preoccupations in American society. He also struck at the missionaries' weakest link, the relationship between missionary efforts and progress. While many Americans firmly believed that conversion and Christianity advanced a progressive vision of historical change, they also seemed ready to believe that race and character excluded certain peoples from that vision. Even a multitude of treaty guarantees would not overcome that cultural deficiency; only character could do that. Thus, if the Indians were too "ignorant and barbarous to submit to the state laws . . . they are too ignorant and barbarous to establish and maintain a government which shall protect its own citizens."[20]

Jeremiah Evarts, busy orchestrating opposition to the removal policy, did not have time to draft a response to Cass, so he commissioned a young colleague at the American Board to do so in his stead. George Cheever combined a review of Evarts's arguments in the "William Penn" essays with a broad attack on the "sophistry" of Lewis Cass. He expressed "astonishment" that Cass would justify the "most unparalleled perfidy and bare injustice" of Jackson's policy. In fact, Cheever was equally astonished that the *North American Review* even published such an article and upbraided the editor as well as the author. Cheever's reply was actually rather feeble in contrast to Cass's effort. He fulminated against those who insisted that the Indians could not be civilized and attacked Cass for misunderstanding the purpose and success of benevolence. But by and large Cheever avoided debate over the history and future of Indian relations, emphasizing instead the centrality of the removal issue for the national character. He rejected the notion that power makes right and urged readers not to be misled by the more superficial (but legal, and important) claims of treaty rights. The issue, Cheever warned, *"far more deeply involves our moral and religious character, by bringing us, in that capacity, to the very eve of the commission of a great and dreadful crime."*[21]

More than half of Cheever's reply to Cass focused on the moral issues involved in Indian removal as well as on the need to rouse the public from its apathy to oppose that policy. As such, Cheever's essay was more formally a part of Evarts's tactics than it was a reply to Cass. The American people, he warned, had become callous to "everything but the stimulus of vanity, and selfishness, and pride." Indian removal was a test of the American spirit, of the American soul. It had implications for the very character of American life, not just for the condition of the Indians. Failure to protect the Indians, Cheever insisted, "will read a mournful lesson to the poor, the ignorant, the weak, and the oppressed, on the insensate folly of throwing themselves for protection on the mercy of those, who are more powerful than they." Better that the Indian tribes take up arms and be exterminated than move west in the vain hope that they would find protection from the tide of "civilized" settlement in western lands.[22]

While Cheever penned his reply to Cass, parties on both sides of the controversy mobilized their forces and sought to shape the outcome. Gov. George Gilmer of Georgia undertook an extensive correspondence not only within his state but with the Washington political community as well. Time and again he resolutely asserted Georgia's claims and pressured the president and Congress to uphold them. Isaac McCoy, who favored Indian removal but for different reasons, lobbied the president, his cabinet, and virtually every congressman he could buttonhole, even speaking before the House Committee on Indian Affairs. Under the leadership of Secretary of War John Eaton, meanwhile, the government solicited estimates for the cost of removal. Even the ABCFM missionaries in Georgia organized, meeting to discuss the prospect of removal. After choosing Daniel Butrick as their chairman and Samuel Worcester as their secretary, they adopted a resolution which stated that Indian removal was a moral rather than a political question and announced their opposition to it. Meanwhile, Mississippi joined Georgia in extending its state laws over the tribes within its boundaries and also asked for their immediate removal.[23]

As these events unfolded, Jeremiah Evarts kept in close contact with his friends in Washington. New Jersey senator Theodore Frelinghuysen was a regular correspondent, giving Evarts a summary of the daily maneuvering within Congress as well as assessments about the bill's chances for passage in the House and Senate. Reports from Thomas McKenney, indicating that the value of the Cherokees' improvements far exceeded preliminary expectations, fueled anti-removal arguments that removal would retard the civilizing process. Press reports excited partisans on all sides, as did public meetings, and opponents of Jackson and removal feared that the controversy would disrupt the union. "What is the Union coming to," wrote one partisan; "Is Georgia to dissolve it for the honor of hanging an Indian?"[24]

The Jackson administration, meanwhile, operated as if removal was a certainty even before the congressional debate had begun. Thomas McKenney planned for settlement of the eastern tribes on lands west of the Mississippi, secret (and not-so-secret) federal agents moved among the tribes valuing improvements and locating boundary lines, and agents of Georgia encouraged (even bribed) Cherokees to remove and then allowed Georgia citizens to move onto these lands literally on the heels of the departing Indians. In the eyes of men like editor Duff Green, the public lands and Indian removal were intimately joined in a powerful political connection—a connection that held the key to future political alignments. "If the *South* will unite with the *West* on this great point conceding the lands to the west," Green wrote, "that great interest will sustain southern men."[25]

To the north, Jeremiah Evarts and other anti-removal advocates organized public meetings to rally opposition to Jackson's policy. Three themes dominated Evarts's efforts: the implications of removal for morality and national honor, the need to observe legal treaty obligations, and a determination that removal not become a party question. Should party loyalty rather than humanitarian sensibility become the prime determinant, Evarts feared that partisanship would overwhelm morality. At public meetings in Boston and elsewhere, he warned against apathy, negligence, and rash measures. "It is for the honor of our country, and for the benefit of all parties, that this important subject should be settled upon correct principles."[26]

In addition, Evarts wrote to many of the missionaries and tribal leaders to suggest a course of action. Insisting that the Cherokees should settle this matter themselves, he nonetheless maintained that the American Board had both a right and an obligation to advise them. His prescription for success was a mixture of three components. First, the treaties of the United States should repeatedly be cited before the Congress and the public. The Indians should not assume that congressmen were familiar with the details of their story. Second, the tribes should send their best men to Washington while Congress was in session. These should be leaders who will not be awed, deceived, or frightened by government officials. Third, these tribal delegations should employ "able counsel," present their case directly to the committees on Indian affairs, and document the condition of their tribes. The Cherokees, in short, should make a stand. This was the time, Evarts warned, for "their best friends throughout the country are firmly of the opinion, that if the government cannot protect the Indians where they are, they cannot protect them any where else."[27]

These views were outlined in great detail in a petition from influential Massachusetts citizens meeting at the State House in Boston that January. The meeting, called to "consider the present relations between the government of the United States and the Indians," adopted nine resolutions without a dissenting vote. The present crisis, the first resolution argued, demanded a public outcry "on the part of all friends of humanity, justice, and their country." The issue was the "preservation of our national character." Removal of the Cherokees violated existing treaties and tarnished the national honor. Many of the other resolutions defended the rights of Indians to their lands and insisted that the tribes possessed at least a qualified sovereignty. Modeled in many respects on the revolutionary committees of correspondence, the meeting not only outlined the nature of the crisis but attempted to create additional committees (including a "Committee of Correspondence") and pass resolutions to inform residents throughout the commonwealth and move them to action. Men of influence and power dominated the committee of correspondence, men like Leverett Saltsonstall, Rufus Choate, Samuel Hoar, Charles Loring, Samuel Worcester, and Jeremiah Evarts. Their vision of American society was a deferential vision, one in which the essence of that society was articulated from above instead of welling up from below.[28]

The underlying problem of the memorial, however, did not stem from the deferential views of its originators. Its arguments were simply too rational to sway partisans of removal. In this respect, the Cherokee crisis was a foretaste of the slavery debates of the 1840s and 1850s. Interested parties to the dispute asserted a position that defied rational argument and was not amenable to compromise. Arguments that if government reports were correct and the western lands were unsuitable for habitation, the Indians would starve, or if they were wrong and western lands held great promise, whites would quickly covet them and intrude once again were wasted in the face of determined advocacy by pro-removal forces. Moral imprecations against staining the national honor went unheeded in the face of stolid opposition from Georgians and Jacksonians alike. Perhaps sensing that this would be the case, anti-removal forces appealed for public pressure on Congress.[29]

They quickly discovered that theirs was not the only pressure being brought to bear on the government. The opening months of the Jackson administration presented a turbulent array of issues and conflicting demands. The Webster-Hayne debates had been but the opening round of a protracted conflict. John Quincy Adams enumerated these issues in his *Memoirs* and then warned that there "are combustibles enough: they only want kindling; and the torches are at hand."[30] Vice-president John Calhoun echoed these sentiments, writing in late January that

> The session commenced with great apparent calmness, but we already have indications that its termination will not be like its beginning. If I do not mistake, it will be one of great excitement; and characterized above all others, for the number and importance of the subjects agitated. In part, our system of legislation, turning inwardly since the end of the late war, and operating unequally on the great interest of the several sections is, I fear, coming into violent conflict in a manner to endanger the Government itself, unless there be great moderation and forbearance, which I trust will be the fact. I have for some years anticipated this conflict of interest, and will, as far as my power extends, aid in carrying the country through it in safety. It has commenced with the subject of publick lands, but will extend to several other subjects not less exciting.[31]

The Indian removal issue contained those very seeds of conflict that Calhoun feared, and contentiousness mounted as parties to the dispute lobbied for support before congressional debates on the removal bill began.

Four—perhaps five—different viewpoints emerged, each representing not only a particular solution to the problem but emanating from a different party to the dispute. Georgia was the ultimate protagonist, for Georgia citizens and politicians had been the most insistent from the outset that there was a problem and that it must be resolved. They wanted, of course, full and immediate removal. Then, in what was a supporting but also somewhat separate argument, the Jackson administration argued for removal on grounds of states' rights and the need to create opportunity through the elimination of limits that bound white settlers. Whether or not Jackson believed this would be in the best interests of the Indians is a matter of debate among historians, but what is clear is Jackson's determination to act without consulting the other parties and in a manner that (he hoped) would remove the issue from national politics.[32]

Similar divisions were apparent in the missionary community. Again, historians differ over their interpretation of the motives behind the policies, but the American Board of Commissioners for Foreign Missions and the Baptist Board of Foreign Missions adopted opposing positions. Led by Jeremiah Evarts, the American Board argued against removal on legal and humanitarian grounds. Evarts solicited funds for the Cherokees to hire legal counsel, and most ABCFM missionaries defended their existing missionary establishments and supported a continuation of their educational and religious endeavors. ABCFM officials believed that removal was not a panacea; similar problems would soon arise in the West. The Baptist Board, pushed by the aggressive actions of Isaac McCoy, disagreed. Only the removal of the Indians from the midst of the white population, they insisted, could preserve the tribes and promote their well-being. Finally, there were the Indians themselves. They sent delegations to Washington, they sought support from various parties interested in their cause, but their views were largely irrelevant to the debate on all sides. The federal government, the state of Georgia, missionary groups for and against removal—all spoke for the Indians rather than with them.[33]

Throughout the early winter Evarts labored from his Boston office to rally congressional as well as public opinion. He believed that a prolonged debate favored the tribes and hoped that the Supreme Court would rule in their favor before its likely conclusion in mid-spring. Memorials poured in to Congress, not only from northerners sympathetic to the Indian cause but from the tribes themselves. A Creek memorial caught their argument most succinctly when it noted that state policies would "grind down the hopes and subdue the spirits of the Indians." The issue, Creek memorialists argued, was as much cultural as political sovereignty.[34]

But men like Thomas McKenney in the Office of Indian Affairs had given up. Although he admitted that the public mind "would be composed" if Congress agreed to continue the civilization program after removal, McKenney had undergone a tortured reassessment of his views on Indian removal. His detailed reconsideration in a letter to ABCFM missionary Cyrus Kingsbury is worth delineating at length:

> I appreciate your labors—and have never done else than wished well to them. I once, like you, hoped for complete success. I had not gone through the country of the Southern Indians, I mean those portions of it, through which I passed, before I was compelled to let go the hope to which I had like you, been so long clinging, as wholly delusive. It is as much impossible to redeem the natives *situated as they are*, and elevate their condition, and place

them on a level with ourselves, as it would be for you, or I, to raise the dead.

Those of us who occupy the two sides of this great question have incurred a terrible responsibility. If those who think nothing but a removal can save the Indians, are right, and the present aspect of things looks very much like it, then those who think otherwise, if they succeed in paralizing [sic] the efforts that are making for their removal, and the Indians remain, and perish, as they will, *if they remain*, will have wrought a work, innocently I know, over which they will have occasion long to mourn.[35]

The benevolent community, however, was far from united, and its divisions extended well beyond the differences between Evarts and McCoy. ABCFM missionaries generally supported their parent organization, arguing, in the words of missionary Isaac Proctor, that "Georgia would never extend her laws if she for once thought that the Indians would be able to live under them." But Evarts's efforts to organize public meetings against removal in upstate New York failed to generate support, and Presbyterian clergyman Ezra Stiles Ely, editor of the *Philadelphian*, voiced his support for removal. In an essay on the "preservation and improvement of the Indians," Ely defended the efforts of the missionaries but argued that conditions prevailing among the tribes frustrated their efforts. His solution, however, was not the assertion of law and a revitalization of republican principles. Instead, he insisted that the path to preservation lay with an application of the principles of free enterprise capitalism and the ethic of individualism. Indians' traditional communal hospitality, he said, undercut the spirit of industriousness. His remedy was to "give individual families estates" so that "each man will realize that he labours for himself." He supported the extension of state laws over the tribes because it promised to accelerate this process.[36]

Amid such debates and divisions in the benevolent community, the controversy over Indian removal moved inexorably forward. Officials of the Jackson administration insisted that opposition to removal stemmed either from a few Indian leaders of mixed blood or from the missionary community and their supporters. Men like John Eaton used the language of democracy to assert that power among the tribes was concentrated in the hands of a few, who failed to represent the "Indians at large." Such governance, Eaton insisted, was not deference but "slavery in disguise." More than three thousand Cherokees contradicted this interpretation, however, signing memorials to Congress opposing removal. Although the effectiveness of these memorials is questionable, they disturbed the administration. Secretary of War Eaton investigated the authority of subsequent Indian delegations to Washington, and hereafter the government often purported to deal with "real chiefs" who were usually elsewhere and were frequently pro-removal.[37]

By mid-February, however, the arguments on each side were largely fixed. Proponents of removal argued that the Indians had failed to make any substantial progress toward civilization, that their culture supported a badly skewed inequality which rewarded a few chiefs at the expense of the masses, that tribal claims to political sovereignty were specious in the face of state sovereignty, that the federal government was incapable of preventing white encroachment on Indian lands, and that only removal would prevent their extinction. Anti-removal advocates quarreled with some of these contentions but based most of their arguments on the twin themes of law and morality. The United States, they insisted, needed to observe its own treaties, and federal law took precedence over state laws. In addition, morality and humanity demanded that the federal government protect the tribes from the greed of settlers and speculators alike. Reports from House and Senate committees as well as memorials from citizens throughout the country echoed these arguments time and again.[38]

What remained was the question of tactics. In these years Congress debated a variety of bills simultaneously, voting on them near the end of the session. One effect of this procedure was that divisions over one bill could, if severe, influence voting on subsequent measures. There was also the possibility that momentum on one issue could carry over to other issues, so timing was important. Sen. Theodore Frelinghuysen, a staunch ally of Evarts and defender of benevolent causes, worried about the effect of Foot's resolution on other legislation. He hoped that the public lands question would be resolved before the Indian removal bill came up for a vote. In late February he proposed to Evarts that they wait on both removal and the Sabbath question until this resolution had occurred. Then, if no action seemed imminent, he would call up the subjects by resolution if necessary.[39]

But there was one other factor that bothered anti-removal advocates. In the words of Senator Frelinghuysen, "I fear the spirit of party—If its dreadful influence can be enlisted in the service of Georgia, resistance on the ground of argument will be almost hopeless." This was not a new fear, but the debates in the Twenty-first Congress gave it focus. Jeremiah Evarts had long opposed the emergence of a party spirit, believing that it ballooned small differences into deep divisions that trampled morality and republican virtue. Party loyalty, Evarts insisted, not only threatened to violate individual rights but emasculated individual judgment. Evarts feared that party spirit would offset his appeals to individual conscience and poison the final debates over Indian removal.[40] The *Journal of Commerce* stated the problem clearly: "We protest against the principle that because Gen. Jackson may have expressed an opinion on the policy which ought to be pursued towards the Indians, it must therefore be made a party question: and we do so, both for his own sake, and because in this way the claims of justice and the honor of the country are in danger of being sacrificed on the altar of political devotion."[41]

When Evarts, Frelinghuysen, and others railed against the dangers of a "party spirit," they did not necessarily mean that two organized and structured parties existed. As historians like William Shade, Herbert Ershkowitz, and Ronald Formisano have demonstrated, modern organized national parties did not exist until the late 1830s or 1840s. But, as voting in the Twenty-first Congress would reveal, the outlines of party support were becoming clear even while the formal organizational structures had yet fully to emerge. What was happening, as historian Robert Shalhope has demonstrated, was that "an assemblage of doctrines and ideologies had emerged."[42]

But while Evarts and his colleagues may have been aware of these developments, they were reacting more to perceptions than to organizational structures. To them, "party" meant a corrupting spirit that robbed men of their individual conscience by insisting on adherence to particular principles or ideas whose determination emanated from "party leaders." This spirit acquired strength from the changing nature of American political culture. In the face of greater demographic and geographic complexity, individuals were less able to win election through personal appeals to the electorate by themselves or a few well-placed friends. Organizational structures, primitive though they were, emerged to become part of the electoral machinery. With that, Evarts feared, men would be elected on the strength of their organization rather than on the power and virtue of their ideas and program. Slogans and campaigns would sway voters rather than morality or Christian republicanism. Public virtue would deteriorate; the scramble for office would push aside individual conscience and tarnish republican virtue.[43]

Whether or not the increasing rhetoric about the rise of party spirit reflected reality is not terribly important for an understanding of the debates in the first Jacksonian Congress. What is certain is that men like Evarts *believed* that partisan motives were at work and acted accordingly. This belief, ironically, gave Evarts hope; for if support for removal could be attributed to party influence among Jacksonians, then individual conviction about removal must remain shallow and subject to change if one could nullify the arguments for party loyalty. From this perspective, Jacksonian political power was more apparent than real. Such an understanding also opened the way for an appeal to conscience and morality. Moreover, if the Second Great Awakening had truly revitalized American society, then its members should be susceptible to such an appeal. Perhaps this was the darkness before the dawn. At the same time, of course, quite the opposite could be true. Should Evarts's appeals be unsuccessful, then revitalization had been limited, and the future looked bleak. These alternative explanations made the fight against Indian removal, at least for Evarts, a struggle whose importance reached well beyond the well-being of a few tribes. It was, for him, a struggle for the soul of America.

An essay in the *Spirit of the Pilgrims* critiquing Lewis Cass's earlier advocacy of removal outlined these sentiments. Blaming most of the Indians' problems on rapacious white settlers and attacking Jackson's proposals for removal, the author argued that the "experiments" of Indian missions hoped to overcome these problems. "They have cherished a strong hope, that the period was at hand, when a part at least of the debt which Americans owe to this much abused people, would be honorably cancelled. But a portentous storm has of late been gathering; and unless God avert the omen, the bolts of desolation seem to be inevitable. A CRISIS now exists, which demands the most serious attention of every patriot and Christian in America."[44] Even proponents of removal within the religious and benevolent community feared the power of this appeal. Groups like the Baptists encouraged a Christian republicanism similar to that advocated by Evarts but also spoke out in favor of removal. Lucius Bolles, corresponding secretary of the Baptist Board of Foreign Missions and a close friend of Evarts, outlined the difficulty in a printed circular favoring removal. "It is to be remembered, too, that large and powerful bodies of Christians are petitioning Congress against the removal of the Indians. This made it the more necessary to be cautious, lest our Memorial should furnish occasion for placing our denomination in array against other Christians, on a question of the utmost importance, whether viewed as a measure of Christian benevolence, or of national policy."[45]

Charges that the Indian Removal Bill had become the target for partisan political attacks and maneuvering were not restricted to the benevolent community. Defenders of Jackson's position attacked their opponents in similar language. The *United States' Telegraph* editorialized against "the *political* philanthropists who oppose this administration!" Other supporters of the administration attacked what one writer called "the politico-ecclesiastical co-alition" that opposed removal. From Georgia, Gov. George Gilmer wrote Sen. Hugh White that he considered it "improbable that our laws can be exercised without acts of violence." The problem, according to Gilmer, was twofold. First, those Indians most able to understand civil government were the most active opponents of state jurisdiction. Second, their actions, "together with the constant abuse which has been poured upon the State & its people by the opposition to the present administration under the guise of sympathy for the Indians, will draw upon them the most rigid enforcement of our laws."[46]

In the face of persistent administration efforts to effect removal, Jeremiah Evarts focused his tactics more sharply. He had been struggling to mobilize public opinion for some time, and the numerous memorials opposing removal that flooded Congress bear testimony to his success, but now he shifted his attention almost exclusively to men of influence and power. It was a tacit admission (as *Niles' Weekly Register* observed) that the struggle now began and ended with power. George Cheever's circular, prepared at Evarts's request, went into the mails. Arguing that "A CRISIS of fearful importance is at hand," the circular broadcast a warning that action was imminent. Its language strained at the boundaries of propriety, for as Cheever admitted to Evarts "it was very difficult to put sufficient force and spirit into it, and yet avoid all appearance of every thing intemperate." Evarts, meanwhile, stepped up his visits to men like Daniel Webster and Edward Everett in the hope that influence would outweigh numbers when Congress opened its final debates. He also solicited letters from ABCFM missionaries among the Cherokees to document Indian progress and offset statements to the contrary from men like Ezra Stiles Ely and from administration officials. But clearly Evarts was on the defensive. Finally, feeling his cause slipping away, at the end of March he left Boston for Washington.[47]

When he arrived in Washington on April third, Jeremiah Evarts found few indicators favorable to his cause. Pro-removal Congressmen dominated the committees on Indian affairs in both the House and Senate. Both committees had issued elaborate reports sustaining the administration's position. Proponents of removal literally bubbled with enthusiasm. In the words of one committee chairman: "Sir, we have *succeeded* in making the Indian subject a party measure. There may be some chicken-hearted fellows at the North, who will not stand by the party; but we shall carry the measure in both Houses; and in the lower House, by a majority of perhaps seventeen or twenty."[48]

Debate on the Indian Bill opened on April sixth, only three days after Evarts's arrival. This gave him little time to prepare the opposition and forced him to divide his time during the month between the congressional galleries where he could monitor the proceedings and congressional offices where he could rally opposition and court allies. At the same time, he had to find time to keep in touch with various ABCFM missionaries in the field as well as initiate and respond to requests for articles on the issue to be published in various journals. Furor still raged in some circles over the publication of Lewis Cass's article "Removal of the Indians" in the *North American Review*. Just as Evarts arrived in Washington, moreover, editorial control of the *Review* passed from Jared Sparks to Alexander Hill Everett. Everett, partly at the urging of his brother Edward and partly on his own account, courted Evarts for an essay that would make clear to the public not only the issues involved but the position of the *Review* in opposition to removal.[49]

At the moment, however, more pressing concerns dominated Evarts's consciousness. The journal he kept in Washington, coupled with a reading of the congressional debates, reveal a man at the center of a political storm—a missionary concerned with the nation's moral consciousness who was trying to leash politically volatile forces that he believed sought to shape and erode that consciousness. While Thomas McKenney and John Eaton quibbled over the geography of the western country and the cost per capita for removal (six cents per day per Indian), Evarts tried to convince congressmen that morality rather than money lay at the heart of the issue. He also had to offset the lobbying efforts of the Baptists, for Isaac McCoy arrived in Washington one day after the debates began. The two men met frequently but never reconciled their views. As McCoy later wrote: "Our interviews were always friendly, but each employed what strength he possessed in opposite directions." Even McCoy later admitted that Evarts's efforts were superb and lamented that advocates of removal agitated the matter "chiefly for the purpose of attaining other ends than the welfare of the Indians."[50]

Evarts not only reported the content of speeches made on the floor of

Congress in his journal; he also characterized the reaction of the various parties to them. The Indians' defense was led in the Senate by Sen. Theodore Frelinghuysen of New Jersey. A close friend of Evarts and steadfast supporter of benevolent causes, Frelinghuysen sought to have the Senate protect the tribes where they were until *they* decided to remove and to encompass any agreements for removal or land sales within the protection of treaty rights. His speech clearly reflected the influence and efforts of Evarts; indeed, Evarts may have written much of it. Scattered throughout his remarks were quotations from War Department correspondence that demonstrated the all-consuming efforts to remove the tribes by any means as well as references to various treaty obligations that these efforts violated. Perhaps more disturbing to southern proponents of removal, however, was Frelinghuysen's assertion that the 1802 Compact with Georgia, the compact so frequently cited by state officials in their effort to compel removal, required all lands west of the current state boundaries to be admitted to the union under the Ordinance of 1787. This meant, he reminded listeners, that slavery would be prohibited. In addition, those states were not to encroach on Indian lands except in time of war. "Do the obligations of justice," he asked, "change with the color of the skin?"[51]

Evarts reported that Georgia senator Forsyth "appeared much troubled" as he listened to Frelinghuysen. Senator Troup, former governor of Georgia, "obviously changed color, becoming quite pale." Although colleagues like Daniel Webster did not believe the speeches would change any votes, Evarts had Frelinghuysen's speech reprinted immediately and circulated throughout the country. If Webster was right and he could not influence the Senate, then perhaps he could change some votes in the House. In fact, immediately following this speech, Evarts spent some time counting heads (and votes) in the House and Senate. He concluded that most if not all the Jacksonians would support the administration in the Senate but there would be many desertions in the House. "Indeed," wrote Evarts, "there was never a question better fitted to break up the party than this, if it could only be brought forward under favorable auspices; that is soon, & before the measure shall have passed the Senate." But efforts to bring the bill to the floor failed. Evarts feared that it would surface at the end of the session for a quick vote, when the moral effect would then be lost.[52]

The best chance to defeat the Indian Bill, Evarts believed, was to have Congress launch a full and open debate that would force representatives to take a public position and would allow anti-removal forces to put his "William Penn" arguments before the Congress. In the words of Senator Frelinghuysen: "I prefer that this latent object should be put fully before us, that we and the nation may look at it, and freely scrutinize it." To encourage such an effort, and to gather additional ammunition for anti-removal forces to use in the debate, Evarts relentlessly made the rounds in Washington, visiting friend and foe alike. He spent some time with Thomas McKenney, much to the latter's embarrassment, and engaged in long discussions with men like John Bell of the Indian Affairs Committee. Discussions such as these revealed to Evarts that Pres. Andrew Jackson was the real stumbling block to success. Bell admitted as much, when he told Evarts that although he believed the Cherokees to be right, "it is not in the power of man to defend them." Evarts vehemently disagreed, asserting that strong presidential statements in defense of treaty rights would be effective. "Is the world to be told," he asked, "that we cannot enforce our laws, and cannot fulfill our most solemn engagements?"[53]

Suffering from a bad cough, Evarts labored through the abnormally cold Washington weather to focus congressional attention on morality rather than politics. Acrimonious Senate debates over patronage matters, however, stalled his efforts. While he rejoiced that the Senate rejected the appointment of New Hampshire editor Isaac Hill to office ("solely on account of his having conducted a lying, prostituted press"), he feared that such debates would excite party feelings. An agreement with the Choctaws for their removal also upset him, for he hoped that if Congress failed to stop removal then the courts would. He had already convinced the Cherokees to appeal to the Supreme Court and had informally presented their case to various justices in his Washington travels. In a letter to missionary Cyrus Kingsbury, he advised the Choctaws to delay removal and place their hopes in a favorable court decision as well. "There cannot be the least doubt that the Court would pronounce the laws of Georgia, Mississippi, and Alabama unconstitutional; and these tribes would have preserved the lands of their fathers; but if they remove, it is impossible that they should ever again have a good title to their lands."[54]

Evarts's tactics were clear. He planned to organize a phalanx of friendly congressmen to present the case against removal on the floor of the House and Senate, hoping to convince enough Jacksonians that the immorality of removal required them to vote against the Indian Removal Bill. At the same time, he would continue to barrage the public with letters, pamphlets, and articles on the Indian question, along with whatever other information might create a groundswell of public opinion against removal. Notwithstanding these efforts, however, Evarts was enough of a realist to understand that they might fail. He recognized the existence of powerful political factions and arguments in favor of removal and knew that Andrew Jackson's leadership of the pro-removal forces would be difficult to counteract. This conviction led him to place his trust in the Supreme Court. Believing that a majority of the justices shared his humanitarian consciousness and worldview and that they would recognize the coincidence of law and morality on the side of the Indians, Evarts felt secure that an appeal to the court would be successful. Even as the battle with the Congress and the president was joined, therefore, he planned a final thrust to provide victory if all else failed.

But in mid-April, Evarts still hoped to defeat the Indian Bill in Congress. Men like Edward Everett, who had long opposed forced removal but had said little in public about it, sought him for information useful in the debates. Evarts needed this support, for advocates of the bill attacked not only its opponents but missionary organizations like the American Board of Commissioners, claiming that these groups controlled Cherokee affairs. They were less interested in civilization, Georgian John Forsyth charged, than in maintaining their "comfortable settlements" and influence among the tribes. Preservation of tribal identity was a mistake, Forsyth argued, because the missionaries' efforts at civilization had failed. "I do not believe that this removal will accelerate the civilization of the tribes. You might as reasonably expect that wild animals, incapable of being tamed in a park, would be domesticated by turning them loose in the forest. This desirable end cannot be obtained without destroying the tribal character, and subjecting the Indians, as individuals, to the regular action of well digested laws. Wild nature never was yet tamed but by coercive discipline."[55]

Although he admitted to his journal that the "administration party calculate on carrying the measure [in the Senate] with great confidence; and they probably know their men better than I do," Evarts nonetheless rallied the opposition. Senators such as Peleg Sprague of Maine relied heavily on Evarts's writings, as they traced a history of the treaties with various tribes and demonstrated that Georgia's assertion of right stemmed from a change of attitude on her part and did not rest on any treaty obligations. Throughout their remarks they returned time and again to the theme that any removal or change in Indian relations must be voluntary and not violent. Peleg Sprague summarized the message:

"It is said that their existence cannot be preserved; that it is the doom of Providence, that they must perish. So, indeed, must we all; but let it be in the course of nature; not by the hand of violence. If, in truth, they are now in the decrepitude of age, let us permit them to live out all their days, and die in peace; not bring down their gray hairs in blood to a foreign grave."[56]

Despite the efforts of Frelinghuysen, Sprague, and others, only ten days after the Senate opened debate Evarts knew that the Cherokee cause was lost in that body. Various amendments to the removal bill surfaced, but all failed. Near the end of April Frelinghuysen confided to Evarts that three influences had been particularly influential in the debates: the "William Penn" essays, the support of the president for southern interests, and the "effort to preserve the integrity of the Jackson party." In his journal Evarts lamented both the willingness of public officials to vote according to the prejudices of their constituents and the emergence of party feeling: "Now what can we do, when men will act in this manner? The question is already as plain in the Senate as any question of human conduct can possibly be. Not one question of theft, robbery or murder in ten thousand is so perfectly free from all doubt, or cavil; not one bond in ten thousand, that are collected or enforced by courts of justice, is so perfectly clear of all dispute; and yet it is expected that men will vote by platoons, in regular rank & file, according to party drilling, on this question of public faith. I have never before seen exactly such a commentary on human depravity."[57] He was outraged that a question of national honor and humanity had become a partisan issue. The country seemed to have lost its moral bearings.

Jeremiah Evarts now turned to the House of Representatives. The removal bill had not yet come up for debate there when the Senate bill arrived in late April. John Bell of the Indian Affairs Committee agreed to place the Senate bill rather than his own bill before the House. Debate began in mid-May. Evarts's hopes in the House rested on faith as well as politics. He believed the House to be more broadly representative of public opinion and thereby more sensitive to the humanitarian sentiments that had emerged from the Second Great Awakening. Yet at the same time, deep in despair over the Senate vote favoring removal, he lamented "how tame and timid, and how vacillating and inconstant—how yielding and compromising—nine tenths of even the religious people are on all political questions which involve moral and religious considerations." The political situation gave him some hope. Close attention to meetings, dinners, and other events convinced him that "the Jackson party in the House is about crumbling to pieces." How ironic! Political action might succeed where moral suasion had failed. The revitalization efforts of the awakening had failed to temper self-interest. Was political virtue now to consist in balancing various self-interest groups to prevent tyranny rather than in inculcating republican virtue in the citizenry at large?[58]

In early May, however, Evarts confided to his journal that a small majority appeared to support removal. He was uncertain that a protest against the Senate removal bill drafted by Edward Everett would change many votes. Pro-administration newspapers, led by the *United States Telegraph*, editorialized for the bill's passage and attacked opponents as "political philanthropists" more interested in opposing the administration than in opposing removal. Gov. George Gilmer of Georgia kept in close touch with a fellow Georgian, Attorney General John Berrien, about the state's claims and the support it might expect from the administration. Discouraged by the size of the Senate majority, Evarts also became distressed at the growing partisanship evident in the Congress. He failed to see that his own efforts had stimulated much of that spirit. At the same time, it became increasingly evident that his best hope to defeat the removal bill lay in the pursuit of that self-interest he lamented. *Niles' Weekly Register* summarized the situation most succinctly: "The lines between parties are evidently *tightening*. There are *many* parties in congress. We cannot predict the *shape* that any will assume hereafter—or how far *oppositions* will extend, or be swallowed up, in particular calculations."[59]

House debate on the Indian Removal Bill opened on May 13, 1830, and Evarts threw himself into the fray. As in the Senate debates, attention focused on the historic rights of the tribes, government efforts to negotiate treaties with them, international law, the doctrine of discovery, and other legal points to prove that Georgia was either justified or unjustified in extending her laws over the Cherokees and that removal was the only option remaining to save the Indians from extinction. But, almost from the outset, other themes emerged that changed the shape of the debate and influenced the outcome. Two such themes that stood out emphasized the nature of the Union and the question of self-interest.

Discussion about the nature of the Union surfaced in a rather oblique manner. Division, secession, nullification—words that had marked the past and would soon emerge again—found little currency except among the administration press which reprinted excerpts from the Hartford Convention throughout the debates. Debate over the nature of the Union in 1830 focused partially on the government's treaty obligations but more centrally on the role of the executive in our system of government. Henry Storrs of Connecticut, the only northerner on the Indian Affairs Committee, attacked Andrew Jackson's use of executive power. Storrs blamed Jackson for helping create the problems before the Congress, attacking his behavior as president as a stain on the national honor.

> I have been a party man, sir, perhaps too much so—and I have contributed nothing to place the present Chief Magistrate in the station which he now holds—as yet under the constitution and not above it. But I should deem it a lesser evil and a more supportable calamity—and I declare to you that I had rather see him or any other man created dictator at once, and let him sway our destinies, for one life at least, than suffer for a single hour the shame of feeling that my country must submit before the christian world to the disgrace of being set down in history as the violator of her treaties, and the oppressor of this helpless people who have trusted so confidently to her faith.[60]

Anti-removal forces had heretofore avoided direct attacks on Jackson, but now Storrs led an assault on the president's misuse of executive power—setting out a theme that increasingly characterized opposition attacks for the remainder of the Jackson presidency. "The States may destroy the Union themselves by open force," Storrs admonished his colleagues, "but the concentration of power in the hands of the Executive leads to despotism, which is worse."[61]

The second theme was that of self-interest. Storrs charged that Georgia, Alabama, and Mississippi adopted their position not because they truly believed it was right but to secure "benefits which they expect to attain to themselves by the removal of the Indians." Such a charge was not really new, of course, but most previous attacks on southern state policies toward the tribes had emphasized the sanctity of treaties and broad national considerations. They had sidestepped insofar as possible the narrow pursuit of self-interest. The arrival of the Jackson administration appeared to have changed that, for the policies of that administration seemed to herald a new boundlessness. Previously defined boundaries—political, social, economic, even moral—threatened to disappear with the liberalization of American culture. Critics of this change charged that *power* was now in the driver's seat, supplanting that Christian republicanism they had cherished and upon which they believed the nation rested.[62]

Wilson Lumpkin of Georgia gave further evidence of this change when he attacked the "christian party in politics" during the debates. Lumpkin singled out "William Penn" in particular, charging that "Penn" advocated a civil war if necessary to block the Indians' removal. Men like Evarts, Lumpkin told his congressional colleagues, condemned everyone who "will not unite with them in all their machinery of societies and schemes for governing public opinion." Their speeches and essays, Lumpkin insisted, "have much more of the character of the politician and lawyer than that of an humble missionary." They were intended to deceive the public and sought to generate the very party feelings they pretended to oppose. Proponents of removal were, in his words, mere "canting fanatics," "the boasted progeny of the pilgrims and puritans," who sought to condemn all who disagreed with them as un-Christian. Such phony philanthropists misled the Indians and advocated policies that guaranteed their destruction. Despite what New Englanders seemed to believe, Lumpkin concluded, the Indians and not the Georgians were the irreligious savages in this affair.[63]

Although Lumpkin sought to disclaim any personal intent, this assault was an unprecedented and sweeping attack on the missionary community and on Jeremiah Evarts in particular. It was an attack that reflected more than opposition to a course of action or a political opponent; it was an attack apparently motivated by fear. What was there to fear? Did not Georgia have the support of the president and the votes of the Jacksonian majority in Congress? Clearly Lumpkin lacked confidence in that political majority. And well he might have worried, for the House debates quickly lost the circumspect character that had marked Senate passage of the bill. Discussions about the avaricious pursuit of self-interest by the southern states soon turned to charges of bribery, speculation, and corruption. Despite the assurances of men like Lumpkin that removal was the most humanitarian course of action, mercenary motives rather than humanitarian sensibilities seemed to lie at the heart of the matter.[64]

As the debates strayed from a narrow view of federal treaties and Indian rights, the position outlined by Georgia and her supporters became more problematic to other congressmen. Particularly disturbing was the determination of Georgia to go her own way regardless of the bill's fate. Lumpkin had hinted at this when he warned that "things can no longer remain in their present state." Action was needed. But Thomas Foster of Georgia sharpened the picture when he announced that Georgia would not be restrained in the exercise of her rights "by the arm of the

General Government." These were not idle threats, for public sentiment in the state had become feverish in its lust for Indian lands. Even the immoderate language of the House debate was insufficient to accommodate this greed, and men like James Wayne found it prudent to add even more vituperative paragraphs to their speeches when they were printed for distribution in Georgia. All this agitation did, of course, was further to excite the populace. To counter it, the Cherokees played a waiting game. As Samuel Worcester told Evarts: "[Mr. Ross] thinks that, in spite of Georgia laws, the Cherokees can outlive here the administration of Gen. Jackson and then, that times will change."[65]

Rep. George Evans of Maine tried to redirect the debate back to the issue of benevolence and humanitarianism, and in the process he defended Evarts from Lumpkin's attacks. "I know him [Evarts]," Evans replied, "only as possessing a reputation for intelligence, philanthropy, benevolence and untiring zeal in the promotion of human happiness, which any one upon this floor might be proud to possess." More to the point, Evans reminded his colleagues that the government itself had asked missionary societies and men like Evarts for their help in formulating their Indian program. Other speakers noted that the government already had more lands than it could sell and that only four years earlier John Eaton himself had defended tribal sovereignty. But it was Evans who focused on the humanitarian implications that seemed so bothersome.

> And, sir, how are they to be removed? The only project I have seen is that contained in the "report from the bureau of Indian Affairs" to the Secretary of War, and by him transmitted to Congress. The proposition is, that they shall be removed "by contract"—and the recommendation of this plan is, that it can be done much cheaper than in any other mode. By contract, sir! What, are sixty thousand human beings—the sick, the aged, the infirm, children, and infants—to be transported hundreds of miles, over mountains and rivers and forests, by contract! By those who will engage to perform the service for the smallest sum!

Such a plan, Edward Everett added, was only a money-making proposition that would destroy many Indians along the way.[66]

But perhaps the most revealing comments came from Richard Wilde of Georgia, comments that exposed the changing cultural and political paradigm that confronted Jeremiah Evarts and the benevolent community. "The earth was given for labor," Wilde asserted, "and to labor it belongs. The gift was not to the red, or to the white, but to the human race—and the inscription was to the wisest—the bravest—to virtue—and to industry." According to this prescription, and in keeping with the spirit of liberal capitalism, industriousness had supplanted virtue as the essence of the American spirit. Society still treasured virtue, but industriousness itself became a measure of virtue regardless of the purposes to which it was applied. Work, labor, the calling—all had long been ingrained in the American spirit; but virtue had been at its soul. Now the "doing" seemed more important than the spirit or purpose behind it. Finally, Wilde went one step further in the direction of liberal capitalism, insisting that "separate property in land is the basis of civilized society."[67]

Throughout the debates in the House only members of the Georgia delegation spoke at length for the Indian Removal Bill. Indeed, few other southerners aside from John Bell and David Crockett of Tennessee spoke at all. Bell, who chaired the House Indian Affairs Committee, introduced the bill and argued for it but then stepped aside for the Georgians' assault. Crockett followed his conscience and broke with the Tennessee Democratic Party to oppose the bill. This opposition led to his defeat at the next election, but four years later he returned to Congress and introduced a bill to remove all whites from eastern Tennessee to lands beyond the Mississippi so as not to impede Georgians' lust for land. Representatives from a variety of states, on the other hand, were outspoken in their opposition to removal. The matter became a heated political issue not only in New England states like Massachusetts and Connecticut but in Indiana, Illinois, Ohio, New York, and Pennsylvania. Even areas that favored removal, indeed that practiced it on their own lands, worried about the costs of a fair removal and the administration's plans simultaneously to force removal and cut costs. What united many of these states was often not so much a broad humanitarianism but a fear that heavy federal expenses for Indian removal would frustrate their plans to secure internal improvement monies from the Congress.[68]

As the House prepared to vote in late May, uncertainty over the fate of the removal bill heightened. Joseph Hemphill of Pennsylvania sought to postpone final action, arguing that the country was not yet ready for definitive action. Too much of the country remained silent because the issue had come to a head so quickly, and that silence, he warned, was "a solemn warning that we ought to act with the greatest caution and circumspection." Daniel Webster, on the other hand, believed that the administration had only recently begun to show its true colors on a variety of issues, including Indian removal. What sustained Webster was the mounting evidence that Jackson opposed internal improvements. His supporters in the Senate had killed a Baltimore railroad bill, and Webster expected Jackson to veto the Maysville Turnpike Bill. He was convinced that these actions would drive a wedge between Jacksonians in states like Ohio and Pennsylvania and the administration. Webster hoped that "the conduct of the President & his friends, on these two measures, should be the means, with Heaven's blessing, of preventing the passage of the Indian Bill."[69]

For almost a week the House struggled to bring the Indian Bill to a vote. On May 24 it refused, ninety-nine to ninety-three. Joseph Hemphill offered an amendment to clarify whether tribes of individual Indians would be paid for improvements. The bill stipulated that individuals would receive payment for any improvements they relinquished upon removal, and Hemphill feared that this opened the way for government to pressure individuals when tribes refused to remove. His substitute bill nearly succeeded; Speaker Andrew Stevenson of Virginia had to cast his vote to break a ninety-eight to ninety-eight tie. Throughout the day maneuvering on the bill was intense, especially by its opponents. After numerous attempts to table the measure, a series of quorum calls, and efforts at adjournment, the House finally voted to consider the bill for a third reading. That effort again produced a deadlock, ninety-nine to ninety-nine, and the Speaker had to cast the deciding vote. After Stevenson voted in the affirmative, the House approved a third reading of the removal bill by a one hundred two to ninety-seven margin. Exhausted, the members then adjourned for the day.

The next two days witnessed continued close maneuvering by partisans on both sides. Further attempts to amend the bill and make removal entirely voluntary or to recommit the bill to the committee of the whole House on the state of the union failed. Efforts to adjourn also failed, and as deliberations on May 25 drew to a close, the House struggled to find a majority to support a final consideration of the measure. A motion to put the previous question (to consider the bill) once again ended with the Speaker breaking a deadlocked House. With this out of the way, the House voted ninety-nine to ninety-eight to bring the Indian Bill to a vote. The next day, May 26, 1830, the Indian Removal Bill passed the House by a margin of one hundred two to ninety-seven. The battle was over.[70]

CHAPTER NINE

The Aftermath

※

Passage of the Indian Removal Bill in May 1830 dashed Jeremiah Evarts's cherished hopes that justice and morality would triumph over political considerations, but it did not end his struggle to implant a Christian republicanism at the center of American life and mores. Two weeks before the vote, Evarts had written in his journal: "As to the issue of the Indian question, I have this only ground of hope left, that God will not leave us as a people to such guilt and infatuation as would be involved in the success of the bill from the Senate. On any calculation of numbers and probabilities, made without reference to what God will do, I cannot sustain a hope that the bill will be defeated. And our views of what God will do, are very dim and short-sighted."[1] Evarts hoped that the bill's passage represented a moment of partisan politics, not the beginning of a movement that would trample national honor. He continued to believe that republican virtue could temper Americans' growing inclination to seize the main chance whatever the moral consequences.

At first glance, the political struggle over removal gave Evarts little comfort. Voting patterns in the House revealed the emergence of a Jacksonian phalanx based on political philosophy and self-interest. The chief support for removal, not surprisingly, came from the South and West. Opposition coalesced in the Northeast and Middle Atlantic states. But just as Evarts and others had charged during the debates, partisan considerations often superseded sectional alignments. New Hampshire representatives, for instance, contradicted the New England opposition to removal and voted unanimously for the bill. Such clusters of votes gave evidence of a Jacksonian coalition, a coalition whose foundation lay in the South and West. Representatives from South Carolina, Georgia, Alabama, Mississippi, and Missouri voted without dissent to endorse Jackson's position. There, self-interest and partisanship coincided; Indian removal was a vital precondition for continued geographic expansion and economic development. Other Southern delegations from Virginia, Maryland, Kentucky, and Tennessee also supported removal.

Elsewhere the pattern was more confusing or, from the Jacksonian perspective, more troubling. Delegations from Indiana, Illinois, Ohio, New York, and Pennsylvania split their votes. Despite the influence of Martin Van Buren, for example, the thirty-four member New York delegation gave but a one vote plurality for removal. Although predominantly Jacksonian by political inclination, these delegations found other factors more compelling. Many of these states had largely removed tribes from within their boundaries and now opposed further federal expenditures for removal. They favored instead internal improvements to develop their regions through the construction of roads and canals or supported the graduation of land prices to encourage settlement. Both promised to promote economic growth, but both were also expensive. Funding Indian removal under a president who supported retrenchment would necessarily curtail these other projects. These were also regions in which the benevolent crusade had found support during the past decade or more, and towns and societies throughout these states participated fully in the anti-removal petition drive to Congress. For men like Jeremiah Evarts such developments left some hope that moral concerns could still mediate self-interest or partisan motives. To his mind, the struggle for the soul of America was not over.[2]

To a large extent, however, that struggle now seemed increasingly dependent on those very partisan and sectional interests Evarts had just condemned. The day after the House passed the Indian Removal Bill, Andrew Jackson vetoed the Maysville Road Bill. The veto shocked representatives from states like Pennsylvania, states which had elected Jacksonians but which also warmly embraced internal improvements. They were shocked not only at the presidential veto but because they believed they had been betrayed. Jacksonian proponents of Indian removal, when they realized how close the House vote would be, had appealed for support from Pennsylvanians and other northerners by promising to accept internal improvements in return for support on Indian removal. Now, in the name of economy and states' rights, they were denied. "The President kindly tells us," observed an editorial in the *Kentucky Reporter*, "that the time *may* come when he can spare a little from the Treasury for Roads and Canals, but not now. Georgia must first be indulged." The timing, of course, was deliberate. Jackson knew what effect a veto would have. As Evarts noted in his journal, an earlier veto would have changed at least ten votes and meant the defeat of Indian removal. Edward Everett agreed, observing that the "veto of the president in the Maysville road bill will cost him, I think, all Ohio & the other N.W. States & finish the destruction of his party in Kentucky."[3]

It was too late to reverse the vote on removal but perhaps not too late to ameliorate the effect of that vote. Evarts hoped to rally the benevolent community yet again, emphasizing the need for a moral ethos to undergird the web of party politics. In an editorial lamenting passage of the removal bill, the *Christian Advocate* gave voice to similar sentiments: "If it shall be such as we fear, the iniquity of this single transaction will overshadow, as with one broad cloud of deepest darkness, the whole lustre of our national glory. We are free citizens of a free country, and on this subject we will speak freely. Into mere party politicks we have never dipped our editorial pen, and we never will. But no fear of being charged with meddling in party politicks, shall make us forget or forego our duty and character as a *Christian Advocate*."[4] From New England the *Missionary Herald* echoed these sentiments and urged its readers to remember the sacrifices of the revolutionary generation. In rhetoric that seemed to sound the clarion call of a new campaign, the *Herald* reminded readers that "Then, it was *a whole people* that rose, like one man, to their work. They breathed united strength. They achieved what they undertook, because, under the blessing of God, they *undertook it on principle; with concentrated effort; and with extensive and harmonious co-operation*."[5]

In early June 1830 Jeremiah Evarts left Washington to return to Boston. On his way he stopped in New York City, meeting with anti-removal advocates to plan a new petition campaign. Back in Boston, he edited a volume of speeches on the Indian Bill. He also prepared a history of the Indian Bill, published in seven installments in the *New York Observer*, wrote an article for the *North American Review*, and prepared other articles under the signature of "William Penn" on Americans' duties toward the Indians. But public opinion in the North had become quiescent on Indian affairs, apparently believing that the cause had been lost to partisan politics. Evarts undertook to reverse that feeling and to revitalize the benevolent spirit; indeed, he seized on portions of the congressional debates to make his point: "Now, we are sluggish, incautious, confident in the success of our republic, and easy as to the operations of government. . . . the mass of the community are absolutely ignorant what is their character in the light of republican principles." Generations had changed, and Evarts charged that popular familiarity with and sensitivity to governmental measures had dimmed. There is, in fact, little evidence that he was correct. More central was a prevailing concern for secular affairs and the divorce of the secular from religion and morality.[6]

Evarts was not so distressed at political divisions (which, after all, were not new) as he was at the apparent subversion of republican principles. Parties appeared to be emerging as engines for governance rather than as rallying points for political dissidence. This would give them an institutional permanence to which individuals would pledge their loyalty, a loyalty that Evarts believed should be attached to particular principles instead. The difference between the two understandings can best be underscored by two commentaries on politics, character, and principles. In 1830, Joel Hawes warned that Christians "are solemnly bound to commit themselves to the dictation of no party, but with an enlightened conscience, and in the fear of God, always to withhold their support from bad men of every name, and to give their votes in favor of such as are best qualified for the duties of office, to whatever denomination or party they belong." Thirteen years later, Henry Ward Beecher characterized individual behavior in a markedly different manner: "All the requisitions of his conscience he obeys in his private character; all the requisitions of his party, he obeys in his political conduct. In one character he is a man of principle; in the other, a man of mere expedients. As a *man* he means to be veracious, honest, moral; as a *politician*, he is deceitful, cunning, unscrupulous,——*anything* for party." Jeremiah Evarts firmly believed that passage of the Indian Removal Bill presaged the future, and he resolutely refused to give up without a struggle. To him, the private and public character should be as one.[7]

In early June, however, Evarts faced much more pressing and immediate problems. First, encouraged by passage of the removal bill and angered by ABCFM opposition to that measure, the Jackson administration terminated funding for several of the American Board's mission stations. In a letter to Georgia governor Gilmer, Secretary of War John Eaton had asked that Georgia restrain settlers on Indian lands because, with passage of the removal bill, he was convinced that the tribes would quickly see immediate removal as in their best interests. He also wrote Indian agents to warn them that a "crisis in Indian Affairs is at hand." But since the removal bill had passed, what was that crisis? It was a marked change in government policy. Hereafter, Eaton wrote, there would be no more partial removals. In addition, the administration decided to shift all monies in the Indian Civilization Fund to missions west of the Mississippi. Eaton hoped that this move would reduce missionary opposition to removal as well as discourage the tribes from remaining on their lands. This decision cost the American Board more than one-half of all monies it received from that fund and placed it in a financial bind. Further to emphasize its commitment to proponents of removal, the War Department extended patronage to Isaac McCoy as a reward for his pro-removal lobbying.[8]

The second matter that seized Evarts's attention was the Cherokees' decision to appeal their case to the United States Supreme Court. They retained William Wirt as their counsel, and Wirt immediately wrote to Governor Gilmer to announce their intent and ask for his understanding. Aware of the excitement over Cherokee lands among Georgians, he sought to defuse their reaction to the Cherokee case. While Wirt made clear to Gilmer that he disagreed with Georgia's interpretation of the law, he also sought a calm and rational solution to the crisis. "We may be wrong," he wrote, "and as infallibility is not the lot of mortals, those who hold the opposite opinion may possibly be wrong." He insisted that the Supreme Court was both rational and impartial and should be able to settle the matter. Wirt repudiated violence and assured Gilmer that the Cherokees shared this conviction. He concluded by asking for Gilmer's support in making a case so as to settle the matter quickly.[9]

Wirt might have considered the Supreme Court neutral, but Chief Justice John Marshall's correspondence reveals that he was not disinterested. During congressional debates over the removal bill, Marshall had met at least once with Jeremiah Evarts. While Evarts maintained that discussion of Marshall's opinion on removal would have been improper, the meeting nonetheless acquainted Marshall with the views of the measure's chief opponent. Then, following the bill's passage, he wrote Edward Everett to thank him for a copy of his speech against removal. In the process, the chief justice revealed his sympathies.

> The speeches with which I have been favored, which are indeed all on one side, abound in arguments which appear to me to be valid and conclusive, and which do very great honour to the heads and hearts of those who made them. You have brought into more open view than any other whose speech I have seen an idea which always appeared to me to be of the first importance and to be peculiarly appropriate. It is the cooperation which exists between

the acts extending state legislation over the Indians and this bill for their removal. You have shown, what is certainly true, that they are part of the same system, and that Congress completes the coercive measures begun by the states.

It has been to me matter of the greatest astonishment that, after hearing the arguments in both houses, Congress could pass the bill.[10]

Of these two developments, Evarts was immediately concerned with the future of the American Board's southern missions. Eaton's order had cut off all federal funds to southern Indians east of the Mississippi. This placed the board's missions and schools among the Cherokees, Choctaws, and Chickasaws in jeopardy. The decision to suspend federal enrollment of individual emigrants was an additional threat, for, together with southern states' renewed efforts to extend and enforce their laws over the tribes, it increased pressure on the tribes to remove. An announcement that the president himself would meet in August with the Cherokee chiefs, but *only* if they wished to remove, tightened the coercive net and joined the two developments. From Boston, Evarts responded to missionary Samuel Worcester's request that he review the course of action that the missionaries in Georgia might take by urging Worcester to dissuade the Indians from selling their lands and to keep them peaceful until the Supreme Court could defend their rights. At the same time, he kept in touch with prominent congressmen about the changes taking place in the board's Indian affairs.[11]

Evarts also wrote William Wirt about his intent to represent the Cherokees before the Supreme Court. He had previously talked with Wirt when he passed through Baltimore on his journey from Washington to Boston. Both men agreed that the case should not come as a surprise either to Georgia or to Jackson, and Evarts had endorsed the effort to have the highest court hear the matter. Now he offered his own advice about the nature of Indian rights and future legal action. Mixing his training as a lawyer with his humanitarian impulses, Evarts admitted that the Indians were not citizens of the United States. They were aliens, but *were* citizens of the Cherokee Nation. Previous treaties, especially the Treaty of Holston, had recognized them as such and had also implied that their lands were not "within the jurisdictions of any state." He urged Wirt to ask the court for an injunction on their behalf and encouraged individual Cherokees to bring private lawsuits to get a hearing before the Supreme Court "as soon as possible."[12] Evarts clearly hoped to move the dispute out of politics and into the courts. He retained a faith, naive in retrospect, that partisan passions and the lust for land would recede in the face of a judgment from the country's highest legal tribunal. He concurred, in effect, with the words of New Hampshire's Sen. Samuel Bell: "The election of Jackson to the Presidency seems to have had a pestilential effect upon the moral and patriotic feelings of a large portion of the people, but there is still room for hope that they are not corrupted beyond a possibility of recovery."[13]

In the meantime Evarts tried to curtail ABCFM expenses at its Indian missions and to stiffen the Cherokees' determination to defend their rights in court. He also sought other means of resistance that might be more immediately fruitful and binding. Henry Clay suggested that Congress reject any removal treaties negotiated under the new law and that it withhold appropriations to carry existing treaties into effect. That would focus new attention on the character of those treaties as well as reveal the enormous public expense of Jackson's removal policy. The *Cincinnati American* suggested a similar course of action: "We presume the Indian bill can only be put into operation by effective treaties. These must be strangled in the Senate. Sixteen new Senators are to be elected for the next Congress, and the people must exert their utmost influence to produce the election of such men as will be opposed to the unparalleled injustice and faithfulness, that would otherwise result from the measures of the administration in regard to this question."[14]

The immediate crisis in Georgia escalated, however, with the discovery of gold on Cherokee lands. Whites, determined to mine that gold whatever the cost, demanded state and federal assistance to drive the Indians off those lands without delay. To further encourage removal, Secretary of War Eaton directed that all future annuities be distributed *only* to individual Indians and their families rather than in common to representatives of the tribes. This measure sought to encourage a breakdown in unity and to weaken the authority of tribal leaders, many of whom led the anti-removal forces.[15]

Hopes for a calm solution to the crisis faded when Governor Gilmer answered Wirt's request for a rational understanding of the Cherokees' legal position. His letter to Wirt was sharp, even nasty, and was drafted with the advice of Jackson's Attorney General John Berrien. Gilmer confessed that he saw no reason why Wirt was compelled to take the case but admitted that he was not surprised at the appeal to the courts. "It is known that the extent of the jurisdiction of Georgia, and the policy of removing the Cherokees and other Indians to the west of the Mississippi,"

Gilmer charged, "have become party questions. It is not therefore surprising," he admitted, "that those who engage in the struggle for power, should find usurpation and faithlessness in the measures of the Government, accordingly as the loss of office, or the hope of its acquisition, may enlighten their understandings." He told Wirt, in essence, to do whatever he wanted, for "Georgia claims no jurisdiction over the lawyers of Maryland." But he also cast a veiled threat toward Wirt. So long as Wirt remained out of the state of Georgia, Gilmer said, state authorities would not interfere with him.[16]

After telling Wirt that he had no need to apologize for his actions, Gilmer then recited the claims of Georgia to Cherokee lands and insisted that whatever leadership and civilizing influences the Cherokees exhibited stemmed from "the children of white men" and not the "real aborigines." They had corrupted the tribes, and now that the "Cherokees have lost all that was valuable in their Indian character," they must fall under state jurisdiction or remove west of the Mississippi. Gilmer rejected any notion that the Supreme Court could nullify what the Georgia legislature had done; to suggest otherwise was insulting and "exceedingly disrespectful to the Government of the State." Then Gilmer went one step further and questioned Wirt's motives. He reminded the Maryland lawyer that his first wife had been the daughter of Dr. George Gilmer, "the brother of my grandfather," and asked if Wirt was trying to take advantage of family connections. He also noted that he understood Wirt's fee to be $20,000.[17]

Wirt's letter created a stir, not only in the Gilmer household but elsewhere as well. The *United States' Telegraph* published a series of editorials opposing Wirt and attacking the "political philanthropists" who supported him for their partisan efforts to discredit the Jackson administration. Gilmer also appointed a superintendent of public lands within Georgia to keep the peace and shore up the state's claims to the gold mines in the event they became the focus of litigation.[18]

Wirt reacted strongly to Gilmer's reply. He was convinced that the Jacksonians intended to make the case a political issue and implored old friend Dabney Carr to discretely ask Chief Justice John Marshall two questions. Wirt wanted to know if Marshall considered the Indians to be aliens and sought his evaluation of President Jackson's declaration that the Cherokees were subject to Georgia law. He sought advice elsewhere as well, from such distinguished lawyers as James Kent, Daniel Webster, Ambrose Spencer, Horace Binney, and John Sergeant. They convinced him to pursue the case, but throughout these preliminary inquiries Wirt clearly feared that Jackson might strike out on his own and even disobey a Court decree if he could gain a political advantage. He tried to protect himself in case this politicization occurred, and his letters to Judge Dabney Carr reveal this determination as well as an unshakable sense of self-importance.

> I saw that I was about to be made instrumental in thwarting or impeding (or trying to do it, perhaps in vain,) a project on which the President and the State of Georgia were bent, and which, but for my interference, might take immediate effect by the removal of the Indians—for they would sooner remove and die in the wilderness, than remain in subjection to the laws of Georgia. But, on the other hand, having been assured by so many distinguished men that the Supreme Court would protect them, and that they had only to secure eminent counsel to effect their object, they have resolved to bear the present oppression of Georgia until the question can be decided by the Supreme Court. . . . I did not think it right to flinch from any considerations of personal ease and safety; and I promised to examine their case and give them my opinion, and, if necessary, my professional services in the Supreme Court.[19]

Wirt was well aware that Jacksonians linked him to the Adams administration, but what he wrote Carr was even more restrained than what he originally intended to say. Before drafting his final letters, he crossed out passages that revealed a thorough distaste and distrust of Andrew Jackson and the men around him—a conviction that corruption as much as conviction had motivated the president during the Indian Removal Bill debates. Despite his belief that the morality of the Cherokees' position was unshakable, Wirt asked Carr's advice about taking the case. He particularly questioned Carr if "there is any thing in the effort I am making which *ought* or *probably will* injure my reputation either as a man, a citizen of the United States, or a lawyer."[20]

When Wirt accepted the case, even as he was defending Judge James Peck from charges of impeachment by the Jacksonians, other friends of the Indians extended support. Correspondence between Ambrose Spencer and Jeremiah Evarts reveals their endorsement of Wirt's actions. Both men hoped that a favorable decision from the Supreme Court would "have a powerful influence in undeceiving those who yet believe in the wisdom or patriotism of the administration of the federal government." But even so stalwart an anti-Jacksonian as John Quincy Adams admitted that the president's personal popularity was stronger than ever. Nonetheless, Evarts firmly believed that the appeal to the Court would succeed, if only because of the righteousness of the cause. To secure broader public support of the Cherokees' case, Evarts devoted the entire summer almost exclusively to their cause, turning over the operation of the board's missionary rooms as well as nearly all responsibility for the *Missionary Herald* to his assistant and son-in-law David Greene.[21]

The effort to prevent removal, then, moved forward on two fronts. On the first, Wirt prepared the Cherokees' case for presentation to the Court, fighting to overcome his fears that John Marshall might not last out Jackson's term or that Jackson would defy any decision with which he disagreed. "I should not be at all surprized," Wirt wrote, "if our learned President and his classical Secretary of War should say that the Supreme Court have no right to meddle with the matter, and that the Indians shall move—so that there will be an end to our government—and yet the people will say 'hurrah for Jackson!'"[22] By the end of June Wirt had also heard from John Marshall (through Dabney Carr). After admonishing Carr not to publish his reply, Marshall declined comment on Wirt's queries but admitted that he had followed congressional debates on Indian removal carefully and wished that the outcome had been different. While this reply gave Wirt no clear-cut answers to his questions, it must have assured him that the Marshall court would be sympathetic to his pleas for the Cherokees.

On the second front, Jeremiah Evarts moved among his influential New England friends and mobilized the machinery of the benevolent network to excite the public throughout the country. With the support and endorsement of Daniel Webster, the speeches on the Indian Bill were published. He hoped to use the volume to present the substance of the anti-removal argument to the public, thereby offsetting the steady outpouring of pro-removal editorials in administration newspapers throughout the country. Led by the *United States' Telegraph*, these papers insisted that removal would be voluntary and was in the best interests of the tribes, that only a few power-hungry chiefs, partisan politicians, and politically inspired missionaries opposed the president's removal policy. The *Albany Argus* warned that anti-removal advocates sought to frustrate the will of the people.[23]

In the face of this opposition and waning public attention to the issue, and amid fears of sectarian divisions, Evarts faced a formidable task. An exchange of letters with Baptist leader Francis Wayland revealed his difficulties. Wayland had written for information, noting that he had kept clear of the Indian issue and suggesting that perhaps matters were not as bad as they appeared. He also expressed concern that Baptist support for removal would mix religion and party rancor so as further to divide the religious community. Evarts replied immediately, informing Wayland that "the case is far worse than you ever conceived of." After detailing how serious the impact of removal had already become for the tribes and noting the support of Methodist missionaries for Choctaw removal, he warned that further sectarian controversy would doom all efforts to ground political behavior in a moral ethos. Opponents of religion, he told Wayland, blamed *all* missionaries for frustrating removal and had "arrayed patriotism against religion." The issue, for Evarts, was not only the removal of the Indians but the future of religion in the republic. He lamented previous Baptist support for removal but expressed a desire to avoid sectarian feelings and indicated his willingness to make "the most charitable allowances" for those who he believed "have been egregiously misled." The Indians' rights could be defended, but Evarts feared that the effort would not be made.[24]

Evarts received some comfort from missionary Cephas Washburn at the Dwight Mission. The removal bill, he agreed, was a disgrace, but he did not believe that future prospects for the Indians were as bleak as Evarts feared. Washburn did not explain the reason for his optimism, but much of it seemed to stem from a belief that perhaps the American Board would be more successful if all its mission stations lay beyond the Mississippi and the political tentacles of states and their citizens. Certainly the actions of Georgia and its governor gave credence to that position. Governor Gilmer continued to oppose Wirt's lawsuit on the basis that Georgia's authority came from a higher source, from power retained when she joined the Union under the Constitution, and because the Indian question was too excitable and partisan "for the interference of the Supreme Court." In fact, by early July Gilmer threatened nullification should the Court rule against Georgia. "There is," he wrote Georgia Judge Augustin Clayton, "no probability that the State of Georgia would submit to the orders of the Court if it should determine that the laws of the State in relation to the Indians were void."[25]

Even as he organized further resistance to the government's removal policy, however, Evarts moved to placate the administration. In a letter to Secretary of War Eaton he expressed his regret that the Civilization Fund had been cut off before the Indians were actually removed and noted his dismay over the current controversy about Indian removal.

Was he being disingenuous, or was there something else behind Evarts's concern? The answer is probably a mixture of the two. Evarts had certainly been the most strenuous and effective opponent of removal, and he clearly intended to continue his opposition to the administration's Indian policy. At the same time, however, he was not about to give up the American Board's Indian missions out of spite. Throughout the crisis he had refused to elaborate the board's intent to follow the tribes and continue its missions west of the Mississippi for fear of weakening opposition to removal. Evarts still firmly believed that the government was morally obligated to uphold its previous treaties and protect the tribes where they lived. But the ABCFM was more than willing to relocate its mission stations should removal occur, and it wanted continued government support from the Indian Civilization Fund to defray the costs of those missions. In effect Evarts was waging two battles simultaneously, one for the present and another for the future. In this spirit he regretted that the current controversy had led the government to endanger future missions.[26]

This threat did not deter him, however, in his efforts to defend the Indians' rights. His difficulties in fomenting further opposition to Jackson's plan for immediate and complete removal were succinctly outlined by a reviewer in London. Reviewing publications by Evarts and Lewis Cass on the removal question, the writer observed with some prescience that the petitioning system was about to be tested to see if public opinion could influence a question in which self-interest "is the antagonist of benevolence, justice, and good faith." "It would seem to be no very easy thing," he concluded, "to rouse the public of America, when their national rights or personal interests are not immediately involved."[27]

During the summer and early fall of 1830 the general and the missionary clashed once again. This time neither was particularly successful. Both men believed that the Indian removal issue went straight to the soul of the republic, and both linked its outcome to the essential character of the citizenry, each in his own way. Evarts wrote Cherokee chief John Ross to advise him about the proper measures to pursue in any meetings with the president. The Cherokees, however, did not want their critics to charge that white men had shaped any of their public acts or documents and asked Evarts and ABCFM missionaries to keep their distance. Ross did ask Evarts to convince either Daniel Webster or William Wirt to take their case to the Supreme Court, confident that the Court was on their side. "The clouds may gather, thunder roar & lightening flash from the acts of Ga. under the approbation of Gen. Jackson's neutrality," Ross wrote Evarts, "but the Cherokees with an honest patriotism & love of country will still remain peaceably and quietly on their own soil." Evarts was less confident, writing New Hampshire Sen. Samuel Bell that the "Indians can be saved, if the apathy of the people is not inexcusably great."[28]

Jackson, meanwhile, lined up support for what he hoped to be the final act of physical removal. Through John Eaton he instructed all Indian agents to inform the tribes that if they delayed their removal they would be responsible for all provisions and costs themselves. In his letter to Cherokee agent Col. Hugh Montgomery, Eaton outlined explicitly the administration's views, not only on Indian affairs but on matters of race, civilization, and the very nature of mankind, progress, and an underlying moral ethos. It was a revealing admission of administration attitudes.

> It is at least but a Utopian thought to think of civilizing Indians. Nature must first be changed. One or two generations at least must pass away under a rigid culture, before these people can be much benefited by science and education. The wild turkey, tho' you shall take the egg and hatch it in your barn yard, will seek the tallest forest tree, at night fall, for his roosting place.... An Almighty hand has stamped upon every creature a particular genius, propensity and leading traits of character. The polish of education may improve, but cannot change, for the imperishable seal is there; bars and dungeons, penitentiaries and death itself, have been found insufficient, even in civilized society, to restrain man from crime, and constrain him to the necessity of moral and virtuous action. How then are we to look for, or expect it, in a community made up of savage and illiterate people?... Their improvement is certainly greatly to be desired, but for the present it must be given up into the hands of care and time.[29]

Jackson also dismissed Thomas McKenney from his post in the Office of Indian Affairs. Although McKenney had attempted to defend and execute the president's removal policy, he had close ties to men like Jeremiah Evarts and John Calhoun, both opponents of Jackson in different arenas. Jackson clearly did not believe that McKenney wholeheartedly supported his policy. As if to confirm that estimate, the *Georgia Journal* praised the removal as "among the best acts of Gen. Jackson's administration."[30]

In the meantime, while many Jacksonian partisans worried that the Maysville veto would erode support for the administration and that opposition to the removal policy among directors of the Bank of the United States would lead that institution to try to embarrass the government,

Andrew Jackson waited at the Hermitage. He expected to receive delegations from the various tribes and negotiate treaties for their removal. Even missionary Cyrus Kingsbury feared that Jackson would succeed, that he was willing to offer the chiefs whatever funds necessary to effect a complete removal, thereby resolving the Indian question and defusing its political implications. Further to encourage the tribes, Baptist missionary and removal advocate Isaac McCoy wrote a series of articles on Indian affairs and removal for the pro-administration *United States' Telegraph* under the pseudonym "Candour."

Beginning with his first essay, McCoy argued that removal of the Indians to lands west of the Mississippi was an essential precondition to their survival and should not become a party question. He reminded readers that he had first spoken out in favor of removal during the administration of James Monroe and that the tribes' condition had only worsened since then. But in many respects, McCoy's essays seemed designed to counter the influence of Jeremiah Evarts's "William Penn" essays within the benevolent community and among the general public. Like Evarts, McCoy spent much of his time examining early Indian treaties and discussing his interpretation of the tribes' rights to the soil. He also defended his position that the Indians did not possess sovereignty. Since whites set the terms of treaties, McCoy argued somewhat ingenuously, the Indians have not *really* been a party to them in contractual terms. To admit that would be to admit that the tribes had a choice as to who and when to treat, and McCoy insisted that this was not the case. This argument led McCoy to a rousing defense of the doctrine of discovery. "Treaties with the Indian tribes are, *in fact*, merely matters of convenience to us, and of humanity towards them. Civilized nations have long since divided the continent of America among themselves. So the nations have adopted the practice of settling their territories without asking the natives to leave it by the formalities of a treaty."[31]

This was not fraud in McCoy's view, because the United States was not seeking the land in treaty negotiations; it already owned it. Instead, the government was merely purchasing the Indians' consent to leave the land or their consent to whites' occupation of it. "The sums, therefore, which we have at different times paid, have varied, not in proportion to the amount or value of the *land* in question, but according to the disposition of the Indians to accede to our terms, or according to other circumstances not connected with the *value* of the *land*."[32] By this argument the tribes were virtual prisoners in their own country. They had the right to leave but had to negotiate to remain.

Isaac McCoy was not, of course, the first person—or even the first missionary—to express such an extreme paternalism. But he did stand out with his blatant assertions of imperial "responsibilities" and his conceptualization of the United States' civilizing mission. Indeed, what is perhaps most striking about many missions to the North American Indians, and particularly ABCFM missions, is the departure by both missionaries and their parent bodies from their larger paradigmatic structure of missionary activity. As one reads through the voluminous correspondence to and from Jeremiah Evarts and missionaries in the field or studies reports of mission stations printed in the *Missionary Herald*, lamentations about the "perishing heathen" leap to the eye. These foreign mission reports document, often in great detail, "barbaric" or "heathen" religious and secular practices which loom as obstacles to the conversion of distant peoples, the civilization of "backward" societies, and the overall success of missions in foreign lands. Scenarios of this sort were, in fact, the essence of the missionary paradigm; foreign peoples were largely objects to be manipulated in the name of religion and progress.

For the American Board of Commissioners, missions to the North American Indian tribes were also foreign missions. Depictions of missionary prospects among those tribes, however, appear much more positive, even from their inception, despite the lack of progress. Even the scenes of degradation and barbarism were drawn more softly than those depicted in India or the Sandwich Islands. When Isaac McCoy told readers of the *United States' Telegraph* that the United States was "now honored in being the first civilized nation, which has fairly, as we believe, entered upon the work of lifting up from the dust, and rescuing from destruction the remnants of the aborigines of our vast continent," he was only saying what others also believed. But he said it with words that men like Jeremiah Evarts usually reserved for the natives of foreign lands. There seemed, in short, to be something special about the tribal missions that precluded such a bald statement of purpose. Was it perhaps a feeling of continental brotherhood? Or was it a reflection that, just perhaps, the North American Indians represented a segment of our own experience, our own civilization?[33]

McCoy believed that removal beyond the Mississippi would place the Indians beyond the reach of whites until they could adjust to the demands of civilization, but he also believed that the government would act to protect them there as it had not in their eastern lands. Nowhere in his scheme of things, however, was there room for an integration of the two societies. To McCoy there were only three choices for the United States (and, by extension, the missionaries): Indian sovereignty, denial of all tribal titles to the soil, or a proper paternalism. And only the latter alternative, he believed, was acceptable. While McCoy's proposal placed him at odds with Jeremiah Evarts and the American Board of Commissioners, it also exposed an underlying dilemma in the ABCFM position. How was it possible, McCoy asked, to argue that Indians should be civilized and given the chance to become citizens while at the same time insisting that they held a separate status from the rest of the American people? Was Evarts interested in protection or preservation? What the tribes needed, in McCoy's estimation, was their own system of political institutions and moral restraints to effect a fundamental change in their character.[34]

Finally, underlying Isaac McCoy's arguments and casting an aura of doubt over his motives, was the matter of politics. Even if he believed that removal would be best for the tribes, McCoy could never quite shake his critics' conviction that a desire to secure government patronage for his own mission stations lay behind his actions and motivated his defense of Jacksonian Indian policy. Whatever the motives, these critics remained suspicious about them. Despite McCoy's insistence that his removal plan represented the best way to protect the tribes, he never really satisfied opponents of removal because he appeared too willing to accede to the Jacksonian argument that treaties were legally meaningless and did not convey rights to the tribes who signed them. At the same time, he seemed oblivious to the implications of removal for the Indians themselves. Underlying moral and logistical complexities seemed to escape him. In the words of frontier Gen. E. P. Gaines: "For my part I would just as soon seek for fame by an attempt to remove the Shakers, or the Quakers, as to break up the Indians, take their land and throw together twenty tribes speaking different languages where the most ferocious savages will cut the throat of the most civilized and orderly."[35]

While McCoy wrote, Jackson waited. By August of 1830 Isaac McCoy's proposals addressed the fact that the Removal Bill *had* passed Congress, while Jeremiah Evarts continued his efforts to repeal that bill or frustrate the removal process. Jackson, on the other hand, impatiently waited at the Hermitage to effect what he believed to be the final act of the removal drama. He intended personally to negotiate treaties with those tribes who wished to remove and to let those who refused to beseech the Great White Father for future protection cast their lot with the state authorities. The Chickasaws appeared to sign a treaty, and Jackson expected the Choctaws to follow. The Creeks and the Cherokees refused to negotiate. Jackson then announced that negotiations were over and told the remaining tribes that their fate was in the hands of their "wicked advisers" and the states. If they wished to remove, they would not only have to find "by their own means, a country, and a home," but bear all removal expenses themselves. "I have exonerated the national character from all imputation," Jackson wrote Maj. William B. Lewis, "and now leave the poor deluded Creeks and Cherokees to their fate, and their annihilation, which their wicked advisers has induced."[36]

In fact, Jackson was not willing to leave the other tribes to their own devices. Within a week John Eaton had written a Cherokee agent to request that he "proceed to the nation and employ all fair arguments you can to induce them to awaken to a sense of their true condition, and remove from the country they occupy." In the meantime, Jackson warned other agents not to execute any part of the removal provisions until he acted. The president himself wanted to control the entire process. In that same vein he rejected the request of ABCFM missionaries Cyrus Kingsbury, Cyrus Byington, Loving Williams, and Colvin Cushman to attend the treaty negotiations with the Choctaws. Replying for the president, John Eaton and John Coffee praised the missionaries for their concern but insisted that "the present" was not "a proper time, place, or occasion, for such undertakings." After a second request from the missionaries, Eaton and Coffee were more direct in their refusal. "We prefer," they wrote, "that you should go away. . . . Your absence may aid civil purposes greatly." Their presence, on the other hand, would not advance religion. They had had their chance to influence the tribe; now it was the government's turn.[37]

Government hostility to the missionaries' influence was even more pronounced in the message of Eaton and Coffee to the Choctaw chiefs on the treaty ground at Dancing Rabbit Creek. They warned the chiefs to heed missionary advice *only* on religious matters; to do otherwise would lead the Indians "to a state of political wretchedness" that the missionaries could not alleviate. With the missionaries excluded and the government insistent, the Choctaws signed a removal treaty. The final treaty provided no compensation for the ABCFM schools and mission stations that had to be relocated or abandoned in its wake, and the extensive reserve granted to the Choctaw leaders led many to suspect bribery. More disturbing to the missionaries, however, was the commissioners' (Eaton and Coffee) use of alcohol and favors to divide the Christian Indians from the remainder of the tribe. Reports from the treaty ground testified that small groups of Choctaws prayed and sang while the rest danced, drank, and gambled in an orgy of dissipation and revelry. Another observer wrote that the Choctaws signed because they were frightened. Eaton had threatened that unless they yielded, white men would come "among them like flocks of blackbirds and swarms of locusts; that they and their children would become paupers and beggars" and that they would cease to exist as a nation. Eaton had then placed the treaty on the table, and the chiefs rushed forward to sign it.[38]

Reaction to the treaty was predictable but pointed, nonetheless. Southern states were ecstatic. In Natchez, Mississippi, a public dinner was held to celebrate; speakers predicted prosperity for the state. Elsewhere, Methodist missionaries signed a resolution supporting removal. At the offices of the American Board, meanwhile, reaction was sharply critical. The treaty represented just what Evarts had long argued, a determination on the part of the Jackson administration to effect removal without respect to fairness and morality, and confirmed his conviction that the removal bill was an unmitigated disaster. The government had cut off all funds for the removal of small parties of Indians, holding out for wholesale removal such as that concluded at Dancing Rabbit Creek. This left the tribes few choices.[39]

While government agents negotiated removal treaties and Georgia's Governor Gilmer warned the administration that he could not much longer restrain gold seekers from invading Cherokee lands in search of their fortune, Jeremiah Evarts continued to cultivate opposition to removal. The *Christian Examiner* and the *Spirit of the Pilgrims* both published extensive commentaries expounding Evarts's views on removal. Both argued that the underlying issue was a moral one that involved the "character of our country for justice and humanity." Individuals must pursue what is right, the *Examiner* instructed readers, and not let "fears of a collision between the General Government and the authorities of any State" obscure the moral dimensions of the question or obstruct the compelling need for justice. This assertion was important and dangerous, for it argued implicitly for obedience to a higher moral law that transcended secular political arrangements. It portended a position that abolitionists would soon embrace. That the anonymous author of the article was well versed on Evarts's intentions, however, is clear from his insistence that the way to avoid such a collision was to send the question to the Supreme Court. The Court, not the president, had the responsibility and power to decide the constitutionality of laws. If Georgia was willing to forego an appeal to the Court, the article concluded, perhaps the state would relinquish her claims to Cherokee lands if Congress authorized a suitable payment. This forlorn suggestion revealed how little the benevolent community understood the perspective of the southern states.[40]

The attack on removal in the *Spirit of the Pilgrims*, meanwhile, began with the warning "ACTUM EST DE REPUBLICA!" Arguing that the removal bill had tarnished the nation's honor, the article reviewed congressional speeches on that bill to insist that morality, honor, and patriotism commanded the public to shake off its "selfish indifference" and recapture a moral ethos. The cruel and inhumane treatment of the Cherokees had stained the soul of the nation; "our disgrace and guilt as a community are great." But while the author found solace in the morality and truth of the Cherokees' cause, the discussion of the tribe's future made clear that the political system had failed to protect the Indians from a variety of predators. Only the Supreme Court remained, and even a favorable court decision might come too late to save the Indians. There was in this experience a larger lesson for the republic and its inhabitants.

> The progress of this bill teems with warning to the United States. It tells, with a power which no eloquence could have commanded, the awful necessity of an enlightened and well-principled public mind, for the perpetuity of our institutions. . . . Just as in proportion as the people become unwary, indifferent, or uninformed, civil liberty will be broken down, and disorders rush in and accumulate on every part of the Constitution. . . . The tendency of the Executive to an unwarrantable extent of its prerogative should keep us on the watch, and cautious in the extreme, how we commit the highest trusts in the Republic to unprincipled hands.[41]

Efforts to rouse the Christian community had failed to prevent the Indians' expulsion. Part of the explanation, according to the article, lay in individuals' failure to become excited about oppression which did not touch them personally. Another factor was the growing power of party. "That the demon of party should have gained such possession of the souls of our Senators and Representatives," the author stated, "as to permit them, in the eyes of all the world, to set their hand and seal to the violation of the Faith of the Republic . . . is indeed a most dark and dreadful fact." While the Supreme Court might yet stay that action, the baneful effects of party fervor remained as a danger to the American spirit. For a third explanation, the author returned to an early theme of Evarts's undergraduate days. A principled chief executive was essential to breathe life into the laws; *"the laws must be executed."* [42] Even as a student at Yale, Jeremiah Evarts had insisted that execution of the laws formed the backbone of the body politic. The confrontation between Georgia and the Cherokees reinforced that conviction. Finally, of course, at least one other explanation remained. Perhaps the majority of adult Americans no longer embraced an underlying moral ethos. Perhaps, indeed, a selfish individualism had seized the soul of America.

Jeremiah Evarts refused to admit the latter possibility and worked feverishly to stir public sentiment and develop a new crusade for morality and justice. His two defeats in the past year, on Sabbatarianism and Indian removal, did not shake his conviction that a residual moral ethos remained within the public at large and that the right appeal would shake it loose. If the article in the *Spirit of the Pilgrims* sounded familiar to readers of Evarts's "William Penn" essays, it was because its author, George Cheever, had prepared the piece with the close advice and assistance of Evarts. Support also came from Henry Clay, who insisted to Evarts that the influence of the "female sex" and the clergy, together with renewed activity by the friends of religion, could have a decisive influence. Although Clay's support was welcome, it was not very significant. For more than two years he had been conferring with Evarts and privately backing his crusade against Indian removal. But Henry Clay had shied away from taking a strong public stance on the question and never delivered a formal address on the subject. Indeed, he seemed more interested in maintaining his ties to the benevolent community in preparation for another run at the presidency than in standing in the front lines of the anti-removal forces.[43]

Uncertain that he could find sufficient support in the political community, Evarts looked elsewhere. He wrote to his network of coworkers to ask their assistance. To Ashbel Green in Philadelphia he outlined the need to prevent removal and asked him to call a meeting and prepare petitions on the subject. Thomas Stuart in South Carolina received a similar plea; petitions to Congress and letters to the president might delay or prevent removal. Although they pledged support to the cause, and although anti-Jackson politicians increasingly linked removal to internal improvements (spending on one would delay implementation of the other), by early fall the best hopes of Evarts and the Cherokees rested with William Wirt and his efforts to carry the case to the Supreme Court.[44]

Wirt, however, seemed an unwilling participant. Despite support from Evarts and many of the day's leading lawyers, he was reluctant to press the Cherokees' case. He continued to be defensive about his decision to take the case and to worry not only about its impact on his reputation but also about the likelihood that he would not be paid. He feared as well that the government would retaliate against him for defending the Cherokees and remove him from a very lucrative land case in Florida in which he represented its interests. On almost all his letters on the matter, and he wrote many of them, he carefully lettered "Not to be Published" across the top margin. Even his correspondence with James Madison was defensive, revealing an obsession with the propriety of his taking the case. Madison supported his decision, but the correspondence is more interesting for its revelation of Wirt's possible real anxiety. Wirt argued, and Madison agreed, that if the Cherokees could obtain an adequate guarantee and lands from the government, they should remove. This argument was at variance with the public views of the anti-removal forces, who not only defended the Indians' right to remain (as did Wirt) but insisted that removal would be a dishonorable disaster for the tribes and the nation.[45]

The issues, for Wirt, were those of happiness and rights. He believed that in the West the Cherokees would not be disturbed by whites but admitted on at least one occasion that party motives had created the case and blamed the governor of Georgia for abusive behavior that forced his hand. "I fear the dangerous and powerful collisions of authority which may arise if the Supreme Court shall be of the opinion that the State of Georgia has no right . . . to extend their rights over them," Wirt wrote. "But what was I to do when these people came to me for a professional opinion, on their rights?"[46] To a friend in Florida he wrote, "I was exceedingly sorry that they came to me, and if I could have put them off, with honor, I would have done so." But that had not been possible, for even under the Indian Removal Bill removal was voluntary, and the Cherokees had a right to remain on their lands. By October Wirt had heard from Chancellor Kent and was convinced both that the Georgia laws were unconstitutional and that the Supreme Court possessed original jurisdiction in the matter. He was ready to move forward.[47]

At the same time, forces on both sides became more combative. Jackson and his advisers rejoiced at the Choctaw treaty, believing that it had broken "the force of the Indian question." Georgians, meanwhile, prepared to take extreme actions should the Supreme Court rule against them—even to the point of prosecuting for treason any person who should "call into question the sovereign jurisdictional or territorial rights of the State." For their part, Cherokee chiefs placed the future of their nation in the hands of the Court. David Vann pleaded for relief from the threat of emigration. "'Hail Columbia happy land!' Yes, happy to aspiring states, unrestrained by law, and who will have the Indian lands free of cost, and the sacrifices of the Indian tears. Sir, compulsion is the practice of the day, and by those who advocated Indian emigration. We and our people are under the screw, and one turn has already forced tears from our eyes. If the Indian bill is not repealed by the next congress, the second turn will draw from our agonized bodies life preserving blood. But let us remain still innocent, and pray the Lord to change the hearts of the rulers of the U. States."[48]

Believing that the next battle would be before the justices of the Supreme Court, Jeremiah Evarts kept the issue before the public but resumed most of his regular duties as corresponding secretary for the American Board. He outlined a three-pronged attack to focus public attention on the Indians' situation, but none of these efforts required his fulltime services. First, lawyers from across the country should publish their opinions on the issue. Not only would they lay a groundwork of legal opinion that might influence the Court, but the focus might also shift from states' rights or political considerations to matters of law. Second, petitions should be circulated asking that Congress either repeal the bill or refuse to make appropriations to carry out its provisions. Finally, friends of the Cherokees and morality should fill the papers with "moving appeals" to stir public sentiment. Evarts now feared more than ever that the government would fail to fulfill its commitments under existing removal treaties and that the Jackson administration simply wanted to get rid of the Indians at any cost. To that end he carefully solicited Cyrus Kingsbury's story of being warned off the treaty grounds so as to publicize the new tone of government negotiations with the tribes. Even if the Indians were going to be destroyed and the nation's honor besmirched, Evarts concluded that the "religious and public-spirited" part of the community should stick to their principles.[49]

In fact, officials of both the state of Georgia and the Jackson administration seemed determined to provoke a confrontation. John Eaton sent his agents out among the Cherokees to urge immediate removal. But despite their advice that delay might be preferable, because if the Supreme Court held against them the Indians would remove, the administration continued to force the issue. Andrew Jackson ordered the existing enrollment plan postponed and indicated to Georgia that it should take whatever steps it felt warranted. The delay, Jackson believed, would split the "common Indians" off from their chiefs; this division would fragment the tribe and erode opposition to removal. Jackson also ordered federal troops withdrawn from their stations on the Cherokee lands, thereby leaving the tribesmen at the mercy of state residents at the very moment that Georgia authorities prepared to survey those lands. "Times are dark, and our case is desperate," Elias Boudinot wrote Evarts; "The Lord have mercy upon the poor Cherokees."[50]

In his annual message that December President Jackson defended these actions. He hoped to remove the Indians as fast as possible, he explained, so as to avoid a collision between state and federal authorities. Removal would free the Indians from the power of the states, particularly Georgia, Mississippi, and Alabama, and enable them "to pursue happiness in their own way and under their own rude institutions." Jackson insisted that removal would retard their decay and let them "cast off their savage habits, and become an interesting, civilized, and Christian community." The efforts of the missionaries had been worthy, he concluded, but had failed. Removal would both stop the inexorable annihilation of the Indians and open the country to continued progress. To critics who insisted that the expediency of removal and the tribes' rights to their lands were different issues, Jackson replied in sweeping tones that mixed progress with patriotism. "Philanthropy could not wish to see this continent restored to the condition in which it was found by our forefathers. What good man would prefer a country covered with forests and ranged by a few thousand savages to our extensive Republic, studded with cities, towns, and prosperous farms, embellished with all the improvements which art can devise or industry execute, occupied by more than 12,000,000 happy people, and filled with all the blessings of liberty, civilization, and religion?"[51] A delegation of Cherokees visiting Washington received essentially the same message from the president. One of their number wrote Evarts that Eaton had told them directly that "we must not expect that the President would 'make war upon his own people.'" They asked Evarts to come to Washington to advance their cause.[52]

By December 1830, however, Jeremiah Evarts was tired and in poor health. He had spent virtually the entire year lobbying against Indian removal, drafting essays, circulating petitions, and attempting to both inform and arouse the public. At the same time, he had retained ultimate responsibility for his other duties as corresponding secretary of the American Board of Commissioners for Foreign Missions. Much of the day-to-day correspondence with the American Board's far-flung foreign missions he had given to assistants David Greene and Rufus Anderson, but he retained the decision-making authority. In addition, he had fought to retain federal support for ABCFM missions to the Indian tribes even while he opposed the administration's removal policy. These efforts not only placed a strain on his personal relations with federal officials, but also created greater tension in his own life and further drained his energies. Finally, throughout these trials there remained not only his interest in other benevolent causes but the fact that he had a wife and family in Charlestown.

Evarts's surviving account books for 1829 and 1830 reveal his continued attention to family matters. He maintained his interest in Illinois lands, buying additional lots when he had the money to do so. He also occasionally hired help for his wife and persisted in his contributions to various charitable causes. His son John was now at Yale, and the father bore the full costs of his tuition expenses. His income from sundry publications for essays on the Indian issue was steady but only helped offset printing costs for the "William Penn" essays, which he bore himself. Although his expenses were steady and high, the Evarts family was well-off by early nineteenth-century standards. In a day when the average American urban family spent about $1,000 a year, in addition to housing costs, Evarts's terse records indicate that he spent several times that amount.[53]

Beyond the sparse notations penciled in his account books, we know little about his family life. Virtually no family letters survive. Surely many were written, for Evarts believed strongly in the educational and nurturing value of family. Family and maternal affection, he wrote at one point, when blended with religion was the backbone of the republic. It invigorated thought and promoted inquiry; it made "knowledge precious" and "incorporates it with the soul." But his continually poor health coupled with his heavy workload and long trips away from home left most of the burden of family life to his wife, Mehitabel. Letters between the two of them were likely among those destroyed (at his instructions) after his death. His private persona remains shadowy.[54]

His public life, however, is well documented. Aside from his primary duties with the American Board of Commissioners, Evarts remained active in numerous benevolent causes. Receipts reveal that in 1830 he not only subscribed to a multitude of journals and magazine that addressed public affairs (such as the *North American Review*), but he also belonged to an array of organizations that included the Park Street Gentlemen's Society, the American Education Society, Massachusetts Society for Promoting Christian Knowledge, Boston Prison Discipline Society, Massachusetts Peace Society, the American Temperance Society, and the Massachusetts Bible Society. He served many of those societies in some official capacity.[55]

Throughout his entire life Jeremiah Evarts had sought to foster a moral ethos in public life. Despite his preoccupation with Indian affairs throughout 1830, he continued to do so. He believed that the essence of the New England character, indeed the soul of the country, lay in the interconnection of morality and behavior with public affairs. He subscribed to what the Reverend Royal Washburn summarized in a public fast sermon: "Righteousness diffuses through a community mutual good will, a love for each other's well-being, and respect for each other's rights. It thus prevents feuds, quarrels of citizen with citizen, and furnishes no aliment for the growth of party spirit,—the volcano, which has poured its desolating fires over republics."[56] Those evils, which Washburn detailed, included neglect of the Sabbath and intemperance, causes dear to Evarts's heart and central to his life's work.

This sort of language, of course, was central to the New England jeremiad tradition. But for Evarts it reflected the world as he understood it in the early nineteenth century. As he looked around at the swirling eddies of political and economic change that were Jacksonian America, Jeremiah Evarts believed firmly that the country, as well as its inhabitants, was in danger of losing its moral compass. Entrepreneurial capitalism, individualism, the resurgence of political parties, the disestablishment of religion—all seemed evidence of decay if not of decline. Indeed, the very secular success of the republic threatened its spiritual well-being. Indian removal was only the most recent demonstration to Evarts that declining moral accountability endangered the republic's stability. Divisiveness and self-interest appeared to have become dominant. "A profligate people cannot long continue free," warned one speaker; "public virtue is an inseparable condition of national freedom."[57]

Despite setbacks, despite his defeat on the Indian removal issue, Evarts remained confident. Only a year earlier he had planned new missions to Greece and China, and he remained convinced that there would be a moral revolution in this country. He believed that organizations such as the Prison Discipline Society had demonstrated "the power of the Bible to awaken an interest in abandoned men and effect a reformation" and that this power could be replicated so as to revitalize the larger society. These convictions, of course, bespoke a belief that the best men should lead society. In the words of the *American Ladies Magazine*: "We are republicans, but we need not be levellers." Although Evarts would recoil at the idea that he represented a sort of noblesse oblige, nonetheless his confidence that benevolent organizations would effectively transform American society rested on a belief that a few virtuous leaders could instigate that transformation when supported by an organizational network that reached throughout the populace. The societies to which he belonged and which he had oftentimes helped form represented just such a network.[58]

The recent experience of the American Board further bolstered Evarts's optimism. After declining during the early 1820s, receipts had climbed steadily since 1824. This success stemmed not only from greater public awareness of ABCFM efforts and improved economic conditions but from the power of the associational web that Evarts had constructed. That web, in the words of William Ellery Channing, had become "a mighty engine." By 1829 there were more than fifteen hundred such organizations throughout the country. Although most of them were in New England and New York, they could be found as far south as Georgia and as far west as Ohio.[59]

By 1831 his cherished causes had suffered a series of setbacks, his health was bad, and Georgia authorities continued to probe the limits of federal acquiesence through relentless attacks on missionary policies and presence. Although the matter was before the Supreme Court, Governor Gilmer of Georgia had made clear his determination to disregard any attempt to countermand his policies. Together with a renewed commitment by the missionaries to resist the intrusions of Georgia and to defend not only Cherokee rights but their own behavior, this resolute behavior spawned yet another crisis for Evarts and the American Board. To start the new year right, the *Cherokee Phoenix* printed a series of resolutions from the missionaries. They said little that was new, seeking to outline the missionaries' position as well as delineate the progress Cherokees had made in the "arts of civilization." What was new, however, and what portended a new phase in the resistance to removal, was the missionaries' decision to enter the public fray themselves. Until now, resolutions of support for the Cherokees from the missionary community had come from ABCFM offices in Boston or in public pronouncements from Evarts as the ABCFM's corresponding secretary. Now missionaries in the field appealed directly to the public. Even though the American Board sanctioned (and even encouraged) their resolutions, the memorial represented a new phase of reform activism. Opposition to removal threatened to move out of middle-class parlors or legislative assemblies and into the arena of direct-action public protest.[60]

Even as these resolutions appeared, the drama over removal heightened. The American Board of Commissioners divided over future policy. In 1831 the Prudential Committee, with a bare majority, agreed to ask missionaries to establish new mission stations west of the Mississippi if their consciences permitted and began to face the likelihood that removal would occur despite their best efforts. Georgia further inflamed public opinion, meanwhile, by her arrest and execution of Corn Tassels, a Cherokee accused of murdering another Cherokee in Indian Territory, despite Chief Justice John Marshall's injunction to stay the execution. Within months ABCFM missionaries themselves would face arrest at the hands of Georgia authorities. Memorials against removal once again flooded Congress. In the words of John Quincy Adams, "the whole head is sick, and the whole heart faint." The president would not support the judiciary, and the legislature would not act. Moral reform appeared ineffective, and Adams believed that anarchy threatened the Union. "To this end," he wrote, "one-third of the people is perverted, one-third slumbers, and the rest wring their hands with unavailing lamentations in the foresight of evil which they cannot avert. The ship is about to flounder. A merciful Providence can save."[61]

From New Echota, Harriet Gold Boudinot wrote that "sometimes I fear the Cherokees will see evil days—but I think they will come off victorious in the end." Boudinot, whose marriage in the mid-1820s to Cherokee Elias Boudinot had caused so much controversy at the American Board's Foreign Mission School, insisted that "that is all they want—they fear nothing; if but their Country & freedom is spared them." Their hopes, and those of Evarts, continued to rest on appeals to morality and the hope that divisions over internal improvements might sufficiently weaken the coalition behind Indian removal to repeal the measure. But differences over policy and the introduction of moral arguments into the legislative process had sparked a dangerous confrontation, not only between Georgia and the federal government, or between partisans on each side, but between entrenched perceptions of right and wrong. In a letter to Gov. Ninian Edwards of Illinois in mid-January, John McLean seconded what John Quincy Adams had said earlier: "The political horizon at this place is overcast. To the man who loves his country there is no pleasing prospect for the future. I cannot state what I see, much less what I fear. I will, however, continue to hope, even against hope. A more important crisis than the present has not occured in the annals of our Government. Parties are arrayed against each other in conflict on questions of National policy, and unless there be magnanimity and forbearance on both sides, there is ground to fear that the contest may end in the dissolution of the Union. If this shall take place, there is no hope for free government." [62]

A steady stream of memorials against removal, meanwhile, agitated the Congress and spurred renewed requests from Georgia that the federal government remove the Indians as quickly as possible and terminate the issue. Fellow southerners favored repeal of the section of the Judiciary Act which allowed the Supreme Court to overturn state laws and rulings, but a bill to that effect failed passage in late January. All the while, congressional foes of removal beseeched Evarts to come to Washington to direct another campaign. Led by Sen. Theodore Frelinghuysen of New Jersey, they hoped for relief from the Supreme Court and believed that the American people would not tolerate any attempt by Jackson to disobey a direct court order. "The truth is," Frelinghuysen wrote Evarts, "he has men flattered into the belief that as he is the greatest, so he is the strongest man that ever held his high office."[63] Poor health inclined Evarts to remain in Boston, however, and to use his pen rather than his presence to lead anti-removal forces.

In the absence of any major piece of legislation on Indian removal, attention turned to the Supreme Court; John Marshall and his fellow justices debated the case of *Cherokees v. Georgia*. The case revolved around the Cherokees' effort to secure an injunction against Georgia to prevent the state from extending her laws over the tribe. In defense of the Indians, lawyers John Sergeant and William Wirt argued that the Cherokee claim to the area long predated that of any white men. Much of the Cherokee defense, however, also rested on the poverty of the land offered them in the west in exchange for their lands in Georgia. That land would become, the Cherokees' brief argued, "the grave not only of their civilization and Christianity, but of their entire nation itself." Central to their argument, however, was their effort to prove that the Supreme Court possessed jurisdiction in the case because the United States through its many treaties had recognized the Cherokees as an independent nation. The imperatives of civilization, justice, Christianity, and humanity cried out for compassion, Wirt insisted. "There is I know not what vague idea among us, that these nations cannot be states, because they are Indians, ignorant savages, wild and wandering hordes, mere heathens, very little if at all superior to the beasts which they chase. . . . It is not the tincture of a skin by which the rights of these peoples are to be tested. We are beginning to recover from our mistake on this ground, with regard to another unfortunate race. Let us not create for ourselves, and place in the hands of a just God, a new scourge of a similar description."[64]

The language of Jeremiah Evarts and "William Penn" coursed through the arguments by Sergeant and Wirt, but to no avail. The Court held that it lacked jurisdiction because the Cherokees were not a foreign nation. John Marshall admitted in his opinion that humanity and sympathy were on the side of the Cherokees but decided that the tribe was not strictly a foreign nation. It was, he concluded, a "domestic dependent" nation. "Their relation to the United States resembles that of a ward to his guardian." Marshall recognized, and worried about, the intent of the case—that the Supreme Court somehow control the legislature of Georgia. That might be too political for the Court, he noted, and a sense of relief pervaded his language when he concluded that such a step was unnecessary since the Court lacked jurisdiction.[65]

The other justices had different thoughts, however. Justice William Johnson shared Marshall's concern that they might be "the instruments to compel another branch of the government to make good the stipulations of treaties." This step would involve the Court in policy, an unwise development. Justice Smith Thompson dissented, insisting that the Court possessed jurisdiction but admitting that full relief would probably require the exercise of political rather than judicial power. To that end he tacitly criticized Pres. Andrew Jackson for his behavior. Marshall's earlier correspondence with Dabney Carr and Evarts indicated his strong support for the Cherokees, and he clearly believed that Georgia had violated the tribe's treaty rights. Justice Joseph Story shared those views. In a brief summary of the case to his wife, Story outlined the two sides' positions and then concluded by noting the "intemperate and indecorous proceedings of Georgia on the question."[66]

Perhaps Thompson revealed what Marshall and some other justices thought, that the issue was inherently political and that Andrew Jackson had already made clear his determination to support the actions of

Georgia. Undoubtedly they hoped that state, federal, and tribal authorities would now resolve the matter and remove the issue from the Court's docket as well as from politics. Story's correspondence reveals an awareness that the Jackson administration not only was hostile to the judiciary but intended to curb its power severely as part of an effort to enhance state rights. "The recent attacks in Georgia, and the recent nullification doctrine in South Carolina, are but parts of the same general scheme, the object of which is to elevate an exclusive State sovereignty upon the ruins of the general Government." Story warned that "the indifference of some, the indolence of others, and the easy good-natured credulity of others, have given a strength to these doctrines, and familiarized them to the people to much, that it will not hereafter be easy to put them down."[67]

Although Marshall quickly regretted his view of the case and agreed with the dissents of Justices Thompson and Story, the Indians' cause was lost. Marshall's fears and Story's perceptions proved correct; Andrew Jackson *was* determined to allow Georgia to extend her laws over the tribes and to force removal. The legal and humanitarian arguments of Jeremiah Evarts and others had been to no avail; the legal arguments or injunctive powers of the Supreme Court would have been to no avail in the face of Jackson's determination. A year later, in *Worcester v. Georgia*, the Supreme Court changed its position. President Jackson, however, would not change his. Georgia, more determined than ever, resolved "to resist and repel any and every invasion, from whatever quarter, upon the administration of the criminal laws of this State."[68] In the aftermath of the court decision, few hopes remained for the Cherokees.

CHAPTER TEN

Epilogue

By the winter of 1831 both the Cherokees' cause and Jeremiah Evarts's health were precarious. Defeat at the hands of the Supreme Court dashed the hopes of the Indians. It also seemed to kill Evarts's attempt to shift the removal question out of politics and into the courtroom. He believed that this move would still controversy while at the same time assert the rule of law. Evarts had clearly expected the Court to rule in favor of the tribe; indeed, he had spent the last few years of his life arguing that point. The decision left him in a difficult position. He wanted neither to oppose the Court nor to abandon the Cherokees. The Prudential Committee, divided over the future of its Cherokee missions, instructed Evarts to tell its missionaries at Carmel, New Echota, Hightower, and Haweis to stand firm and hope for the best. Evarts wrote Samuel Worcester to that effect, asking that he not obtain the license required under Georgia law or do anything that might imply that the state possessed jurisdiction over Cherokee territory. At the same time, however, Evarts revealed that the Prudential Committee could not decide on any authoritative directions to give the missionaries. They should act according to their conscience. Herein lay the American Board's dilemma: to resist state authority would further politicize the process; to acquiesce before that authority would appear to abandon the Indians and indicate that their cause was hopeless.[1]

Jeremiah Evarts quietly developed his own strategy, however, and his closing words to Samuel Worcester revealed it: "If Georgia should carry some of you to prison, the fact would rouse this whole country, in a manner totally unlike anything which has yet been experienced. It would call forth the prayers of all God's people for you & the Indians. It would call forth petitions to the President and to the next Congress, & very possibly to the governor of Georgia. I cannot believe you would be detained in prison long."[2] But if Evarts's hopes rested on the imprisonment of the missionaries, a new campaign for public support, and the belief that the Supreme Court would subsequently reverse its decision, then a postscript added by his son-in-law David Greene revealed a major hurdle to such an effort. Jeremiah Evarts was gravely ill, so ill that Greene had to finish the letter to Worcester and detail the missionaries' course of action should the Georgia authorities act against them. In a letter to Edward Everett the next day, Evarts promised to set out for Washington as soon as he got the strength. He would never make the trip.[3]

Throughout the winter months the network of benevolent societies that Evarts had so diligently cultivated during the past three decades roused their members and sent a stream of petitions and memorials to Washington. Each resembled the other, praying for the repeal of the removal bill and asking Congress to protect the Indians on their own lands. But without Evarts's driving force to spearhead the campaign, there was little concerted leadership, and even strong proponents of the Indians' cause grew discouraged. As one correspondent wrote David Greene: "I am out of all patience with human nature. The truth is the majority of mankind dont care a grat [sic] deal for the interests of humanity or justice, provided they can obtain bread & beef, and as somebody said, 'pretty good clothes.'"[4]

By mid-February the dilemma of the anti-removal forces was manifest. The stream of memorials had become a flood. Edward Everett initiated a new debate on Indian affairs in the House. But little public enthusiasm was evident, and Jeremiah Evarts was seriously ill. Debilitated by disease, Evarts left his family on February 15, 1831, and sailed to Havana, Cuba, to try to recover his health. His shipboard letters, although few and far between, reveal his conviction that he would not long survive. "Whether I make my grave on the land, or in the ocean," Evarts wrote, "I submit cheerfully to Him." Friends like Edward Everett, Daniel Webster, and Theodore Frelinghuysen worried about his health and moved to fill the breach. They advanced the old causes in Congress, especially Indian affairs and sabbatarianism, but the jeremiad that "private vice always keeps pace with public immorality" seemed to fall on deaf ears. Writing for the Prudential Committee, David Greene warned that "It is in character for the selfish & ambitious politician to forget to what laws, & treaties

& the immutable principles of justice binds him, & to let his mind dwell exclusively on expediency."[5]

In mid-March the crisis that Evarts had anticipated, and on which he had based his hopes, arrived. The Georgia Guard arrested missionaries Isaac Proctor, Samuel Worcester, and John Thompson for living on Cherokee property without swearing allegiance to the state of Georgia and for failing to secure a permit from the governor. Superior Court Judge Augustin Clayton ordered them released on the grounds that they were agents of the federal government (since the ABCFM received federal funds), but Governor Gilmer opposed their release and demanded to know if the federal government claimed such an immunity for them. Secretary of War John Eaton replied that they were not agents, since the American Board no longer received federal funds for its Cherokee missions in Georgia. The American Board criticized Georgia authorities for the arrests and insisted that the men's missionary status did not deprive them of their right to express their opinion on "an important moral question."[6]

Despite the position of the American Board, however, the arguments of Evarts and other members of the Prudential Committee were too political for many of the missionaries. More concerned about spiritual and missionary matters than about political disputes, more conversant with religious than with legal issues, Isaac Proctor and John Thompson left with Daniel Butrick for the ABCFM's Tennessee missions. They believed that their mission was to Christianize and civilize the Cherokees rather than to defend their legal rights against state laws or federal policies. This split distressed Samuel Worcester, but he supported Evarts's plan and decided to remain and provide a test case.[7]

While Worcester awaited arrest in Georgia, a wait that would last well past the spring and beyond the lifetime of Jeremiah Evarts, the man whose energies and insights had fueled much of the campaign for Cherokee rights was slowly dying in Havana. He spent about six weeks at the estate of a friend near Matanzas, but his health only improved marginally. "As I am so weak, & have so little flesh," he wrote his wife in mid-March, "it is to be expected that my progress will at first be slow." He admitted that he would probably never be healthy enough to return to work in the missionary rooms. His son John, a student at Yale, anxiously inquired about his father's health in a series of letters to his mother. That he wrote his mother rather than his father perhaps reflects the crucial nurturing role Mehitabel Evarts had filled for her children while Jeremiah was away on business for the American Board. For her part, Mehitabel worried that her husband would die in Cuba. In late March she urged him to return home unless he had made significant strides toward recovery. "Your restoration may be slow, and gradual, and require nice attention," she wrote lovingly, "which you could have better at home in our pleasant chamber, than you could have elsewhere."[8]

As soon as he received his wife's letter, Jeremiah made plans to return home. His health was still not good, but his spirits had picked up to the point that he proposed to visit England as soon as he was in better health to advance the cause of missions. Evarts arrived in Charleston, South Carolina, on May 3. He was very tired from the ocean voyage, in poor health, and suffering from recurrent bouts with diarrhea. Unable to write, Evarts knew that he was a very sick man. The Reverend Joseph Brown warned that he would not live long. But despite his inability to leave his bed, three days later Evarts met with several local ministers to discuss missionary matters. These efforts further exhausted him, and his feeble health declined precipitously. On Tuesday, May 10, 1831, Jeremiah Evarts died in Charleston. An autopsy revealed that death came from pulmonary consumption. "All the viscera, except the lungs, were perfectly sound. The lungs were almost completely decayed." Following a funeral service the next afternoon, his remains were sent to Boston. After another service and a funeral oration preached by Lyman Beecher, Jeremiah Evarts was buried in the family vault beneath Park Street Church. Additional services were later held at Andover Theological Seminary. Jeremiah Evarts had died as he had lived, among friends to the missionary cause and apart from his family.[9]

During the next month, as the various societies Evarts had nurtured held their annual meetings, torrents of praise illuminated his character and chronicled his life. At the annual meeting of the Boston Prison Discipline Society, he drew praise for his "countenance, patronage, and a letter of credit which would have furnished Bibles for all the Prisons of the land," traits which reflected his confidence in the ability of benevolent societies to sponsor measures not only to ameliorate problems but to reform individuals. The *Missionary Herald* marked his passing with a black-bordered notice on the "DECEASE OF THE CORRESPONDING SECRETARY." The story that followed detailed Evarts's last days and his enduring commitment to the missionary cause. It was as much the depiction of a behavioral model as it was a memorial. In October at its twenty-second annual meeting, the American Board of Commissioners passed a lengthy resolution which highlighted Evarts's contributions to missions and religious reform, noting that few if any individuals ever exceeded his labors for that cause. Evarts's nephew, John Todd, recorded in his diary that he "never before knew any such effect produced by the fall of a man in Israel as there was in Boston by the tidings of his death." Todd also observed that he "fell, too, just after having made his greatest efforts; as if the sun should sink suddenly away, after having just thrown up his most golden beams."[10]

The various journals published by and for the benevolent crusade also praised Jeremiah Evarts's accomplishments and commitment. They seized upon his death not only to chronicle his life but to instruct readers about the life of a model Christian. Perhaps the *Christian Advocate and Journal* said it most succinctly: "As a writer and philanthropist, he needs no other eulogy than the simple statement—'He was the author of the essays signed William Penn.'" Other publications echoed this praise and observed that Evarts had been the true patriot. Not only had he sought to advance Christian principles; he worried about "how this might become a nation of holy men, fearing God, keeping his commandments, and enjoying his favor."[11]

This underlying national morality was, to Jeremiah Evarts, the soul of America. He had envisioned a nation that was at once progressive, expansive, and worldly but also instructive and moral. "I will not believe," he had told the Reverend Gardiner Spring, "that the nation is yet lost to truth and honor." This conviction had sustained him throughout his defense of the Cherokees, and it remained with him until his death. Indeed, the final blows to his health came from his labors in the Cherokee cause and his insistence that he travel to New Bedford, Massachusetts, in frigid and stormy December weather to deliver the final instructions to the third reinforcement of missionaries to the Sandwich Islands.[12]

Even his will reflected a determination to place Christian republicanism at the center of his life. He left his Bibles, along with $200 worth of books from his personal library, to his wife Mehitabel. The rest of his library went to the American Board, with a proviso that his family could keep it *if* they paid the ABCFM $500 plus interest from a year after his death. In death as in life Jeremiah Evarts placed his commitment before his family. This reflected his conviction that institutional life had a morphology similar to that of human life. Each had its beginning, maturity, and decline. But while he believed that human life was in the hands of God, Evarts was convinced that, although institutional life was not eternal, committed individuals and proper precautions could prolong its vitality. Herein lay the essence of the conservative republicanism so attractive to Evarts. Indeed, two days after Evarts's death the *Boston Daily Advertiser* reported a speech by Alexander Hill Everett before the Massachusetts Bible Society which could well have served as his epitaph. Everett called the age one of revolutions and lamented that "Established institutions have lost their influence and authority." He noted that deference had largely disappeared: "There is . . . an effort . . . to reduce the action of Government within the narrowest possible limits, and to give the widest possible extent to individual liberty." The cure for this boundless individualism, Everett concluded, was religion and self-restraint. "The citizen who is released in a great measure from the control of positive authority must possess within his own mind the strong curb of an enlightened conscience—a well-grounded, deeply-felt, rational and practical Piety."[13]

Just before his death, Jeremiah Evarts wrote "Contingent Prospects of Our Country," an article that could just as well be a self-composed epitaph. Optimistic as usual, Evarts noted the happy prospects facing the United States with its rapid population growth and expanding influence. But, also typical of Evarts, he warned readers that "gigantic accretions" had attached themselves to fundamental institutions and threatened to undermine the "foundation and structure of our society." Once again his metaphor was that of human morphology. Skillful political surgery was needed, he said, to correct these ills and control "epidemics." "There are," he warned, "the seeds of numerous and hurtful diseases, lurking in the blood; there are, in short, many symptoms of no very remote decline, many and powerful tendencies to a dissolution of our fabric, and a blasting of our hopes." The United States was at a crisis, Evarts insisted, and there was only one sure solution. "To pursue an upright and honorable course, notwithstanding the defects of our institutions, so as to work off all the unseemly accretions and morbid affections from the body politic, *public virtue* is the only and the essential requisite. And that cannot exist independently of *private* virtue, possessed to such an extent, as to form the public character. And the only nurse of virtue, private and public, on a secure and permanent basis, is *Christianity*. Christianity alone embodies all the elements of virtue; and consequently, in the pervading influence of Christianity is all our hope."[14]

Evarts believed that self-discipline, individual virtue, and Christian principles were essential to harness the centrifugal tendencies evident in

American life. He feared that the "seeds of civil discord" were increasing throughout the land and was convinced that if left unchecked they would infect and agitate "our whole political body" until its very fabric dissolved. The Indian removal controversy and the rising debate over slavery seemed to him to represent two such evils. "The former of these evils is a gangrene of monstrous growth," he wrote, "entering into the muscle, bone, and very marrow of our Republic. The latter is fast becoming so—though not with the same chance of dangerous increase."[15]

Political conservative that he was, however, Jeremiah Evarts's embrace of moral principles to cure temporal problems and promote stability ironically introduced a destabilizing element into American political culture. Since the ratification of the Constitution, politicians had sought compromise on vexing issues as a deterrent to conflict. But as Evarts's stand on Indian removal demonstrated, commitment to moral principles led one to stand firm and refuse to compromise those principles. Perhaps, therefore, it should be no surprise that many abolitionists in the 1830s and 1840s came out of Federalist households. Nor should it have been surprising that in 1830, when William Lloyd Garrison prepared to found an antislavery newspaper, he sought out the corresponding secretary of the American Board of Commissioners for help. Garrison and Evarts embraced very different methods, but they sought the same goal. The words of one petition to Congress opposing Sunday mail delivery summed up their intent: "We feel that we have a right to look to the government of our country for example; and that those whom the people have clothed with power will not permit a practice which is continually undermining the morals, and consequently endangering the liberties, of the nation."[16]

This sort of expression also revealed another transformation effected by the work of men like Jeremiah Evarts during the preceding three decades. At the height of the Second Great Awakening, benevolent reformers urged citizens to undergo personal conversion and looked to God for signs of declension and for moral warnings. By the 1820s, however, these same individuals, perhaps to accommodate the new liberal individualism of that age, looked to moral associations and citizen watchfulness for these signs and warnings. The more perceptive among them seemed to understand the new race for riches and power and the lure of liberal capitalism and boundless individualism. To temper the ethos of acquisitiveness and self-interest, they looked increasingly to a gospel of self-restraint rather than institutional constraints and to the influence of groups (women, for instance) who remained outside that race. Jacob Abbott, in a lecture on moral education, sounded this theme most succinctly:

> There must be in the generation which is to come upon the stage, a greater portion of social virtue than will come spontaneously, or the dangers which even now threaten our country will thicken into deeper and deeper gloom. To be mild and gentle in spirit, kind and conciliatory in temper and conduct, and submissive to proper authority, are not the natural characteristics of Americans. The stern unbending spirit of freedom which prevails in this land is with difficulty retained in union with the gentler and more peaceful virtues of social life. We must then earnestly exert ourselves to sustain the latter, or else this extended government over our immensely varied country will soon become a very unstable equilibrium of the fierce elements of whirlwind and storm.[17]

In the end, Jeremiah Evarts's search for the soul of America led him to his death. He had sacrificed his health for his conscience and had drawn on that conscience to articulate a synthetic vision of American culture at the very moment when centrifugal forces were creating a dynamic landscape of competing and conflicting visions. His search was the search of a conservative in an age of liberal transformation. In his "William Penn" essays and elsewhere, Evarts had argued that the law should restrain and bind men together through their compacts, to provide a fettered freedom that reflected moral purpose and preserved underlying rights. But Americans in the Jacksonian years no longer wished to be fettered, particularly in their pursuit of the main chance. In the same manner that the Foot Resolution reflected a progressive but conservative expansion, so too did the Indian Removal debates reflect that new boundless spirit that animated so many citizens in Andrew Jackson's America.

Jeremiah Evarts was only one of many individuals who, in their own ways, searched for the soul of America during the early years of the nineteenth century. Few others, however, touched so many elements of the American social, political, and ideological spectrum as did Evarts. That he devoted his life to religious and moral causes, yet was not a minister, itself represented evidence of a significant transition. Organized religion had never been able totally to control local society, although it had always possessed the shadow of ideological and even institutional hegemony. As disestablishment proceeded apace throughout New England, men like Evarts tried to marry religious conviction to social and political virtue through benevolent societies so as to advance the ideological hegemony of Christian republicanism. As they did so they confronted the stirrings of liberal individualism and in turn sought to harness that individualism to the ideal of behavioral virtue. They came to grips with a new concept of citizenship—activist, participatory, increasingly non-deferential. From that confrontation they sought to mold a proto-Victorian synthesis. Evarts refused to uncouple individual freedom in the marketplace from moral self-restraint, seeking instead a fusion of republicanism, capitalism, and revivalism. He had hoped that the revivals of the Second Great Awakening would spawn a humanitarian sensibility sufficiently pervasive to advance a Christian republicanism. He gradually came to understand (but never to admit) that it had not and turned to moral reform societies and missionary enterprises to stimulate inner moral imperatives that might, in turn, foster such a sensibility.[18]

Jeremiah Evarts himself underwent a similar transformation. In 1816 he had bemoaned the lack of leadership to promote a disinterested benevolence. "We want such a man set forth," he wrote, "as an instrument of good to mankind. . . . It is a notorious truth . . . that there is not in Massachusetts a single man capable of leading the moral exertions of the friends of religion and morality."[19] Sixteen years later, one year after Evarts's death, the Cherokee Council instructed John Ridge to "go to the cities of the North, and let them know of our distress. Go to the land of that great man who had buckled on the armour of truth and eloquence, and nobly defended the Cherokees on the floor of Congress; go to the land of Edward Everett—Go to the city of the man who struggled for our rights to the last, and died in the cause of the Cherokees: the city of Jeremiah Evarts."[20]

Had Evarts lived even one more year, he would have witnessed the Supreme Court's affirmation of his arguments in *Worcester v. Georgia*. On the one hand, the decision would have encouraged him to hope that a respect for the law and a moral humanitarianism were yet alive in Jacksonian America. On the other hand, however, Andrew Jackson's determination to ignore the decision of the Marshall Court and to forcibly remove the Cherokees would have reinforced his fears that contrary values were ascendant. With the death of Evarts and the failure of the Cherokees' cause, moral outrage over Indian removal faded quickly. After his death, the ABCFM acceded to the inevitability of removal.[21] The American Board's failure to prevent removal dramatized the problem of Christian republicanism and consensus. The Second Great Awakening had clearly transformed much of the American cultural landscape, but it had not revitalized that society to the extent of creating a new political consensus formulated from its underlying principles. During the next few years moral outrage would simmer once again, this time over the slavery issue. Slavery was more pervasive as a political and cultural issue; its leaders were far more radical than men of Jeremiah Evarts's generation. Within two decades that simmering controversy would boil over; appeals to conscience, morality, and a Higher Law echoed once again in the halls of Congress and throughout the land. The American people would be forced to confront the question of an underlying moral ethos. A civil war would lay bare the soul of America.

Abbreviations

AAS   American Antiquarian Society, Worcester, Massachusetts
ABC   Archives of the American Board of Commissioners for Foreign Missions, Houghton Library, Harvard University, Cambridge, Massachusetts
ABCFM   American Board of Commissioners for Foreign Missions
AHR   American Historical Review
EFP   Evarts Family Papers, Sterling Library, Yale University, New Haven, Connecticut
HSP   Historical Society of Pennsylvania, Philadelphia, Pennsylvania
IA, LR Office of Indian Affairs, Letters Received
IA, LS Office of Indian Affairs, Letters Sent
LC   Library of Congress, Washington, D.C.
SW, LS Secretary of War, Letters Sent
WMQ   William and Mary Quarterly

Notes

NOTES FOR PROLOGUE

1. John Ross to the Senate and House of Representatives, September 28, 1836, in Gary Moulton, ed., *The Papers of Chief John Ross* 1:460.
2. Ross to the Senate and House of Representatives, June 21, 1836, ibid., 427–28.
3. See Gordon Wood, "Conspiracy and the Paranoid Style: Causality and Deceit in the Eighteenth Century," *WMQ* 3d series, 39 (1982): 401–41; Karen Halttunen, *Confidence Men and Painted Women: A Study of Middle-Class Culture in America, 1830–1870*, pp. 201–2; and Daniel Walker Howe, "Victorian Culture in America," in *Victorian America*, Daniel Walker Howe, ed., pp. 3–28.
4. These topics have generated a voluminous literature. The following works have particularly influenced my thinking: Joyce Appleby, *Capitalism and a New Social Order: The Republican Vision of the 1790s*; Richard Beeman, *The Evolution of the Southern Backcountry: A Case Study of Lunenburg County, Virginia, 1746–1832*; Robert Shalhope, "Republicanism and Early American Historiography," *WMQ* 3d series, 39 (1982): 334–56. See also Sean Wilentz, *Chants Democratic: New York City and the Rise of the American Working Class, 1788–1850*; Thomas Brown, *Politics and Statesmanship: Essays on the American Whig Party*; and Richard Holmes, *Communities in Transition: Bedford and Lincoln, Massachusetts, 1729–1850*. A stimulating analysis of the post-revolutionary years is in Michael Zuckerman, "A Different Thermidor: The Revolution Beyond the American Revolution" (Paper presented to the Philadelphia Center for Early American Studies, May 23, 1986).
5. Thomas Haskell has pointed to a number of other connections in two insightful essays, "Capitalism and the Origins of the Humanitarian Sensibility," *AHR* 90 (1985): 339–61, 547–66.
6. From the Woodstock, Vermont, newspaper, *Liberal Extracts*, August 1829,

quoted in Randolph Roth, "Whence This Strange Fire? Religious and Reform Movements in the Connecticut River Valley of Vermont, 1791–1843" (Ph.D. diss., Yale University, 1981), p. 289.

7. Quoted in Richard Hofstadter, "Andrew Jackson and the Rise of Liberal Capitalism," *The American Political Tradition*, p. 57.

8. Walton Felch, *The Manufacturer's Pocket-Piece; or the Cotton-Mill Moralized*, pp. 12–14. For a discussion of the transition from piety to morality in the early nineteenth century, see Kathryn Sklar, *Catharine Beecher: A Study in American Domesticity*, pp. 78, 83.

NOTES FOR CHAPTER ONE

1. Ebenezer C. Tracy, *Memoir of the Life of Jeremiah Evarts, Esq.*, p. 13. This remains an essential source, for Evarts left few papers detailing his early life.

2. C. Y. A., "On the Execution of the Laws," *Panoplist* 2 (December 1806): 321. A list of pseudonyms under which Evarts wrote is in Tracy, *Memoir*, p. 45n. My discussion is based on this essay; quotations are from pp. 319, 321, 322, and 323.

3. The Connecticut background is pieced together from Bruce Daniels, *The Connecticut Town: Growth and Development, 1635–1790*, pp. 53–63; Bernard Steiner, *A History of the Plantation of Menunkatuck and of the Original Town of Guilford, Connecticut, comprising the Present Towns of Guilford and Madison*, pp. 148–49; John J. Waters, "Patrimony, Succession, and Social Stability: Guilford, Connecticut, in the Eighteenth Century," *Perspectives in American History* 10 (1976): 131–61; John J. Waters, "Family, Inheritance, and Migration in Colonial New England: The Evidence from Guilford, Connecticut," *WMQ*, 3d series, 39 (1982): 64–86; Ralph Smith, *The History of Guilford, Connecticut, from its First Settlement in 1639*, p. 13; Ralph Smyth, "John Evarts of Guilford, Conn., and His Descendants," *New England Historic & Genealogical Register* 61 (1907): 25–30, 307. I want to thank Ella Greene of Schenectady, New York, for providing additional material on the Evarts family.

4. Tracy, *Memoir*, p. 9; Nathan Perkins, *Narrative of a Tour Through the State of Vermont, From April 27 to June 12, 1789*, pp. 13–14; Wallace Lamb, *The Lake Champlain and Lake George Valleys*, 1:345–46; Abby Hemenway, ed., *The Vermont Historical Gazetteer*, pp. 239, 241.

5. Zadock Thompson, *A Gazetteer of the State of Vermont*, pp. 130, 306; John Haywood, *A Gazetteer of Vermont*, pp. 129–30; Lamb, *Lake Champlain*, 2:487–88; "Sketch of the Life and Character of Jeremiah Evarts," *Missionary Herald* 27 (October 1831): 305. On the spread of New England villages, see Joseph Wood, "The Origin of the New England Village" (Ph.D. diss., Pennsylvania State University, 1978), pp. 1–8, 58.

6. "Miss Thoughtful," *Instructive and Entertaining Emblems*, quoted in Jay

Fliegelman, *Prodigals and Pilgrims: The American Revolution Against Patriarchal Authority, 1750–1800*, pp. 94–95; Tracy, *Memoir*, pp. 9–10.

7. Joseph Kett, *Rites of Passage: Adolescence in America, 1790 to the Present*, p. 5. Evarts left orders that most of his private papers be destroyed upon his death. Those orders were carried out; few survive. That perhaps bespeaks deep personal or family conflicts, probably over his choice of a career, at which the surviving evidence only hints.

8. Gardiner Spring, *A Tribute to the Memory of the Late Jeremiah Evarts, Esq., Secretary of the American Board of Commissioners for Foreign Missions*, p. 7; Hemenway, *Vermont Historical Gazeteer*, p. 241; John Tracy, ed., "Diary of a Yale Student in 1798 (Jeremiah Evarts)," *Yale Alumni Weekly* 38 (1928): 159; "Review of Sketches of the Life and Character of Jeremiah Evarts Esq.," *Spirit of the Pilgrims* 4 (November 1831): 601; "Sketch of Evarts," p. 305; Franklin Dexter, *Biographical Sketches of the Graduates of Yale College with Annals of the College History*, 5:483–87; David Field, comp., *Brief Memoirs of the Members of the Class Graduated at Yale College in September, 1802*.

9. Ralph Gabriel, *Religion and Learning at Yale: The Church of Christ in the College and University, 1757–1957*, p. 54; Brooks Kelley, *Yale: A History*, pp. 118–22.

10. Steven Novak, *The Rights of Youth: American Colleges and Student Revolt, 1798–1815*, p. 70; Peter Slater, *Children in the New England Mind in Death and in Life*, p. 125; Maxwell Bloomfield, *American Lawyers in a Changing Society, 1776–1876*, pp. 39–40.

11. Nathaniel Emmons, "God Never Forsakes His People," in Jacob Ide, ed., *The Works of Nathaniel Emmons, D.D., Late Pastor of the Church in Franklin, Mass., with a Memoir of His Life*, 2:179–80. Delivered November 27, 1800.

12. This work was published in several volumes and went through multiple editions. I have used the twelfth edition.

13. Dwight, *Theology*, 2:427–28.

14. Ibid., 3:135.

15. Ibid., 345–46 (Sermon 109: "The Duty of Subjects"). For a discussion of Dwight's theology see Wayne C. Tyner, "The Theology of Timothy Dwight in Historical Perspective" (Ph.D. diss., University of North Carolina, 1971). See also John Fitzmier, "The Godly Federalism of Timothy Dwight, 1752–1817: Society, Doctrine, and Religion in the Life of New England's 'Moral Legislator'" (Ph.D. diss., Princeton University, 1986).

16. Hemenway, *Vermont Historical Gazeteer*, p. 241; Tracy, *Memoir*, p. 11. See Christopher Jedrey, *The World of John Cleaveland: Family and Community in Eighteenth-Century New England*, pp. 28–29, for eighteenth-century Yale; as well as Peter Dobkin Hall, *The Organization of American Culture, 1700–1900: Private Institutions, Elites, and the Origins of American Nationality*, p. 161. Those who did not in some way escape often suffered the economic consequences; see Nancy

Folbre, "The Wealth of Patriarchs: Deerfield, Massachusetts, 1760–1840," *Journal of Interdisciplinary History* 16 (1985): 199–200.

17. Tracy, "Diary," p. 159.
18. Ibid.; Dexter, *Biographical Sketches*, 5:342.
19. Tracy, "Diary," p. 159.
20. Ibid.
21. Franklin Dexter, "Student Life at Yale College Under the First President Dwight (1795–1817)," *Proceedings of the American Antiquarian Society* 27 (1917): 320. See also Novak, *Rights of Youth* and Tracy, "Diary," p. 160.
22. Tracy, "Diary," p. 160; Dexter, *Biographical Sketches*, 5:342.
23. Tracy, "Diary," pp. 160, 187–88.
24. Jeremiah Evarts, "A Dissertation on *Amor Patriae*," Box 5, folder 190, Evarts Family Papers, Yale. Hereafter these will be designated EFP.
25. Jeremiah Evarts, "Are the Abilities of Females Inferior to those of Males?" Box 5, folder 191, EFP.
26. Tracy, "Diary," p. 202. Evarts's entries are in cipher. See also Novak, *Rights of Youth*, pp. 73–74; and Charles Keller, *The Second Great Awakening in Connecticut*, pp. 136–37.
27. J. Evarts, Journal, October 5, 1801, Box 5, folder 192, EFP.
28. Ibid.; Tracy, "Diary," p. 203; J. Evarts, Journal, November 5, 1801, Box 5, folder 192, EFP; Evarts to John White, Jr., Box 3, folder 126, EFP. There are numerous letters to White, 1801–5, concerning literary criticism and poetry. His poetry is published in the *Connecticut Evangelical Intelligencer* 2 (September 1801): 119–20.
29. Charles Backus, *A Sermon, Delivered Jan. 1, 1801: Containing a Brief Review of Some of the Distinguishing Events of the Eighteenth Century*, p. 11; Timothy Dwight, *A Discourse on Some Events of the Last Century, Delivered in the Brick Church in New Haven, on Wednesday, January 7, 1801*, p. 35; Timothy Alden, Jr., *The Glory of America: A Century Sermon Delivered at the South Church, in Portsmouth, New Hampshire, 4 January 1801*, p. 22; Thomas Cary, *A Sermon, Delivered to the First Religious Society in Newburyport, September 27, 1801*, p. 12. For the revival of politics see David H. Fischer, *The Revolution of American Conservatism: The Federalist Party in the Era of Jeffersonian Democracy*.
30. Journal entry for January 9, 1802, in Tracy, *Memoir*, p. 18. See also Kett, *Rites of Passage*, p. 68; Oliver Elsbree, *The Rise of the Missionary Spirit in America, 1790–1815*, p. 36.
31. Kelley, *Yale*, p. 124; David Allmendinger, *Paupers and Scholars: The Transformation of Student Life in Nineteenth-Century New England*, p. 119. The Porter quote is in Kelley, *Yale*, pp. 122–23. Also see Chauncey Goodrich, "Narrative of Revivals of Religion in Yale College, From Its Commencement to the Present Time," *Journal of the American Education Society* 10 (1838): 295; Gabriel, *Religion and Learning*, pp. 71–72; Novak, *Rights of Youth*, p. 135; "Review of Sketches," pp. 601–2. For

Evarts see David Field to the Rev. E. C. Tracy, Box 3, EFP.

32. Benjamin Silliman to his mother, June 11, 1802, in George Fisher, *Life of Benjamin Silliman*, 1:83. For the state of New Haven at this time, see Evarts to Rosewell Swan, October 2, 1802, Box 3, folder 113, EFP.

33. Spring, *Tribute*, pp. 7–8.

34. Tracy, *Memoir*, p. 29; Timothy Dwight, "Ministers and Their Converts: A Mutual Rejoicing in the Day of Christ," in *Sermons*, pp. 417–18; Samuel Spring, *A Sermon, Delivered Before the Massachusetts Missionary Society, At Their Annual Meeting, May 25, 1802*, pp. 12–13; Hemenway, *Vermont Historical Gazeteer*, pp. 241–42; Dexter, *Biographical Sketches*, 5:483–87. Samuel Worcester, Leonard's brother, would later be Evarts's superior at the American Board of Commissioners for Foreign Missions; and one of Leonard's sons, also a Samuel, would figure prominently in the 1830–32 dispute between Georgia and the Cherokees.

35. Evarts to Eleazer Foster, March 27, 1803, Box 2, folder 52, EFP; Fischer, *Revolution of American Conservatism*; Edmund B. Thomas, Jr., "Politics in the Land of Steady Habits: Connecticut's First Political Party System, 1789–1820" (Ph.D. diss., Clark University, 1972), pp. 133, 213–14; Linda Kerber, *Federalists in Dissent: Imagery and Ideology in Jeffersonian America*, pp. viii–ix, 95–96, 212; Michael Kammen, *A Season of Youth: The American Revolution and the Historical Imagination*, p. 98.

36. Evarts to Rosewell Swan, June 27, 1803, Box 3, folder 113, EFP. See also Tracy, *Memoir*, pp. 30–31, and Randolph Roth, *The Democratic Dilemma: Religion, Reform, and the Social Order in the Connecticut Valley of Vermont, 1791–1850*, for conditions in Peacham.

37. Tracy, *Memoir*, pp. 32–40; Evarts to Sarah Evarts, May 3, 1803; Evarts to Rosewell Swan, June 27, 1803; J. Evarts, Journal, May 22–September 12, 1803, Boxes 3 and 5, folders 123, 113, 193, EFP. Also Evarts to R. Swan, December 5, 1803, in Tracy, *Memoir*, pp. 39–40. Swan had been a classmate of Evarts at Yale.

38. Evarts to Swan, December 5, 1803, in Tracy, *Memoir*, pp. 39–40.

39. Lyman Beecher, *The Practicability of Suppressing Vice, By Means of Societies Instituted for that Purpose. A Sermon, Delivered Before the Moral Society, in East-Hampton, September 21, 1803*, pp. 7, 9, 20; Samuel Austin, *Christians Bound to Spread the Gospel Among all Descriptions of Their Fellow Men: A Sermon, Preached Before the Massachusetts Missionary Society, May 24, 1803*, p. 11; Evan Johns, *The Happiness of American Christians. A Thanksgiving Sermon, Preached On Thursday the 24th of November, 1803*, p. 8; T. Dwight, "Ministers and Their Converts," p. 412.

40. Evarts's journal entry for April 18, 1804, in Tracy, *Memoir*, p. 43. For the legal profession see Kett, *Rites of Passage*, p. 32.

41. Spring, *Tribute*, pp. 7–8; Kett, *Rites of Passage*, pp. 33, 45.

42. Gerard Gawalt, *The Promise of Power: The Legal Profession in Massachusetts, 1760–1840*, pp. 173–76, 200–207.

43. Tracy, *Memoir*, pp. 44–45; Christopher Collier, *Roger Sherman's Connecticut:*

Yankee Politics and the American Revolution, pp. 322–23; Andrew Peabody, "Hopkinsianism," *Proceedings of the American Antiquarian Society* 5 (1888):444; Dexter, *Biographical Sketches*, 5:483–87. All of Roger Sherman's daughters married well: Martha to Jeremiah Day, later president of Yale; Rebecca to Simeon Baldwin; another sister to Samuel Hoar of Massachusetts.

44. C. Y. A., "Fame," *Panoplist* 1 (January 1806): 349–50.

45. Ibid., pp. 397–400.

46. C. Y. A., "On the Reasonableness of an Immediate Repentance," *Connecticut Evangelical Magazine* 4 (March 1804): 345–48; (April 1804): 380–83; 5 (August 1804): 76–79; 6 (May 1806): 412–16; 7 (August 1806): 48–50; (December 1806): 205–7; (June 1807): 447–49.

47. Jonathan French, *A Discourse, Delivered in the South Parish in Andover, December 1, 1801, On the Anniversary Thanksgiving in Massachusetts*, p. 17.

48. Orsamus C. Merrill, *The Happiness of America. An Oration, Delivered at Shaftsbury, On the Fourth of July, 1804. Being the Twenty-ninth Anniversary of American Independence*, p. 23; Luther Richardson, *An Address, Delivered Before the Roxbury Charitable Society, At their Anniversary Meeting, September 17, 1804*, pp. 11, 17–18.

49. Jotham Waterman, *National Righteousness National Security. A Discourse, Delivered April 5, 1804. The Day Appointed for Fast. By His Excellency, Caleb Strong, Esq., Governor of the Commonwealth of Massachusetts*, pp. 8, 24; Daniel Waldo, *The Causes and Remedies of National Divisions, Illustrated in A Discourse, Delivered in Suffield, 1st Society. July 4th, 1804*, passim; Daniel Dana, *The Importance of Virtue and Piety as Qualifications of Rulers: A Discourse Delivered March 31, 1805*, passim.

50. Daniel Dana, *A Discourse Delivered May 22, 1804, Before the Members of the Female Charitable Society of Newburyport, Organized June 8, 1803*, p. 21. *Christian Intelligencer* 9 (September 1, 1838), reprinted an 1804 sermon of John Livingston that argued the same point.

51. Edward D. Griffin, *The Kingdom of Christ: A Missionary Sermon, Preached Before the General Assembly of the Presbyterian Church, in Philadelphia, May 23d, 1805*, pp. 24–25; *Panoplist* 2 (September 1806): 171; William Lyman, *The Happy Nation. A Sermon, Preached at the Anniversary Election, in Hartford, May 8th, 1806*, pp. 6, 27; Peter Wendover, *National Deliverance. An Oration, Delivered in the New Dutch Church, in the City of New York, on the Fourth of July, 1806, Being the Thirtieth Anniversary of American Independence*, p. 14. For Evarts's own feelings see Tracy, *Memoir*, pp. 43–44, and material in Box 6, folder 202, EFP.

52. Dana, *Importance of Virtue*, pp. 22–23; Joseph Gleason, Jr., *An Oration, Pronounced on the Thirtieth Anniversary of American Independence, Before the Young Democratic Republicans, of the Town of Boston, at the Second Baptist Meeting House, July 4, 1806*, p. 12.

53. Natalie Naylor, "Raising a Learned Ministry: The American Education Society, 1815–1860" (Ph.D. diss., Columbia University, 1971), pp. 29–30; "Jeremiah Evarts," *American Quarterly Register* 4 (1831): 74.

54. C. Y. A., "On the State of Literature in New England," *Panoplist* 2 (March 1807): 471–73; (April 1807): 522–24; (May 1807): 565–72. The following discussion is drawn from this article.

55. Ibid., p. 522.

56. Ibid., pp. 523, 566–69.

57. Ibid., pp. 569–70.

58. Ibid., p. 572.

59. Coke, "On the Profession of the Law," *Literary Cabinet* 1 (November 15, 1806): 12; (December 27, 1806): 29–30. For a similar experience that produced greater despair, see Richard Rollins, *The Long Journey of Noah Webster*, p. 4. See also Tracy, *Memoir*, pp. 45, 48.

60. Evarts to Worcester, December 8, 1806, in Tracy, *Memoir*, p. 51. See also *A Brief History of the American Tract Society, instituted at Boston, 1814, and its relations to the American Tract Society at New York, instituted 1825*, p. 5.

61. Jonathan T. Evarts to J. Evarts, February 1, 1807, Box 1, folder 37, EFP. See the *Panoplist* 3 (July 1807): 63–64 and above notes 2, 40, and 42 for his earlier publications. See also the Reverend S. Worcester to Mrs. Zervia Worcester, June 13, 1807, ABC 1.5, vol. 2, Houghton Library, Harvard. This standard abbreviation for the Archives of the American Board of Commissioners for Foreign Missions will be used throughout.

62. Letter of August 19, 1808, in Tracy, *Memoir*, p. 53.

63. Elsbree, *Rise of Missionary Spirit*, pp. 65–66. For Evarts's decision see John E. Todd, *John Todd: The Story of His Life, Told Mainly by Himself*, p. 45; Evarts to Morse, January 16, 1809, Simon Gratz Collection, Historical Society of Pennsylvania (hereafter HSP). There are also numerous letters between Evarts and Morse in the Morse Family Papers, Yale.

64. For Morse, see Joseph Phillips, "Jedidiah Morse: An Intellectual Biography" (Ph.D. diss., University of California, Berkeley, 1978), pp. 9–30. This has since been published as *Jedidiah Morse and New England Congregationalism*.

65. Evarts to Morse, November 27, 1809, Simon Gratz Collection, HSP. See also several letters in Box 8, the Morse Family Papers, Yale; Evarts to Morse, February 17, 1809, Simon Gratz Collection, HSP; William Sprague, *The Life of Jedidiah Morse, D.D.*, pp. 71–72.

66. Tracy, *Memoir*, p. 55.

67. Ibid., pp. 55–56; James F. Hunnewell, *A Century of Town Life: A History of Charlestown, Massachusetts, 1775–1887*, p. 202.

68. For a good summary of these changes, see Gerard Gawalt, "Sources of Anti-Lawyer Sentiment in Massachusetts, 1740–1840," *American Journal of Legal History* 14 (1970): 283–307. A summary of these cultural indices is found in Howe, "Victorian Culture," pp. 3–13, 21.

NOTES FOR CHAPTER TWO

1. *Connecticut Evangelical Magazine* 1 (July 1800): 19. From an account of a religious revival in Somers, Connecticut, in 1797.

2. Thomas Jefferson, *Notes on Virginia*, quoted in Robert Bellah, "The Revolution and Civil Religion," in Jerald Brauer, ed., *Religion and the American Revolution*, pp. 61–62. A fine discussion of the awakening's scope is in Richard Shiels, "The Scope of the Second Great Awakening: Andover, Massachusetts, as a Case Study," *Journal of the Early Republic* 5 (1985): 223–46.

3. This discussion leans heavily on Jack P. Greene, "An Uneasy Connection: An Analysis of the Preconditions of the American Revolution," in Stephen Kurtz and James Hutson, eds., *Essays on the American Revolution*, pp. 54–55; Timothy Smith, "Righteousness and Hope: Christian Holiness and the Millennial Vision in America, 1800–1900," *American Quarterly* 31 (1979): 21; Kenneth Lockridge, "Social Change and the Meaning of the American Revolution," *Journal of Social History* 6 (1973): 431; and John Shy, "The American Revolution: The Military Conflict Considered as a Revolutionary War," in Kurtz and Hutson, *Essays on the American Revolution*, pp. 154–55. See also Charles Dickson, "Jeremiads in the New American Republic: The Case of National Fasts in the John Adams Administration," *New England Quarterly* 60 (1987): 187–207.

4. A good summary is in Nathan Hatch, *The Sacred Cause of Liberty: Republican Thought and the Millennium in Revolutionary New England*; see especially pp. 105ff.

5. Ibid., pp. 112–13. Stephen Davis, "From Plowshares to Spindles: Dedham, Massachusetts, 1790–1840" (Ph.D. diss., University of Wisconsin, 1973), pp. 17, 23, discusses local changes after 1790. See also Richard Bushman, "'This New Man': Dependence and Independence, 1776," in Richard Bushman et al., *Uprooted Americans: Essays to Honor Oscar Handlin*, pp. 91–92; Catherine Albanese, *Sons of the Fathers: The Civil Religion of the American Revolution*, p. 33; and Mark Noll, "Common Sense Traditions and American Evangelical Thought," *American Quarterly* 37 (1985): 216–38.

6. Gordon Wood, *The Creation of the America Republic, 1776–1787*, p. 59; John F. Berens, *Providence and Patriotism in Early America, 1640–1815*, pp. ix–x, iii; Sacvan Bercovitch, *The American Jeremiad*, pp. 135, 154; Richard D. Brown, "Modernization: A Victorian Climax," *American Quarterly* 27 (1975): 214; Richard D. Brown, "The Emergence of Urban Society in Rural Massachusetts, 1760–1820," *Journal of American History* 61 (1974): 36.

7. Thomas Danforth, *A Discourse, Before the Humane Society, of the Commonwealth of Massachusetts, Boston, June 14, 1808*, pp. 14–15; Wood, *Creation of American Republic*, pp. 68, 395; Lockridge, "Social Change," p. 436; and Bellah, "The Revolution and Civil Religion," pp. 57–61.

8. Joseph Lathrop, *The Signs of Perilous Times. A Sermon. Delivered at the Public Fast, in West-Springfield, April 7, 1808*, p. 9. Wood, *Creation of American Republic*,

p. 421, has a good breakdown of these two positions. See also Martha Blauvelt, "Society, Religion and Revivalism: The Second Great Awakening in New Jersey, 1780–1830," (Ph.D. diss., Princeton University, 1975), p. 76; and Robert Shalhope, *John Taylor of Caroline: Pastoral Republican*, pp. 8–9.

9. Eighteenth-century ideas about self-love are discussed in Joseph Conforti, "Samuel Hopkins and the New Divinity: Theology, Ethics, and Social Reform in Eighteenth-Century New England," *WMQ* 3d series, 34 (1977): 583–85. See also Stephen Berk, *Calvinism versus Democracy: Timothy Dwight and the Origins of American Evangelical Orthodoxy*, pp. 103, 110; Shiels, "Connecticut Clergy," pp. 116–17.

10. Timothy Dwight, "Address to the Ministers of the Gospel of Every Denomination in the United States," *American Museum* 4 (July 1788), p. 30. For a discussion of this point and its connection to the American Board of Commissioners for Foreign Missions, see Alan Perry, "The American Board of Commissioners for Foreign Missions and the London Missionary Society in the 19th Century: A Study of Ideas" (Ph.D. diss., Washington University, 1974), p. 52n. For an analysis of this and related concerns see William McLoughlin, "The Role of Religion in the Revolution: Liberty of Conscience and Cultural Cohesion in the New Nation," in Kurtz and Hutson, *Essays on the American Revolution*, pp. 197–255 *passim*.

11. See William McLoughlin, ed., *Isaac Backus on Church, State, and Calvinism: Pamphlets, 1754–1789*, pp. 17, 30–31, for the issue of dissenting sects; and William McLoughlin, *New England Dissent, 1630–1833: The Baptists and the Separation of Church and State*; Theodore Linn, "Religion and Nationalism: American Methodism and the New Nation in the Early National Period, 1766–1844" (Ph.D. diss., Drew University, 1971), p. 68; and William Maxwell, *A Memoir of the Rev. John H. Rice, D.D.*, p. 50.

12. George Kirsch, "Clerical Dismissals in Colonial and Revolutionary New Hampshire," *Church History* 49 (1980): 163–64, 171.

13. James Sullivan, *Strictures on the Rev. Mr. Thacher's Pamphlet*, p. 4.

14. See the 1784 election sermon of Samuel McClintock in Richard Hudson, "The Challenge of Dissent: Religious Conditions in New Hampshire in the Early Nineteenth Century" (Ph.D. diss., Syracuse University, 1970), pp. 19, 23; Fred Hood, "Presbyterianism and the New American Nation, 1783–1826" (Ph.D. diss., Princeton University, 1968), p. 8; T. Dwight, "Address," p. 30.

15. Peter Thacher, *A Reply to the Strictures of Mr. J. S., a Layman, Upon the Pamphlet Entitled Observations Upon the Present State of the Clergy of New-England*; Blauvelt, "Society," pp. 66–68, 75; William McLoughlin, "The Relevance of Congregational Christianity: Barrington Congregational Church, 1717–1967," *Rhode Island History* 29 (1970): 71; Hatch, *Sacred Cause*, p. 12; Carl Peterson, "The Politics of Revival, 1783–1815" (Ph.D. diss., Stanford University, 1974), p. 203.

16. Thacher, *Reply*, p. 7.

17. Isaac Lewis (1799), quoted in Peterson, "Politics of Revival," pp. 249–

50; Barbara Wingo, "Politics, Society, and Religion: The Presbyterian Clergy of Pennsylvania, New Jersey, and New York, and the Formation of the Nation, 1775–1808" (Ph.D. diss., Tulane University, 1976), p. 16; Joseph Ellis, *After the Revolution: Profiles of Early American Culture*, p. 34.

18. Dwight, "Address," p. 30; Rush to John Adams, August 8, 1777, quoted in G. Howard Miller, *The Revolutionary College: American Presbyterian Higher Education, 1707–1837*, p. 109. See also pp. 142, 194–97.

19. Instructive here is Edward Tiryakian, "A Model of Societal Change and its Lead Indicators," in Samuel Klausner, ed., *The Study of Total Societies*, pp. 69–97. That all three of his indicators for revolution were present (large increase in the rates of urbanization, growing corruption in society, and the outbreak of noninstitutional religious phenomena) indicates the potential of this response.

20. William McLoughlin, *Revivals, Awakenings, and Reform: An Essay on Religion and Social Change in America, 1607–1977*, p. xiii; Richard Shiels, "The Myth of the Second Great Awakening" (Paper delivered at the American Historical Association meetings, December 1977); and John A. Andrew III, *Rebuilding the Christian Commonwealth: New England Congregationalists and Foreign Missions, 1800–1830*, chapter 1.

21. My thinking in this matter has been greatly influenced by Anthony F. C. Wallace, "Revitalization Movements," *American Anthropologist* 58 (1956): 264–81; and McLoughlin, *Revivals*.

22. Danforth, *Discourse*, p. 5. For elaboration of the concepts underlying this analysis, see Wallace, "Revitalization Movements"; Tiryakian, "Model of Societal Change"; and Anthony F. C. Wallace, *Religion: An Anthropological View*.

23. Nathan Perkins, *The Benign Influence of Religion on Civil Government and National Happiness*, p. 8.

24. Rev. Asa Cummings, comp., *Memoir, Select Thoughts and Sermons of the Late Rev. Edward Payson, D.D. Pastor of the Second Church in Portland*, 1:150. From a letter to his mother, March 28, 1808.

25. The primary sources are, of course, the volumes of these two periodicals. But also see Phillips, "Jedidiah Morse," p. 143; Shiels, "Second Great Awakening," p. 5; Andrew, *Rebuilding the Christian Commonwealth*, chapter 1.

26. Joseph Lathrop, *A Sermon, Preached in Putney, (Vt.) June 25, 1807. At the Ordination of Reverend Elisha D. Andrews, over the Congregational Church and Charitable Christian Society, in that Town*, p. 4. See also John Hammond, *The Politics of Benevolence: Revival Religion and American Voting Behavior*, p. 52; Richard Shiels, "The Connecticut Clergy in the Second Great Awakening" (Ph.D. diss., Boston University, 1976), chapter 1; Donald Mathews, "Religion in the Old South: Speculation on Methodology," *South Atlantic Quarterly* 73 (1974): 36; Nathan Hatch, "The Christian Movement and the Demand for a Theology of the People," *Journal of American History* 67 (1980): 546, 567; Lois Banner, "The Protestant Crusade: Religious Missions, Benevolence, and Reform in the United States, 1790–1840"

(Ph.D. diss., Columbia University, 1970), p. 10; McLoughlin, *New England Dissent*, 2:984. For some English parallels see Bernard Semmel, *The Methodist Revolution*, pp. 8–9; Niel Gunson, *Messengers of Grace: Evangelical Missionaries in the South Seas, 1797–1860*, p. 48; and Gregory Clark, "Timothy Dwight's 'Travels in New England and New York' and the Rhetoric of Puritan Public Discourse" (Ph.D. diss., Rensselaer Polytechnic Institute, 1985), p. 104.

27. Nathan Strong, *On the Universal Spread of the Gospel, a Sermon delivered January 4th, the First Sabbath in the 19th Century of the Christian Era*, p. 20. For influences on the revivals, see Rev. Isaac Parsons, *Memoir of the Life and Character of Rev. Joseph Vaill, Late Pastor of the Church of Christ in Hadlyme*, p. 188, and Richard Carwardine, *Trans-Atlantic Revivalism: Popular Evangelicalism in Britain and America, 1790–1865*, p. 56.

28. See Eliphalet Nott's 1801 Fourth of July address in Hood, "Presbyterianism," p. 86; and William B. Sprague, *Lectures on Revivals of Religion*, pp. 210–11. For moral agency see C. Y. A., "Execution of Laws," p. 321; William Breitenbach, "The Consistent Calvinism of the New Divinity Movement," *WMQ* 3d series, 41 (April 1984): 241–64. Also see "Letter XVI. From the Rev. Asahel Hooker, of Goshen," *Connecticut Evangelical Magazine and Religious Intelligencer* 1 (March 1801): 343–44. An extensive reading of public addresses from 1800 to 1830 indicates that references to the national covenant remained common after 1800. What does seem to emerge is an increasingly partisan use of the covenant idea; see Dietrich Buss, "The Millennial Vision as Motive for Religious Benevolence and Reform: Timothy Dwight and the New England Evangelicals Reconsidered," *Fides et Historia* 16 (1983): *passim*. Rhys Isaac noted relationships between individualism and evangelicalism in *The Transformation of Virginia, 1740–1790*, p. 171n.

29. Edward C. Lyrene, Jr., "The Role of Prayer in American Revival Movements, 1740–1860" (Ph.D. diss., Southern Baptist Theological Seminary, 1985), p. 87; Daniel Scott Smith, "A Perspective on Demographic Methods and Effects on Social History," *WMQ* 3d series, 39 (July 1982): 447; and Sandra Wagner, "Sojourners Among Strangers: The First Two Companies of Missionaries to the Sandwich Islands" (Ph.D. diss., University of Hawaii, 1986), pp. 62–65, 72. For a discussion of disinterested benevolence see Joseph Conforti, *Samuel Hopkins and the New Divinity Movement: Calvinism, The Congregational Ministry, and Reform in New England Between the Great Awakenings*, pp. 192–93; John Giltner, "The Fragmentation of New England Congregationalism and the Founding of Andover Seminary," *Journal of Religious Thought* 20 (1963–64): 27–42 *passim*; and William C. Dennis II, "A Federalist Persuasion: The American Ideal of the Connecticut Federalists" (Ph.D. diss., Yale University, 1971), pp. 17–18. A broader, more political perspective is in John Diggins, *The Lost Soul of American Politics: Virtue, Self-Interest, and the Foundations of Liberalism*, pp. 4–5, 16.

30. See the early volumes of *Connecticut Evangelical Magazine* for accounts

of these revivals and some early missionary activity. For an assessment of preaching in these revivals, see Shiels, "Connecticut Clergy," pp. 33–59, 67–68; Richard Shiels, "The Second Great Awakening in Connecticut: Critique of the Traditional Interpretation," *Church History* 49 (1980): 401–15; Douglas Sweet, "Church Vitality and the American Revolution: Historiographical Consensus and Thoughts Towards a New Perspective," *Church History* 45 (1976): 346–47.

31. Bennet Tyler, *New England Revivals as they existed At the Close of the Eighteenth, and the Beginning of the Nineteenth Centuries*, p. 32.

32. Shiels, "Connecticut Clergy," p. 228.

33. For English activities see Perry, "American Board," pp. 54, 105–6; Semmel, *Methodist Revolution*, pp. 147–48, 167; Carwardine, *Trans-Atlantic Revivalism*; Joan Brumberg, *Mission for Life*, pp. 25–26; and Andrew, *Rebuilding the Christian Commonwealth*, pp. 19–20. Paul Johnson, *A Shopkeeper's Millennium: Society and Revivals in Rochester, New York, 1815–1837*, pp. 5–6, notes the middle-class nature of the Rochester revival, as do Fischer, *Revolution of American Conservatism*, p. 49, and Mary Ryan, *Cradle of the Middle Class: The Family in Oneida County, New York, 1790–1865*, pp. 11–15, 102–3. For other revivals see Tyler, *New England Revivals*.

34. Elias Smith to William Gridley, July 18, 1803, in Hudson, "Challenge of Dissent," p. 14.

35. Shiels, "Connecticut Clergy," pp. 128, 160–61; Berk, *Calvinism*, p. 110; Johnson, *Shopkeeper's Millennium*, p. 8.

36. Rev. Asa Packard to Rev. Hezekiah Packard, November 7, 1808, Packard Family Letters, AAS. For some instances of revivals as a cohesive force, see Carwardine, *Trans-Atlantic Revivalism*, pp. 25, 49–50; Cyrus Eaton, *Annals of the Town of Warren: with the Early History of St. George's, Broad Bay, and the Neighboring Settlements of the Waldo Patent*, pp. 321–22; Johnson, *Shopkeeper's Millennium*, pp. 33–36, 55, 78–79, 93, 137–38; Anthony Wallace, *Rockdale, passim*; Blauvelt, "Society," pp. 49–50, 93. On the small-town nature of the revivals, see Joshua Bradley, *Accounts of Religious Revivals in Many Parts of the United States from 1815 to 1818, passim*.

37. Samuel Waterman of Plymouth, Connecticut, on public reaction during the Second Great Awakening, quoted in Phillips, "Jedidiah Morse," pp. 144–45.

38. Revival narratives emphasize this point; see for instance the *Connecticut Evangelical Magazine*. Also see Conforti, "Samuel Hopkins," pp. 588–89; Linn, "Religion and Nationalism," pp. 132–33; Marie Caskey, *Chariot of Fire: Religion and the Beecher Family*, p. 380.

39. For some description and other analysis of this point see Philip Greven, Jr., "Youth, Maturity, and Religious Conversion: A Note on the Ages of Converts in Andover, Massachusetts, 1711–1749," *Essex Institute Historical Collections* 108 (1972): 129–30; Donald Scott, *From Office to Profession: The New England Ministry, 1750–1850*, p. 37; Johnson, *Shopkeeper's Millennium*, p. 32; Hillel Schwartz, "Adolescence and Revivals in Ante-Bellum Boston," *Journal of Religious History* 8 (1974): 144ff; Blauvelt, "Society," pp. iii–iv; and Kett, *Rites of Passage*, pp. 69–70.

40. *Panoplist* 3 (December 1807): 325. See also Kett, *Rites of Passage*, pp. 69–70, 107; Joseph Kett, "Growing Up in Rural New England, 1800–1840," in Tamara Hareven, ed., *Anonymous Americans: Explorations in Nineteenth-Century Social History*, pp. 4–11; Barbara Epstein, *The Politics of Domesticity: Women, Evangelism, and Temperance in Nineteenth-Century America*, pp. 45–50; Phillips, "Jedidiah Morse," p. 164.

41. Quoted in Nancy Cott, *The Bonds of Womanhood: "Woman's Sphere" in New England, 1780–1835*, pp. 147–48. For women see Richard Shiels, "The Feminization of American Congregationalism, 1730–1835," *American Quarterly* 33 (1981): 46–62.

42. Timothy Dwight, *The Charitable Blessed* (1810), quoted in Phillips, "Jedidiah Morse," pp. 163–64.

43. Joseph Lathrop, *The Importance of Female Influence in the Support of Religion. A Sermon, Delivered to a Charitable Female Association in West-Springfield. May 15, 1810*, p. 5. See also Blauvelt, "Society," p. 203; Nancy Cott, "Young Women in the Second Great Awakening in New England," *Feminist Studies* 3 (1975): 16.

44. Lyman, *A Virtuous Woman the Bond of Domestic Union, and the Source of Domestic Happiness* (1802), quoted in Cott, *Bonds of Womanhood*, p. 85. Also see Blauvelt, "Society," pp. 192–93, 211.

45. Johnson, *Shopkeeper's Millennium*, p. 108. For a case study that reflects this separation of roles, see Mary Ryan's analysis of the Utica, New York, revivals: "A Woman's Awakening: Evangelical Religion and the Families of Utica, New York, 1800–1840," *American Quarterly* 30 (1978), especially pp. 618–19. To take this separation a step further, she notes that 66 percent of these women were married to men who kept a business address that was separate from their home address.

46. Some examples are in Brumberg, *Mission for Life*, p. 37; Davis, "Plowshares to Spindles," pp. 148–49; Anne Boylan, "The Role of Conversion in Nineteenth-Century Sunday Schools," *American Quarterly* 20 (1979): 42–43; Ryan, "Woman's Awakening," p. 623; Kett, *Rites of Passage*, pp. 75–76; Slater, *Children in New England Mind*, p. 100; and Blauvelt, "Society," pp. 190–91.

47. Amariah Brigham, *Observations on the Influence of Religion Upon the Health and Physical Welfare of Mankind*, p. 275. See also pp. 169, 268–69.

48. See for example Menzies Rayner, *A Dissertation upon Extraordinary Awakenings*, pp. 6, 12; Berk, *Calvinism*, pp. 189–90.

49. Carroll Smith Rosenberg, *Religion and the Rise of the American City: The New York City Mission Movement, 1812–1870*, pp. 44–45; Blauvelt, "Society," pp. 263–64; Sweet, "Church Vitality," p. 349; Perry Miller, "From the Covenant to the Revival," in James Smith and A. L. Jamison, eds., *The Shaping of American Religion*, p. 354.

50. Somewhat the same thing occurred in England, as indeed the missionary movements in both countries paralleled one another. See Gordon Taylor, *The*

Angel-Makers: A Study in the Psychological Origins of Historical Change, 1750–1850, pp. 36, 50–51, 83–84, 248. For the United States see Hammond, *Politics of Benevolence,* p. 65; William Gribbin, *The Churches Militant: The War of 1812 and American Religion,* pp. 2, 18–19; Banner, "Protestant Crusade," pp. 12–13; Brown, "Modernization," pp. 537–38; Philip Greven, *The Protestant Temperament: Patterns of Child-Rearing, Religious Experience, and the Self in Early America,* pp. 12–13. See Samuel Brazer, Jr., *An Oration, Pronounced at Springfield, on July 4th, 1809, in Commemoration of American Independence,* p. 12, for a declaration that the Fourth of July was a "political *Sabbath.*"

51. John Dann, "Humanitarian Reform and Organized Benevolence in the Southern United States, 1780–1830" (Ph.D. diss., William and Mary, 1975), pp. 28, 30; Shiels, "Connecticut Clergy," p. 270. Also see George Marsden, *The Evangelical Mind and the New School Presbyterian Experience,* pp. 3–4; Donald Mathews, "The Second Great Awakening as an Organizing Process, 1780–1830: An Hypothesis," *American Quarterly* 21 (1969): 28; Daniel W. Howe, *The Political Culture of the American Whigs,* p. 9; Bercovitch, *American Jeremiad,* p. xi; Bernard Wishy, *The Child and the Republic: The Dawn of Modern American Child Nurture,* pp. 4–5.

52. Berk, *Calvinism,* p. 172; David Davis, *The Problem of Slavery in the Age of Revolution, 1770–1823,* p. 289; Lois Banner, "Presbyterians and Voluntarism in the Early Republic," *Journal of Presbyterian History* 50 (1972): 192. For a detailed discussion of moral philosophy and its influence, see Donald Meyer, *The Instructed Conscience: The Shaping of the American National Ethic.*

NOTES FOR CHAPTER THREE

1. Evarts to the Reverend Joseph Lyman, January 2, 1810, Simon Gratz Collection, HSP.

2. For the larger issue see the discussion in James M. Banner, Jr., *To The Hartford Convention: The Federalists and the Origin of Party Politics in Massachusetts, 1789–1815,* pp. 65–68, 81–82.

3. Fischer, *Revolution of American Conservatism,* p. xi; Banner, *Hartford Convention,* p. 25; *Proceedings of a Convention of Moral Societies, in the County of Litchfield, Holden May 30th, 1815, at Goshen: An Abstract of the Laws of Connecticut, and an Address to the Public, on the Promotion of Virtue and Good Morals,* pp. 21, 35.

4. James G. Blaine II, "The Birth of a Neighborhood: Nineteenth-Century Charlestown, Massachusetts" (Ph.D. diss., University of Michigan, 1978).

5. Banner, *Hartford Convention,* pp. 26–33.

6. Griffin to Evarts, April 16, 1810, Box 2, folder 58, EFP.

7. See Tracy, *Memoir,* pp. 65–69. Also see Jedidiah Morse, *Signs of the Times. A Sermon, Preached Before the Society for Propagating the Gospel Among the Indians and Others in North America, At Their Anniversary, Nov. 1, 1810,* p. 19.

8. Agenor, "On the Duty of Educating Children for the Arduous Duties of

the Present Times," *Panoplist* 9 (August 1813): 153–54. Also see A. M., "Meditation VI," *Panoplist* 9 (August 1813): 126–27; and Hunnewell, *Century of Town Life*, p. 229, for the baptism of John Jay Evarts.

9. Agenor, "On the Encouragements to Give Children a Strictly Religious Education," *Panoplist* 9 (September 1813): 249–50. For remarks supportive of these points, also see Agenor, "Educating Children," pp. 153–54; A. B., "Thoughts on the Loss of Near Relatives," *Panoplist* 9 (August 1813): 160–64; John Chester, *A Sermon, Delivered Before the Berkshire and Columbia Missionary Society, at Their Annual Meeting in Canaan, September 21st, 1813*.

10. Among the best analyses of this change are Cott, *Bonds of Womanhood*, and Sklar, *Catharine Beecher*.

11. Fanny Woodbury to B. K. and R. K. (1813), in Joseph Emerson, ed., *Writings of Miss Fanny Woodbury*, p. 120. See also A. B., "On Praying for the Holy Spirit," *Panoplist* 8 (April 1813): 507–11; Nathan Strong, *The Character of a Virtuous and Good Woman. A Discourse Delivered By the Desire and in the Presence of the Female Benevolent Society in Hartford, October 4th, A.D. 1809*, p. 6.

12. Daniel Chapin's sermon before the Charitable Female Society in Groton, Massachusetts, October 19, 1814, quoted in Keith Melder, "The Beginnings of the Women's Rights Movement in the United States, 1800–1840" (Ph.D. diss., Yale University, 1963), p. 89.

13. This notion had become increasingly prevalent by 1813; see Rev. Benjamin Wisner, *Memoirs of the Late Mrs. Susan Huntington, of Boston, Mass.*, pp. 69, 108–9; Hervey Wilbur, *Female Piety Demanding Assistance. Two Sermons, Delivered in Bradford, Second Parish, January 5, 1812, and Afterwards in Two Other Places*; Timothy Gillet, *Charity Profitable; or, God a Surety for the Poor. A Sermon, Delivered Before the Female Charitable Society, in Guilford, January 6, 1813*, pp. 12–13. Evarts insisted that they remain separate. See A. B., "On Religious Conferences," *Panoplist* 9 (August 1813): 109. The extreme dedication of one woman is noted in Wisner, *Memoirs of Mrs. Huntington*, pp. 118n, 121–22.

14. Philalethes, "Plain Scripture Readings," *Panoplist* 9 (June 1813): 17. Also see A. B., "On Religious Conferences," *Panoplist* 9 (July 1813): 73–78; (August 1813): 109–10; and A. B., "On Singing Praises to God," *Panoplist* 9 (June 1813), 21–23.

15. A. B., "Thoughts on Harvest," *Panoplist* 9 (October 1813): 303. Also see A. B., "On Covetousness, or a Reliance upon Riches for Happiness," *Panoplist* 9 (September 1813): 258–63; A. B., "On the Misconduct of Professed Christians, and the Use Which is Made of it by the Men of the World," *Panoplist* 9 (October 1813): 346–49; A. B., "Abuse of the Late Harvest," *Panoplist* 9 (October 1813): 358–60. On this same subject see A. B., "Magnitude of the Evil of Intemperance," *Panoplist* 9 (August 1813): 105–6; Antipas, "On Drinking Healths," *Panoplist* 9 (July 1813): 78–79; A. M., "On the Duty of Admonition," *Panoplist* 9 (November 1813): 450–52.

16. "Address to the Public," *Panoplist* 6 (June 1810): 4. See Evarts to Rev. Edward D. Griffin, August 20, 1810, Simon Gratz Collection, HSP, for a discussion of publication practices.

17. Jeremiah Evarts, "Review of the Dorchester Controversy," *Panoplist* 10 (June 1814): 257, 269–70.

18. The early history of the NETS is in Elizabeth Twaddel, "The American Tract Society, 1814–1860," *Church History* 15 (1946): 116–32. See also *Proceedings of the First Ten Years of the American Tract Society* and *The Address of the Executive Committee of the American Tract Society to the Christian Public: Together with a Brief Account of the Formation of the Society, its Constitution and Officers*, both reprinted in *The American Tract Society Documents, 1824–1925*. Also see Sprague, *Life of Jedidiah Morse*, p. 156.

19. Twaddel, "American Tract Society," pp. 117–18, 120–22.

20. Rice to Rev. Archibald Alexander, January 28, 1810, in Maxwell, *Memoir*, p. 50. Also see Tracy, *Memoir*, p. 90.

21. William Bannister, *An Oration, Delivered at Newburyport, on the 34th Anniversary of American Independence*, p. 10.

22. A. B., "A Hint to the Benevolent," *Panoplist* 6 (December 1810): 306. Boston women organized the Corban Society in 1811 to aid divinity students. See Naylor, "Raising a Learned Ministry," p. 30; Brumberg, *Mission for Life*, p. 240n.

23. A. B., "Hint to Benevolent," p. 307.

24. Ibid., pp. 307–8.

25. John F. Schermerhorn and Samuel J. Mills, *A Correct View of that Part of the United States which lies West of the Allegany Mountains, with Respect to Religion and Morals*; Naylor, "Raising a Learned Ministry," p. 1; *Panoplist* 10 (July 1814): 330. For criticism of Beecher see *A Letter to the Rev. Lyman Beecher. By a Layman*. The survey of the West is in Samuel J. Mills and Daniel Smith, *Report of a Missionary Tour Through that Part of the United States which lies West of the Allegany Mountains; Performed Under the Direction of the Massachusetts Missionary Society*; see especially p. 47.

26. Phillips, "Jedidiah Morse," p. 195.

27. See Banner, *Hartford Convention*, p. 187, for a discussion of the Suffolk County (Massachusetts) bar's decision to keep charges high. For the formation of the AES and Evarts's central role, see *Panoplist* 11 (October 1815): 481; *An Address of the Charitable Society for the Education of Indigent Pious Young Men, for the Ministry of the Gospel*. Also see Naylor, "Raising a Learned Ministry," p. 234. For earlier years see James Schmotter, "Ministerial Careers in Eighteenth-Century New England: The Social Context, 1700–1760," *Journal of Social History* 9 (1975): 249–67.

28. Anson Phelps Stokes, *Church and State in the United States*, 2: 13; Ronald Formisano, *The Birth of Mass Political Parties: Michigan, 1827–1861*, p. 122; A. B., "The Sabbath," *Panoplist* 7 (May 1812): 539–40.

29. Gideon Granger to the House of Representatives, January 31, 1811, American State Papers, Class 7: *Post Office*, No. 26, pp. 44–55. Also see Hood, "Presbyterianism," pp. 99–100.

30. A. B., "The Sabbath," pp. 540ff.

31. *Panoplist* 10 (April 1814): 160.

32. A. B., "Thoughts on the Late Measures of the Legislature of Massachusetts in Relation to the Sabbath," *Panoplist* 10 (August 1814): 354–55. Also see T., "Outrages on the Sabbath," *Panoplist* 10 (April 1814): 159.

33. "Sketch of Evarts," pp. 338–39; John Jentz, "Artisans, Evangelicals and the City: A Social History of Abolition and Labor Reforms in Jacksonian New York," (Ph.D. diss., CUNY, 1977), p. 105n; Banner, "Protestant Crusade," p. 245.

34. Meigs to the House of Representatives, January 20, 1815, American State Papers, Class 7: *Post Office*, No. 29, p. 46. A rather caustic view is in Gribbin, *Churches Militant*, pp. 140, 144. A discussion of various types of reform is in W. David Lewis, "The Reformer as Conservative: Protestant Counter-Subversion in the Early Republic," in Stanley Coben and Lorman Ratner, eds., *The Development of an American Culture*, pp. 79–80.

35. Benevolus, "Arithmetic Applied to Moral Purposes," *Panoplist* 6 (October 1810): 211–14. For British efforts see Gordon Taylor, *Angel-Makers*, p. 95. Also see Frank Crow, "The Age of Promise: Societies for Social and Economic Improvement in the United States, 1783–1815" (Ph.D. diss., University of Wisconsin, 1952), p. 500; Tracy, *Memoir*, p. 75.

36. Benevolus, "Arithmetic Applied," pp. 211–14.

37. Nathan Strong, *Character of a Virtuous and Good Woman*, p. 7. Also see Benevolus, "Arithmetic Applied," *Panoplist* 7 (June 1811): 21; William Rorabaugh, *The Alcoholic Republic: An American Tradition*, pp. 191–92. For Evarts's early committee work in this effort, see Tracy, *Memoir*, p. 75; Samuel Worcester, *The Life and Labors of Rev. Samuel Worcester, D.D.*, 2:253–54; John Krout, *The Origins of Prohibition*, p. 90.

38. *Fourth Report of the American Temperance Society, Presented At the Meeting in Boston, May 1831*, p. 68; *Panoplist* 8 (September 1812): 183–87.

39. Ebenezer Porter, *The Fatal Effects of Ardent Spirits. A Sermon*, p. 3.

40. Ibid., p. 4; A. Jones Cook, *The Student's Companion*, p. 127, quoted in Epstein, *Politics of Domesticity*, p. 69; Benjamin Wood, *Labourers Needed in the Harvest of Christ. A Sermon: Delivered at Sutton, (S.P.) March 18, 1812. As A Preliminary to the Formation of a Society, in the County of Worcester, for the Aid of Pious Young Men, With a View to the Ministry*, p. 20.

41. *Address of the Cumberland Association, to the Several Churches and Societies, with Which They are Connected*, p. 5. For comments on the meeting at Dexter's house, also see the *Proceedings of the American Antiquarian Society* 9 (1895): 472. A formative work on the organizing impulse is Mathews, "Second Great Awakening," pp. 23–43.

42. *Panoplist* 8 (February 1813): 421; Jentz, "Artisans," pp. 304–17, 445–46; *A Directory, Containing Names, Places of Business, and Residence, of the Members of the Washington Benevolent Society, of Massachusetts, from its Commencement.* See also Robert Hampel, "Influence and Respectability: Temperance and Prohibition in Massachusetts, 1813–1852" (Ph.D. diss., Cornell University, 1979), chapter 1. Hampel estimates that 40 percent of the Boston society were Unitarians.

43. Paul Meyer, "The Transformation of American Temperance: The Popularization and Radicalization of a Reform Movement, 1813–1860" (Ph.D. diss., University of Iowa, 1976), pp. 21–22, 27–28; Ian Tyrrell, "Drink and the Process of Social Reform: From Temperance to Prohibition in Ante-Bellum America, 1813–1860" (Ph.D. diss., Duke University, 1974), pp. 12, 14. See also Rorabaugh, *Alcoholic Republic* for a provocative summary of the alcohol question. In the Paxton, Massachusetts, Papers, AAS, there is a survey of that town's drinking habits by household. Almost every family seems to have harbored at least one drunkard. Also significant is that between 1800 and 1820 Massachusetts's population rose 24 percent but the costs of pauper support tripled. The parallel increase in drinking made the connection seem plausible. Further details are in the *Fourth Report of the American Temperance Society*, p. 68.

44. Meyer, "Transformation," pp. 35ff.

45. Ibid., p. 49. Rorabaugh's argument in *The Alcoholic Republic* that the temperance movement was linked to a larger market revolution is interesting, but until some local studies are undertaken it remains largely speculative; see p. 90 for a clear statement of his argument. For one such local study see Hampel, "Influence," table 2 in chapter 1, where he provides an occupational breakdown for the Concord, Massachusetts, society. Only 1.5 percent of its members were unskilled laborers.

46. For a more detailed discussion see Andrew, *Rebuilding the Christian Commonwealth*, pp. 18–24; Tracy, *Memoir*, pp. 96–97. The best discussion of the broader organizing impulse is in Mathews, "Second Great Awakening," pp. 23–43. See also Valentin Rabe, "Evangelical Logistics: Mission Support and Resources to 1920," in *The Missionary Enterprise in China and America*, ed. John K. Fairbank, p. 57.

47. See Andrew, *Rebuilding the Christian Commonwealth*, chapter 5; Clifton Phillips, "Protestant America and the Pagan World: The First Half Century of the American Board of Commissioners for Foreign Missions, 1810–1860" (Ph.D. diss., Harvard University, 1954), p. 240 and *passim*; and Henry W. Bowden, "An Overview of Cultural Factors in the American Protestant Missionary Enterprise," in *American Missions in Bicentennial Perspective*, ed. R. Pierce Beaver, p. 41. The ABCFM drew most of its local auxiliaries' and fund-raising support from the Northeast. See Perry, "American Board," p. 567, for the geographic origins of its financial support.

48. "Concern for the Salvation of the Heathen," *Panoplist* 5 (May 1810): 546.

49. See for instance Timothy Dwight, *The Charitable Blessed. A Sermon. Preached in the First Church in New-Haven, August 8, 1810*, p. 27. Some indication of the demands for his attention are in the *Panoplist* 6 (November 1810): 259–62; see also Henry May, *The Enlightenment in America*, p. 318.

50. "Address to the Public," *Panoplist* 7 (June 1811): 3. Similar concerns were expressed in the South; see Rev. John Rice to Rev. Archibald Alexander, May 3, 1811, in Maxwell, *Memoir*, pp. 64–65. Also see Jotham Fairchild, *An Oration, Pronounced at the Meeting-house in the Vicinity of Dartmouth College, on the Fourth of July, 1811*, p. 11.

51. Tracy, *Memoir*, p. 98; *Panoplist* 4 (September 1811): 185; Leslie Dunstan, *A Light to the City: 150 Years of the City Missionary Society of Boston, 1816–1966*, p. 13; ABCFM, *Address to the Christian Public*, p. 6.

52. Jeremiah Evarts, Jedidiah Morse, and Samuel Worcester, "An Address to the Christian Public, Prepared and Published by a Committee of the American Board of Commissioners for Foreign Missions," *Panoplist* 7 (November 1811): 241–42, 245–46; A. B., "On the Association of Ideas," *Panoplist* 7 (December 1811): 300–302; A. B., "On Dispensations and Indulgences," *Panoplist* 7 (October 1811): 201; V. A., "On Examination for Admission into the Church," *Panoplist* 7 (March 1811): 449–51.

53. "To the Patrons of the Panoplist," *Panoplist* 7 (November 1811): 286; Worcester to Evarts, December 16, 1811, Box 3, EFP.

54. Worcester to Evarts, December 16, 1811, Box 3, EFP. Notices of other salaries are in Anne Loveland, *Southern Evangelicals and the Social Order, 1800–1860*, p. 58.

55. His Franklin County bar certificate is in Box 6, folder 202, EFP. For his wife's description of his trip, see Mehitabel Evarts to Elizabeth Baldwin, February 9, 1812, Box 15, Baldwin Family Papers, Yale.

56. Porter to the Reverend Zephania Swift, March 12, 1812, in Lyman Matthews, *Memoir of the Life and Character of Ebenezer Porter, D.D.*, p. 290. For the background of this mission see Clifton Phillips, *Protestant America and the Pagan World: The First Half-Century of the American Board of Commissioners for Foreign Missions, 1810–1860*, chapter 2.

57. *Panoplist* 7 (February 1812): 431. For notice of the local Boston society, see ibid., p. 427, and ABC 8.5, no. 17. Evarts's March essay is under A. B., "Foreign Missions," *Panoplist* 7 (March 1812): 445–48, and the series on Asia is in the *Panoplist* 7 (April 1812).

58. Leonard Woods, *A Sermon, delivered at the Tabernacle in Salem, Feb. 6, 1812, on Occasion of the Ordination of the Rev. Messrs. Samuel Newall, Adoniram Judson, Samuel Nott, Gordon Hall, and Luther Rice, Missionaries to the Heathen in Asia, Under the Direction of the Board of Commissioners for Foreign Missions*, p. 15.

59. Joseph Lathrop, *The Angel Preaching the Everlasting Gospel. A Sermon Delivered in Springfield, April 21st, 1812, at the Institution of a Society for the Encouragement*

of Foreign Missions, p. 18; Thomas Baldwin, *The Knowledge of the Lord Filling the Earth. A Sermon, Delivered in Boston, June 4, 1812, Before the Massachusetts Bible Society, Being Their Third Anniversary*, p. 15. Also see William Paton, ed., *The Missionary Motive*, p. 159; Andrew, *Rebuilding the Christian Commonwealth*, pp. 77–82.

60. *Panoplist* 8 (October 1812): 228. Also see Jeremiah Evarts, Jedidiah Morse, and Samuel Worcester, "An Address to the Christian Public on the Subject of Missions to the Heathen and Translation of the Scriptures," *Panoplist* 8 (November 1812): 249–56.

61. ABCFM, "Address to the Christian Public," quoted in Tracy, *Memoir*, p. 101.

62. Murray Rubinstein, "'Go Ye Unto the World': The Defining of the Missionary's Task in America and China, 1830–1850," *Academia Sinica* 10 (1980): 379.

63. *Panoplist* 9 (June 1813): 43. For the *Panoplist*, see "Address to the Public," *Panoplist* 9 (June 1813): 4. Evarts's comment on the costs of war is in A. B., "Calculations on the Expenses of War," *Panoplist* 9 (November 1813): 444–48.

64. "Address to the Public on the Subject of Missions," *Panoplist* 9 (October 1813): 315–25.

65. Quoted in Tracy, *Memoir*, p. 106.

66. "Address to the Public," (October 1813): 325. Also see John Jay to Evarts, January 12, 1813, Jeremiah Evarts Papers, LC; as well as Bennet Tyler, *A Sermon, Preached at Litchfield, Before the Foreign Mission Society of Litchfield County. At their Annual Meeting, February 10, 1813*, p. 9.

67. "Address to the Public," *Panoplist* 10 (June 1814): 4.

68. James Richards, *The Spirit of Paul the Spirit of Missions. A Sermon Preached at New Haven, (Con.) before the American Board of Commissioners for Foreign Missions, at Their Annual Meeting, Sept. 15, 1814*, p. 23.

69. Evan Johns, *A Sermon Preached at Northampton, Before the Foreign Missionary Society, of Northampton and the Neighboring Towns, at their First Meeting, March 31, 1812*, pp. 17–18.

70. A. B., "On the Good Uses, Which Might Be Made of the Money Now Expended in War," *Panoplist* 10 (April 1814): 175. The same theme is expressed in A. B., "On Religious Charities," *Panoplist* 10 (May 1814): 224–27.

71. Letter for the *Panoplist*, August 24, 1814, Box 4, EFP. A good summary statement is in Clark Brown, *The Utility of Moral and Religious Societies, and of the Masonick in Particular. A Sermon, Delivered in Putney, Vt. on the Anniversary of St. John the Baptist, June 24th, 1814*, p. 10.

72. For Cornelius's attitude see his March 14, 1814, diary entry in Bela Bates Edwards, ed., *Memoir of Elias Cornelius*, p. 29. One such warning of this sort is in Joseph Lathrop, *A Sermon, Preached in Springfield. Before the Bible Society, and the Foreign Mission Society, in the County of Hampden, at Their Annual Meeting, August 31, 1814*, p. 10. The larger issue is in Bertram Wyatt-Brown, "The Antimission Movement in the Jacksonian South: A Study in Regional Folk Culture," *Journal of Southern History* 36 (1970): 501–29.

73. Spring, *Tribute*, p. 19; Evarts to Hezekiah Howe, January 15, 1811, Roger Sherman Papers, LC; V. A., "On Human Depravity," *Panoplist* 6 (January 1811): 357–61; (February 1811): 396–403; (March 1811): 447–52; (April 1811): 494–502; (May 1811): 553–61; 7 (September 1811): 150–54; (October 1811): 203–6; (December 1811): 302–10. See also Tracy, *Memoir*, pp. 76–77.

74. "Address to the Public," *Panoplist* 8 (June 1812): 3; Jeremiah Evarts, *An Oration, Delivered at Charlestown, (Mass.), on the Fourth of July, 1812, in Commemoration of American Independence*, pp. 3–4.

75. Evarts, *Oration*, pp. 7–11.

76. Ibid., pp. 14–17.

77. Ibid., pp. 19, 28.

78. Ibid., pp. 23–24; Otis Thompson, *"Signs of the Times!" A Sermon, Preached at Attleborough, West Parish, on the Annual Fast in Massachusetts, April 9th, A.D. 1812*, p. 22. Also see Gribbin, *Churches Militant*, pp. 32–34; Paul Nagel, *The Sacred Trust: American Nationality, 1798–1898*, pp. 43–44.

79. Tracy, *Memoir*, pp. 78–79. The quotation is from Timothy Dwight, *A Discourse in Two Parts, Delivered July 23, 1812, On the Public Fast in the Chapel of Yale College*, quoted in Peterson, "Politics of Revival," p. 76.

80. For other expressions of this concern see Winthrop Bailey, *National Glory. A Discourse, Delivered at Brunswick, On the Day of the National Fast, August 20, 1812*; and James Van Hoeven, "Salvation and Indian Removal: The Career Biography of the Rev. John Freeman Schermerhorn, Indian Commissioner" (Ph.D. diss., Vanderbilt University, 1972), p. 51.

81. Evarts to Samuel F. B. Morse, October 7, 1812, quoted in Edward L. Morse, ed., *Samuel F. B. Morse: His Letters and Journals*, 1:86–87. For a discussion of the role of rhetoric and public discourse, see Clark, "Timothy Dwight's Travels," p. 17.

82. *The Charlestown Association for the Reformation of Morals*, p. 5.

83. Jesse Appleton, *A Discourse. Delivered at Bath, May 11th, 1813, Before the Society for Discountenancing and Suppressing Public Vices*, p. 4. See also Elijah Parish, *A Discourse, Delivered at Byfield, on the Annual Fast, April 8, 1813*; Society for Suppression of Vice and Immorality, *Articles of Association, of the Society for the Suppression of Vice and Immorality*.

84. Peter Eaton, *A Sermon, Delivered at Topsfield, (Mass.), June 20, 1815. Before the Moral Society of Boxford and Topsfield*, p. 11. See also pp. 10–11 for a longer justification of these societies.

85. Quoted in Dennis, "Federalist Persuasion," p. 52. Also see Richard Beeman, "The New Social History and the Search for 'Community' in Colonial America," *American Quarterly* 29 (1977): 442; and John Garrison, "Surviving Strategies: In Commercialization of Life in Rural Massachusetts, 1790–1860" (Ph.D. diss., University of Pennsylvania, 1985), p. 384.

86. Josiah Bartlett, *An Historical Sketch of Charlestown, in the County of Middlesex*,

and *Commonwealth of Massachusetts, Read to an Assembly of Citizens at the Opening of Washington Hall, Nov. 16, 1813*, p. 16n; John Church, *The Progress of Divine Truth. A Discourse Delivered at the Eighth Annual Meeting of the New England Tract Society in Boston, May 29, 1822*, p. 25; New England Tract Society, *First Report, May 29, 1815*, p. 30; *Report of the Executive Committee of the Bible Society of Massachusetts, June 2, 1814*, p. 11; *Panoplist* 10 (May 1814): 235. For an overview see Richard D. Brown, "The Emergence of Voluntary Associations in Massachusetts, 1760–1830," *Journal of Voluntary Action Research* 2 (1973): 64–73.

87. A. B., "Thoughts on the Manner in Which Nations Declare and Conduct War," *Panoplist* 11 (July 1815): 303–5.

NOTES FOR CHAPTER FOUR

1. Webster to William Rowland(?), January 11, 1815, Charles Wiltse, ed., *The Papers of Daniel Webster*, 1:181–82.

2. Ibid.

3. Quoted in O. F. Lewis, *The Development of American Prisons and Prison Customs*, p. 73. See also Augustus Alden, *An Address, Delivered at Augusta, on the Thirty-fourth Anniversary of American Independence, July Fourth, 1809*, p. 8; Andrew Scull, "The Discovery of the Asylum Revisited: Lunacy Reform in the New American Republic," in Andrew Scull, ed., *Madhouses, Mad-Doctors, and Madmen: The Social History of Psychiatry in the Victorian Era*, p. 148; Stanley Schultz, "Temperance Reform in the Antebellum South: Social Control and Urban Order," *South Atlantic Quarterly* 83 (1984): *passim*; Shalhope, *John Taylor*, p. 70; Tyrrell, "Drink and Social Reform," p. 2; Fred Somkin, *Unquiet Eagle: Memory and Desire in the Idea of American Freedom, 1815–1860*, pp. 6–7; and Steven Watts, *The Republic Reborn: War and the Making of Liberal America, 1790–1820*, pp. xvii, 10–11, 114.

4. *An Address, to the Emigrants from Connecticut, and from New England Generally, in the New Settlements of the United States*, p. 9. A thorough discussion of virtue, Republicanism, and liberalism is in the exchange between Appleby and Lance Banning. See Joyce Appleby, "Republicanism in Old and New Contexts," and Lance Banning, "Jeffersonian Ideology Revisited: Liberal and Classical Ideas in the New American Republic," *WMQ* 43 (1986): 20–34 and 1–19. Also see Rowland Berthoff, "Independence and Attachment, Virtue and Interest: From Republican Citizen to Free Enterpriser, 1787–1837," in Richard Bushman et al., *Uprooted Americans*, pp. 106–7; and Appleby, *Capitalism*, pp. ix–x.

5. "Address to the Public," *Panoplist* 11 (January 1815): 2.

6. "Sketch of Evarts," p. 309; *Panoplist* 11 (August 1815): 379; *Report of the Executive Committee of the Bible Society of Massachusetts, June 8, 1815*, p. 14; Edwin Rice, *The Sunday-School Movement and the American Sunday-School Union*, pp. 55–56. For Mrs. Evarts see the *Panoplist* 11 (August 1815): 196; Gribbin, *Churches Militant*, p. 149.

7. Heman Humphrey, "Union is Strength," in *Miscellaneous Discourses and Reviews*, p. 23; Timothy Dwight, *Greenfield Hill*, p. 134.

8. Todd, *John Todd*, pp. 53, 56. Additional notes on Evarts's family life are in Hunnewell, *Century of Town Life*, p. 231; Field, *Brief Memoirs*, p. 39. Evarts maintained an interest in Todd's life during his later struggles with studies and ill health at Yale.

9. Hunnewell, *Century of Town Life*, p. 188; Evarts to S. Worcester, August 14, 1815, ABC 11, vol. 1, no. 132.

10. Detailed analyses of the economic shifts that precipitated much of this are in Robert F. Dalzell, Jr., "The Rise of the Waltham-Lowell System and Some Thoughts on the Political Economy of Modernization in Ante-Bellum Massachusetts," *Perspectives in American History* 9 (1975); T. M. Adams, *Prices Paid by Vermont Farmers for Goods and Services and Received by Them for Farm Products, 1790–1940: Wages of Vermont Farm Labor, 1780–1940*, pp. 91, 104, 106–7; Robert Zevin, *The Growth of Manufacturing in Early Nineteenth Century New England*, pp. 310–33. For the nature of urban growth in these years, see Allan Pred, *Urban Growth and the Circulation of Information: The United States System of Cities, 1790–1840*, pp. 81–82, 108–9, 200–201. See also Lance Banning, *The Jeffersonian Persuasion: Evolution of a Party Ideology*, p. 302; Stanley Schultz, *The Culture Factory: Boston Public Schools, 1789–1860*, pp. 234–35.

11. From a Fast Day sermon in 1815, quoted in J. Earl Thompson, Jr., "A Perilous Experiment: New England Clergymen and American Destiny, 1796–1826" (Ph.D. diss., Princeton University, 1966), p. 204. See Gen. Ebenezer Elmer, *Oration Delivered Before the Washington Whig Society and Other Citizens of the County of Cumberland, (N.J.) April 11, 1815, passim*, for expression of this general concern.

12. Abel Flint, *A Discourse, Occasioned by the News of Peace, Delivered at the South Meeting-house in Hartford, February 14, 1815*, pp. 10–11.

13. Daniel Sanders, *An Address, Delivered in Sherburne, 28th February, 1815. Occasioned by the Celebration of the Peace of Ghent, 24th December, 1814*, pp. 5–6.

14. *The Crisis: On the Origin and Consequences of Our Political Dissensions. By a Citizen of Vermont*, p. 14.

15. Hiram Bingham Journal, November 30, 1816, in Char Miller, "'Teach Me O My God': The Journal of Hiram Bingham (1815–1816)," *Vermont History* 48 (1980): 231; "Address to the Public," *Panoplist* 12 (January 1816): 3; [Jeremiah Evarts], "Thoughts on Publishing Charitable Donations," *Panoplist* 12 (February 1816): 30–33; Merle Curti, *The American Peace Crusade, 1815–1860*, p. 9; "Peace Societies Compared with Other Benevolent Institutions," *Friend of Peace* 2 (1816): 6–7; Evarts to Samuel Worcester, June 1816, in Banner, *Hartford Convention*, p. 165n; Abel Flint, *A Sermon, Preached at the Anniversary Election, Hartford, May 9, 1816*, pp. 7–8.

16. Ward Cotton, *Causes and Effects of Female Regard to Christ, Illustrated in A Sermon, Delivered before the Female Society in Boylston, for the Aid of Foreign Missions,*

at their request, October 1, 1816, pp. 12–13; Todd, *John Todd*, p. 63; David Thurston, *A Sermon Delivered in Saco, June 26, 1816, Before the Maine Missionary Society, at their Ninth Annual Meeting*, p. 5; S. Worcester to Edward Payson, February 28, 1816, in C. Phillips, "Protestant America," p. 237; *Constitution and Address of the American Society for Educating Pious Youth*, pp. 19, 29; Evarts to Joseph Lyman, March 3, 1816, Simon Gratz Collection, HSP. See also Humphrey, "Union is Strength," p. 23; Norman Jacobson, "The Concept of Equality in the Assumptions and the Propaganda of Massachusetts Conservatives, 1790–1840" (Ph.D. diss., University of Wisconsin, 1951), pp. 133–34; Samuel Miller, Jr., *The Life of Samuel Miller*, 2:41. A valuable discussion of some related issues is in Bertram Wyatt-Brown, "Prelude to Abolitionism: Sabbatarian Politics and the Rise of the Second Party System," *Journal of American History* 58 (1971): 320–23, 328–29.

17. Good summaries are in Phillips, "Jedidiah Morse," pp. 220–23, and Conrad Wright, "Institutional Reconstruction in the Unitarian Controversy," in Conrad Wright, ed., *American Unitarianism, 1805–1865*, pp. 3–30.

18. Jeremiah Evarts, *Review of American Unitarianism*, pp. 8–9.

19. Ibid., p. 23. See also pp. 10–22.

20. Ibid., p. 25. See also A. A., "Letter of Pliny to Trajan," *Panoplist* 12 (April 1816): 152–53.

21. Quoted in Florence Hayes, *Daughters of Dorcas*, pp. 12–13.

22. Dunstan, *Light to the City*, p. 21; Phillips, "Jedidiah Morse," p. 248; Raymond Mohl, "Education as Social Control in New York City, 1784–1825," *New York History* 51 (1970): 233–34; Paul Boyer, *Urban Masses and Moral Order in America, 1820–1920*, p. 36; *Report of the Executive Committee of the Bible Society of Massachusetts, June 6, 1816*, p. 8; *Constitution of the American Bible Society, Formed by a Convention of Delegates, Held in the City of New York, May, 1816. Together With Their Address to the People of the United States*, pp. 3–13; W. P. Strickland, *History of the American Bible Society, from its Organization to the Present Time*, p. 33.

23. *Address to the Public on the Use of Ardent Spirits*, pp. 16–17. Also see William Cogswell, *A Discourse, Delivered before the Dedham Auxiliary Society for the Suppression of Intemperance, at Their Anniversary Meeting, Feb. 2, 1818, passim*; Dr. Noah Fifield, *An Address Delivered Before the Society for the Reformation of Morals, in Weymouth and Braintree, At Their Annual Meeting, April 13, 1818*, p. 5 and *passim*; [Jeremiah Evarts], "Address to the Public, at the Commencement of a New Year," *Panoplist* 13 (January 1817): 1–3; Micah Stone, *Address, Delivered Before the Moral Society in Brookfield, April 15, 1817*, p. 11; Levi Frisbie, "Professor Frisbie's Inaugural Address," *North American Review* 6 (January 1818): 229, 236–37.

24. A. B., "On Atheism," *Panoplist* 13 (December 1817): 548–49; A. B., "On the Duty of Praying for the Salvation of Relatives and Friends," *Panoplist* 13 (October 1817): 453–54; A. B., "President Edwards' First Resolution," *Panoplist* 13 (September 1817): 404–7; A. M., "On the Intercourse of Christians with the World," *Panoplist* 13 (August 1817): 352–59; A. B., "Massachusetts Missionary Society,"

Panoplist 13 (April 1817): 161–63; A. E., "The Corban Society," *Panoplist* 13 (April 1817): 163–65.

25. Samuel Etheridge, *The Christian Orator; or, A Collection of Speeches. Delivered on Public Occasions before Religious Benevolent Societies*, p. iii; Heman Humphrey, *On Doing Good to the Poor*, p. 20. A long exegesis of this theme is in Mighill Blood, *Moral Duty and Improvement. A Discourse Delivered in Bucksport (Me.) Before the Felicity Lodge of Free and Accepted Masons; On the Festival of St. John the Baptist. 24th June, Anno Lucis, 5818.—A.D. 1818*, pp. 3–13.

26. Joshua Bates, *A Discourse Delivered in Castleton, at the Organization of the Vermont Juvenile Missionary Society, September 16, 1818*, pp. 8–9. See also Thomas Adams, *A Sermon, Delivered at Farmington (Maine), December 4, 1817; Being the Day Set Apart by the Governor and Council, As a Day of Public Thanksgiving and Prayer*, pp. 12–13; *An Address to the Citizens of Windham County, On the Importance of Forming a County Society for Charitable Purposes, By the Consociation of Said County*, pp. 4–5; Daniel Dana, *An Address, Delivered August 16, 1818, at a Public Meeting of the Sabbath Schools under the patronage of the Newburyport Sabbath School and Tract Society*, pp. 3, 8; John Keep, *Nature and Operations of Christian Benevolence. A Sermon, Delivered Oct. 21, 1818, Before the Directors of the Domestic Missionary Society, of Massachusetts Proper, at their first meeting in Northampton*, pp. 17–20. For expressions of nationalism see Frisbie, "Professor Frisbie's," p. 239; John Everett, *An Oration on the Prospects of the Young Men of America*, passim.

27. Humphrey, *On Doing Good*, pp. 18–19; Benjamin L. Oliver, Jr., *Hints for an Essay on the Pursuit of Happiness*, pp. 57–58, 206–7.

28. Louis Billington, "'Female Laborers in the Church': Women Preachers in the Northeastern United States, 1790–1840," *Journal of American Studies* 19 (1985): 369–94; Joseph Chickering, *A Sermon, Preached in Boston, Before the American Society for Educating Pious Youth for the Gospel Ministry, at their Second Anniversary, Oct. 15, 1817*, pp. 34–35; Anne Boylan, "Evangelical Womanhood in the Nineteenth Century: The Role of Women in Sunday Schools," *Feminist Studies* 4 (1978): 64–71; Anne Boylan, "Timid Girls, Venerable Widows and Dignified Matrons: Life Cycle Patterns Among Organized Women in New York and Boston, 1797–1840," *American Quarterly* 38 (1986): 779–81; Jan Lewis, "The Republican Wife: Virtue and Seduction in the Early Republic," *WMQ* 44 (1987): 689–721; *A Brief Account of the Origin and Progress of the Boston Female Society for Missionary Purposes*, p. 3; Tucker's diary entry for November 30, 1817, in John Codman, ed., *The Hidden Life of a Christian, Exemplified in the Character and Writings of Mrs. Susannah H. Tucker, Late of Milton, Mass.*, p. 95. Nancy Hewitt, in *Women's Activism and Social Change: Rochester, New York, 1822–1872*, found three separate networks of female activists: benevolent women, perfectionists, and those who worked to change the social structure. The bonds of womanhood were not unitary. For a comparative view of the English experience, see Brian Harrison, "A Genealogy of Reform in Modern Britain," in *Anti-Slavery, Religion, and Reform: Essays in Memory of Roger*

Anstey, ed. Christine Bolt and Seymour Drescher, pp. 119–48. Also see James Bean, *The Christian Minister's Affectionate Advice to a Married Couple*, p. 1; Benjamin Wadsworth, *Female Charity an Acceptable Offering. A Sermon, Delivered in the Brick Meeting House in Danvers, At the Request of the Charitable Female Cent Society in Danvers and Middleton, for Promoting Christian Knowledge*, p. 25; New Hampshire Missionary Society officials as quoted in Melder, "Beginnings of Women's Rights Movement," p. 80.

29. *Panoplist* 14 (May 1818): 212–13. Also see Forrest McDonald, *Novus Ordo Seclorum: The Intellectual Origins of the Constitution*, pp. 70–71.

30. J. Evarts to S. Worcester, June 18, 1816, ABC 11, vol. 1, no. 139; Tracy, *Memoir*, p. 109. See also A. B., "On the Present Want of Faithful and Able Ministers of the Gospel," *Panoplist* 12 (November 1816): 503–5; A. A., "On the Significance of the Word Atonement, As Used in Scripture," *Panoplist* 12 (March 1816): 98; 12 (July 1816): 324–38.

31. Noah Porter, *A Sermon, Delivered at the Meeting for the Connecticut Society for the Promotion of Good Morals, in New-Haven, October 16, 1816*, p. 19; Charles Lowell, *A Discourse, Delivered Before the Society for Promoting Christian Knowledge, Piety, and Charity: May 27, 1816*, p. 17; David D. Field, *The Sabbath. A Sermon, Preached at Hartford, on the Evening of May 15, 1816. Before the Connecticut Society for the Promotion of Good Morals, passim*; A. B., "The Sabbath Made for Man," *Panoplist* 13 (April 1817): 157–61. Also important are Rev. Zephaniah S. Moore, *The Sabbath a Permanent and Benevolent Institution. A Sermon, Preached at the Annual Election, May 27, 1818, Before His Excellency John Brooks, Esq. Governor; His Honor William Phillips, Esq. Lieutenant Governor; The Honorable Council; and the Legislature of Massachusetts*, pp. 15, 20; *Second Report of the American Bible Society, Presented May 14, 1818, passim*; *An Address to the Children of the North Parish Sabbath School, in Portsmouth, By a Teacher, passim*; *Annals of Congress*, 14th Cong. 1st sess., pp. 1046–47; A. B., "Laws Respecting the Observance of the Sabbath," *Panoplist* 13 (July 1817): 303–8; A. B., "Laws of Connecticut in Reference to the Sabbath," *Panoplist* 13 (August 1817): 363–66.

32. John Butler, *A Sermon Delivered April 28, 1817, Before the Association for the Suppression of Intemperance, and the Promotion of Morality in the Town of Hanover, Massachusetts*, p. 9; Abiel Holmes, *A Discourse, Delivered at the Opening of the New Almshouse in Cambridge, passim*; John Codman, *A Discourse, Delivered before the Roxbury Charitable Society, at their Anniversary, Sept. 24, 1817*, p. 10.

33. Quoted in A. D. Jones, *Memoir of Elder Abner Jones*, pp. 194–95. See also Reuben Emerson, *A Sermon, Delivered at S. Reading, November 23, 1820. Being A Day of Public Thanksgiving Throughout the Commonwealth*, p. 14.

34. Frederick Marryat, *A Diary in America, with Remarks on Its Institutions*, pp. 310–11; Evarts to S. Worcester, March 31, 1815, in Tracy, *Memoir*, p. 107.

35. For a much fuller discussion see Andrew, *Rebuilding the Christian Commonwealth*, chapter 5. Also see Joseph Harvey, *A Sermon, Preached at Litchfield, Before*

the *Foreign Mission Society of Litchfield County, at Their Annual Meeting, February 15, 1815,* p. 25; Jeremiah Evarts to S. Worcester, April 1, 1815, ABC 11, vol. 1, no. 125; Zebulon Ely, *Revelation Necessary to Salvation. A Sermon, Delivered in Thompson, At a Meeting of the Foreign Mission Society of Windham County, Oct. 4, 1815,* p. 5; Edwards, *Memoir of Cornelius,* p. 37.

36. S. Worcester to J. Evarts, July 1, 1815, ABC 1.5, vol. 2.

37. Return J. Meigs to William H. Crawford (secretary of war), November 30, 1815, American State Papers, *Indian Affairs,* 2: 86. Also see Ronald Miriani, "Lewis Cass and Indian Administration in the Old Northwest, 1815–1836" (Ph.D. diss., University of Michigan, 1974), p. 207.

38. For a succinct statement of government policy, see A. J. Dallas (secretary of war) to Richard Graham (Indian agent, Illinois Territory), July 14, 1815, Clarence Carter, ed., *The Territorial Papers of the United States,* vol. 17, *The Territory of Illinois, 1814–1818,* pp. 199–200. The volumes of the territorial papers are filled with examples of this pressure; see particularly vol. 11, *The Territory of Michigan, 1820–1829,* and vol. 17, *The Territory of Illinois, 1814–1818.*

39. Joseph Harvey, Charles Prentice, and James Morris to ABCFM, August 20, 1816, ABC 12.1, vol. 2; "Second Quarterly Circular of the Prudential Committee of the American Board of Commissioners for Foreign Missions," *Panoplist* 12 (April 1816): 186–90; the report of the Prudential Committee in *Panoplist* 12 (October 1816): 444–55; "On Educating Heathen Youth in Our Own Country," *Panoplist* 12 (July 1816): 299; Joseph Harvey and James Morris to Samuel Worcester, June 25, 1816, ABC 12.1, vol. 2. For a discussion of the many factors involved in establishing this school, see John A. Andrew III, "Educating the Heathen: The Foreign Mission School Controversy and American Ideals," *Journal of American Studies* 12 (1978): 331–42.

40. *Panoplist* 12 (January 1816): 41. For Cornwall see Edward Starr, *A History of Cornwall, Connecticut,* pp. 64, 90; Percy Bidwell, "Rural Economy in New England at the Beginning of the Nineteenth Century," Connecticut Academy of Arts and Sciences, *Transactions* 20 (1916): 264; Theodore Gold, comp., *Historical Records of the Town of Cornwall, Litchfield County, Connecticut,* p. 30.

41. Gordon Chappell, "The Life and Activities of John Coffee" (Ph.D. diss., Vanderbilt University, 1941), pp. 149–52; Thomas P. Abernathy, *From Frontier to Plantation in Tennessee,* pp. 270–71; Andrew Jackson to John Coffee, February 2, 1816, Box 8, folder 19, John Coffee Papers, Tennessee Historical Society. Coffee was a confidant of Jackson and had married one of Rachel Jackson's nieces. For government reaction see Secretary of War William Crawford to Jackson, January 21, 1816, in John Spencer Bassett, ed., *Correspondence of Andrew Jackson,* 2:227–28. See also J. Orin Oliphant, ed., *Through the South and West with Jeremiah Evarts in 1826,* p. 21; Marion Starkey, *The Cherokee Nation,* p. 30; Robert Walker, *Torchlights to the Cherokees: The Brainerd Mission,* p. 16; Jack Gregory and Rennard Strickland, *Starr's History of the Cherokees,* p. 248.

42. K. C., "What are the Motives Which Should Induce the Churches in the United States to Attempt the Conversion and Civilization of the Indians?" *Panoplist* 12 (March 1816): 118–22; K. C., "Sketch of a Plan for Instructing the Indians," *Panoplist* 12 (April 1816): 150–52.

43. William Crawford to Sen. John Gaillard, March 13, 1816, in American State Papers, *Indian Affairs*, 2:26–28. The Jackson formula is in Jackson to Gen. Edmund Gaines, April 8, 1816, in Bassett, *Correspondence of Jackson*, 2:238–39. See also *Annals of Congress*, 14th Cong., 1st sess. (1816), p. 196.

44. Cyrus Kingsbury to William Crawford, May 4, 1816, Box 1, no. 29, Cherokee Collection, Brainerd Mission Manuscripts, Tennessee State Library and Archives.

45. Andrew Jackson to William Crawford, June 10, 1816, American State Papers, *Indian Affairs*, 2:111; Jackson to Crawford, June 10, 13, July 1, 1816, in Bassett, *Correspondence of Andrew Jackson*, 2:245, 248, 250–51; Cass to Crawford, June 6, 1816, in Carter, *Territorial Papers of Michigan, 1805–1820*, 10:648–49; Alexander McNair to Josiah Meigs, August 16, 1816, in Carter, *Territorial Papers*, 15:171; editorial in *Liberty Hall and Cincinnati Gazette*, March 18, 1816, quoted in Richard Farrell, "Internal-Improvement Projects in Southwestern Ohio, 1815–1834," *Ohio History* 80 (1971): 6. See also *Annals of Congress*, 14th Cong., 1st sess. (1816), p. 111.

46. Crawford to the Indian Commissioners, September 17, 1816, in Carter, ed., *Territorial Papers*, 15:175.

47. William McLoughlin, *Cherokees and Missionaries, 1789–1839*, p. 102. For the initial uncertainty of the missionaries, see Cyrus Kingsbury to Samuel Worcester, October 15, 1816, in Walker, *Torchlights*, p. 20. See also Mary Peacock, "Methodist Mission Work Among the Cherokee Indians before the Removal," *Methodist History* 3 (1965): 27.

48. J. Evarts to his wife (1818), Box 2, folder 40, EFP; Mrs. M. Evarts to Elizabeth Baldwin, November 17, 1817, Box 10, Baldwin Family Papers, Yale; Tracy, *Memoir*, pp. 110–11. Evarts's activities have been studied in Oliphant, *Through the South and the West*. Before he left, the Evarts family switched its membership from First Church in Charlestown to Park Street Church in Boston. See *The Articles of Faith, and the Covenant, of Park Street Church, Boston; With a List of the Members*.

49. Tracy, *Memoir*, p. 111; from his journal, February 11, 1818.

50. Evarts to his wife, February 28, March 13, 1818, EFP; Tracy, *Memoir*, p. 113; Brainerd Dyer, *The Public Career of William M. Evarts*, p. 1. For a commentary on personal letters in these years, see Pauline Maier, *The Old Revolutionaries: Political Lives in the Age of Samuel Adams*, pp. xiv–xv. We want to know more than the writers were willing to reveal. For the nurture of children see the quotation from Evarts's essay "On Educating Children for the Present Times" in Dyer, *Public Career*, pp. 2–3; and John Frisch, "Youth Culture in America, 1790–1865" (Ph.D. diss., Uni-

versity of Missouri–Columbia, 1970), pp. 42–52. See also Evarts's journal entry for March 13, 1818, in Tracy, *Memoir*, p. 116.

51. Evarts to his wife, April 24, 1818, Box 2, folder 41, EFP.

52. Journal entry for April 6, 1818, in Tracy, *Memoir*, pp. 116–17.

53. Evarts to S. Worcester, May 22, 1818, ABC 11, vd. 1. See also Tracy, *Memoir*, pp. 119–23; Cephas Washburn, *Reminiscences of the Indians*, p. 82. The nineteenth-century missionary veneration of David Brainerd is analyzed in Joseph Conforti, "David Brainerd and the Nineteenth Century Missionary Movement," *Journal of the Early Republic* 5 (1985): 308–29.

54. Evarts's journal for May and June 1818, quoted in Tracy, *Memoir*, 125–26; J. Evarts to his wife, June 5, 1818, Box 2, folder 41, EFP.

55. J. Evarts to Thomas McKenney, November 26, 1818, ABC 1.01, vol. 2. See also Tracy, *Memoir*, pp. 127–28.

56. Elias Cornelius to Cyrus Kingsbury, August 31, 1818, ABC 18.4.5, vol. 1; McLoughlin, *Cherokees and Missionaries*, p. 116; Joseph Harvey, *The Banner of Christ Set Up. A Sermon Delivered at the Inauguration of the Rev. Hermon [sic] Daggett, as Principal of the Foreign Mission School in Cornwall, Connecticut, May 6, 1818*, pp. 16, 24. In a letter to Samuel Worcester, Evarts voiced his fears that the missionary spirit would quickly wane and noted that receipts had fallen by 33 percent; see Evarts to Worcester, December 8, 1818, Letters From Officers of the Board, ABC 11.

57. William McLoughlin, *The Cherokee Ghost Dance: Essays on the Southeastern Indians, 1789–1861*, p. xiii. The tribes themselves were beginning to respond to these changes in nonmilitary ways; see William McLoughlin, "The Cherokee Ghost Dance Movement of 1811–1813," in McLoughlin, *Cherokee Ghost Dance*, pp. 111–51.

58. James D. Richardson, *Messages and Papers of the Presidents*, 2:9; Jackson to Monroe, March 4, 1817, in Bassett, *Correspondence of Jackson*, 2:279–80; Josiah Meigs to John Coffee, March 18, 1817, in Carter, *Territorial Papers*, 6:781. Coffee, with Jackson's support, became an inveterate land speculator. See Jackson to Coffee, June 21, 1817, John Coffee Papers, Box 8, folder 33, Tennessee State Library and Archives; Chappell, "Life of John Coffee," pp. 157–59.

59. The best analysis of this trial is in William McLoughlin, "Experiment in Cherokee Citizenship, 1817–1829," *American Quarterly* 33 (1981): 3–25.

60. Monroe to Jackson, October 5, 1817, in Bassett, *Correspondence of Jackson*, 2:331–32.

61. Calhoun to Joseph McMinn, July 29, 1818, in W. Edwin Hemphill, ed., *The Papers of John Calhoun*, 2:437. Evolution of this policy can be traced in the following: George Graham to William Clarke and Ninian Edwards, 1817, SW, LS (M-15), reel 4, pp. 94–95; Monroe's "Annual Message," in Richardson, *Messages and Papers*, 2:16–17; Calhoun to McMinn, January 19, 1818, in Hemphill, *Papers*

of Calhoun, 2:81; Calhoun to Isaac Shelby and Andrew Jackson, May 2, 1818, and C. C. Vandeventer to Lewis Cass, June 29, 1818, in SW, LS (M-15), reel 4, pp. 150, 176–79; Calhoun to Clark, May 8, 1818, in Carter, *Territorial Papers*, 15:391. Tribal opposition is noted in Hugh Young to Andrew Jackson, September 1, 1818, Carter, *Territorial Papers*, 18:407–8. See also Calhoun to Henry Clay, December 5, 1818, in Hemphill, *Papers of Calhoun*, 3:355.

62. See McKenney to Isaac Thomas, December 14, 1817, in Ora Peake, *A History of the United States Indian Factory System, 1795–1822*, p. 281; David Mitchell to Calhoun, February 3, 1818, in Hemphill, *Papers of Calhoun*, 2:15; and various letters about applicants in ABC 13, vol. 1. Other religious groups, like the Baptists, increased their Indian missions as well; see James Patterson, "Motives in the Development of Foreign Missions Among American Baptists, 1810–1826," *Foundations* 19 (1976): 313. For a study of the impact of change upon the tribes, see Richard White, *The Roots of Dependency: Subsistence, Environment, and Social Change Among the Choctaws, Pawnees, and Navajos*, pp. xix, 114–19, 130, 144, and *passim*.

63. Samuel Worcester to Calhoun, February 6, Calhoun to McKenney, February 16, Meigs to Calhoun, June 10, Cornelius to Calhoun, July 9, John Joyce to Calhoun, July 13, 1818, in Hemphill, *Papers of Calhoun*, 2:124–25, 141, 335–36, 369, 372–73; McKenney to John McKee, April 15, 1818, in Carter, *Territorial Papers*, 18:303.

64. Monroe's "Annual Message," November 16, 1818, is in Richardson, *Messages and Papers*, 2:45–46. See also Journal of the Mission at Brainerd, November 25, 1818, in *Panoplist* 15 (January 1819): 46; Hall to Evarts, December 4, 1818, ABC 18.3.1, vol. 3.

65. Robert Blackson, "Helping Those Who Help Themselves: Benevolent Organizations in the Early Nineteenth Century" (Paper delivered at the forty-ninth meeting of the Pennsylvania Historical Association, 1980), p. 12; Michael Holt, *The Political Crisis of the 1850s*, pp. 17–21; George Nielsen, "The Indispensable Institution: The Congressional Party During the Era of Good Feelings" (Ph.D. diss., University of Iowa, 1968), p. 103; Watts, *Republic Reborn*, p. 319; Andrew Cayton, *The Frontier Republic: Ideology and Politics in the Ohio Country, 1780–1825*, p. 111. For a provocative symbolic interpretation see James McLachlan, "The 'Choice of Hercules': American Student Societies in the Early 19th Century," in Lawrence Stone, ed., *The University in Society*, 2:450, 462, 493.

66. Ronald Satz, *American Indian Policy in the Jacksonian Era*, p. 247; Tracy, *Memoir*, pp. 127–28; Michael Green, *The Politics of Indian Removal: Creek Government and Society in Crisis*, p. 47; McLoughlin, *Cherokees and Missionaries*, p. 129; William McLoughlin, "The Missionary Dilemma," *Canadian Review of American Studies* 16 (1985): 398.

67. Evarts to Worcester, February 3 and 16, 1819, in Tracy, *Memoir*, pp. 128–30; see also pp. 131–32.

68. Evarts to Worcester, February 3, 1819, ABC 11, vol. 1, no. 182; Meigs to

Calhoun, February 10, 1819; Calhoun to the Cherokee Delegation, February 17, 1819; Charles Hicks to Calhoun, February 19, 1819, all in Hemphill, *Papers of Calhoun*, 3:561–63, 588–89.

69. Evarts to Worcester, February 16, 1819, ABC 11, vol. 1, no. 190; Worcester to Evarts, February 28, 1819, ABC 11, vol. 1, no. 23; Calhoun to J. H. Hobart, March 24, 1819, in Hemphill, *Papers of Calhoun*, 3:686–87; Calhoun to the Creek Deputation, March 28, 1819, SW, LS (M-15), reel 4, pp. 279–80; Jackson to Henry Atkinson, May 15, 1819, Hemphill, *Papers of Calhoun*, 4:63.

70. Massachusetts Peace Society, *Fourth Report*, p. 6.

71. *Catharine Brown, The Converted Cherokee: A Missionary Drama, Founded on Fact*, p. 9. The Cass quote is in Robert Unger, "Lewis Cass: Indian Superintendent of the Michigan Territory, 1813–1831, A Survey of Public Opinion as Reported by the Newspapers of the Old Northwest Territory" (Ph.D. diss., Ball State University, 1967), p. 86. See also Bernard Sheehan, *Seeds of Extinction: Jeffersonian Philanthropy and the American Indian*, pp. 122–29; Arthur H. DeRosier, Jr., "Cyrus Kingsbury—Missionary to the Choctaws," *Journal of Presbyterian History* 50 (1972): 271–72; Arthur Cole, "Cyclical and Sectional Variations in the Sale of Public Lands, 1816–1860," *Review of Economic Statistics* 9 (1927): 41–53; Norval Luxon, *Niles' Weekly Register: News Magazine of the Nineteenth Century*, pp. 233–34; Jack Averitt, "The Democratic Party in Georgia, 1824–1837" (Ph.D. diss., University of North Carolina, 1956), pp. 16–17; Arthur H. DeRosier, Jr., "John C. Calhoun and the Removal of the Choctaw Indians," *Proceedings of the South Carolina Historical Association* (1957): 36–38; Louis R. Harlan, "The Public Career of William Berkeley Lewis," *Tennessee Historical Quarterly* 7 (1948): 10–11.

72. The report is in *Panoplist* 15 (December 1819): 551–52.

73. Thomas Gallaudet, *An Address, Delivered at a Meeting for Prayer, with Reference to the Sandwich Mission, in the Brick Church in Hartford, October 11, 1819*, p. 8. For a fuller history of the Sandwich Islands mission, see Andrew, *Rebuilding the Christian Commonwealth*, especially chapter 6.

74. Quoted in *Religious Intelligencer* 4 (October 30, 1819): 344. See also Miron Winslow, *A Sermon Delivered at the Old South Church, Boston, June 7, 1819, on the Evening Previous to the Sailing of the Rev. Miron Winslow, Levi Spaulding, and Henry Woodward, & Dr. John Scudder, as Missionaries to Ceylon*, pp. 16–17.

75. Heman Humphrey, *The Promised Land. A Sermon, delivered at Goshen, (Conn.) at the Ordination of the Rev. Messrs. Hiram Bingham & Asa Thurston, as Missionaries to the Sandwich Islands, Sept. 29, 1819*, p. 10. See also Andrew, *Rebuilding the Christian Commonwealth*, chapter 9.

76. Quoted in Tracy, *Memoir*, pp. 79–80.

77. "Letters on the Eastern States," *North American Review* 11 (July 1820): 74.

78. Webster to Henry Baldwin, February 15, 1820, in Wiltse, *Papers of Daniel Webster*, 1:269–70. See also Tracy, *Memoir*, p. 81; Glover Moore, *The Missouri Controversy, 1819–1821*, pp. 15–16.

79. William Crafts, *Address Delivered Before the New-England Society of South-Carolina. On the 22d December, 1820*, pp. 15–16.

80. "The Missouri Question," *Panoplist* 16 (January 1820): 15–21.

81. Ibid., pp. 21–24, 59–68. Evarts actually did not believe Congress would act soon. See Evarts to S. Worcester, March 2, 1820, ABC 11, Vol. 1.

82. "The Missouri Question," pp. 69–71.

83. "On the Condition of Blacks in This Country," *Panoplist* 16 (June 1820): 242.

84. Ibid., pp. 242–45. See also Tracy, *Memoir*, p. 87; and, for a hostile view of these efforts, Gribbin, *Churches Militant*, p. 142.

85. "On the Condition of Blacks" (November 1820): 481–85.

86. Quoted in Tracy, *Memoir*, pp. 85–86.

87. "Slavery and the Missouri Question," *North American Review* 10 (January 1820): 144. For the idea of power and proxy, see Otto Pflanze, "Toward a Psychoanalytic Interpretation of Bismarck," *AHR* 77 (1972): 424; and Martin Wangh, "The 'Evocation of a Proxy': A Psychological Maneuver, Its Use as a Defense, Its Purpose and Genesis," *Psychoanalytic Study of the Child* 17 (1962): 456. See also Lyman Beecher, *The Means of National Prosperity. A Sermon, Delivered at Litchfield, On the Day of the Anniversary Thanksgiving, December 2, 1819*, pp. 16–25.

88. For an explanation of Evarts's resignation see *Panoplist* 16 (August 1820): 357.

89. J. Evarts to Sarah Greene, April 26, 1820, Box 3, folder 124, EFP.

90. J. Evarts to his father, March 3, July 8, August 27, 1820, Box 1, folder 1, EFP.

91. Tracy, *Memoir*, pp. 132–33; S. Worcester to Evarts, March 2, 11, 1820, Letters to Officers of the Board, to September 1824, ABC; *Panoplist* 16 (March 1820): 140–41. See also Andrew, *Rebuilding the Christian Commonwealth*, chapter 7.

92. Richardson, *Messages and Papers*, 2:92. For some background see Calhoun to Rev. Abraham Steiner, May 9, 1820, Hemphill, *Papers of Calhoun*, 5:108; Calhoun to Cherokee agent R. J. Meigs, May 23, 1820, SW, LS (M-15), reel 4; Meigs to Calhoun, May 30, 1820; Calhoun to Meigs, July 19, 1820, in Hemphill, *Papers of Calhoun*, 5:147–52, 269. The ABCFM initially received $1,000 each for its Brainerd and Elliott Missions. By 1820 the value of board property at Brainerd alone was more than $11,000. See ABC 18.3.1, vol. 2, and Evarts to Calhoun, June 9, 1820, Hemphill, *Papers of Calhoun*, 5:169–70.

93. Eliphalet Gillet, *Evils of Intemperance. A Sermon Preached at Hallowell, on the Day of the Annual Fast in Maine, April 12, 1821*, p. 8; Paul Willard, *An Oration, Pronounced at Charlestown, On the 4th of July, 1821, At the Request of the Republican Citizens of that Town, in Commemoration of the Anniversary of National Independence*, pp. 9–11; Noah Porter, *Memorial of a Revival. A Sermon, Delivered in Farmington, At the Anniversary Thanksgiving, December 6, 1821*, p. 23; [F. Collins], *The Advan-*

tages and Disadvantages of Drunkenness: Containing a Variety of Plain and Important Maxims, Well Worthy of Being Remembered by Every Man in the Nation, p. 6.

94. Alexander Hill Everett, *America, or a General Survey of the Political Situation of the Several Powers of the Western Continent with Conjectures on Their Future Prospects*, p. 19. See also Susan Geib, "'Changing Works': Agriculture and Society in Brookfield, Massachusetts, 1785–1820" (Ph.D. diss., Boston University, 1981), pp. 202–3; James Essig, *The Bonds of Wickedness: American Evangelicals Against Slavery, 1770–1808*, p. 163; and Watts, *Republic Reborn*, pp. 68, 250–51.

NOTES FOR CHAPTER FIVE

1. Tracy, *Memoir*, p. 184; Evarts to Benjamin Swift, January 14, 27, 1823, Jeremiah Evarts Letterbook, pp. 69, 71–72, Box 1, folder 1, EFP. Additional family material is in ABC 34.

2. Evarts's note for August 23, 1823, ABC 34. He would later take much the same position toward the Cherokees.

3. There are many expressions of this concern. See Joseph R. Anthony, *Life in New Bedford A Hundred Years Ago*, p. 8; James Sabine, *The Relation the Present State of Religion Bears to the Expected Millennium. A Sermon, Delivered in the Old South Church, Boston, Before the Foreign Mission Society, of Boston and the Vicinity, Jan. 8, 1823*, p. 4; Ebenezer Porter, *Signs of the Times. A Sermon Preached in the Chapel of the Theological Seminary, Andover, on the Public Fast, April 3, 1823*, pp. 5–6; Nathaniel W. Taylor, *A Sermon, Addressed to the Legislature of the State of Connecticut, at the Annual Election in Hartford, May 7, 1823*, p. 34; Homer Babbidge, Jr., ed., *Noah Webster: On Being American, Selected Writings, 1783–1828*, pp. 160–61; O. Pearson, "How Shall a Student Ascertain His Personal Duty as to Engaging as a Missionary?" Society of Inquiry, Student Dissertations, vol. 16, ms. Andover-Newton Theological Seminary, p. 22; Samuel Allen, *An Oration Delivered on the Anniversary of American Independence; At Blackstone Village, Mendon, Massachusetts, July 4, 1823*, p. 13; Henry Colman, *A Discourse on the Character Proper to a Christian Society. Delivered at the Opening of the Second Congregational Church in Lynn, Massachusetts, 30 April 1823*, passim; Selden [pseud.], *Letters Addressed to the Members of the Eighteenth Congress*, p. 5; Gardiner Spring, *An Appeal to the Citizens of New-York, in Behalf of the Christian Sabbath*, p. 24; Wilde, *An Oration*, p. 14.

4. For discussion of these matters see Stuart Piggin, "Assessing Nineteenth-Century Missionary Motivation: Some Considerations of Theory and Method," in *Religious Motivation: Biographical and Sociological Problems for the Church Historian*, ed. Derek Baker, pp. 328–36; Andrew, *Rebuilding the Christian Commonwealth*, chapter 8; Justin Edwards, *A Sermon, Delivered at the Fourth Anniversary, of the Auxiliary Education Society, of the Young Men of Boston, February 12, 1823*, p. 17.

5. Hosea Hildreth, *Two Discourses on the Most Important Duties of Townsmen*, p. 6;

Merritt's remarks are in the *Methodist Magazine* for June 1824, quoted in Linn, "Religion and Nationalism," p. 141. See also the remarks of New York Rep. Silas Wood in Rush Welter, *The Mind of America, 1820–1860*, p. 48; and Mohl, *Poverty in New York, 1783–1825*, pp. 87–88.

6. Andrew Emerson, *An Oration Delivered at Portland, July 5, 1824. On the Celebration of the 48th Anniversary of American Independence*, p. 5.

7. A suggestive discussion of this change is in Watts, "Masks," especially p. 128. For some contemporary views see Orville Holley, *An Oration on the Permanency of Republican Institutions; Delivered at Troy, July 5, 1824*, pp. 21–22; and Alpheus Cary, *An Address, Delivered Before the Massachusetts Charitable Mechanic Association, October 7, 1824*, p. 9.

8. Yale College Society of Inquiry Respecting Missions, *A Missionary Catechism. For the Use of Children; Containing a Brief View of the Moral Condition of the World, and the Progress of Missionary Efforts Among the Heathen*, p. 39. See also Humphrey Moore, *A Sermon Preached at Leominster, January 24, 1821, at the Ordination of the Rev. Abel Conant to the Pastoral Care of the Church at that Place*, pp. 18–19. Broader commentary on foreign missions is in William Hutchison, "New England's Further Errand: Millennial Belief and the Beginnings of Foreign Missions," *Proceedings of the Massachusetts Historical Society* 94 (1982): 49–64, and Andrew, *Rebuilding the Christian Commonwealth*, passim.

9. January 1, 1822, quoted in David Calhoun, "The Last Command: Princeton Theological Seminary and Missions, 1812–1862" (Ph.D. diss., Princeton Theological Seminary, 1983), p. 308. See also Yale College Society, *A Missionary Catechism*, p. 39.

10. For these problems see Evarts to Parsons and Fisk, February 19, 1821, and Evarts to William Goodell, January 19, 1821, in Tracy, *Memoir*, pp. 134, 137–38.

11. *Boston Recorder* (February 17, 1821): 31.

12. Codman, *Hidden Life*, pp. 200–201. For Bingham's report see Bingham to Samuel Worcester, May 13, 1820, in Hawaiian Historical Society, *Sixteenth Annual Report* (1951), p. 18, as well as the *Boston Recorder* (June 9, 1821): 95. A fuller description of the arrival is in Andrew, *Rebuilding the Christian Commonwealth*, chapter 7.

13. From the board's *Annual Report* of 1821, quoted in Tracy, *Memoir*, pp. 153–54. For the changed atmosphere see Joshua Bates, *A Sermon, Preached on the Day of General Election, at Montpelier, October 11, 1821, Before the Honourable Legislature of Vermont*, pp. 16, 25; Charles Stewart to Evarts, August 30, 1821, Testimonials, vol. 4, ABC; Joseph Harvey to Evarts, November 14, 1821, Foreign Mission School, pre-September 1824, no. 32, ABC.

14. Evarts to Adam Hodgson in Liverpool, April 20, 1823, in Tracy, *Memoir*, pp. 186–87. For Douglas see James Douglas, *Hints on Missions*, p. 85. Evarts's other views on cooperation with the London Missionary Society are in Tracy, *Memoir*, p. 156, and ABC 13, vol. 1. See also Alexander Proudfit, *The Universal*

Extension of Messiah's Kingdom. A Sermon, Delivered in the North Church, New-Haven, Con. Sept. 12, 1822. Before the American Board of Commissioners for Foreign Missions, At Their Thirteenth Annual Meeting, pp. 24–25. For applicants' circumstances see Artemas Bishop to Evarts, January 30 and March 13, 1822; Charles Stewart to Evarts, March 5, 1822; and James Ely to Evarts, July 27, 1822, in Testimonials, vol. 4, ABC. Despite many monographs on foreign missions, however, there remains a lack of social theory in these studies; see T. O. Beidelman, "Social Theory and the Study of Christian Missions in Africa," *Africa* 44 (1974): 235–49.

15. Letter of April 15, 1823, in Tracy, *Memoir*, p. 185.

16. Ibid., pp. 185–86; *Missionary Herald* 19 (July 1823): 233–39. The last quotation is from Evarts's resolution before the Foreign Mission Society of Boston and Vicinity.

17. *Missionary Herald* 19 (November 1823): 365. See also the notes for a meeting of October 1, 1823, in ABC 8.5, no. 74; and Andrew, *Rebuilding the Christian Commonwealth*, chapter 7.

18. ABCFM, *View of the Missions of the American Board of Commissioners for Foreign Missions*, pp. 9–10; *Missionary Herald* 19 (November 1823): 366.

19. ABCFM, *The Necessity and Utility of Employing Agents to Solicit Money for the Support of Missions*, pp. 1–2, 11. Evidence of the appeal to community leaders is in Edward Byers, *The Nation of Nantucket: Society and Politics in an Early Commercial Center, 1660–1820*, p. 308.

20. Evarts to Henry Hill, January 12, 1824, ABC 11, vol. 1, no. 259. Evarts's itinerary is in the *Missionary Herald* 20 (November 1824): 367–68. For criticism of his salary ($2,000 per year) see the *Reformer* 5 (July 1, 1824): 159–60. The larger problems inherent in these efforts are noted in James Moorhead, "Between Progress and Apocalypse: A Reassessment of Millennialism in American Religious Thought, 1800–1880," *Journal of American History* 71 (1984); see especially pp. 527–29. For societies' coordination of their meetings see James Fraser, *Pedagogue for God's Kingdom: Lyman Beecher and the Second Great Awakening*, p. 34.

21. The best summaries of these tensions are in two works by William McLoughlin, *Cherokees and Missionaries* and *Cherokee Renascence in the New Republic*. See also R. Pierce Beaver, ed., *American Missions in Bicentennial Perspective*, p. viii; Calhoun, "The Last Command," pp. 302–3; Herman Viola, "Thomas L. McKenney and the Administration of Indian Affairs, 1824–1830" (Ph.D. diss., Indiana University, 1970), p. 205; and Sheehan, *Seeds of Extinction*, pp. 129–30, 249–50.

22. Samuel Jarvis, "A Discourse on the Religion of the Indian Tribes of North America: Delivered before the New-York Historical Society, December 20, 1819," in *New-York Historical Society Collections*, 3 (1821): 183; Phillips, "Jedidiah Morse," pp. 294–95.

23. Jackson to Calhoun, January 18, 1821, American State Papers, *Indian Affairs*, 2:503. For state requests see Thomas H. Benton and David Barton to Cal-

houn, March 3, 1821, in Carter, *Territorial Papers*, 15:706. Further details are in Perry McCandless, *A History of Missouri*, 2:54–55.

24. Evarts to Kingsbury, March 8, 1821, and Evarts to Hoyt, March 14, 1821, in Tracy, *Memoir*, pp. 139–40; Evarts to S. Worcester, April 2, 1821, in Tracy, *Memoir*, p. 141.

25. Thomas McKenney to Matthew Lyon, May 18, 1821, in Carter, *Territorial Papers*, 19:292.

26. The most succinct statement of this change is in Jackson to the Secretary of State, October 6, 1821, in Carter, *Territorial Papers*, 22:233. A broader discussion is in McLoughlin, *Cherokee Renascence*, passim, and Sheehan, *Seeds of Extinction*, pp. 250–56.

27. For the Report of a Joint Select Committee of the Tennessee Legislature, November 17, 1821, see Robert White, *Messages of the Governors of Tennessee, 1821–1825*, 2:28. Alabama's reply is in Gov. Israel Pickens to Gov. John Clark, December 13, 1821, Alabama: Executive Letter-Book, pp. 9–10. See also Calhoun to Clark, December 26, 1821, in Hemphill, *Papers of Calhoun*, 6:587–58; Hicks to Clark, January 29, 1822, ABC 18.3.1, vol. 3.

28. Rev. Cyrus Kingsbury to John Calhoun, January 31, 1822, ABC 18.3.4, vol. 1.

29. Calhoun to Monroe, February 8, 1822, in Hemphill, *Papers of Calhoun*, 6:680–82. See also *Annals of Congress*, 17th Cong., 1st sess., pp. 984–86, and Meigs to Calhoun, Hemphill, *Papers of Calhoun*, 6:691.

30. *Missionary Herald* 18 (March 1822): 93. See also Montgomery, "Jeremiah Evarts," pp. 10–11; and *The Christian Spectator* 4 (March 1822): 113–20.

31. Porter to his wife, March 18, 1822, in Matthews, *Memoir*, pp. 112–13; "Sketch of Evarts," pp. 311–12; Oliphant, *Through the South and the West*, pp. 27–28; Henry Malone, *Cherokees of the Old South: A People in Transition*, p. 102; Evarts to Rev. Calvin Chapin, April 17, 1821, in Tracy, *Memoir*, p. 142.

32. Evarts's diary entries for March 23 and April 6, 1822, in Tracy, *Memoir*, pp. 166–67.

33. Ibid., April 6, 1822.

34. Evarts to ABCFM, May 1822, in Tracy, *Memoir*, pp. 177–78. See also Evarts's memos of the Cherokee mission, May 21, 1822, ABC 18.3.1, vol. 2; and Mary Higginbotham, "The Creek Path Mission," *Journal of Cherokee Studies* 1 (1976): 78–79.

35. Evarts to the board, May 1822, in Tracy, *Memoir*, p. 179. See also *Missionary Herald* 18 (July 1822): 235.

36. *Letter to a Member of Congress in relation to Indian Civilization. By the domestic Secretary of the United Foreign Missionary Society*, pp. 13–14. Evarts's letters to the board in May 1822 contain the elements of this moral equality; see Tracy, *Memoir*, pp. 177–78.

37. For evidence on this point see Calhoun to Rep. W. D. Rochester, April 15,

1822, SW, LS (M-15), reel 5, p. 233; Robert Troup to Calhoun, June 10, 1822, Hemphill, *Papers of Calhoun*, 7:158; Henry Conway to Edmund P. Gaines, June 25, 1822, in Carter, *Territorial Papers*, 19:445; Evarts to S. Worcester, July 3, 1822, ABC 11, vol. 1; Crawford to Charles J. Ingersoll, July 4, 1822, Charles Jared Ingersoll Collection, HSP.

38. For John Ross and the Cherokee perspective, see John Ross to David Brown, July 13, 1822, in Moulton, *Papers of Ross*, 1:42–43; and Cherokee National Committee to Calhoun, October 24, 1822, Hemphill, *Papers of Calhoun*, 7:351. For changes among the Cherokees see McLoughlin, *Cherokees and Missionaries*, p. 126.

39. For Morse see Phillips, "Jedidiah Morse," p. 213; and Calhoun to Morse, October 28, 1822, SW, LS (M-15), reel 5, p. 349. Evarts's views are in a letter to Rev. Cyrus Kingsbury, August 1822, in Tracy, *Memoir*, p. 183.

40. Statement of May 5, 1823, quoted in Robert F. Berkhofer, Jr., *The White Man's Indian: Images of the American Indian from Columbus to the Present*, p. 151. See also Moody Hall to Evarts, February 17, 1823, ABC 18.3.1, vol. 3; Boudinot to Gold, April 7, 1823, Vaill Collection, Yale. War Department policy is summarized in Calhoun to Louis McLane, February 15, 1823, SW, LS (M-15), reel 5, pp. 387–88.

41. McCoy's plan is outlined in Yeager, "Indian Enterprises," pp. 245–49; and William Miles, "'Enamoured with Colonization': Isaac McCoy's Plan of Indian Reform," *Kansas Historical Quarterly* 38 (Autumn 1972): 269–79. See especially McCoy to Lewis Cass, June 23, 1823, in Miles, pp. 271–72.

42. Evarts to Rufus Anderson, December 20, 1823, ABC 11, vol. 1; Robert Lewitt, "Indian Missions and Anti-Slavery Sentiment: A Conflict of Evangelical and Humanitarian Ideals," *Mississippi Valley Historical Review* 50 (1963): 44; Tracy, *Memoir*, p. 187. See also John Andrew, "Betsey Stockton: Stranger in a Strange Land," *Journal of Presbyterian History* 52 (1974): 157–66.

43. Finney to ABCFM, October 17, 1823, *Missionary Herald* 20 (February 1824): 46–47; Memorial of the Georgia Legislature to Monroe, December 18, 1823, American State Papers, *Indian Affairs*, 2:491; Calhoun to McMinn, December 10, 1823, Hemphill, *Papers of Calhoun*, 8:401; Tracy, *Memoir*, p. 188.

44. Dickerson quoted in Herbert Ershkowitz, "New Jersey Politics During the Era of Andrew Jackson, 1829–1837" (Ph.D. diss., New York University, 1965), p. 1. For political changes see also John McLean to George P. Torrence, February 12, 1823, Isaac Cox, "Selections from the Torrence Papers," *Quarterly Publications of the Historical and Philosophical Society of Ohio* 2 (1907): 7; Daniel Webster to his brother Ezekiel, December 4, 1823, Fletcher Webster, ed., *The Private Correspondence of Daniel Webster*, 1:331; John McLean to Ohio governor Allen Trimble, January 31, 1823, *Autobiography and Correspondence of Allen Trimble, Governor of Ohio*, p. 133. Evarts's activities are in Anderson to Evarts, November 7, 1822, Box 1, folder 5, EFP; Tracy, *Memoir*, p. 188.

45. *The First Annual Report of the American Society for Promoting the Civilization and General Improvement of the Indian Tribes in the United States*, p. 22; "Application of the Board of Commissioners for Foreign Missions for Pecuniary Aid in Civilizing the Indians," American State Papers, *Indian Affairs*, 2:446–48.

46. Evarts's notes are in Box 4, folder 151, EFP. See also J. Fraser Cocks, III "From Boarding School to Demonstration Farm: Protestant Missionaries and the Plains Indians, 1825–1835," p. 13; Phillips, "Jedidiah Morse," pp. 303–4; and Mary Young, "Congress Looks West: Liberal Ideology and Public Land Policy in the Nineteenth Century," in David Ellis, ed., *The Frontier in American Development*, p. 79.

47. Evarts to Brown, January 6, 1824, ABC 1.01, vol. 5; Evarts to a friend, January 17, 1824, in Tracy, *Memoir*, pp. 189–90.

48. Cherokee delegation to the president, January 19, 1824, and Calhoun to the Cherokee delegation, January 30, 1824, American State Papers, *Indian Affairs*, 2:473. William McLoughlin has a full discussion of the many factors behind this shift in *Cherokee Renasence*; see especially pp. 366–67.

49. Evarts to Kingsbury, February 1, 1824, in Tracy, *Memoir*, p. 190. His discussions with government officials are noted in his Journal, Box 5, EFP. For his views on forcible removal see Evarts to Henry Hill, February 7, 1824, ABC 11, vol. 1. Evarts also had several long talks with Gen. Andrew Jackson during this visit.

50. Troup to Calhoun, February 28, 1824, in Edward Harden, *The Life of George M. Troup*, pp. 203–4. Cabinet discussions are noted in Hemphill, *Papers of Calhoun*, 8:xx. Other state petitions are in American State Papers, *Public Lands*, 4; see documents no. 414 and 422. Georgia's attack is in Georgia Congressional Delegation to President Monroe, March 10, 1824, American State Papers, *Indian Affairs*, 2:476–77. For one Cherokee's ambition see David Brown to Evarts, March 15, 1824, ABC 18.3.1, vol. 1.

51. *Missionary Herald* 20 (April 1824): 131–32. See also *Missionary Herald* 20 (June 1824): 186; Evarts to H. Hill, April 3, 1824, ABC 11, vol. 1; and Calhoun to Monroe, March 29, 1824, American State Papers, *Indian Affairs*, 2:462. Monroe's message of March 30, 1824, is in Richardson, *Messages and Papers*, 2:235–36.

52. Forsyth chaired a House select committee to study the Georgia claims; see his report in American State Papers, *Indian Affairs*, 2:498. Evarts's itinerary is in Tracy, *Memoir*, pp. 199–200. Concerns about the moral issue are raised in "View of Publick Affairs," *Christian Advocate* 2 (May 1824): 240.

53. Evarts to Washburn, May 28, 1824, Tracy, *Memoir*, pp. 200–201. For government views see Thomas McKenney to Indian Agent John Johnston, May 11, 1824, IA, LS (M-21), reel 1, p. 70; James Monroe to the Chickasaw chiefs, May 24, 1824, Hemphill, *Papers of Calhoun*, 9:112.

54. Evarts to Calhoun, July 27, 1824; see also Rev. T. Charleton Henry to Calhoun, May 28, 1824, Hemphill, *Papers of Calhoun*, 9:247, 120–21. Also see

Thomas McKenney to Henry, June 8, 1824, and Calhoun to Rev. William H. Barr, July 2, 1824, IA, LS (M-21), reel 1, pp. 103, 128.

55. See Troup's message to the Georgia legislature, November 2, 1824, in Harden, *Life of Troup*, pp. 222-23. Government attitudes are in Calhoun to the Piankashaw Delegation, August 1, 1824, and McKenney to Evarts, August 5, 1824, Hemphill, *Papers of Calhoun*, 9:258, 266-67; McKenney's Circular to all Indian Agents, August 7, 1824, IA, LS (M-21), reel 1, p. 170; Calhoun to John Crowell, August 12, 1824, Hemphill, *Papers of Calhoun*, 9:279-80; Evarts to Calhoun, August 12, 1824, ABC 1.01, vol. 5.

56. Evarts to Kingsbury, December 7, 1824, ABC 1.01, vol. 5. A recent discussion of this conflict between expansion through space as opposed to change over time is in Myra Jehlen, *American Incarnation: The Individual, the Nation, and the Continent*; see especially p. 6.

57. Evarts to Ceylon missionaries, February 7, 1825, in Tracy, *Memoir*, pp. 214-15. The *New York Observer* comment is quoted in the *Reformer* 7 (May 1, 1826): 67. See also Oliphant, *Through the South and the West*, p. 34; Tracy, *Memoir*, p. 208; and Evarts to Erastus Dean, January 14, 1825, ABC 1.01, vol. 5.

58. Timothy Flint, *Recollections of the Last Ten Years*, pp. 375-76. For efforts to organize and revitalize local societies, see J. Evarts's note, June 30, 1825, ABC 1.01, vol. 5; G. Cowles to Evarts, July 11, 1825, Miscellaneous Letters—Agents, 1822-91, ABC; Evarts to Henry Hill, July 21, 1825, quoted in Banner, "Protestant Crusade," p. 323; J. Walker, "Associations for Benevolent Purposes," *Christian Examiner* 2 (1825): 241, 245; Auxiliary Foreign Mission Society of Boston and Vicinity, *Thirteenth Anniversary, January 3, 1825*, p. 31; *Missionary Herald* 21 (September 1825): 301; Ornan Eastman to Evarts, October 5, 1825, Agencies, September 1824-September 1831, ABC. Criticism of these efforts is in the *Reformer* 6 (March 1, 1825): 1, 37.

59. Warren Fay, *The Obligations of Christians to the Heathen World. A Sermon, Delivered at the Old South Church in Boston, before the Auxiliary Foreign Mission Society of Boston and Vicinity, at the Annual Meeting, January 3, 1825*, pp. 6-7. For the ABCFM meeting see the *Missionary Herald* 21 (October 1825): 335 and ibid. (December 1825): 396.

60. "Reasonable Expectations in Relation to the Palestine Mission," *Missionary Herald* 22 (July 1826): 212-14. See also Tracy, *Memoir*, p. 223.

61. Quoted in Hood, "Presbyterianism," p. 233. See also Dann, "Humanitarian Reform," pp. 345-46; Dean May and Maris Vinovskis, "A Ray of Millennial Light: Early Education and Social Reform in the Infant School Movement in Massachusetts, 1826-1840," in *Family and Kin in Urban Communities, 1700-1930*, ed. Tamara Hareven, pp. 76-77. Masonic ideas are discussed in Dorothy Lipson, *Freemasonry in Federalist Connecticut, 1789-1835*, p. 120. See also Evarts to agents of the board, August 13, 1826, in Tracy, *Memoir*, p. 251.

NOTES FOR CHAPTER SIX

1. For a full discussion of the school and these problems, see Andrew, "Educating the Heathen," (1978): 331–42.
2. The agents' circular is in the *Foreign Mission School Catalogue*, June 1825, ABC 18.8, vol. 1. See also Stephen Gold to Rev. Herman Vaill, June 11, 1825, Vaill Collection.
3. Harriet Gold to unknown, n.d., Mary B. Church typescript, ABC 18.8, vol. 1.
4. Vaill to Harriet Gold, June 29, 1825, Vaill Collection.
5. Thomas Cooper, *Strictures Addressed to James Madison on the Celebrated Report of Wm. H. Crawford Recommending the Intermarriage of Americans with the Indian Tribes*, pp. iii–iv, 5–6, 10–11. William McLoughlin has argued that this racism was a major factor in the shift of American Indian policy in the Age of Jackson; see McLoughlin, "Red Indians, Black Slavery and White Racism: America's Slaveholding Indians," *American Quarterly* 26 (1974): 378.
6. Evarts to Dr. Chapin, July 5, 1825, ABC 1.01, vol. 5; Butrick's remarks are in Butrick to Evarts, October 12, 1824, ABC 18.3.1, vol. 4. For other ABCFM comments on race see the *Missionary Herald* 20 (November 1824): 355–56.
7. Evarts to Rev. Charles Prentice, July 26, 1825, ABC 8.6, vol. 5; Evarts to Rev. Timothy Stone, August 26, 1825, ABC 1.01, vol. 5. The "romantic valley" reference is in Adam Hodgson, *Remarks During a Journey Through North America in the Years 1819, 1820, and 1821*, pp. 244–45.
8. *Report of the American Board of Commissioners for Foreign Missions. Compiled from Documents Laid Before the Board, at the Seventeenth Annual Meeting, Which was held in Middletown, (Con.) Sept. 14, and 15, 1826*, p. 105. For Evarts's correspondence see Evarts to Kingsbury, September 8, 1825; Evarts to Chamberlain, September 16, 1825; and Evarts to Butrick, September 16, 1825, in ABC 1.01, vol. 5. Also see Brown to Evarts, September 29, 1825, ABC 18.3.1, vol. 5; and Butrick to Evarts, October 26, 1825, ABC 18.3.1, vol. 4.
9. *Report, ABCFM, 1826*, pp. 103–4, 106; Evarts to Rev. Amos Bassett, November 10, 1826, and Evarts to Rev. Charles Boardman, October 7, 1826, ABC 1.01, vol. 6. Other changes made by the board are noted in McLoughlin, *Cherokees and Missionaries*, pp. 195–96.
10. Evarts to Kingsbury, March 7, 1825, ABC 1.01, vol. 5.
11. For the Choctaw treaty see Hemphill, *Papers of Calhoun*, 9:xxix. Calhoun's survey is in Calhoun to Monroe, January 24, 1825, Hemphill, *Papers of Calhoun*, 9:516–7; and Monroe's message is in Richardson, *Messages and Papers*, 2:280–83. For Benton's remarks see Benton to Calhoun, January 28, 31, 1825, Hemphill, *Papers of Calhoun*, 9:523, 531–32. Other state reactions are in Calhoun to Louis McLane, February 1, 1825, Hemphill, *Papers of Calhoun*, 9:537; *Western Sun* [Indiana], March 5, 1825, quoted in Logan Esarey, *Internal Improvements in Early Indiana*, p. 74; and Carol Pingel, "The Disorder of American Indian Policy: The Old

Northwest, 1825–1829" (M.A. thesis, University of Wisconsin–Milwaukee, 1968), pp. 22–23.

12. McKenney to Evarts, February 7, 1825, ABC 10, vol. 10; Evarts to McKenney, February 14, 1825, ABC 1.01, vol. 5.

13. Georgia politics can best be followed in Averitt, "Democratic Party in Georgia," pp. 17–19, 54–59, 159–74; Ronald Faircloth, "The Impact of Andrew Jackson in Georgia Politics, 1828–1840" (Ph.D. diss., University of Georgia, 1971), pp. 8–9; and Paul Murray, *The Whig Party in Georgia, 1825–1853*, pp. 4–6, 34, 193. See also Marie Mahoney, "American Public Opinion of Andrew Jackson's Indian Policy, 1824–1835" (M.A. thesis, Clark University, 1935), pp. 19–20; and Michael Green, "Federal-State Conflict in the Administration of Indian Policy: Georgia, Alabama, and the Creeks, 1828–1834" (Ph.D. diss., University of Iowa, 1973), p. 160.

14. Starkey, *Cherokee Nation*, pp. 61–62; McLoughlin, *Cherokees and Missionaries*, p. 132; William Crouch, "Missionary Activities Among the Cherokee Indians, 1757–1838" (M.A. thesis, University of Tennessee, 1932), p. 121; McLoughlin, *Cherokee Renascence*, pp. xvii, 348, 376–79; and Ronald Satz, "Cherokee Traditionalism, Protestant Evangelism, and the Trail of Tears," *Tennessee Historical Quarterly* 44 (1985): *passim*. For a similar reaction from another tribe, see Jacob Jimeson to Calhoun, July 15, 1824, Hemphill, *Papers of Calhoun*, 9:275–78.

15. Cherokee delegation to the secretary of war, March 12, 1825, Carter, *Territorial Papers*, 20:4–5. See also Troup to the chiefs and headmen of Tuckanbatchee and Cussetah, February 26, 1825, American State Papers, *Indian Affairs*, 2:763; Calhoun to the Arkansas Cherokees, March 2, 1825, IA, LS (M-21), reel 1, pp. 353–54.

16. *Christian Advocate* 3 (March 1825): 143–44. For a territorial view kinder than that of Georgia officials, see Henry Conway to James Barbour, March 15, 1825, Carter, *Territorial Papers*, 20:9.

17. Ross, Lowrey, and Hicks to Adams, March 12, 1825, American State Papers, *Indian Affairs*, 2:775.

18. Kingsbury to Evarts, April 14, August 8, 1825, ABC 18.3.4, vol. 3.

19. Evarts to Worcester, August 29, 1825, ABC 1.01, vol. 5. For another example of this dilemma see Andrew, *Rebuilding the Christian Commonwealth*, chapter 9. For examples of federal persuasion see McKenney to the Wyandot chiefs, March 24, 1825, and McKenney to Cherokee chief Charles Hicks, March 29, 1825, IA, LS (M-21), reel 1, pp. 424–25, 432–33. Troup's comments are in his message to the Georgia legislature, May 23, 1825, in Hardin, *Life of Troup*, 298–99. For Pickens see Pickens to Gen. E. P. Gaines, July 28, 1825, Alabama: Executive Letterbooks, pp. 59–60. Hutchison's comments are in his *Errand to the World: American Protestant Thought and Foreign Missions*, p. 1.

20. Delineations of government policy are in McKenney to Rev. James B. Finley, September 10, 1825, and McKenney to Capt. Jasper Parrish, Sept. 29,

1825; McKenney to Barbour, December 13, 1825; McKenney to Rev. W. F. Vaill, December 15, 1825, IA, LS (M-21), reel 2, pp. 146, 170–71, 298–306, 317. See also Royce McCrary, "John MacPherson Berrien of Georgia (1781–1856): A Political Biography" (Ph.D. diss., University of Georgia, 1971), pp. 18–19; and Pingel, "Disorder," pp. 48, 76–77, 99–100.

21. Charles Francis Adams, ed., *Memoirs of John Quincy Adams Comprising Portions of His Diary from 1795 to 1848*, 7:89–90.

22. Adams, *Memoirs*, 7:92. For the political situation in Congress see Nielsen, "Indispensable Institution," pp. 203–4, 208.

23. Leonard Bacon, *The Social and Civil Influence of the Christian Ministry. A Sermon, Preached at the Sixth Anniversary of the Auxiliary Education Society of the Young Men of Boston: February 6, 1825*, pp. 18–19. See also *Examination of the Controversy Between Georgia and the Creeks*, p. 1; Joshua Bates, *Influence of Christian Truth. A Sermon, Preached in Northampton, Mass., Sept. 21, 1825, at the Sixteenth Meeting of the American Board of Commissioners for Foreign Missions*, p. 19.

24. *Missions Will Not Impoverish the Country*, p. 9; Auxiliary Foreign Mission Society of Essex County, *Proceedings at the Organization of, April 11, 1826*, pp. 9–10, 12, 17–18, 26. See also the Eastern Auxiliary Foreign Mission Society of Rockingham County, New Hampshire, *First Annual Report, Presented at Kingston, June 22, 1826*, p. 7; Beriah Green, *A Sermon, Preached in Poultney, June 29, 1826, at the First Annual Meeting of the Rutland County Foreign Missionary Society*, pp. 5, 8.

25. Evarts to his wife, April 7, 1825, Box 2, folder 43, EFP; *Reformer* 6 (January 1, 1825): 4. For Evarts's relations with his family in Vermont, see Evarts to J. T. Evarts, February 9 and March 1, 1825, Box 1, EFP; Evarts to Henry Hill, July 21, 1825, ABC 11, vol. 2; and various personal notes in ABC 34. His Illinois landholdings are noted in Evarts to John Tillson, Jr., August 21, 1826, J. Evarts Letterbook, p. 98, Box 1, folder 1, EFP.

26. Evarts Cash Books, 1826, New York Public Library.

27. J. Evarts to H. Hill, January 24, 1826, in Oliphant, *Through the South and the West*, p. 68; Evarts to Mrs. M. Evarts, May 8, 1825, Box 2, EFP.

28. "Sketch of Evarts," p. 312; Dann, "Humanitarian Reform," p. 205. For developments in other locales see Frederick Norwood, "Strangers in a Strange Land: Removal of the Wyandot Indians," *Methodist History* (1975): 48; McCrary, "John Berrien," pp. 121–22; Green, "Federal-State Conflict," pp. 171–72; Murray, *Whig Party in Georgia*, p. 6; and Willie Mangum to Bartlett Yancey, January 15, 1826, in Henry T. Shanks, ed., *The Papers of Willie Person Mangum*, 1:231.

29. [Lewis Cass], "Indians of North American," *North American Review* 22 (January 1826): 58–59, 115–19; Harry Scheiber, *Ohio Canal Era: A Case Study of Government and the Economy, 1820–1861*, p. 39. Cass's other activities are detailed in Miriani, "Lewis Cass," pp. 125–26, 143, 187–88.

30. Isaac Darneille, *A Discourse or Lecture on the Subject of Civilizing the Indians*, pp. 7–9, 15, 19.

31. Evarts to Hill, January 28, 1826, in Oliphant, *Through the South and the West*, pp. 70–71.

32. *Missionary Herald* 22 (February 1826): 49; McKenney to Kingsbury, April 10, 1826, IA, LS (M-21), reel 3, p. 20. See also Henry Schoolcraft, *Personal Memoirs of a Residence of Thirty Years with the Indian Tribes of the American Frontiers*, p. 240.

33. Evarts to Rufus Anderson, February 22, 1826, ABC 11, vol. 2; Evarts to Hill, February 25, 1826, ABC 11, vol. 2. Brandon is quoted in Claude Fike, "The Gubernatorial Administrations of Governor Gerard Chittocque Brandon, 1825–1832," *Journal of Mississippi History* 35 (1973): 252–53; and the report of the joint select committee is in American State Papers, *Indian Affairs*, 2:645.

34. Adams's remarks are in *Memoirs*, 7:113. For Barbour see his letter to John Cocke, February 21, 1826, quoted in Charles Lowery, *James Barbour: A Jeffersonian Republican*, pp. 287–88.

35. McKenney to Folsom, May 9, 1826, IA, LS (M-21), reel 3, p. 66. These same records contain similar letters to agents and other tribes. See also Phillips, "Jedidiah Morse," pp. 305–6; and the circular letter of William Hendricks of Indiana, May 13, 1826, in Noble Cunningham, Jr., *Circular Letters of Congressmen to Their Constituents, 1789–1829*, 3:1327.

36. Tracy, *Memoir*, pp. 236–37, 249–51, 261–63; Evarts to Rev. Joshua Bates, June 28, 1826, ABC 1.01, vol. 6. Evarts's Journal entry for May 15, 1826, in Oliphant, *Through the South and the West*, pp. 137–39, discusses his visit with Blackburn, whom he revered as a missionary pioneer but whose character he now considered defective.

37. Coffee's remarks and the Chickasaws' reply are in American State Papers, *Indian Affairs*, 2:721–22. See also Jackson to Col. John Terrill, July 29, 1826, in Bassett, *Correspondence of Jackson*, 3:308; Troup to Barbour, August 26, 1826, American State Papers, *Indian Affairs*, 2:743.

38. Ray to Clay, November 10, 1826; Ray to Indiana General Assembly, December 8, 1826, in Dorothy Riker and Gayle Thornbrough, *Messages and Papers Relating to the Administration of James Brown Ray, Governor of Indiana, 1825–1831*, pp. 148–49, 168.

39. Butrick to Ridge and Boudinot, November 26, 1826, ABC 18.3.3, vol. 2. Also see the Georgia Legislature to Barbour, November 28, 1826, IA, LR (M-234), reel 72, Cherokee Agency (East); McKenney to Barbour, December 27, 1826, American State Papers, *Indian Affairs*, 2:700; McKenney to McCoy, October 13, 1826, IA, LS (M-21), reel 3, p. 188; Yeager, "Indian Enterprises," 161–62, 287–88; George A. Schultz, *An Indian Canaan: Isaac McCoy and the Vision of an Indian State*, pp. 82–85; McKenney to Barbour, November 20, 1826, IA, LS (M-21), reel 3, pp. 229–34.

40. For a discussion of McKenney's role see Viola, "Thomas L. McKenney," pp. 244–45. An analysis of political changes is in Nielsen, "Indispensable Institution," pp. 217–18, 225–26, 260–61. For a somewhat different interpretation

see Vincent Lacey, "The United States Senate in the Age of Jackson, 1825–1837: Regional Coalitions and the Development of the Two-Party System" (Ph.D. diss., Southern Illinois University at Carbondale, 1985), p. 9.

41. Richard Latner, *The Presidency of Andrew Jackson: White House Politics, 1829–1837*, p. 123; Susan Conrad, *Perish the Thought: Intellectual Women in Romantic America, 1830–1860*, p. 21; Rudolph Forderhase, "Jacksonianism in Missouri From Predilection to Party, 1820–1836," (Ph.D. diss., University of Missouri, 1968), pp. 311–12; Whitman Ridgway, *Community Leadership in Maryland, 1720–1840: A Comparative Analysis of Power in Society*, pp. 98, 103; Holt, *Political Crisis*, p. 22; Harry Watson, "'Bitter Combinations of the Neighbourhood': The Second American Party System in Cumberland County, North Carolina" (Ph.D. diss., Northwestern University, 1976), p. 137; Jonathan Mills Thornton III, "Politics and Power in a Slave Society: Alabama, 1806–1860" (Ph.D. diss., Yale University, 1974), p. 74; Alvin W. Lynn, "Party Formation and Operation in the House of Representatives, 1824–1837" (Ph.D. diss., Rutgers University, 1972), p. 247.

42. McKenney to John Cocke, January 23, 1827, McKenney to King & Owens, January 26, 1827, IA, LS (M-21), reel 3, pp. 326–29; Lewis Cass, "Remarks on the Policy and Practice of the United States and Great Britain in Their Treatment of the Indians," *North American Review* 24 (1827): 408–9 and *passim*.

43. Evarts to Rev. T. S. Harris, February 3, 1827, ABC 1.01, vol. 6; McCrary, "John Berrien," pp. 128–29. Adams's message is in Richardson, *Messages and Papers*, 2:373. For Georgia's politics see Wilson Lumpkin, *The Removal of the Cherokee Indians from Georgia*, 1:42–46. See also Elisha Whittlesey's letter to his wife, February 17, 1827, in Kenneth Davison, "Forgotten Ohioan: Elisha Whittlesey, 1783–1863" (Ph.D. diss., Western Reserve University, 1953), p. 56.

44. Evarts to Kingsbury, February 6, 1827, ABC 1.01, vol. 6; Thomas McKenney to James Barbour, February 20, 1827, IA, LS (M-21), reel 3, p. 390. See also the 1827 circular letters of Lewis Williams and Burwell Bassett in Cunningham, *Circular Letters*, 3:1367, 1373. The problems behind these attitudes are discussed more fully in James Axtell, "Some Thoughts on the Ethnohistory of Missions," *Ethnohistory* 29 (1982): 35–41; and Robert Berkhofer, "Protestants, Pagans, and Sequences Among the North American Indians, 1760–1860," *Ethnohistory* 10 (1963): 201–32.

45. Rufus Anderson to Rev. Charles Jenkins, February 29, 1827, ABC 1.01, vol. 7; McCrary, "John Berrien," pp. 128–29; Romulus Saunders to Bartlett Yancey, February 26, 1827, in A. R. Newsome, ed., "Letters of Romulus M. Saunders to Bartlett Yancey, 1821–1828," *North Carolina Historical Review* 8 (1931): 460–61; Montgomery, "Jeremiah Evarts," pp. 17–34.

46. Evarts to Anderson, March 3, 1827, ABC 11, vol. 2. See also Evarts to Henry Hill, March 9, 1827, ABC 11, vol. 2.

47. Evarts to Anderson, March 12, 1827, ABC 11, vol. 2; Evarts to Washburn, March 13, 1827, ABC 8.6, vol. 5.

48. McKenney to Evarts, March 23, 1827, ABC 13, vol. 1.

49. Evarts to Rufus Anderson, March 31, 1827, ABC 11, vol. 2.

50. Evarts to Anderson, April 5, 1827, ABC 11, vol. 2; Evarts to Kingsbury, April 5, 1827, in Tracy, *Memoir*, pp. 274–75.

51. See the extract from Baptist missionary Evan Jones's journal, April 1, 1827, in the *American Baptist Magazine* 7 (October 1827): 198–99. Also see Theophilus, "Indian Government," *Christian Advocate and Journal* 1 (April 21, 1827): 129.

52. Evarts to John Hastings, Jr., April 27, 1827, ABC 1.01, vol. 7. For a discussion of the Cherokee position and the antecedents of this nationalism, see McLoughlin, *Cherokee Renascence*, pp. xvi, 109–110, 132–33, 226, 278–87.

53. William Chamberlain to Evarts, May 3, 1827, and Isaac Proctor to Evarts, May 10, 1827, ABC 18.3.1, vol. 4. For Cherokee sentiment see William McLoughlin, "Cherokee Anti-Mission Sentiment, 1824–1828," *Ethnohistory* 21 (1974): 361–65; McLoughlin, *Cherokees and Missionaries*, pp. 212–17; and Moulton, *Papers of Ross*, 1:5. Similar problems in the Choctaw Nation are noted in Arthur DeRosier, Jr., "Pioneers with Conflicting Ideals: Christianity and Slavery in the Choctaw Nation," *Journal of Mississippi History* 21 (1959): 182. The Sandwich Islands material is discussed in Andrew, *Rebuilding the Christian Commonwealth*, chapter 9.

54. The full story of White Path's Rebellion is told in McLoughlin, *Cherokee Renascence*, chapter 19.

55. Alvin Duckett, *John Forsyth: Political Tactician*, p. 114; Journal of the Commissioners to Treat with the Cherokees, 1827, IA, LR (M-234), reel 72, Cherokee Agency (East); Butler to Evarts, August 3, 1827, ABC 18.3.1, vol. 4. For similar problems in Mississippi see J. F. H. Claiborne, *Life and Correspondence of John A. Quitman*, pp. 92–93.

56. Evarts to Rev. Alvan Coe, October 1, 1827, ABC 1.01, vol. 7; Pixley to Evarts, October 24, 1827, in *Missionary Herald* 24 (March 1828): 79; *Missionary Herald* 23 (November 1827): 358–59; *Missionary Paper No. 1*, p. 6. The ABCFM collected the lion's share of the Indian Civilization Fund; see S. S. Hamilton to Rev. J. Emory, July 9, 1827, IA, LS (M-21), reel 4, p. 90.

57. McKenney to Barbour, November 29, 1827, IA, LS (M-21), reel 4, pp. 153–57. See also Evarts to Washburn, November 28, 1827, ABC 1.01, vol. 8; James F. Hopkins, et al., eds., *Papers of Henry Clay*, 6:509n; Memorial of the Baptist Board of Foreign Missions, November 26, 1827, in the Isaac McCoy Papers (microfilm), reel 6, Kansas State Historical Society; *Niles' Weekly Register* 33 (November 24, 1827): 196 and (December 1, 1827): 214; Isaac McCoy, *History of Baptist Indian Missions*, pp. 323–24.

58. Bolles to McCoy, December 20, 1827, McCoy Papers, reel 6. For McCoy's views see McCoy to Johnson Lykins and Robert Simervall, December 19, 1827, McCoy Papers, reel 6; Schultz, *Indian Canaan*, pp. 96–98; Sheehan, *Seeds of Extinction*, pp. 262–63.

59. McKenney to Compere, January 2, 1828, IA, LS (M-21), reel 4, pp. 220–

22. See also McKenney to T. L. Ogden, January 2, 1828, 4:223; McKenney to Barbour, January 4, 1828, 4:229–32; Potter to Evarts, January 5, 1828, ABC 18.3.1, vol. 4; Mary Hargreaves, *The Presidency of John Quincy Adams*, chapter 9.

60. A concise summary of these efforts is in William McLoughlin, "Georgia's Role in Instigating Compulsory Indian Removal," *Georgia Historical Quarterly* 70 (1986): 609–11. See also Gov. John Forsyth to John Quincy Adams, January 16, 1828, IA, LR (M-234), reel 72, Cherokee Agency (East).

61. John McCarty to Samuel Martin, January 11, 1821, IA, LR, Cherokee Emigration, 1828–1836 (M-234), reel 113; McKenney to Rep. Charles Miner, January 18, 1828, IA, LS (M-21), reel 4, p. 258; Evarts to Kingsbury, January 18, 1828, ABC 1.01, vol. 8; Adams, *Memoirs*, 7:410–11 (entry for January 23, 1828).

62. See Adams, *Memoirs*, 7:437; Lumpkin, *Removal*, 1:47–53; *Cherokee Phoenix*, February 21, 1828.

63. *Cherokee Phoenix*, March 13, 1828. Evarts's lobbying is detailed in Evarts to R. Anderson, March 13, 1828, ABC 11, vol. 2; and Tracy, *Memoir*, p. 306.

64. McCoy journal entry, March 15, 1828, quoted in *American Baptist Magazine* 8 (August 1828): 239; Evarts to R. Anderson, March 21, 1828, ABC 11, vol. 2. McCoy worked closely with pre-removal forces; see Wilson Lumpkin to McCoy, April 5 and 14, 1828, McCoy Papers, microfilm reel 6.

65. Evarts to Washburn, March 29, 1828, ABC 8.6, vol. 5; Washburn to Evarts, May 28, 1828, ABC 18.3.1, vol. 6; Daniel Feller, *The Public Lands in Jacksonian Politics*, p. 79. See Welter, *Mind of America*, p. 299, for Richard Johnson's speech.

66. McLoughlin, *Cherokee Renascence*, pp. 416–23.

67. William McLean to McCoy, June 25, 1828, McCoy Papers, microfilm reel 6; McKenney to Gen. William Clark, June 10, 1828, and McKenney to Capt. John Rogers, May 31, 1828, IA, LS (M-21), reel 5, p. 7, and reel 4, p. 477; Lela Barnes, "Journal of Isaac McCoy for the Exploring Expedition of 1828," *Kansas Historical Quarterly* 5 (1936): 230–31 (entry for July 6, 1828); *Cherokee Phoenix*, July 9, 1828.

68. For one expression of this see McKenney to J. C. Mitchell, July 10, 1828, IA, LS (M-21), reel 5, pp. 34–35.

69. Requa to Evarts, July 12, 1828, Grant Foreman Papers, Gilcrease Institute Library, Tulsa, Oklahoma, pp. 227–28.

70. Evarts to William Hudson, July 17, 1828, ABC 1.01, vol. 8. Further discussion of these developments is in "Georgia Controversy," *Southern Review* 2 (November 1828): 541–82; "Review . . . Mr. M'Coy's Indian Reform," *American Baptist Magazine* 8 (May 1828): 147–55; Elizabeth Sanders, *Conversations, Principally on the Aborigines of North America*, pp. 1–179, *passim;* "Removal of the Indians Beyond the Mississippi," *Christian Advocate and Journal* 3 (December 19, 1828): 62; and Althea Bass, *Cherokee Messenger*, pp. 102–3.

71. McKenney to Hugh Montgomery, Cherokee agent, July 22, 1828; McKenney to John Crowell, Creek agent, July 23, 1828; and Porter to David Brearley,

Creek agent, July 30 and August 6, 1828, IA, LS (M-21), reel 5, pp. 47–48, 50–51, 67–68, 76–77; *Cherokee Phoenix*, July 23, 1828.

72. Evarts to Washburn, August 9, 1828, and Evarts to McKenney, August 18, 1828, ABC 1.01, vol. 8; *Missionary Herald* 24 (July 1828): 216–17; McKenney to Evarts, July 22, 1828, IA, LS (M-21), reel 5, p. 50.

73. *Cherokee Phoenix*, September 17, 1828. For enrollment figures see Col. Hugh Montgomery, Cherokee agent, to Porter, October 10, 1828, IA, LR (M-234), reel 72, Cherokee Agency (East).

74. Marshall to Story, October 29, 1828, in the *Proceedings of the Massachusetts Historical Society* 14, 2d series (1900–1901): 337–38.

75. See McKenney to Porter, November 1, 28, December 1, 1828, and McKenney to Major E. W. Duval, Cherokee agent, November 17, 1828, IA, LS (M-21), reel 5, pp. 162–63, 188, 209–11, 214–15. Schoolcraft's observations are in Schoolcraft, *Personal Memoirs*, pp. 318–19.

76. Evarts to Vaill, December 19, 1828, ABC 1.01, vol. 9.

77. Templin Ross to Porter, November 22, 1828, IA, LR (M-234), reel 72, Cherokee Agency (East); Evarts to Porter, December 18, 1828, and Evarts to Worcester, December 19, 1828, ABC 1.01, vol. 9.

78. William C. Dawson, *A Compilation of the Laws of the State of Georgia, Passed by the General Assembly, Since the Year 1819 to the Year 1829, Inclusive*, pp. 197–98; Duckett, *John Forsyth*, pp. 115–16.

79. Evarts to R. Anderson, December 30, 1828, ABC 11, vol. 2; Evarts's notes, December 19 and 20, 1828, ABC 1.01, vol. 9; Evarts to Stuart, December 26, 1828, ABC 1.01, vol. 9.

80. See Evarts's journal entry for March 18, 1827, in Tracy, *Memoir*, p. 274; Evarts to J. C. Ellsworth, January 5, 1827, ABC 1.01, vol. 6; *Missionary Herald* 23 (February 1827): 58; *Boston Recorder* (June 29, 1827): 102; *American Quarterly Register* 1 (July 1827): 14.

81. For the school's closing see the *Missionary Herald* 23 (January 1827): 24–26; Evarts to Connecticut governor John Smith, January 8, 1827, and Evarts to Edward Newton, January 20, 1827, ABC 1.01, vol. 6; David Greene to John Smith, March 13, 1827, and Evarts to L. Loomis, May 4, 1827, ABC 1.01, vol. 7.

82. ABCFM, *An Appeal to the American Churches in Behalf of Missions*, p. 7. See also D. Greene to Josiah Kilpatrick, June 26, 1827, ABC 1.01, vol. 7; Jared Sparks to Evarts, July 31, 1827, Jeremiah Evarts Papers, LC; Evarts to Sparks, August 1 and October 25, 1827, no. 153, Jared Sparks Papers, Houghton Library, Harvard University; Evarts to Josiah Bissell, Jr., July 15, 1827, and Evarts to Eleazar Lord, November 30, 1827, in Tracy, *Memoir*, pp. 279–80, 286–87; Evarts to Rev. Mark Tucker, December 24, 1827, Simon Gratz Collection, HSP; Phillips, *Protestant America*, pp. 80–81. A description of the duties of the corresponding secretary is in the *Missionary Herald* 24 (January 1828): 4. For an analysis of the impact of

these societies see Russell Handsman, "Historical Archaeology and Capitalism, Subscriptions and Separations: The Production of Individualism," *North American Archaeologist* 4 (1983): 63–79.

83. Evarts to Anderson, November 28, 1828, quoted in Phillips, *Protestant American*, p. 142. See also Tracy, *Memoir*, pp. 292–93.

84. Evarts to David Perry, January 12, 1828, ABC 1.01, vol. 8. See also Evarts's Cash Books for 1827 and 1828, New York Public Library; and Evarts's letter to his wife, November 4, 1828, Box 2, folder 45, EFP.

NOTES FOR CHAPTER SEVEN

1. John Davis to Eliza Davis, December 11, 1829, John W. Davis Papers, AAS.

2. James Curtis, *Andrew Jackson and the Search for Vindication*, pp. 92–94. Also see John William Ward, *Andrew Jackson: Symbol for an Age*; George Forquer to Illinois governor Ninian Edwards, December 1, 1829, in E. B. Washburne, ed., *The Edwards Papers; Being a Portion of the Collection of the Letters, Papers, and Manuscripts of Ninian Edwards*, 3:460–61; Elisha Whittlesey to Henry Clay, September 1829, in Davison, "Forgotton Ohioan," p. 62; and Michael Rogin, *Fathers and Children: Andrew Jackson and the Subjugation of the American Indian*, p. 267.

3. American State Papers, Class 7: *Post Office*, pp. 211–12. See also Heman Lincoln to Evarts, January 6, 1829, ABC 10, vol. 9; Evarts to Josiah Bissell, Jr., January 20, 1829, ABC 1.01, vol. 9; *Niles' Weekly Register* 35 (January 10, 1829): 313; *United States Telegraph*, January 17, 1829; Stokes, *Church and State*, 2:19–20.

4. "Sunday Mails," *Niles' Weekly Register* 35 (February 14, 1829): 405–6; American State Papers, Class 7: *Post Office*, pp. 212–15; *Magazine of the Reformed Dutch Church* 3 (February 1829): 349; Leland Meyer, *The Life and Times of Colonel Richard M. Johnson of Kentucky*, pp. 258–59.

5. Jeremiah Evarts, *The Logic and the Law of Col. Johnson's Report to the Senate, on Sabbath Mails*, pp. 3–15.

6. Ibid., pp. 15–21; Evarts to David Greene, February 16, 25, 1829, ABC 11, vol. 2.

7. "Mr. Johnson's Report on Sabbath Mails," *Spirit of the Pilgrims* 2 (March 1829): 143, 157, 165–66.

8. Tracy, *Memoir*, pp. 330–33; *Magazine of the Reformed Dutch Church* 4 (April 1829): 31. See James Rohrer, "Sunday Mails and the Church-State Theme in Jacksonian America," *Journal of the Early Republic* 7 (1987): 53–74, for a summary of the Sunday mail issues. A good summary discussion of virtue and its varieties is in Diggins, *The Lost Soul*, pp. 98, 136–37, 163–64.

9. The *Philadelphia Gazette* item is in *Niles' Weekly Register* 36 (May 2, 1829): 148, and the Evarts remark is in a letter of July 4, 1829, in Tracy, *Memoir*, p. 335. See also "View of Publick Affairs," *Christian Advocate* 7 (May 1829): 240; *Magazine of the Reformed Dutch Church* 4 (May 1829): 62.

10. (Boston, 1829). The printed September circular is in Box 5, EFP.

11. [Jeremiah Evarts], *An Account of Memorials Presented to Congress During Its Last Session, By Numberous Friends of Their Country and Its Institutions; Praying that the Mails May Not Be Transported, Nor Post-Offices Kept Open, on the Sabbath,* p. 4; Jentz, "Artisans," pp. 78, 82–83; Wilentz, *Chants Democratic,* pp. 146–48; Lawrence Friedman, *Gregarious Saints: Self and Community in American Abolitionism, 1830–1870,* pp. 20, 36; Royal Washburn, *Evils Which Threaten Our Country. A Sermon Delivered in Amherst First Parish, (Mass.) on Thursday, April 9, 1829. The Day of Public Fast,* p. 13.

12. See the Marietta, Pennsylvania, *Pioneer,* quoted in *Reformer* 10 (September 1829): 131. Also see *Reformer* 10 (December 1829): 180, 189–90; and Roth, "Whence This Fire?" pp. 143–44, 333–34, 440.

13. Richard Latner's "A New Look at Jacksonian Politics," *Journal of American History* 61 (1975): 943–69, and his book *The Presidency of Andrew Jackson* place Indian removal at the center of Jacksonian Democracy, but he is virtually alone. Most historians have taken their cue from Arthur Schlesinger, Jr., in *The Age of Jackson,* whether or not they agree with his thesis. Schlesinger barely mentions the issue. See also David Russo, "The Major Political Issues of the Jacksonian Period: The Development of Party Loyalty in Congress, 1830–1840," *Transactions of the American Philosophical Society* 62, part 5 (1972). For the relationship of liberalism and property rights to Indian removal, see John Nelson, Jr., *Liberty and Property: Political Economy and Policymaking in the New Nation, 1789–1812,* pp. 164–65.

14. John Peters, "The Influence of the Missionaries to the Cherokee Indians, 1800–1860" (M.A. thesis, University of Oklahoma, 1938), p. 48; Montgomery, "Jeremiah Evarts," pp. 39–40.

15. Caleb Atwater, *Remarks Made on a Tour to Prairie Du Chien Thence to Washington City in 1829,* pp. 33, 36, 75ff, 134, 142–46; Benjamin Wisner, *The Proper Mode of Conducting Missions to the Heathen. A Sermon Delivered Before the Society for Propagating the Gospel among the Indians and Others in North America, November 5, 1829, passim.*

16. Atwater, *Remarks,* p. 147; "Removal of the Indians," p. 75; McCoy, *History of Baptist Indian Missions,* pp. 377–78; Schultz, *Indian Canaan,* pp. 124–26; Isaac McCoy, *Remarks on the Practicability of Indian Reform, Embracing Their Colonization; with an Appendix,* pp. 8–14, 17–25, 29–32, 41–42, 51–52.

17. For Knox see Knox to Washington, July 7, 1789, American State Papers, Indian Affairs, 1: 53–54. Evarts's new efforts are noted in Evarts to Rev. William Potter, January 5, 1829, ABC 1.01, vol. 9, and William Chamberlain to Evarts, January 8, 1829, ABC 18.3.1, vol. 4. For Porter see Porter to Arkansas governor John Murphy, January 9, 1829, IA, LS (M-21), reel 5, p. 261, and John Quitman to Franklin Plummer, January 12, 1829, in Claiborne, *Life and Correspondence,* p. 94. The *Cherokee Phoenix* editorialized against these views and reprinted editorials from other papers opposing them; see the *Phoenix,* January 14, 1829, and

Theda Purdue, "Rising from the Ashes: *The Cherokee Phoenix* as an Ethnohistorical Source," *Ethnohistory* 24 (1977): 207–18. For the impact on ABCFM missions see Cyrus Kingsbury to ABCFM, January 28, 1829, ABC 18.3.1, vol. 3.

18. *Missionary Herald* 25 (February 1829): 37.

19. Evarts to his wife, February 17, 1829, Box 2, folder 46, EFP; Heman Lincoln to McKenney, February 19, 1829, IA, LR, Misc., 1829 (M-234). For Georgia's actions see John Coffee, Private Remarks on the Testimony Given Between the State of Georgia and the Cherokee Nation, Box 3, no. 6, Cherokee Collection, Tennessee State Library and Archives; Circular from McKenney to superintendents and agents, February 17, 1829, IA, LS (M-21), reel 5, p. 309; Evarts to David Greene, February 21, 1829, ABC 11, vol. 2; W. F. Vaill to Evarts, February 21, 1829, Grant Foreman Papers, Gilcrease Institute Library, pp. 237–38.

20. Evarts to D. Greene, February 23, 25, 1829, ABC 11, vol. 2; Daniel Webster to Ezekiel Webster, February 23, 26, 1829, in C. H. Van Tyne, ed., *The Letters of Daniel Webster from Documents Owned Principally by the New Hampshire Historical Society*, pp. 141–42, 144–45; Evarts's journal entry for February 25, 1829, in Tracy, *Memoir*, p. 324.

21. Evarts to D. Greene, February 26, March 5, 1829, ABC 11, vol. 2; John Ross to the Congress, February 27, 1829, Moulton, *Papers of Ross*, 1:155; Green, "Federal-State Conflict," pp. 245–46; Satz, *American Indian Policy*, p. 12; Averitt, "Democratic Party in Georgia," pp. 234–36.

22. Evarts to Greene, March 10, 20, 1829, and Evarts to H. Hill, March 28, 1829, ABC 11, vol. 2; D. Greene to William Potter, March 28, 1829, ABC 1.01, vol. 9; Tracy, *Memoir*, pp. 328–29.

23. "Civilization and Conversion of the Indians," *North American Review* 28 (April 1829): 364–66.

24. Evarts to Greene, April 6, 1829, ABC 11, vol. 2; Eaton to Lewis Cass, March 10, 1829; McKenney to Eaton, March 11, 1819; McKenney to Evarts, March 23, 1829, all in IA, LS, roll 5, pp. 326, 328–31, 363–4.

25. Evarts to Greene, April 11, 1829, ABC 11, vol. 2; McKenney to Hobart, April 7, 1829, ABC 13, vol. 1; McKenney to the Cherokee Delegation, April 11, 1829, IA, LS (M-21), reel 5, p. 402.

26. Eaton to the Cherokee delegation, April 18, 1829, IA, LS (M-21), reel 5, pp. 408–12; Ross to Evarts, May 6, 1829, ABC 10, vol. 12; McKenney to Stephen Van Rensselaer, May 9, 1829, Simon Gratz Collection, HSP.

27. Thomas L. McKenney, *Memoirs, Official and Personal*, pp. 224–29, 240–41; McKenney to Rev. Eli Baldwin, June 27, 1829, IA, LS (M-21), reel 6, pp. 30–32; Satz, *American Indian Policy*, pp. 14–18; Van Hoeven, "Salvation," p. 113n; Francis Paul Prucha, "Thomas L. McKenney and the New York Indian Board," *Mississippi Valley Historical Review* 48 (1962): 636–55; Viola, "Thomas L. McKenney," pp. 250n, 251–52.

28. Eaton to the governors of Tennessee, Mississippi, and Alabama, May 21,

1829; Eaton to Gen. William Carroll, May 30, 1829; McKenney to Col. John Crowell, June 15, 1829; all in IA, LS (M-21), reel 5, p. 438, 456–59 and reel 6, pp. 13–14. See also Eaton to Carroll and Coffee, May 30, 1829, *Senate Documents*, 21st Cong., 1st sess., doc. no. 1, pp. 178–80; *American Baptist Magazine* 9 (June 1829): 210–11; *Cherokee Phoenix*, June 10, 1828; *Niles' Weekly Register* 36 (June 13, 1829): 250; *Georgia Journal*, May 30, 1829, in Mahoney, "American Public Opinion," p. 25.

29. *Cherokee Phoenix*, July 1, 1829. Also see William Carroll to Jackson, June 29, 1829, in *Correspondence on the Subject of the Emigration of the Indians*, 23d Cong., 1st sess., Senate doc. no. 512, 2:76–77.

30. Evarts to Rev. T. C. Stuart, June 6, 1829; Evarts to James Holmes, June 6, 1829, ABC 1.01, vol. 9; Worcester to Evarts, July 1, 1829, ABC 18.3.1, vol. 5.

31. See McKenney to Heman Lincoln, July 6, 1829, IA, IS (M-21), reel 6, p. 41; Evarts to McKenney, July 7, 1829, ABC 1.01, vol. 9; *Christian Advocate* 7 (July 1829): 336.

32. See the *Cherokee Phoenix*, July 8, 1829, and Loring Williams's report from his Choctaw mission in the *Missionary Herald* 25 (August 1829): 251.

33. Kingsbury to Evarts, July 23, 1829, ABC 18.3.1, vol. 3. See also Montgomery, "Jeremiah Evarts," p. 43.

34. Quoted in Philip McFarland, "Removal of the Cherokee Indians from the State of Georgia, 1824–1835: An Analysis of Rhetorical Strategy," (Ph.D. diss., Stanford University, 1973), pp. 54–55. See also Evarts to Levi Beebee, July 23, 1829; Evarts to Rev. Richard Brown, August 1829; Evarts to Eleazar Lord, August 11, 1829; all in ABC 1.01, vol. 9; Lord to Evarts, August 15, 1829, ABC 10, vol. 9; Evarts to Simeon Baldwin, August 10, 1829, and to Eleazar Lord, August 18, 1829, EFP; Roberts Vaux to Joseph Gales, October 1, 1829, ABC 10, vol. 14. Also see Michael Rogin, "Liberal Society and the Indian Question," *Politics and Society* 1 (1971): 304–5n; Montgomery, "Jeremiah Evarts," pp. 67, 73; "Jeremiah Evarts," p. 75; and Mary Young, *Redskins, Ruffleshirts and Rednecks: Indian Allotments in Mississippi and Alabama, 1830–1860*, p. 18. Evarts himself wrote publishers to seek publication of his essays, although he usually spoke as an interested third party.

35. William Penn [Jeremiah Evarts], *Essays on the Present Crisis in the Condition of the American Indians*, reprinted in Francis Paul Prucha, ed., *Cherokee Removal: The "William Penn" Essays and Other Writings by Jeremiah Evarts*, pp. 49–51. Because this volume is much more readily available than the original pamphlet, all citations will refer to it.

36. Ibid., pp. 55–56.
37. Ibid., pp. 57–71 *passim*.
38. Ibid., p. 73.
39. Ibid., pp. 81–82.
40. Ibid., pp. 96, 113.

41. Ibid., p. 113.
42. Ibid., p. 128. See also p. 140.
43. Ibid., p. 151.
44. Ibid., pp. 174–75, 177.
45. Ibid., pp. 178–95.
46. Tracy, *Memoir*, pp. 347–49.
47. Jeremiah Evarts, *A Brief View of the Present Relations Between the Government and People of the United States and the Indians within Our National Limits*, reprinted in Prucha, *Cherokee Removal*, p. 204.
48. Ibid., pp. 208–10.
49. *Examination of the Relations Between the Cherokees and the Government of the United States, passim*.
50. Heman Humphrey, *Indian Rights & Our Duties. An Address Delivered at Amherst, Hartford, etc. December 1829*, pp. 6–7, 10–11, 13–14.
51. Ibid., pp. 16, 19, 23.
52. Ibid., pp. 14–15.
53. Eaton to Forsyth, September 15, 1829, IA, LS (M-21), reel 6, p. 86. See also Duckett, *John Forsyth*, pp. 120–21; Gen. William Carroll to Eaton, September 2, 1829, IA, LR, Cherokee Emigration, 1828–36 (M-234), reel 113; *Cherokee Phoenix*, September 9, 1829.
54. Greene to Worcester, September 26, 1829, ABC 1.01, vol. 9. See also Evarts to James Holmes, October 24, 1829, ABC 1.01, vol. 9.
55. McKenney to Heman Lincoln, September 28, 1829, IA, LS (M-21), reel 6, pp. 97–101. See also *Niles' Weekly Register* 37 (October 3, 1829): 81; *Magazine of the Reformed Dutch Church* 4 (October 1829): 222, (November 1829): 248–50.
56. McKenney to Lincoln, September 28, 1829; McKenney to Rev. Eli Baldwin, October 8, 23, 1829, IA, LS (M-21), reel 6, pp. 104–6, 132–36.
57. The laws are quoted in John Brown, *Old Frontiers: The Story of the Cherokee Indians from the Earliest Times to the Date of Their Removal to the West, 1838*, p. 491. See also the Cherokee National Council to John Eaton, November 4, 1829, IA, LR, Cherokee Agency (East), 1829 (M-234), reel 113.
58. See the editorial in the *Cherokee Phoenix*, November 18, 1829. For the public campaign see Roberts Vaux to Evarts, November 9, 1829, ABC 10, vol. 14; Sidney Morse to Evarts, November 13, 1829, ABC 10, vol. 10; Eleazar Lord to Evarts, November 14, 1829, ABC 10, vol. 9; Evarts's note of November 27, 1829, ABC 1.01, vol. 9; Sklar, *Catharine Beecher*, p. 99. For the commissioners see *Niles' Weekly Register* 37 (November 21, 1829): 197, and Carroll to Eaton, November 19, 1829, IA, LR, Cherokee Emigration, 1828–36 (M-234), reel 113.
59. Andrew Jackson, "First Annual Message," December 8, 1829, in Richardson, *Messages and Papers*, 2:442–62. See also Eli Baldwin to McKenney, November 26, 1829, IA, LR, Misc., 1829 (M-234), reel 432; *Magazine of the Reformed*

Dutch Church 4 (December 1829): 287; John Bell to Isaac McCoy, December 2, 1829, Isaac McCoy Papers, microfilm, reel 7.

60. Quoted in Sanders, *Conversations*, p. 23.

61. Washburn to Evarts, December 9, 1829, ABC 18.3.1, vol. 6; Gilmer to the Georgia Legislature, December 11, 1829, in *Correspondence*, 2:222–23; George Gilmer, *Sketches of some of the First Settlers of Upper Georgia, of the Cherokees, and the Author*, p. 319; Gilmer to Jackson, December 29, 1829, in Gilmer, *Sketches*, p. 335.

62. Lord to Evarts, December 16, 1829, and Evarts to Lord, December 19, 1829, in Tracy, *Memoir*, pp. 349–52. See reprints of newspaper comment in the *Cherokee Phoenix*, December 16, 1829, *Christian Advocate and Journal* 4 (December 18, 1829): 63, and *Niles' Weekly Register* 37 (December 19, 1829): 257. Also see the *House Journal*, 21st Cong., 1st sess., p. 61; and the Report of the Joint Committee on the State of the Republic, Georgia House of Representatives, December 12, 1829, in IA, LR, Cherokee Agency (East), 1829 (M-234), reel 73.

63. Mrs. Eliza Baldwin to Evarts, December 26, 1829, Box 1, folder 8, EFP. Georgia's laws are in Dawson, *A Compilation*, p. 199. See also the *Cherokee Phoenix*, December 23, 1829; E. Lord to Evarts, December 24, 25, 26, 1829, Box 3, folder 83, EFP; and the December 26, 1829, entry in the *Diary of Charles Francis Adams*, 3:115.

64. Evarts to Lord, December 31, 1829, in Tracy, *Memoir*, pp. 352–53. Gilmer's letters are in the Executive Letterbooks of the Governor of Georgia, reel 3, and *Correspondence*, vol. 2.

NOTES FOR CHAPTER EIGHT

1. McLoughlin, *Cherokees and Missionaries*, p. 69. For brief discussions of missionary assumptions see Richard Slotkin, *Regeneration Through Violence: The Mythology of the American Frontier, 1600–1860*, p. 427; Henry Bowden, *American Indians and Christian Missions: Studies in Cultural Conflict*, pp. 164–65; and Roy Pearce, *The Savages of America: A Study of the Indian and the Idea of Civilization*, p. 104.

2. The best summary of these changes is in McLoughlin, *Cherokees and Missionaries*, pp. 124–25, 134–35, 179–86. See also Young, *Redskins*, pp. 5–6; Robert F. Berkhofer, Jr., *Salvation and the Savage: An Analysis of Protestant Missions and American Indian Response, 1787–1862*, pp. 16, 74, 107; and Hutchison, *Errand*, p. 68.

3. For a discussion of these problems on a theoretical level, see Calvin Martin, ed., *The American Indian and the Problem of History*, pp. 10, 12; Mary Young, "Pagans, Converts, and Backsliders, All: A Secular View of the Metaphysics of Indian-White Relations," in Martin, *The American Indian*, p. 81; and Young, *Redskins*, p. 11.

4. Henry Stevens, "Character of a Democrat," November 7, 1828, quoted in Roth, "Whence This Strange Fire?" p. 521. A good summary of the missionaries' problem is in McLoughlin, "The Missionary Dilemma." Also see Evarts to

Rev. Luther Humphrey, October 21, 1830, ABC 1.01, vol. 10; *Missionary Herald* 26 (January 1830): 21; and Mary Young, "The Cherokee Nation: Mirror of the Republic," *American Quarterly* 33 (1981): 503–4. Historians themselves have been divisive in their interpretations of character and motive. See Francis Prucha, "Andrew Jackson's Indian Policy: A Reassessment," *Journal of American History* 56 (1969): 527–39; Francis Prucha, *American Indian Policy in the Formative Years: The Indian Trade and Intercourse Acts, 1790–1834*; Satz, *American Indian Policy*; Rogin, *Fathers and Children*; Sheehan, *Seeds of Extinction*; Berkhofer, *Salvation*; and Young, *Redskins*. Summary and criticism of these conflicting interpretations are in Wilcomb Washburn, "Indian Removal Policy: Administrative, Historical and Moral Criteria for Judging Its Success or Failure," *Ethnohistory* 12 (1965): 274–78; and Reginald Horsman, *The Origins of Indian Removal*.

5. *Register of Debates*, 21st Cong., 1st sess., pp. 3–4, 22–24, 30; Welter, *Mind of America*, p. 299.

6. *Register of Debates*, 21st Cong., 1st sess., pp. 31–34.

7. Ibid., pp. 36–39.

8. Ibid., pp. 48–50.

9. Ibid., pp. 58–108. The quotation is on p. 108.

10. Ibid., p. 146.

11. See Frelinghuysen to Evarts, February 1, 1830, Jeremiah Evarts Papers, LC; *House Reports*, 21st Cong., 1st sess., vol. 2, doc. no. 271; *Niles' Weekly Register* 37 (February 6, 1830): 399; *United States Telegraph* (February 11, 1830); Edward Everett to Thaddeus Spaulding, February 25, 1830, Edward Everett Papers, reel 25, frames 773–74; Joseph Blau, "The Christian Party in Politics," *Review of Religion* 11 (1946): 32; *Magazine of the Reformed Dutch Church* 4 (March 1830): 383; and American State Papers, Class 7: *Post Office*, pp. 226–29.

12. Alexander Hill Everett, "Sunday Mails," *North American Review* 31 (July 1830): 162. Also see American State Papers, Class 7: *Post Office*, pp. 229–41; "Sunday Mails," *Niles' Weekly Register* 38 (March 20, 1830): 78; Boyer, *Urban Masses*, p. 61; and Jentz, "Artisans," pp. 66, 73.

13. These views are reflected in a variety of sources. See *An Expose of the Rise and Proceedings of the American Bible Society, During the Thirteen Years of Its Existence, By a Member*, pp. 28–29; Frelinghuysen to Evarts, March 24, 1830, Box 2, folder 53, EFP; *United States Telegraph* (March 27, 1830); J. Evarts Journal, April 11 and May 8, 1830, ABC 11, vol. 2; *Register of Debates*, 21st Cong., 1st sess., 6: 427; Schlesinger, *Age of Jackson*, p. 143. A list of names from a Connecticut petition is in the *Reformer* 10 (May 1830): 72–73.

14. *Letters and Conversations on the Cherokee Mission, passim*; "Circular, Addressed to benevolent Ladies of the U. States," *Christian Advocate and Journal* 4 (December 25, 1829): 65–66.

15. *A Vindication of the Cherokee Claims, Addressed to the Town Meeting in Philadel-*

phia, On the 11th of January, 1830, pp. 4, 8. See also the *Memorial from Citizens of Pennsylvania to Congress, passim.*

16. *Plea for the Indians, passim*; Simeon Baldwin, *Life and Letters of Simeon Baldwin*, p. 327.

17. [Lewis Cass], "Considerations on the Present State of the Indians, and Their Removal to the West of the Mississippi," *North American Review* 30 (January 1830): 64–67.

18. Ibid., pp. 67–75.

19. Ibid., pp. 76–92.

20. Ibid., p. 102; Miriani, "Lewis Cass," pp. 84–85.

21. [George Cheever], *The Removal of the Indians*, pp. 1–7. See Evarts to Cheever, March 10, 1830, Box 3, folder 2, Cheever Family Papers, AAS.

22. Cheever, *Removal of the Indians*, pp. 8–14. See also "Notes of Recent Publications," *Spirit of the Pilgrims* 3 (January 1830): 51–52; and Evarts to Eleazar Lord, January 8, 1830, Box 3, folder 83, EFP.

23. Gilmer to George Troup, January 1, 1830, Executive Letterbooks of the Governor of Georgia, reel 3, p. 25; Yeager, "Indian Enterprises," p. 415; E. W. Duval to John Eaton, January 1, 1830, IA, LR, Cherokee Emigration, 1828–1836 (M-234), reel 113; *Cherokee Phoenix* (January 1, 1830); Fike, "Gubernatorial Administrations," p. 253; John Quitman to J. F. H. Claiborne, January 8, 1830, in Claiborne, *Life and Correspondence*, pp. 103–4.

24. Robert Stoddard to Josiah Johnston, January 12, 1830, Josiah S. Johnston Papers, HSP. Also see Frelinghuysen to Evarts, January 11, 1830, J. Evarts Papers, LC; McKenney to Major E. W. Duval, January 6, 1830, IA, LS (M-21), reel 6, p. 222; *United States' Telegraph* (January 12, 1830); Eleazar Lord to Evarts, January 12, 1830, Box 3, folder 83, EFP.

25. Green to James Hamilton, January 20, 1830, Duff Green Papers, reel 4, vol. 4. See also McKenney to Gen. William Clark, January 14, 1830, IA, LS (M-21), reel 6, p. 234; and John Coffee to John Eaton, January 15, 1830, IA, LR, Cherokee Agency (East), 1830–31 (M-234), reel 74.

26. See Tracy, *Memoir*, pp. 353–56; as well as Rebecca Gratz to Maria Gist Gratz, January 14, 1830, in David Philipson, ed., *Letters of Rebecca Gratz*, pp. 112–13.

27. Quoted in Tracy, *Memoir*, p. 356. For an opposing view, that northerners should remain quiet and let the South solve the problem, see the editorial in the *Boston Courier*, January 21, 1830, quoted in Montgomery, "Jeremiah Evarts," p. 103.

28. Massachusetts Citizens, *Rights of the Indians*, pp. 1–12 *passim.*

29. Ibid., pp. 9–12. For the situation in Washington see Isaac McCoy to his wife, Christiania, January 23, 1830, McCoy Papers, reel 7; and Schoolcraft, *Personal Memoirs*, p. 331.

30. Adams, *Memoirs*, 8:180. See also a comment in the *New York Evening Post*, January 26, 1830, quoted in Feller, *Public Lands*, p. 111.

31. Calhoun to Micah Sterling, January 30, 1830, *Papers of Calhoun*, 11:109.

32. These views are found throughout the correspondence for 1830 in IA, LS (M-21), reel 6.

33. Expressions of these views can be found in Evarts to Eleazar Lord, January 30, 1830, Box 3, folder 84, EFP; *American Baptist Magazine* 10 (February 1830): 55; Cephas Washburn to Thomas McKenney, February 2, 1830, in Carter, *Territorial Papers*, 21:182–83; Ezra Styles Ely, "Preservation and Improvement of the Indians," *Philadelphian* (February 12, 1830): *passim*; and Isaac McCoy to Rev. Eben Galusha, February 5, 1830, McCoy Papers, reel 7.

34. Evarts to Webster, February 6, 1830, in Charles Wiltse and David Allen, eds., *The Papers of Daniel Webster, Correspondence, Volume 3: 1830–1834*, p. 17; Cyrus Kingsbury to Thomas McKenney, February 8, 1830, in Ruby Lee Culp, "The Missions of the American Board and Presbyterian Church Among the Five Civilized Tribes, 1803–1860" (M.A. thesis, George Washington University, 1934), p. 15; *House Reports*, 21st Cong., 1st sess., vol. 1, doc. no. 169.

35. McKenney to James McDonald, February 9, 1830; McKenney to H. L. White, February 24, 1830; and McKenney to Kingsbury, March 8, 1830, IA, LS (M-21), reel 6, pp. 259–60, 287, 315–16.

36. Proctor to Evarts, February 11, 1830, ABC 18.3.1, vol. 5; Rev. Edward Kirk to Evarts, February 12, 1830, ABC 10, vol. 9; *Philadelphian* (February 12, 1830); Jack Kilpatrick and Anna Kilpatrick, eds., *New Echota Letters: Contributions of Samuel A. Worcester to the Cherokee Phoenix*, pp. 70–74.

37. Eaton to Rep. John Bell, February 13, 1830; McKenney to Eaton, February 16, 1830; McKenney to the Creek chiefs in Washington, February 16, 1830, IA, LS (M-21), reel 6, pp. 267–70, 272–75. Memorials are in *House Reports*, 21st Cong., 1st sess., vol. 3.

38. See, for example, the Senate report on Indian affairs, February 22, 1830, in Nancy Scott, ed., *A Memoir of Hugh Lawson White*, pp. 154–57; *Register of Debates*, 6, part 2 (appendix), pp. 991–94. The memorials are in *House Reports*, 21st Cong., 1st sess., vol. 2.

39. Frelinghuysen to Evarts, February 22, 1830, J. Evarts Papers, LC.

40. For specific references to party see the *National Intelligencer* (March 4, 1829) in Nielsen, "Indispensable Institution," p. 262; Henry Clay to J. S. Johnston, July 18, 1829, in Calvin Colton, ed., *The Private Correspondence of Henry Clay*, p. 239; Evarts to "S. G.", August 6, 1828, in Tracy, *Memoir*, p. 314; Frelinghuysen to Evarts, February 24, 1830, Box 2, folder 53, EFP; James Campbell to James Findlay, February 25, 1830, Cox, "Selections from the Torrence Papers," 6:86–87; D. Webster to Jeremiah Mason, February 27, 1830, Wiltse and Allen, *Papers of Webster*, 3:19; Duff Green to Mordecai Noah, February 27, 1830, Duff Green

Papers, reel 24, vol. 4; and Rep. Isaac Bates to Evarts, February 26, 1830, Box 1, folder 12, EFP.

41. Printed in the *Cherokee Phoenix* (March 3, 1830).

42. A good survey of historians' views is in Robert Shalhope, "Jacksonian Politics in Missouri: A Comment on the McCormick Thesis," *Civil War History* 15 (1969): 210–25. See also Rosa Wirt to her mother, January 18, 1829, William Wirt Papers, reel 12. For questions of party see especially Herbert Ershkowitz and William Shade, "Consensus or Conflict? Political Behavior in the State Legislatures during the Jacksonian Era," *Journal of American History* 58 (1971): 591–621; Ronald Formisano, "Deferential-Participant Politics: The Early Republic's Political Culture, 1789–1840," *American Political Science Review* 68 (June 1974): 473–87; and Ronald Formisano, *The Transformation of Political Culture: Massachusetts Parties, 1790s–1840s*.

43. For cautionary remarks against relying only on roll-call analysis to determine the rise of parties, see Banning, *Jeffersonian Persuasion*, p. 161n. Various letters from 1830 in the Edward Everett Papers demonstrate this rising concern about party influence.

44. "Review of an Article in the *North American Review* for January 1830," *Spirit of the Pilgrims* 3 (March 1830): 143.

45. A copy of the circular, dated March 6, 1830, is in the Isaac McCoy Papers, reel 7.

46. *United States Telegraph* (March 5, 1830); Cornelius Westbrook to John Eaton, March 7, 1830, IA, LR, Misc., 1830 (M-234), reel 433; Gilmer to White, March 11, 1830, Executive Letterbooks of the Governor of Georgia, reel 3, pp. 86–87.

47. *Niles' Weekly Register* 38 (March 20, 1830): 67; Cheever to Evarts, March 13, 1830, Box 1, EFP; Edward Everett Diary, March 15, 1830, Edward Everett Papers, reel 36, p. 434; Adams, *Memoirs*, 8:206; Rev. Samuel Worcester to Ely, March 10, 1830, in Kilpatrick and Kilpatrick, *New Echota Letters*, pp. 76–77; Worcester to David Greene, March 29, 1830, ABC 18.3.1, vol. 5; Greene to Rev. Thompson Harris, March 30, 1830, ABC 1.01, vol. 10; Evarts to Greene, March 31, 1830, ABC 11, vol. 2.

48. Quoted in Tracy, *Memoir*, p. 354. He was quoting Churchill C. Cambreleng of New York.

49. *Register of Debates*, 21st Cong., 1st sess., 6, part 1. The controversy over the *North American Review* is detailed in Edward Everett to A. H. Everett, March 24 and April 5, 1830, Everett Papers, reel 4, frames 158, 195–96; and in A. H. Everett to Evarts, April 5, 1830, Box 3, folder 92, EFP.

50. McKenney to Eaton, April 6, 1830, IA, LS (M-21), reel 6, pp. 373–77; McCoy, *History of Baptist Indian Missions*, pp. 399–400.

51. Theodore Frelinghuysen, *Speech of Mr. Frelinghuysen, of New Jersey, Delivered in the Senate of the United States, April 6, 1830, on the Bill for an Exchange of*

Lands with the Indians Residing in any of the States or Territories, and For Their Removal West of the Mississippi, pp. 3, 5–9, 22, 25–26.

52. J. Evarts Journal, April 8, 9, 1830, ABC 11, vol. 2. Evarts also had made contact with several Supreme Court justices, who voiced support for his position.

53. Frelinghuysen's speech is in the *Register of Debates*, 21st Cong., 1st sess., 6, part 1, p. 309. See also J. Evarts Journal, April 10, 1830, ABC 11, vol. 2; and D. Webster to Joseph Story, April 10, 1830, in the *Proceedings of the Massachusetts Historical Society*, 14, 2d series (1900), p. 406.

54. J. Evarts Journal, April 12, 1830, ABC 11, vol. 2; Evarts to Kingsbury, April 12, 1830, in Tracy, *Memoir*, pp. 362–63. For Mississippi see M. Philip Lucas, "The Development of the Second Party System in Mississippi, 1817–1846" (Ph.D. diss., Cornell University, 1983), p. 78.

55. *Register of Debates*, 21st Cong., 1st sess., 6, part 1, pp. 327, 329. See also E. Everett to Evarts, April 13, 1830, Box 2, folder 50, EFP; J. Evarts Journal, April 14, 1830, ABC 11, vol. 2.

56. *Speeches on the Passage of the Bill for the Removal of the Indians, Delivered in the Congress of the United States, April and May, 1830*, p. 66. See also J. Evarts Journal, April 16, 1830, ABC 11, vol. 2.

57. J. Evarts Journal, April 17, 25, 1830, ABC 11, vol. 2; *United States Telegraph* (April 26, 1830); Satz, *American Indian Policy*, pp. 21, 43. See also the *Cherokee Phoenix* (April 21, 1830) for commentary and support from the *National Intelligencer* and *The Journal of Humanity*. For another dismal assessment of the times, see Daniel Webster to Chancellor James Kent, April 27, 1830, in Van Tyne, *Letters of Daniel Webster*, p. 158. Evarts's commentary on the Senate vote is in his journal for April 28, 1830, ABC 11, vol. 2.

58. Satz, *American Indian Policy*, p. 26; J. Evarts Journal, April 18, 21, 1830, ABC 11, vol. 2; Tracy, *Memoir*, p. 367. Isaac McCoy, meanwhile, dreamed of patronage should the bill pass Congress; see McCoy to his wife, April 18, 1830, McCoy Papers, reel 7.

59. *Niles' Weekly Register* 38 (May 8, 1830): 202–3. See also J. Evarts Journal, May 5, 1830, ABC 11, vol. 2; E. Everett to A. H. Everett, May 4, 1830, Everett Papers, reel 4, frame 259; Everett Diary, May 4, 1830, Everett Papers, reel 36, frame 439; *United States Telegraph* (May 5, 1830); G. Gilmer to J. Berrien, May 6, 1830, Executive Letterbooks of the Governor of Georgia, reel 3, pp. 121–22; *House Reports*, 21st Cong., 1st sess., 3:397; S. Worcester to Evarts, May 11, 1830, ABC 18.3.1, vol. 5.

60. *Register of Debates*, 21st Cong., 1st sess., 6, part 2, p. 1015. Also see *Speeches on the Passage of the Bill*, pp. 89–90, 93–97, 126–27; and Everett Diary, May 13, 1830, Everett Papers, reel 36, frame 441. Members of the House Committee on Indian Affairs included Storrs (Connecticut), Bell (Tennessee), Lewis (Alabama), Lumpkin (Georgia), Gaither (Kentucky), and Hinds (Mississippi).

61. *Register of Debates*, 21st Cong., 1st sess., 6, part 2, p. 1002.
62. *Speeches on the Passage of the Bill*, pp. 86, 136, 138. One example of this theme is starkly expressed in John Eaton to the Creek Indians East of the Mississippi, May 1830, IA, LS (M-21), reel 6, pp. 422–23.
63. Lumpkin's speech is in *Register of Debates*, 21st Cong., 1st sess., 6, part 2; see especially pp. 1020–22. Also see Lumpkin, *Removal*, 1:82.
64. See for example the speeches of Ellsworth of Connecticut and Lumpkin of Georgia in *Register of Debates*, 21st Cong., 1st sess., 6, part 2, pp. 1026–27; and Lumpkin, *Removal*, 1:57, 65–66.
65. *Register of Debates*, 21st Cong., 1st sess., 6, part 2, pp. 1025, 1037; Alexander Lawrence, *James Moore Wayne, Southern Unionist*, pp. 44–45; Worcester to Evarts, May 17, 1830, ABC 18.3.1, vol. 5.
66. *Register of Debates*, 21st Cong., 1st sess., 6, part 2, pp. 1037–49, 1076–77. The quotation is on p. 1048. See also *Speeches on the Passage of the Bill*, pp. 148–49, 181, 219, 225.
67. *Register of Debates*, 21st Cong., 1st sess., 6, part 2, pp. 1093–94, 1103.
68. Betty Hayes, "An Investigation of the Congressional Delegation of Georgia, 1829–1837" (M.A. thesis, Emory University, 1950), pp. 50–53; Satz, *American Indian Policy*, p. 65; *Speeches on the Passage of the Bill*, pp. 251–53; Norman Parks, "The Career of John Bell of Tennessee in the United States House of Representatives" (Ph.D. diss., Vanderbilt University, 1942), pp. 78–79; Starkey, *Cherokee Nation*, p. 125; John Stephens, "Removal as the Solution to the Indian Problem in the Old Northwest, 1825–1840" (M.A. thesis, Louisiana State University, 1968), pp. 21–23, 52–53, 145; Young, *Redskins*, p. 19; Mahoney, "American Public Opinion," p. 96.
69. Webster to James Barbour, May 24, 1830, Wiltse and Allen, *Papers of Webster*, 3:74–75. For Hemphill's remarks see the *Register of Debates*, 21st Cong., 1st sess., 6, part 2, p. 1132.
70. Voting on the bill can be followed in the *Register of Debates*, 21st Cong., 1st sess., 6, part 2, especially pp. 1123, 1133, 1135; and in the *House Journal*, 21st Cong., 1st sess., pp. 707–12, 716–22, 726–30. See also Satz, *American Indian Policy*, pp. 29–30.

NOTES FOR CHAPTER NINE

1. Entry for May 16, 1830, quoted in Tracy, *Memoir*, p. 371. In her *Domestic Manners of the Americans*, Mrs. Frances Trollope chastised Americans for this act, noting that it revealed a serious defect in the American character. See pp. 221–22. See also Mehitabel Evarts to Elizabeth Baldwin, June 8, 1830, Box 30, Baldwin Family Papers, Yale.
2. For the voting on the Removal Bill see the *House Journal*, 21st Cong., 1st

sess., pp. 729–30. Evarts's own tabulation of votes is in Box 5, folder 188, EFP. For additional analysis of this measure see Lynn Parsons, "'A Perpetual Harrow Upon My Feelings': John Quincy Adams and the American Indian," *New England Quarterly* 46 (1973): 339–79 *passim*; Latner, *Presidency of Andrew Jackson*, p. 94; Russo, "Major Political Issues," pp. 13–14; and Everett Kindig, "Western Criticism of Jackson's Indian Removal Policy: The Ohio Valley as a Case Study" (Paper delivered at the Phi Alpha Theta Convention, San Francisco, 1973). Also see Sheehan, *Seeds of Extinction*, p. 261; and Satz, *American Indian Policy*, p. 25. Historians of the second party system have often confused the mechanisms of party governance with parties; see Thornton, "Politics and Power," p. 57n; and Joel Silbey, *The Partisan Imperative: The Dynamics of American Politics Before the Civil War*, pp. 18–19.

3. Hayes, "An Investigation," pp. 8–9; Philip Klein, *Pennsylvania Politics, 1817–1832: A Game Without Rules*, pp. 341–42; Tracy, *Memoir*, p. 380. The editorial from the *Kentucky Reporter* is quoted in Everett Kindig, "Western Criticism of Jackson's Indian Removal Policy," p. 16. The Everett remark is in Edward Everett to Alexander Hill Everett, May 28, 1830, reel 4, frame 316, Everett Papers. See also D. Webster to H. Clay, May 29, 1830, Wiltse and Allen, *Papers of Webster*, 3:78.

4. *Christian Advocate* 8 (May 1830): 263. See also Young, *Redskins*, p. 20.

5. *Missionary Herald* 26 (June 1830): 197.

6. Tracy, *Memoir*, pp. 382–83; Mahoney, "American Public Opinion," p. 101; "Speeches on the Indian Bill," *Spirit of the Pilgrims* 3 (October 1830): 526; Brown, *Politics and Statesmanship*, pp. 7–8.

7. Hawes is quoted in Peterson, "Politics of Revival," p. 81; and Beecher in Halttunen, *Confidence Men*, p. 14. See also Formisano, *Transformation*, pp. 84–96.

8. Eaton to Gilmer, June 1, 1830; Eaton to Col. John Crowell, Creek agent, June 4, 1830; Eaton to McKenney, June 7, 1830, and McKenney to Evarts, June 7, 1830, in IA, LS (M-21), reel 6, pp. 436–39, 449–51, 456, 459; I. McCoy to his wife, June 3, 1830, McCoy Papers, reel 7. See also Satz, *American Indian Policy*, p. 252. For ABCFM finances see Evarts to J. Elsworth, June 19, 1830, ABC 1,01, vol. 10.

9. Wirt to Gilmer, June 4, 1830, reel 13, Wirt Papers.

10. Marshall to Everett, June 5, 1830, reel 4, frames 330–31, Everett Papers.

11. McKenney to Evarts, June 9, 1830, ABC 13, vol. 1; McKenney to Col. Hugh Montgomery, Cherokee agent, June 9, 1830, IA, LS (M-21), reel 6, pp. 469–71; J. Evarts notes June 9 and 10, 1830, ABC 1.01, vol. 10.

12. Evarts to Wirt, June 12, 1830, ABC 1.01, vol. 10.

13. Samuel Bell to William Plumer, June 10, 1830, folder 3, Samuel Bell Papers, New Hampshire Historical Society.

14. *Cincinnati American*, June 17, 1830, quoted in Mahoney, "American Public Opinion," p. 116. Also see Everett Diary, June 15, 1830, reel 36, frame 448, Everett Papers; Evarts to Samuel Newton, June 15, 1830, ABC 1.01, vol. 10; and

Clay to E. Everett, June 16, 1830, reel 4, frame 337, Everett Papers.

15. Gov. Gilmer to Jackson, June 15, 1830, Executive Letterbooks of the Governor of Georgia, reel 3, p. 146; Gilmer to Jackson, June 17, 1830, IA, LR, Cherokee Agency (East), 1830–31 (M-234), reel 74; McKenney to Superintendents of Indian Affairs, June 18, 1830, IA, LS (M-21), reel 6, p. 486.

16. Gilmer to Wirt, June 19, 1830, Executive Letterbooks of the Governor of Georgia, reel 3, pp. 141–44.

17. Ibid.; Gilmer, *Sketches*, 354. For Berrien's help see Berrien to Andrew Jackson, June 25, 1830, IA, LR, Cherokee Agency (East), 1830–31 (M-234), reel 74.

18. *United States Telegraph*, June 17, 19, 1830; Gilmer to Col. Yelverton King, June 21, 1830, Executive Letterbooks of the Governor of Georgia, reel 3, pp. 144–45.

19. Wirt to Carr, June 21, 1830, in John Kennedy, *Memoirs of the Life of William Wirt, Attorney-General of the United States* (2 vols., Philadelphia, 1850), 2:254–55. Also see Marvin Cain, "William Wirt Against Andrew Jackson: Reflections of an Era," *Mid-America* 47 (1965): 125–35.

20. Wirt to Carr, June 21, 1830, reel 13, Wirt Papers.

21. Cain, "William Wirt," p. 126; A. Spencer to Evarts, June 21, 1830, Jeremiah Evarts Papers, LC; Adams, *Memoirs*, 8:232; D. Greene to the Rev. Hugh Wilson, June 22, 1830, and Greene to the Rev. Erastus Maltby, June 23, 1830, ABC 1.01, vol. 10.

22. Wirt to Mr. Pope, June 25, 1830, and John Marshall to Dabney Carr, June 26, 1830, reel 13, Wirt Papers.

23. Webster to Perkins Marvin, June 28, 1830, Jeremiah Evarts Papers, LC; *United States Telegraph*, June 28, 29, 30, 1830; "The Indian Question," *Albany Argus Extra*, June 19, 1830, *passim*.

24. Wayland to Rufus Anderson, June 27, 1830, ABC 10, vol. 15; Evarts to Wayland, July 1, 1830, ABC 1.01, vol. 10.

25. Washburn to Evarts, July 5, 1830, ABC 18.3.1, vol. 6; Gilmer to Clayton, July 6, 1830, in Gilmer, *Sketches*, pp. 356–57.

26. Evarts to Eaton, July 8, 1830, ABC 1.01, vol. 10.

27. "Condition of the American Indians," *Eclectic Review* 52 (July 1830): 85–86.

28. Everett Diary, July 20, 1830, reel 36, frame 458, Everett Papers; S. Worcester to Evarts, July 16, 1830, ABC 18.3.1, vol. 5; Ross to Evarts, July 24, 1830, Box 3, folder 105, EFP; Evarts to Bell, July 23, 1830, folder 3, Samuel Bell Papers. See also letters from Jackson to Van Buren and Moses Dawson in Bassett, *Correspondence of Jackson*, 4:160–61.

29. Eaton to Montgomery, July 29, 1830, printed in *Niles' Weekly Register* 39 (November 18, 1830): 200; Jackson to Van Buren, July 12, 1830, reel 9, Martin Van Buren Papers, LC.

30. McKenney's views are quoted in Viola, "Thomas L. McKenney," pp. 254–

58. For the *Georgia Journal* see *Niles' Weekly Register* 39 (October 9, 1830): 106. For the political relationship see Azariah C. Flagg to Oran Follett, August 4, 1830, in L. Belle Hamlin, ed., "Selections from the Follett Papers," *Quarterly Publication of the Historical and Philosophical Society of Ohio* 5 (1910): 42–43; Abel C. Pepper to John Tipton, August 5, 1830, in Nellie Robertson and Dorothy Riker, *The John Tipton Papers*, 2:318; and John Calhoun to Virgil Maxcy, August 6, 1830, *Papers of John Calhoun*, 11:214. Also see Jackson to John Pitchlynn, August 5, 1830, Bassett, *Correspondence of Jackson*, 4:169; Jackson to Van Buren, August 12, 1830, reel 9, Van Buren Papers, LC; and C. Kingsbury to Evarts, August 11, 1830, ABC 18.3.1, vol. 3.

31. "Candour," *United States Telegraph*, August 19, 1830. Also see the first essay in the August 18, 1830, issue; and Yeager, "Indian Enterprises," p. 441.

32. "Candour," *United States Telegraph*, August 19, 1830.

33. Ibid., August 23, 1830.

34. Ibid., August 24, September 2, 7, 1830.

35. Gaines to a Mr. Miller, August 20, 1830, in James Silver, "A Counter-Proposal to the Indian Removal Policy of Andrew Jackson," *Journal of Mississippi History* 4 (1942): 214.

36. Jackson to Lewis, August 25, 1830, Bassett, *Correspondence of Jackson*, 4:177. Also see Jackson to James K. Polk, August 31, 1830, Herbert Weaver and Paul Bergeron, eds., *Correspondence of James K. Polk* (Nashville, 1969–), 1:330; and Jackson's talk to the Chickasaws, in *Niles' Register* 39 (September 18, 1830): 68.

37. Eaton to Col. John Lowrey, September 1, 1830, *Correspondence* (Senate doc. 512), 2:98–99; P. G. Randolph to John Tipton, September 8, 1830, IA, LS (M-21), reel 7, p. 29; Eaton and Coffee to Kingsbury, Byington, Williams, and Cushman, September 18, 1830, *Correspondence*, 2:253, 255.

38. Talk to the Choctaws by John Eaton and John Coffee, September 18, 1830, *Correspondence*, 2:256. For discussion of the treaty negotiations see Young, *Redskins*, p. 33; and H. S. Halbert, "Story of the Treaty of Dancing Rabbit," *Mississippi Valley Historical Society Publications* 6 (1903): 373–402. Eaton's words are in Halbert, p. 395.

39. Edwin Miles, *Jacksonian Democracy in Mississippi*, pp. 55–56; Culp, "Missions of the American Board," p. 65; Kilpatrick and Kilpatrick, *New Echota Letters*, pp. 82–83; Samuel Hamilton to Col. John McElvam, September 30, 1830, *Correspondence*, 2:36.

40. Gilmer to P. G. Randolph, September 18, 1830, IA, LR, Cherokee Agency (East), 1830–31 (M-234), reel 74; "Indian Controversy," *Boston Christian Examiner and General Review* 9 (September 1830): 108, 111–15, 119, 152–53, 158.

41. "Speeches on the Indian Bill," p. 525. See also pp. 492–93, 495–97, 499–500.

42. Ibid., pp. 528, 531–32.

43. Enoch Pond to Cheever, August 4, 1830, Box 3, folder 2, Cheever Family

Papers, AAS; Cheever to Evarts, August 23, 1830, Box 1, folder 20, EFP; Clay to Evarts, August 23, 1830, Box 1, folder 21, EFP.

44. Evarts to Green, September 3, 1830, Simon Gratz Collection, HSP; Evarts to Stuart, September 7, 1830, ABC 1.01, vol. 10; Green to Evarts, September 10, 1830, ABC 10, vol. 7; Address by William Stanberry, September 8, 1830, quoted in Stephens, "Removal," p. 177.

45. Wirt to Dabney Carr, September 29, 1830, and Wirt to Thomas Swann, September 30, 1830, reel 13, Wirt Papers; Madison to Wirt, October 1, 1830; Wirt to Madison, October 5, 1830; Madison to Wirt, October 12, 1830, in Kennedy, *Memoirs of Wirt*, 2:260–63; *Niles' Register* 39 (September 18, 1830): 58.

46. Wirt to Swann, October 4, 1830, reel 13, Wirt Papers.

47. Wirt to Judge Thomas Randall, October 7, 1830, and Wirt to Carr, October 9, 1830, reel 13, Wirt Papers.

48. Vann to the *Cherokee Phoenix*, reprinted in *Niles' Register* 39 (October 2, 1830): 99. See also Martin Van Buren to James Hamilton, October 17, 1830, in James Hamilton, *Reminiscences of James A. Hamilton; or, Men and Events, at Home and Abroad, During Three Quarters of a Century*, p. 190; and George Troup to Dr. W. C. Daniell, October 6, 1830, Harden, *Life of Troup*, pp. 512–13; "Removal of the Indians," *North American Review* 31 (October 1830): 396–400, 439.

49. Evarts to Eleazar Lord, October 13, 1830, Tracy, *Memoir*, pp. 400–401; Evarts to Kingsbury, October 19, 1830, ABC 1.01, vol. 10; Evarts to George Cheever, October 28, 1830, Box 3, folder 2, Cheever Family Papers, AAS; Evarts to Lord, November 24, 1830, Tracy, *Memoir*, pp. 402–3.

50. John Lowry to Eaton, November 7, 1830, IA, LR, Cherokee Agency (East), 1830–31 (M-234), reel 74; Jackson to Eaton, November 18, 1830, IA, LR, Cherokee emigration, 1828–36 (M-234), reel 113; Boudinot to Evarts, November 27, 1830, ABC 10, vol. 5.

51. Jackson, "Second Annual Message," December 6, 1830, in Richardson, *Messages and Papers*, 2:519–23. Also see [Roger Williams], "Removal of the Indians," *American Baptist Magazine* 10 (December 1830): 364; William Wirt to Thomas Swann, December 6, 1830, reel 13, Wirt Papers.

52. William S. Coody to Evarts, December 23, 1830, Box 1, folder 24, EFP. For the report of the Cherokee delegation, see their arguments to John Eaton, December 22, 1830, in *Correspondence*, 2:202–6.

53. Evarts Cash Books, 1829, 1830, New York Public Library. For living standards in 1830 see William Pease and Jane Pease, *The Web of Progress: Private Values and Public Styles in Boston and Charleston, 1828–1843*, pp. 32–33.

54. Antipas, "The Comparative Importance of Moral and Intellectual Culture," *Spirit of the Pilgrims* 3 (November 1830): 573, 575. Also see Mary Gordon, "Patriots and Christians: A Reassessment of Nineteenth-Century School Reformers," *Journal of Social History* 11 (1978): 554.

55. For Evarts's memberships see Box 6, folder 218, EFP. Also see the *Fifth*

Annual Report of the Board of Managers of the Prison Discipline Society, Boston, 1830, passim; *Missionary Herald* 26 (October 1830): 335; and Tracy, *Memoir*, pp. 403–4.

56. Washburn, *Evils*, p. 4.

57. James T. Austin, *An Oration, Delivered on the Fourth of July, 1829, At the Celebration of American Independence, in the City of Boston*, p. 16. Also see David Damon, *Address Delivered at Amesbury, August 2, 1829, Previous to the Organization of the Salisbury and Amesbury Society for Promoting Temperance*, pp. 5–6; Benjamin Hill, *The Moral Responsibility of Civil Rulers: A Sermon, Addressed to the Legislature of the State of Connecticut, at the Annual Election in Hartford, May 6, 1829*, p. 6; Alexander McLean, *An Oration, Pronounced at Ludlow Factory Village, Mass., July 4th, 1829, Being the Fifty-Third Anniversary of American Independence*, passim; Joseph Allen, *The Sources of Public Prosperity. A Discourse, Delivered in Northborough, April 9, 1829, on the Day of the Public Fast*, pp. 9, 16.

58. For the Greece mission see Rufus Anderson to Evarts, July 13, 1829, ABC 1.5, vol. 2. A summary of the China mission is in Murray Rubinstein, "Zion's Corner: Origins of the American Protestant Missionary Movement in China, 1827–1839" (Ph.D. diss., New York University, 1976). Also see the *American Ladies Magazine* 2 (August 1829): 377; Elipha White, *A Moral Revolution. A Sermon, Preached Before the Associations for Foreign Missions in Charleston, S.C., June 7th, 1829*, pp. 4–5, 10–11; Carl Kaestle and Maris Vinovskis, "From Apron Strings to ABCs: Parents, Children, and Schooling in Nineteenth-Century Massachusetts," *American Journal of Sociology* 84 (Supplement): 52–53. The Prison Discipline Society Report is excerpted in the *Missionary Herald* 25 (November 1829): 359.

59. *American Quarterly Register* 2 (August 1829): 26; William Ellery Channing, "Associations," *Christian Examiner* 7 (September 1829): 106; ABCFM, *Brief View of the American Board of Foreign Missions and Its Operations*, p. 27.

60. Gilmer's announcement is in *Niles' Register* 39 (January 8, 1831): 338. For the missionaries' resolutions see the *Cherokee Phoenix* 3 (January 1, 1831); and Kilpatrick and Kilpatrick, *New Echota Letters*, pp. 83–92.

61. Adams, *Memoirs*, 8: 261–63. Also see Edward Everett Diary, January 4, 1831, reel 36, frame 485, Everett Papers; and Cocks, "From Boarding School to Demonstration Farm," pp. 15–16.

62. Harriet G. Boudinot to Rev. H. Vaill, January 7, 1831, Vaill Collection; Archibald Yell to James K. Polk, January 10, 1831, Weaver and Bergeron, *Correspondence of James K. Polk*, 1:380; McLean to Edwards, January 16, 1831, in Washburne, *Edwards Papers*, pp. 562–63.

63. Frelinghuysen to Evarts, January 24, 1831, Box 2, EFP. Also see Gilmer to John Eaton, January 18, 1831, in Gilmer, *Sketches*, pp. 370–71; Albert Beveridge, *The Life of John Marshall*, 4:515–17; *Journal of the Senate*, 21st Cong., 2d sess., pp. 96, 98, 101, 106.

64. Richard Peters, *The Case of the Cherokee Nation against the State of Georgia*;

Argued and Determined at the Supreme Court of the United States, January Term, 1831. With an Appendix, p. 95. See also pp. 3, 20, 38–39, 87–88.

65. Ibid., pp. 159, 161, 164.

66. Ibid., pp. 174, 194–95, 197–98, 220–21; Story to his wife, January 28, 1831, in William Story, ed., *Life and Letters of Joseph Story*, 2:44–45.

67. Story to Professor Ashmun, January 30, 1831, Story, *Life and Letters*, 2:47–88.

68. Resolutions of the Georgia Legislature, 1831, in Gilmer, *Sketches*, p. 374. Also see Satz, *American Indian Policy*, p. 46.

NOTES FOR CHAPTER TEN

1. Evarts to Worcester, February 1, 1831, ABC 1.01, vol. 10.

2. Ibid.

3. Evarts to Everett, February 2, 1831, ABC 1.101, vol. 10.

4. Prof. S. M. Worcester to Greene, February 6, 1831, ABC 10, vol. 15. For the petitions see the *Journal of the Senate*, 21st Cong., 2d sess. Also see William Wirt to his wife, February 10, 1831, reel 13, Wirt Papers.

5. Greene to Rev. W. Vaill, February 18, 1831, ABC 1.01, vol. 10. Wirt's remarks are in *Speeches of Messrs. Webster, Frelinghuysen and Others, at the Sunday School Meeting in the City of Washington, February 16, 1831*, p. 5; and Evarts's letter is quoted in "Review of Sketches," p. 609. See also Edward Everett's Diary for February 13, 14, and 15, 1831, reel 36, frame 493, Everett Papers. For comments on the voting see Everett to Evarts, February 21, 1831, Box 2, folder 50, EFP.

6. *Missionary Herald* 27 (March 1831): 79. See also Culp, "Missions of the American Board," p. 42; and Crouch, "Missionary Activities," pp. 166–67. Sanford's remarks are in Sanford to Gilmer, May 5, 1831, IA, LR, Cherokee emigration, 1828–36 (M-234), reel 113.

7. The best summary of this maneuvering is in McLoughlin, *Cherokees and Missionaries*, pp. 258–62. Also see William McLoughlin, "Civil Disobedience and Evangelism Among the Missionaries to the Cherokees, 1829–1839," *Journal of Presbyterian History* 51 (1973): 125.

8. Mehitabel Evarts to her husband, March 26, 1831, Box 2, folder 48, EFP. Also see J. Evarts to Mehitabel Evarts, March 12, 1831, Box 2, folder 48, EFP. John's letters are in Box 44, folder 13, EFP. Ironically, John died two years later at age twenty-one.

9. Evarts to Hill, April 1, 1831, and Brown to David Greene, May 5, 1831, ABC 11, vol. 2; "Review of Sketches," pp. 610–11; Tracy, *Memoir*, p. 417; "Jeremiah Evarts," p. 79.

10. "Sixth Annual Report of the Board of Managers of the Prison Discipline Society, Boston, May 24, 1831," in *Reports of the Prison Discipline Society, Boston:*

1826–1835, 1:431–32; *Missionary Herald* 27 (June 1831): 197 and (November 1831): 361; Todd, *John Todd*, p. 223.

11. *Christian Advocate and Journal* 5 (May 27, 1831): 155; "Review of *A Tribute to the Memory of the Late Jeremiah Evarts*. By Gardiner Spring," *New England Magazine* 1 (September 1831): 265; "Review of Sketches," p. 605.

12. Spring, *Tribute*, pp. 8–10; "Sketch of Evarts," p. 344; *Missionary Herald* 27 (February 1831): 60.

13. Everett is quoted in Redmond Barnett, "The Movement Against Imprisonment for Debt in Massachusetts, 1811–1834," (Senior thesis, Harvard University, 1965), chapter 4, pp. 7–8. For Evarts's will see ABC 34.5. An excellent summary of the conservative republican philosophy, although in a different context, is in Dickson Bruce, Jr., *The Rhetoric of Conservatism: The Virginia Convention of 1829–30 and the Conservative Tradition in the South*, p. 82. In addition to his wife and son, John, who died in 1833, Evarts left one other son, William Maxwell Evarts (later secretary of state in the Hayes administration) and two daughters. One daughter, Mary, married David Greene, who worked with Evarts at ABCFM headquarters. The other daughter, Martha, married E. C. Tracy of Windsor, Vermont, author of the *Memoir of Jeremiah Evarts*.

14. Antipas, "Contingent Prospects of Our Country," *Spirit of the Pilgrims* 4 (April 1831): 183–84.

15. Ibid., pp. 184–85; "Jeremiah Evarts," p. 80.

16. Quoted in Lewis Tappan, *Letter to Eleazar Lord, Esq. in Defense of Measures for Promoting the Observance of the Christian Sabbath*, p. 7. For Garrison's approach to Evarts see Friedman, *Gregarious Saints*, p. 23. For other links between these groups see Roth, "Whence This Strange Fire?" pp. 129–30; Bertram Wyatt-Brown, "Conscience and Career: Young Abolitionists and Missionaries," in *Anti-Slavery, Religion, and Reform: Essays in Memory of Roger Anstey*, ed. Christine Bolt and Seymour Drescher, pp. 183–203; Bertram Wyatt-Brown, *Yankee Saints and Southern Sinners*, p. 68. Also see *The Eleventh Annual Report of the Auxiliary Foreign Missionary Society of New Haven County (West), at a Meeting Held at Humphreysville, (Derby), October 11, 1831*, p. 8.

17. Quoted in Daniel Calhoun, *The Intelligence of a People*, p. 157. For a strong defense of the new spirit and a warning about its consequences, see *Interesting Correspondence, Letter from Mr. Rush, on the Policy of the American System*, p. 8.

18. Although my thinking on these matters has been shaped by virtually every item mentioned in these notes, a few secondary sources touch on similar issues. See Rowland Berthoff, "Writing a History of Things Left Out," *Reviews in American History* 14 (1986): 9; David Davis, "Reflections on Abolitionism and Ideological Hegemony," *AHR* 92 (1987): 797–812; John Ashworth, "The Relationship Between Capitalism and Humanitarianism," *AHR* 92 (1987): 813–28; Thomas Haskell, "Convention and Hegemonic Interest in the Debate over Antislavery: A Reply to Davis and Ashworth," *AHR* 92 (1987): 829–78; Formisano, *Transforma-*

tion, p. 8; and Louis Gerteis, *Morality & Utility in American Antislavery Reform*, pp. 20–24.

19. Tracy, *Memoir*, p. 109.

20. Quoted in William Strickland, "The Rhetoric of Removal and the Trail of Tears: Cherokee Speaking Against Jackson's Indian Removal Policy, 1828–1832," *Southern Speech Communication Journal* 47 (1982): 301–2.

21. For a study of the American Board's position by the time of *Worcester v. Georgia*, see Edwin Miles, "After John Marshall's Decision: *Worcester v. Georgia* and the Nullification Crisis," *Journal of Southern History* 39 (1973):519–44.

Bibliography

Research for this study rests on an extensive variety of primary sources, manuscript and printed. Both were essential to piece together the story of Jeremiah Evarts and the changing temper of early nineteenth century America. Since Evarts left few personal papers, apparently by design, one must rely on E. C. Tracy's memoir, which reprints many letters, some of which do not seem to have survived that endeavor. (Tracy was Evarts's son-in-law.) While the editorial commentary in that volume is usually worshipful, the printed primary sources appear accurate when checked against surviving copies and one has, therefore, to assume that the others are also accurate. Three collections of Evarts's Papers are extant. His account books at the New York Public Library and the papers at the Library of Congress both constitute small collections. The Evarts Family Papers at Yale are much more useful, especially for insights into his personal life. The remainder of Evarts's letters can be found scattered throughout the extensive and very rich archives of the American Board of Commissioners for Foreign Missions at Houghton Library, Harvard University. There is one small collection of Evarts's personal papers here also. Various other manuscript collections, listed below in the bibliography, provide further insight into Evarts or the causes that consumed his life.

Of particular note among the manuscript materials is the substantial collection at the ABCFM Archives. These are critical not only for a narrative history of ABCFM activities, but also for evaluating the objectives of the American Board and the responses of its officers and missionaries to cultural, political, and social change in the early republic. Especially useful for my study were the many volumes of letters to and from domestic correspondents, the letters from ABCFM officers, and the volumes relating to specific Indian missions.

Printed primary materials were essential to this study, not only for providing the broader context for Evarts's efforts and those of his colleagues in the religious and reform communities, but for the galaxy of ideas that pervaded these efforts and informed the language of the early nineteenth century. The *Panoplist*, later renamed the *Missionary Herald*, published numerous reports from local societies as well as articles penned by Evarts while he was editor. I have tried to indicate in the bibliography below specific articles that can be identified with Evarts. As Tracy indicates in his memoir, Evarts wrote under various pseudonyms. They include: Coke, C.Y.A. [Collegii Yalensis Alumnus], Philalethes, A.B., A.M., V.A., Agenor, Antipas, Benevolus. (See Tracy's note in *Memoir of the Life of Jeremiah Evarts, Esq.*, p. 45.) I have followed Tracy's lead to track them down. Other pieces that appeared without an alias, but which he surely wrote, are cited in the notes and the likelihood of his authorship noted in the text. The most complete collection of printed primary materials relevant to this work is at the American Antiquarian Society in Worcester, Massachusetts. Sermons and public addresses were particularly useful, as were reports from the many reform societies of the day. A particularly strong collection of these reports is at the Congregational Library, Boston, Massachusetts. The *Cherokee Phoenix*, available on microfilm, is an essential source for understanding many of the political and cultural perceptions and conflicts that buffeted the United States in the early nineteenth century.

PRIMARY SOURCES

Manuscripts

Alabama. Executive Letter-Book, November 17–December 13, 1822 (microfilm), Library of Congress.

Executive Letter-Book, December 18, 1822–May 18, 1836 (microfilm), Library of Congress.

American Board of Commissioners for Foreign Missions Archives, Houghton Library, Harvard University.

ABC 1.01: Letters to Domestic Correspondents, 11 vols., 1816–32.

ABC 1.5, vol. 1: Memorials to the United States Government regarding the Indians, 1831–32.

ABC 1.5, vol. 2: Letters of Early Secretaries, 1803–64.

ABC 2.01, vol. 1: Letters to Foreign Correspondents, 1827–32.

ABC 5.4, vol. 1: Contracts for Printing the Panoplist, 1811–14.

ABC 5.4, vol. 2: Miscellaneous Papers Relating to the Missionary Herald, 1822–44.

ABC 8.5: Valuable Documents.

ABC 8.6, vol. 5: J. Evarts Letters, 1823–28.

ABC 10: Letters Received from Domestic Correspondents, 15 vols., 1824–30.

ABC 11, vol. 1: Letters from Officers of the Board, Previous to September 1824.

ABC 11, vol. 2: Letters from Officers of the Board, September 13, 1824–May 11, 1831, Part I.
ABC 11, vol. 3: Letters from Officers of the Board, September 13, 1824–May 11, 1831, Part II.
ABC 13, vol. 1: Letters from Government Officials, 1824–31.
ABC 18.3.1, vol. 1: Arkansas Mission, previous to September 1824.
ABC 18.3.1, vol. 2: Cherokee Mission, previous to September 1824.
ABC 18.3.1, vol. 3: Cherokee Mission, from individual missionaries.
ABC 18.3.1, vol. 4: Cherokee Mission, September 1824–31, Part 1.
ABC 18.3.1, vol. 5: Cherokee Mission, September 1824–31, Part 2.
ABC 18.3.1, vol. 6: Cherokee Mission: New York Indians, 1824–31.
ABC 18.3.3, vol. 2: Cherokee Mission, Miscellaneous.
ABC 18.3.4, vol. 1: Choctaw Mission, previous to September 1824.
ABC 18.3.4, vol. 2: Choctaw Mission, from individual missionaries.
ABC 18.3.4, vol. 3: Choctaw Mission, 1824–30, Part 1.
ABC 18.3.4, vol. 4: Choctaw Mission, 1824–30, Part 2.
ABC 18.4.5, vol. 1: Chickasaw Mission Miscellaneous: Papers of Cyrus Kingsbury.
ABC 18.8, vol. 1: North American Indians, Miscellaneous Letters.
ABC 18.8, vol. 2: North American Indians, Miscellaneous (biographical notes on missionaries).
ABC 34: Personal Papers of Jeremiah Evarts, 1817–30.
ABC 34.5: Papers Relating to the Legacy of the Library of Jeremiah Evarts to the ABCFM, 1832.

Baldwin Family Papers, Sterling Library, Yale University.
Samuel Bell (1770–1850) Papers, 1789–1876, New Hampshire Historical Society, Concord, New Hampshire.
John MacPherson Berrien Papers (microfilm), Southern Historical Collection, University of North Carolina Library.
Chamberlain Collection, Boston Public Library, Boston, Massachusetts.
Cheever Family Papers, American Antiquarian Society.
Cherokee Collection, Tennessee State Library and Archives, Nashville, Tennessee.
John Coffee Papers, Tennessee State Library and Archives, Nashville, Tennessee.
William H. Crawford to Samuel Smith, November 21, 1826, Autograph File, Houghton Library, Harvard University.
John W. Davis Papers, American Antiquarian Society.
Day Family Collection, Sterling Library, Yale University.
J. Evarts to Howe & Deforest, October 18, 1813, Autograph File, Houghton Library, Harvard University.
Jeremiah Evarts Papers, Library of Congress.

Jeremiah Evarts Account Books, 1826–30 (5 vols.), New York Public Library.
Evarts Family Papers, Manuscripts and Archives, Yale University Library.
Edward Everett Papers (microfilm), Massachusetts Historical Society, Boston.
Grant Foreman Papers, Thomas Gilcrease Institute of American History and Art, Tulsa, Oklahoma.
Georgia. Executive Letter-Books of the Governor (microfilm).
Gilman Family Papers, Sterling Library, Yale University.
Simon Gratz Autograph Collection, Historical Society of Pennsylvania, Philadelphia.
Duff Green Papers (microfilm), Southern Historical Collection, Library of the University of North Carolina, Chapel Hill.
Isaac Hill Papers, New Hampshire Historical Society, Concord, New Hampshire.
Hillhouse Family Papers, Sterling Library, Yale University.
Charles Jared Ingersoll Collection, Historical Society of Pennsylvania, Philadelphia.
Andrew Jackson to Rachel Jackson, September 30, 1820, Autograph File, Houghton Library, Harvard University.
Andrew Jackson Papers (microfilm), Library of Congress.
Josiah S. Johnston Papers, Historical Society of Pennsylvania, Philadelphia.
Kingsley Memorial Collection, Sterling Library, Yale University.
Edward and William Lucas Manuscripts, Perkins Library, Duke University.
Isaac McCoy Papers (microfilm), Kansas State Historical Society.
M. D. McHenry to John McHenry, April 2, 1830, Hardin Collection, Chicago Historical Society.
Letters from Thomas L. McKenney, from Various Collections in the New York Historical Society (microfilm), courtesy of Dr. Herman Viola, Smithsonian Institution.
McKenney-Lewis Correspondence, Huntington Library, San Marino, California (microfilm), courtesy of Dr. Herman Viola.
Jotham Meeker Papers (microfilm), Kansas State Historical Society.
Memorandum Book of the Book Committee of the Massachusetts Missionary Society, Congregational Library, Boston, Massachusetts.
Pliny Merrick Correspondence, American Antiquarian Society.
Mississippi. The Proceedings of the Governor as Superintendent of Indian Affairs (microfilm).
Morse Family Papers, Sterling Library, Yale University.
Packard Family Letters, 1796–1853, American Antiquarian Society.
Leonard Moody Parker Papers, 1811–37, American Antiquarian Society.
Paxton, Massachusetts Papers, 1779–1861, American Antiquarian Society.
Records of the Office of Indian Affairs, National Archives. Letters Received, 1826–36; Letters Sent, vol. 1–7, 1824–31.

Records of the Office of the Secretary of War, National Archives. Letters Sent, Indian Affairs, 1817–1824.
Scituate, Massachusetts, Records of the Society for the Suppression of Intemperance, 1817–36, American Antiquarian Society.
Roger Sherman Papers, Library of Congress.
Silliman Family Papers, Sterling Library, Yale University.
Society of Inquiry Papers, Andover-Newton Theological Seminary.
Jared Sparks Papers, Houghton Library, Harvard University.
Herman L. Vaill Collection, Manuscripts and Archives, Yale University Library.
Martin Van Buren Papers (microfilm), Library of Congress.
Daniel Webster Papers (microfilm), Massachusetts Historical Society.
Eli Whitney Papers, Sterling Library, Yale University.
William Wirt Papers (MS 1011, microfilm edition), Maryland Historical Society.
Wolf Papers, Historical Society of Pennsylvania, Philadelphia.

Published Material

A. A. "Letter of Pliny to Trajan." *Panoplist* 12 (April 1816): 152–53.
———. "On the Significance of the Word Atonement, As Used in Scripture." *Panoplist* 12 (March 1816): 97–103, 12 (July 1816): 324–38.
A. B. "Abuse of the Late Harvest." *Panoplist* 9 (October 1813): 358–60.
———. "Avarice of Professing Christians." *Panoplist* 15 (December 1819): 529–31.
———. "Calculations on the Expenses of War." *Panoplist* 9 (November 1813): 444–48.
———. "Caution Against Promoting Intemperate Drinking." *Panoplist* 12 (October 1816): 460–62.
———. "Centurial Celebration." *Panoplist* 16 (April 1820): 155.
———. "Concert of Prayer." *Panoplist* 11 (January 1815): 19–20.
———. "The Execution of the Pirates." *Panoplist* 15 (March 1819): 110–19.
———. "Foreign Missions." *Panoplist* 7 (March 1812): 445–48.
———. "A Hint to the Benevolent." *Panoplist* 6 (December 1810): 306–9.
———. "Laws of Connecticut in Reference to the Sabbath." *Panoplist* 13 (August 1817): 363–66.
———. "Laws Respecting the Observance of the Sabbath." *Panoplist* 13 (July 1817): 303–8.
———. "Magnitude of the Evil of Intemperance." *Panoplist* 9 (August 1813): 105–6.
———. "Massachusetts Missionary Society." *Panoplist* 13 (April 1817): 161–63.
———. "On the Association of Ideas." *Panoplist* 7 (December 1811): 300–302.
———. "On Atheism." *Panoplist* 13 (December 1817): 548–49.
———. "On Being Stewards of God." *Panoplist* 15 (December 1819): 539–42.
———. "On Covetousness, or a Reliance upon Riches for Happiness." *Panoplist* 9 (September 1813): 258–63.

———. "On the Deceitfulness of Riches." *Panoplist* 14 (December 1818): 546–50.

———. "On Dispensations and Indulgences." *Panoplist* 7 (October 1811): 199–201.

———. "On the Duty of Praying for the Salvation of Relatives and Friends." *Panoplist* 13 (October 1817): 453–54.

———. "On the Execution of Criminals." *Panoplist* 15 (January 1819): 19–22.

———. "On the Good Uses, Which Might Be Made of the Money Now Expended in War." *Panoplist* 10 (April 1814): 169–75.

———. "On the Means of Averting National Calamities." *Panoplist* 8 (September 1812): 177–79.

———. "On Mendacity." *Panoplist* 16 (March 1820): 115–17.

———. "On a Minister's Intercourse with His People." *Panoplist* 16 (July 1820): 296–300.

———. "On the Misconduct of Professed Christians, and the Use Which is Made of it by the Men of the World." *Panoplist* 9 (October 1813): 346–49.

———. "On Praying for the Holy Spirit." *Panoplist* 8 (April 1813): 507–11.

———. "On the Present Want of Faithful and Able Ministers of the Gospel." *Panoplist* 12 (November 1816): 503–5.

———. "On the Private Intercourse of Ministers with their People." *Panoplist* 7 (January 1812): 354–55.

———. "On Religious Charities." *Panoplist* 10 (May 1814): 224–27.

———. "On Religious Conferences." *Panoplist* 9 (July 1813): 73–78; (August 1813): 106–10.

———. "On the Salaries of Ministers." *Panoplist* 7 (November 1811): 270–75.

———. "On Singing Praises to God." *Panoplist* 9 (June 1813): 21–23.

———. "On the Word *Brethren* as Applied in the Holy Scriptures to Christians." *Panoplist* 8 (December 1812): 306–10.

———. "President Edwards' First Resolution." *Panoplist* 13 (September 1817): 404–7.

———. "The Sabbath." *Panoplist* 7 (May 1812): 539–43.

———. "The Sabbath Made for Man." *Panoplist* 13 (April 1817): 157–61.

———. "Thoughts on Harvest." *Panoplist* 9 (October 1813): 299–304.

———. "Thoughts on the Late Measures of the Legislature of Massachusetts in Relation to the Sabbath." *Panoplist* 10 (August 1814): 354–62.

———. "Thoughts on the Loss of Near Relatives." *Panoplist* 9 (August 1813): 160–64.

———. "Thoughts on the Manner in Which Nations Declare and Conduct War." *Panoplist* 11 (July 1815): 303–5.

Abbot, Abiel. *A Discourse, Delivered before the Bible Society of Salem and Its Vicinity, on Their Anniversary, June 11, 1817*. Salem: Thomas Cushing, 1817.

———. *An Address, Delivered Before the Massachusetts Society for Suppressing Intem-*

perance, At their Anniversary Meeting, June 2, 1815. Cambridge, Mass.: Hilliard & Metcalf, 1815.

Abbott, Warren. *Address to the Danvers Auxiliary Society for Suppressing Intemperance and other Vices, and Promoting Temperance and General Morality, April 30, 1822.* Salem: John Cushing & Brothers, 1822.

An Account of Memorials Presented to Congress During Its Last Session. By Numerous Friends of their Country and Its Institutions; Praying that the Mails May Not be Transported Nor Post-Offices Kept Open, on the Sabbath. New York: T. R. Marvin, 1829.

The Act of Incorporation, Regulations, and Members of the Massachusetts Congregational Charitable Society; With a Brief Sketch of its Origin, Progress, and Purpose. Boston: John Eliot, 1815.

Adams, Charles Francis, ed. *Memoirs of John Quincy Adams, Comprising Portions of His Diary From 1795 to 1848.* 12 vols. Philadelphia: J. B. Lippincott & Co., 1875.

Adams, George W. *An Oration Delivered At Quincy, on the Fifth of July, 1824.* Boston: Ezra Lincoln, 1824.

Adams, John Quincy. *An Oration Addressed to the Citizens of the Town of Quincy, on the Fourth of July, 1831, the Fifty-fifth Anniversary of the Independence of the United States of America.* Boston: Richardson, Lord & Holbrook, 1831.

Adams, Josiah. *An Address Delivered Before the Society of Middlesex Husbandmen and Manufacturers, on Their Anniversary at Concord, October 2, 1823.* Concord, Mass.: William Gould, 1823.

Adams, Thomas. *A Sermon, Delivered at Farmington, (Maine) December 4, 1817: Being the Day Set Apart by the Governor and Council, As a Day of Public Thanksgiving and Prayer.* Hallowell: E. Goodale, 1818.

——. *A Sermon on Intemperance.* Hallowell: Glazier & Co., 1827.

An Address of a Minister to the Youth of His Congregation. Hartford: W. Hudson & L. Skinner, 1826.

An Address of the Charitable Society for the Education of Indigent Pious Young Men, for the Ministry of the Gospel. N.p., [1814].

Address of the Connecticut Society for the Encouragement of American Manufactures. Middletown: T. Dunning, 1817.

Address of the Cumberland Association to the Several Churches and Societies, with Which They are Connected. Portland: Arthur Shirley, 1813.

Address to Mothers. Simsbury, Conn.: N.p., 1817.

An Address to Parents. Amherst, N.H.: Joseph Cushing, 1804.

An Address to the Children of the North Parish Sabbath School, in Portsmouth. By a Teacher. Portsmouth: Whidden, 1818.

Address to the Christian Public. Boston: N.p., 1809.

An Address to the Citizens of Windham County, On the Importance of Forming a County Society for Charitable Purposes, By the Consociation of Said County. Hartford: Peter Gleason, 1818.

An Address, To the Emigrants from Connecticut, and from New England Generally, in the New Settlements of the United States. Hartford: Peter B. Gleason & Co., 1817.

An Address to the Inhabitants of the State of Vermont, On the Use of Ardent Spirits. Montpelier: E. P. Walton, 1817.

Address to the Public on the Use of Ardent Spirits. Concord, N.H.: Daniel Cooledge, 1818.

Aderman, Ralph, ed. *The Letters of James Kirke Paulding.* Madison: Univ. of Wisconsin Press, 1962.

A. E. "The Corban Society." *Panoplist* 13 (April 1817): 163–65.

Agenor. "On the Duty of Educating Children for the Arduous Duties of the Present Times." *Panoplist* 9 (August 1813): 153–58.

———. "On the Encouragements to Give Children a Strictly Religious Education." *Panoplist* 9 (September 1813): 248–50.

Aiken, Solomon. *The Rise and Progress of the Political Dissension in the United States. A Sermon, Preached in Dracutt, May 11, 1811. It Being the Annual Fast.* Haverhill: William B. Allen, 1811.

Alden, Augustus. *An Address, Delivered at Augusta, on the Thirty-fourth Anniversary of American Independence, July Fourth, 1809.* Augusta: Peter Edes, 1809.

Alden, Timothy, Jr. *The Glory of America. A Century Sermon Delivered at the South Church in Portsmouth, New Hampshire, 4 January, 1801.* Portsmouth: William Treadwell & Co., 1801.

Allen, Joseph. *The Sources of Public Prosperity. A Discourse. Delivered in Northborough, April 9, 1829, on the Day of the Public Fast.* Worcester: Griffin & Morrill, 1829.

Allen, Morrill. *A Sermon, Delivered in Hanson, Lord's Day December 26, 1824.* Plymouth, Mass.: Allen Danforth, 1825.

Allen, Samuel. *An Oration Delivered on the Anniversary of American Independence; At Blackstone Village, Mendon, Massachusetts, July 4, 1823.* Providence: John Miller, 1823.

Allen, William. *An Account of the Separation in the Church and Town of Pittsfield, with Remarks on Some Ecclesiastical Proceedings, Which Seem to Have Violated the Principles of the Congregational and Independent Churches of New England.* Pittsfield: P. Allen, 1809.

———. *A Farewell Sermon, Preached at Pittsfield, Feb. 23, 1817, Being the Last Sabbath of His Ministry.* Pittsfield: Phinehas Allen, 1817.

———. *Memoir of John Codman, D. D.* Boston: T. R. Marvin and S. K. Whipple & Co., 1853.

———. *A Sermon, Preached Before the Auxiliary Society for Promoting Good Morals, and the Female Charitable Society of Williamstown, June 7, 1815.* Pittsfield: Phinehas Allen, 1815.

Allen, William S. *An Oration, Delivered in Newburyport, on the Fifty-fourth Anniversary of the Declaration of American Independence.* Newburyport: The Herald Office, 1830.

A. M. "Concert of Prayer." *Panoplist* 11 (March 1815): 124–25.
———. "Meditation VI." *Panoplist* 9 (August 1813): 126–27.
———. "On the Duty of Admonition." *Panoplist* 9 (November 1813): 450–52.
———. "On the Intercourse of Christians with the World." *Panoplist* 13 (August 1817): 352–59.
Ambler, Charles. *The Life and Diary of John Floyd*. Richmond: Richmond Press, 1918.
American Bible Society. *Annual Reports*. New York, 1817–1825.
American Board of Commissioners for Foreign Missions
  An Appeal to the American Churches in Behalf of Missions. Boston: Crocker & Brewster, 1828.
  An Address to the Christian Public. N.p., n.d. [1811]
  Brief View of the American Board of Foreign Missions, and Its Operations. Boston: Crocker & Brewster, 1829.
  Missionary Paper, No. 7. Containing a Brief Memoir of Asaud Shidiak; an Arab Young Man, of the Maronite Roman Catholic Church in Syria. Boston: Crocker & Brewster, 1827.
  Report of. Compiled from Documents Laid Before the Board, at the Seventeenth Annual Meeting, Which was held in Middletown, (Con.) Sept. 14, and 15, 1826. Boston: Crocker & Brewster, 1826.
  The Necessity and Utility of Employing Agents to Solicit Money for the Support of Missions. Boston: Crocker & Brewster, 1824.
  Statements Respecting the Necessities and Claims of the Missions and Missionaries, Under the Direction of the American Board of Commissioners for Foreign Missions, April 1831. New York: Sleight & Robinson, 1831.
  View of the Missions, Funds, Expenditures and Prospects of the American Board of Commissioners for Foreign Missions. Boston: Crocker & Brewster, 1820.
  View of the Missions of . . . . Boston: Crocker & Brewster, 1824.
American Education Society. *Annual Reports of the Directors*. 1818–1830.
American Society for Promoting the Civilization and General Improvement of the Indian Tribes in the United States. *First Annual Report*. New Haven: S. Converse, 1824.
American State Papers. Class 2: *Indian Affairs*. 2 vols. Washington, D.C. Gales & Seaton, 1834.
———. Class 7: *Post Office*. Washington, D.C.: Gales & Seaton, 1834.
American Temperance Society. *Annual Reports*. 1828–1832.
American Tract Society. *The Address of the Executive Committee of the American Tract Society To The Christian Public: Together with a Brief Account of the Formation of the Society, Its Constitution and Officers*. New York: D. Fanshaw, 1825.
———. *Proceedings of the First Ten Years of the American Tract Society*. Boston: Flagg & Gould, 1824.
Andros, Thomas. *The Grand Era of Ruin to Nations From Foreign Influences. A Dis-*

course, Delivered Before the Congregational Society in Berkley, Nov. 26, 1812. Boston: Samuel T. Armstrong, 1812.

Annals of the Congress of the United States, 1815–23. Washington, D.C.: Gales & Seaton, 1854.

Anthony, Joseph R. *Life in New Bedford A Hundred Years Ago.* New Bedford: George H. Reynolds, 1940.

"Anti-Masonry." *American Quarterly Review* 7 (March 1830): 162–88.

Antipas. "The Comparative Importance of Moral and Intellectual Culture." *Spirit of the Pilgrims* 3 (November 1830): 572–75.

———. "Contingent Prospects of Our Country." *Spirit of the Pilgrims* 4 (April 1831): 181–85.

———. "The Favorableness of the Present Age for the Success of the Christian Enterprise." *Spirit of the Pilgrims* 1 (December 1828): 617–24.

———. "Hints on the Relative Importance of New England to the Rest of the United States, in a Moral and Religious View." *Spirit of the Pilgrims* 1 (July 1828): 337–43.

———. "Hints on the Relative Importance of the United States to the Rest of the World, in a Moral and Religious View." *Spirit of the Pilgrims* 1 (June 1828): 281–84.

———. "A Novel Habit in Public Prayer." *Panoplist* 9 (August 1813): 110.

———. "On Drinking Healths." *Panoplist* 9 (July 1813): 78–79.

An Appeal to the Moral & Religious of All Denominations; or, An Exposition of Some of the Indiscretions of General Andrew Jackson, as Copied From the Records, and Certified by the Clerk of Mercer County, Kentucky. New York: R. Johnson, 1828.

Appleton, Jesse. *An Address, Delivered Before the Massachusetts Society for Suppressing Intemperance, At their Anniversary Meeting, May 31, 1816.* Boston: John Eliot, 1816.

———. *A Discourse, Delivered at Bath, May 11th, 1813, Before the Society for Discountenancing and Suppressing Public Vices.* Boston: Printed for the Society, 1813.

———. *A Sermon, Delivered at Portland, November 19, 1818. At the Formation of the Maine Branch of the American Society for Educating Pious Youth for the Gospel Ministry.* Hallowell: E. Goodale, 1819.

Appleton, William. *Selections from the Diaries of William Appleton, 1786–1862.* Boston: Privately printed, 1922.

The Articles of Faith, and the Covenant, of Park Street Church, Boston: With a List of the Members. Boston: T. R. Marvin, 1825.

Atmore, Charles. *Serious Advice from a Father to His Children, Respecting Their Conduct in the World; Civil, Moral, and Religious.* Philadelphia: J. H. Cunningham, 1819.

Atwater, Caleb. *Remarks Made on a Tour to Prairie Du Chien Thence to Washington City in 1829.* Columbus, Ohio: Isaac Whiting, 1831.

Austin, James T. *Address Delivered Before the Massachusetts Society for the Suppression of Intemperance, May 27, 1830.* Boston: John Eastburn, 1830.

———. *An Oration, Delivered on the Fourth of July, 1829, At the Celebration of American Independence, in the City of Boston.* Boston: John Eastburn, 1829.

———. "The Proposed New Tariff." *North American Review* 12 (January 1821): 60–88.

———. "Punishment of Crimes." *North American Review* 10 (April 1820): 235–59.

Austin, Samuel. *An Address, Pronounced in Worcester, (Mass.) on the Fourth of July, 1825, Being the Forty-ninth Anniversary of the Independence of the United States.* Worcester: William Manning, 1825.

———. *An Oration, Pronounced at Newport, Rhode Island, July 4, 1822, the Forty-sixth Anniversary of the Independence of the United States of America.* Newport: William Simons, 1822.

———. *Christians Bound to Spread the Gospel Among all Descriptions of Their Fellow Men: A Sermon, Preached Before the Massachusetts Missionary Society, at Their Annual Meeting in Boston, May 24, 1803.* Salem: Joshua Cushing, 1803.

Autobiography and Correspondence of Allen Trimble, Governor of Ohio. Columbus: Ohio Archaeological and Historical Society, 1909.

Auxiliary Foreign Mission Society of Boston and Vicinity. *Thirteenth Anniversary, January 3, 1825.* Boston: Crocker & Brewster, 1825.

Auxiliary Foreign Mission Society of Essex County (Massachusetts). *Proceedings at the Organization of, April 11, 1826.* Salem: Warwick Palfrey, Jr., 1826.

Auxiliary Foreign Missionary Society of New Haven County (West). *The Eleventh Annual Report of, at a Meeting Held at Humphreysville, (Derby), October 11, 1831.* New Haven: Hezekiah Howe, 1831.

Babbidge, Homer Jr., ed. *Noah Webster: On Being American, Selected Writings, 1783–1828.* New York: Frederick Praeger, 1967.

Babcock, Rufus Jr. *The Claims of Education Societies; Especially on the Young Men of Our Country. A Sermon, Delivered in the First Baptist Meeting House in Boston, on the Evening of November 8, 1829, Before the Boston Young Men's Baptist Auxiliary Education Society.* Boston: William Collier, 1829.

Backus, Charles. *A Sermon, Delivered Jan. 1, 1801; Containing a Brief Review of Some of the Distinguishing Events of the Eighteenth Century.* Hartford: Hudson & Goodwin, 1801.

Backus, Samuel. *Courage in Doing Good. A Sermon, Delivered Before the Windham County Charitable Society, At Their Annual Meeting, in Ashford, June 3, 1823.* Worcester: William Manning, 1823.

Bacon, Leonard. *A Plea for Africa; Delivered in New-Haven, July 4, 1825.* New Haven: T. G. Woodward and Co., 1825.

———. *The Social and Civil Influence of the Christian Ministry. A Sermon, Preached at the Sixth Anniversary of the Auxiliary Education Society of the Young Men of Boston; February 6, 1825.* Boston: T. R. Marvin, 1825.

———. *Total Abstinence from Ardent Spirits; An Address Delivered, By Request of the*

Young Men's Temperance Society, of New Haven, in the North Church, June 24th, 1829. New Haven: Sidney's Press, 1829.

Bailey, Benjamin. *An Oration, Delivered at Burlington, Vt., on the Fourth of July 1828, Being the Fifty-second Anniversary of American Independence*. Burlington: E. & T. Miller, 1828.

Bailey, Luther. *A Sermon Delivered at Randolph, Before the Norfolk Auxiliary Education Society, At their Annual Meeting, June 9, 1824*. Boston: Lincoln & Edmands, 1824.

Bailey, Rufus. *God the Proper Object of Gratitude; and Thanksgiving a Necessary Evidence of Its Sincerity. A Sermon, Preached in Pittsfield, Mass. on the Day of the State Thanksgiving, December 3, 1824*. Pittsfield: Phinehas Allen, 1825.

Bailey, Winthrop. *National Glory. A Discourse, Delivered at Brunswick, on the Day of the National Fast, August 20, 1812*. Portland: Arthur Shirley, 1812.

Baldwin, Simeon. *Life and Letters of Simeon Baldwin*. New Haven: Tuttle, Morehouse & Taylor, 1919.

Baldwin, Thomas. *On the Duty of Parents to Children. A Sermon, Delivered in the Meeting-house of the Second Baptist Church and Society in Boston, On the Afternoon of Lord's-Day, March 17, 1822*. Boston: Lincoln & Edmands, 1822.

———. *The Knowledge of the Lord Filling the Earth. A Sermon, Delivered in Boston, June 4, 1812, Before the Massachusetts Bible Society, Being Their Third Anniversary*. Boston: Lincoln & Edmands, 1812.

Bancroft, Aaron. *A Discourse on Conversion*. Worcester: William Manning, 1818.

———. *The Nature and Worth of Christian Liberty. Illustrated in a Sermon Delivered Before the Second Congregational Church and Society in Worcester, on the Twenty-third Day of June, 1816*. Worcester: William Manning, 1816.

———. *A Sermon Delivered at the Dedication of the Second Congregational Church, in Worcester, Aug. 20, 1829*. Worcester: Griffin and Morrill, 1829.

Bancroft, George. *An Oration Delivered on the Fourth of July, 1826, At Northampton, Mass*. Northampton: T. Watson Shepard, 1826.

Bannister, William. *An Oration, Delivered at Newburyport, on the 34th Anniversary of American Independence*. Newburyport: E. W. Allen, 1809.

Barbour, I. Richmond. *A Statistical Table, Showing the Influence of Intemperance on the Churches*. Boston: Perkins & Marvin, 1831.

Barck, Dorothy, ed. *Letters from John Pintard to His Daughter Eliza Noel Pintard Davidson, 1816–1833*. 4 vols. New York: New-York Historical Society, 1940–41.

Bard, Simeon. *An Oration, Pronounced at Francestown, New-Hampshire, July Fourth, 1820*. Amherst, N.H.: Elijah Mansur, 1820.

Barker, Eugene, and Amelia Williams, eds. *The Writings of Sam Houston, 1813–1863*. Austin: Univ. of Texas Press, 1938.

Barnes, Lela, ed. "Journal of Isaac McCoy for the Exploring Expedition of 1828." *Kansas Historical Quarterly* 5 (August 1936): 227–77.

———. "Journal of Isaac McCoy for the Exploring Expedition of 1830." *Kansas Historical Quarterly* 5 (November 1936): 339–77.

Bartlett, John. *God. Not the Author of Sin. A Discourse, Delivered before the Second Congregational church and Society in Marblehead, June 20, 1819.* Salem: John Cushing, 1819.

Bartlett, Josiah. *An Address to the Charlestown Branch of the Washington Benevolent Society of Massachusetts, on the Twenty-second of February, 1813.* Charlestown: Samuel Etheridge, 1813.

——— . *An Historical Sketch of Charlestown, in the County of Middlesex, and Commonwealth of Massachusetts. Read to an Assembly of Citizens at the Opening of Washington Hall, Nov. 16, 1813.* Boston: John Eliot, 1814.

Barton, Ira. *An Oration, Delivered at Oxford, on the Forty-sixth Anniversary of American Independence.* Cambridge, Mass.: Hilliard & Metcalf, 1822.

Bassett, Francis. *An Oration, Delivered on Monday, the Fifth of July, 1824, in Commemoration of American Independence, Before the Supreme Executive of the Commonwealth, and the City Council and Inhabitants of the City of Boston.* Boston: Wells & Lilly, 1824.

Bassett, John Spencer, ed. *Correspondence of Andrew Jackson.* 7 vols. Washington, D.C.: Carnegie Institute, 1926–33.

Bates, Isaac. *Speech of Mr. Bates, of Massachusetts, On the Indian Bill.* N.p.: [1830].

Bates, Joshua. *A Discourse, Delivered in Castleton, At the Organization of the Vermont Juvenile Missionary Society, September 16, 1818.* Middlebury: Francis Burnap, 1818.

——— . *Influence of Christian Truth. A Sermon, Preached in Northampton, Mass., Sept. 21, 1825, at the Sixteenth Meeting of the American Board of Commissioners for Foreign Missions.* Boston: Crocker & Brewster, 1825.

——— . *A Sermon, Preached on the Day of General Election, at Montpelier, October 11, 1821, Before the Honourable Legislature of Vermont.* Montpelier: P. Walton, 1821.

Bean, James. *The Christian Minister's Affectionate Advice to a Married Couple.* Andover: Flagg & Gould, 1817.

Beard, James, ed. *The Letters and Journals of James Fenimore Cooper.* Cambridge, Mass.: Belknap Press, 1964.

Beecher, Lyman. *Autobiography.* 2 vols. New York: Harper & Brothers, 1864.

——— . *The Design, Rights, and Duties of Local Churches. A Sermon Delivered at the Installation of the Rev. Elias Cornelius as Associate Pastor of the Tabernacle Church in Salem, July 21, 1819.* Andover: Flagg & Gould, 1819.

——— . *The Means of National Prosperity. A Sermon, Delivered at Litchfield, On the Day of the Anniversary Thanksgiving, December 2, 1819.* Hartford: Lincoln & Stone, 1820.

——— . *The Practicability of Suppressing Vice, By Means of Societies Instituted for That Purpose. A Sermon, Delivered Before the Moral Society, in East-Hampton, (Long Island) September 21, 1803.* New London, Conn.: Samuel Green, 1804.

——— . *A Reformation of Morals Practicable and Indispensable. A Sermon Delivered at New-Haven on the Evening of October 27, 1812.* New Haven: Eli Hudson, 1813.

———. *Something Has Been Done, During the Last Forty Years.* N.p., 1830.
Benedict, George. *An Oration, Delivered at Burlington, Vt. on the Fourth of July 1826, Being the Fiftieth Anniversary of American Independence.* Burlington: E. & T. Mills, 1826.
Benevolus. "Arithmetic Applied to Moral Purposes." *Panoplist* 6 (October 1810): 211–14; 7 (June 1811), 18–21.
Bent, Josiah Jr. *National Jubilee. An Oration Delivered at Braintree, July 4, 1826, in Presence of the Citizens of Braintree and Weymouth; on the Fiftieth Anniversary of American Independence.* Boston: E. Bellamy, 1826.
Bigelow, Andrew. *A Farewell Discourse Preached to the First Congregational Society in Eastport, on Sunday May 27, 1821.* Boston: Wells & Lilly, 1821.
———. *Signs of the Moral Age. A Sermon Preached in Reading, North Parish, on Lord's Day, January 6, 1828.* Boston: Bowles & Dearborn, 1828.
Bigelow, Tyler. *Address, Delivered at the Eighth Anniversary of the Massachusetts Peace Society, December 25, 1823.* Boston: John B. Russell, 1824.
Binns, John. *Recollections of the Life of John Binns.* Philadelphia: Parry & M'Millan, 1854.
Bird, Jonathan. *Discourse, Delivered to the Freemen Collected in the Second Society in Saybrook, April 11th, A.D. 1803.* Middletown: T. & J. B. Dunning, 1803.
Blake, Caleb. *Unweariness in Well Doing Urged in A Sermon, Preached Before the Charitable Female Society in Westford, in November, 1814.* Boston: Samuel T. Armstrong, 1815.
Blakely, William, comp. *American State Papers Bearing on Sunday Legislation.* Reprint. New York: DaCapo, 1970.
Blanchard, Joseph. *Address Delivered at the Thirteenth Anniversary of the Massachusetts Peace Society, December 25, 1828.* Boston: Wait, Greene & Co., 1829.
Blood, Mighill. *Moral Duty and Improvement. A Discourse Delivered in Bucksport, (Me.) Before the Felicity Lodge of Free and Accepted Masons; On the Festival of St. John the Baptist, 24th June, Anno Lucis, 5818—A.D. 1818.* Hallowell: E. Goodale, 1818.
Boardman, Charles. *The Agency of God, Illustrated in the Achievement of the Independence of the United States. A Sermon, Delivered at New-Preston, Connecticut, July 4, 1826, Being a Religious Celebration of That Day.* New Haven: Treadway & Adams, 1826.
Bonney, Catharina, ed. *A Legacy of Historical Gleanings.* 2 vols. Albany: J. Munsell, 1875.
The Boston Directory. Boston: John Frost & Charles Stimpson, Jr., 1826.
Boston Prison Discipline Society.
    Fifth Annual Report of the Board of Managers of the Prison Discipline Society, Boston, 1830. Boston: N.p., 1830.
    Sixth Annual Report of the Board of Managers of the Prison Discipline Society, Boston, May 24, 1831. Boston: Perkins & Marvin, 1831.
Boston Society for the Moral and Religious Instruction of the Poor.

Report, Presented at the Annual Meeting, Oct. 1817. Boston: N.p., 1817.

Fourth Annual Report, Presented at Their Anniversary, Oct. 11, 1820. Boston: George Clark & Co., 1820.

Fifth Annual Report, Presented at Their Anniversary, Oct. 17, 1821. Charlestown: S. Etheridge, 1821.

Sixth Annual Report, Presented at Their Anniversary, Nov. 6, 1822. Boston: Crocker & Brewster, 1822.

Bound, John. *The Means of Curing & Preventing Intemperance.* New York: Charles Baldwin, 1820.

Bouton, Nathaniel. *Christian Patriotism. An Address Delivered at Concord. July the Fourth, 1825.* Concord, N.H.: Shepard & Bannister, 1825.

Bradford, Gamaliel. *An Address Delivered Before the Massachusetts Society for the Suppression of Intemperance, June, 1826.* Boston: Isaac R. Butts and Co., 1826.

Bradford, John. *The Word of Life: A Light Held Forth by the Bible Societies.* Albany: Webster & Skinners, 1817.

Brazer, Samuel, Jr. *An Oration, Pronounced at Springfield, on July 4th, 1809, in Commemoration of American Independence.* Springfield: Thomas Dickman, 1809.

Brewer, John. *An Address, Delivered Before the New Bedford Auxiliary Society for the Suppression of Intemperance, At Their Annual Meeting, January 1, 1816.* New Bedford: Benjamin Lindsey, 1816.

A Brief Account of the Origin and Progress of the Boston Female Society for Missionary Purposes. Boston: Lincoln & Edmands, 1818.

A Brief View of the American Education Society, With the Principles Upon Which it is Conducted and an Appeal to the Christian World on its Behalf. Andover: Flagg & Gould, 1826.

Briggs, Charles. *A Discourse Delivered at Concord, October the Fifth, 1825.* Concord, Mass.: John G. Allen, 1825.

Brigham, Amariah. *Observations on the Influence of Religion Upon the Health and Physical Welfare of Mankind.* Reprint. New York: Arno Press, 1973.

Brodhead, Jacob. *A Plea for the Poor. A Sermon, Delivered in the Independent Tabernacle, in Philadelphia, on Sabbath Evening, the 18th December, 1814. For the Benefit of the Female Hospitable Society.* Philadelphia: Printed for the Society, 1815.

Brown, Clark. *The Utility of Moral and Religious Societies, and of the Masonick in Particular. A Sermon, Delivered in Putney, Vt. on the Anniversary of St. John the Baptist, June 24th, 1814.* Keene, N.H.: John Prentiss, 1814.

Brown, Everett, ed. *The Missouri Compromises and Presidential Politics, 1820–1825.* Reprint. New York: DaCapo, 1970.

Brown, Solyman. *An Address to the People of Litchfield County.* New Haven: T. G. Woodward, 1818.

———. *A Second Address to the People of Litchfield County.* New Haven: Flagg & Gould, 1818.

Brownson, Orestes. "Ultraism." *Boston Quarterly Review* 1 (July 1838): 377–84.

Bryant, William, and Thomas Voss, eds. *The Letters of William Cullen Bryant*, Vol. 1. New York: Fordham Univ. Press, 1975.

Buchan, William. *Advice to Mothers, on the Subject of Their Own Health; and of the Means of Promoting the Health, Strength, and Beauty of Their Offspring.* Boston: Joseph Bumstead, 1809.

Buckingham, Joseph T. *An Address Delivered Before the Massachusetts Charitable Mechanic Association, At the Public Celebration of Their Third Triennial Festival, December 21, 1815.* Boston: N.p., 1816.

———. *An Address Delivered Before the Massachusetts Charitable Mechanic Association, At the Celebration of Their Eighth Triennial Festival, October 7, 1830.* Boston: John Cotton, 1830.

Burder, Henry. *Mental Discipline; or, Hints on the Cultivation of Intellectual and Moral Habits: Addressed Particularly to Students in Theology and Young Preachers.* Andover: Flagg & Gould, 1827.

Butler, John. *A Sermon Delivered April 28, 1817, Before the Association for the Suppression of Intemperance, and the Promotion of Morality in the Town of Hanover, Massachusetts.* Boston: Lincoln & Edmands, 1817.

Byars, William, ed. *B. and M. Gratz: Merchants in Philadelphia, 1754–1798.* Jefferson City, Mo.: Hugh Stephens Printing Co., 1916.

Calhoun, John C. *The Papers of John C. Calhoun.* 20 vols. to date. Ed. Robert Meriwether *et al.* Columbia: Univ. of South Carolina Press, 1959–.

Calhoun, William. *An Address Delivered in Springfield, July 4, 1825, in Commemoration of American Independence.* Springfield: A. G. Tannatt & Co., 1825.

Cannon, Josiah. *A Sermon, Delivered in Gill, Massachusetts, August 6, 1817, Occasioned by Laudable Exertions and Liberal Donations, Recently Made, in Repairing and Ornamenting the House of God.* Greenfield: Denio & Phelps, 1817.

Carson, James. *An Oration, On the Past and Present State of Our Country; Delivered Before the Tammany Society, or Columbian Order, on Their Anniversary, the 12th of May, 1802.* Philadelphia: Robert Cochran, 1802.

Carter, Clarence, ed. *The Territorial Papers of the United States.* 26 vols. Washington, D.C.: GPO, 1934–62.

Cary, Alpheus. *An Address, Delivered Before the Massachusetts Charitable Mechanic Association, October 7, 1824.* Boston: Munroe & Francis, 1824.

Cary, Thomas. *A Sermon, Delivered to the First Religious Society in Newburyport, September 27, 1801.* Newburyport: Allen & Stickney, 1801.

[Cass, Lewis]. "Considerations on the Present State of the Indians, and Their Removal to the West of the Mississippi." *North American Review* 30 (1830): 62–121.

[———]. "Indians of North America." *North American Review* 22 (January 1826): 53–119.

———. *Inquiries, Respecting the History, Traditions, Languages, Manners, Customs, Religion, & of the Indians, Living within the United States.* Detroit, 1823.

[———]. "Remarks on the Policy and Practice of the United States and Great Britain in Their Treatment of the Indians." *North American Review* 24 (1827): 365–442.

A Catalogue of the Officers and Members of the Massachusetts Peace Society, Including Nine Branches and Auxiliaries, March 1, 1819. Cambridge, Mass.: Hilliard & Metcalf, 1819.

A Catalogue of the Officers and Members of the Massachusetts Peace Society. Including Nine Branches and Auxiliaries, March 1, 1820. Cambridge, Mass.: Hilliard & Metcalf, 1820.

Catharine Brown, The Converted Cherokee: A Missionary Drama, Founded on Fact. New Haven: S. Converse, 1819.

Chalmers, Thomas. *The Influence of Bible Societies, on the Temporal Necessities of the Poor.* New York: Kirk & Mercein, 1817.

Chandler, Amariah. *A Discourse; Delivered at Waitsfield, January 1, 1826.* Montpelier: E. P. Walton, 1826.

Channing, William Ellery. "Associations." *Christian Examiner* 7 (September 1829): 105–40.

Chapin, Seth, *Duty and Dependence of Sinners.* Boston: Samuel T. Armstrong, 1819.

Chapin, Stephen. *The Duty of Living for the Good of Posterity. A Sermon, Delivered at North-Yarmouth, December 22, 1820, in Commemoration of the Close of the Second Century From the Landing of the Forefathers of New-England.* Portland: Thomas Todd & Co., 1821.

———. *Moral Education. An Address, Delivered at China, June 25th, 1825, At the Installation of Central Lodge.* Waterville, Me.: William Hastings, 1825.

The Charlestown Association for the Reformation of Morals. Boston: Samuel T. Armstrong, 1813.

[Cheever, George]. *The Removal of the Indians.* Boston: Peirce & Williams, 1830.

"The Cherokee Case." *North American Review* 33 (July 1831): 136–53.

Chester, John. *Knowledge and Holiness the Sources of Morality. A Sermon, Delivered by Appointment, Before the Albany Moral Society, in the North Dutch Church, October 5th, 1821, and by request, on the following Sabbath, to the people of his charge.* Albany: E. & E. Hosford, 1821.

———. *A Sermon, Delivered before the Berkshire and Columbia Missionary Society, at Their Annual Meeting in Canaan, September 21st, 1813.* Hudson: A. Stoddard, 1813.

Chester, Leonard. *Federalism Triumphant in the Steady Habits of Connecticut Alone. Or, The Turnpike Road to a Fortune. A Comic Opera, Or, Political Farce in Six Acts, As Performed at the Theatres Royal and Aristocratic in Hartford and New Haven, October, 1801.* New York (?), 1802.

Chickering, Joseph. *A Sermon, Preached in Boston, Before the American Society for Educating Pious Youth for the Gospel Ministry, at their Second Anniversary, Oct. 15, 1817.* Dedham: Abel Alleyne, 1817.

Child, David. *An Oration Pronounced Before the Republicans of Boston, July 4, 1826, The Fiftieth Anniversary of American Independence*. Boston: Josiah B. Clough, 1826.

The Choice of a Free People. N.p., 1830.

Church, John. *The Progress of Divine Truth. A Discourse Delivered at the Eighth Annual Meeting of the New England Tract Society in Boston, May 29, 1822*. N.p., n.d.

A Circular Address from the Bible Society of Massachusetts. Boston: J. Belcher, 1809.

"Circular, Addressed to benevolent Ladies of the U. States." *Christian Advocate and Journal* 4 (December 25, 1829): 65–66.

Circular Addressed to the Members of the Massachusetts Society for Suppressing Intemperance. Boston: Samuel T. Armstrong, 1814.

A Circular Letter from the Massachusetts Peace Society. Cambridge, Mass.: Hilliard & Metcalf, 1816.

City Missionary Society, Boston. *Third Annual Report of the Boston Society for the Moral and Religious Instruction of the Poor; presented at Their Anniversary, Nov. 8th, 1819*. Boston, 1819.

"Civilization and Conversion of the Indians." *North American Review* 28 (April 1829): 354–68.

Claiborne, J. F. H., ed. *Life and Correspondence of John A. Quitman*. 2 vols. New York: Harper & Brothers, 1860.

Clark, Daniel A. "The Influence of a Good Taste Upon the Moral Affections." In Rev. Frederick Clark, ed., *The Works of Rev. Daniel A. Clark*, pp. 882–897. New York: Ivison, Blakeman, Taylor & Co., 1872.

Clarke, Samuel. *The Character and Reward of the Righteous. A Sermon, Occasioned by the Death of John Adams: Preached in Princeton, July 16, 1826*. Worcester: William Manning, 1826.

"Classes of American Society." *Christian Examiner and General Review* 9 (November 1830): 250–68; (December 1830): 269–90.

Clay, Henry. *Papers of Henry Clay*. Ed. James F. Hopkins, et al. 10 vols. to date. Lexington: Univ. of Kentucky Press, 1959–.

Codman, John. *A Discourse, Delivered before the Roxbury Charitable Society, at Their Anniversary, Sept. 24, 1817*. Boston: Munroe & Francis, 1817.

———. *An Oration on the Fiftieth Anniversary of American Independence*. Boston: Crocker & Brewster, 1826.

———. *The Hidden Life of a Christian, Exemplified in the Character and Writings of Mrs. Susannah H. Tucker, Late of Milton, Mass.* Boston: Perkins, Marvin & Co., 1835.

———. *Home Missions. A Sermon Delivered Before the Massachusetts Society for Promoting Christian Knowledge, in Park Street Church, Boston, May 31, 1826*. Boston: Crocker & Brewster, 1826.

Cogswell, William. *A Discourse, Delivered before the Dedham Auxiliary Society for the Suppression of Intemperance, at Their Anniversary Meeting, Feb. 2, 1818*. Dedham: Alleyne, 1818.

———. *Religious Liberty. A Sermon, Preached on the Day of the Annual Fast in Massachusetts, April 3, 1828.* Boston: Peirce & Williams, 1828.

Coke. "On the Profession of the Law." *Literary Cabinet* 1 (November 15, 1806): 11–14; (December 13, 1806): 17–20; (December 27, 1806): 27–30; (January 10, 1807): 35–38; (February 7, 1807): 41–43; (February 21, 1807): 50–51; (March 7, 1807): 59–61; (March 21, 1807): 67–68; (April 18, 1807): 83–84.

[Collins, F.]. *The Advantages and Disadvantages of Drunkenness; Containing A Variety of Plain and Important Maxims, Well Worthy of Being Remembered By Every Man in the Nation.* Cambridge, Mass.: Hilliard & Metcalf, 1821.

Colman, Henry. *A Discourse, Addressed to the Plymouth and Norfolk Bible Society, At Their First Annual Meeting in Hanover, 11 September 1816.* Boston: John Eliot, 1816.

———. *A Discourse on the Character Proper to a Christian Society, Delivered at the Opening of the Second Congregational Church in Lynn, Massachusetts, 30 April, 1823.* Cambridge, Mass.: Hilliard & Metcalf, 1823.

Colton, Calvin, ed. *The Private Correspondence of Henry Clay,* New York: A. S. Barnes & Co., 1856.

Colton, Simeon. *The Gospel a Message of Glad Tidings. A Sermon Preached Before the Union Charitable Society, at Their First Annual Meeting in Monson, September 8, 1818.* Hartford: Goodwin, 1818.

"Condition of the American Indians." *Eclectic Review* 52 (July 1830). 77–86.

"The Congregational Churches of Massachusetts." *Spirit of the Pilgrims* 1 February 1828): 57–74; (March 1828): 113–40.

Connecticut Education Society. *Annual Reports.* New Haven: N.p., 1820–26.

Constitution and Address of the American Society for Educating Pious Youth. N.p., [1816].

Constitution and Circular Address of the Female Society of Boston and its Vicinity, Auxiliary to the American Education Society. Boston: Ezra Lincoln, 1819.

Constitution of the American Bible Society, Formed by a Convention of Delegates. Held in the City of New York, May, 1816, Together With Their Address to the People of the United States. New York: G. F. Hopkins, 1816.

Constitution of the Massachusetts Society, for Suppressing Intemperance. And Report of the Board of Council, Prepared for the Anniversary of the Society, May 28, 1813. Boston: Samuel T. Armstrong, 1813.

The Constitution of the Massachusetts Society for the Suppression of Intemperance, as Revised and Altered, together with Their Annual Report for the Year 1818. Boston: Sewell Phelps, 1818.

"Conversation Between a Clergyman and His Parishioner." *Christian Spectator* 1 (June 1819): 292–96.

Cooke, Phinehas. *Reciprocal Obligations of Religion and Civil Government. A Discourse, Delivered at Concord, Before the Constituted Authorities of the State of New-Hampshire, on the Day of the Anniversary Election, June 2, 1825.* Concord, N.H.: Jacob B. Moore, 1825.

Cooper, James F., ed. *Correspondence of James Fenimore Cooper.* Vol. 1. New Haven: Yale Univ. Press, 1922.

Cooper, James Fenimore. *Notions of the Americans.* 2 vols. Reprint. New York: Frederick Ungar, 1963.

Cooper, Thomas. *Strictures Addressed to James Madison on the Celebrated Report of Wm. H. Crawford recommending the Intermarriage of Americans with the Indian Tribes.* Philadelphia: Jesper Harding, 1824.

Correspondence on the Subject of the Emigration of Indians, Between the 30th November, 1831, and 27th December, 1833, With Abstracts of Expenditures by Disbursing Agents, in the Removal and Subsistence of Indians. 5 vols. Washington, D.C.: Duff Green, 1835.

Cotton, Ward. *Causes and Effects of Female Regard to Christ, Illustrated in A Sermon. Delivered before the Female Society in Boylston, for the Aid of Foreign Missions, at their request, October 1, 1816.* Worcester: William Manning, 1817.

Cox, Isaac, ed. "Selections from the Torrence Papers." *Quarterly Publications of the Historical and Philosophical Society of Ohio* 1 (July–September 1906): 61–96; 2 (January–March 1907): 1–36; (July–September 1907): 93–120; 3 (July–September 1908): 63–102; 4 (July–September 1909): 91–138; 6 (April–June 1911): 1–44; (July–September 1911): 45–88.

Crafts, William. *Address Delivered Before the New-England Society of South-Carolina, On the 22d December 1820.* Charleston: Thomas B. Stephens, 1820.

———. *An Oration on the Influence of Moral Causes on National Character, delivered before the Phi Beta Kappa Society (at Cambridge, Mass.) on their Anniversary, 28 August, 1817.* Charleston: Courier Office, 1818.

The Crisis: On the Origin and Consequences of Our Political Dissensions. By a Citizen of Vermont. Albany: E. & E. Hosford, 1815.

The Crisis. To the People of Connecticut. Hartford, 1819.

Cross, Robert. *An Oration Delivered at Newburyport, on the Forty-sixth Anniversary of American Independence, July 4, 1822.* Newburyport: W. & J. Gilman, 1822.

Crosswell, Harry. *A Sober Appeal to the Christian Public.* New Haven: Flagg & Gray, 1819.

Cumming, John, ed. "A Missionary Among the Senecas: The Journal of Abel Bingham, 1822–1828." *New York History* 60 (April 1979): 157–93.

Cummings, Abraham. *The Harmony of Christians, The Glory of God. A Sermon, Delivered at Sullivan. (Me.) September, 1820.* Hallowell: Goodale, Glazier & Co., 1822.

Cummings, Rev. Asa, comp. *Memoir, Select Thoughts and Sermons of the Late Rev. Edward Payson, D.D. Pastor of the Second Church in Portland.* 3 vols. Philadelphia: William S. & Alfred Martien, 1859.

Cunningham, Nobel, Jr., ed. *Circular Letters of Congressmen to Their Constituents. 1789–1829.* 3 vols. Chapel Hill: Univ. of North Carolina Press, 1978.

Curtis, Charles P. *An Oration, Delivered on the Fourth of July, 1823, in Commemoration of American Independence, Before the Supreme Executive of the Commonwealth,* and the City Council and Inhabitants of the City of Boston. Boston: Joseph W. Ingraham, 1823.

Cutler, Julia, ed. *Life and Times of Ephraim Cutler: Prepared From His Journals and Correspondence.* Cincinnati: Robert Clarke & Co., 1890.

C. Y. A. "Fame" *Panoplist* 1 (January 1806): 349–52; (February 1806): 397–401.

———. "On the Execution of the Laws." *Panoplist* 2 (December 1806): 318–24.

———. "On the Reasonableness of an Immediate Repentance." *Connecticut Evangelical Magazine* 4 (March 1804): 345–48; (April 1804): 380–83; 5 (August 1804): 76–79; 6 (May 1806): 412–16; 7 (August 1806): 48–50; (December 1806): 205–7; (June 1807): 447–49.

———. "On the State of Literature in New England." *Panoplist* 2 (March 1807): 471–73; (April 1807): 522–24; (May 1807): 565–72.

Damon, David. *Address Delivered at Amesbury, August 2, 1829, Previous to the Organization of the Salisbury and Amesbury Society for Promoting Temperance.* Boston: Examiner Press, 1829.

———. *A Sermon, Preached at Charlton, Massachusetts, Sept. 14, 1826, At the Annual Meeting of the Auxiliary Bible Society in the County of Worcester.* Worcester: William Manning, 1826.

Dana, Daniel. *An Address, Delivered August 16, 1818, at a Public Meeting of the Sabbath Schools under the patronage of the Newburyport Sabbath School and Tract Society.* Newburyport: Gilmans, 1818.

———. *A Discourse Delivered May 22, 1804, Before the Members of the Female Charitable Society of Newburyport, Organized June 8, 1803.* Newburyport: Edmund Blunt, 1804.

———. *Evangelical Preaching is Rational Preaching. A Sermon, Delivered November 2, 1825, At the Ordination of the Rev. William K. Talbot, as Pastor of the Presbyterian Church in Nottingham-West.* Concord, N.H.: Isaac Hill, 1826.

———. *The Importance of the Christian Ministry. A Sermon Preached Before the American Society for Educating Pious Youth for the Gospel Ministry.* Andover: Flagg & Gould, 1818.

———. *The Importance of Virtue and Piety as Qualifications of Rulers: A Discourse Delivered March 31, 1805.* Newburyport: Edmund Blunt, 1805.

———. *A Sermon Delivered Before the Female Benevolent Society in Exeter, At Their Anniversary Meeting, July 30, 1820.* Newburyport: W. & J. Gilman, 1820.

Dana, Samuel. *Observations on Public Principles and Characters; With Reference to Recent Events.* Washington, D.C.: Gales & Seaton, 1820.

———. *A Sermon. Delivered to His Society, April 6, 1809, the Day of Annual Fast in Massachusetts.* Charlestown: Hastings, Etheridge & Bliss, 1809.

[———]. *A Specimen of Republican Institutions.* Philadelphia: H. Maxwell, 1802.

Danforth, Thomas. *A Discourse, Before the Humane Society, of the Commonwealth of Massachusetts, Boston, June 14, 1808.* N.p.: Russell and Cutler, 1808.

Darling, William. *An Oration, Delivered Before the Washington Benevolent Society of*

Canaan, Columbia County, February 22, 1816—Being the Birthday of the Immortal Washington. Hudson, N.Y.: William L. Stone, 1816.

Darneille, Isaac. *A Discourse or Lecture on the Subject of Civilizing the Indians.* Washington, D.C., 1826.

Dawes, Thomas. *An Address to the Massachusetts Peace Society, At Their Second Anniversary, December 25, 1817.* Boston: Joseph T. Buckingham, 1818.

Dawson, William C. *A Compilation of the Laws of the State of Georgia, Passed By the General Assembly, Since the Year 1819 to the Year 1829, Inclusive.* Milledgeville: Grantland & Orme, 1831.

Deane, Samuel. *A Discourse on the Good and Evil Principles of Human Nature, Delivered Before the First Congregational Society in Situate, on the Lord's Day, February 18, 1827.* Boston: Office of the Christian Register, 1827.

Diary of Charles Francis Adams. Vols. 2 and 3. Cambridge, Mass.: Belknap Press, 1964, 1968.

"Difficulties in Parishes." *Christian Examiner* 10 (September 1830): 1–20.

Dimmick, Luther F. *Intemperance: A Sermon, Delivered at the North Church in Newburyport, On the Occasion of the Publick Fast, April 1, 1824.* Newburyport: Charles Whipple, 1824.

A Directory, Containing Names, Places of Business, and Residence, of the Members of the Washington Benevolent Society, of Massachusetts, From its Commencement. Boston: C. Stebbins, 1813.

"Documents." *Ethnohistory* 4 (Spring 1957): 198–217.

Douglas, James. *Hints on Missions.* Boston: Samuel T. Armstrong, 1823.

Drake, Daniel. *An Oration on the Intemperance of Cities: Including Remarks on Gambling, Idleness, Fashion, and Sabbath-Breaking, Delivered in Philadelphia, January 24th, 1831.* Philadelphia: Griggs & Dickinson, 1831.

Dreadful Effects of Intemperance. Providence: D. White, 1827.

Dunham, Josiah. *Address Delivered in Publick, at the First Quarterly Meeting of the Windsor Union Sunday-School Society, January 1, 1819.* Windsor, Vt.: W. Spooner, 1819.

Dunlap, Andrew. *An Oration, Delivered at the Request of the Republicans of Boston, at Faneuil Hall, on the Fourth of July, 1822.* Boston: True & Greene, 1822.

Dwight, Sereno. *The Greek Revolution. An Address, Delivered in Park Street Church. Boston, on Thursday, April (?), and Repeated at the Request of the Greek Committee, in the Old South Church, on the Evening of April 14, 1824.* Boston: Crocker & Brewster, 1824.

———. *Thy Kingdom Come; A Sermon, Delivered in the Old South Church, Boston, before the Foreign Mission Society of Boston and the Vicinity, January 3, 1820.* Boston: Crocker & Brewster, 1820.

Dwight, Timothy. "Address to the Ministers of the Gospel of Every Denomination in the United States." *American Museum* 4 (July 1788): 30–33.

―――. *The Charitable Blessed. A Sermon, Preached in the First Church in New-Haven. August 8, 1810*. New Haven: Sidney's Press, 1810.

―――. *A Discourse on Some Events of the Last Century, Delivered in the Brick Church in New Haven, on Wednesday, January 7, 1801*. New Haven: Ezra Read, 1801.

―――. *Greenfield Hill*. Reprint. New York: AMS Press, 1970.

―――. *Sermons of Timothy Dwight*. 2 vols. New Haven: Hezekiah Howe, 1828.

―――. *Theology Explained and Defended. In a Series of Sermons*. 4 vols. New York: Harper & Brothers, 1849.

East, T. *The Memoirs of the Late Miss Emma Humphries, of Frome, England, with a Series of Letters to Young Ladies on the Influence of Religion, in the Formation of Their Moral and Intellectual Character*. Boston: Samuel T. Armstrong, 1819.

Eastern Auxiliary Foreign Mission Society of Rockingham County, New Hampshire. *First Annual Report. Presented at Kingston, June 22, 1826*. Portsmouth: T. H. Miller and C. W. Brewster, 1826.

Eaton, Peter. *A Sermon, Delivered at Topsfield, (Mass.) June 20, 1815, Before the Moral Society of Boxford and Topsfield*. Andover: Flagg & Gould, 1816.

Edwards, Bela Bates, ed. *Memoir of Elias Cornelius*. Boston: Perkins & Marvin, 1833.

Edwards, Justin. *Joy in Heaven Over the Penitent. A Sermon, Delivered in Park Street Church, Before the Penitent Females' Refuge Society, on the Evening of Sabbath, December 18, 1825*. Boston: T. R. Marvin, 1826.

―――. *A Sermon, Delivered at the Fourth Anniversary, of the Auxiliary Education Society, of the Young Men of Boston, February 12, 1823*. Andover: Flagg & Gould, 1823.

Eichelberger, Lewis. *Two Sermons on National Blessings and Obligations*. Winchester, Va.: Samuel H. Davis, 1830.

Ellingwood, John W. *The Duty of Using Means for the Reformation of Immoral Persons. A Sermon, Delivered at Bath, May 9, 1815, Before "The Bath Society for Discountenancing and Suppressing Public Vices;" Also, at Union, May 31, 1815 . . . Before "The Union Society for Discountenancing and Suppressing Public Vices."* Boston: N. Willis, 1815.

―――. *Nothing Too Precious for Christ. A Sermon Delivered in Norridgewock, June 25, 1817; Before the Maine Missionary Society, at Their Tenth Annual Meeting*. Hallowell: N. Cheever, 1817.

Ellis, Ferdinand. *A Discourse, Adapted to the Present Situation of Our National Concerns, Preached at Marblehead, Mass. July 23, 1812, Appointed by the Executive of this Commonwealth as a Day of Fasting, Humiliation and Prayer*. Salem: Warwick Palfray, Jr., 1812.

Elmer, Gen. Ebenezer. *Oration Delivered Before the Washington Whig Society and Other Citizens of the County of Cumberland (N.J.) April 11, 1815*. Philadelphia: Printed for the Society, 1815.

Ely, Ezra Stiles. "The Duty of Christian Freemen to Elect Christian Rulers; A

Discourse on the Fourth of July, 1827, in the Seventh Presbyterian Church, in Philadelphia." In Joseph Blau, ed. *American Philosophic Addresses, 1700–1900*, pp. 551–62. New York: Columbia Univ. Press, 1946.

———. "Preservation and Improvement of the Indians." *Philadelphian*, February 12, 1830.

Ely, Zebulon. *Revelation Necessary to Salvation. A Sermon, Delivered in Thompson, At a Meeting of the Foreign Mission Society of Windham County, Oct. 4, 1815*. Hartford: Peter B. Gleason, 1815.

———. *The Wisdom and Duty of Magistrates. A Sermon, Preached at the General Election, May 10th, 1804*. Hartford: Hudson & Goodwin, 1804.

Emerson, Andrew. *An Oration Delivered at Portland, July 5, 1824, On the Celebration of the 48th Anniversary of American Independence*. Portland: Adams & Paine, 1824.

Emerson, George B. *An Address, Delivered at the Opening of the Boston Mechanics' Institution, February 7, 1827*. Boston: Hilliard, Gray, Little & Wilkins, 1827.

Emerson, Joseph, ed. *Writings of Miss Fanny Woodbury*. Boston: Samuel T. Armstrong, 1816.

Emerson, Ralph Waldo. "New England Reformers," in Lewis Mumford, ed., *Ralph Waldo Emerson: Essays and Journals*, pp. 365–82. New York: Doubleday, 1968.

Emerson, Reuben. *A Sermon, Delivered at S. Reading, November 23, 1820. Being a Day of Public Thanksgiving Throughout the Commonwealth*. Boston: True & Weston, 1820.

An Enquiry into the Causes of the Present Commercial Embarrassments in the United States, with a Plan of Reform of the Circulating Medium. N.p.: 1819.

Etheridge, Samuel. *The Christian Orator; or, A Collection of Speeches, Delivered on Public Occasions before Religious Benevolent Societies*. Charlestown: Samuel Etheridge, 1818.

Evans, Elizabeth, ed. *Alexander Hill Everett: Prose Pieces and Correspondence*. Saint Paul: John Colet Press, 1975.

Evarts, Jeremiah, Jedidiah Morse, and Samuel Worcester. "An Address to the Christian Public, Prepared and Published by a Committee of the American Board of Commissioners for Foreign Missions." *Panoplist* 7 (November 1811): 241–47.

———. "An Address to the Christian Public on the Subject of Missions to the Heathen and Translations of the Scriptures." *Panoplist* 8 (November 1812): 249–56; 9 (October 1813): 315–28.

[Evarts, Jeremiah]. "Address to the Public." *Panoplist* 11 (January 1815): 1–6.

———. "Address to the Public, at the Commencement of a New Year." *Panoplist* 13 (January 1817): 1–7.

———. *An Account of Memorials Presented to Congress During Its Last Session, By Numerous Friends of Their Country and Its Institutions: Praying that the Mails May Not be Transported, Nor Post-Offices Kept Open, on the Sabbath*. Boston: T. R. Marvin, 1829.

———. "American Missionaries at the Sandwich Islands." *North American Review* 58 (January 1828): 59–111.

———. *Essays on the Present Crisis in the Condition of the American Indian.* Philadelphia: Thomas Kite, 1830.

———. *An Oration, Delivered at Charlestown, (Mass.) On the Fourth of July, 1812, in Commemoration of American Independence.* Charlestown: Samuel Etheridge, 1812.

———. *The Logic and the Law of Col. Johnson's Report to the Senate, on Sabbath Mails.* Utica: G. S. Wilson, 1829.

[———]. *The Removal of the Indians. An Article from the "American Monthly Magazine"; An Examination of an Article in the "North American Review," and an Exhibition of the Advancement of the Southern Tribes in Civilization and Christianity.* Boston: Peirce & Williams, 1830.

———. *Review of American Unitarianism.* Boston: Samuel T. Armstrong, n.d.

———. "Review of the Dorchester Controversy." *Panoplist* 10 (June 1814): 256–81; (July 1814): 289–307.

———. "Thoughts on Publishing Charitable Donations." *Panoplist* 12 (February 1816): 30–33.

Everett, Alexander Hill. *America, or a General Survey of the Political Situation of the Several Powers of the Western Continent with Conjectures on Their Future Prospects.* Reprint. New York: Augustus Kelley, 1970.

———. *The Conduct of the Administration.* Boston: Stimson & Clapp, 1832.

———. "Sunday Mails." *North American Review* 31 (July 1830): 154–67.

Everett, Edward. *An Address Delivered at Charlestown, August 1, 1826, in Commemoration of John Adams and Thomas Jefferson.* Boston: William L. Lewis, 1826.

———. *An Oration Delivered at Concord, April the Nineteenth, 1825.* Boston: Cummings, Hilliard & Co., 1825.

———. "The Tariff Question," *North American Review* 19 (July 1824): 223–53.

Everett, John. *An Oration on the Prospects of the Young Men of America.* Boston: Wells & Lilly, 1818.

Ewell, Thomas. *Letters to Ladies, Detailing Important Information, Concerning Themselves and Infants.* Philadelphia: N.p., 1817.

Ewing, Thomas. "Autobiography of Thomas Ewing." *Ohio Archaeological and Historical Quarterly* 22 (1912): 126–204.

Examination of the Controversy Between Georgia and the Creeks. New York, 1825.

"An Examination of the Indian Question." *Washington Globe,* March 31, 1832.

Examination of the Relations Between the Cherokees and the Government of the United States. New York, 1829.

An Explanation of the Views of the Society for Employing the Female Poor. Boston: John Cotton, 1826.

Explanation of the Views of the Society for Employing the Poor. Boston, 1820.

An Expose of the Rise and Proceedings of the American Bible Society, During the Thirteen Years of Its Existence. By a Member. New York, 1830.

An Exposition of the Principles and Views of the Middling Interest, in the City of Boston. Boston, 1822.

Extracts Concerning the Importance of Religion and Public Worship to Civil Society. Hallowell: E. Goodale, 1820.

Fairchild, Jotham. *An Oration, Pronounced at the Meeting-house in the Vicinity of Dartmouth College, on the Fourth of July, 1811.* Hanover: Charles Spear, 1811.

Farkas, Alexander. *Journey in North America.* Reprint. Philadelphia: American Philosophical Society, 1977.

Farley, Stephen. *Letters Addressed to the Rev. Noah Worcester.* Windsor, Vt.: Thomas Pomroy, 1813.

Fay, Warren. *The Obligations of Christians to the Heathen World. A Sermon, Delivered at the Old South Church in Boston, before the Auxiliary Foreign Mission Society of Boston and Vicinity, at the Annual Meeting, January 3, 1825.* Boston: Crocker & Brewster, 1825.

Felch, Walton. *The Manufacturer's Pocket-Piece; or the Cotton-Mill Moralized.* Newburyport: Samuel Allen, 1816.

Fessenden, William. *An Oration, Delivered Before the Young Men of Portland, July 4, 1827.* Portland: James Adams, Jr., 1827.

Field, David D. *The Sabbath. A Sermon, Preached at Hartford, on the Evening of May 15, 1816. Before the Connecticut Society for the Promotion of Good Morals.* Hartford: Benjamin Hamlen, 1816.

Fifield, Dr. Noah. *An Address Delivered Before the Society for the Reformation of Morals, in Weymouth and Braintree, At Their Annual Meeting, April 13, 1818.* Boston: Parmenter & Norton, 1818.

Fifteenth Annual Report of the Massachusetts Society for the Suppression of Intemperance, with Resolutions Passed at a Public Meeting Held March 8, 1830. Boston: N. S. & S. G. Simpkins, 1830.

Finney, Charles G. *Lectures on Revivals of Religion.* Reprint. Cambridge, Mass.: Belknap Press, 1960.

The First Annual Report of the American Society for Promoting the Civilization and General Improvement of the Indian Tribes in the United States. New Haven: S. Converse, 1824.

Fisk, Elisha. *A Sermon, Preached in Braintree. Before the Norfolk Auxiliary Society for the Education of Pious Youth for the Gospel Ministry, at Their Third Annual Meeting, June 9, 1819.* Dedham: H. & W. H. Mann, 1819.

Fisk, Wilbur. *Future Rewards and Punishments. The Substance of a Discourse Delivered Before the New England Conference of Methodist Ministers, Providence, June 17, 1823.* New York: T. Mason & G. Lane, 1836.

Fitch, Eleazar. *National Prosperity Perpetuated: A Discourse, Delivered in the Chapel of Yale College; on the Day of the Annual Thanksgiving, November 29, 1827.* New Haven: Treadway & Adams, 1828.

Fitzpatrick, John, ed. *The Autobiography of Martin Van Buren*. Washington, D.C.: GPO, 1920.

Fletcher, Nathaniel. *A Discourse, Delivered at Kennebunk, May 6th, 1827, On the Following Subject: How Far Unanimity in Religious Opinions is Necessary in Order to Christian Communion*. Kennebunk: James K. Remick, 1827.

Flint, Abel. *A Charity Sermon, Delivered in the North Presbyterian Meeting-house in Hartford, on the Evening of October 7th, 1810; By Desire of the Female Beneficent Society*. Hartford: Charles Hosmer, 1810.

———. *A Discourse, Occasioned by the News of Peace, Delivered at the South Meeting-house in Hartford, February 14, 1815*. Hartford: Sheldon & Goodwin, 1815.

———. *A Sermon, Preached at the Anniversary Election, Hartford, May 9, 1816*. Hartford: George Goodwin & Sons, 1816.

Flint, Joshua. *An Address Delivered Before the Massachusetts Society for the Suppression of Intemperance, May 29, 1828*. Boston: Bowles & Dearborn, 1828.

Flint, Timothy. *Recollections of the Last Ten Years*. Reprint. New York: Alfred A. Knopf, 1932.

Foster, Edmund. *A Sermon, Preached Before His Excellency the Governor. His Honor the Lieutenant-Governor, and the Two Branches of the Legislature of Massachusetts, May 27, 1812, Being the Day of Annual Election*. Boston: Russell & Cutler, 1812.

Foster, Festus. *An Oration, Pronounced at Hardwick, July 4th, 1812, Being the Thirty-sixth Anniversary of American Independence*. Brookfield: E. Merriam & Co., 1812.

Frelinghuysen, Theodore. *Speech of Mr. Frelinghuysen, of New Jersey, Delivered in the Senate of the United States, April 6, 1830, on the Bill for an Exchange of Lands with the Indians Residing in any of the States or Territories, and For Their Removal West of the Mississippi*. Washington, D.C.: Office of the National Journal, 1830.

French, Jonathan. *A Discourse, Delivered in the South Parish in Andover, December 1, 1801, on the Anniversary Thanksgiving in Massachusetts*. Newburyport: E. M. Blunt, 1804.

Frisbie, Levi. "Professor Frisbie's Inaugural Address." *North American Review* 6 (January 1818): 224–41.

Full and Authentic Report of the Debates in Faneuil Hall, Dec. 31, Jan. 1, & 12, 1821–22; on Changing the Form of Government of the Town of Boston. Boston: William Emmons, 1822.

Fuller, Timothy. *Address, Delivered at the Eleventh Anniversary of the Massachusetts Peace Society, December 25, 1826*. Boston: C. S. Hamilton, 1827.

———. *An Oration Pronounced at Lexington, Massachusetts, on the Fourth of July, A.D. 1814, By Request of the Republican Citizens of Middlesex County, Being the Thirty-eighth Anniversary of American Independence*. Boston: Rowe & Hooper, 1814.

[Gaines, George S.]. "Removal of the Choctaws." Alabama State Department of Archives and History, *Historical and Patriotic Series* 10 (1928): 9–24.

Gallaudet, Thomas. *An Address, Delivered at a Meeting for Prayer, with Reference to the Sandwich Mission, in the Brick Church in Hartford, October 11, 1819*. Hartford: Lincoln & Stone, 1819.

———. *A Sermon Delivered at the Opening of the Connecticut Asylum for the Education and Instruction of Deaf and Dumb Persons*. Hartford: Hudson & Co., 1817.

Gallison, John. *Address, Delivered at the Fourth Anniversary of the Massachusetts Peace Society, December 25, 1819*. Cambridge, Mass.: Hilliard & Metcalf, 1820.

"Georgia Controversy." *Southern Review* 2 (November 1828): 541–82.

Giles, John. *An Address, Delivered Before the Republican Citizens of Newburyport, and the Neighbouring Towns, . . . on the Fourth of July, 1809*. Newburyport: W. & J. Gilman, 1809.

Gillet, Eliphalet. *Evils of Intemperance. A Sermon Preached at Hallowell, on the Day of the Annual Fast in Maine, April 12, 1821*. Hallowell: Goodale, Glazier & Co., 1821.

———. *Thanksgiving. A Discourse, Delivered at Hallowell, on the Day of the Thanksgiving in Massachusetts, Dec. 2, 1819*. Hallowell: E. Goodale, 1819.

Gillett, Timothy. *Causes, Which Render the Gospel Ministry Ineffectual, Stated and Remedies Suggested. A Sermon, Delivered at the Installation of the Rev. Saul Clark, A.M. Over the Congregational Church in Barkhamsted, January 13, 1819*. New Haven: A. H. Maltby & Co., 1819.

———. *Charity Profitable; or, God a Surety for the Poor. A Sermon, Delivered Before the Female Charitable Society, in Guilford, January 6, 1813*. New Haven: Oliver Steele, 1813.

Gilman, Samuel. *Address Delivered at the Anniversary Meeting of the South-Carolina Society for the Promotion of Temperance, May 18th, 1831*. Charleston: A. E. Miller, 1831.

Gilmer, George. *Sketches of Some of the First Settlers of Upper Georgia, of the Cherokees, and the Author*. New York: D. Appleton & Co., 1855.

Gleason, Benjamin. *Anniversary Oration, In Commemoration of American Independence, Pronounced Before the Republican Citizens of Charlestown, July 5, 1819*. Charlestown: T. Green, 1819.

Gleason, Joseph, Jr. *An Oration, Pronounced on the Thirtieth Anniversary of American Independence, Before the Young Democratic Republicans, of the Town of Boston, at the Second Baptist Meeting House, July 4, 1806*. Boston: Oliver & Munroe, 1806.

Goff, John, ed. "Land Cessions of the Cherokee Nation in Tennessee, Mississippi, North Carolina, Georgia, Alabama, 1785–1835." In *Cherokee and Creek Indians*. New York: Garland Publishing Co., 1974.

Gold, Theodore, comp. *Historical Records of the Town of Cornwall, Litchfield County, Connecticut*. Hartford: Case, Lockwood & Brainerd Co., 1877.

Goldman, Perry, and James Young, eds. *United States Congressional Directories, 1789–1840*. New York: Columbia Univ. Press, 1974.

Goodale, Ezekial, comp. *Extracts Concerning the Importance of Religion and Public Worship to Civil Society*. Hallowell: E. Goodale, 1820.

Gray, Thomas. *A Sermon, On the Religious Opinions of the Present Day, Delivered in Two Parts, Morning and Afternoon, on Lord's Day, Sept. 23, 1821, to the Church and Congregation on Jamaica Plain, Roxbury.* Boston: R. M. Peck, 1822.

Green, Beriah. *A Sermon, Preached in Poultney, June 29, 1826, at the First Annual Meeting of the Rutland County Foreign Missionary Society.* Castleton, Vt.: Published by the Society, 1826.

Greene, Albert. *Oration Pronounced on the Fifty-first Anniversary of American Independence, Before the Young Men of the Town of Providence, July 4, 1827.* Providence: Smith & Parmenter, 1827.

Greene, Evarts B., and Clarence Alvord, eds. *The Governors' Letter-Books, 1818–1834.* Springfield: Illinois State Historical Society, 1909.

Greenwood, Francis. *A Sermon, Delivered on the Twenty-fifth Anniversary of the Boston Female Asylum, September 23, 1825.* Boston: Christian Register, 1825.

Gregg, Daniel. *An Address Delivered Before the Newton Temperance Society, July 4, 1828.* Boston: True & Greene, 1828.

Griffin, Edward D. *An Address, Delivered to the Class of Graduates of Williams College.* Pittsfield: Phinehas Allen, 1822.

―――. *The Kingdom of Christ: A Missionary Sermon, Preached Before the General Assembly of the Presbyterian Church, in Philadelphia, May 23d, 1805.* Greenfield: John Denio, 1808.

Griscom, John. *A Discourse, on the Importance of Character and Education. In the United States.* New York: Mahlon Day, 1823.

Griswold, Alexander. *A Sermon, on the Blessedness of Charitable Giving; Preached Before the Prayer-Book and Tract Association, of Trinity Church, Boston.* Boston: R. P. & C. Williams, 1817.

Grosvenor, Cyrus. *National Blessings of Christianity. A Discourse Delivered in the Meeting House of the First Baptist Church and Society, Union Street, Boston, on the Day of Public Thanksgiving, November 26, 1829.* Boston: True & Greene, 1829.

Grout, Jonathan. *An Oration, Delivered in Heath, on the Anniversary of American Independence, July the 4th, 1803.* Greenfield: John Denio, 1803.

Gurley, Ralph. *A Discourse, Delivered on the Fourth of July, 1825, in the City of Washington.* Washington, D.C.: Gales & Seaton, 1825.

Haig, James. *An Oration, Delivered on the Fifth of July, 1824, Before the Cincinnati and Revolution Societies.* Charleston: A. E. Miller, 1824.

Hamilton, J. G. DeRoulhac, ed. *The Papers of Thomas Ruffin.* 4 vols. Reprint. New York: AMS Press, 1973.

Hamilton, James A. *Reminiscences of James A. Hamilton; or, Men and Events, at Home and Abroad, During Three Quarters of a Century.* New York: Charles Scribner & Co., 1869.

Hamlin, L. Belle, ed. "Selections from the Follett Papers." *Quarterly Publication of the Historical and Philosophical Society of Ohio* 5 (April–June 1910): 33–76.

Handlin, Oscar, and Mary Handlin, eds. *The Popular Sources of Political Authority: Documents on the Massachusetts Constitution of 1780.* Cambridge, Mass.: Belknap Press, 1966.

Happy Poverty, or The Story of Poor Blind Ellen. Hartford: Hudson, 1817.

Harrington, Joseph. *Address, Delivered at Roxbury, Before the Roxbury Auxiliary Society for the Suppression of Intemperance, June 30, 1820.* Boston: Joseph T. Buckingham, 1820.

Harvey, Joseph. *A Sermon, Preached at Litchfield, Before the Foreign Mission Society of Litchfield County, at Their Annual Meeting, February 15, 1815.* New Haven: Hudson & Woodward, 1815.

———. *The Banner of Christ Set Up. A Sermon Delivered at the Inauguration of the Rev. Hermon [sic] Daggett, as Principal of the Foreign Mission School in Cornwall, Connecticut, May 6, 1818.* Elizabethtown, N.J.: Edson Hart, 1819.

Haswell, Charles. *Reminiscences of New York by an Octogenarian.* New York: Harper & Brothers, 1896.

Hawes, Joel. "What Hath God Wrought!" *A Sermon, Delivered in Hartford, on the Last Sabbath of the Year, 1822.* Hartford: W. Hudson & L. Skinner, 1823.

Hawley, Zerah. *A Journal of a Tour Through Connecticut, Massachusetts, New-York, the North Part of Pennsylvania and Ohio.* New Haven: S. Converse, 1822.

Hazard, Caroline, ed. *Nailer Tom's Diary: The Journal of Thomas B. Hazard of Kingstown, Rhode Island, 1778 to 1840.* Boston: The Merrymount Press, 1930.

Herttell, Thomas. *Remarks on the Law of Imprisonment for Debt; Showing its Unconstitutionality, and Its Demoralizing Influence on the Community.* New York: Gould & Banks, 1823.

Heywood, Levi. *An Oration, Delivered at Worcester, Mass. on the Anniversary of American Independence, July 4th, 1810.* Worcester: M. Rogers, 1810.

Hildreth, Hosea. *Two Discourses on the Most Important Duties of Townsmen.* Exeter: J. & P. Williams, 1824.

Hill, B. T., ed. *The Diary of Isaiah Thomas, 1805–1828.* 2 vols. Worcester: American Antiquarian Society, 1909.

Hill, Benjamin. *The Moral Responsibility of Civil Rulers: A Sermon, Addressed to the Legislature of the State of Connecticut, at the Annual Election in Hartford, May 6, 1829.* New Haven: Baldwin & Treadway, 1829.

Hilliard, Francis. *An Address, Delivered Before the Lowell Temperance Society, Jan. 2, 1831.* Lowell: T. Billings, 1831.

Hilliard, William. *An Address, Delivered Before the Massachusetts Charitable Mechanic Association, October 4, 1827.* Cambridge, Mass.: Hilliard, Metcalf & Co., 1827.

Hines, William. *An Address, Delivered at the Methodist Chapel, in Norwich, December 22, 1827, At the Request of the Norwich Falls Society for the Promotion of Temperance.* Norwich: J. Dunham, 1828.

Hinton, John. *The Means of a Religious-Revival.* Boston: Lincoln and Edmands, 1831.

Hoadly, Loammi. *An Address, Delivered at the Union Celebration of Independence, at Sutton, Mass. July 5, 1824.* Worcester: William Manning, 1824.

Hodgson, Adam. *Remarks During a Journey Through North America in the Years 1819, 1820, and 1821.* New York: Samuel Whiting, 1823.

Holley, Orville. *An Oration on the Permanency of Republican Institutions; Delivered at Troy, July 5, 1824.* Troy, N.Y.: Tuttle & Richards, 1824.

Holmes, Abiel. *A Discourse, Delivered at the Opening of the New Almshouse in Cambridge.* Cambridge, Mass.: Hilliard & Metcalf, 1818.

Howard Benevolent Society, Organized in Boston, June 1, 1812, Incorporated, February 16, 1818. Boston: Henry Bowen, 1822.

Hoyt, William, ed. *The Papers of Archibald D. Murphey.* 2 vols. Raleigh: E. M. Uzzell & Co., 1914.

Hubbard, Henry. *An Oration, Delivered at Pittsfield, on the Fourth of July, 1826, Being the Fiftieth Anniversary of the Independence of the United States.* Pittsfield: J. M. Beckwith, 1826.

Hughs, Mrs. Mary. *An Affectionate Address to the Poor.* Boston: Wells & Lilly, 1820.

Humphrey, Heman. *Indian Rights & Our Duties. An Address Delivered at Amherst, Hartford, etc., December 1829.* Amherst: J. S. & C. Adams, 1830.

———. *On Doing Good to the Poor.* Pittsfield: Phinehas Allen, 1818.

———. *Parallel Between Intemperance and the Slave Trade. An Address Delivered at Amherst College, July 4, 1828.* Amherst: J. S. and C. Adams, 1828.

———. *The Promised Land. A Sermon, Delivered at Goshen, (Conn.) at the Ordination of the Rev. Messrs. Hiram Bingham & Asa Thurston, as Missionaries to the Sandwich Islands, Sept. 29, 1819.* Boston: Samuel T. Armstrong, 1819.

———. "Union is Strength." In *Miscellaneous Discourses and Reviews,* pp. 9–32. Amherst: J. S. & C. Adams, 1874.

Hunt, Ebenezer. *Address, Delivered Before the Danvers Auxiliary Society for the Suppression of Intemperance, At the Annual Meeting, April 5, 1827.* Salem: Office of the Essex Register, 1827.

Hunt, Gaillard, ed. *The Writings of James Madison.* 10 vols. New York: G. P. Putnam's, 1910.

Hunter, William. *Oration Pronounced Before the Citizens of Providence, on the Fourth of July, 1826, Being the Fiftieth Anniversary of American Independence.* Providence: Smith & Parmenter, 1826.

Huntington, Daniel. *An Intolerant Spirit, Hostile to the Interests of Society: A Sermon, Delivered . . . on the Anniversary Election, May 29, 1822.* Boston: Russell & Gardner, 1822.

Ide, Jacob, ed. *The Works of Nathaniel Emmons, D.D., Late Pastor of the Church in Franklin, Mass., with a Memoir of His Life.* 6 vols. Boston: Crocker & Brewster, 1842.

"Imprisonment for Debt." *North American Review* 32 (April 1831): 490–508.

"Indian Affairs." *American Annual Register* 5 (1829–30): 43–61.

"Indian Controversy." *Boston Christian Examiner and General Review* 9 (September 1830): 107–60.

"The Indian Question." *Albany Argus Extra*, June 19, 1830.

"The Indians, and Our Relations with Them." *Boston Quarterly Review* 2 (April 1839): 228–59.

Ingersoll, Charles J. "A Discourse Concerning the Influence of America on the Mind: Being the Annual Oration Delivered Before the American Philosophical Society, at the University of Pennsylvania, on the 18th October, 1823." In Joseph Blau, ed. *American Philosophic Addresses, 1700–1900*, pp. 20–59. New York: Columbia Univ. Press, 1946.

Interesting Correspondence. Letter from Mr. Richard Rush, on the Policy of the American System. Washington, D.C.: National Journal, 1830.

Jackson, Donald, ed. *Letters of the Lewis and Clark Expedition with Related Documents, 1783–1854.* 2 vols. Urbana: Univ. of Illinois Press, 1978.

James, William. *The Moral Responsibility of the American Nation: A Discourse, Delivered in Rochester, July 4, 1828.* Rochester: E. Peck & Co., 1828.

Jameson, J. Franklin, ed. "Correspondence of John C. Calhoun." *American Historical Association Annual Report for 1899.* Vol. 2. Washington, D.C. GPO, 1900.

Jarvis, Russell. *An Oration, Delivered Before the Republicans of Boston, on the Fourth of July, 1823.* Boston: True & Greene, 1823.

Jarvis, Samuel. "A Discourse on the Religion of the Indian Tribes of North America: Delivered before the New-York Historical Society, December 20, 1819." In *New-York Historical Society Collections*. Vol. 3, pp. 181–268. New York: E. Bliss & E. White, 1821.

———. *A Sermon, Preached Before the Auxiliary Education Society of the Young Men of Boston, January 23, 1822, on Occasion of Their Third Anniversary.* Boston: Joseph W. Ingraham, 1822.

Jarvis, William. *The Republican; or, A Series of Essays on the Principles and Policy of Free States. Having a Particular Reference to the United States of America and the Individual States.* Pittsfield: Phinehas Allen, 1820.

Jenkins, Joseph. *An Address Delivered before the Massachusetts Charitable Mechanick Association, December 17, 1818, Being the Anniversary of the Choice of Officers, and Fourth Triennial Celebration of their Public Festival.* Boston: Munroe & Francis, 1819.

"Jeremiah Evarts." *American Quarterly Register* 4 (November 1831): 73–85.

Johns, Evan. *The Happiness of American Christians. A Thanksgiving Sermon, Preached on Thursday the 24th of November 1803.* Hartford: Hudson & Goodwin, 1804.

———. *A Sermon Preached at Northampton, Before the Foreign Missionary Society, of Northampton and the Neighboring Towns, at their First Meeting, March 31, 1812.* Northampton: William Butler, 1812.

Johnson, William. "A Young Man's Journal of 1800–1813." *New Jersey Historical Society Proceedings, n.s. 7 (1922): 49–59, 122–34, 211–26, 305–14; 8 (1923): 150–54, 219–25, 313–20.

Johnson and Graham's Lessee v. William M'Intosh. 8 Wheaton 543 (1823).

Journal of Debates and Proceedings in the Massachusetts Constitutional Convention, 1820–1821. Reprint. New York: DaCapo Press, 1970.

The Juvenile Story Teller, A Collection of Original Moral Tales. New Haven: Sidney's Press, 1817.

Kappler, Charles, comp. Indian Affairs: Laws and Treaties. 2 vols. Washington, D.C.: GPO, 1904.

K. C. "Sketch of a Plan for Instructing the Indians." Panoplist 12 (April 1816): 150–52.

———. "What are the Motives Which Should Induce the Churches in the United States to Attempt the Conversion and Civilization of the Indians?" Panoplist 12 (March 1816): 118–22.

Keep, John. Nature and Operations of Christian Benevolence. A Sermon, Delivered Oct. 21, 1818, Before the Directors of the Domestic Missionary Society, of Massachusetts Proper, at their first meeting in Northampton. Northampton: Thomas W. Shepard & Co., 1818.

Kelly, Albert. An Oration, Delivered at Portland, July 4, 1825. Portland: Printed at the Mirror Office, 1825.

Kennedy, John P. Quodlibet. Philadelphia: Lea & Blanchard, 1840.

Kent, William, ed. Memoirs and Letters of James Kent. Reprint. New York: DaCapo, 1970.

Kilpatrick, Jack, and Anna Kilpatrick, eds. New Echota Letters: Contributions of Samuel A. Worcester to the Cherokee Phoenix. Dallas: Southern Methodist Univ. Press, 1968.

Kimball, David. The Obligation and Disposition of Females to Promote Christianity. An Address, Delivered June 15, 1819, Before the Female Education and Charitable Societies, in the First Parish in Ipswich. Newburyport: Ephraim W. Allen, 1819.

King, Charles, ed. The Life and Correspondence of Rufus King. 6 vols. Reprint. New York: DaCapo, 1971.

King, Thomas. An Oration, Delivered on the 4th of July, 1821, Before the Tammany, Hibernian, Stone Cutters, Tailors, and Cordwainers Societies, in the Mulberry-Street Church. New York: B. Young, 1821.

Kittredge, Jonathan. An Address, Upon the Effects of Ardent Spirits, Delivered in the Town Hall of Lyme, N.H., January 8, 1827. Canandaigua, N.Y.: Bemis, Morse & Ward, 1827.

Knapp, Samuel. An Address Delivered in Chauncey Place Church, Before the Young Men of Boston, August 2, 1826, in Commemoration of the Death of Adams and Jefferson. Boston: Ingraham & Hewes, 1826.

Knowles, James. Perils and Safeguards of American Liberty. Address, Pronounced July 4,

1828, in the Second Baptist Meetinghouse in Boston, At the Religious Celebration of the Anniversary of American Independence. By the Baptist Churches and Societies in Boston. Boston: Lincoln & Edmands, 1828.

———. *Spiritous Liquors Pernicious and Useless. An Address, Delivered in the Second Baptist Meeting House, Boston, April 9, 1829, The Day of the Annual Fast*. Boston: Lincoln & Edmands, 1829.

Ladd, William. *Address, Delivered at the Tenth Anniversary of the Massachusetts Peace Society, December 25, 1825*. Boston: Isaac R. Butts & Co., 1826.

Lathrop, Joseph. *The Angel Preaching the Everlasting Gospel. A Sermon Delivered in Springfield, April 21st, 1812, at the Institution of a Society for the Encouragement of Foreign Missions*. Springfield: Thomas Dickman, 1812.

———. *The Importance of Female Influence in the Support of Religion. A Sermon, Delivered to a Charitable Female Association in West-Springfield, May 15, 1810*. Springfield: Thomas Dickman, 1810.

———. *A Sermon, Preached in Putney, (Vt.) June 25, 1807. At the Ordination of Reverend Elisha D. Andrews, over the Congregational Church and Charitable Christian Society, in That Town*. Brattleboro: William Fessenden, 1807.

———. *A Sermon, Preached in Springfield, Before the Bible Society, and the Foreign Mission Society, in the County of Hampden, at Their Annual Meeting, August 31, 1814*. Springfield: Thomas Dickman, 1814.

———. *The Signs of Perilous Times. A Sermon, Delivered at the Public Fast, in West-Springfield, April 7, 1808*. Springfield: Henry Brewer, 1808.

Lawrence, Barbara and Nedra Branz, eds. *The Flagg Correspondence: Selected Letters, 1816–1854*. Carbondale: Southern Illinois Univ. Press, 1986.

A Layman. *An Address to the Clergy of New-England, On Their Opposition to the Rulers of the United States*. Concord, N.H.: I. & W. R. Hill, 1814.

Letter to a Member of Congress in relation to Indian Civilization. By the domestic Secretary of the United Foreign Missionary Society. New York: Daniel Fanshaw, 1822.

A Letter to the Rev. Lyman Beecher. By a Layman. N.p., 1814.

"Letter XVI. From the Rev. Asahel Hooker, of Goshen." *Connecticut Evangelical Magazine and Religious Intelligencer* 1 (March 1801): 341–47.

Letters and Conversations on the Cherokee Mission. 2 vols. Boston: T. R. Marvin, 1830.

"Letters of Andrew Jackson to Roger Brooke Taney." *Maryland Historical Magazine* 4 (December 1909): 297–313.

"Letters of William C. Rives, 1823–1829." *Tyler's Quarterly Historical & Genealogical Magazine* 5 (1923–24): 223–31; 6 (1924–25): 6–15, 97–105.

"Letters on the Eastern States." *North American Review* 11 (July 1820): 68–103.

Lincoln, William. *An Oration, Pronounced at Worcester, Massachusetts, July 4th, 1816, in Commemoration of American Independence. Before an Assembly of Youth*. Worcester: Henry Rogers, 1816.

Linsley, Joel H. *Lectures on the Relations and Duties of the Middle Aged*. Hartford: Hudson & Skinner, 1828.

Little, Robert. *The Duty of Public Usefulness. A Sermon Preached in the Hall of the House of Representatives in the Capitol of the United States, Washington City, on Sunday, February 16, 1823.* Washington, D.C.: Way & Gideon, 1823.

Lowell, Charles. *A Discourse, Delivered Before the Society for Promoting Christian Knowledge, Piety, and Charity; May 27, 1816.* Boston: Munroe & Francis, 1816.

———. *A Sermon. Preached at the State Prison, in Massachusetts, November 29th, 1812.* Boston: Joshua Belcher, 1812.

Lucas, John, ed. *Letters of Honorable John B. C. Lucas from 1815 to 1836.* Saint Louis: Privately printed, 1905.

Lumpkin, Wilson. *The Removal of the Cherokee Indians from Georgia.* 2 vols. Reprint. New York: Arno Press, 1969.

Lyman, William. *The Happy Nation. A Sermon, Preached at the Anniversary Election, in Hartford, May 8th, 1806.* Hartford: Hudson & Goodwin, 1806.

McCoy, Isaac. *History of Baptist Indian Missions.* Washington, D.C.: W. M. Morrison, 1840.

———. *Remarks on the Practicability of Indian Reform, Embracing Their Colonization; with an Appendix.* New York: Gray & Bunce, 1829.

McKean, Joseph. *A Sermon, Preached at Dorchester, June 25, 1817, On Occasion of Organizing the Third Church, in that Town, and the Installation of the Rev. Edward Richmond, D.D. as its Pastor.* Dedham: Abel Alleyne, 1817.

McKee, Irving, ed. *The Trail of Death: Letters of Benjamin Marie Petit.* Indianapolis: Indiana Historical Society, 1941.

McKenney, Thomas L. *Memoirs, Official and Personal.* Lincoln: Univ. of Nebraska Press, 1973.

McLean, Alexander. *An Oration, Pronounced at Ludlow Factory Village, Mass., July 4th, 1829, Being the Fifty-third Anniversary of American Independence.* Belchertown, Mass.: Warner & Wilson, 1829.

McLoughlin, William, ed. *Isaac Backus on Church, State, and Calvinism: Pamphlets, 1754–1789.* Cambridge: Belknap Press, 1968.

McPherson, Elizabeth, ed. "Unpublished Letters of North Carolinians to Andrew Jackson." *North Carolina Historical Review* 14 (1937): 361–92.

Macy, Thomas. *An Address, Delivered Before the Nantucket Society for the Suppression of Intemperance, Vice and Immorality, Second Month, 26, 1820.* New Bedford: Benjamin Lindsay, 1820.

Madison, James. *Selections from the Private Correspondence of James Madison, from 1813 to 1836.* Washington, D.C.: J. C. McGuire, 1823.

Mann, Mary Lee, ed. *A Yankee Jeffersonian: Selections from the Diary and Letters of William Lee of Massachusetts, Written from 1796 to 1840.* Cambridge, Mass.: Harvard Univ. Press, 1958.

Manwaring, Christopher. *Individual and National Dependance and Independence. Considered. Together with Observations on the Present State of the Times. Exhibited in an Address, Delivered at New-London, July 4, 1808.* Hartford: E. Babcock, 1808.

Marryat, Frederick. *A Diary in America, with Remarks on Its Institutions.* Reprint. New York: Alfred Knopf, 1962.

Marshall, Thomas, ed. *The Life and Papers of Frederick Bates.* 2 vols. Saint Louis: Missouri Historical Society, 1926.

Mason, Ebenezer, ed. *The Complete Works of John Mason, D.D.* 4 vols. New York: Baker & Scribner, 1849.

Massachusetts Bible Society. *Reports of the Executive Committee.* Boston, 1812–25, 1829–30.

Massachusetts Citizens. *Rights of the Indians.* Boston: N.p., 1830.

Massachusetts Peace Society. *Reports.* N.p. [1818–22, 1826].

Massachusetts Society for the Suppression of Intemperance. *Fourteenth Annual Report, with Resolutions passed at a Public Meeting Held November 5, 1827.* Boston: N. S. Simpkins & Co., 1827.

Maxwell, William. *A Memoir of the Rev. John H. Rice, D.D.* Philadelphia: J. Whetham, 1835.

Mayo, Robert. *Political Sketches of Eight Years in Washington.* Baltimore: John Toy, 1839.

Mead, Asa. *A Sermon. Addressed to the Temperate.* Portland: Shirley & Hyde, 1827.

Memoir and Correspondence of Jeremiah Mason. Cambridge, Mass.: Riverside Press, 1873.

"Memoir and Journals of Rev. Paul Coffin, D.D." *Collections of the Maine Historical Society.* Vol. 6, pp. 235–407. Portland: Brown, Thurston, 1856.

"Memoirs, The Reverend Benjamin Wooster." *Vermont Historical Society Proceedings* 4, n.s. (1936): 215–51.

Memorial from Citizens of Pennsylvania to Congress. N.p., n.d.

Memorial of a Delegation from the Cherokee Indians, Presented to Congress, January 18, 1831. N.p. [1831].

"Memorial of the American Board of Commissioners for Foreign Missions." *House Documents,* vol. 87, no. 102, 18th Cong., 1st sess. Washington, D.C.: Gales & Seaton, 1824.

"Memorial to Congress." *Christian Advocate and Journal* 4 (January 8, 1830): 73.

Merrill, Orsamus C. *The Happiness of America. An Oration, Delivered at Shaftsbury, on the Fourth of July, 1804. Being the Twenty-ninth Anniversary of American Independence.* Bennington, Vt.: Anthony Haswell, 1804.

Message from the President of the United States, in compliance With a Resolution of the Senate, relative to the execution of the act to regulate trade and intercourse with the Indian tribes, and to preserve peace on the frontiers, passed the 30th March, 1802. Document no. 65 in *Senate Documents,* 21st Cong., 2d sess. Washington, D.C.: Duff Green, 1831.

Miller, Char, ed. "'Teach Me O My God': The Journal of Hiram Bingham (1815–1816)." *Vermont History* 48 (Fall 1980): 225–35.

Mills, Samuel J., and Daniel Smith. *Report of a Missionary Tour Through that Part of* the United States which lies West of the Allegany Mountains; Performed Under the Direction of the Massachusetts Missionary Society. Reprint. New York: Arno Press, 1972.

Minutes of the General Assembly of the Presbyterian Church in the United States of America, From A.D. 1821 to A.D. 1837 Inclusive. Philadelphia: Presbyterian Board of Publication and Sabbath-School Work, 1821–37.

Missionary Paper No. 1. Boston: Crocker & Brewster, 1827.

Missions Will Not Impoverish the Country. N.p. [1826?].

"The Missouri Question." *Panoplist* 16 (January 1820): 15–24; (February 1820): 59–72.

Moore, Humphrey. *A Sermon Preached at Leominster, January 24th, 1821, at the Ordination of the Rev. Abel Conant, to the Pastoral Care of the Church at that Place.* Amherst, N.H.: Elijah Mansur, 1821.

Moore, John B., ed. *The Works of James Buchanan.* 12 vols. Philadelphia: J. B. Lippincott Co., 1908.

Moore, John H., ed. "The Abiel Abbot Journals: A Yankee Preacher in Charleston Society, 1818–1827." *South Carolina Historical Magazine* 68 (1967): 51–73, 115–39, 232–54.

Moore, Rev. Zephaniah S. *The Sabbath a Permanent and Benevolent Institution. A Sermon, Preached at the Annual Election, May 27, 1818, Before His Excellency John Brooks, Esq. Governor; His Honor William Phillips, Esq. Lieutenant Governor; The Honorable Council; and the Legislature of Massachusetts.* Boston: Russell, Cutler & Co., 1818.

Morse, Edward L., ed. *Samuel F. B. Morse: His Letters and Journals.* 2 vols. Boston: Houghton Mifflin, 1914.

Morse, Jedidiah. *A Discourse Delivered at the African Meeting House, in Boston, July 14, 1808.* Boston, 1808.

———. *Signs of the Times. A Sermon, Preached Before the Society for Propagating the Gospel Among the Indians and Others in North America, At Their Anniversary, Nov. 1, 1810.* Charlestown: Samuel T. Armstrong, 1810.

Moseley, Jonathan W., Jr., ed. *A Record of Missionary Meetings Held in the Chahta and Chikesha Nations and the Records of Tombigbee Presbytery, From 1825 to 1838.* N.p., n.d.

Mott, James. *Hints to Young People on the Duties of Civil Life.* New York: Mahlon Day, 1826.

Moulton, Gary, ed. *The Papers of Chief John Ross.* 2 vols. Norman: Univ. of Oklahoma Press, 1985.

"Mr. Johnson's Report on Sabbath Mails." *Spirit of the Pilgrims* 2 (March 1829): 142–66.

Munsell, Joel. *Reminiscences of Men and Things in Northfield as I knew them from 1812 to 1825.* Albany: J. Munsell, 1876.

Nevins, Allan, ed. *The Diary of John Quincy Adams.* New York: Longmans, Green & Co., 1929.

Newell, Jonathan. *An Aged Minister's Review of the Events and Duties of Fifty Years; A Sermon, Preached at Stow, Oct. 11, 1824.* Concord, Mass.: Allen & Lamson, 1825.

New England Tract Society. *First Report, May 29, 1815.* N.p., n.d.

New England Tract Society. *Sixth Annual Report, May, 1820.* Andover: Flagg & Gould, 1820.

Newsome, A. R., ed. "Letters of Romulus M. Saunders to Bartlett Yancy, 1821–1828." *North Carolina Historical Review* 8 (October 1931): 427–62.

Nichols, Ichabod. *Address Delivered Before the Portland Association for the Promotion of Temperance, February 22, 1828.* Portland: Hill & Edwards, 1828.

Norton, Jacob. *The Duty of Religious Toleration, Mutual Sympathy, and Fellowship among Christians of Different Denominations, Exhibited in A Sermon, Delivered in the South Meeting House in Weymouth, Nov. 8, 1821, On a Peculiarly Interesting and Important Occasion.* Boston: John Cotton, Jr., 1822.

"Notes of Recent Publications." *Spirit of the Pilgrims* 3 (January 1830): 51–52.

Nott, Samuel, Jr. *The Freedom of the Mind, Demanded of American Freemen; Being Lectures to the Lyceum, on the Improvement of the People.* Boston: Crocker & Brewster, 1830.

Novanglus. "Review of Rev. C. G. Finney's Sermon." *Christian Advocate* 5 (December 1827): 553–68; 6 (January 1828): 29–36.

Noyes, Thomas. *A Sermon, Preached in the South Parish in Weymouth, Before the Norfolk Auxiliary Society for the Education of Pious Youth for the Gospel Ministry, At Their Sixth Annual Meeting, June 12, 1822.* Dedham: B. Field, 1822.

"Obituary Notice [Jeremiah Evarts]." *Spirit of the Pilgrims* 4 (June 1831): 347–48.

Oliphant, J. Orin, ed. *Through the South and West with Jeremiah Evarts in 1826.* Lewisburg, Pa.: Bucknell Univ. Press, 1956.

Oliver, Benjamin L., Jr. *Hints for An Essay on the Pursuit of Happiness.* Cambridge, Mass.: Hilliard & Metcalf, 1818.

"On the Condition of Blacks in This Country." *Panoplist* 16 (June 1820): 241–45; (November 1820): 481–94.

"On Educating Heathen Youth in Our Own Country." *Panoplist* 12 (July 1816): 299.

Otis, George. *Perfectability. An Address Delivered Sept. 1, 1818, Before the Humane Society of Newburyport.* Newburyport: William Hastings, 1818.

Parish, Elijah. *A Discourse, Delivered at Byfield, on the Annual Fast, April 8, 1813.* Newburyport: E. W. Allen, 1813.

———. *A Sermon Preached Before the Members of the Female Charitable Society of Newburyport, It Being Their Fifth Anniversary, May 17, 1808.* Newburyport: E. W. Allen, 1808.

[Park, John]. *An Address to the Citizens of Massachusetts, on the Causes and Remedy of our National Distress. By a Fellow Sufferer.* Boston: Printed at the Repertory Office, 1808.

Parker, Joel. *The Signs of the Times; A Sermon, Delivered in Rochester, December 4, 1828, Being the Day of Publick Thanksgiving.* Rochester: E. Peck & Co., 1829.

Parker, Theodore. *A Discourse on the Transient and Permanent in Christianity; Preached at the Ordination of Mr. Charles C. Shackford, in the Hawes Place Church in Boston, May 19, 1841.* Boston: Printed for the Author, 1841.

The Patriot; or People's Companion: Consisting of Five Essays on the Law and Politics of Our Country. Hudson: A. Stoddard, 1828.

Patriotism and Piety: The Speeches of Caleb Strong, 1800–1807. Newburyport: Edmund M. Blunt, 1808.

"Peace Societies Compared with Other Benevolent Institutions." *Friend of Peace* 2, no. 6 (1816): 1–8.

Pearson, Eliphalet. *A Sermon Delivered in Boston Before the American Society for Educating Pious Youth for the Gospel Ministry, Oct. 26, 1815.* Andover: Flagg & Gould, 1815.

Pease, Zephaniah, ed. *The Diary of Samuel Rodman: A New Bedford Chronicle of Thirty-seven Years, 1821–1859.* New Bedford, Mass.: Reynolds Printing Co., 1927.

"Penitentiary System." *North American Review* 13 (October 1821): 417–40.

Pepper, Calvin. *An Oration, Pronounced at Wilbraham on the 4th of July 1810.* Palmer, Mass.: E. Terry, 1810.

Perdue, Theda, ed. *Cherokee Editor: The Writings of Elias Boudinot.* Knoxville: Univ. of Tennessee Press, 1983.

Perkins, Elisha. *Address Delivered Before the Peace Society of Windham County. At Its Annual Meeting in Brooklyn, August 20th, 1828.* Brooklyn, Conn.: William H. Bigelow, 1828.

Perkins, Nathan. *The Benign Influence of Religion on Civil Government and National Happiness; Illustrated in A Sermon, Preached Before His Excellency Jonathan Trumbull, Esq. Governor; His Honor John Treadwell, Esq. Lieutenant Governor; The Honorable the Council; and House of Representatives of the State of Connecticut, on the Anniversary Election, May 12th, 1808.* Hartford: Hudson & Goodwin, 1808.

———. *Narrative of a Tour Through the State of Vermont, From April 27 to June 12, 1789.* Woodstock, Vt.: The Elm Tree Press, 1920.

Perry, David. *The Spiritual Temple. A Sermon, Delivered at the Annual Exhibition of the Foreign Mission School, in Cornwall, May 17, 1820.* Hartford: Peter B. Gleason & Co., 1820.

Peters, Richard. *The Case of the Cherokee Nation against the State of Georgia; Argued and Determined at the Supreme Court of the United States, January Term, 1831, With an Appendix.* Philadelphia: John Grigg, 1831.

[Phelps, John]. *The Present State of Our Country Considered, In an Address to the Freemen of Vermont, By a Farmer of Windham County.* N.p., 1808.

Philalethes. "Plain Scripture Readings." *Panoplist* 8 (January 1813): 352–58; (February 1813): 393–97; (March 1813): 454–59; (April 1813): 495–99; (May 1813): 552–56; 9 (June 1813): 15–18; (July 1813): 58–62; (August 1813): 121–26, 164–81.

Philipson, David, ed. *Letters of Rebecca Gratz*. Reprint. New York: Arno Press, 1975.

Plea for the Indians. N.p. [1830?].

The Political Mirror: or Review of Jacksonism. New York: J. P. Peaslee, 1835.

Polk, James K. *Correspondence of James K. Polk*. 4 vols. to date. Ed. Herbert Weaver and Paul Bergeron. Nashville: Vanderbilt Univ. Press, 1969–.

Pond, Enoch. *Short Missionary Discourses, or Monthly Concert Lectures*. Worcester: Dorr & Howland, 1824.

Porter, Ebenezer. *The Fatal Effects of Ardent Spirits, A Sermon*. Middlebury, Vt.: T. C. Strong, 1812.

———. *Great Effects Result from Little Causes. A Sermon, Delivered Sept. 13, 1815, At the Anniversary of the Moral Society in Andover*. Newark, N.J.: John Tuttle & Co., 1816.

———. *A Sermon, Delivered in Boston, on the Anniversary of the American Education Society, Oct. 4, 1820*. Andover: Flagg & Gould, 1821.

———. *A Sermon preached in Boston, November 1, 1827, before the Society for Propagating the Gospel Among the Indians, and others in North America*. Andover: Flagg & Gould, 1827.

———. *Signs of the Times. A Sermon Preached in the Chapel of the Theological Seminary, Andover, on the Public Fast, April 3, 1823*. Andover: Flagg & Gould, 1823.

Porter, Kenneth. *The Jacksons and the Lees: Two Generations of Massachusetts Merchants, 1765–1844*. 2 vols. Cambridge, Mass.: Belknap Press, 1937.

Porter, Noah. *Memorial of a Revival. A Sermon, Delivered in Farmington, At the Anniversary Thanksgiving, December 6, 1821*. Hartford: G. Goodwin & Sons, 1822.

———. *A Sermon. Delivered at the Meeting for the Connecticut Society for the Promotion of Good Morals, in New-Haven, October 16, 1816*. New Haven: F. G. Woodward, 1816.

"Prevention of Crimes." *North American Review* 9 (September 1819): 288–322.

Proceedings of a Convention of Moral Societies, in the County of Litchfield, Holden May 30th, 1815, at Goshen: An Abstract of the Laws of Connecticut, and an Address to the Public, on the Promotion of Virtue and Good Morals. New Haven: Printed at the Journal Office, 1816.

Proceedings of the First Ten Years of the American Tract Society, Instituted at Boston, 1814. Andover: Flagg & Gould, 1824.

Proctor, John W. *Address to the Danvers Auxiliary Society, for Suppressing Intemperance and other Vices, and Promoting Temperance and General Morality, April 24, 1821*. Salem: John D. Cushing, 1822.

Proudfit, Alexander. *The Universal Extension of Messiah's Kingdom. A Sermon. Delivered in the North Church, New-Haven, Con. Sept. 12, 1822, Before the American Board of Commissioners for Foreign Missions, At their Thirteenth Annual Meeting.* Boston: Crocker & Brewster, 1822.

Prucha, Francis Paul, ed. *Cherokee Removal: The "William Penn" Essays and Other Writings by Jeremiah Evarts.* Knoxville: Univ. of Tennessee Press, 1981.

"Punishment of Crimes." *North American Review* 10 (April 1820): 235–59.

Quandary, Christopher [pseud.]. *Some Serious Considerations on the Present State of Parties, with Regard to the Presidential Election.* Richmond: T. W. White, 1827.

Quincy, Josiah. *Address, Delivered at the Fifth Anniversary of the Massachusetts Peace Society, December 25, 1820.* Cambridge, Mass.: Hilliard & Metcalf, 1821.

———. *An Oration. Delivered on Tuesday, the Fourth of July, 1826, It Being the Fiftieth Anniversary of American Independence, Before the Supreme Executive of the Commonwealth, and the City Council and Inhabitants of the City of Boston.* Boston: True & Greene, 1826.

———. *Remarks on Some of the Provisions of the Laws of Massachusetts Affecting Poverty, Vice, and Crime.* Cambridge, Mass.: Hilliard & Metcalf, 1822.

Rayner, Menzies. *A Dissertation upon Extraordinary Awakenings.* New Haven: Herald Office, 1816.

Read, Alexander. *An Address, Delivered Before the New Bedford Auxiliary Society for the Suppression of Intemperance, at their annual meeting, Jan. 6, 1817.* New Bedford: Benjamin Lindsey, 1817.

Register of Debates in Congress. Washington, D.C.: Gales & Seaton, 1830.

Remarks on State Rights. By A Citizen of Massachusetts. Boston: Richardson & Lord, 1824.

Remarks on the Existing State of the Laws of Massachusetts, Respecting Violations of the Sabbath. Boston: Nathaniel Willis, 1816.

"Removal of the Indians." *North American Review* 31 (October 1830): 396–442.

"Removal of the Indians Beyond the Mississippi." *Christian Advocate and Journal* 3 (December 19, 1828): 62.

Report of the Board of Counsel to the Massachusetts Society for the Suppression of Intemperance, Presented at their Eighth Anniversary, June 2, 1820. Boston: Sewell Phelps, 1820.

Report of the Committee on the Subject of Pauperism and A House of Industry in the Town of Boston. N.p., 1821.

Report of the Directing Committee of the Connecticut Bible Society; Exhibited to the Society, At their Meeting, May 14, 1818. Hartford: Hudson & Co., 1818.

Reports of the Prison Discipline Society, Boston, 1826–1835. Boston: T. R. Marvin, 1855.

"Review . . . Mr. M'Coy's Indian Reform." *American Baptist Magazine* 8 (May 1828): 147–55.

"Review of an Article in the *North American Review* for Jan. 1830." *Spirit of the Pilgrims* 3 (March 1830): 141–61.

"Review of *A Tribute to the Memory of the Late Jeremiah Evarts.* By Gardiner Spring."

New England Magazine 1 (September 1831): 265–67.
"Review of Sketches of the Life and Character of Jeremiah Evarts, Esq." *Spirit of the Pilgrims* 4 (November 1831): 599–613.
Rezneck, Samuel, ed. "Letters from a Massachusetts Federalist to a New York Democrat, 1823–1839." *New York History* 48 (July 1967): 255–74.
Rice, John Holt. *The Power of Truth and Love. A Sermon Preached at Philadelphia, Oct. 1, 1828, at the Nineteenth Annual Meeting of the American Board of Commissioners for Foreign Missions.* Boston: Crocker & Brewster, 1828.
Richards, James. *The Spirit of Paul the Spirit of Missions. A Sermon Preached at New Haven, (Con.) before the American Board of Commissioners for Foreign Missions, at Their Annual Meeting, Sept. 15, 1814.* Boston: Samuel T. Armstrong, 1814.
Richardson, James D., ed. *Messages and Papers of the Presidents.* 11 vols. Washington, D.C.: GPO, 1896.
Richardson, Joseph. *The Progress of Christianity Retarded by its Friends. A Sermon Delivered to the First Parish in Hingham, Lord's Day, August 1, 1824.* Boston: J. P. Orcutt, 1824.
Richardson, Luther. *An Address, Delivered Before the Roxbury Charitable Society, At their Anniversary Meeting, September 17, 1804.* Boston: Munroe & Francis, 1804.
Rights of the Indians. N.p., n.d. [1830].
"The Rights of the Indians Ascertained." *Christian Advocate* 8 (February 1830): 73–78.
Riker, Dorothy, ed. *Executive Proceedings of the State of Indiana, 1816–1836.* Indianapolis: Indian Historical Bureau, 1947.
Riker, Dorothy, and Gayle Thornbrough, eds. *Messages and Papers Relating to the Administration of Noah Noble, Governor of Indiana, 1831–1837.* Indianapolis: Indiana Historical Bureau, 1958.
———. *Messages and Papers Relating to the Administration of James Brown Ray, Governor of Indiana, 1825–1831.* Indianapolis: Indiana Historical Bureau, 1954.
Robbins, Thomas. *An Address Delivered at the Retreat for the Insane, in Hartford, at the Dedication of that Institution, April 1, 1824.* Hartford: Goodwin & Co., 1824.
Robertson, Nellie, and Dorothy Riker, eds. *The John Tipton Papers.* 3 vols. Indianapolis: Indiana Historical Bureau, 1942.
Rohrbach, Lewis, ed. *Boston Taxpayers in 1821.* Camden, Me.: Picton Press, 1988.
Royall, Anne. *Letters from Alabama, 1817–1822.* University: Univ. of Alabama Press, 1969.
Sabine, James. *The Great Moral Duties of a Free and Independent People. A Sermon Delivered on Fast Day, April 6, 1826, in the Presbyterian Church, Boston.* Boston: Dutton & Wentworth, 1826.
———. *The Relation the Present State of Religion Bears to the Expected Millennium. A Sermon, Delivered in the Old South Church, Boston, Before the Foreign Mission Society, of Boston and the Vicinity, Jan. 8, 1823.* Boston: Crocker & Brewster, 1823.
Sanders, Daniel. *An Address. Delivered in Sherburne, 28th February, 1815, Occasioned*

by the Celebration of the Peace of Ghent. 24th December, 1814. Dedham: Printed at the Gazette Office, 1815.

Sanders, Mrs. Elizabeth. *Conversations Principally on the Aborigines of North America*. Salem: W. & S. B. Ives, 1828.

Schermerhorn, John F., and Samuel J. Mills. *A Correct View of that Part of the United States which lies West of the Allegany Mountains, with Respect to Religion and Morals*. Reprint. New York: Arno Press, 1972.

Schmucker, Samuel S. *A Plea for the Sabbath-School System. Delivered Feb. 2, 1830, At the Anniversary of the Gettysburg Sunday-School*. Gettysburg: H. C. Neinstedt, 1830.

Schoolcraft, Henry. *Personal Memoirs of a Residence of Thirty Years with the Indian Tribes of the American Frontiers*. Philadelphia: Lippincott, Grambo & Co., 1851.

Second Annual Report of the Committee of Inquiry of the Massachusetts Peace Society. Cambridge, Mass.: Hilliard & Metcalf, 1819.

The Second Annual Report of the Massachusetts Society for the Suppression of Intemperance. N.p., n.d.

"Second Quarterly Circular of the Prudential Committee of the American Board of Commissioners for Foreign Missions." *Panoplist* 12 (April 1816): 186–90.

Sedgwick, Catharine. *Clarence; or, A Tale of Our Own Times*. 2 vols. Philadelphia: Carey & Lea, 1830.

Selden [pseud.]. *Letters Addressed to the Members of the Eighteenth Congress*. Washington, D.C., 1823.

Shanks, Henry T. (ed.). *The Papers of Willie Person Mangum*. 2 vols. Raleigh, N.C.: State Department of Archives and History, 1950.

Sharp, Daniel. *A Discourse, Pronounced Before His Excellency William Eustis, Esq. Governor, The Honorable Council, and the Two Houses, Composing the Legislature of Massachusetts, May 26, 1824. Being the Anniversary Election*. Boston: True & Greene, 1824.

Shirreff, Patrick. *A Tour Through North America; Together With a Comprehensive View of the Canadas and the United States. As Adapted for Agricultural Emigration*. Edinburgh: Ballantyne & Co., 1835.

Sinclair, William. *A Sermon on Universal Charity, Preached at the Maryland Institute*. Baltimore: Benjamin Edes, 1827.

Sixth Annual Report of the New England Tract Society. May. 1820. Andover: Flagg & Gould, 1820.

"Sketch of the Life and Character of Jeremiah Evarts." *Missionary Herald* 27 (October 1831): 305–13; (November 1831): 337–46.

"Slavery and the Missouri Question." *North American Review* 10 (January 1820): 137–68.

Smith, Elias. *The Loving Kindness of God Displayed in the Triumph of Republicanism in America; Being a Discourse, Delivered at Taunton, (Mass.) July Fourth, 1809; At the Celebration of American Independence*. N.p., 1809.

Society for the Suppression of Vice and Immorality. *Articles of Association, of the Society for the Suppression of Vice and Immorality.* Newburyport: W. B. & H. G. Allen, 1813.

Southern Opposition. *An Address to the People of the Eastern States, Developing the Causes of Their Oppression. By a Friend to Freedom.* New York: John Forbes, 1813.

Speeches of Messrs. Webster, Frelinghuysen and Others, At the Sunday School Meeting in the City of Washington, February 16, 1831. Philadelphia: American Sunday School Union, 1831.

"Speeches on the Indian Bill." *Spirit of the Pilgrims* 3 (September 1830): 492–500; (October 1830): 517–32.

Speeches on the Passage of the Bill for the Removal of the Indians, Delivered in the Congress of the United States, April and May, 1830. Boston: Perkins & Marvin, 1830.

Sprague, Charles. *Address Delivered Before the Massachusetts Society for the Suppression of Intemperance, May 31, 1827.* Boston: Bowles & Dearborn, 1827.

Sprague, Peleg. *Speeches and Addresses.* Boston: Phillips, Sampson & Co., 1858.

Sprague, William. *Intemperance, A Just Cause for Alarm and Execution. A Sermon, Preached at West Springfield, April 5th, 1827, The Day of the Annual Fast.* New York: J. Seymour, 1827.

———. *Lectures on Revivals of Religion.* New York: D. Appleton & Co., 1833.

———. *Religious Celebration of Independence. A Discourse Delivered at Northampton, on the Fourth of July, 1827.* Hartford: Goodwin & Co., 1827.

Spring, Gardiner. *An Appeal to the Citizens of New-York, in Behalf of the Christian Sabbath.* New York: J. Seymour, 1823.

———. *Essays on the Distinguishing Traits of Christian Character.* New York: Dodge & Sayre, 1813.

———. *A Tribute to the Memory of the Late Jeremiah Evarts, Esq., Secretary of the American Board of Commissioners for Foreign Missions.* New York: Sleight & Robinson, 1831.

———. "Wealth a Fearful Snare to the Soul." *American National Preacher* 4 (May 1830): 369–80.

Spring, Samuel. *A Charity Sermon, Delivered at the Request of the Howard Benevolent Society, in the First Presbyterian Church of Newburyport, October 4, 1818.* Newburyport: W. & J. Gilman, 1818.

———. *A Sermon, Delivered Before the Massachusetts Missionary Society, At Their Annual Meeting, May 25, 1802.* Newburyport: E. M. Blunt, 1802.

Stark, Andrew. *Charitable Exertions an Evidence of a Gracious State: A Sermon, Preached in the Associate Presbyterian Church in the City of New-York, on Sabbath Evening, January 2, 1825.* Albany: Webster & Wood, 1825.

Stickney, William, ed. *Autobiography of Amos Kendall.* Boston: Lee & Shepard, 1872.

Stone, Micah. *Address, Delivered Before the Moral Society in Brookfield, April 15, 1817.* Brookfield: E. Merriam & Co., 1817.

———. *The Duty of Men's Serving Their Generation. A Sermon Preached at Brookfield, South Parish, on Lord's Day, July 1st, 1810; Being the Sabbath After the Interment of Phinehas Upham, Esq.* Brookfield: E. Merriam & Co., 1810.

Storrs, Richard. *The Mutability of Created Things A Reason for Active Benevolence. Sermon, Delivered Before the Howard Benevolent Society of Boston, January 12, 1820.* Boston: Munroe & Francis, 1820.

Story, William, ed. *Life and Letters of Joseph Story.* 2 vols. Boston: Little & Brown, 1851.

Strong, Nathan. *The Character of a Virtuous and Good Woman, A Discourse, Delivered by the Desire and in the Presence of the Female Beneficient Society, in Hartford, October 4th, A.D. 1809.* Hartford: Hudson & Goodwin, 1809.

———. *On the Universal Spread of the Gospel, a Sermon Delivered January 4th, the First Sabbath in the 19th Century of the Christian Era.* Hartford: Hudson & Goodwin, 1801.

———. *A Sermon, On the Use of Time; Addressed to Men in the Several Ages of Life. Delivered at Hartford, January 10, 1813.* Hartford: Peter Gleason & Co., 1813.

Sullivan, James. *Strictures on the Rev. Mr. Thacher's Pamphlet.* Boston: Benjamin Edes & Sons, 1784.

Sullivan, Richard. *Address, Delivered at the Seventh Anniversary of the Massachusetts Peace Society, December 25th, 1822.* Cambridge, Mass.: Hilliard & Metcalf, 1823.

Sullivan, William. *Familiar Letters on Public Characters and Public Events; From the Peace of 1783, to the Peace of 1815.* Boston: Russell, Odiorne, & Metcalf, 1834.

Sumner, Bradford. *An Address Delivered Before the Massachusetts Peace Society: Together with a Report Made at Their Fifteenth Anniversary, 1831.* Boston: Samuel Dickinson, 1831.

"Sunday Mails." *Niles' Register* 35 (January 24, 1829): 352–53; (February 14, 1829): 405–7; (March 20, 1830): 74–7.

Sunday Mails; or, Inquiries into the Origin, Institution, and Proper Mode of Observance, of the First Day of the Week, or Christian Sabbath. Philadelphia: Published for the Benefit of Sunday Mails, 1830.

Sutherland, David. *Christian Benevolence. A Sermon, Delivered at Newbury, Vt. Before the Washington Benevolent Society, at the Celebration of the Anniversary of the National Independence, July 4, 1812.* Windsor, Vt.: Thomas Pomroy, 1812.

T. "Outrages on the Sabbath." *Panoplist* 10 (April 1814): 159–62.

Tappan, Lewis. *Letter to Eleazar Lord, Esq. in Defense of Measures for Promoting the Observance of the Christian Sabbath.* New York: Sleight & Robinson, 1831.

———. *Remarks on Prisons and Prison Discipline.* Boston: Isaac R. Butts & Co., 1826.

Taylor, Nathaniel W. *A Sermon, Addressed to the Legislature of the State of Connecticut, at the Annual Election in Hartford, May 7, 1823.* New Haven: A. H. Maltby & Co., 1823.

Thacher, Peter. *A Reply to the Strictures of Mr. J. S., a Layman, Upon the Pamphlet Entitled Observations Upon the Present State of the Clergy of New-England*. Boston: Norman, White & Freeman, 1784.

Theophilus. "Indian Government." *Christian Advocate and Journal* 1 (April 21, 1827): 129.

Thomas, Daniel. *The Mode to Insure a Reformation of Morals, Pointed Out, and Its Adoption Urged, in a Sermon, Delivered January 1, 1818, on the First Anniversary of "The Abington Moral Society"*. Boston: Thomas Rowe, 1818.

Thompson, Otis. *A Sermon Preached on the National Thanksgiving for the Restoration of Peace, April 13, 1815*. Providence: Goddard & Mann, 1815.

———. *"Signs of the Times!" A Sermon, Preached at Attleborough, West Parish, on the Annual Fast in Massachusetts, April 9th, A.D. 1812*. Providence: David Hawkins, Jr., 1812.

Thornbrough, Gayle, ed. *The Correspondence of John Badollet and Albert Gallatin, 1804–1836*. Indianapolis: Indiana Historical Society, 1963.

Thurston, David. *A Sermon. Delivered at Winthrop. April 7, 1825. The Annual Fast in Maine*. Augusta: Eaton & Severance, 1825.

———. *A Sermon, Delivered Before the Somerset Association for the Reformation of Morals, At Their Annual Meeting in Norridgewock, February 17, 1819*. Hallowell: E. Goodale, 1819.

———. *A Sermon Delivered in Saco, June 26, 1816, Before the Maine Missionary Society, at their Ninth Annual Meeting*. Hallowell: N. Cheever, 1816.

To All of Every Station, Who Love Zion, The Prudential Committee of the American Board of Commissioners for Foreign Missions, Address Themselves in Behalf of the Missionary Herald. N.p., 1821.

To The Friends of Christ in Our Colleges. [Boston, 1827].

Todd, John. *John Todd: The Story of His Life, Told Mainly by Himself*. New York: Harper & Brothers, 1876.

Torrey, William. *A Discourse, Delivered Before the Charitable Society of Plymouth, January, 1822*. Boston: Crocker & Brewster, 1822.

Tracy, John Evarts, ed. "Diary of a Yale Student in 1798 (Jeremiah Evarts)." *Yale Alumni Weekly* 38 (October 26–November 9, 1928): 159–60, 187–89, 222–23.

Trollope, Mrs. Frances. *Domestic Manners of the Americans*. Reprint. New York: Vintage, 1949.

Trumbull, Henry. *Address on the Importance of Charity. Delivered Before the Brothers Charitable Society, At the Second Congregational Church, Providence—on the Anniversary of Said Society, Wednesday, Nov. 18, 1829*. Providence: Marshall & Hammond, 1829.

T. S. "Methodist Missionaries Among the Indians." *Christian Advocate and Journal* 2 (July 18, 1828): 181.

Tyler, Bennet. *A Sermon, Preached at Litchfield, Before the Foreign Mission Society, of*

Litchfield County, At Their Annual Meeting, February 10, 1813. New Haven: Eli Hudson, 1813.

V. A. "A Question to Universalists." *Panoplist* 7 (May 1812): 538–39.

———. "On Examination for Admission into the Church." *Panoplist* 7 (March 1811): 449–51.

———. "On Human Depravity." *Panoplist* 6 (January 1811): 357–61; (February 1811): 396–403; (March 1811): 447–52; (April 1811): 494–502; (May 1811): 553–61; 7 (September 1811): 150–54; (October 1811): 203–6; (December 1811): 302–10.

Van Tyne, C. H., ed. *The Letters of Daniel Webster from Documents Owned Principally by the New Hampshire Historical Society*. New York: McClure, Phillips & Co., 1902.

"Vindication of the Baptist Foreign Mission." *American Baptist Magazine* 7 (1827): 130–39.

A Vindication of the Cherokee Claims, Addressed to the Town Meeting in Philadelphia, On the 11th of January, 1830. N.p., n.d.

Wadsworth, Benjamin. *Female Charity an Acceptable Offering. A Sermon, Delivered in the Brick Meeting House in Danvers, At the Request of the Charitable Female Cent Society in Danvers and Middleton, for Promoting Christian Knowledge*. Andover: Flagg & Gould, 1817.

Waldo, Daniel. *The Causes and Remedies of National Divisions. Illustrated in a Discourse, Delivered in Suffield, 1st Society, July 4th, 1804*. Suffield: Edward Gray, 1804.

Walker, J. "Associations for Benevolent Purposes." *Christian Examiner* 2 (July and August 1825): 241–52.

Ware, John. *Address Delivered Before the Massachusetts Peace Society, At Their Ninth Anniversary, December 25, 1824*. Boston: F. Y. Carlile, 1825.

———. *An Address Delivered Before the Massachusetts Society for the Suppression of Intemperance at their Annual Meeting, May, 1825*. Boston: Isaac R. Butts & Co., 1826.

Warfel, Harry, ed. *Letters of Noah Webster*. New York: Library Publishers, 1953.

Warren, Charles. *An Address, in Commemoration of American Independence. Delivered at Palmyra, July 4, 1823*. Hallowell, Me.: S. K. Gilman, 1823.

Warren, Henry. *An Address Delivered at Roxbury, Before the Roxbury Auxiliary Society for the Suppression of Intemperance, October 25, 1821*. Boston: Russell & Gardner, 1821.

Washburn, Cephas. *Reminiscences of the Indians*. Richmond: Presbyterian Committee of Publication, 1869.

Washburn, Royal. *Evils Which Threaten Our Country. A Sermon Delivered in Amherst First Parish, (Mass.) on Thursday, April 9, 1829. The Day of Public Fast*. Amherst: J. S. and C. Adams, 1829.

Washburne, E. B., ed. *The Edwards Papers; Being a Portion of the Collection of the Letters, Papers, and Manuscripts of Ninian Edwards*. Chicago: Fergus Printing Co., 1884.

Waterbury, Jared B. *Influence of Religion on National Prosperity: A Sermon. Delivered in Portsmouth, N.H., April 1, 1830, Being the Day of the Annual Fast*. Portsmouth: John W. Shepard, 1830.

Waterman, Jotham. *National Righteousness National Security. A Discourse. Delivered April 5, 1804. The Day Appointed for Fast, by His Excellency, Caleb Strong, Esq. Governor of the Commonwealth of Massachusetts*. Boston: Manning & Loring, 1804.

Wayland, Francis. *The Duties of an American Citizen. Two Discourses. Delivered in the First Baptist Meeting House in Boston, on Thursday, April 7, 1825. The Day of Public Fast*. Boston: James Loring, 1825.

———. *The Moral Dignity of the Missionary Enterprise. A Sermon Delivered Before the Boston Baptist Foreign Mission Society, on the Evening of October 26, and before the Salem Bible Translation Society on the Evening of November 4, 1823*. Boston: James Loring, 1824.

Webster, Daniel. *A Discourse in Commemoration of the Lives and Services of John Adams and Thomas Jefferson, Delivered in Faneuil Hall, Boston, August 2, 1826*. Boston: Cummings, Hilliard & Co., 1826.

———. *The Papers of Daniel Webster: Correspondence*. Vol. 1, *1798–1824*; vol. 2, *1825–1829*. Ed. Charles Wiltse. Vol. 3, *1830–1834*. Ed. Charles Wiltse and David Allen. Hanover: Univ. Press of New England.

———. *Speeches and Forensic Arguments*. Boston: Perkins & Marvin, 1830.

Webster, Fletcher, ed. *The Private Correspondence of Daniel Webster*. 2 vols. Boston: Little Brown & Co., 1857.

Wells, Thomas. *An Address Delivered Before the Massachusetts Charitable Mechanic Association, October 4, 1821*. Boston: J. T. Buckingham, 1821.

Wendover, Peter. *National Deliverance. An Oration, Delivered in the New Dutch Church, in the City of New York, on the Fourth of July, 1806, Being the Thirtieth Anniversary of American Independence*. New York, 1806.

Weston, John E. *Claims of the Poor. A Discourse Delivered at Charlestown, on the Evening of November 8, 1829, Before the Female Benevolent Society, and at East Cambridge, on the Evening of December 18, 1829, Before the Female Charitable Society*. Boston: True & Greene, 1830.

White, Elipha. *A Moral Revolution. A Sermon, Preached Before the Associations for Foreign Missions in Charleston, S.C. June 7th, 1829*. Boston: Crocker & Brewster, 1829.

White, John. *An Address, Delivered before the Dedham Auxiliary Society for the Suppression of Intemperance, at their annual meeting, Feb. 10, 1817*. Dedham: Abel Alleyne, 1817.

White, Robert, ed. *Messages of the Governors of Tennessee, 1821–1835*. Nashville: Tennessee Historical Commission, 1952.

Whitman, Bernard. *A Letter to an Orthodox Minister, on Revivals of Religion*. Boston: Gray & Bowen, 1831.

———. *A Thanksgiving Discourse, on the Means of Increasing Public Happiness*. Cambridge, Mass.: Hilliard & Brown, 1828.
Wilbur, Hervey. *Female Piety Demanding Assistance. Two Sermons, Delivered in Bradford, Second Parish, January 5, 1812, and Afterwards in Two Other Places*. Haverhill: William B. Allen, 1812.
Wilde, George C. *An Oration, Delivered in Newburyport, on the Forty-Seventh Anniversary of American Independence, July 4, 1823*. Newburyport: E. W. Allen, 1823.
Wilde, Richard H. *Speech of Mr. Wilde. of Georgia, on the Bill for Removing the Indians from the East to the West Side of the Mississippi, Delivered in the House of Representatives, on the 20th of May, 1830*. Washington, D.C.: Gales & Seaton, 1830.
Willard, Joseph. *An Oration Delivered at Lancaster, Mass. in Celebration of American Independence, July, 1825*. Boston: Cummings, Hilliard & Co., 1825.
Williard, Paul. *An Oration, Pronounced at Charlestown, on the 4th of July, 1821, At the Request of the Republican Citizens of that Town, in Commemoration of the Anniversary of National Independence*. Boston: E. Bellamy, 1821.
Williams, Roger (pseud.). "Removal of the Indians." *American Baptist Magazine* 10 (December 1830): 362–64.
Williams, Samuel P. *An Address Delivered and Published at the Request of the Young Men's Auxiliary Education Society of Newburyport, Sept. 1822*. Newburyport: W. & J. Gilman, 1822.
Willis, William. *An Address, Delivered Before the New-Bedford Auxiliary Society for the Suppression of Intemperance, At Their Annual Meeting, First Month 4, 1819*. New-Bedford: Benjamin Lindsey, 1819.
Williston, Seth. *A Fast Sermon, On the National Profanation of the Sabbath. in Which it is Shown, That the Nation is Exposed to the Wrath of God, By a Contemptuous Disregard of His Holy Day; Preached in the Spring of 1825*. Albany: Webster & Wood, 1825.
———. *A Sermon on Revivals of Religion: Containing a Caution to the Church, in the Nineteenth Century, to Beware of the Device of Satan in Corrupting Them*. New York: D. Fanshaw, 1827.
Winslow, Miron. *A Sermon Delivered at the Old South Church, Boston. June 7, 1819, on the Evening Previous to the Sailing of the Rev. Miron Winslow, Levi Spaulding, and Henry Woodward, & Dr. John Scudder, as Missionaries to Ceylon*. Andover: Flagg & Gould, 1819.
Wisner, Benjamin. *Memoirs of the Late Mrs. Susan Huntington, of Boston, Mass.* Edinburgh: Waugh and Innes, 1828.
———. *The Proper Mode of Conducting Missions to the Heathen. A Sermon Delivered Before the Society for Propagating the Gospel among the Indians and Others in North America, November 5, 1829*. Boston: Putnam & Hunt, 1829.
Wood, Benjamin. *Labourers Needed in the Harvest of Christ. A Sermon; Delivered at Sutton, (S.P.) March 18, 1812, As A Preliminary to the Formation of a Society, in the County of Worcester, for the Aid of Pious Young Men, With a View to the Ministry*. Worcester: Isaac Sturtevant, 1812.

Woods, Alva. *Intellectual and Moral Culture. A Discourse, Delivered at His Inauguration as President of Transylvania University, October 13, 1828.* Lexington, Ky.: Joseph G. Norwood, 1828.

Woods, John. *The Importance of Preserving our Civil and Religious Institutions from Destruction, Illustrated, in a Sermon, Preached at Warner, New Hampshire, March 9, 1815, At the Organization of a Moral Society in That Town.* Concord, N.H.: George Hough, 1815.

Woods, Leonard. "Duties of the Rich." *American National Preacher* 2 (April 1827): 161–76.

——— . *A Sermon delivered at the Tabernacle in Salem, Feb. 6, 1812, on Occasion of the Ordination of the Rev. Messrs. Samuel Newell, Adoniram Judson, Samuel Nott, Gordon Hall, and Luther Rice, Missionaries to the Heathen in Asia. Under the Direction of the Board of Commissioners for Foreign Missions.* Boston: Samuel T. Armstrong, 1812.

Worcester, Leonard. *Sermon, Preached at Peacham, Lord's Day, November 15th, 1801.* Peacham, Vt.: Samuel Goss, 1801.

Worcester, Samuel. *The Drunkard a Destroyer. A Discourse, Delivered Before the Massachusetts Society for Suppressing Intemperance, At their Anniversary Meeting, May 30, 1817.* Boston: John Eliot, 1817.

——— . *True Liberality. A Sermon, Preached in Boston on the First Anniversary of the American Society for Educating Pious Youth for the Gospel Ministry, Oct. 23, 1816.* Andover: Flagg & Gould, 1816.

Yale College Society of Inquiry Respecting Missions. *A Missionary Catechism, For the Use of Children; Containing a Brief View of the Moral Condition of the World, and the Progress of Missionary Efforts Among the Heathen.* New Haven: S. Converse, 1821.

Yale University. *Student Catalogue. 1801.* New Haven: T. Greene & Son, 1801.

Newspapers and Periodicals

American Baptist Magazine (Boston).
Boston Recorder (Boston).
Cherokee Phoenix and Indians' Advocate (New Echota).
Christian Advocate (Philadelphia).
Christian Advocate and Journal (New York).
Christian Intelligencer (New York).
Columbian Centinel (Boston).
Connecticut Evangelical Magazine (Hartford).
Connecticut Evangelical Magazine and Religious Intelligencer (Hartford).
Literary Cabinet (New Haven).
Magazine of the Reformed Dutch Church (New York).
Missionary Herald (Boston).
Niles' Weekly Register (Baltimore).
North American Review (Boston).

Panoplist (Boston).
Reformer and Christian (Philadelphia).
Spirit of the Pilgrims (Boston).
United States Telegraph (Washington).

SECONDARY SOURCES

Books

Abernathy, Thomas P. *From Frontier to Plantation in Tennessee.* Chapel Hill: Univ. of North Carolina Press, 1932.

Abzug, Robert. *Passionate Liberator: Theodore Dwight Weld and The Dilemma of Reform.* New York: Oxford Univ. Press, 1980.

Adams, T. M. *Prices Paid by Vermont Farmers for Goods and Services and Received by Them for Farm Products, 1790–1940: Wages of Vermont Farm Labor, 1780–1940.* Burlington: Vermont Agricultural Experiment Station, 1944.

Ahlstrom, Sydney. *A Religious History of the American People.* New Haven: Yale Univ. Press, 1972.

Albanese, Catherine. *Sons of the Fathers: The Civil Religion of the American Revolution.* Philadelphia: Temple Univ. Press, 1976.

Allmendinger, David. *Paupers and Scholars: The Transformation of Student Life in Nineteenth-Century New England.* New York: St. Martin's Press, 1975.

Andrew, John A., III. *Rebuilding the Christian Commonwealth: New England Congregationalists and Foreign Missions, 1800–1830.* Lexington: Univ. of Kentucky Press, 1976.

Appleby, Joyce. *Capitalism and A New Social Order: The Republican Vision of the 1790s.* New York: New York Univ. Press, 1984.

Axtell, James. *The Invasion Within: The Contest of Cultures in Colonial North America.* New York: Oxford Univ. Press, 1985.

Bailey, Hugh. *John Williams Walker: A Study in the Political, Social, and Cultural Life of the Old Southwest.* University: Univ. of Alabama Press, 1964.

Banner, James M., Jr. *To The Hartford Convention: The Federalists and the Origins of Party Politics in Massachusetts, 1789–1815.* New York: Knopf, 1970.

Banning, Lance. *The Jeffersonian Persuasion: Evolution of a Party Ideology.* Ithaca: Cornell Univ. Press, 1978.

Bass, Althea. *Cherokee Messenger.* Norman: Univ. of Oklahoma Press, 1936.

Beaver, R. Pierce, ed. *American Missions in Bicentennial Perspective.* South Pasadena: William Carey Library, 1977.

———. *Church, State, and the American Indians.* Saint Louis: Concordia Publishing House, 1966.

———. *Pioneers in Mission: The Early Missionary Ordination Sermons, Charges, and Instructions.* Grand Rapids: William Eerdmans, 1966.

Beeman, Richard. *The Evolution of the Southern Backcountry: A Case Study of Lunen-*

burg County, Virginia, 1746–1832. Philadelphia: Univ. of Pennsylvania Press, 1984.

Bercovitch, Sacvan. *The American Jeremiad.* Madison: Univ. of Wisconsin Press, 1978.

Berens, John F. *Providence and Patriotism in Early America, 1640–1815.* Charlottesville: Univ. Press of Virginia, 1978.

Berk, Stephen. *Calvinism versus Democracy: Timothy Dwight and the Origins of American Evangelical Orthodoxy.* Hamden, Ct.: Archon Books, 1974.

Berkhofer, Robert F., Jr. *Salvation and the Savage: An Analysis of Protestant Missions and American Indian Response, 1787–1862.* New York: Atheneum, 1972.

——— . *The White Man's Indian: Images of the American Indian from Columbus to the Present.* New York: Knopf, 1978.

Beveridge, Albert. *The Life of John Marshall.* 4 vols. Boston: Houghton Mifflin, 1919.

Binder, Frederick. *The Color Problem in Early National America as Viewed by John Adams, Jefferson and Jackson.* The Hague: Mouton, 1968.

Bloch, Ruth. *Visionary Republic: Millennial Themes in American Thought, 1756–1800.* New York: Cambridge Univ. Press, 1985.

Bloomfield, Maxwell. *American Lawyers in a Changing Society, 1776–1876.* Cambridge, Mass.: Harvard Univ. Press, 1976.

Blumenthal, Walter. *American Indians Dispossessed: Fraud in Land Cessions Forced Upon the Tribes.* Philadelphia: George McManus, 1955.

Blumin, Stuart. *The Urban Threshold: Growth and Change in a Nineteenth-Century American Community.* Chicago: Univ. of Chicago Press, 1976.

Bowden, Henry. *American Indians and Christian Missions: Studies in Cultural Conflict.* Chicago: Univ. of Chicago Press, 1981.

Boyer, Paul. *Urban Masses and Moral Order in America, 1820–1920.* Cambridge, Mass.: Harvard Univ. Press, 1978.

Bradley, Ian. *The Call to Seriousness: The Evangelical Impact on the Victorians.* New York: Macmillan, 1976.

Bradley, Joshua. *Accounts of Religious Revivals in Many Parts of the United States from 1815 to 1818.* Albany: G. J. Loomis, 1819.

A Brief History of the American Tract Society, instituted at Boston, 1814, and its relations to the American Tract Society at New York, instituted 1825. Boston: T. R. Marvin, 1857.

Brooke, John. *The Heart of the Commonwealth: Society and Political Culture in Worcester County, Massachusetts, 1713–1861.* New York: Cambridge Univ. Press, 1989.

Brown, John. *Old Frontiers: The Story of the Cherokee Indians from the Earliest Times to the Date of Their Removal to the West, 1838.* Kingsport, Tenn.: Southern Publishers, 1938.

Brown, Thomas. *Politics and Statesmanship: Essays on the American Whig Party.* New York: Columbia Univ. Press, 1985.

Browne, Gary. *Baltimore in the Nation, 1789–1861*. Chapel Hill: Univ. of North Carolina Press, 1980.

Bruce, Dickson D., Jr. *The Rhetoric of Conservatism: The Virginia Convention of 1829–30 and the Conservative Tradition in the South*. San Marino: Huntington Library, 1982.

Brumberg, Joan. *Mission for Life*. New York: Free Press, 1980.

Bushman, Richard, et al. *Uprooted Americans: Essays to Honor Oscar Handlin*. Boston: Little, Brown, 1979.

Byers, Edward. *The Nation of Nantucket: Society and Politics in an Early American Commercial Center, 1660–1820*. Boston: Northeastern Univ. Press, 1987.

Calhoun, Daniel. *The Intelligence of a People*. Princeton: Princeton Univ. Press, 1973.

Carwardine, Richard. *Trans-Atlantic Revivalism: Popular Evangelicalism in Britain and America, 1790–1865*. Westport, Ct.: Greenwood Press, 1978.

Caskey, Marie. *Chariot of Fire: Religion and the Beecher Family*. New Haven: Yale Univ. Press, 1978.

Cayton, Andrew. *The Frontier Republic: Ideology and Politics in the Ohio Country, 1780–1825*. Kent: Kent State Univ. Press, 1986.

Clark, Christopher. *The Roots of Rural Capitalism: Western Massachusetts, 1780–1860*. Ithaca: Cornell Univ. Press, 1990.

Cole, Donald. *Jacksonian Democracy in New Hampshire, 1800–1851*. Cambridge, Mass.: Harvard Univ. Press, 1970.

Coleman, Peter. *The Transformation of Rhode Island: 1790–1860*. Providence: Brown Univ. Press, 1969.

Collier, Christopher. *Roger Sherman's Connecticut: Yankee Politics and the American Revolution*. Middletown: Wesleyan Univ. Press, 1971.

Conforti, Joseph. *Samuel Hopkins and the New Divinity Movement: Calvinism, The Congregational Ministry, and Reform in New England Between the Great Awakenings*. Grand Rapids: Christian Univ. Press, 1981.

Conrad, Susan. *Perish the Thought: Intellectual Women in Romantic America, 1830–1860*. New York: Oxford Univ. Press, 1976.

Cott, Nancy. *The Bonds of Womanhood: "Woman's Sphere" in New England, 1780–1835*. New Haven: Yale Univ. Press, 1977.

Cotterill, R. S. *The Southern Indians: The Story of the Civilized Tribes Before Removal*. Norman: Univ. of Oklahoma Press, 1954.

Curti, Merle. *The American Peace Crusade, 1815–1860*. Reprint. New York: Octagon, 1973.

Curtis, James. *Andrew Jackson and the Search for Vindication*. Boston: Little, Brown, 1976.

Daniels, Bruce. *The Connecticut Town: Growth and Development, 1635–1790*. Middletown: Wesleyan Univ. Press, 1979.

Davis, David. *The Problem of Slavery in the Age of Revolution, 1770–1823*. Ithaca: Cornell Univ. Press, 1975.

Dexter, Franklin. *Biographical Sketches of the Graduates of Yale College with Annals of the College History*. New York: Henry Holt, 1911.

Diggins, John. *The Lost Soul of American Politics: Virtue, Self-Interest, and the Foundations of Liberalism*. New York: Basic Books, 1984.

Duckett, Alvin. *John Forsyth: Political Tactician*. Athens: Univ. of Georgia Press, 1962.

Dunstan, Leslie. *A Light to the City: 150 Years of the City Missionary Society of Boston, 1816–1966*. Boston: Beacon Press, 1966.

Dyer, Brainerd. *The Public Career of William M. Evarts*. Berkeley: Univ. of California Press, 1933.

Eaton, Cyrus. *Annals of the Town of Warren; with the Early History of St. George's, Broad Bay, and the Neighboring Settlements of the Waldo Patent*. Hallowell: Masters, Smith & Company, 1851.

Eaton, Rachel. *John Ross and the Cherokee Indians*. Menasha, Wis.: George Banta Publishing Company, 1914.

Ellis, Joseph. *After the Revolution: Profiles of Early American Culture*. New York: W. W. Norton, 1979.

Ellis, Richard. *The Union At Risk: Jacksonian Democracy, States' Rights, and the Nullification Crisis*. New York: Oxford Univ. Press, 1987.

Elsbree, Oliver. *The Rise of the Missionary Spirit in America, 1790–1815*. Williamsport: Williamsport Printing and Binding Co., 1928.

Epstein, Barbara. *The Politics of Domesticity: Women, Evangelism, and Temperance in Nineteenth-Century America*. Middletown: Wesleyan Univ. Press, 1981.

Esarey, Logan. *Internal Improvements in Early Indiana*. Indianapolis: Edward J. Hecker, 1912.

Essig, James. *The Bonds of Wickedness: American Evangelicals Against Slavery, 1770–1808*. Philadelphia: Temple Univ. Press, 1982.

Faler, Paul. *Mechanics and Manufacturers in the Early Industrial Revolution: Lynn, Massachusetts, 1780–1860*. Albany: State Univ. of New York Press, 1981.

Feller, Daniel. *The Public Lands in Jacksonian Politics*. Madison: Univ. of Wisconsin Press, 1984.

Field, David, comp. *Brief Memoirs of the Members of the Class Graduated at Yale College in September, 1802*. New Haven: Privately printed, 1863.

Fischer, David H. *The Revolution of American Conservatism: The Federalist Party in the Era of Jeffersonian Democracy*. New York: Harper, 1965.

Fisher, George. *The Life of Benjamin Silliman*. 2 vols. New York: Charles Scribner & Co., 1866.

Fliegelman, Jay. *Prodigals and Pilgrims: The American Revolution Against Patriarchal Authority, 1750–1800*. Cambridge, Mass.: Cambridge Univ. Press, 1982.

Formisano, Ronald. *The Birth of Mass Political Parties: Michigan, 1827–1861.* Princeton: Princeton Univ. Press, 1971.

———. *The Transformation of Political Culture: Massachusetts Parties, 1790s–1840s.* New York: Oxford Univ. Press, 1983.

Fraser, James. *Pedagogue for God's Kingdom: Lyman Beecher and the Second Great Awakening.* Lanham, Md.: University Press of America, 1985.

Friedman, Lawrence. *Gregarious Saints: Self and Community in American Abolitionism, 1830–1870.* Cambridge, Eng.: Cambridge Univ. Press, 1982.

Gabriel, Ralph. *Religion and Learning at Yale: The Church of Christ in the College and University, 1757–1957.* New Haven: Yale Univ. Press, 1958.

Gawalt, Gerard. *The Promise of Power: The Legal Profession in Massachusetts, 1760–1840.* Westport, Conn.: Greenwood Press, 1979.

Gerteis, Louis. *Morality & Utility in American Antislavery Reform.* Chapel Hill: Univ. of North Carolina Press, 1987.

Gibb, George. *The Saco-Lowell Shops: Textile Machinery Building in New England, 1813–1949.* Reprint. New York: Russell & Russell, 1969.

Gilmore, William. *Reading Becomes a Necessity of Life: Material and Cultural Life in Rural New England, 1780–1835.* Knoxville: Univ. of Tennessee Press, 1989.

Ginzberg, Lori. *Women and the Work of Benevolence: Morality, Politics, and Class in the Nineteenth-Century United States.* New Haven: Yale Univ. Press, 1990.

Goodman, Paul. *Towards A Christian Republic: Antimasonry and the Great Transition in New England, 1826–1836.* New York: Oxford Univ. Press, 1988.

Green, Michael. *The Politics of Indian Removal: Creek Government and Society in Crisis.* Lincoln: Univ. of Nebraska Press, 1982.

Gregory, Frances. *Nathan Appleton: Merchant and Entrepreneur, 1779–1861.* Charlottesville: Univ. Press of Virginia, 1975.

Gregory, Jack, and Rennard Strickland, eds. *Starr's History of the Cherokees.* Reprint. Fayetteville: Indian Heritage Association, 1967.

Greven, Philip. *The Protestant Temperament: Patterns of Child-Rearing, Religious Experience, and the Self in Early America.* New York: Knopf, 1977.

Gribbin, William. *The Churches Militant: The War of 1812 and American Religion.* New Haven: Yale Univ. Press, 1973.

Gunson, Niel. *Messengers of Grace: Evangelical Missionaries in the South Seas, 1797–1860.* Melbourne: Oxford Univ. Press, 1978.

Hall, Peter Dobkin. *The Organization of American Culture, 1700–1900: Private Institutions, Elites, and the Origins of American Nationality.* New York: New York Univ. Press, 1982.

Halttunen, Karen. *Confidence Men and Painted Women: A Study of Middle-Class Culture in America, 1830–1870.* New Haven: Yale Univ. Press, 1982.

Hammond, John. *The Politics of Benevolence: Revival Religion and American Voting Behavior.* Norwood, N.J.: Ablex Publishing Corporation, 1979.

Hampel, Robert. *Temperance and Prohibition in Massachusetts, 1813–1852*. Ann Arbor: UMI Research Press, 1982.
Harden, Edward. *The Life of George M. Troup*. Savannah: E. J. Purse, 1859.
Hargreaves, Mary. *The Presidency of John Quincy Adams*. Lawrence: Univ. Press of Kansas, 1985.
Hatch, Nathan. *The Democratization of American Christianity*. New Haven: Yale Univ. Press, 1989.
——— . *The Sacred Cause of Liberty: Republican Thought and the Millennium in Revolutionary New England*. New Haven: Yale Univ. Press, 1977.
Hawaiian Historical Society. *Sixteenth Annual Report*. N.p., 1951.
Hayes, Florence. *Daughters of Dorcas*. New York: Presbyterian Board of National Missions, 1952.
Haywood, John. *A Gazetteer of Vermont*. Boston: Tappan, Whittemore, & Mason, 1849.
Heath, Milton. *Constructive Liberalism: The Role of the State in Economic Development in Georgia to 1860*. Cambridge, Mass.: Harvard Univ. Press, 1954.
Hemenway, Abby, ed. *The Vermont Historical Gazetteer*. Burlington: A. Hemenway, 1867.
Hewitt, Nancy. *Women's Activism and Social Change: Rochester, New York, 1822–1872*. Ithaca: Cornell Univ. Press, 1984.
Hindus, Michael. *Prison and Plantation: Crime, Justice, and Authority in Massachusetts and South Carolina, 1767–1878*. Chapel Hill: Univ. of North Carolina Press, 1980.
The History of the American Education Society. Boston: Massachusetts Sabbath School Society, 1835.
Hofstadter, Richard. *The American Political Tradition and the Men Who Made It*. New York: Knopf, 1948.
Holmes, Richard. *Communities in Transition: Bedford and Lincoln, Massachusetts, 1729–1850*. Ann Arbor: UMI Press, 1980.
Holt, Michael. *The Political Crisis of the 1850s*. New York: John Wiley & Sons, 1978.
Horsman, Reginald. *Expansion and American Indian Policy, 1783–1812*. East Lansing: Michigan State Univ. Press, 1967.
——— . *The Origins of Indian Removal*. East Lansing: Michigan State Univ. Press, 1970.
Horwitz, Richard. *Anthropology Toward History: Culture and Work in a 19th-Century Maine Town*. Middletown: Wesleyan Univ. Press, 1978.
Howe, Daniel W. *The Political Culture of the American Whigs*. Chicago: Univ. of Chicago Press, 1979.
Hunnewell, James F. *A Century of Town Life: A History of Charlestown, Massachusetts, 1775–1887*. Boston: Little, Brown, 1888.
Hutchison, William. *Errand to the World: American Protestant Thought and Foreign Missions*. Chicago: Univ. of Chicago Press, 1987.

Isaac, Rhys. *The Transformation of Virginia, 1740–1790.* Chapel Hill: Univ. of North Carolina Press, 1982.
Jaher, Frederic. *The Urban Establishment: Upper Strata in Boston, New York, Charleston, Chicago, and Los Angeles.* Urbana: Univ. of Illinois Press, 1982.
Jedrey, Christopher. *The World of John Cleaveland: Family and Community in Eighteenth-Century New England.* New York: W. W. Norton, 1979.
Jehlen, Myra. *American Incarnation: The Individual, The Nation, and The Continent.* Cambridge, Mass.: Harvard Univ. Press, 1986.
Johnson, Curtis. *Islands of Holiness: Rural Religion in Upstate New York, 1790–1860.* Ithaca: Cornell Univ. Press, 1989.
Johnson, Paul. *A Shopkeeper's Millennium: Society and Revivals in Rochester, New York, 1815–1837.* New York: Hill & Wang, 1978.
Jones, A. D. *Memoir of Elder Abner Jones.* Boston: William Crosby & Co., 1842.
Kammen, Michael. *A Season of Youth: The American Revolution and the Historical Imagination.* New York: Knopf, 1978.
Keller, Charles. *The Second Great Awakening in Connecticut.* Reprint. New York: Archon Books, 1968.
Kelley, Brooks. *Yale: A History.* New Haven: Yale Univ. Press, 1974.
Kennedy, John. *Memoirs of the Life of William Wirt, Attorney-General of the United States.* 2 vols. Philadelphia: Lea & Blanchard, 1850.
Kerber, Linda. *Federalists in Dissent: Imagery and Ideology in Jeffersonian America.* Ithaca: Cornell Univ. Press, 1970.
Kett, Joseph. *Rites of Passage: Adolescence in America, 1790 to the Present.* New York: Basic Books, 1977.
Klein, Philip. *Pennsylvania Politics, 1817–1832: A Game Without Rules.* Philadelphia: Historical Society of Pennsylvania, 1940.
Kohl, Lawrence. *The Politics of Individualism: Parties and the American Character in the Jacksonian Era.* New York: Oxford Univ. Press, 1989.
Krout, John. *The Origins of Prohibition.* New York: Knopf, 1925.
Kulik, Gary, Roger Parks, Theodore Penn, eds. *The New England Mill Village, 1790–1860.* Cambridge, Mass.: MIT Press, 1982.
Lamb, Wallace. *The Lake Champlain and Lake George Valleys.* 3 vols. New York: American Historical Company, Inc., 1940.
Lamplugh, George. *Politics on the Periphery: Factions and Parties in Georgia, 1783–1806.* Newark: Univ. of Delaware Press, 1986.
Laslett, Peter. *The World We Have Lost: England Before the Industrial Age.* New York: Scribners, 1971.
Latner, Richard. *The Presidency of Andrew Jackson: White House Politics, 1829–1837.* Athens: Univ. of Georgia Press, 1979.
Laurie, Bruce. *Working People of Philadelphia, 1800–1850.* Philadelphia: Temple Univ. Press, 1980.

Lawrence, Alexander. *James Moore Wayne: Southern Unionist*. Chapel Hill: Univ. of North Carolina Press, 1943.

Lewis, O. F. *The Development of American Prisons and Prison Customs*. Albany: J. B. Lyon, 1922.

Lipson, Dorothy. *Freemasonry in Federalist Connecticut, 1789–1835*. Princeton: Princeton Univ. Press, 1977.

Loveland, Anne. *Southern Evangelicals and the Social Order, 1800–1860*. Baton Rouge: Louisiana State Univ. Press, 1980.

Lowery, Charles. *James Barbour, A Jeffersonian Republican*. University: Univ. of Alabama Press, 1984.

Luxon, Norval. *Niles' Weekly Register: News Magazine of the Nineteenth Century*. Baton Rouge: Louisiana State Univ. Press, 1947.

Lyons, Emory. *Isaac McCoy: His Plan of and Work for Indian Colonization*. Topeka: Kansas State Univ. Press, 1945.

McCandless, Perry. *A History of Missouri*. Vol. 2. Columbia: Univ. of Missouri Press, 1972.

McCormick, Richard. *The Second American Party System: Party Formation in the Jacksonian Era*. Chapel Hill: Univ. of North Carolina Press, 1966.

McCoy, Drew. *The Elusive Republic: Political Economy in Jeffersonian America*. Chapel Hill: Univ. of North Carolina Press, 1980.

McDonald, Forrest. *Novus Ordo Seclorum: The Intellectual Origins of the Constitution*. Lawrence: Univ. Press of Kansas, 1985.

McLoughlin, William. *Champions of the Cherokees: Evan and John B. Jones*. Princeton: Princeton Univ. Press, 1990.

———. *The Cherokee Ghost Dance: Essays on the Southeastern Indians, 1789–1861*. Macon: Mercer Univ. Press, 1984.

———. *Cherokee Renascence in the New Republic*. Princeton: Princeton Univ. Press, 1986.

———. *Cherokees and Missionaries, 1789–1839*. New Haven: Yale Univ. Press, 1984.

———. *New England Dissent, 1630–1833: The Baptists and the Separation of Church and State*. 2 vols. Cambridge, Mass.: Harvard Univ. Press, 1971.

———. *Revivals, Awakenings, and Reform: An Essay on Religion and Social Change in America, 1607–1977*. Chicago: Univ. of Chicago Press, 1978.

Maier, Pauline. *The Old Revolutionaries: Political Lives in the Age of Samuel Adams*. New York: Knopf, 1980.

Malone, Henry. *Cherokees of the Old South: A People in Transition*. Athens: Univ. of Georgia Press, 1956.

Marsden, George. *The Evangelical Mind and the New School Presbyterian Experience*. New Haven: Yale Univ. Press, 1970.

Martin, Calvin, ed. *The American Indian and the Problem of History*. New York: Oxford Univ. Press, 1987.

Matthews, Lyman. *Memoir of the Life and Character of Ebenezer Porter, D.D.*. Boston: Perkins & Marvin, 1837.

May, Henry. *The Enlightenment in America*. New York: Oxford Univ. Press, 1976.

Meyer, Donald. *The Instructed Conscience: The Shaping of the American National Ethic*. Philadelphia: Univ. of Pennsylvania Press, 1972.

Meyer, Leland. *The Life and Times of Colonel Richard M. Johnson of Kentucky*. New York: Columbia Univ. Press, 1932.

Miles, Edwin. *Jacksonian Democracy in Mississippi*. Chapel Hill: Univ. of North Carolina Press, 1960.

Miller, Char. *Fathers and Sons: The Bingham Family and the American Mission*. Philadelphia: Temple Univ. Press, 1982.

Miller, G. Howard. *The Revolutionary College: American Presbyterian Higher Education, 1707–1837*. New York: New York Univ. Press, 1976.

Miller, Samuel, Jr. *The Life of Samuel Miller*. 2 vols. Philadelphia: Claxton, Remsen, & Haffelfinger, 1869.

Mohl, Raymond. *Poverty in New York, 1783–1825*. New York: Oxford Univ. Press, 1971.

Mooney, Chase. *William H. Crawford, 1772–1834*. Lexington: Univ. of Kentucky Press, 1973.

Moore, Glover. *The Missouri Controversy, 1819–1821*. Lexington: Univ. of Kentucky Press, 1953.

Murray, Paul. *The Whig Party in Georgia, 1825–1853*. Chapel Hill: Univ. of North Carolina Press, 1948.

Nagel, Paul. *This Sacred Trust: American Nationality, 1798–1898*. New York: Oxford Univ. Press, 1971.

Nelson, John, Jr. *Liberty and Property: Political Economy and Policymaking in the New Nation, 1789–1812*. Baltimore: Johns Hopkins Univ. Press, 1987.

Nissenbaum, Stephen. *Sex, Diet, and Debility in Jacksonian America: Sylvester Graham and Health Reform*. Westport, Conn.: Greenwood Press, 1980.

Noll, Mark. *Princeton and the Republic, 1768–1822: The Search for a Christian Enlightenment in the Era of Samuel Stanhope Smith*. Princeton: Princeton Univ. Press, 1989.

Novak, Steven. *The Rights of Youth: American Colleges and Student Revolt, 1798–1815*. Cambridge, Mass.: Harvard Univ. Press, 1977.

Park, Edwards. *Memoir of Nathaniel Emmons; with Sketches of His Friends and Pupils*. Boston: Congregational Board of Publication, 1861.

Parks, Joseph. *Felix Grundy: Champion of Democracy*. Baton Rouge: Louisiana State Univ. Press, 1940.

Parsons, Rev. Isaac. *Memoir of the Life and Character of Rev. Joseph Vaill, Late Pastor of the Church of Christ in Hadlyme*. New York: Taylor & Dodd, 1839.

Paton, William, ed. *The Missionary Motive*. London: Student Christian Movement, 1913.

Peake, Ora. *A History of the United States Indian Factory System, 1795–1822*. Denver: Sage Books, 1954.

Pearce, Roy. *The Savages of America: A Study of the Indian and the Idea of Civilization*. Baltimore: Johns Hopkins Univ. Press, 1953.

Pease, William, and Jane Pease. *Ladies, Women & Wenches: Choice & Constraint in Antebellum Charleston & Boston*. Chapel Hill: Univ. of North Carolina Press, 1990.

———. *The Web of Progress: Private Values and Public Styles in Boston and Charleston, 1828–1843*. New York: Oxford Univ. Press, 1985.

Perry, Lewis, and Michael Fellman, eds. *Antislavery Reconsidered: New Perspectives on the Abolitionists*. Baton Rouge: Louisiana State Univ. Press, 1979.

Phillips, Clifton. *Protestant America and the Pagan World: The First Half-Century of the American Board of Commissioners for Foreign Missions, 1810–1860*. Cambridge, Mass.: Harvard Univ. Press, 1969.

Phillips, Joseph. *Jedidiah Morse and New England Congregationalism*. New Brunswick: Rutgers Univ. Press, 1983.

Poulson, Barry. *Value Added in Manufacturing, Mining, and Agriculture in the American Economy From 1809 to 1839*. Reprint. New York: Arno Press, 1975.

Pred, Allan. *Urban Growth and the Circulation of Information: The United States System of Cities, 1790–1840*. Cambridge, Mass.: Harvard Univ. Press, 1973.

Proceedings of the Massachusetts Historical Society, 2nd series, 14 (1900–1901). Boston: Published by the Society, 1901.

Prucha, Francis. *American Indian Policy in the Formative Years: The Indian Trade and Intercourse Acts, 1790–1834*. Lincoln: Univ. of Nebraska Press, 1962.

Prude, Jonathan. *The Coming of Industrial Order: Town and Factory Life in Rural Massachusetts, 1810–1860*. Cambridge, Eng.: Cambridge Univ. Press, 1983.

Remini, Robert. *Andrew Jackson and the Course of American Freedom, 1822–1832*. New York: Harper & Row, 1981.

Rice, Edwin. *The Sunday-School Movement and the American Sunday-School Union*. Philadelphia: Union Press, 1917.

Ridgway, Whitman. *Community Leadership in Maryland, 1790–1840: A Comparative Analysis of Power in Society*. Chapel Hill: Univ. of North Carolina Press, 1979.

Rogin, Michael. *Fathers and Children: Andrew Jackson and the Subjugation of the American Indian*. New York: Knopf, 1975.

Rohrbough, Malcolm. *The Trans-Appalachian Frontier: People, Societies, and Institutions, 1775–1850*. New York: Oxford Univ. Press, 1978.

Rollins, Richard. *The Long Journey of Noah Webster*. Philadelphia: Univ. of Pennsylvania Press, 1980.

Rorabaugh, William. *The Alcoholic Republic: An American Tradition*. New York: Oxford Univ. Press, 1979.

Rosenberg, Carroll Smith. *Religion and the Rise of the American City: The New York*

City Mission Movement, 1812–1870. Ithaca: Cornell Univ. Press, 1971.
Roth, Randolph. *The Democratic Dilemma: Religion, Reform, and the Social Order in the Connecticut River Valley of Vermont, 1791–1850*. New York: Cambridge Univ. Press, 1987.
Ryan, Mary. *Cradle of the Middle Class: The Family in Oneida County, New York, 1790–1865*. Cambridge, Eng.: Cambridge Univ. Press, 1981.
Satz, Ronald. *American Indian Policy in the Jacksonian Era*. Lincoln: Univ. of Nebraska Press, 1975.
Scheiber, Harry. *Ohio Canal Era: A Case Study of Government and the Economy, 1820–1861*. Athens: Ohio Univ. Press, 1969.
Schlesinger, Arthur, Jr. *The Age of Jackson*. Boston: Little, Brown, 1945.
Schultz, George A. *An Indian Canaan: Isaac McCoy and the Vision of an Indian State*. Norman: Univ. of Oklahoma Press, 1972.
Schultz, Stanley. *The Culture Factory: Boston Public Schools, 1789–1860*. New York: Oxford Univ. Press, 1973.
Scott, Donald. *From Office to Profession: The New England Ministry, 1750–1850*. Philadelphia: Univ. of Pennsylvania Press, 1978.
Scott, Nancy, ed. *A Memoir of Hugh Lawson White*. Philadelphia: J.B. Lippincott, 1856.
Semmel, Bernard. *The Methodist Revolution*. New York: Basic Books, 1973.
Shalhope, Robert. *John Taylor of Caroline: Pastoral Republican*. Columbia: Univ. of South Carolina Press, 1980.
Sheehan, Bernard. *Seeds of Extinction: Jeffersonian Philanthropy and the American Indian*. Chapel Hill: Univ. of North Carolina Press, 1973.
Silbey, Joel. *The Partisan Imperative: The Dynamics of American Politics Before the Civil War*. New York: Oxford Univ. Press, 1985.
Silverman, Kenneth. *Timothy Dwight*. New York: Twayne, 1969.
Siracusa, Carl. *A Mechanical People: Perceptions of the Industrial Order in Massachusetts, 1815–1880*. Middletown: Wesleyan Univ. Press, 1979.
Sklar, Kathryn. *Catharine Beecher: A Study in American Domesticity*. New Haven: Yale Univ. Press, 1973.
Slater, Peter. *Children in the New England Mind in Death and in Life*. Hamden, Conn.: Archon Books, 1977.
Slotkin, Richard. *Regeneration Through Violence: The Mythology of the American Frontier, 1600–1860*. Middletown: Wesleyan Univ. Press, 1973.
Smith, Ralph. *The History of Guilford, Connecticut, from its First Settlement in 1639*. Albany: J. Munsell, 1877.
Somkin, Fred. *Unquiet Eagle: Memory and Desire in the Idea of American Freedom, 1815–1860*. Ithaca: Cornell Univ. Press, 1967.
Sprague, William. *The Life of Jedidiah Morse, D.D.* New York: Anson D. F. Randolph & Company, 1874.

Starkey, Marion. *The Cherokee Nation*. New York: Knopf, 1946.

Starr, Edward. *A History of Cornwall, Connecticut*. New Haven: Tuttle, Morehouse, & Taylor, 1926.

Steiner, Bernard. *A History of the Plantation of Menunkatuck and of the Original Town of Guilford, Connecticut, comprising the Present Towns of Guilford and Madison*. Baltimore: Published by the Author, 1897.

Stewart, James B. *Wendell Phillips: Liberty's Hero*. Baton Rouge: Louisiana State Univ. Press, 1986.

Stokes, Anson Phelps. *Church and State in the United States*. 3 vols. New York: Harper & Brothers, 1950.

Strickland, W. P. *History of the American Bible Society, from its Organization to the Present Time*. New York: Harper & Brothers, 1849.

Taylor, Gordon. *The Angel-Makers: A Study in the Psychological Origins of Historical Change, 1750–1850*. London: Heinemann, 1958.

Taylor, James. *Memoir of Rev. Luther Rice, One of the First American Missionaries to the East*. Baltimore: Armstrong & Berry, 1841.

Thompson, Zadock. *A Gazetteer of the State of Vermont*. Montpelier: E. P. Walton, 1824.

Thornton, Tamara. *Cultivating Gentlemen: The Meaning of Country Life Among the Boston Elite, 1785–1860*. New Haven: Yale Univ. Press, 1989.

Tracy, Ebenezer C. *Memoir of the Life of Jeremiah Evarts, Esq*. Boston: Crocker & Brewster, 1845.

Tuveson, Ernest. *Redeemer Nation: The Idea of America's Millennial Role*. Chicago: Univ. of Chicago Press, 1968.

Tyler, Bennet. *Memoir of the Life and Character of Rev. Asahel Nettleton, D. D.* Boston: Congregational Board of Publication, 1856.

———. *New England Revivals as they existed At the Close of the Eighteenth, and the Beginning of the Nineteenth Centuries*. Boston: Massachusetts Sabbath School Society, 1846.

Viola, Herman. *Thomas L. McKenney: Architect of America's Early Indian Policy, 1816–1830*. Chicago: Swallow Press, 1974.

Walker, Robert. *Torchlights to the Cherokees: The Brainerd Mission*. New York: Macmillan, 1931.

Wallace, Anthony F. C. *Religion: An Anthropological View*. New York: Random House, 1966.

———. *Rockdale*. New York: Knopf, 1978.

Ward, John William. *Andrew Jackson: Symbol for an Age*. New York: Oxford Univ. Press, 1955.

Watson, Harry. *Jacksonian Politics and Community Conflict: The Emergence of the Second American Party System in Cumberland County, North Carolina*. Baton Rouge: Louisiana State Univ. Press, 1981.

Watts, Steven. *The Republic Reborn: War and the Making of Liberal America, 1790–1820*. Baltimore: Johns Hopkins Univ. Press, 1987.
Weisenburger, Francis. *The Life of John McLean: A Politician on the United States Supreme Court*. Columbus: Ohio State Univ. Press, 1937.
Wellington, Raynor. *The Political and Sectional Influence of the Public Lands, 1828–1842*. Cambridge: Riverside Press, 1914.
Welter, Rush. *The Mind of America, 1820–1860*. New York: Columbia Univ. Press, 1975.
Whipple, Charles. *Relation of the American Board of Commissioners for Foreign Missions to Slavery*. Boston: R. F. Wallent, 1861.
White, Richard. *The Roots of Dependency: Subsistence, Environment, and Social Change Among the Choctaws, Pawnees, and Navajos*. Lincoln: Univ. of Nebraska Press, 1983.
Wilentz, Sean. *Chants Democratic: New York City and the Rise of the American Working Class, 1788–1850*. New York: Oxford Univ. Press, 1984.
Wiltse, Charles. *John C. Calhoun: Nullifier, 1829–1839*. Indianapolis: Bobbs-Merrill Co., 1949.
Wishy, Bernard. *The Child and the Republic: The Dawn of Modern American Child Nurture*. Philadelphia: Univ. of Pennsylvania Press, 1968.
Wood, Gordon. *The Creation of the American Republic, 1776–1787*. New York: W. W. Norton, 1972.
Worcester, Samuel. *The Life and Labors of Rev. Samuel Worcester, D. D.* 2 vols. Boston: Crocker and Brewster, 1852.
Wright, Conrad, ed. *American Unitarianism, 1805–1865*. Boston: Northeastern Univ. Press, 1989.
Wyatt-Brown, Bertram. *Yankee Saints and Southern Sinners*. Baton Rouge: Louisiana State Univ. Press, 1985.
Wyman, Thomas. *The Genealogies and Estates of Charlestown, Massachusetts, 1629–1818*. 2 vols. Boston: David Clapp & Son, 1879.
Young, Mary. *Redskins, Ruffleshirts and Rednecks: Indian Allotments in Mississippi and Alabama, 1830–1860*. Norman: Univ. of Oklahoma Press, 1961.
Zevin, Robert. *The Growth of Manufacturing in Early Nineteenth Century New England*. Reprint. New York: Arno Press, 1975.

Articles and Essays

Anderson, Hattie. "Frontier Economic Problems in Missouri, 1815–1828, Part II." *Missouri Historical Review* 34 (January 1940): 182–203.
Andrew, John A., III. "Betsey Stockton: Stranger in a Strange Land." *Journal of Presbyterian History* 52 (Summer 1974): 157–66.
―――. "Educating the Heathen: The Foreign Mission School Controversy and American Ideals." *Journal of American Studies* 12 (December 1978): 331–42.

Andrews, Edward. "The County Grammar Schools and Academies of Vermont." *Vermont Historical Society Proceedings*, n.s., 4 (1936): 117–211.

Appleby, Joyce. "Republicanism and Ideology." *American Quarterly* 37 (Fall 1985): 461–73.

———. "Republicanism in Old and New Contexts." *WMQ*, 3d series, 43 (January 1986): 20–34.

Ashworth, John. "The Relationship Between Capitalism and Humanitarianism." *AHR* 92 (October 1987): 813–28.

Axtell, James. "Some Thoughts on the Ethnohistory of Missions." *Ethnohistory* 29 (1982): 35–41.

Baird, W. David. "The Reduction of a People: The Quapaw Removal, 1824–1834." *Red River Valley Historical Review* 1 (Spring 1974): 21–36.

Banner, Lois. "Presbyterians and Voluntarism in the Early Republic." *Journal of Presbyterian History* 50 (Fall 1972): 187–205.

Banning, Lance. "Jeffersonian Ideology Revisited: Liberal and Classical Ideas in the New American Republic." *WMQ*, 3d series, 43 (January 1986): 1–19.

Beeman, Richard. "The New Social History and the Search for 'Community' in Colonial America." *American Quarterly* 29 (Fall 1977): 422–43.

Beidelman, T. O. "Social Theory and the Study of Christian Missions in Africa." *Africa* 44 (July 1974): 235–49.

Bellah, Robert. "The Revolution and Civil Religion." In Jerald Brauer, ed., *Religion and the American Revolution*, pp. 55–73. Philadelphia: Fortress Press, 1976.

Berkhofer, Robert F., Jr. "Protestants, Pagans, and Sequences Among the North American Indians, 1760–1860." *Ethnohistory* 10 (Summer 1963): 201–32.

Berthoff, Rowland. "Independence and Attachment, Virtue and Interest: From Republican Citizen to Free Enterpriser, 1787–1837." In Richard Bushman et al., *Uprooted Americans*, pp. 97–124. Boston: Little, Brown, 1979.

———. "Writing a History of Things Left Out." *Reviews in American History* 14 (March 1986): 1–16.

Bidwell, Percy. "Rural Economy in New England at the Beginning of the Nineteenth Century." *Connecticut Academy of Arts and Sciences Transactions* 20 (1916): 241–399.

Billington, Louis. "'Female Laborers in the Church': Women Preachers in the Northeastern United States, 1790–1840." *Journal of American Studies* 19 (December 1985): 369–94.

Blau, Joseph. "The Christian Party in Politics." *Review of Religion* 11 (November 1946): 18–35.

Bowden, Henry. "An Overview of Cultural Factors in the American Protestant Missionary Enterprise." In R. Pierce Beaver, ed., *American Missions in Bicentennial Perspective*, pp. 40–62. South Pasadena: William Carey Library, 1977.

Boylan, Anne. "Evangelical Womanhood in the Nineteenth Century: The Role of Women in Sunday Schools." *Feminist Studies* 4 (October 1978): 62–80.

——— . "The Role of Conversion in Nineteenth-Century Sunday Schools." *American Quarterly* 20 (Spring 1979): 35–48.

——— . "Sunday Schools and Changing Evangelical Views of Children in the 1820s." *Church History* 48 (September 1979): 320–33.

——— . "Timid Girls, Venerable Widows and Dignified Matrons: Life Cycle Patterns Among Organized Women in New York and Boston, 1797–1840." *American Quarterly* 38 (Winter 1986): 779–97.

——— . "Women in Groups: An Analysis of Women's Benevolent Organizations in New York and Boston, 1797–1840." *Journal of American History* 71 (December 1984): 497–523.

Breitenbach, William. "The Consistent Calvinism of the New Divinity Movement." *WMQ*, 3d series, 41 (April 1984): 241–64.

Brown, G. Gordon. "Missions and Cultural Diffusion." *American Journal of Sociology* 50 (November 1944): 214–19.

Brown, Richard D. "The Emergence of Urban Society in Rural Massachusetts, 1760–1820." *Journal of American History* 61 (June 1974): 29–51.

——— . "The Emergence of Voluntary Associations in Massachusetts, 1760–1830." *Journal of Voluntary Action Research* 2 (1973): 64–73.

——— . "Modernization: A Victorian Climax." *American Quarterly* 27 (December 1975): 533–48.

Buss, Dietrich. "The Millennial Vision as Motive for Religious Benevolence and Reform: Timothy Dwight and the New England Evangelicals Reconsidered." *Fides et Historia* 16 (Fall–Winter 1983): 18–34.

Cain, Marvin. "William Wirt Against Andrew Jackson: Reflections of an Era." *Mid-America* 47 (April 1965): 113–38.

Cayton, Andrew. "The Fragmentation of 'A Great Family': The Panic of 1819 and the Rise of a Middling Interest in Boston, 1818–1822." *Journal of the Early Republic* 2 (Summer 1982): 143–67.

Clark, Christopher. "Household Economy, Market Exchange, and the Rise of Capitalism in the Connecticut Valley: 1800–1860." *Journal of Social History* 13 (Winter 1979): 169–89.

Cole, Arthur. "Cyclical and Sectional Variations in the Sale of Public Lands, 1816–1860." *Review of Economic Statistics* 9 (January 1927): 41–53.

Coleman, Louis. "Cyrus Byrington: Missionary to the Choctaws." *Chronicles of Oklahoma* 62 (1984–85): 360–87.

Conforti, Joseph. "David Brainerd and the Nineteenth Century Missionary Movement." *Journal of the Early Republic* 5 (Fall 1985): 308–29.

——— . "Samuel Hopkins and the New Divinity: Theology, Ethics, and Social Reform in Eighteenth-Century New England." *WMQ*, 3d series, 34 (October 1977): 572–89.

Cott, Nancy. "Young Women in the Second Great Awakening in New England." *Feminist Studies* 3 (Fall 1975): 15–29.

Dalzell, Robert F., Jr. "The Rise of the Waltham-Lowell System and Some Thoughts on the Political Economy of Modernization in Ante-Bellum Massachusetts." *Perspectives in American History* 9 (1975): 229–68.

Davis, David. "Reflections on Abolitionism and Ideological Hegemony." *AHR* 92 (October 1987): 797–812.

Dawley, Alan, and Paul Faler. "Working Class Culture and Politics in the Industrial Revolution: Sources of Loyalism and Rebellion." *Journal of Social History* 10 (June 1976): 466–80.

DeRosier, Arthur H., Jr. "Cyrus Kingsbury—Missionary to the Choctaws." *Journal of Presbyterian History* 50 (Winter 1972): 267–87.

———. "John C. Calhoun and the Removal of the Choctaw Indians." *Proceedings of the South Carolina Historical Association* (1957): 33–45.

———. "Pioneers with Conflicting Ideals: Christianity and Slavery in the Choctaw Nation." *Journal of Mississippi History* 21 (1959): 174–89.

Dexter, Franklin. "Student Life at Yale College Under the First President Dwight (1795–1817)." *Proceedings of the American Antiquarian Society* 27 (October 1917): 318–35.

Dickson, Charles. "Jeremiads in the New American Republic: The Case of National Fasts in the John Adams Administration." *New England Quarterly* 60 (June 1987): 187–207.

Ershkowitz, Herbert, and William Shade. "Consensus or Conflict? Political Behavior in the State Legislatures during the Jacksonian Era." *Journal of American History* 58 (December 1971): 591–621.

Farnum, Anne. "A Society of Societies: Associations and Voluntarism in Early Nineteenth-Century Salem." *Essex Institute Historical Collections* 113 (July 1977): 181–90.

———. "Uncle Varnum's Farm: Refuge or Workhouse for Salem's Poor?" *Essex Institute Historical Collections* 109 (January 1973): 60–86.

Farrell, Richard. "Internal-Improvement Projects in Southwestern Ohio, 1815–1834." *Ohio History* 80 (Winter 1971): 4–23.

Field, Alexander. "Sectoral Shift in Antebellum Massachusetts: A Reconsideration." *Explorations in Economic History* 15 (April 1978): 146–71.

Fike, Claude. "The Gubernatorial Administrations of Governor Gerard Chittocque Brandon, 1825–1832." *Journal of Mississippi History* 35 (August 1973): 247–65.

Folbre, Nancy. "The Wealth of Patriarchs: Deerfield, Massachusetts, 1760–1840." *Journal of Interdisciplinary History* 16 (Autumn 1985): 199–220.

Formisano, Ronald. "Deferential-Participant Politics: The Early Republic's Political Culture, 1789–1840." *American Political Science Review* 68 (June 1974): 473–87.

Foster, Stephen. "A Connecticut Separate Church: Strict Congregationalism in Cornwall, 1780–1809." *New England Quarterly* 39 (1966), 309–33.

Freeman, John. "The Indian Convert: Theme and Variation." *Ethnohistory* 12 (Spring 1965): 113–28.

Gawalt, Gerard. "Sources of Anti-Lawyer Sentiment in Massachusetts, 1740–1840." *American Journal of Legal History* 14 (1970): 283–307.

Giltner, John. "The Fragmentation of New England Congregationalism and the Founding of Andover Seminary." *Journal of Religious Thought* 20 (1963–64): 27–42.

Goodheart, Lawrence, and Richard Curry, eds. "The Trinitarian Indictment of Unitarianism: The Letters of Elizur Wright, Jr., 1826–1827." *Journal of the Early Republic* 3 (Fall 1983): 281–96.

Goodman, Paul. "The Social Basis of New England Politics in Jacksonian America." *Journal of the Early Republic* 6 (Spring 1986): 23–58.

[Goodrich, Chauncey]. "Narrative of Revivals of Religion in Yale College, From Its Commencement to the Present Time." *Journal of the American Education Society* 10 (February 1838): 289–310.

Gordon, Mary. "Patriots and Christians: A Reassessment of Nineteenth-Century School Reformers." *Journal of Social History* 11 (Summer 1978): 554–73.

Greene, Jack. "An Uneasy Connection: An Analysis of the Preconditions of the American Revolution." In Stephen Kurtz and James Hutson, eds., *Essays on the American Revolution*, pp. 32–80. New York: W. W. Norton, 1973.

Greven, Philip, Jr. "Youth, Maturity, and Religious Conversion: A Note on the Ages of Converts in Andover, Massachusetts, 1711–1749." *Essex Institute Historical Collections* 108 (1972): 119–34.

Gribbin, William. "Antimasonry, Religious Radicalism, and the Paranoid Style of the 1820's." *The History Teacher* 7 (February 1974): 239–54.

———. "The Covenant Transformed: The Jeremiad Tradition and the War of 1812." *Church History* 40 (September 1971): 297–305.

Gross, Robert. "Lonesome in Eden: Dickinson, Thoreau and the Problem of Community in Nineteenth-Century New England." *Canadian Review of American Studies* 14 (Spring 1983): 1–17.

Grossbart, Stephen. "Seeking the Divine Favor: Conversion and Church Admission in Eastern Connecticut, 1711–1832." *WMQ*, 3d series, 46 (October 1989): 696–740.

Halbert, H. S. "Story of the Treaty of Dancing Rabbit." *Mississippi Valley Historical Society Publications* 6 (1903): 373–402.

Handsman, Russell. "Historical Archaeology and Capitalism, Subscriptions and Separations: The Production of Individualism." *North American Archaeologist* 4 (1983): 63–79.

Harlan, Louis R. "The Public Career of William Berkeley Lewis." *Tennessee Historical Quarterly* 7 (1948): 3–37, 118–51.

Harrison, Brian. "A Genealogy of Reform in Modern Britain." In Christine Bolt and Seymour Drescher, eds., *Anti-Slavery, Religion, and Reform: Essays in Memory of Roger Anstey,* pp. 119–48. Hamden, Conn.: Archon Books, 1980.

Haskell, Thomas. "Capitalism and the Origins of the Humanitarian Sensibility." Parts 1, 2. *AHR* 90 (April, June, 1985): 339–61, 547–66.

———. "Convention and Hegemonic Interest in the Debate over Antislavery: A Reply to Davis and Ashworth." *AHR* 92 (October 1987): 829–78.

Hatch, Nathan. "The Christian Movement and the Demand for a Theology of the People." *Journal of American History* 67 (December 1980): 545–67.

Heale, M. J. "The New York Society for the Prevention of Pauperism, 1817–1823." *New York Historical Society Quarterly* 55 (April 1971): 153–76.

Hendricks, Rickey. "Henry Clay and Jacksonian Indian Policy: A Political Anachronism." *The Filson Club History Quarterly* 60 (April 1986): 218–38.

Henretta, James. "Families and Farms: *Mentalite* in Pre-Industrial America." *WMQ*, 3d series, 35 (January 1978): 3–32.

Higginbotham, Mary. "The Creek Path Mission." *Journal of Cherokee Studies* 1 (1976): 72–86.

Howe, Daniel. "Victorian Culture in America." In Daniel Howe, ed., *Victorian America*, pp. 3–28. Philadelphia: University of Pennsylvania Press, 1976.

Hutchison, William. "New England's Further Errand: Millennial Belief and the Beginnings of Foreign Missions." *Proceedings of the Massachusetts Historical Society* 94 (1982): 49–64.

John, Richard. "Taking Sabbatarianism Seriously: The Postal System, the Sabbath, and the Transformation of American Political Culture." *Journal of the Early Republic* 10 (Winter 1990): 517–67.

Johnson, Parkes. "Lucius Bolles: Pastor and Friend of Missions." *Foundations* 22 (October–December 1979): 306–12.

Johnson, Paul. "The Modernization of Mayo Greenleaf Patch: Land, Family, and Marginality in New England, 1766–1818." *New England Quarterly* 55 (October 1982): 488–516.

Juster, Susan. "'In a Different Voice': Male and Female Narratives of Religious Conversion in Post-Revolutionary America." *American Quarterly* 41 (March 1989): 34–62.

Kaestle, Carl, and Maris Vinovskis. "From Apron Strings to ABCs: Parents, Children, and Schooling in Nineteenth-Century Massachusetts." *American Journal of Sociology* 84 (Supplement): 39–80.

Kafer, Peter. "The Making of Timothy Dwight: A Connecticut Morality Tale." *WMQ*, 3d series, 47 (April 1990): 189–209.

Kett, Joseph. "Growing Up in Rural New England, 1800–1840." In Tamara Hareven, ed., *Anonymous Americans: Explorations in Nineteenth-Century Social History*, pp. 1–16. Englewood Cliffs: Prentice-Hall, 1971.

Kirsch, George. "Clerical Dismissals in Colonial and Revolutionary New Hampshire." *Church History* 49 (June 1980): 160–77.

Kloppenberg, James. "The Virtues of Liberalism: Christianity, Republicanism, and Ethics in Early American Political Discourse." *Journal of American History* 74 (June 1987): 9–33.

Kohl, Lawrence. "The Concept of Social Control and the History of Jacksonian America." *Journal of the Early Republic* 5 (Spring 1985): 21–34.

Latner, Richard. "A New Look at Jacksonian Politics." *Journal of American History* 61 (March 1975): 943–69.

Lewis, Jan. "The Republican Wife: Virtue and Seduction in the Early Republic." *WMQ*, 3d series, 44 (October 1987): 689–721.

Lewis, W. David. "The Reformer as Conservative: Protestant Counter-Subversion in the Early Republic." In Stanley Coben and Lorman Ratner, eds., *The Development of an American Culture*, pp. 64–91. Englewood Cliffs: Prentice-Hall, 1970.

Lewitt, Robert. "Indian Missions and Anti-Slavery Sentiment: A Conflict of Evangelical and Humanitarian Ideals." *Mississippi Valley Historical Review* 50 (1963): 39–55.

Lockridge, Kenneth. "Social Change and the Meaning of the American Revolution." *Journal of Social History* 6 (1973): 403–39.

McDermott, John, ed. "Isaac McCoy's Second Exploring Trip in 1828." *Kansas Historical Quarterly* 13 (August 1945): 400–62.

McLachlan, James. "The 'Choice of Hercules': American Student Societies in the Early 19th Century." In Lawrence Stone, ed. *The University in Society* (2 vols.), 2: 449–94. Princeton: Princeton Univ. Press, 1974.

McLoughlin, William. "Cherokee Anti-Mission Sentiment, 1824–1828." *Ethnohistory* 21 (Fall 1974): 361–70.

———. "Civil Disobedience and Evangelism Among the Missionaries to the Cherokees, 1829–1839." *Journal of Presbyterian History* 51 (Summer 1973): 116–39.

———. "Experiment in Cherokee Citizenship, 1817–1829." *American Quarterly* 33 (Spring 1981): 3–25.

———. "Georgia's Role in Instigating Compulsory Indian Removal." *Georgia Historical Quarterly* 70 (Winter 1986): 605–32.

———. "The Missionary Dilemma." *Canadian Review of American Studies* 16 (Winter 1985): 395–409.

———. "Red Indians, Black Slavery and White Racism: America's Slaveholding Indians." *American Quarterly* 26 (October 1974): 367–85.

———. "The Relevance of Congregational Christianity: Barrington Congregational Church, 1717–1967." *Rhode Island History* 29 (Summer and Fall 1970): 63–81.

———. "The Role of Religion in the Revolution: Liberty of Conscience and Cultural Cohesion in the New Nation." In Stephen Kurtz and James Hutson, eds., *Essays on the American Revolution*, pp. 197–255. New York: W. W. Norton, 1973.

Malone, Henry. "The *Cherokee Phoenix:* Supreme Expression of Cherokee Nationalism." *Georgia Historical Quarterly* 34 (September 1950): 163–86.

Mathews, Donald. "Religion in the Old South: Speculation on Methodology." *South Atlantic Quarterly* 73 (Winter 1974): 34–52.

———. "The Second Great Awakening as an Organizing Process, 1780–1830: An Hypothesis." *American Quarterly* 21 (Spring 1969): 23–43.

May, Dean, and Maris Vinovskis. "A Ray of Millennial Light: Early Education and Social Reform in the Infant School Movement in Massachusetts, 1826–1840." In Tamara Hareven, ed., *Family and Kin in Urban Communities, 1700–1930*, pp. 62–99. New York: New Viewpoints, 1977.

Miles, Edwin. "After John Marshall's Decision: *Worcester v. Georgia* and the Nullification Crisis." *Journal of Southern History* 39 (1973): 519–44.

Miles, William. "'Enamored with Colonization': Isaac McCoy's Plan of Indian Reform." *Kansas Historical Quarterly* 38 (Autumn 1972): 268–86.

Miller, Perry. "From the Covenant to the Revival," in James Smith and A. L. Jamison, eds., *The Shaping of American Religion* (4 vols.), 1: 322–68. Princeton: Princeton Univ. Press, 1961.

Mohl, Raymond. "Education as Social Control in New York City, 1784–1825." *New York History* 51 (March 1970): 219–37.

Moorhead, James. "Between Progress and Apocalypse: A Reassessment of Millennialism in American Religious Thought, 1800–1880." *Journal of American History* 71 (December 1984): 524–42.

Moss, Richard. "Republicanism, Liberalism, and Identity: The Case of Jedidiah Morse." *Essex Institute Historical Collections* 126 (October 1990): 209–36.

Nettels, Curtis. "The National Cost of the Inland Frontier, 1820–1830." *Wisconsin Academy of Sciences, Arts and Letters, Transactions* 25 (1930): 1–37.

Noll, Mark. "Common Sense Traditions and American Evangelical Thought." *American Quarterly* 37 (Summer 1985): 216–38.

Norwood, Frederick. "Strangers in a Strange Land: Removal of the Wyandot Indians." *Methodist History* 14 (April 1975): 45–60.

Pargellis, Stanley. "The Problem of American Indian History." *Ethnohistory* 4 (Spring 1957): 113–24.

Parsons, Lynn. "'A Perpetual Harrow Upon My Feelings': John Quincy Adams and the American Indian." *New England Quarterly* 46 (September 1973): 339–79.

Patterson, James. "Motives in the Development of Foreign Missions Among American Baptists, 1810–1826." *Foundations* 19 (October–December 1976): 298–319.

Peabody, Andrew. "Hopkinsianism." *Proceedings of the American Antiquarian Society* 5 (October 1888): 437–61.

Peacock, Mary. "Methodist Mission Work Among the Cherokee Indians before the Removal." *Methodist History* 3 (1965): 20–39.

Pendleton, Othneill, Jr. "Temperance and the Evangelical Churches." *Journal of the Presbyterian Historical Society* 25 (1947): 14–45.

Perdue, Theda. "The Conflict Within: The Cherokee Power Structure and Removal." *Georgia Historical Quarterly* 73 (Fall 1989): 467–91.

———. "John Ross and the Cherokees." *Georgia Historical Quarterly* 70 (Fall 1986): 456–76.

———. "Rising from the Ashes: *The Cherokee Phoenix* as an Ethnohistorical Source." *Ethnohistory* 24 (Summer 1977): 207–18.

Pflanze, Otto. "Toward a Psychoanalytic Interpretation of Bismarck." *AHR* 77 (April 1972): 419–44.

Phillips, Kim. "The Pennsylvania Origins of the Jackson Movement." *Political Science Quarterly* 91 (Fall 1976): 489–508.

Piggin, Stuart. "Assessing Nineteenth-Century Missionary Motivation: Some Considerations of Theory and Method." In Derek Baker, ed., *Religious Motivation: Biographical and Sociological Problems for the Church Historian*, pp. 327–37. Oxford: Basil Blackwell, 1978.

Prucha, Francis. "Andrew Jackson's Indian Policy: A Reassessment." *Journal of American History* 56 (December 1969): 527–39.

———. "Thomas L. McKenney and the New York Indian Board." *Mississippi Valley Historical Review* 48 (March 1962): 635–55.

Rabe, Valentin. "Evangelical Logistics: Mission Support and Resources to 1920." In John Fairbank, ed., *The Missionary Enterprise in China and America*, pp. 56–90. Cambridge: Harvard Univ. Press, 1974.

Rogin, Michael. "Liberal Society and the Indian Question." *Politics and Society* 1 (May 1971): 269–312.

Rohrer, James. "Sunday Mails and the Church-State Theme in Jacksonian America." *Journal of the Early Republic* 7 (Spring 1987): 53–74.

Rose, Anne. "Social Sources of Denominationalism Reconsidered: Post-Revolutionary Boston as a Case Study." *American Quarterly* 38 (Summer 1986): 243–64.

Rubinstein, Murray. "'Go Ye Unto the World': The Defining of the Missionary's Task in America and China, 1830–1850." *Academia Sinica* 10 (1980): 377–400.

Russo, David. "The Major Political Issues of the Jacksonian Period: The Development of Party Loyalty in Congress, 1830–1840." *Transactions of the American Philosophical Society* 62 (1972), part 5.

Ryan, Mary. "A Women's Awakening: Evangelical Religion and the Families of Utica, New York, 1800–1840." *American Quarterly* 30 (Winter 1978): 602–23.

Satz, Ronald. "Cherokee Traditionalism, Protestant Evangelism, and the Trail of Tears." *Tennessee Historical Quarterly* 44 (1985): 285–301, 380–401.

Schmotter, James. "Ministerial Careers in Eighteenth-Century New England: The Social Context, 1700–1760." *Journal of Social History* 9 (Winter 1975): 249–67.

Schultz, Stanley. "Temperance Reform in the Antebellum South: Social Control and Urban Order." *South Atlantic Quarterly* 83 (Summer 1984): 323–39.

Schwartz, Hillel. "Adolescence and Revivals in Ante-Bellum Boston." *Journal of Religious History* 8 (December 1974): 144–58.

Scull, Andrew. "The Discovery of the Asylum Revisited: Lunacy Reform in the New American Republic." In Andrew Scull, ed., *Madhouses, Mad-Doctors, and Madmen: The Social History of Psychiatry in the Victorian Era*, pp. 144–65. Philadelphia: Univ. of Pennsylvania Press, 1981.

———. "Humanitarianism or Control? Some Observations on the Historiography of Anglo-American Psychiatry." In Martin Wiener, ed., *Humanitarianism or Control: A Symposium on Aspects of Nineteenth-Century Social Reform in Britain and America*, pp. 21–41. Rice Univ. Studies, v. 67: Winter 1981.

Shalhope, Robert. "Jacksonian Politics in Missouri: A Comment on the McCormick Thesis." *Civil War History* 15 (September 1969): 210–25.

———. "Republicanism and Early American Historiography." *WMQ*, 3d series, 39 (April 1982): 334–56.

Shiels, Richard. "The Feminization of American Congregationalism, 1730–1835." *American Quarterly* 33 (Spring 1981): 46–62.

———. "The Scope of the Second Great Awakening: Andover, Massachusetts, as a Case Study." *Journal of the Early Republic* 5 (Summer 1985): 223–46.

———. "The Second Great Awakening in Connecticut: Critique of the Traditional Interpretation." *Church History* 49 (December 1980): 401–15.

Shy, John. "The American Revolution: The Military Conflict Considered as a Revolutionary War." In Stephen Kurtz and James Hutson, eds., *Essays on the American Revolution*, pp. 121–56. New York: Norton, 1973.

Silver, James. "A Counter-Proposal to the Indian Removal Policy of Andrew Jackson." *Journal of Mississippi History* 4 (1942): 207–15.

Sloan, Herbert, and Peter Onuf. "Politics, Culture, and the Revolution in Virginia." *Virginia Magazine of History and Biography* 91 (July 1983): 259–84.

Smith, Daniel Scott. "A Perspective on Demographic Methods and Effects on Social History." *WMQ*, 3d series, 39 (July 1982): 442–68.

Smith, Timothy. "Righteousness and Hope: Christian Holiness and the Millennial Vision in America, 1800–1900." *American Quarterly* 31 (Spring 1979): 21–45.

Smyth, Ralph. "John Evarts of Guilford, Conn., and His Descendants." *New England Historic & Genealogical Register* 61 (1907): 25–30, 307.

Snyder, K. Alan. "Foundations of Liberty: The Christian Republicanism of Timothy Dwight and Jedidiah Morse." *New England Quarterly* 56 (1983): 382–97.

Stommel, Henry, and Elizabeth Stommel. "The Year Without a Summer." *Scientific American* 240 (June 1979): 176–86.

Streifford, David. "The American Colonization Society: An Application of Republican Ideology to Early Antebellum Reform." *Journal of Southern History* 45 (May 1979): 201–20.

Strickland, William. "The Rhetoric of Removal and the Trail of Tears: Chero-

kee Speaking Against Jackson's Indian Removal Policy, 1828–1832." *Southern Speech Communication Journal* 47 (Spring 1982): 292–309.
Sweet, Douglas. "Church Vitality and the American Revolution: Historiographical Consensus and Thoughts Towards a New Perspective." *Church History* 45 (September 1976): 341–57.
Thornton, Tamara. "Between Generations: Boston Agricultural Reform and the Aging of New England, 1815–1830." *New England Quarterly* 59 (June 1986): 189–211.
Tiryakian, Edward. "A Model of Societal Change and its Lead Indicators." In Samuel Klausner, ed., *The Study of Total Societies*, pp. 69–97. New York: Praeger, 1967.
Twaddell, Elizabeth. "The American Tract Society, 1814–1860." *Church History* 15 (1946): 116–32.
Valliere, Kenneth. "Benjamin Currey, Tennessean Among the Cherokees: A Study of the Removal Policy of Andrew Jackson, Part I." *Tennessee Historical Quarterly* 41 (Summer 1982): 140–58.
Wallace, Anthony F. C. "Revitalization Movements." *American Anthropologist* 58 (April 1956): 264–81.
Wangh, Martin. "The 'Evocation of a Proxy': A Psychological Maneuver, Its Use as a Defense, Its Purposes and Genesis." *Psychoanalytic Study of the Child* 17 (1962): 451–69.
Washburn, Wilcomb. "Indian Removal Policy: Administrative, Historical and Moral Criteria for Judging Its Success or Failure." *Ethnohistory* 12 (Summer 1965): 274–78.
Waters, John. "Family, Inheritance, and Migration in Colonial New England: The Evidence from Guilford, Connecticut." *WMQ*, 3d series, 39 (January 1982): 64–86.
———. "Patrimony, Succession, and Social Stability: Guilford, Connecticut, in the Eighteenth Century." *Perspectives in American History* 10 (1976): 131–60.
Watts, Steven. "Masks, Morals, and the Market: American Literature and Early Capitalist Culture, 1790–1820." *Journal of the Early Republic* 6 (Summer 1986): 127–49.
Wood, Gordon. "Conspiracy and the Paranoid Style: Causality and Deceit in the Eighteenth Century." *WMQ*, 3d series, 39 (July 1982): 401–41.
Wyatt-Brown, Bertram. "The Antimission Movement in the Jacksonian South: A Study in Regional Folk Culture." *Journal of Southern History* 36 (November 1970): 501–29.
———. "Conscience and Career: Young Abolitionists and Missionaries." In Christine Bolt and Seymour Drescher, eds., *Anti-Slavery, Religion, and Reform: Essays in Memory of Roger Anstey*, pp. 183–203. Hamden, Conn.: Archon Books, 1980.
———. "Prelude to Abolitionism: Sabbatarian Politics and the Rise of the Second

Party System." *Journal of American History* 58 (September 1971): 316–41.

Young, Mary. "The Cherokee Nation: Mirror of the Republic." *American Quarterly* 33 (Winter 1981): 502–24.

———. "Congress Looks West: Liberal Ideology and Public Land Policy in the Nineteenth Century." In David Ellis, ed., *The Frontier in American Development*, pp. 74–112. Ithaca: Cornell Univ. Press, 1969.

———. "The Exercise of Sovereignty in Cherokee Georgia." *Journal of the Early Republic* 10 (Spring 1990): 43–63.

———. "Indian Removal and the Attack on Tribal Autonomy: The Cherokee Case." In John Mahon, ed., *Indians of the Lower South: Past and Present*, pp. 125–42. Pensacola: Gulf Coast History and Humanities Conference, 1975.

———. "Indian Removal and Land Allotment: The Civilized Tribes and Jacksonian Justice." *AHR* 64 (October 1958): 31–45.

———. "Pagans, Converts, and Backsliders, All: A Secular View of the Metaphysics of Indian-White Relations," in Calvin Martin, ed., *The American Indian and the Problem of History*, pp. 75–83. New York: Oxford Univ. Press, 1987.

Zachary, Alan. "Social Disorder and the Philadelphia Elite Before Jackson." *Pennsylvania Magazine of History and Biography* 99 (July 1975): 299–309.

Zevin, Robert. "The Growth of Cotton Textile Production After 1815." In Robert Fogel and Stanley Engerman, eds., *The Reinterpretation of American Economic History*, pp. 122–47. New York: Harper & Row, 1971.

Zuckerman, Michael. "The Fabrication of Identity in Early America." *WMQ*, 3d series, 34 (April 1977): 183–214.

Unpublished Works

Averitt, Jack. "The Democratic Party in Georgia, 1824–1837." Ph.D. diss., University of North Carolina, 1956.

Baghdadi, Mania, "Protestants, Poverty and Urban Growth. A Study of the Organization of Charity in Boston and New York, 1820–1865." Ph.D. diss., Brown University, 1975.

Banner, Lois. "The Protestant Crusade: Religious Missions, Benevolence, and Reform in the United States, 1790–1840." Ph.D. diss., Columbia University, 1970.

Barnett, Redmond. "The Movement Against Imprisonment for Debt in Massachusetts, 1811–1834," Senior thesis, Harvard University, 1965.

Blackson, Robert. "Helping Those Who Help Themselves: Benevolent Organizations in the Early Nineteenth Century." Paper delivered at the 49th meeting of the Pennsylvania Historical Association, 1980.

Blaine, James G., II. "The Birth of a Neighborhood: Nineteenth-Century Charlestown, Massachusetts." Ph.D. diss., University of Michigan, 1978.

Blauvelt, Martha. "Society, Religion and Revivalism: The Second Great Awakening in New Jersey, 1780–1830." Ph.D. diss., Princeton University, 1975.

Bollman, Oscar. "The Foreign Mission School of Cornwall, Connecticut." Master of Sacred Theology thesis, Yale Divinity School, 1939.

Calhoun, David. "The Last Command: Princeton Theological Seminary and Missions, 1812–1862." Ph.D. diss., Princeton University, 1983.

Chappell, Gordon. "The Life and Activities of John Coffee." Ph.D. diss., Vanderbilt University, 1941.

Chatfield, John H. "'Already We Are a Fallen Country': The Politics and Ideology of Connecticut Federalism, 1797–1812." Ph.D. diss., Columbia University, 1988.

Clark, Gregory. "Timothy Dwight's 'Travels in New England and New York' and the Rhetoric of Puritan Public Discourse." Ph.D. diss., Rensselaer Polytechnic Institute, 1985.

Cocks, J. Fraser, III. "From Boarding School to Demonstration Farm: Protestant Missionaries and the Plains Indians, 1825–1835." Unpublished paper lent to author.

Crouch, William. "Missionary Activities Among the Cherokee Indians, 1757–1838." M.A. thesis, University of Tennessee, 1932.

Crow, Frank. "The Age of Promise: Societies for Social and Economic Improvement in the United States, 1783–1815." Ph.D. diss., University of Wisconsin, 1952.

Culp, Ruby Lee. "The Missions of the American Board and Presbyterian Church Among the Five Civilized Tribes, 1803–1860." M.A. thesis, George Washington University, 1934.

Danforth, Brian. "The Influence of Socio-Economic Factors Upon Political Behavior: A Quantitative Look at New York City Merchants, 1828–1844." Ph.D. diss., New York University, 1974.

Dann, John. "Humanitarian Reform and Organized Benevolence in the Southern United States, 1780–1830." Ph.D. diss., William and Mary, 1975.

Davis, Stephen. "From Plowshares to Spindles: Dedham, Massachusetts, 1790–1840." Ph.D. diss., University of Wisconsin, 1973.

Davison, Kenneth. "Forgotten Ohioan: Elisha Whittlesey, 1783–1863." Ph.D. diss., Western Reserve University, 1953.

Dennis, William C., II. "A Federalist Persuasion: The American Ideal of the Connecticut Federalists." Ph.D. diss., Yale University, 1971.

Dillon, Timothy. "Jedidiah Morse's Christian Republicanism: Reform and the Young Nation." Ph.D. diss., University of Wisconsin, 1987.

Ershkowitz, Herbert. "New Jersey Politics During the Era of Andrew Jackson, 1829–1837." Ph.D. diss., New York University, 1965.

Faircloth, Ronald. "The Impact of Andrew Jackson in Georgia Politics, 1828–1840." Ph.D. diss., University of Georgia, 1971.

Feldblum, Mary. "The Formation of the First Factory Labor Force in the New England Cotton Textile Industry, 1800–1848." Ph.D. diss., New School for Social Research, 1977.

Fitzmier, John. "The Godly Federalism of Timothy Dwight, 1752–1817: Society, Doctrine, and Religion in the Life of New England's 'Moral Legislator.'" Ph.D. diss., Princeton University, 1986.

Forbes, Bruce. "Beyond Caricature: Motivations of Missionaries to American Indians." Paper delivered at the annual meeting of the Organization of American Historians, 1986.

Forderhase, Rudolph. "Jacksonianism in Missouri, From Predilection to Party, 1820–1836." Ph.D. diss., University of Missouri, 1968.

Frisch, John. "Youth Culture in America, 1790–1865." Ph.D. diss., University of Missouri–Columbia, 1970.

Garrison, John. "Surviving Strategies: In Commercialization of Life in Rural Massachusetts, 1790–1860." Ph.D. diss., University of Pennsylvania, 1985.

Geib, Susan. "'Changing Works': Agriculture and Society in Brookfield, Massachusetts, 1785–1820." Ph.D. diss., Boston University, 1981.

Green, Michael. "Federal-State Conflict in the Administration of Indian Policy: Georgia, Alabama, and the Creeks, 1824–1834." Ph.D. diss., University of Iowa, 1973.

Grigg, Susan. "The Dependent Poor of Newburyport, 1800–1830." Ph.D. diss., University of Wisconsin, 1978.

Hampel, Robert. "Influence and Respectability: Temperance and Prohibition in Massachusetts, 1813–1852." Ph.D. diss., Cornell University, 1979.

Hayes, Betty. "An Investigation of the Congressional Delegation of Georgia, 1829–1837." M.A. thesis, Emory University, 1950.

Hood, Fred. "Presbyterianism and the New American Nation: 1783–1826." Ph.D. diss., Princeton University, 1968.

Hudson, Richard. "The Challenge of Dissent: Religious Conditions in New Hampshire in the Early Nineteenth Century." Ph.D. diss., Syracuse University, 1970.

Jacobson, Norman. "The Concept of Equality in the Assumptions and the Propaganda of Massachusetts Conservatives, 1790–1840." Ph.D. diss., University of Wisconsin, 1951.

Jentz, John. "Artisans, Evangelicals, and the City: A Social History of Abolition and Labor Reforms in Jacksonian New York." Ph.D. diss., City University of New York, 1977.

Kidwell, Clara. "Choctaws and Missionaries in Mississippi Before 1830." Paper presented at the Newberry Library, 1986.

Kindig, Everett. "Western Criticism of Jackson's Indian Removal Policy: The Ohio Valley as a Case Study." Paper presented at the annual meeting of Phi Alpha Theta, 1973.

Lacey, Vincent. "The United States Senate in the Age of Jackson, 1825–1837: Regional Coalitions and the Development of the Two-Party System." Ph.D. diss., Southern Illinois University at Carbondale, 1985.

Linn, Theodore. "Religion and Nationalism: American Methodism and the New Nation in the Early National Period, 1766–1844." Ph.D. diss., Drew University, 1971.

Lucas, M. Philip. "The Development of the Second Party System in Mississippi, 1817–1846." Ph.D. diss., Cornell University, 1983.

Lynn, W. Alvin. "Party Formation and Operation in the House of Representatives, 1824–1837." Ph.D. diss., Rutgers University, 1972.

Lyrene, Edward C., Jr. "The Role of Prayer in American Revival Movements, 1740–1860." Ph.D. diss., Southern Baptist Theological Seminary, 1985.

McCrary, Royce. "John MacPherson Berrien of Georgia (1781–1856): A Political Biography." Ph.D. diss., University of Georgia, 1971.

McFarland, Philip. "The Removal of the Cherokee Indians from the State of Georgia, 1824–1835: An Analysis of Rhetorical Strategy." Ph.D. diss., Stanford University, 1973.

McLoughlin, William. "Two Bostonian Missions to the Frontier Indians, 1810–1860." Paper presented at the Massachusetts Historical Society, 1990.

Mahoney, Marie. "American Public Opinion of Andrew Jackson's Indian Policy, 1828–1835." M.A. thesis, Clark University, 1935.

Melder, Keith. "The Beginnings of the Women's Rights Movement in the United States, 1800–1840." Ph.D. diss., Yale University, 1963.

Meyer, Paul. "The Transformation of American Temperance: The Popularization and Radicalization of a Reform Movement, 1813–1860." Ph.D. diss., University of Iowa, 1976.

Miriani, Ronald. "Lewis Cass and Indian Administration in the Old Northwest, 1815–1836." Ph.D. diss., University of Michigan, 1974.

Montgomery, Dean. "Jeremiah Evarts and Indian Removal." M.A. thesis, University of Maryland, 1971.

Naylor, Natalie. "Raising a Learned Ministry: The American Education Society, 1815–1860." Ph.D. diss., Columbia University, 1971.

Nielsen, George. "The Indispensable Institution: The Congressional Party During the Era of Good Feelings." Ph.D. diss., University of Iowa, 1968.

Parks, Norman. "The Career of John Bell of Tennessee in the United States House of Representatives." Ph.D. diss., Vanderbilt, 1942.

Perry, Alan. "The American Board of Commissioners for Foreign Missions and the London Missionary Society in the 19th Century: A Study of Ideas." Ph.D. diss., Washington University, 1974.

Peters, John L. "The Influence of the Missionaries to the Cherokee Indians, 1800–1860." M.A. thesis, University of Oklahoma, 1938.

Peterson, Carl. "The Politics of Revival, 1783–1815." Ph.D. diss., Stanford University, 1974.

Phillips, Clifton J. "Protestant America and the Pagan World: The First Half Century of the American Board of Commissioners for Foreign Missions, 1810–1860." Ph.D. diss., Harvard University, 1954.

Phillips, Joseph. "Jedidiah Morse: An Intellectual Biography." Ph.D. diss., University of California, Berkeley, 1978.

Pingel, Carol. "The Disorder of American Indian Policy: The Old Northwest, 1825–1829." M.A. thesis, University of Wisconsin–Milwaukee, 1968.

Prude, Jonathan. "The Social System of Early New England Textile Mills: A Case Study, 1812–1840." Paper lent to the author.

Rabinowitz, Richard. "Soul, Character and Personality: An Experimental History of New England Religion During the Age of Industrialization, 1790–1860." Ph.D. diss., Harvard University, 1977.

Roth, Randolph. "Whence This Strange Fire? Religious and Reform Movements in the Connecticut River Valley of Vermont, 1791–1843." Ph.D. diss., Yale University, 1981.

Rubinstein, Murray. "Zion's Corner: Origins of the American Protestant Missionary Movement in China, 1827–1839." Ph.D. diss., New York University, 1976.

Schmidt, Gregory. "Republican Visions: Constitutional Thought and Constitutional Revision in the Eastern United States, 1815–1830." Ph.D. diss., University of Illinois, 1981.

Shiels, Richard. "The Connecticut Clergy in the Second Great Awakening." Ph.D. diss., Boston University, 1976.

———. "The Myth of the Second Great Awakening." Paper delivered at the American Historical Association Meeting, 1977.

———. "The Social Origins of Religious Revival: Goshen, Connecticut, in 1798–99." Paper delivered at the annual meeting of the Society for Historians of the Early American Republic, 1985.

Smith, Ralph. "'In Every Destitute Place': The Mission Program of the American Sunday School Union, 1817–1834." Ph.D. diss., University of Southern California, 1973.

Stephens, John. "Removal as the Solution to the Indian Problem in the Old Northwest, 1825–1840." M.A. thesis, Louisiana State University, 1968.

Thomas, Edmund B., Jr. "Politics in the Land of Steady Habits: Connecticut's First Political Party System, 1789–1820." Ph.D. diss., Clark University, 1972.

Thompson, J. Earl, Jr. "A Perilous Experiment: New England Clergymen and American Destiny, 1796–1826." Ph.D. diss., Princeton University, 1966.

Thorton, J. Mills, III. "Politics and Power in a Slave Society: Alabama, 1806–1860." Ph.D. diss., Yale University, 1974.

Tyner, Wayne C. "The Theology of Timothy Dwight in Historical Perspective." Ph.D. diss., University of North Carolina, 1971.

Tyrrell, Ian. "Drink and the Process of Social Reform: From Temperance to Prohibition in Ante-Bellum America, 1813–1860." Ph.D. diss., Duke University, 1974.

Unger, Robert. "Lewis Cass: Indian Superintendent of the Michigan Territory, 1813–1831: A Survey of Public Opinion as Reported by the Newspapers of the Old Northwest Territory." Ph.D. diss., Ball State University, 1967.

Van Hoeven, James. "Salvation and Indian Removal: The Career Biography of the Rev. John Freeman Schermerhorn, Indian Commissioner." Ph.D. diss., Vanderbilt University, 1972.

Viola, Herman. "Thomas L. McKenney and the Administration of Indian Affairs, 1824–30." Ph.D. diss., Indiana University, 1970.

Wagner, Sandra. "Sojourners Among Strangers: The First Two Companies of Missionaries to the Sandwich Islands." Ph.D. diss., University of Hawaii, 1986.

Watson, Harry. "'Bitter Combinations of the Neighborhood': The Second American Party System in Cumberland County, North Carolina." Ph.D. diss., Northwestern University, 1976.

Wingo, Barbara. "Politics, Society, and Religion: The Presbyterian Clergy of Pennsylvania, New Jersey, and New York, and the Formation of the Nation, 1775–1808." Ph.D. diss., Tulane University, 1976.

Wish, Judith. "From Yeoman Farmer to Industrious Producer: The Relationship Between Classical Republicanism and the Development of Manufacturing in America from the Revolution to 1850." Ph.D. diss., Washington University, 1976.

Wood, Joseph. "The Origin of the New England Village." Ph.D. diss., Pennsylvania State University, 1978.

Yeager, Randolph. "Indian Enterprises of Isaac McCoy, 1817–1846." Ph.D. diss., University of Oklahoma, 1954.

Zuckerman, Michael. "A Different Thermidor: The Revolution Beyond the American Revolution." Paper presented to the Philadelphia Center for Early American Studies, 1986.

Index

Abbott, Abiel, 58, 60
Abbott, Jacob, 266
ABC. *See* American Board of Commissioners for Foreign Missions
ABCFM. *See* American Board of Commissioners for Foreign Missions
Abolitionism, 5, 123, 175, 203, 265, 268. *See also* Indian removal: debates over, a foretaste of slavery debates; Slavery
Account of Memorials Presented to Congress During its Last Session . . . Praying that the Mails may not be Transported, nor Post-Offices kept open, on the Sabbath, 175
Acculturation. *See* Assimilation
Acquisitiveness. *See* Self-interest
Adams, John, 16
Adams, John Quincy, 211, 237; as possible presidential candidate, 124; Indian policy of, 126, 142–43, 148, 151–53, 155, 158, 160, 164, 178, 179; reelection defeat of, 168; on state of nation under Jackson, 255, 256
Address of the Charitable Society for the Education of Indigent Pious Young Men for the Ministry of the Gospel (Beecher), 55
"Address to the Christian Public" (ABCFM), 65
Africa: ABC's inability to fund missions in, 130
Ahmohee Mission, 90

Alabama: missions to Cherokees in, 87; and Indian removal, 117, 141, 182, 195, 220, 230, 251; criticism of, 224
Albany Argus, 238
Alcohol: Jackson's use of, in treaty negotiations, 246. *See also* Temperance
American Bible Society, 80, 82
American Board of Commissioners for Foreign Missions (ABCFM), 173; Evarts's work for, 6, 8, 61, 83, 84, 107, 111, 144, 145, 153, 156, 164–67, 176–77, 184, 195, 198, 205, 207–28, 231–35, 237–41, 244, 246–47, 250, 252, 259–60; foreign missions of, 64, 66, 68, 96, 98–100, 113, 123–24, 166; goals of, 66, 199, 244; Evarts's positions with, 73, 107, 132; and missions to North American Indians, 85, 88–89, 92–95, 99, 121–22, 141, 150, 152, 156, 162, 239–40, 255; finances of, 96, 105, 109–10, 115, 160, 232–35, 245–46, 254; and government policy toward North American Indians, 105, 128, 129, 157–58; auxiliaries of, 112, 144, 166; Evarts's fundraising efforts for, 112–13, 125, 126, 130–31, 165, 167, 254; merges with United Foreign Missionary Society, 131; racism at, 133–37; and Foreign Mission School, 136, 165; debates by, about national character and Indian removal, 143–44, 200–201; criticism of,

419

American Board of Commissioners for
 Foreign Missions (ABCFM) (cont'd)
 144, 221, 225; opposition of, to Cherokee syllabary, 147; and policy on Indian removal, 180, 182–84, 190–91, 193, 194, 212–13, 239–40; Jacksonian fear of power of, 182, 232; fears of, about Indian removal, 208, 246; as Cherokees' advisor, 209–10, 212, 240–41, 251; on Evarts's death, 263; and slavery issue, 265. *See also* Evarts, Jeremiah; Foreign missions; Foreign Mission School; Indian Civilization Fund; Missionaries; Missionary work; Missions; Prudential Committee
American Education Society, 55, 253
American Home Missionary Society, 132
American Ladies Magazine, 254
American Revolution: impact of, on later generations, 2–4, 31–32, 34–35, 39, 69
American Society for Promoting the Civilization and General Improvement of the Indian Tribes Within the United States, 118, 124
American Society for Promoting the Civilization of the Indians, 122
American Temperance Society, 253
American Tract Society (ATS), 53
American Unitarianism: Evarts's review of, 78–80
Anderson, Rufus, 123, 153, 154, 165, 167, 252
Andover Academy, 54
Andover Theological Seminary, 53, 61, 262
Antislavery efforts. *See* Abolitionism
Appleby, Joyce, 75
Appleton, Jesse, 72
"Are the Abilities of Females Inferior to Those of Males?" (Evarts), 16
"Arithmetic Applied to Moral Purposes" (Evarts), 57
Arkansas: missions to Cherokees in, 87, 92, 159; and Choctaw treaty, 138
Arkansas River: proposals to move Cherokees to, 94, 96
Artisans: role of, in Sabbatarian efforts, 175

Assimilation: as whites' goal for North American Indians, 89, 97–98, 120, 121, 138, 147, 153, 199; Cherokees' resistance to, 155. *See also* Civilization programs; Education: for Indians; Indian Civilization Fund; Integration; Nationalism
ATS. *See* American Tract Society
Atwater (Evarts's tutor at Yale), 15
Atwater, Caleb, 177
Awakenings: compared to revivals, 35–36. *See also* First Great Awakening; Revitalization; Second Great Awakening

Bacon, Leonard, 143–44
Baldwin, Thomas, 65
Banking: as social concern of Evarts's time, 77, 176
Bank of the United States, 241
Baptist Board of Foreign Missions, 212, 216
Baptist General Convention for Foreign Missions, 156
Baptists, 11, 53, 154; doctrinal divisions among, 33; growth of, 34, 54; salaries of ministers of, 64; Indian missions of, 156; and Sabbatarianism, 204; and Indian removal, 216, 218, 238–39. *See also* Interdenominational competition; McCoy, Isaac
Barbour, James, 141–43, 148–50, 153, 154, 160
Barnes, Daniel, 22
Barnes, Mehitabel Sherman. *See* Evarts, Mehitabel
Barton, David, 203
Bates, Joshua, 81, 143
Beecher, Catharine, 195
Beecher, Henry Ward, 2, 232
Beecher, Lyman, 2, 55, 57, 82, 144, 262; and intermarriage, 134
Behavior: changes in beliefs about, 2–5, 7, 27, 31–33, 36, 45–46, 69, 81–82, 201; Evarts's beliefs about, 120. *See also* Character; Morality; Private vs. public morality
Bell, John, 220, 222, 227
Bell, Samuel, 235, 241

Benevolence: Dwight's views of, 14, 17; in early nineteenth-century America, 21; Evarts's views of, 23, 51, 67–68, 71, 75, 80, 108; and revitalization movement, 39–41, 82–83; and patriotism, 108, 239. *See also* Benevolent societies; Moral reform

Benevolent societies: Evarts's work with, 4, 6; and Second Great Awakening, 35, 47, 82; and women, 44, 50; split in, over Indian removal, 122–23, 143–44, 163, 211–13. *See also* Moral reform

Benton, Thomas Hart, 138, 201, 203

Berrien, John, 169, 179–81, 223, 235

Bigelow, Timothy, 60

Bingham, Hiram, 100, 109, 110

Binney, Horace, 236

Blackburn, Gideon, 86, 149

Blacks. *See* Slavery

Bolles, Lucius, 156, 157, 216

Boston, 49, 210; Evarts's life in, 6–7, 27. *See also* American Board of Commissioners for Foreign Missions; Park Street Church

Boston Daily Advertiser, 264

Boston Female Bible Society, 76

Boston Foreign Mission Society. *See* Foreign Mission Society of Boston and the Vicinity

Boston Prison Discipline Society, 253, 254, 262

Boston Recorder, 85, 100, 110

Boudinot, Elias, 122, 150, 164, 251; marriage of, 133, 135–36, 255

Boudinot, Harriet Gold. *See* Gold, Harriet

Bowdoin College, 72

Brainerd Mission, 88, 90, 92, 95, 98, 107, 115, 118; President Monroe visits, 96

Brief View of the Present Relations Between the Government and People of the United States and the Indians Within our National Limits, A (Evarts), 189–92

Brigham, Amariah, 44–45

British East India Company, 111

Brothers' Society, 16

Brown, David, 125, 136

Brown, Joseph, 262

Buckminster, Joseph, 43

Burlington (Vt.): Evarts's education in, 11–12

Butler, Elizur, 156

Butrick, Daniel, 135, 136, 150, 261

Byington, Cyrus, 245

Caledonia County Grammar School, 19–20

Calhoun, John, 94–97, 241; letters to, 114, 128–29; on Indian policy, 117–18, 121, 123, 140; as possible presidential candidate, 124; and Indian removal, 126, 211; and Indian survey, 138

Canals. *See* Internal improvements

"Candour." *See* McCoy, Isaac

Candy's Creek Mission, 90

Capitalism: influence of, on Evarts's society, 2–3, 5, 7, 93, 104, 182, 253, 267; and Indians' future success, 213, 227

Carmel Mission, 90, 259

Carr, Dabney, 236–37, 238, 257

Carroll, William, 195

Cass, Lewis, 240; and Indian policy, 85, 89, 98, 146, 152, 177, 206–8, 216, 218

Catherine Brown, The Converted Cherokee, 98

Ceylon: missions to, 66, 98–99, 110, 111, 113, 130

Chamberlain, William, 136

Channing, William Ellery, 78, 254

Chapin, Calvin, 131

Character: views about, in Evarts's time, 3, 75, 80, 141, 207; Dwight's views of, 12, 19; Evarts's views of, 69, 83, 120, 173; allegations about Indian, 97, 206–7, 236, 244; Indian removal and nature of American, 143–44, 150, 196, 200–201, 207–8, 210, 232, 246–47, 265; Jackson's concern about national, 245. *See also* Behavior; Morality; Private vs. public morality; Racism

Charleston (S.C.), 91, 131, 145, 262

Charleston Society in Aid of Missions to the Heathen, 146, 147

Charlestown (Mass.), 28–29, 48, 49, 64, 73, 252

Charlestown Association for the Reformation of Morals, 71, 73

Chauncey, Charles, 20, 21
Cheever, George, 207–8, 217, 248
Cherokee Constitution, 155–57, 159, 199
Cherokee Council, 139, 194–95, 199, 267
Cherokee Indians: Evarts's failures concerning, 1–2, 248, 267; missions to, 85, 87, 92, 96, 119–20, 142, 146, 234; Calhoun on removal of, 94, 140; missionaries' support for, 96, 254–55; ceding of some land by, 97; anti-removal strategies of, 121, 147, 250; refusal of, to sign treaties or cede lands, 122, 125–26, 162, 245; Monroe on removal of, 127; threats to, 128; printing press of, 146, 147; syllabary of, 147; divisions among, 155; refuse to leave voluntarily, 156, 159, 181, 213; as model Indian nation for ABC, 156, 161, 162, 184, 199, 208; Evarts's work on behalf of, 179–80, 184–91, 205, 209–10, 240; intrusions on, 193, 209; and Congressional debate over removal, 217–28. *See also* Cherokee Constitution; Civilization programs; Corn Tassels; Georgia; Gold; Indian lands; Indian removal; Indians; Nationalism; Ross, John; Sovereignty; Supreme Court; Treaties
Cherokee Nation, 234
Cherokee Phoenix, 159–64, 183, 192, 195, 254
Cherokees v. Georgia, 256
Chickamauga Mission, 88, 90, 92. *See also* Brainerd Mission
Chickasaw Indians: missions to, 96, 127, 146, 165, 234; Coffee's approach to, 149; treaty with, 245
Children: nurturing of, 49–50
China: missions to, 113, 124, 166, 253
Choate, Rufus, 210
Choctaw Indians: missions to, 87, 92, 96, 120, 121, 146, 234; treaty with, 138, 245–46, 249; Evarts on, 152; agree to remove, 220; Methodist support for removal of, 239
Christian Advocate, 140, 231
Christian Advocate and Journal, 263
Christian Examiner, 246

Christianity: and civilization, 125, 180; and racism, 135–37; Cherokees' resistance to, 199–200
Christian republicanism: Evarts's desire for, 1–4, 5, 7, 8, 10, 17, 29, 30, 37, 39, 69–71, 80–81, 103–4, 190, 199, 229, 267; threats to, 81–82, 173–74, 205; politicization of approach to, 133–68. *See also* Benevolence; Moral reform; Sabbatarianism
Churches: growth of, 34, 41–42; revitalization concerns about, 40
Cincinnati American, 235
Civilization: and Christianity, 125, 180; alleged impossibility of, for Indians, 143; whites' poor example of, 153. *See also* Civilization programs
Civilization Fund. *See* Indian Civilization Fund
Civilization programs: as goal of missions, 85, 87, 89–90, 94–95, 109, 146–47, 149, 243; opposition to, 93, 95; needed to prevent extermination, 97, 122, 124, 180; slow progress of, 116, 119–20, 123, 128, 141, 158, 177, 214; difficulties of removal after, 127, 140–41, 192; alleged failure of, 160, 161, 177–78, 206–7; and loss of cultural identity, 194, 200. *See also* Assimilation; Education: for Indians; Indian Civilization Fund; Indian mission policy; Integration; Missions: goals of
Clark, John, 117, 139
Clay, Henry, 124, 150; on Indian removal, 142–43, 235; motives of, 248
Clayton, Augustin, 239, 261
Codman, John, 52, 78
Coffee, John, 87, 149, 195, 245–46
Community: Evarts's emphasis on, 10. *See also* Christian republicanism; Morality
Compact of 1802, 116, 127, 158, 188, 219
Concord (Mass.): temperance efforts in, 59
Congregationalists, 11; doctrinal divisions among, 33, 34, 76–77; and moral reform issues, 53, 56, 68; and missions, 110, 154. *See also* Interdenominational competition
Congress: Ross addresses, 1; Evarts's battle

with, 8, 92–93, 217–28; and Sunday mail delivery, 55, 57, 83, 173–75; efforts to enlist, in evangelical reform, 82–83, 105–6; and its authority to make territorial laws, 101; and possibility of its buying Cherokee lands for Cherokees, 126; debates Indian matters, 152–53, 217–28; and costs of Indian removal, 158; funds expedition to explore Western lands, 160; and Indian removal, 193, 197, 198, 217–28; Evarts's strategy for Cherokees' case before, 209–10; suggestions to stall implementation of Indian Removal Bill by, 235, 250. *See also* House Committee on Indian Affairs; Indian Civilization Fund

Connecticut: Evarts's early life in, 6, 10–12; Indian removal issue in, 227. *See also* Cornwall; East Guilford; Guilford; Hartford; New Haven

Connecticut Evangelical Magazine, 23, 30–31, 36, 39

Connecticut Religious Tract Society, 26, 27

"Contingent Prospects of Our Country" (Evarts), 264

Conversion: importance of, 18–19, 23–24, 31, 38, 45, 78, 265; narratives of, 39–40; and social status, 40–41; vs. civilizing, 115. *See also* Converts

Converts: nature of, 41–42; as leaders, 120

Cooper, Thomas, 135

Cornelius, Elias, 68, 86, 92, 95

Corn Tassels, 255

Cornwall (Conn.), 85–88, 122. *See also* Foreign Mission School

Corruption: allegations of, in Jackson administration, 237, 246

Cotton, Ward, 78

Cowles, George, 130

Crawford, William H., 88, 89, 92, 121, 124; and intermarriage, 135

Creek Indians: need to "civilize," 97; opposition of, to removal, 117, 212; 1825 treaty with, 139, 142, 143, 153; Georgia's designs on lands of, 147–48, 152–53, 179; government pressure on, to remove, 162; refusal of, to sign treaty with Jackson, 245

Creek Path Mission, 90, 158

Crockett, David, 227

Cultural pluralism, 200. *See also* Assimilation; Integration

Cushman, Colvin, 245

Daily National Journal, 153

Dan, Nathan, 60

Dana, Daniel, 24, 81

Dancing Rabbit Creek, 245

Danforth, Thomas, 32, 36

Darneille, Isaac, 146–47

Deference: waning of, in American society, 34, 60; Evarts's belief in, 210. *See also* Democracy; Elitism; Equality

Democracy: concerns about, 5, 15, 41; Evarts's views on, 25, 254; and the ABCFM, 61, 63. *See also* Deference; Equality

Denison, Charles, 16

Dexter, Samuel, 60

Dickerson, Mahlon, 124

Discovery: doctrine of, 242

"Dissertation on *Amor Patriae*, A" (Evarts), 16

Douglas, James, 111

Dwight, Timothy: influence of, on Evarts, 9, 12–14, 17–19, 39, 51; on liberalism, 33; religious concerns of, 35, 73; on education of children, 76; and benevolent societies, 82; and Obookiah, 99

Dwight Mission (Arkansas Territory), 153, 159, 239

East Guilford (Conn.), 12

Eaton, John, 169, 179–83, 187–88, 193, 208, 213–14, 218, 226, 232–35, 238, 239, 241, 261; and Jackson's treaty signing with Indians, 245–46; and aggression toward Cherokees, 250–51

Eaton, Peter, 72

Education: Evarts's views concerning, 25, 49, 50, 54–55, 119, 149, 191; for Indians,

Education (cont'd)
85–88, 94, 96. *See also* Foreign Mission School
Edwards, Jonathan, 13, 36
Edwards, Jonathan, Jr., 28
Edwards, Justin, 53
Edwards, Ninian, 94, 256
Elitism: Evarts's, 68, 120, 254. *See also* Deference; Democracy; Leaders
Elliott, John, 12, 14
Ely, Ezra Stiles, 213, 217
Embargo Act, 36, 62
Emmons, Nathaniel, 13, 39, 45
Episcopalians, 53
Equality: whites reject notion of Indians', 93; Evarts's idea of moral, 120
Ershkowitz, Herbert, 215
Etheridge, Samuel, 81
"Evangelical Exertions in Asia" (Evarts), 64
Evangelism. *See* Benevolence; Foreign missions; Missionaries; Revivals; Second Great Awakening
Evans, George, 226
Evarts, James, 10–12, 14, 16, 64, 105; financial problems of, 107–8, 144–45
Evarts, Jeremiah, characterization of, 9; early life of, 10–29; health problems of, 11, 22, 90, 108, 118, 131, 145, 251–52, 255, 260–62; and his interest in politics, 15, 17, 19–20, 26; conversion of, 18–19, 42; makes covenant with Yale friends, 19, 22, 24, 30; as schoolteacher, 19–20; as lawyer, 20–28, 64; personal finances of, 64, 144–45, 168, 252; family life of, 90, 145, 167–68, 252, 263; death of, 262; will of, 263–64

—AS MORAL REFORMER: failures of, 1, 248, 267; his differences with Jackson, 2, 169–98, 240–41; his efforts to define the soul of America, 4–10, 48–49, 68, 76, 205, 207–8, 216, 229–30, 240, 247–48, 253, 263–68; official positions held by, 26–28, 53, 62, 64, 66, 71, 73, 80–81, 104, 107, 118, 131, 167, 253; issues supported by, 49–50, 60, 172–73, 203–4, 253; as corresponding secretary for ABCFM, 109, 250, 252; advising abstinence from politics for missionaries, 142

—AND INDIAN AFFAIRS: his visits to North American Indian missions, 90–93, 113–14, 118, 123, 127–28, 131, 146–49; fears Indian removal, 96, 97, 98, 148, 152, 162; as critic of federal Indian policy, 116, 138–39; his lobbying for Indian missions, 124–25, 128–29, 146, 152–54, 159, 164–65, 176–81, 240; on intermarriage, 135; proposed as Indian agent, 138–39; favors voluntary Indian removal, 153, 154, 157; opposes Indian removal, 159–60, 164–65, 179–91, 205–28; criticism of, 225–26; and Marshall, 233; as advisor to Cherokees, 209–10, 212, 240–41, 251; Cherokees' respect for, 267

See also American Board of Commissioners for Foreign Missions; "William Penn" essays

Evarts, John Jay, 50, 252, 261
Evarts, Jonathan Todd, 27, 144
Evarts, Mehitabel (Mrs. Jeremiah), 22, 64; joins church, 26, 29; family responsibilities of, 76, 90, 145–46, 252; letters from Jeremiah to, 90–91, 144–46, 168, 261; letters to Jeremiah from, 262; after Jeremiah's death, 263
Evarts, Sarah (Jeremiah's daughter), 76, 145–46
Evarts, Sarah (Jeremiah's mother), 11, 16
Evarts, Sarah (Jeremiah's sister), 27, 104–5, 145
Evarts, William Maxwell, 2, 91
Everett, Alexander Hill, 204, 218, 264
Everett, Edward, 217, 218, 221, 223, 226, 231, 233, 260, 267
Examination of the Relations Between the Cherokees and the Government of the United States, 191
Executive branch of government: role of, 224, 247–48, 255, 267
Exeter Academy, 54
Extinction (of Indians): convictions about inevitability of, 142–43, 205; removal as

way of preventing, 152, 154, 177, 183, 196, 206, 212, 214, 251; fears of, from removal, 222. *See also* Civilization programs: needed to prevent extermination
Extinguishment (of Indian land titles), 115, 126, 148, 244

Fame: Evarts's views of, 22–23
Family: revitalization concerns about, 40; Evarts's convictions about, 50
Fay, Warren, 131
Federalists, 3, 49, 265; Dwight's support for, 13, 17; Evarts's support for, 69; and *North American Review*, 207
Female Missionary Society, 80
First Church (Charlestown, Mass.), 29, 76
First Church (New Haven, Conn.), 26
First Great Awakening, 36, 39, 41
Fischer, David, 19
Fisk, Pliny, 110
Flint, Abel, 77, 78
Flint, Timothy, 130–31
Florida: U.S. annexation of, 95
Folsom, David, 148
Foot Resolution, 201–4, 214, 266
Foreign missions: Evarts's concern about, 40, 61–68; goals of, 99, 109; contrasted with missions to North American Indians, 141, 243. *See also* American Board of Commissioners for Foreign Missions; Ceylon; China; Greece; India; Palestine; Sandwich Islands
Foreign Mission School (Cornwall, Conn.), 85–86, 88, 92, 93, 130; foreigners at, 99, 131; controversy over intermarriage at, 133–37, 142, 149, 255; closing of, 165–66
Foreign Mission Society of Boston and the Vicinity, 64, 73, 83, 131
Formisano, Ronald, 215
Forsyth, John, 128, 155, 164, 193, 219, 221
Foster, Thomas, 225
Frelinghuysen, Theodore, 204, 208, 214, 215, 219, 220, 256, 260
French Revolution, 25
Frey, Samuel, 130

Gaines, E. P., 244
Gambold, John, 92
Garrison, William Lloyd, 265
Gender. *See* Women
General Association of Massachusetts, 58, 61
Georgia: missions to Cherokees in, 87; extension of laws of, over Cherokees, 96, 164, 181, 182, 188–90, 213, 256; and its insistence on Indian removal, 116–17, 121, 123, 126, 139, 142, 147–48, 152–54, 158, 159, 162, 192–93, 208, 210–12, 230, 231, 239, 241, 246–47, 256; and Jackson, 143, 195, 257–58; and Cherokee Constitution, 155–56; and its attempts to gain Indian lands, 179, 209, 236–37, 254; criticisms of, 188–89, 220, 221, 224–27; opposition to claims of, 195; limits rights of Indians, 198; discovery of gold on Cherokee lands in, 235–36; aggression by, against Cherokees, 250–51, 255; arrest of missionaries by, 259–60, 261. *See also Cherokees v. Georgia*; Clark, John; Compact of 1802; Gilmer, George (Gov.); Lumpkin, Wilson; Troup, George; *Worcester v. Georgia*
Georgia (Vt.), 11, 19, 83, 105, 144; Evarts buys land in, 107
Georgia Journal, 241
Gilmer, George (Doctor), 236
Gilmer, George (Governor): and Indians in Georgia, 197, 198, 208, 217, 223, 232, 233, 235, 239, 246–47, 254, 261; and Wirt, 236, 249
Gold, Benjamin, 133–34
Gold, Eleanor, 133, 134
Gold, Flora, 135
Gold, Franklin, 122
Gold, Harriet, 133–35, 255
Gold, Stephen, 134
Gold: discovery of, on Cherokee lands, 235–36, 246
Government: revitalization concerns about, 40. *See also* Executive branch of government; Morality: vs. politics; Party politics; States' rights

Granger, Gideon, 56
Greece: missions in, 123–24, 166, 253
Green, Ashbel, 248
Green, Duff, 209
Green, Michael, 96
Greene, David, 165, 181, 193, 238, 252, 260–61
Griffin, Edward Dorr, 49
Grund, Francis J., 7
Guilford (Conn.), 10–11

Hall, Moody, 95, 122
Hartford (Conn.), 205
Hartford Convention, 176, 223
Harvard University, 28; Unitarianism at, 27, 52, 79
Harvey, Joseph, 86, 134
Hawaii. *See* Sandwich Islands
Haweis Mission, 90, 259
Hawes, Joel, 232
Hayne, Robert Y., 201–3, 211
Hemphill, Joseph, 227–28
Hicks, Charles, 117
Hicks, Elijah, 141
Hightower Mission, 90, 259
Hill, Henry, 113, 147, 148
Hill, Isaac, 220
Hints on Missions (Douglas), 111
Hoar, Samuel, 210
Hobart, Bishop, 181
Hooker, John, 131
Hopefield Village Mission, 161
Hopkins, Samuel, 61; followers of, 27, 39
House Committee on Indian Affairs, 96, 197, 208, 217, 220, 222, 224
Howe, Daniel Walker, 3
Hoyt, Ard, 115
Humane Society of Massachusetts, 32
Humphrey, Heman, 81, 100, 191–92
Hutchison, William, 109, 141

Illinois: land availability in, 160, 227; and Indian removal, 230
India: foreign missions to, 64, 66, 98–99, 110, 111, 113, 130, 243

Indiana: and Indian lands, 126, 150, 227; and Indian removal, 230
Indian Affairs Committee. *See* House Committee on Indian Affairs
Indian Civilization Fund: Congress's creation of, 96, 97, 98, 100, 105–6; ABCFM as major recipient of, 114, 129, 181, 184, 261; southern efforts to repeal, 125; Cass's views of, 146, 152, 206–7; government lack of enthusiasm for, 163, 194; Jackson cuts funding to, 232–33, 239–40. *See also* Civilization programs
Indian lands: white avarice for, 87–89, 93, 94, 114–17, 138, 140, 152, 155, 188–89, 205, 250; missionaries' views on, 92–93, 96, 242–44; federal government's avarice for, 149; state governments' avarice for, 150, 226, 232, 233; Frelinghuysen's proposals for, 219; Georgia's avarice for, 232, 233. *See also* Extinguishment; Gold; Land
Indian mission policy, 85, 88–89, 113–14, 118–21. *See also* Civilization programs; Indian Civilization Fund; Missions: goals of
Indian Nations. *See* Cherokee; Chickasaw; Choctaw; Creek; Sovereignty
Indian policy (federal government's), 8, 85, 87–88, 105–6, 116–17, 120, 129, 130, 142, 150–57, 162–64, 182
Indian removal: as social issue, 5, 77, 128, 133–68, 176–77, 246–47, 253; motives for, 85–86, 88, 114–15, 147, 237; without force, 138, 141, 142, 148–51, 221, 228, 249; by force, 177, 180, 191, 194, 197, 250, 258, 267; logistical problems and costs of, 191, 208, 218, 226, 227, 241; debates over, a foretaste of slavery debates, 210, 246–47, 265. *See also* Character: Indian removal; Cherokee Indians; Evarts, Jeremiah: and Indian affairs; Extinction; Indian lands; Indian Removal Bill; Missions: threat to, of Indian removal; Supreme Court
Indian Removal Bill, 217–29, 231, 237, 249, 250

Indians: their view of missionaries' goals, 94–95, 106, 136–39; political rights of, 121–22, 142, 158, 164, 198; making American citizens of, 142; slaves owned by, 160; differences among, 161, 244; factionalism among, 183–84, 200; their views of removal, 184, 189, 192, 212, 250; government attempts to undercut, 235. *See also* Leaders: Indian; Nationalism; Sovereignty; Treaties

"Indians of North America" (Cass), 146

Individualism. *See* Self-interest

Individuals: transformation of, as means of transforming society, 14. *See also* Conversion

Industriousness: as essence of American spirit, 227

Institutions: Evarts's belief in, 4; revitalization concerns about, 40; women and, 43–44. *See also* Government

Integration: lack of commitment to Indian and white, 98, 149, 169, 186; ABCFM missionaries' belief in, 120–22, 128, 166; Cherokees' lack of interest in, 125, 139–40; federal government abandons policy of, 162; McCoy on, 244. *See also* Assimilation; Indian mission policy; Intermarriage

Interdenominational competition, 35, 154, 238–39

Interdenominational cooperation, 53, 58, 173

Intermarriage: issues of Indian and white, 88, 133–37

Internal improvements: and Indian removal, 77, 85, 89, 125, 146, 227, 228, 230, 248–49

Jackson, Andrew, 139, 143; Evarts's conflicts with, 2, 8, 169–98, 220–21, 240–42; Indian policy of, 2, 85, 87, 88, 93–94, 116, 128, 146, 159, 171, 176, 182–83, 192–98, 207, 211–12, 215, 250–51, 267; motivations for, 196; and moral reformers' faith in virtuous leaders, 56–57; southern and western support for, 74, 222; on Indian character, 97; on Indian sovereignty, 114; as presidential candidate, 124, 152, 162; morality of, 151, 171; background of, 151, 169, 171; as president, 168, 224; and Cherokee chiefs, 234; and question of abiding by Supreme Court decisions, 237, 238, 255, 257–58, 267; waits to sign treaties with Indians, 244–46. *See also* Corruption; Executive branch of government; Maysville Turnpike Bill

Jacksonians, 3, 229–30

Jarvis, Samuel, 114

Jefferson, Thomas, 13, 17, 31, 36, 124

Jentz, John, 175

Johns, Evan, 67

Johnson, Paul, 44

Johnson, Richard, 160, 169, 171–72, 204

Johnson, William, 257

Journal of Commerce, 164, 215

Judiciary Act, 256

Judson, Adoniram, 61

Kamehameha, King, 100

Kent, James, 236, 249

Kentucky: and Indian removal, 230, 231

Kentucky Reporter, 230

Kett, Joseph, 12, 21

Kingsbury, Cyrus: as missionary to Cherokees, 86, 88–89, 117, 123; and Indian Civilization Fund, 96; Evarts's letters to, 115, 126, 129, 136–38, 152, 154, 158, 220; stops opposing Indian removal, 141; McKenney's letters to, 147, 212–13; opposes Jackson's policies, 184, 242; asks to attend treaty negotiations with Choctaws, 245, 250

Kirkland, John, 60

Knapp, Samuel Lorenzo, 153

Knox, Henry, 178

Land: availability of, 160, 201–2, 214, 226; Georgians' lust for, 227. *See also* Indian lands

Language: Cherokee, 147; necessity of missionaries' learning native, 149
Lathrop, Joseph, 33, 43, 65
Latner, Richard, 151
Law: Evarts's concerns with, 5, 9, 186–90, 193, 205; as lynchpin of anti-removal arguments, 121–22, 214. *See also* Cherokee Constitution; Evarts: as lawyer; Treaties
Leaders: Evarts's concern about quality of, 56–57, 69; Evarts's ideal of, 68, 254; Indian, 150, 200, 209, 234; criticism of, 213–14
Lewis, John C., 134
Lewis, William B., 245
Liberal capitalism. *See* Capitalism
Lincoln, Heman, 156, 164, 179
Litchfield *Eagle*, 133
Literary societies, 16
Logic and the Law of Col. Johnson's Report to the Senate, on Sabbath Mails (Evarts), 172
London Missionary Society, 64, 99, 110, 111
Lord, Eleazar, 197, 198
Loring, Charles, 210
Lowrey, George, 141
Lumpkin, Wilson, 159, 169, 180, 225–26
Lyman, William, 44
Lyrene, Edward, 38–39

McCoy, Isaac: and Indian removal, 122–23, 140, 150–52, 166, 177–78, 181, 206, 208, 212, 213, 218, 242–44; and Evarts, 159, 177; receives government funding, 233
McIntosh, William, 142, 143
McKenney, Thomas: and Evarts, 92, 94, 138, 153, 154, 164, 179, 220, 241; on "civilizing" of Indians, 115–16, 129, 147, 208; supports removal of Indians, 142, 150, 154, 158, 163, 166, 178, 181, 182, 212–13; promises to Indians by, 148–49, 181; racism of, 152, 156–57, 194, 212–13; and plans for removal of Indians, 209, 218; dismissal of, by Jackson, 241
McLean, John, 256

McLoughlin, William, 35, 89, 93, 155, 160, 199
McMinn, Joseph, 95, 123
Madison, James, 249
Mail. *See* Sabbatarianism
Manifest destiny, 177
Marshall, John: and Indian removal, 163, 233–34, 236, 238, 256–58; and Corn Tassels, 255
Maryland: and Indian removal, 230
Massachusetts: Indian removal issue in, 227. *See also* Boston; Charlestown; Concord; Salem
Massachusetts Bible Society, 65, 73, 80, 253, 264
Massachusetts Missionary Magazine, 27
Massachusetts Missionary Society, 55, 66, 73, 83
Massachusetts Peace Society, 83, 97, 253
Massachusetts Society for Promoting Christian Knowledge, 253
Massachusetts Society for the Suppression of Intemperance, 58–60, 83
Massachusetts State Prison: Board of Visitors of, 75
Mayhew Mission, 136, 184
Maysville Turnpike Bill, 228, 230–31, 241
Meigs, Return J., Jr.: as postmaster, 57; as Indian agent, 95, 96–97
Memoirs (Adams), 211
Merritt, Timothy, 108
Methodists, 154; doctrinal divisions among, 33; growth of, 34, 54; salaries of ministers of, 64; and Indian removal, 239, 246
Middlebury College, 81, 143
Middle-class status: and conversions, 40–41, 43; and temperance, 57, 59–60; and Evarts's vision of a perfect society, 68. *See also* Artisans
Middlesex Bible Society, 73
Millennialism: Evarts's belief in, 2, 24, 33, 62, 71, 73, 81; and revivals, 37, 38, 39; and missionaries, 65, 67, 109; Troup on, 129
Mills, Samuel J., Jr., 54–55, 61

Ministers: supply of, 49, 53–55, 110
Missionaries: sponsored by ABCFM, 61, 110–11, 140, 166–67; theology of, 65; government antipathy toward, 122, 126, 140, 160, 245–46; and Indian removal, 138, 183, 217, 254–55; government support for, 150; descriptions of the heathen by, 243; dilemma of, following Supreme Court decision, 259. *See also* Benevolent societies; Civilization programs; Indian Civilization Fund; Missionary work; Missions
Missionary catechism, 109
Missionary Herald, 92, 231; Evarts's work on, 6, 111, 126–27, 165, 178, 238; as mouthpiece for ABCFM, 62, 64, 104, 105, 147, 162, 166, 167, 243, 262; on Sandwich Island mission, 110
"Missionary Republic," 130
Missionary work: Evarts's involvement with, 5, 29, 110–16; difficulties of, among North American Indians, 87, 116, 119–20, 137–38, 155
Missions: goals of, 85, 87, 89–90, 98, 128, 140, 146–47, 177, 191–92, 261; dilemmas of, 137, 200, 244; expense vs. success of, 156, 162, 190, 200; threat to, of Indian removal, 177, 178, 181; funding for, cut by Jackson, 232–35, 245, 252. *See also* Civilization programs; Foreign missions; Indian mission policy
Mississippi: missions to Choctaws in, 87; white avarice for Indian lands in, 126; and Indian removal, 182, 208, 220, 230, 251; criticism of, 224; reaction to Choctaw treaty in, 246
Missouri: land availability in, 160; and Indian removal, 230
Missouri Crisis, 96, 100–102, 105, 106
Monroe, James, 242; Indian policy of, 93–96, 105–6, 117, 121, 126, 127, 138; meets with Cherokees, 125
Monroe Mission, 165
Montgomery, Hugh, 241
Moore, Zephaniah, 83

Morality: Evarts's concerns with, 5–6, 9–10, 20, 24–26, 100–104, 108, 132, 171, 186–90, 193, 209, 232, 253; Dwight's emphasis on, 13–14, 17, 33; vs. politics, 77–78, 103, 220, 229; contending definitions of, between Jackson and Evarts, 151, 155, 176; as lynchpin of anti-removal arguments, 214, 227. *See also* Behavior; Character; Industriousness; Private vs. public morality
Moral reform: Evarts's commitment to, 29, 46, 48–73, 100–104, 267; and women, 44; views of advocates of, 71–73, 75; linked to conspiracy against West and South, 203. *See also* Awakenings; Benevolence; Christian republicanism; Morality; Revivals
Moral Society. *See* Yale Moral Society
Morris, James, 86
Morse, Jedidiah, 27–29, 53, 58, 66, 71–72, 118, 122
Morse, Samuel, 71
Motives: contention about, 3, 200–201, 215–16, 244. *See also* Indian removal: motives for; Party politics; Self-interest
MSSI. *See* Massachusetts Society for the Suppression of Intemperance

Narrative of Five Youths from the Sandwich Islands, 99
National Intelligencer, 185
Nationalism: among Indians, 106, 114, 125–26, 139–40, 147, 155. *See also* Sovereignty
New Echota Mission, 90, 183, 193, 255, 259
Newell, Samuel, 61
New England Religious Tract Society, 53
New England Tract Society, 53, 73
New Hampshire: and Indian removal policy, 229
New Hampshire Missionary Society, 82
New Haven (Conn.), 206; Evarts's experiences in, 15, 18, 20–22, 24, 27, 28. *See also* First Church

New York: Indian removal issue in, 227, 230
New York Board for the Emigration, Preservation, and Improvement of the Aborigines of North America. *See* New York Indian Board
New York Historical Society, 114
New York Indian Board, 181, 182, 193, 195
New York Observer, 130, 231
New York Review, 143
Niles' Weekly Register, 195, 217, 223
North American Indians. *See* Cherokee Indians; Chickasaw Indians; Choctaw Indians; Creek Indians; Indians
North American Review, 100, 104, 146, 180, 204, 206–7, 218, 231, 253
Northrup, John, 133
Northrup, Sarah, 133, 134, 136
Nott, Samuel, 61
Novels: Evarts's view of, 25
Nullification doctrine, 258

Obookiah, Henry, 99
Office of Indian Affairs, 178, 181, 212, 241; secret agents of, 160. *See also* McKenney, Thomas
Ohio: land availability in, 160; Indian removal issue in, 227, 228, 230, 231
Oliver, Benjamin, 81
"On Atheism" (Evarts), 80
"On Human Depravity" (Evarts), 69
"On Personal Happiness" (Dwight), 13, 14
"On President Edwards' First Resolution" (Evarts), 80
"On the Condition of Blacks" (Evarts), 102
"On the Duty of Praying for the Salvation of Relatives and Friends" (Evarts), 80
"On the Execution of the Laws" (Evarts), 9–10, 38, 189, 190, 248
"On the Intercourse of Christians with the World" (Evarts), 80
Ordinance of 1787, 219
Oregon: missions to, 166
Osage Mission, 156

Packard, Asa, 41

Palestine: missions to, 99, 110, 113, 131
Panic of 1819, 95, 106
Panoplist, 24, 52, 83, 167; Evarts's work on, 6, 8, 27–30, 47–49, 64, 68–69, 73, 77; accounts of revivals in, 36; temperance views of, 57; as mouthpiece for foreign missions, 61–65, 99, 100; on missionaries, 87–88; as mouthpiece for North American Indian missions, 92; on Missouri Crisis, 101; dropped by American Board, 104. *See also Missionary Herald*
Park Street Church, 7, 145, 262
Park Street Gentlemen's Society, 253
Parliament (Great Britain), 111
Parsons, Levi, 110
Party politics: under Jackson, 5, 124, 214–18, 221–24, 235–36, 247–49; Evarts's distrust of, 23, 26, 69–71, 209, 214–16, 229–30, 232, 235; pastoral denunciation of, 77, 253; general distrust of, 204, 256; Evarts criticized for promoting, 225, 236
Paternalism, 242–44; in Supreme Court decision, 257. *See also* Racism
Patriotism. *See* Benevolence: and patriotism
Payne, Rufus, 134
Payson, Edward, 36
Peacham (Vt.), 19–20
Peck, James, 237
Pennsylvania: Indian removal issue in, 227, 228, 230
Perkins, Nathan, 36
Phi Beta Kappa, 17, 28
Philadelphia Gazette, 174
Philadelphian, 213
Phoenix. *See Cherokee Phoenix*
Pickens, Israel, 141
Pixley, Benton, 156
Politics: Evarts's fascination with, 15, 17, 19–20, 26. *See also* Christian republicanism; Jacksonians; Morality: vs. politics; Party politics
Porter, Ebenezer, 53, 58, 64, 118
Porter, Noah, 18
Porter, Peter B., 160–62, 164, 178, 179
Portland (Maine), 36

Post offices. *See* Sabbatarianism
Potter, William, 158
Prentice, Charles, 86
Presbyterians, 53, 56, 64
Press: Evarts's concerns about, 69–70; Evarts's reliance on, 185
Princeton (N.J.), 174
Princeton University Society of Inquiry, 109
Prison Discipline Society. *See* Boston Prison Discipline Society
Private vs. public morality: in Evarts's time, 2–4, 204–5; Dwight's views of, 12–14; Evarts's concerns about, 19, 26–27, 49, 232. *See also* Behavior; Morality
Proctor, Isaac, 213, 261
Prudential Committee (ABCFM), 61, 64, 67, 84, 105, 164, 165, 167, 255, 259, 260; Evarts as a member of, 62, 107, 119–20; and Foreign Mission School, 86, 136–37; and Cherokee Treaty negotiations, 98

Racism: at the Foreign Mission School, 135, 166; against Indians, 140–43, 152, 163, 177, 206–7, 236, 241. *See also* Paternalism
Ray, James, 150
Red Clay Mission, 90
Reformed Dutch Church, 182, 195
"Regeneration: Its Nature" (Dwight), 13
Religious liberals. *See* Unitarians
Religious Tract Society. *See* Connecticut Religious Tract Society
"Remarks on Indian Reform" (McCoy), 206
Remarks on the Practicability of Indian Reform (McCoy), 177
"Removal of the Indians" (Cass), 206–8, 216, 218
Republicanism, 2–3, 13
Requa, William, 161
Revitalization: and the Second Great Awakening, 31, 36, 38, 115, 216; and education, 119; government's impatience with pace of, 161; and cultural transformation, 178

Revivals, 2; at Yale, 18–19, 30, 35; during the Second Great Awakening, 30–31, 35–41; compared to awakenings, 35–36; doctrines of, 38–39; effects of, 41–47, 74–75; opposition to, 44–45
Rice, John, 53
Richards, James, 67
Ridge, John, 133, 134, 136, 150, 155, 267
Roads. *See* Internal improvements
Ross, John, 1, 121, 136, 141, 155, 179, 181, 226, 240–41
Running Water Mission, 90
Rush, Benjamin, 35

Sabbatarianism, 5, 83, 203, 265; Evarts's concern about, 49, 55–57, 69, 171–76, 178, 248, 253
Salem (Mass.), 49, 65
Saltonstall, Leverett, 210
Sanders, Daniel, 77
Sandwich Islands: missions to, 96, 99–100, 105, 110, 113, 131, 190, 243, 263; missionaries in, 123; rebellion in, 155; Evarts's recommendations concerning, 165
Savannah (Ga.): slave auction at, 90–91, 100
Schermerhorn, John F., 54
Schoolcraft, Henry, 163
Schools: revitalization concerns about, 40
Second Great Awakening: Evarts's hope for, 4, 125, 216; impact of, on Evarts, 8; causes of, 28, 30–35; description of, 35–41; effects of, 41–47, 61, 65, 74–75, 120, 180, 222, 265; limitations of, 267–68
Second Quarterly Circular (ABCFM), 85
Secret agents, 160, 183, 209
Sectarianism. *See* Interdenominational competition
Self-interest: concerns about, in Evarts's time, 3, 5, 7, 33–35, 37–38, 40, 108–9, 182, 223–25, 229–30, 240, 253, 265–66
Seminaries: Evarts's proposals for, 54–55
Senate Committee on Indian Affairs, 217
Sergeant, John, 236, 256–57
Shade, William, 215

Shalhope, Robert, 3, 215
Sherman, Roger, 22
Silliman, Benjamin, 16
Slavery: as social concern of Evarts's time, 77, 96, 125, 210; Evarts's views on, 90–91, 100–104, 118–19, 123; and Indians, 160; under Compact of 1802, 219. *See also* Abolitionism
Smith, Daniel, 55
Social status. *See* Middle-class status
Society for the Suppression of Intemperance, 58–60, 83
Socinians, 78
South: political orientation of, 87, 89, 125, 169, 171, 176, 203–4, 209, 229–30; and Indian removal, 127–28, 151–53; benevolent societies' failure to understand, 247
South Carolina: Evarts's travels through, 90, 91; and Indian removal, 230; nullification doctrine in, 258. *See also* Charleston
Sovereignty: question of Indian, 106, 114, 117, 121, 152, 181, 184, 186, 188, 210, 214, 226, 242, 244, 256–57; Evarts's views of Indian, 234. *See also* Georgia: extension of laws of, over Cherokees
Sparks, Jared, 218
Spencer, Ambrose, 236, 237
Spirit of the Pilgrims, 167, 173, 216, 246, 247, 248
Sprague, Peleg, 221–22
Spring, Gardiner, 263
Statehood: and Indian lands, 114–15
States' rights: to remove Indians, 106, 138, 140–41, 155; Georgia's emphasis on, 139, 148, 149, 164, 225–26, 236, 239, 256; Jackson's support for, 159, 211, 257–58; Evarts's criticism of, 188; rejection of notion of, by anti-removal forces, 214. *See also* Georgia
Stevenson, Andrew, 228
Stiles, Ezra, 12
Stockton, Betsey, 123
Stone, Timothy, 134

Storrs, Henry, 224
Story, Joseph, 163, 257–58
Story, Mrs. Joseph, 257
Strong, Nathan, 37–38, 58
Stuart, Moses, 18, 26, 53
Stuart, Thomas, 164–65, 248
Student's Companion, The, 58
Suffrage, 41
Sunday School movement, 80, 83, 103
Sunderland (Vt.), 10–11
Supreme Court: Cherokees look to, for help, 193, 197, 212, 220–21, 233–38, 240, 247–50; threats that Georgia would not obey rulings of, 239, 256; considers *Cherokees v. Georgia*, 256–58; effects of decision of, 259; and *Worcester v. Georgia*, 267. *See also* Jackson, Andrew: and question of abiding by Supreme Court decisions
Swift, Philo, 134

Tamoree, George P., 155
Temperance: as social concern of Evarts's period, 5, 77; Evarts's concern about, 49, 57–61, 83–84, 253
Tennessee: missions to Cherokees in, 87; extending laws of, to Cherokees, 96; and Indian removal, 117, 182, 227, 230
Theology Explained and Defended (Dwight), 13–14
Thompson, John, 261
Thompson, Smith, 257, 258
Thurston, Asa, 100
Todd, John (Evarts's nephew), 76, 78, 263
Todd, John (Evarts's uncle), 16
Todd, Timothy, 11
Trail of Tears, 1
Transcontinental Treaty: with Spain, 95
Treaties, 210, 214, 221; Evarts's views concerning, 1, 186–88, 190, 209, 219, 220; Cherokee, 93, 97, 98; and Jackson, 93, 196, 244–45; federal policy on, 105–6, 161; Adams's view of, 126; with Choctaws, 138, 245–46, 249–50; with Creeks, 139, 142, 143, 153; growing Indian re-

sistance to, 162; Cass's view of, 206, 207; suggestions concerning, after passage of Indian Removal Bill, 235; McCoy's view of, 242, 244. *See also* Character; Compact of 1802; Indians: political rights of; Law
Treaty of Holston, 234
Treaty of Indian Springs (1825 Creek treaty), 142, 143, 153
Treaty of Washington (1826 Creek Treaty), 142
Troup, George, 126, 129, 139–42, 149, 219; wants Creek lands surveyed, 152–53
Tucker, James, 77
Tucker, Susannah, 82
Twenty-first Congress, 214–25. *See also* Congress

Union: nature of, 3–4, 223–24
Unitarians: Evarts's opposition to views of, 27, 49, 52–53, 78–80, 83; Evarts's temperance cooperation with, 59
United Foreign Missionary Society, 121, 122, 131
United States: differing visions of, 3–4, 223–24. *See also* Capitalism; Character; Christian republicanism; Evarts, Jeremiah: as moral reformer; Government; Morality; Self-interest
United States' Telegraph, 217, 223, 236, 238, 242, 243
University of Georgia, 13

Vaill, Herman, 135
Vaill, William, 163, 164
Van Buren, Martin, 2, 230
Vann, David, 250
Van Rensselaer, Stephen, 122
Vaux, Roberts, 189
Vermont: Evarts's early life in, 6, 10–11; Evarts's determination not to return to, 27. *See also* Burlington; Georgia (Vt.); Peacham; Sunderland
Victoria (Queen of England), 2
Virginia: slavery law in, 103; and Indian removal, 230

Voluntary societies. *See* Benevolent societies

War: Evarts's opposition to, 70–71, 75
War of 1812, 8, 64–67, 69, 70, 175, 176; opening of the West after, 116, 117
Washburn, Cephas: Evarts's letters to, 128, 153, 156, 159–60, 162; letters of, to Evarts, 197, 239
Washburn, Royal, 253
Washington, George, 178
Wayland, Francis, 164, 238–39
Wayne, James, 226
Webster, Daniel, 74, 217, 219, 227–28, 236, 238, 240, 260; on Missouri Crisis, 101; and debate with Hayne, 201–3, 211
West: need for religious influence in, 54, 78; political orientation of, 87, 125, 169, 171, 176, 203–4, 209, 229–30; and Indian lands, 114–15, 127–28
Whigs, 3
White Path's Rebellion, 155
White settlers: attitudes of eastern, toward Indians, 114; inability of U.S. government to prevent encroachment of, 214. *See also* Indian lands
White, Hugh, 217
Wilde, Richard, 226–27
"William Penn" essays: Evarts's, 5, 184–89, 191, 193, 200, 206, 207, 220, 222, 231, 248, 257, 263, 266; responses to, 206–8, 225, 242–43; expense of, 252
Williams, Loving, 245
Willstown Mission, 90
Wirt, William, 233–40, 249, 256–57
Women: Evarts's views of, 16, 22, 50–51; as converts, 41, 43–44, 50; in moral reform movement, 62, 82, 266; opposition to Indian removal by, 198; segregation of, in ABCFM auxiliaries, 112
Woodbury, Fanny, 50
Woods, Leonard, 26, 27, 53, 65
Worcester, Samuel (corresponding secretary of ABCFM), 8, 58, 60, 63–64, 66, 78, 85, 95; Evarts's letters to, 90, 115;

Worcester, Samuel (corresponding secretary of ABCFM) (cont'd)
and Indian removal plans, 96, 97, 98; death of, 107, 132
Worcester, Samuel A. (missionary son), 142, 164, 183, 191, 193, 210, 226, 234, 259–61
Worcester v. Georgia, 258, 267

Yale Corporation: rules of, 15
Yale Missionary Catechism, 109
Yale Moral Society, 12, 16–17, 30, 35
Yale University, 28; Evarts's senior address at, 5, 9–10, 38, 189, 190, 248; Evarts's studies at, 12–19; revivals at, 18–19, 30, 35; Evarts's son attends, 252. *See also* New Haven
Young adults: as converts, 41–43, 54
"Young Beaver," 163
"Youth of Nain, The" (Dwight), 18

Zuckerman, Michael, 82

www.ingramcontent.com/pod-product-compliance
Lightning Source LLC
Chambersburg PA
CBHW052338230426
43664CB00041B/2189